A Reader
in
Recent Catholic
Philosophy

ALAN VINCELETTE

En Route Books and Media, LLC
St. Louis, MO

⊕*ENROUTE*
Make the time

En Route Books and Media, LLC
5705 Rhodes Avenue
St. Louis, MO 63109

Cover credit: Alan Vincelette

Library of Congress Control Number: 2020950756

ISBN-13: 978-1-952464-35-5

DEDICATION

I dedicate this text to all of the students who have grappled with the great texts of contemporary Catholic thought with me over the years.

CONTENTS

ACKNOWLEDGMENTS

I would like to express gratitude to my student Ian Hollick for proofreading portions of the text, to my student Edgar Avendano for research assistance, and to the students of St. John's Seminary and Holy Apostles College and Seminary for lively conversations about these thinkers over the years.

The modified cover photos of Max Scheler, Pierre Rousselot, Elizabeth Anscombe, Bernard Lonergan, and Louis Lavelle, are based on originals found at Wikimedia Commons (commons.wikimedia.org) and used via the Creative Commons Attribution 2.0 Generic license (creativecommons.org/licenses /by/2.0/deed.en). The photo of Scheler was originally posted at http://www.phenomenologycenter.org/ gallery.htm. The Rousselot portrait was uploaded by Branor. The Anscombe image was posted by Clever Hans/Metrokles. The Lonergan photograph was posted by BCLonergan and the Lavelle image by Sébastien Robert.

I thank Cambridge University Press, Crossroad Publishing, Fordham University Press, Harvard University Press, ICS Publications, Ignatius Press, Indiana University Press, Marquette University Press, Northwestern University Press, Orbis Books, Oxford University Press, Pontifical Institute of Medieval Studies, Routledge, University of California Press, University of Toronto Press, Wiley-Blackwell, and Yale University Press for permission to republish the excerpts made use of here and noted in the various chapters. The other writings are in the Public Domain.

The readings are chronologically ordered within movements, however for those interested in approaching the texts thematically: readings which deal with epistemology are those by Newman, Gilson A, Maritain B (science), Pieper, Maréchal, Lonergan (science), Duhem (science), Dummett (prayer), and Van Fraassen (science); readings which deal with ethics are by Scheler, Von Hildebrand, Dussel, Wojtyła A and B (love), Rousselot A (love), Lavelle, Anscombe A and B, MacIntyre A and B, Taylor, and De Certeau; anthropological concerns are found in Stein A and B, Henry A and B, Spaemann, Falque, and Marcel; and readings treating the philosophy of religion include those by Chateaubriand, Newman, Blondel A and B (apologetics), Garrigou-Lagrange A and B (apologetics), Gilson B and C, Maritain A, Haldane, Rousselot B (apologetics), De Lubac, Chrétien (prayer), Ulrich, Caputo, Marion A, B, and C (apologetics), Lacoste, and Kearney.

PREFACE

Catholic philosophy has exploded in its amount and variety in the last century. This reader in Recent Catholic Philosophy attempts to convey the strength and diversity of this tradition. To do so it includes key readings by major thinkers in the fields of romanticism, voluntarism, integralism, phenomenology, Neo-Thomism, Transcendental Thomism, existentialism, analytical philosophy, and postmodernism.

Several of the thinkers in the volume have won major philosophical prizes, such as Taylor, Dummett, Anscombe, Føllesdal, Rescher, and Marion. Some have been included in major references works in philosophy, namely Anscombe, Blondel, Chateaubriand, De Certeau, Dummett, Garrigou-Lagrange, Gilson, Lavelle, Lonergan, MacIntyre, Maréchal, Marcel, Maritain, Newman, Rescher, Scheler, Stein, Taylor, and Van Fraassen. All of them have had their work translated into foreign languages, including English, some recently such as Henry, Dussel, Marion, Ulrich, and Falque. Hence they represent the pinnacle of influence of contemporary Catholic thought (though of course there is not a straight correlation between influence and truth or value).

Each entry contains a short biography of the individual, a brief summary of the included reading, and a short guide for further reading, before containing the philosopher's reading at hand. It is the hope that these readings will lead to fruitful discussions and/or reflections on the key ideas of these things, their usefulness for the development of a Catholic philosophy and theology, and the central pillars of Catholic philosophy.

This book is meant to accompany my other work, *Recent Catholic Philosophy: The Twentieth Century*, published through Marquette University Press (1st edition) or Enroute Books (2nd edition), which presents the thought of many of the key thinkers above, in addition to others not included in this volume. This volume also includes the writings of a few figures not in those volumes. So they mutually supplement each other. I have also included four authors of the nineteenth-century (Chateaubriand, Bautain, Newman, and Blondel) whose influence is still being felt.

1

1 19TH CENTURY PHILOSOPHY: ROMANTICISM, FIDEISM, INTEGRALISM, AND VOLUNTARISM

FRANÇOIS-RENÉ DE CHATEAUBRIAND (1768-1848)

Chateaubriand was born in St. Malo, Brittany, France in 1768. He came from a noble family, one recently reinstated in its luster by the purchase of the Château de Combourg. Though educated and spiritually formed by priests at the Collège de Dol, Collège de Rennes, and the Collège de Dinan, Chateaubriand forwent becoming a priest and embraced the liberalism of Locke, Abbé de Mably, and Abbé de Raynal, the deism of Montesquieu and Rousseau, and the politics of the French Revolution.

The violent turn of the Enlightenment-inspired revolution, however, and the suffering it caused to his family, prompted Chateaubriand to reembrace political conservatism and Catholicism. In response to the rationalistic and anti-Christian temper of the French Revolution, Chateaubriand thus penned his romantic novels *Atala* (1801) and *René* (1802), his apologetical work *Le Génie du christianisme* (1802), as well as articles in the journals *Mercure* and *Le Conservateur*. These works led to great literary acclaim for Chateaubriand, and in 1811 he was elected into the French Academy. The Bourbon Restoration of the monarchy saw Chateaubriand rise to political prominence as well, and he became French Minister of State in 1815, Ambassador to Berlin and London in 1821, and French Minister of Foreign Affairs in 1822. Chateaubriand died in 1848 and he was buried in an isolated grave on the island of Grand Bé, just off the coast of Saint-Malo.

Among the works on Chateaubriand consult: Dempsey, Madeleine, *A Contribution to the Study of the Sources of the Génie du Christianisme* (Paris: Champion, 1928); Richard, *Chateaubriand* (New York: Twayne, 1971); Despland, Michel, *Reading an Erased Code: Romantic Religion and Literary Aesthetics in France* (Toronto: University of Toronto Press, 1994); Scott, Malcolm, *Chateaubriand: The Paradox of Change* (Oxford: Peter Lang, 2014); as well as his autobiography *Memoirs from Beyond the Tomb* (London: Penguin, 2014).

The following selection is from Chateaubriand's *The Genius of Christianity: Or the Spirit and Beauty of the Christian Religion* (1802), translated by Charles I. White (Baltimore: John Murphy, 1871): I:I, 1: 46-51; I:V, 1-12: 139-140, 171-172; I: VI, 1-5: 190, 201-202. In it Chateaubriand criticizes the more radical deists, such as Voltaire, who charged that the Catholic Church was harmful to society. Chateaubriand sets forth, by way of contrast, all the benefits that Christianity has bestowed on civilization. He also enters into a romantic apologetic against the atheists, and, partially inspired by his journey through the forests of North America in 1791, argues that the best way to find God is through the beauties of nature and the moral conscience, that is through sentiment, more than reason.

The Genius of Christianity (1802)[1]

Mysteries and Sacraments

[46] While the Church was yet enjoying her triumph, Voltaire renewed the persecution of Julian. He possessed the baneful art of making infidelity fashionable among a capricious but amiable people. Every species of self-love was pressed into this insensate league. Religion was attacked with every kind of weapon, from the pamphlet to the folio, from the epigram to the sophism. No sooner did a religious book appear than the author was overwhelmed with ridicule, while works which Voltaire was the first to laugh at among his friends were extolled to the skies. [47] Such was his superiority over his disciples, that sometimes he could not forbear diverting himself with their irreligious enthusiasm. Meanwhile the destructive system continued to spread throughout France. It was first adopted in those provincial academies, each of which was a focus of bad taste and faction. Women of fashion and grave philosophers alike read lectures on infidelity. It was at length concluded that Christianity was no better than a barbarous system, and that its fall could not happen too soon for the liberty of mankind, the promotion of knowledge, the improvement of the arts, and the general comfort of life. ... Every author blessed his good fortune for having been born in the glorious age of the Diderots and d'Alemberts, in that age when all the attainments of the human mind were ranged in alphabetical order in the *Encyclopedia*, that Babel of the sciences and of reason. ...

[48] The defenders of the Christians fell into an error which had before undone them: they did not perceive that the question was no longer to discuss this or that particular tenet since the very foundation on which these tenets were built was rejected by their opponents. By starting from the mission of Jesus Christ, and descending from one consequence to another, they established the truths of faith on a solid basis; but this mode of reasoning, which might have suited the seventeenth century extremely well, when the groundwork was not contested, proved of no use in our days. It was necessary to pursue a contrary method, and to ascend from the effect to the cause; not to prove that *the Christian religion is excellent because it comes from God, but that it comes from God because it is excellent. ...*

---

[1] [François-René Chateaubriand, *The Genius of Christianity: Or the Spirit and Beauty of the Christian Religion*, translated by Charles I. White (Baltimore: John Murphy, 1871). Public Domain.]

For not having made this remark, much time and trouble were thrown away by those who undertook the vindication of Christianity. Their object should have been to reconcile to religion, not the sophists, but those whom they were leading astray. They had been seduced by being told that Christianity was the offspring of barbarism, an enemy of the arts and sciences, of reason and refinement; a religion whose only tendency was to encourage bloodshed, to enslave mankind, to diminish their happiness, and to retard the progress of the human understanding.

It was, therefore, necessary to prove that, on the contrary, the Christian religion, of all the religions that ever existed, is the most humane, the most favorable to liberty and to the arts and [49] sciences; that the modern world is indebted to it for every improvement, from agriculture to the abstract sciences from the hospitals for the reception of the unfortunate to the temples reared by the Michael Angelos and embellished by the Raphaels. It was necessary to prove that nothing is more divine than its morality nothing more lovely and more sublime than its tenets, its doctrine, and its worship; that it encourages genius, corrects the taste, develops the virtuous passions, imparts energy to the ideas, presents noble images to the writer, and perfect models to the artist; that there is no disgrace in being believers with Newton and Bossuet, with Pascal and Racine. In a word, it was necessary to summon all the charms of the imagination, and all the interests of the heart, to the assistance of that religion against which they had been set in array.

The reader may now have a clear view of the object of our work. All other kinds of apologies are exhausted, and perhaps they would be useless at the present day. Who would now sit down to read a work professedly theological? Possibly a few sincere Christians who are already convinced. But, it may be asked, may there not be some danger in considering religion in a merely human point of view? Why so? Does our religion shrink from the light? Surely one great proof of its divine origin is, that it will bear the test of the fullest and severest scrutiny of reason. Would you have us always open to the reproach of enveloping our tenets in sacred obscurity, lest their falsehood should be detected? Will Christianity be the less true for appearing the more beautiful? Let us banish our weak apprehensions; let us not, by an excess of religion, leave religion to perish. We no longer live in those times when you might say, "Believe without inquiring." People *will* inquire in spite of us; and our timid silence, in heightening the triumph of the infidel, will diminish the number of believers.

It is time that the world should know to what all those charges of absurdity, vulgarity, and meanness, that are daily alleged against Christianity, may be reduced. It is time to demonstrate, that, instead of debasing the ideas, it encourages the soul to take the most daring flights, and is capable of enchanting the imagination as divinely as the deities of Homer and Virgil. Our arguments will at least have this advantage, that they will be [50] intelligible to the world at large, and will require nothing but common sense to determine their weight and strength. In works of this kind authors neglect, perhaps rather too much, to speak the language of their readers. It is necessary to be a scholar with a scholar, and a poet with a poet. The Almighty does not forbid us to tread the flowery path, if it serves to lead the wanderer once more to him; nor is it always by the steep and rugged mountain that the lost sheep finds its way back to the fold.

We think that this mode of considering Christianity displays associations of ideas which are but imperfectly known. Sublime in the antiquity of its recollections, which go back to the creation of the world, ineffable in its mysteries, adorable in its sacraments, interesting in its history, celestial in its morality, rich and attractive in its ceremonial, it is fraught with every species of beauty. Would you follow it in poetry? Tasso, Milton, Corneille, Racine, Voltaire, will depict to you its miraculous effects. In the belles-lettres, in eloquence, history, and philosophy, what have not Bossuet, Fénélon, Massillon, Bourdaloue, Bacon, Pascal, Euler, Newton, Leibnitz, produced by its divine inspiration! In the arts, what master-pieces! If you examine it in its worship, what ideas are suggested by its antique Gothic churches, its admirable prayers, its impressive ceremonies! Among its clergy, behold all those scholars who have handed down to you the languages and the works of Greece and Rome; all those anchorets of Thebais; all those asylums for the unfortunate; all those missionaries to China, to Canada, to Paraguay; not forgetting the military orders whence chivalry derived its origin. ... Sometimes, with the Maronite monk, we dwell on the summits of Carmel and Lebanon; at others we watch with the Daughter of Charity at the bedside of the sick. ... [51] Homer takes his place by Milton, and Virgil beside Tasso; the ruins of Athens and of Memphis form contrasts with the ruins of Christian monuments, and the tombs of Ossian with our rural churchyards. At St. Dennis we visit the ashes of kings; and when our subject requires us to treat of the existence of God, we seek our proofs in the wonders of Nature alone. ...

The Existence of God Demonstrated by the Works of Nature

A General Survey of the Universe
[139] There is a God. The plants of the valley and the cedars of the mountain bless his name; the insect hums his praise; the elephant salutes him with the rising day; the bird glorifies him among the foliage; the lightning bespeaks his power, and the ocean declares his immensity. Man alone has said, "There is no God."

Has he then in adversity never raised his eyes toward heaven? has he in prosperity never cast them on the earth? Is Nature so far from him that he has not been able to contemplate its wonders; or does he consider them as the mere result of fortuitous causes? But how could chance have compelled crude and stubborn materials to arrange themselves in such exquisite order?

It might be asserted that man is the *idea of God displayed*, and the universe *his imagination made manifest*. They who have admitted the beauty of nature as a proof of a supreme intelligence, ought to have pointed out a truth which greatly enlarges the sphere of wonders. It is this: motion and rest, darkness and light, the seasons, the revolutions of the heavenly bodies, which give variety to the decorations of the world, are successive only in appearance, and permanent in reality. The scene that fades upon our view is painted in brilliant colors for another people; it is not the spectacle that is changed, but the spectator. Thus God has combined in his work absolute duration and progressive duration. The first is placed in time, the second in space; by means of the former, the beauties of the universe are one, infinite, and invariable; by means of the latter, [140] they are multiplied, finite, and perpetually renewed. Without the one, there would be no grandeur in the creation; without the other, it would exhibit nothing but dull uniformity.

Here time appears to us in a new point of view; the smallest of its fractions becomes a complete whole, which comprehends all things, and in which all things transpire, from the death of an insect to the birth of a world; each minute is in itself a little eternity. Combine, then, at the same moment, in imagination, the most beautiful incidents of nature; represent to yourself at once all the hours of the day and all the seasons of the year, a spring morning and an autumnal morning, a night spangled with stars and a night overcast with clouds, meadows enamelled with flowers, forests stripped by the frosts, and fields glowing with their golden harvests; you will then have a just idea of the prospect of the universe. While you are gazing with admiration upon the sun sinking beneath the western arch, another beholds it emerging from the regions of Aurora. By what inconceivable magic does it come, that this aged luminary, which retires to rest, as if weary and heated, in the dusky arms of night, is at the very same moment that youthful orb which awakes bathed in dew, and sparkling through the gray curtains of the dawn? Every moment of the day the sun is rising, glowing at his zenith, and setting on the world; or rather our senses deceive us, and there is no real sunrise, noon, or sunset. The whole is reduced to a fixed point, from which the orb of day emits, at one and the same time, three lights from one single substance. This triple splendor is perhaps the most beautiful incident in nature; for, while it affords an idea of the perpetual magnificence and omnipresence of God, it exhibits a most striking image of his glorious Trinity. ...

Two Views of Nature

[171] The vessel in which we embarked for America having passed the bearing of any land, space was soon enclosed only by the two fold azure of the sea and of the sky. ... Oh! how sublime, how awful, at such times, is the aspect of the ocean! Into what reveries does it plunge you, whether imagination transports you to the seas of the north, into the midst of frosts and tempests, or wafts you to southern islands, blessed with happiness and peace!

We often rose at midnight and sat down upon deck, where we found only the officer of the watch and a few sailors silently smoking their pipes. No noise was heard, save the dashing of the prow through the billows, while sparks of fire ran with a white foam along the sides of the vessel. God of Christians! It is on the waters of the abyss and on the vast expanse of the heavens that thou hast particularly engraven the characters of thy omnipotence! Millions of stars sparkling in the azure of the celestial dome—the moon in the midst of the firmament—a sea unbounded by any shore-infinitude in the skies and on the waves—proclaim with most impressive effect the power of thy arm! Never did thy greatness strike me with profounder awe than in those nights, [172] when, suspended between the stars and the ocean, I beheld immensity over my head and immensity beneath my feet!

I am nothing; I am only a simple, solitary wanderer, and often have I heard men of science disputing on the subject of a Supreme Being, without understanding them; but I have invariably remarked, that it is in the prospect of the sublime scenes of nature that this unknown Being manifests himself to the human heart. ...

The Immortality of the Soul Proved by the Moral Law and the Feelings

Desire of Happiness in Man

[184] Were there no other proofs of the existence of God than the wonders of nature, these evidences are so strong that they would convince any sincere inquirer after truth. But if they who deny a Providence are, for that very reason, unable to explain the wonders of the creation, they are still more puzzled when they undertake to answer the objections of their own hearts. By renouncing the Supreme Being, they are obliged to renounce a future state. The soul nevertheless disturbs them; she appears, as it were, every moment before them, and compels them, in spite of their sophistry, to acknowledge her existence and her immortality.

Let them inform us, in the first place, if the soul is extinguished at the moment of death, whence proceeds the desire of happiness which continually haunts us? All our passions here below may easily be gratified; love, ambition, anger, have their full measure of enjoyment: the desire of happiness is the only one that cannot be satisfied, and that fails even of an object, as we know not what that felicity is which we long for. It must be admitted, that if every thing is *matter*, nature has here made a strange mistake, in creating a desire without any object.

Certain it is that the soul is eternally craving. No sooner has it attained the object for which it yearned, than a new wish is formed; and the whole universe cannot satisfy it. Infinity is the only field adapted to its nature; it delights to lose itself in numbers, to conceive the greatest as well as the smallest dimensions, and to multiply without end. Filled at length, but not satisfied with all that it has devoured, it seeks the bosom of the Deity, in [185] whom centre all ideas of infinity, whether in perfection, duration, or space.

But it seeks the bosom of Deity only because he is a being full of mystery, "a hidden God." If it had a clear apprehension of the divine nature, it would undervalue it, as it does all other objects that its intellect is capable of measuring; for, if it could fully comprehend the eternal principle, it would be either superior or equal to this principle. It is not in divine as it is in human things. A man may understand the power of a king without being a king himself; but he cannot understand the divinity without being God. The inferior animals are not agitated by this hope which manifests itself in the heart of man; they immediately attain their highest degree of happiness; a handful of grass satisfies the lamb, a little blood is sufficient for the tiger. If we were to assert, with some philosophers, that the different conformation of the organs constitutes all the difference between us and the brute, this mode of reasoning could, at the farthest, be admitted only in relation to purely material acts. But of what service is my hand to my mind, when amid the silence of night I soar through the regions of boundless space, to discover the Architect of so many worlds? Why does not the ox act in this respect as I do? His eyes are sufficient; and if he had my legs or my arms, they would for this purpose be totally useless to him. He may repose upon the turf, he may raise his head toward the sky, and by his bellowing call upon the unknown Being who fills the immense expanse. But no: he prefers the grass on which he treads; and while those millions of suns that adorn the firmament furnish the strongest evidences of a Deity, the animal consults them not; he is insensible to the prospect of nature, and unconscious that he is himself thrown beneath the tree at the foot of which he lies, as a slight proof of a divine Intelligence.

Man, therefore, is the only creature that wanders abroad, and looks for happiness out of himself. The vulgar, we are told, feel not this mysterious restlessness. They are undoubtedly less unhappy than we, for they are diverted by laborious occupations from attending to their desires, and drown the thirst of felicity in the sweat of their brow. But when you see them toil six [186] days in the week that they may enjoy a little pleasure on the seventh, when, incessantly hoping for repose and never finding it, they sink into the grave without ceasing to desire, will you say that they share not the secret aspiration of all men after an unknown happiness? You may reply, that in the class of which we are speaking this wish is at least limited to terrestrial things; but your assertion remains to be proved. Give the poorest wretch all the treasures in the world, put an end to his toils, satisfy all his wants, and you will observe that, before a few months have elapsed, his heart will conceive new desires and new hopes. ...

If it is impossible to deny that man cherishes hopes to the very tomb,–if it is certain that all earthly possessions, so far from crowning our wishes, only serve to increase the void in the soul,– we cannot but conclude that there must be a something beyond the limits of time. ... [187] Providence has placed beyond the fatal boundary a charm which attracts us, in order to diminish our horror of the grave: thus, the affectionate mother who wishes her child to cross a certain limit, holds some pleasing object on the other side to encourage him to pass it. ...

Remorse and Conscience

Conscience furnishes a second proof of the immortality of the soul. Each individual has within his own heart a tribunal, where he sits in judgment on himself till the Supreme Arbiter shall confirm the sentence. If vice is but a physical consequence of our organization, whence arises this dread which embitters the days of prosperous guilt? Why is remorse so terrible that many would choose rather to submit to poverty and all the rigors of virtue than enrich themselves with ill-gotten goods? What is it that gives a voice to blood and speech to stones? The tiger devours his prey, and slumbers quietly; man takes the life of his fellow-creature, and keeps a fearful vigil! He seeks some desert place, and yet this solitude affrights him; he skulks about the tombs, and yet the tombs fill him with horrors. His eyes are wild and restless; he dares not fix them on the wall of the banqueting-room, for fear he should discover there some dreadful signs. All his senses seem to become more acute in order to torment him: he perceives at night threatening confiscations; he is always surrounded by the smell of carnage; he suspects the taste of poison in the food which he has himself prepared; his ear, now wonder fully sensitive, hears a noise where for others there is profound silence; and when embracing his friend, he fancies that he feels under his garments a hidden dagger.

Conscience! is it possible that thou canst be but a phantom of [188] the imagination, or the fear of the punishment of men? I ask my own heart, I put to myself this question: "If thou couldst by a mere wish kill a fellow-creature in China, and inherit his fortune in Europe, with the supernatural conviction that the fact would never be known, wouldst thou consent to form such a wish?" In vain do I exaggerate my indigence; in vain do I attempt to extenuate the murder, by supposing that through the effect of my wish the Chinese expires instantaneously and without pain; that, had he even died a natural death, his property, from the situation of his affairs, would have been lost to the state; in vain do I figure to myself this stranger overwhelmed with disease and affliction; in vain do I urge that to him death is a blessing, that he himself desires it, that he has but a moment longer to live: in spite of all my useless subterfuges, I hear a voice in the recesses of my soul, protesting so loudly against the mere idea of such a supposition, that I cannot for one moment doubt the reality of conscience.

It is a deplorable necessity, then, that compels a man to deny remorse, that he may deny the immortality of the soul and the existence of an avenging Deity. Full well we know, that atheism, when driven to extremities, has recourse to this disgraceful denial. The sophist, in a paroxysm of the gout, exclaimed, "pain! never will I acknowledge that thou art an evil!" Were it even true that there exist men so unfortunate as to be capable of stifling the voice of conscience, what then? We must not judge of him who possesses the perfect use of his limbs by the paralytic who is deprived of his physical strength. Guilt, in its highest degree, is a malady which sears the soul. By overthrowing religion we destroy the only remedy capable of restoring sensibility in the morbid regions of the heart. This astonishing religion of Christ is a sort of supplement to the deficiency of the human mind. Do we sin *by excess*, by too great prosperity, by violence of temper? she is at hand to warn us of the fickleness of fortune and the danger of angry excitement. Are we exposed, on the contrary, to sin by defect, by indigence, by indifference of soul? she teaches us to despise riches, at the same time warms our frigid hearts, and, as it were, kindles in us the fire of the passions. Toward the criminal, in particular, her charity is inexhaustible; no man is so depraved but she admits him to repentance, no [189] leper so disgusting but she cures him with her pure hands. For the past she requires only remorse, for the future only virtue: "where sin abounded," she says, "grace did much more abound." Ever ready to warn the sinner, Jesus Christ established his religion as a second conscience for the hardened culprit who should be so unfortunate as to have lost the natural one,—an evangelical conscience, full of pity and indulgence, to which the Son of God has given the power to pardon, which is not possessed by the conscience of man.

Having spoken of the remorse which follows guilt, it would be unnecessary to say anything of the satisfaction attendant on virtue. The inward delight which we feel in doing a good action is no more a combination of matter than the accusation of conscience, when we commit a bad one, is fear of the laws.

If sophists maintain that virtue and pity are but self-love in disguise, ask them not if they ever felt any secret satisfaction after relieving a distressed object, or if it is the fear of returning to the state of childhood that affects them when contemplating the innocence of the new-born infant. Virtue and tears are for men the source of hope and the groundwork of faith; how then should he believe in God who believes neither in the reality of virtue nor in the truth of tears? It would be an insult to the understanding of our readers, did we attempt to show how the immortality of the soul and the existence of God are proved by that inward voice called conscience. ...

There Can Be No Morality If There Be No Future State

[190] Morality is the basis of society; but if man is a mere mass of matter, there is in reality neither vice nor virtue, and of course morality is a mere sham. Our laws, which are ever relative and variable, cannot serve as the support of morals, which are always absolute and unalterable; they must, therefore, rest on something more permanent than the present life, and have better guarantees than uncertain rewards or transient punishments. Some philosophers have supposed that religion was *invented* in order to uphold morality: they were not aware that they were taking the effect for the cause. It is not religion that springs from morals, but morals that spring from religion; since it is certain, as we have just observed, that morals cannot have their principle in *physical* man or *mere matter*; and that men no sooner divest themselves of the idea of a God than they rush into every species of crime, in spite of laws and of executioners.

Danger and Inutility of Atheism

[201] Such being the state of things, he must be extremely obstinate who would not espouse the cause in behalf of which not only reason finds the most numerous evidences, but to which morals, happiness, and hope, nay, even instinct itself, and all the desires of the soul, naturally impel us; for if it were as true as it is false, that the understanding keeps the balance even between God and atheism, still it is certain that it would preponderate much in favor of the former; for, besides half of his reason, man puts the whole weight of his heart into the scale of the Deity. ...

Religion ... founds her judgment only on the harmony of the heavens and the immutable laws of the universe; she views only the graces of nature, the charming instincts of animals, and their exquisite conformities with man. Atheism sets before you nothing but hideous exceptions; it seek naught but calamities, unhealthy marshes, destructive volcanoes, noxious animals; and, as if it were anxious to conceal itself in the mire, it interrogates the reptiles and insects that they may furnish it with proofs against God. [202] Religion speaks only of the grandeur and beauty of man. Atheism is continually setting the leprosy and plague before our eyes. Religion derives her reasons from the sensibility of the soul, from the tenderest attachments of life, from filial piety, conjugal love, and maternal affection. Atheism reduces everything to the instinct of the brute, and, as the first argument of its system, displays to you a heart that naught is capable of moving. Religion comforts us, promises another life. ... Human woes are the incense of atheism.

LOUIS BAUTAIN (1796–1867)

Bautain was born in Paris in 1796 and studied philosophy with Victor Cousin at the École Normale Supérieure from 1813 to 1816, after which he came to embrace Cousin's eclecticism. Upon receiving his doctorate in philosophy Bautain taught at the University of Strasbourg where he came under the sway of Louise Humann and returned to the Catholic faith and switch allegiances to the fideism of Kant and Jacobi. Thus also commenced Bautain's ongoing trouble with secular and ecclesiastical authorities. Bautain first was suspended from teaching at the University of Strasbourg in 1824 on account of his rejection of reason's ability to know metaphysical truths. After two years of the study of medicine and two years at the seminary of Molsheim Bautain was ordained a priest in 1828 and became director of the minor seminary of Strasbourg in 1830. Once again, however, on account of his fideism Bautain was removed from his position in 1834 by the local bishop.

In order to regain the trust of the secular and ecclesiastical authorities Bautain traveled to Rome and signed statements affirming that reason can establish the existence of God and the credibility of the faith in 1835, 1840, and 1844 (DH 2751-2756, 2765-2769). With his graces restored, Bautain served as Dean of the Faculty of Letters at the University of Strasbourg from 1838 to 1849, professor of philosophy at the Collège de Juilly in Paris from 1841 to 1849, Vicar General of Paris in 1849, and finished his career teaching moral theology at the Sorbonne from 1853 to 1863, and in addition founded the Sisters of St. Louis.

For more on Bautain consult: Horton, Walter M., *The Philosophy of the Abbé Bautain* (New York: New York University Press, 1929); Kselman, Thomas, "The Bautain Circle and Catholic-Jewish Relations in Modern France," *The Catholic Historical Review* 92 (July 2006): 177–196; Nichols, Aidan, *The Conversation of Faith and Reason: Modern Catholic Thought from Hermes to Benedict XVI* (Leominster: Hildenbrand Books, 2009): 60–72, 81–86; Reardon, Bernard, *Liberalism and Tradition: Aspects of Catholic Thought in Nineteenth-Century France* (Cambridge: Cambridge University Press, 1975), pp. 116–137; Vincelette, Alan, *Recent Catholic Philosophy: The Nineteenth Century* (Milwaukee: Marquette University Press, 2009), pp. 34–41.

The text below is my translation of Letter 14 from Volume 1 of Bautain's *La philosophie du christianisme* (Paris: Dérivaux, 1835), pp. 184-196 which defends the view that faith alone is capable of giving humans knowledge of God as God's nature is beyond the scope of reason. Bautain's fideism was officially rejected at the First Vatican Council in 1870 which affirmed contrary to Bautain that God could be known from created things by the natural light of human reason (DH 3004).

The Philosophy of Christianity (1835)[2]

[184] The Christian who believes in one God alone, also believes, with the whole Church, that this unique God is known in his absolute unity only by Himself; that God, in His divine essence, in the purity and simplicity of His Being, is inaccessible to all created intelligence, [and] absolutely incomprehensible to man ... of whom neither idea nor image can be formed. ...

[185] The human, in his current state, is incapable of elevating himself by himself to the science of any principle. Intelligent creature placed, as it were, at the center of the physical region, he sees what he can reach by his gaze; its visual radius measures the heavens and the stars; he perceives the forms that exist around him in space; he sees sensitive existences; he conceives their images or types; he distinguishes them, knows them insofar as they appear to him, and recognizes them insofar as he has seen, perceived, conceived and known them. But his gaze does not penetrate into the interior of these forms; he does not grasp the principle of existences, nor the life which animates them. ...

[187] And if he cannot contemplate the One who dwells in an inaccessible light; if he cannot see being; how will he conceive by himself a pure, true, [and] adequate idea of Being? And if, on the other hand, the science of God and that of his own nature form his dignity and his felicity; if he is only human by virtue of the sacred character which renders him capable of this science; and if he cannot, in his current state, grasp its objective principle by means of vision, is it not necessary that he receive it by word and by means [188] of hearing? For what would be a science without principle and without idea? And what word can give the human the principle, the idea and the science of God, if not the word of God? ... [Such is] the single source, where you can draw with security the principle of science, the true knowledge of the true God. ... No, friend, it is not in natural phenomena, in the objects of a world which is only a perishable figure, that you will find the immutable and eternal principle. It will not be your reason which will establish in a decisive manner the unity of this principle; for reason everywhere finds evil alongside good. It is not the dictates

---

2 [Louis Bautain, *La philosophie du christianisme* (Paris: Dérivaux, 1835), volume 1. Public Domain. Translated by Alan Vincelette.]

of common sense that will give you the conviction and certainty of metaphysical things. An objective principle is necessary for science, and I affirm to you with the deepest conviction, this principle is found for the current human in the books of divine revelations and [189] nowhere else. ... [193] [Rational authority] can lead to the door of the sanctuary; but it cannot open it, it cannot enter into it, much less teach about it. It is divine grace which attracts the human; it is the divine word which announces the mystery of [194] God and eternity to him, who gives him the key of metaphysical science, and it is the Church who teaches him to make use of it. ...

Before an attempt had been made to erect common sense into a sovereign authority, a power had been accorded to individual reason which it never had and which it will never have, that of elevating itself by itself and by the natural light to the certainty of the existence of the true God, of the single God. Nature, it was said, proclaims the power and the wisdom of its Author. This is very true. But what is important for the human to know is not just the Author of nature, the great Architect, the soul of the world, etc. : it is above all his own Author, his God, the God of the human; and nature is silent on this point. It leaves the human entangled with all the purely natural products. Besides, nature is finite, limited, and the infinitude of the worker cannot be reached from a finite work. Reason, it is said, can elevate itself by induction from effect to cause. For sure. But between finite effects and an infinite cause, between contingent and temporary existences and absolute and eternal Being, there is an abyss that reason will never cross. ...

[195] The prejudice that grants to reason the power to establish by itself, or to prove by arguments, the truth of the existence of one God alone, does nothing less than to propagate among us the crime of idolatry. ... Reason, proud of the power that it attributes to itself to ascertain the truth about God, deifies without scruple the conceptions of natural sense: it believes with confidence in a being that it has laboriously abstracted from forms of [196] nature, and which is only a logical entity. It creates for itself a dynamic God, a supreme being, to whom it lends power according to its measure, wisdom according to its views, justice in its interest; and it is ... especially attached to its philosophical idol.

JOHN HENRY NEWMAN (1801-1890)

Newman was born in London in 1801. He studied at Trinity College, Oxford from 1816-1820 and was elected a fellow of Oriel College, Oxford in 1822, aligning himself with the rational Anglicanism of the Oriel Noetics Richard Whately and Edward Copleston, even assisting the former in writing the *Elements of Logic* (London: J. Mawman, 1827). In 1828 Newman was appointed vicar of the University Church, St. Mary's the Virgin, delivering famous sermons to the students of Oxford. He also joined forces with John Keble, Edward Pusey, and Hurrell Froude in initiating Tractarian Movement. Certain of his writings, however, caused Newman to be censured and he resigned his posts and retired to his benefice of Littlemore where he founded a semi-monastic community.

In 1845 Newman converted to Catholicism and he was ordained a Catholic priest in 1847, after acquiring a doctorate in theology from the Urban College of the Propoganda Fide in Rome. Newman eventually joined the Oratorians and established a community in 1850 near Birmingham. The 1850s were a trying time for Newman. He was accused and found guilty of libel by the former Dominican Giacinto Achilli and attacked in print by the Anglican Charles Kingsley, which spurred Newman to write his religious autobiography, *Apologia pro vita sua* (1865-1866). Newman ultimately was made a Cardinal in 1879 by Leo XIII, just a year before he died. Newman is buried in Oratorian cemetery of Rednal, sharing a tomb with his fellow Oratorian Ambrose St. John.

The following selection is from Newman main philosophical work, *An Essay in Aid of a Grammar of Assent* (London: Burns, Oates, and Company, 1870): IV, 89-93; V, 98-102, 104-107, 110-111; VI, 166-171; VIII, 276, 280, 306-307; IX, 332. In it Newman defends the possibility of certitude in knowledge of concrete facts and not just of abstract syllogisms. Hence, he introduces his famous distinctions between notional and real assent and the illative sense. For besides notional assents to formal deductive truths, there can be real assents to concrete truths based on an accumulation of probabilities allowing for a moral certitude, wherein, even if there is a slight chance one is in error, one has solid grounds for asserting that something is certain, such as believing Great Britain is an island, that one is mortal, or coming to believe that God exists and is good based on one's moral conscience. Here one trusts one's faculties, and the drift and slope of the evidence, as it were grasped, by the illative sense. And if we trust the deliverings of our conscience we have a basis for belief in God as well.

For more on Newman see: Casey, Gerard, *Natural Reason* (Frankfurt: Peter Lang, 1984); Grave, Selwyn, *Conscience in Newman's Thought* (Oxford: Clarendon Press, 1989); Aquino, Frederick, *Communities of Informed Judgment* (Washington: Catholic University of America Press, 2004); Laurence, Richardson, *Newman's Approach to Knowledge* (Leominster: Gracewing, 2007); Rupert, Jane, *John Henry Newman on the Nature of the Mind* (Lanham: Lexington Books, 2011).

An Essay in Aid of a Grammar of Assent (1870)[3]

Notional and Real Assent

Notional and Real Assents Contrasted

[89] The heart is commonly reached, not through the reason, but through the imagination, by means of direct impressions, by the testimony of facts and events, by history, by description. Persons influence us, voices melt us, looks subdue us, deeds inflame us. [90] Many a man will live and die upon a dogma: no man will be a martyr for a conclusion. A conclusion is but an opinion; it is not a thing which *is*, but which *we are* 'certain *about*;' and it has often been observed, that we never say we are sure and certain without implying that we doubt. To say that a thing *must* be, is to admit that it *may* not be. No one, I say, will die for his own calculations: he dies for realities. ...

[91] Logic makes but a sorry rhetoric with the multitude; first shoot round corners, and you may not despair of converting by a syllogism. Tell men to gain notions of a Creator from His works, and, if they were to set about it (which nobody does) they would be jaded and wearied by the labyrinth they were tracing. Their minds would be gorged and surfeited by the logical operation. Logicians are more set upon concluding rightly, than on right conclusions. They cannot see the end for the process. Few men have that power of mind which may hold fast and firmly a variety of thoughts. We ridicule 'men of one idea,' but a great many of us are born to be such, and we should be happier if we knew it. To most men argument makes the point in hand only more doubtful, and considerably less impressive. After all, man is *not* a reasoning animal; he is a seeing, feeling, contemplating, acting animal. He is influenced by what is direct and precise. It is very well to freshen our impressions and convictions from physics, but to create them we must go elsewhere. ...

Life is not long enough for a religion of inferences; we shall never have done beginning, if we determine to begin with proof. We shall ever be laying our [92] foundations; we shall turn theology into evidences, and divines into textuaries. We shall never get at our first principles. Resolve to believe nothing, and you must prove your proof and analyze your elements, sinking farther and farther, and finding 'in the lowest depth a lower deep,'

---

3 [John Henry Newman, *An Essay in Aid of a Grammar of Assent* (New York: The Catholic Publication Society, 1870). Public Domain.]

till you come to the broad bosom of scepticism. I would rather be bound to defend the reasonableness of *assuming* that Christianity is true, than to *prove* a moral governance from the physical world. Life is for action. If we insist on proof for every thing, we shall never come to action: to act you must assume, and that assumption is faith.

Let no one suppose, that in saying this I am maintaining that all proofs are equally difficult, and all propositions equally debatable. Some assumptions are greater than others, and some doctrines involve postulates larger than others, and more numerous. I only say, that impressions lead to action, and that reasonings lead from it. Knowledge of premisses, and inferences upon them,–this is not to *live*. It is very well as a matter of liberal curiosity and of philosophy to analyze our modes of thought: but let this come second, and when there is leisure for it, and then our examinations will in many ways even be subservient to action. But if we commence with scientific knowledge and argumentative proof, or lay any great stress upon it as the basis of personal Christianity, or attempt to make man moral and religious by libraries and museums, let us in consistency take chemists for our cooks, and mineralogists for our masons.

Now I wish to state all this as matter of fact, to be judged by the candid testimony of any persons [93] whatever. Why we are so constituted that faith, not knowledge or argument, is our principle of action, is a question with which I have nothing to do; but I think it is a fact, and, if it be such, we must resign ourselves to it as best we may, unless we take refuge in the intolerable paradox, that the mass of men are created for nothing, and are meant to leave life as they entered it.

So well has this practically been understood in all ages of the world, that no religion yet has been a religion of physics or of philosophy. It has ever been synonymous with revelation. It never has been a deduction from what we know; it has ever been an assertion of what we are to believe. It has never lived in a conclusion; it has ever been a message, a history, or a vision. No legislator or priest ever dreamed of educating our moral nature by science or by argument. There is no difference here between true religions and pretended. Moses was instructed not to reason from the creation, but to work miracles. Christianity is a history supernatural, and almost scenic: it tells us what its Author is, by telling us what He has done. ...

Apprehension and Assent in the Matter of Religion

Belief in One God

[98] When it is said that we cannot see God, this is undeniable; but in what sense have we a discernment of His creatures, of the individual beings which surround us? The evidence which we have of their presence lies in the phenomena which address our senses, and our warrant for taking these for evidence is our instinctive certitude that they are evidence. By the law of our nature we associate those sensible phenomena or impressions with certain units, [99] individuals, substances, whatever they are to be called, which are outside and out of the reach of sense, and we picture them to ourselves in those phenomena. The phenomena are as if pictures; but at the same time they give us no exact measure or character of the unknown things beyond them;–for who will say there is any uniformity between the impressions which two of us would respectively have of some third thing, supposing one of us had only the sense of touch, and the other only the sense of hearing? Therefore, when we speak of our having a picture of the things which are perceived through the senses, we mean a certain representation, true as far as it goes, but not adequate.

And so of those intellectual and moral objects which are brought home to us through our senses:–that they exist, we know by instinct; that they are such and such, we apprehend from the impressions which they leave upon our minds. Thus the life and writings of Cicero or Dr. Johnson, of St. Jerome or St. Chrysostom, leave upon us certain impressions of the intellectual and moral character of each of them, *sui generis*, and unmistakable. We take up a passage of Chrysostom or a passage of Jerome; there is no possibility of confusing the one with the other; in each case we see the man in his language. And so of any great man whom we may have known: that he is not a mere impression on our senses, but a real being, we know by instinct; that he is such and such, we know by the matter or quality of that impression.

Now certainly the thought of God, as Theists entertain it, is not gained by an instinctive association of His presence with any sensible phenomena; but the office [100] which the senses directly fulfil as regards creation that devolves indirectly on certain of our mental phenomena as regards the Creator. Those phenomena are found in the sense of moral obligation. As from a multitude of instinctive perceptions, acting in particular instances, of something beyond the senses, we generalize the notion of an external world, and then picture that world in and according to those particular phenomena from which we started, so from the perceptive power which identifies the intimations of conscience with the reverberations or echoes (so to say) of an external admonition, we proceed on to the notion of a Supreme Ruler and Judge, and then again we image Him and His attributes in those recurring intimations, out of which, as mental phenomena, our recognition of His existence was originally gained. And, if the impressions which His creatures make on us through our senses oblige us to regard those creatures as *sui generis* respectively, it is not wonderful that the notices, which He indirectly gives us through our conscience, of His own nature are such as to make us understand that He is like Himself and like nothing else.

I have already said I am not proposing here to prove the Being of a God; yet I have found it impossible to avoid saying where I look for the proof of it. For I am looking for that proof in the same quarter as that from which I would commence a proof of His attributes and character,–by the same means as those by which I show how we apprehend Him, not merely as a notion, but as a reality. The last indeed of these three investigations alone concerns me here, but I cannot altogether exclude the two former from my [101] consideration. However, I repeat, what I am directly aiming at, is to explain how we gain an image of God and give a real assent to the proposition that He exists. And next, in order to do this, of course I must start from some first principle;–and that first principle, which I assume and shall not attempt to prove, is that which I should also use as a foundation in those other two inquiries, viz. that we have by nature a conscience.

I assume, then, that Conscience has a legitimate place among our mental acts; as really so, as the action of memory, of reasoning, of imagination, or as the sense of the beautiful; that, as there are objects which, when presented to the mind, cause it to feel grief, regret, joy, or desire, so there are things which excite in us approbation or blame, and which we in consequence call right or wrong; and which, experienced in ourselves, kindle in us that specific sense of pleasure or pain, which goes by the name of a good or bad conscience. This being taken for granted, I shall attempt to show that in this special feeling, which follows on the commission of what we call right or wrong, lie the materials for the real apprehension of a Divine Sovereign and Judge.

The feeling of conscience (being, I repeat, a certain keen sensibility, pleasant or painful,–self-approval and hope, or compunction and fear,–attendant on certain of our actions, which in consequence we call right or wrong) is twofold:—it is a moral sense, and a sense of duty; a judgment of the reason and a magisterial dictate. Of course its act is indivisible; still it has two aspects, distinct from each other, and admitting of a separate consideration. Though I lost my sense of the obligation which I lie under to abstain from acts of dishonesty, I should not in consequence [102] lose my sense that such actions were an outrage offered to my moral nature. Again; though I lost my sense of their moral deformity, I should not therefore lose my sense that they were forbidden to me. Thus conscience has both a critical and a judicial office, and though its promptings, in the breasts of the millions of human beings to whom it is given, are not in all cases correct, that does not necessarily interfere with the force of its testimony and of its sanction: its testimony that there is a right and a wrong, and its sanction to that testimony conveyed in the feelings which attend on right or wrong conduct. Here I have to speak of conscience in the latter point of view, not as supplying us, by means of its various acts, with the elements of morals, such as may be developed by the intellect into an ethical code, but simply as the dictate of an authoritative monitor bearings upon the details of conduct as they come before us, and complete in its several acts, one by one. ...

[104] So much for the characteristic phenomena, which conscience presents, nor is it difficult to determine what they imply. I refer once more to our sense of the beautiful. This sense is attended by an intellectual enjoyment, and is free from whatever is of the nature of emotion, except in one case, viz. when it is excited by personal objects; then it is that the tranquil feeling of admiration is exchanged for the [105] excitement of affection and passion. Conscience too, considered as a moral sense, an intellectual sentiment, is a sense of admiration and disgust, of approbation and blame: but it is something more than, a moral sense; it is always, what the sense of the beautiful is only in certain cases; it is always emotional. No wonder then that it always implies what that sense only sometimes implies; that it always involves the recognition of a living object, towards which it is directed. Inanimate things cannot stir our affections; these are correlative with persons. If, as is the case, we feel responsibility, are ashamed, are frightened, at transgressing the voice of conscience, this implies that there is One to whom we are responsible, before whom we are ashamed, whose claims upon us we fear. If, on doing wrong, we feel the same tearful, broken-hearted sorrow which overwhelms us on hurting a mother; if, on doing right, we enjoy

the same sunny serenity of mind, the same soothing, satisfactory delight which follows on our receiving praise from a father, we certainly have within us the image of some person, to whom our love and veneration look, in whose smile we find our happiness, for whom we yearn, towards whom we direct our pleadings, in whose anger we are troubled and waste away. These feelings in us are such as require for their exciting cause an intelligent being: we are not affectionate towards stone, nor do we feel shame before a horse or a dog; we have no remorse or compunction on breaking mere human law: yet, so it is, con-science excites all these painful emotions, confusion, foreboding, self-condemnation; and on the other hand it sheds upon us a deep peace, a sense of security, a [106] resignation, and a hope, which there is no sensible, no earthly object to elicit. "The wicked flees, when no one pursueth;" then why does he flee? whence his terror? Who is it that he sees in solitude, in darkness, in the hidden chambers of his heart? If the cause of these emotions does not belong to this visible world, the Object to which his perception is directed must be Supernatural and Divine; and thus the phenomena of Conscience, as a dictate, avail to impress the imagination with the picture of a Supreme Governor, a Judge, holy, just, powerful, all-seeing, retributive, and is the creative principle of religion, as the moral sense is the principle of ethics.

And let me here refer again to the fact, to which I have already drawn attention, that this instinct of the mind recognizing an external Master in the dictate of conscience, and imaging the thought of Him in the definite impressions which conscience creates, is parallel to that other law of, not only human, but of brute nature, by which the presence of unseen individual beings is discerned under the shifting shapes and colours of the visible world. Is it by sense, or by reason, that brutes understand the real unities, material and spiritual, which are signified by the lights and shadows, the brilliant ever-changing kaleidoscope, as it may be called, which plays upon their *retina*? Not by reason, for they have not reason; not by sense, because they are transcending sense; therefore it is an instinct. This faculty on the part of brutes, unless we were used to it, would strike us as a great mystery. It is one peculiarity of animal natures to be susceptible of phenomena through the channels of sense; it is another to have in those sensible phenomena a [107] perception of the individuals to which this or that group of them belongs. This perception of individual things, amid the maze of shapes and colours which meets their sight, is given to brutes in large measures, and that, apparently from the moment of their birth. It is by no mere physical instinct, such as that which leads him to his mother for milk, that the new-dropped lamb recognizes each of his fellow-lambkins as a whole, consisting of many parts bound up in one, and, before he is an hour old, makes experience of his and their rival individualities. And much more distinctly do the horse and dog recognize even the personality of their masters. How are we to explain this apprehension of things, which are one and individual, in the midst of a world of pluralities and transmutations, whether in the instance of brutes or again of children? But until we account for the knowledge which an infant has of his mother or his nurse, what reason have we to take exception at the doctrine, as strange and difficult, that in the dictate of conscience, without previous experiences or analogical reasoning, he is able gradually to perceive the voice, or the echoes of the voice, of a Master, living, personal, and sovereign? ...

[110] How far this initial religious knowledge comes from without, and how far from within, how much is natural, how much implies a special divine aid which is above nature, we have no means of determining, nor is it necessary for my present purpose to determine. [111] I am not engaged in tracing the image of God in the mind of a child or a man to its first origins, but showing that he can become possessed of such an image, over and above all mere notions of God, and in what that image consists. Whether its elements, latent in the mind, would ever be elicited without extrinsic help is very doubtful; but whatever be the actual history of the first formation of the divine image within us, so far at least is certain, that, by informations external to ourselves, as time goes on, it admits of being strengthened and improved. It is certain too, that, whether it grows brighter and stronger, or, on the other hand, is dimmed, distorted, or obliterated, depends on each of us individually, and on his circumstances. It is more than probable that, in the event, from neglect, from the temptations of life, from bad companions, or from the urgency of secular occupations, the light of the soul will fade away and die out. Men transgress their sense of duty, and gradually lose those sentiments of shame and fear, the natural supplements of transgression, which, as I have said, are the witnesses of the Unseen Judge. And, even were it deemed impossible that those who had in their first youth a genuine apprehension of Him, could ever utterly lose it, yet that apprehension may become almost undistinguishable from an inferential acceptance of the great truth, or may dwindle into a mere notion of their intellect. ...

Assent and Inference

Simple Assent

[166] Treating the subject then, not according to *à priori* fitness, but according to the facts of human nature, as they are found in the concrete action of life, I find numberless cases in which we do not assent at all, none in which assent is evidently conditional;–and many, as I shall now proceed to show, in which it is unconditional, and these in subject-matters which admit of nothing higher than probable reasoning. If human nature is to be its own witness, there is no medium between assenting and not assenting. Locke's theory of the duty of assenting more or less according to degrees of evidence, is invalidated by the testimony of high and low, young and old, ancient and modern, as continually given in their ordinary sayings and doings. Indeed, as I have [167] shown, he does not strictly maintain it himself; yet, though he feels the claims of nature and fact to be too strong for him in certain cases, he gives no reason why he should violate his theory in these, and yet not in many more.

Now let us review some of those assents, which men give on evidence short of intuition and demonstration, yet which are as unconditional as if they had that highest evidence.

First of all, starting from intuition, of course we all believe, without any doubt, that we exist; that we have an individuality and identity all our own; that we think, feel, and act, in the home of our own minds; that we have a present sense of good and evil, of a right and a wrong, of a true and a false, of a beautiful and a hideous, however we analyze our ideas of them. We have an absolute vision before us of what happened yesterday or last year, so as to be able without any chance of mistake to give evidence upon it in a court of justice, let the consequences be ever so serious. We are sure that of many things we are ignorant, that of many things we are in doubt, and that of many things we are not in doubt.

Nor is the assent which we give to facts limited to the range of self-consciousness. We are sure beyond all hazard of a mistake, that our own self is not the only being existing; that there is an external world, that it is a system with parts and a whole, a universe carried on by laws; and that the future is affected by the past. We accept and hold with an unqualified assent, that the earth, considered as a phenomenon, is a globe; that all its regions see the sun by turns; that there are vast tracts on it of land and water; [168] that there are really existing cities on definite sites, which go by the names of London, Paris, Florence, and Madrid. We are sure that Paris or London, unless swallowed up by an earthquake or burned to the ground, is to-day just what it was yesterday, when we left it.

We laugh to scorn the idea that we had no parents, though we have no memory of our birth; that we shall never depart this life, though we can have no experience of the future; that we are able to live without food, though we have never tried; that a world of men did not live before our time, or that that world has had no history; that there has been no rise and fall of states, no great men, no wars, no revolutions, no art, no science, no literature, no religion.

We should be either indignant or amused at the report of our intimate friend being false to us; and we are able sometimes, without any hesitation, to accuse certain parties of hostility and injustice to us. We may have a deep consciousness, which we never can lose, that we on our part have been cruel to others, and that they have felt us to be so, or that we have been, and have been felt to be, ungenerous to those who love us. We may have an overpowering sense of our moral weakness, of the precariousness of our life, health, wealth, position, and good fortune. We may have a clear view of the weak points of our physical constitution, of what food or medicine is good for us, and what does us harm. We may be able to master, at least in part, the course of our past history; its turning-points, our hits, and our great mistakes. We may have a sense of the presence of a Supreme Being, which never has been dimmed [169] by even a passing shadow, which has inhabited us ever since we can recollect any thing, and which we cannot imagine our losing. We may be able, for others have been able, so to realize the precepts and truths of Christianity, as deliberately to surrender our life, rather than transgress the one or to deny the other.

On all these truths we have an immediate and an unhesitating hold, nor do we think ourselves guilty of not loving truth for truth's sake, because we cannot reach them through a series of intuitive propositions. Assent on reasonings not demonstrative is too widely recognized an act to be irrational, unless man's nature is irrational, too familiar to the prudent and clear-minded to be an infirmity or an extravagance. None of us can think or act without the acceptance of truths, not intuitive, not demonstrated, yet sovereign. If our nature has any constitution, any laws, one of them is this absolute reception of propositions as true, which lie outside the narrow range of conclusions to which logic, formal or virtual, is tethered ...

[171] My own opinion is, that the class of writers of whom I have been speaking, have themselves as little misgiving about the truths which they pretend to weigh out and measure, as their unsophisticated neighbours; but they think it a duty to remind us, that since the full etiquette of logical requirements has not been satisfied, we must believe those truths at our peril. They warn us, that an issue which can never come to pass in matter of fact, is nevertheless in theory a possible supposition. They do not, for instance, intend for a moment to imply that there is even the shadow of a doubt that Great Britain is an island, but they think we ought to know, if we do not know, that there is no proof of the fact, in mode and figure, equal to the proof of a proposition of Euclid; and that in consequence they and we are all bound to suspend our judgment about such a fact, though it be in an infinitesimal degree, lest we should seem not to love truth for truth's sake. Having made their protest, they subside without scruple into that same absolute assurance of only partially-proved truths, which is natural to the illogical imagination of the multitude. ...

Inference

Informal Inference
[276] It is plain that formal logical sequence is not in fact the method by which we are enabled to become certain of what is concrete; and it is equally plain, from what has been already suggested, what the real and necessary method is. It is the cumulation of probabilities, independent of each other, arising out of the nature and circumstances of the particular case which is under review; probabilities too fine to avail separately, too subtle and circuitous to be convertible into syllogisms, too numerous and various for such conversion, even were they convertible. As a man's portrait differs from a sketch of him, in having, not merely a continuous outline, but all its details filled in, and shades and colours laid on and harmonized together, such is the multiform and intricate process of ratiocination, necessary for our reaching him as a concrete fact, compared with the rude operation of syllogistic treatment. ...
[280] This I conceive to be the real method of reasoning in concrete matters; and it has these characteristics:–First, it does not supersede the logical form of inference, but is one and the same with it; only it is no longer an abstraction, but carried out into the realities of life, its premisses being instinct with the

substance and the momentum of that mass of probabilities, which, acting upon each other in correction and confirmation, carry it home definitely to the individual case, which is its original scope.

Next, from what has been said it is plain, that such a process of reasoning is more or less implicit, and without the direct and full advertence of the mind exercising it. As by the use of our eyesight we recognize two brothers, yet without being able to express what it is by which we distinguish them; as at first sight we perhaps confuse them together, but, on better knowledge, we see no likeness between them at all; as it requires an artiste's eye to determine what lines and shades make a countenance look young or old, amiable, thoughtful, angry or conceited, the principle of discrimination being in each case real, but implicit;—so is the mind unequal to a complete analysis of the motives which carry it on to a particular conclusion, and is swayed and determined by [281] a body of proof, which it recognizes only as a body, and not in its constituent parts.

And thirdly, it is plain, that, in this investigation of the method of concrete inference, we have not advanced one step towards depriving inference of its conditional character; for it is still as dependent on premises, as it is in its elementary idea. On the contrary, we have rather added to the obscurity of the problem; for a syllogism is at least a demonstration, when the premises are granted, but a cumulation of probabilities [sic], over and above their implicit character, will vary both in their number and their separate estimated value, according to the particular intellect which is employed upon it. It follows that what to one intellect is a proof is not so to another, and that the certainty of a proposition does properly consist in the certitude of the mind which contemplates it. And this of course may be said without prejudice to the objective truth or falsehood of propositions, since it does not follow that these propositions on the one hand are not true, and based on right reason, and those on the other not false, and based on false reason, because not all men discriminate them in the same way. ...

[306] This certitude and this evidence are often called moral; a word which I avoid, as having a very vague meaning; but using it here for once, I observe that moral evidence and moral certitude are all that we can attain, not only in the case of ethical and spiritual subjects, such as religion, but of terrestrial and cosmical questions also. So far, physical Astronomy and Revelation stand on the same footing. ...

[307] This being the state of the case, the question arises,

whether, granting that the personality (so to speak) of the parties reasoning is an important element in proving propositions in concrete matter, any account can be given of the ratiocinative process in such [308] proofs, over and above that analysis into syllogism which is possible in each of its steps in detail. I think there can; though I fear, lest to some minds it may appear far-fetched or fanciful; however, I will hazard this imputation. I consider, then, that the principle of concrete reasoning is parallel to the method of proof which is the foundation of modern mathematical science, as contained in the celebrated lemma with which Newton opens his "Principia." We know that a regular polygon, inscribed in a circle, its sides being continually diminished, tends to become that circle, as its limit; but it vanishes before it has coincided with the circle, so that its tendency to be the circle, though ever nearer fulfilment, never in fact gets beyond a tendency. In like manner, the conclusion in a real or concrete question is foreseen and predicted rather than actually attained; foreseen in the number and direction of accumulated premises, which all converge to it, and approach it, as the result of their combination, more nearly than any assignable difference, yet do not touch it logically, (though only not touching it,) on account of the nature of its subject-matter, and the delicate and implicit character of at least part of the reasonings on which it depends. It is by the strength, variety, or multiplicity of premises, which are only probable, not by well-connected syllogisms,–by objections overcome, by adverse theories neutralized, by difficulties gradually clearing up, by exceptions proving the rule, by unlooked-for correlations found with received truths, by suspense and delay in the process issuing in triumphant reactions,–by all these ways, and many others, the practised and experienced mind [309] is able to make a sure divination that a conclusion is inevitable, of which his lines of reasoning do not actually put him in possession. This is what is meant by a proposition being "as good as proved," a conclusion as undeniable "as if it were proved," and by the reasons for it "amounting to a proof," for a proof is the limit of probabilities. ...

[332] The sole and final judgment on the validity of an inference in concrete matter is committed to a mental faculty, which I have called the Illative Sense.

MAURICE BLONDEL (1861-1949)

Blondel was born in Dijon, France in 1861. He studied with Émile Boutroux and Léon Ollé-Laprune at the École Normale Supérieure from 1881-1886. After receiving his aggregation in 1886, he taught at several lycées throughout France and then at St. Stanislas College in Paris from 1891-1892. He received a doctorate in philosophy from the Sorbonne in 1893, and eventually settled in at the University of Aix-en-Provence where he was professor from 1897-1927. Blondel came under suspicion during the Modernist Crisis and felt it best to shutter, in 1913, the journal he had purchased some years earlier–the *Annales de Philosophie Chrétienne*. Blondel died in Aix-en-Provence in 1949. Some hold that the encyclical *Pascendi dominici gregis* (1907), nn. 7-13, 19-22, 32-39 of Pius X targets Blondel's thought, or at least positions similar to his own, when it condemns vital immanentism (see also *Humani generis* (1950), nn. 25-26). Despite this Blondel's thought was influential on Transcendental Thomists, such as Karl Rahner, and proponents of Nouvelle Théologie or Ressourcement, such as Henri de Lubac.

The following selections are from Blondel's *Action (1893)*, trans. James M. Somerville (Washington: Corpus Books, 1968), IV:ii:2, pp. 237-246; and *The Letter on Apologetics and History and Dogma* (New York: Holt, Rinehart, and Winston, 1964): I, 6, pp. 145-150; II, 1-2, pp. 151-160. In these works Blondel presents his method of immanence wherein we come to God as the satisfaction of our deepest desires–that is, seeing God as the "one thing necessary" to bring the quest for ultimate fulfillment to an end, the quest of what Blondel calls the "willing will." In the end this means choosing concretely with our "willed will" to renounce the sufficiency of the natural order, embracing the mortification of the self, and turning our will wholly to God, ultimately substituting the divine will for our own, an act that only divine grace can ultimately perform. Blondel sees this immanent method of apologetics, i.e. showing how God's revelation answers our deepest needs, as the best method for the modern mind (see his *Letter on Apologetics*, p. 193). Or as he puts it: "It is therefore asking too much of philosophy to wish to introduce it into questions of detail about the 'Christian fact' and to make it ratify or confirm, in its own way, the autonomous conclusions of historical apologetics. But, on the other hand, it is to ask too little of it if we restrict it to the purely negative function of dismissing the objections of naturalism and procure from it the mere statement of a possibility. If the fact is to be accepted by our minds and even impose upon our reason, an inner need and a sort of imperious appetite must prepare us for it ... [and we must show] the profound affinities between Christianity and our human nature, its perfect adaptation to our needs and its internal harmony" (*The Letter on Apologetics*, 1964, pp. 135-136).

On Blondel see: Blanchette, Oliva, *Maurice Blondel: A Philosophical Life* (Grand Rapids: William B. Eerdmans, 2010); Koerpel, Robert, *Maurice Blondel* (Notre Dame: University of Notre Dame Press, 2018).

Action: Essay on a Critique of Life and a Science of Practice (1893)[4]

The Necessary Being of Action: The Life of Action

[237] One thing is certain: action cannot be enclosed within the natural order, that is, within the order of phenomena. It comes from and has repercussions in a region that transcends all temporal dimensions. Yet, by himself, man cannot recover the source of his own spontaneity. If he presumes to limit himself to those things that are within his power, he can never hope to be fully what he [238] already is at the source of his action. By doing his own will, he only succeeds in making it impossible to equal his true will.

The beginning of wisdom, as already pointed out, is the discovery and acknowledgment of this powerlessness to will all that one wills. And yet something in us continues to aspire to what is a human impossibility. Assistance is needed. It can come neither from ourselves nor from the world of phenomena. Yet we cannot commandeer the mysterious presence in things and in ourselves in order to force from it what it alone can give. How then can a man "move" the unmovable so that it may accord the gift of life? We must be ready to break our hearts rather than our heads to win this secret mediation. This means that we must see the truth of our situation: that we are ignorant, weak, and helpless, and that in spite of this the natural order is full enough to point the way to something more but insufficient to provide it. Yet, even this realization is insufficient. ...

The Necessary Condition for Moral Rectitude

The primary rule for moral action is a simple one: act according to your lights; give yourself to what you sincerely believe to be good. But suppose one's conscience is involuntarily and invincibly in error? Even then one must adhere to the good as one knows it or run the risk of being condemned by one's own higher judgment. Superstitious rites are sanctified by the intention which carries beyond the symbolic act, so that it can become the vehicle of expression for the good will. In obeying the light that we have, we remain open to a more complete truth. There is no substitute for the generosity of the sincere will.

---

4 [Maurice Blondel, *Total Commitment: Blondel's L'Action,* translated by James Somerville (Washington: Corpus Books, 1968). Public Domain.]

[239] But this generosity, while it represents the triumph of the will, is inseparable from sacrifice; it embodies the agony and the ecstasy of our human condition. The triumph of the will lies in its adherence to the order of values that has emerged in the course of the investigation; for the hierarchy of goods manifests the deepest desire of the authentic will. But conformity to the order involves an apparent sacrifice, even though fidelity to moral obligation is, in fact, conformity to our own best interests.

It is an error to suppose that man is called on to accomplish all possible good: *bona omnino facere*. The sacrifice which the moral life requires concerns the quality of our acts rather than the quantity. It is more important to do well the little good that we do accomplish: *bene omnia facere*, than to equate rectitude with the desire of an ambitious will to exhaust every human possibility. Since we are not self-sufficient, we translate more faithfully our real situation when we are ready to subordinate our own desires to the sovereign authority of another will, whether we discover the precepts of that will by a more profound analysis of our own volitional life or in the accumulated wisdom of the ages expressed in the moral axioms of one's society. The task of the moral philosopher is to show that man's true interests are safeguarded only when he is faithful to the universal order. If we do only what pleases us or seems to have an immediate cash value, we do not go far in the moral life. And they do not even enter it who feel that their dignity is slighted if they submit to any obligations which they do not impose on themselves. While there are instances when fulfilling an obligation is a pleasure, for the most part obedience to the light requires humility, abnegation, and a victory over self. It is a question of integrating the individual into the universal order, ... subordinating our will to a will other than our own.

A constant illusion in human action is the notion that, in sacrificing the attractions that promise an immediate satisfaction, we are cutting ourselves off from the possibility of self-realization. What we renounce seems to be forever lost. But fidelity to duty opens our eyes to another world. A decision that brings a moment [240] of anguish is like the pain of childbirth; it offers an apparent nothing to the senses, only to bring us into contact with a superior presence and a new life that rewards us for our travail. The only way to encounter the absolute is to be willing to annihilate everything else before it. And then its presence can be found everywhere. Moral disinterestedness is the art of having nothing in order to have all.

This detachment does not mean that we disdain particular

values; for the infinite is only available to us under its finite manifestations. What it does mean is that when alternatives solicit our adherence, we consult, not our personal preference, not our immediate satisfaction, but the imperative of obligation. No doubt, in spuming every other real or apparent good in favor of the value that duty prescribes, we seem to sacrifice the universe. But this limitation of our choice to what is, morally speaking, the one thing necessary, restores the universal and the infinite to the particular; for by surrendering to the determinism of obligation, human action participates in the free necessity of God. If this seems like a kind of death to the sensual and the proud, it is because duty immolates the passions. But it also brings with it the indispensable liberation from the determinism of the appetites. One must die in order to live. By exchanging one determinism for another, we move from darkness to light. Every time that we respond to the imperative of duty, we allow a new life and a new will to act in us. Thus, the martyrdom of the acquisitive will not only enables us to see how suffering and death enter into the original aspiration of the sincere will–because "where there is less of ourselves, there is more of Him"–but it takes its place as one of the means in the determinism of action. What is a scandal for the secular and the profane, becomes an instrument of liberation for those who are generous. But only those who practice self-renunciation and generosity are in a position to understand "what reason demands when it goes as far as it ought to go."

Love and Suffering

If, at the source of every good action, there is an element of renunciation and a perpetual dying to self, [241] there should be no cause for surprise that suffering and sacrifice are inseparable from the development of the whole moral life. It is no secret that those who achieve something in this life usually undergo a painful apprenticeship. But it is one thing to endure the hardships that nature imposes and quite another to consent to suffering, to love it, and to look upon it as a gift. Yet in this light even the act of dying can be embraced with affection; for it then appears as but the last act, the act *par excellence*, in the long series of means for the expansion of the will as it seeks to make explicit all the content that was hidden at the source of action.

The measure of the human heart is the welcome that it accords to suffering, for it impresses on man something that is other than himself. But let there be no mistake about our natural revulsion against it. No matter how well prepared we are for it, when it comes it is always other than what we expected. Under its austere discipline even those who stand up to it and accept it gracefully cannot refrain from hating it. It kills something in us in order to replace it with something that does not come from ourselves. So it is not really suffering that we love but this "other" that is revealed to us through its agency. Suffering enters into us like a seed that is buried in the ground; we seem to share in the corruption and decomposition of the seed, but this incipient death is only the herald of a new life and resurrection. While suffering "spoils, embitters, and hardens those it does not soften", when it is welcomed as a vehicle for expressing one's devotion, it introduces an element of tenderness and becomes a proof of love as well as a trial. Unless we have suffered for something or from something, we cannot really know or love it. Love always exacts a painful surrender of self and a willingness to become passive before the action of another. Taken as a necessary stage in the expanding logic of life, suffering prevents us from acclimatizing ourselves in this world and finding an equilibrium. "The worst possible thing would be not to suffer, as though one's equilibrium had been found and the problem already resolved." It is easy to pretend that the course of life is satisfactory when we have all we need, but let [242] real pain show its face and all our theories and speculations seem empty and absurd. Suffering then becomes the intruder, the inexplicable, the unknown, the infinite, and it cuts through life like a revealing sword.

Love acts on the soul as suffering and death act on the body: they dispossess us and leave us open to the action of the unknown. But once we understand that it is only on this condition that we can awaken to the mysterious presence of the infinite within us, suffering ceases to be the scandal of reason. It then comes to us as a gift which enables us to will and to ratify all things. "When one has learned the secret of finding sweetness in bitterness itself, everything is sweet."

Pain, patiently endured, is much more than the practical proof of a generous will; it is so inseparable from the act of loving that everything that is not the beloved becomes painful. How can the exile sing the canticle of the Lord on an alien soil? "One is more where one loves than where one is." No personal satisfaction can enrich the one who loves the good more than his good. He can more easily deprive himself of all things than content himself with what is less than all. To love and to suffer are so much a part of human life that even those who seem not to love anything but themselves suffer from the inquietude that besets the most generous hearts. Even those who think that they have achieved equilibrium through good fortune are unable to rest in their possessions. Rarely are they satisfied with what they have; for it seems a mere nothing compared with what they still desire. And so it is. Human action and its range are measured, not by what man achieves, but in terms of what he does not yet have. If we want to direct our lives in the way of truth, we must learn to love each disappointment and deception that reminds us of our grandeur, always looking for the truth and reality that lie hidden in privation. No doubt it is hard to find satisfaction in the experience of want, but nothing is more instructive or salutary. For the less we have, the more easily do we understand that our true happiness lies in the possession of all that we are able to get along without.

Active Religious Expectancy

[243] The willingness to accept suffering and sacrifice is a necessary condition for the achievement of action. But by themselves they have no magic power to enable man to realize his destiny. Alone, we cannot complete the great work of salvation because we have not begun it. After having striven as though everything depends on ourselves, we must await as though everything comes from God. It is not merely a question of recognizing that abnegation and the painful renunciation of our own will are insufficient; we must also see that this renunciation itself is not entirely man's own work. Human action proceeds from man, but it is sustained by a superior action. ... The deed is not the result of two component forces; it proceeds, rather, from an active communion in which two wills achieve a common work. Each acts in virtue of the whole, yet each needs the other; so that if it is true to say that man can do nothing without God, it is also true that only man can perform a human act.·

But having made this distinction, it must be qualified by another. Man does not have within him the power to will and to accomplish. We cannot move from desire to execution without drawing upon the divine assistance. But this does not excuse us from the need to act, as though, having conceived a good and noble intention, we might then withdraw from active engagement on the assumption that God will do the rest. Two extremes must be avoided: the notion that what man is able to accomplish is in every sense the product of an autonomous will, and the equally fatuous belief that he is able to accomplish anything without voluntary effort. So, as far as effort is concerned, it is not out of place to repeat that we must always act as though everything depended on ourselves. This does not imply a return to the old illusion that man is self-sufficient. Life is too precarious and the future too uncertain to warrant any undue confidence in man's ability to control them.

Indeed, it is precisely man's fear of the future that convince [244] him of his contingency. Action always involves a risk. No matter how carefully we plan, we can never be certain of the outcome of our decisions. Yet action is still a necessity, for we cannot live on dreams and good intentions. Fortunately, our weakness and fallibility are also the source of our strength; for if we cannot do anything without the divine assistance, we may also be sure that it will never be lacking in all that we do attempt in good faith. Thus, while the element of risk is never absent because of our lack of knowledge, we should never lack the confidence that is essential if our projects are to be undertaken with courage. Courage is not the virtue of one who acts blindly but of one who ... trusts in the assistance of one who is more than himself.

Since man's destiny lies in the future and since it cannot be realized without action and effort, we die the moment we pretend that we have arrived at the goal. We must begin anew at every moment, carrying into the battle the brave assurance of the young soldier and the timidity of the novice, eager to perform well but with the detachment that liberates us from the illusion that man's only duty is to prolong his earthly life in order to enjoy its delicacies. If this detachment, which is indispensable for the moral life, seems like a burden, it is good to consult the experience of those who have borne it faithfully. At first it appears to be uninviting and hard to endure, but as one advances it grows lighter, until, at the end, it carries us more than we carry it. Strange burden, which gives wings to the soul, like the swallow's wings which are a liability when it is on the ground; but once aloft, they bear the creature of song beyond the clouds. ...

Similarly, the onus of duty carries human action beyond time and space and all that is finite. But it does not relieve us of the persistent inquietude that is experienced as a hunger for all that we do not have. In the drama of human action, to be satisfied with the perishable goods of fortune or the senses is to begin to die to the life of action. It means that the ardor of desire is burning low, that the will has abandoned the quest. It is necessary, then, not only to desire, but to desire to desire more than we can achieve [245] by ourselves. There is no limit to what we can achieve once we have learned the art of receiving.

Even to our desire for good desires, we must place beyond

ourselves the origin of this voluntary movement. Even when we ask nothing more than to have something to give, this prayer does not come entirely from us, and it is a prayer only to the extent that we implicitly acknowledge it. To the absolute initiative of man it is necessary to substitute freely–even as it is necessarily present–the absolute initiative of God. It is not up to us to give it to ourselves, nor even to give ourselves to ourselves. Our role is to bring it about that God be in us entirely, as indeed He is, and to recover at the very source of our consent to His sovereign action His efficacious presence. The true will of man is the divine willing. For man, the perfection of activity is to acknowledge one's profound passivity. Whoever recognizes that God does all, receives from God the gift of having done all. Not to appropriate anything as one's own is the unique method of acquiring the infinite.

To fill in the bare outline of the creature that we are, we need only persevere in sincerity and act according to our best lights. No knowledge of abstract science is necessary, nor is there any need to be able to name the unknown presence whose abode is prepared when man empties himself of himself. If truth is only poured out into empty vessels, the measure of the void within us, and therefore of the presence of what is not ourselves, is the acute sense of need. And this experience, in turn, supposes an initial generosity and rectitude. We can give the impression by this kind of analysis that what we are describing is highly complex, but in reality the disposition of active religious expectancy is a very simple one. A secret movement of the heart or a sudden burst of authentic desire is often enough to produce it, yet it is capable of making the infinite a vital reality in our lives.

But, suppose that one has sacrificed all that one has and is, loving the invisible above all, ready to suffer the loss of all things and to die, if need be, since it now appears to be impossible to touch being without passing through death: all this indicates man's willingness to bear witness to the absolute and to prefer it to what is passing. Nevertheless, it is of little value unless we are conscious, not only of our natural impotence, but of the [246] impossibility of achieving our necessary end by any of the means that have been uncovered so far.

It [the supernatural] too takes its place in the dynamism of action. Human science does not have to discover whether it is real or even possible; it ought to show, in the name of the determinism, that it is necessary. ... Absolutely impossible and absolutely necessary for man that is the proper notion of the supernatural.

Letter on Apologetics (1896)[5]

The Various Methods of Apologetics and Their Import

Of the Services Rendered by the Old Method and Its Inconsistency from the Standpoint of Philosophy

[145] This form of argument [called objective, scientific, or the doctrinal method of traditional apologetics], that which is 'always given at the beginning of theology in the treatise on religion' has been rightly summed up for us as follows:[6] 'Reason proves the existence of God It is possible that he has revealed himself. History shows that he has done so, and it also proves the authenticity of the Scriptures and the authority of the Church. Catholicism is thus established upon a truly scientific rational basis'. ...

[146] Thomism seems to many an exact but, if I may so put it, a *static* account: as a building-up of elements, but one in which our passage from one to another remains something external to us; as an inventory, but not as an invention capable of justifying advances in thought by the dynamism which it communicates. Once a man has entered this system, he is himself assured; and from the centre of the fortress he can defend himself against all assaults and rebut all objections on points of detail. But first he must effect his own entrance.

And since the Thomist starts from principles which, for the most part, are disputed in our time; since he does not offer the means of restoring them by his method; since he presupposes a host of assertions which are just those which are nowadays called in question; since he cannot provide, in his system, for the new requirements of minds which must be approached on their own ground, one must not tend to treat this triumphant exposition as the last word. We are still in the life of struggle and suffering; and to understand this is itself a good and a gain. We must not exhaust ourselves refurbishing old arguments and presenting an *object* for acceptance while the *subject* is not disposed to listen. It is not divine truth which is at fault but human preparation, and it is here that our effort should be concentrated. And it is not just an affair of adaptation or temporary expediency; for this function of

---

[5] [Maurice Blondel, *The Letter on Apologetics and History and Dogma*, translated by Alexander Dru and Illtyd Trethowan. Copyright © 1964 by Holt, Rinehart, and Winston. Public Domain.]

[6] See *Le Monde*, 20th May, 1895. The report of a conference at Issy on the conditions of modern apologetics.

subjective preparation is of first importance; it is essential and permanent, if [147] it is true that man's action co-operates all along the line with that of God. ...

What do we find, from this point of view, if we look at the history of human thought since the time when our doctrinal apologetics, which have not been overhauled fundamentally in the meanwhile, corresponded to the mental climate in which men really live?

At first, that is, when scholasticism was in the ascendant, the natural and the supernatural orders were placed one above the other, [148] but in touch, in an ascending hierarchy. There were three zones, as it were, on different levels: on the lowest, reason was in sole charge, *mundus traditur disputationibus hominum* [the world is handed over to the disputations of humans]; on the highest, faith alone revealed to us the mystery of divine life and that of our summons to the feast of God; between the two was a meeting-ground where reason discovered in an incomplete way the more important of natural truths, and these were confirmed and further explained by faith. By thus bearing upon certain common *objects*, these two currents, flowing from different sources, mingled their waters without losing their identities. But there was hardly any thought of examining in a critical spirit what might be called the subjective possibility or the formal compatibility of these two orders.

Soon, however, this dualism began to appear less as a solution than as a statement of the problem, which is, in fact, the great philosophical and religions problem. In a spirit of violent reaction against Aristotelian and Scholastic intellectualism, Protestantism rejected any idea of a rational preparation for faith and began by pulling down the whole edifice of reason and liberty only to build it up again in an independent integrity, no longer regarded as a mere ground floor. Thus there was no longer any middle zone, which might now have become a battle ground rather than a meeting-place. The orders were no longer *hierarchically arranged* but merely *juxtaposed* without any possible communication or intelligible relation between them; they were supposed to be united only in the mysterious intimacy of an individual's faith. As a result, when reason, left sole mistress of the knowable world, claimed to find immanent in herself all the truths needed for the life of man, the world of faith found itself totally excluded; juxtaposition led to *opposition* and incompatibility.

Faced by this rationalism which makes immanence the condition of all philosophy, we have to ask whether, in the only order which remains, there does not reappear an imperious need for the other one. ...

[150] If, then, doctrinal apologetics, in its old form, leaves intact the problem which seems to us today the very basis of religious philosophy, how is the problem to be put, by what method is it to be approached? What can be said on a subject of such complexity and delicacy which will strike home and remain strictly philosophical?

The Really Philosophical Point in the Religious Problem and the Right Method of Approaching It

How the Philosophical Problem Should Be Put If Religion Is Not To Be Simply a Philosophy and Philosophy Is Not To Be Absorbed in Any Way by Religion

[151] „, In a phrase which must be explained but which indicates at once the seriousness of the conflict, modern thought, with a jealous susceptibility, considers the notion of *immanence* as the very condition of [152] philosophizing; that is to say, if among current ideas there is one which it regards as marking a definite advance, it is the idea, which is at bottom perfectly true, that nothing can enter into a man's mind which does not come out of him and correspond in some way to a need for development and that there is nothing in the nature of historical or traditional teaching or obligation imposed from without which counts for him, no truth and no precept which is acceptable, unless it is in some sort autonomous and autochthonous. On the other hand, nothing is Christian and Catholic unless it is *supernatural*, not only transcendent in the simple metaphysical sense of the word, because there could be truth or beings superior to ourselves which we could nevertheless affirm immanently by the use of our own powers, but strictly supernatural, that is to say, beyond the power of man to discover for himself and yet imposed on his thought and on his will.

Thus, it seems, the chief and indeed the unique aim of philosophy is to assure the full liberty of mind, to guarantee the autonomous life of thought, and to determine in complete independence the conditions which establish its sway. Can there be, then, any possible connection between philosophy and Christianity, since the one seems to exclude the other? The first step, if their very coexistence is to be conceivable, is to show that they can meet and collide; it will be less difficult to show, after that, that this collision is not possible unless there is agreement at the heart of the conflict. The initial effort, without which no other has any philosophical value, is to indicate the point of encounter–that and nothing else. ...

[154] ... If Christianity were a belief and a way of life added to our nature and our reason as something optional, if we could develop in our integrity without this addition and we could refuse deliberately and with impunity the crushing weight of the supernatural gift, there would be no intelligible [155] connection between these two levels, one of which, from the rational point of view, might just as well not exist. Not to climb upwards would not be to fall down; and to renounce the higher vocation would be simply to remain on the lower level where men could grow spontaneously–so that no philosophical problem about a Revelation could conceivably arise. But as soon as this Revelation seeks us out, so to speak, on our own ground and pursues us into our inner fastnesses, as soon as it regards a neutral or negative attitude as a positive backsliding and a sort of culpable hostility, as soon as the poverty of our limited being can contract a debt which must be paid for in eternity, then the encounter takes place, the difficulty stares us in the face and the problem is set. For if it is true that the demands of Revelation are well-founded, then we are no longer simply on our own ground; and there must be some trace of this insufficiency, this impotence, this demand in man simply as man, and an echo of it even in the most autonomous philosophy. ...

Of the Right Method of Pinning Down the Precisely Philosophical Point of the Religious Problem

[156] ... The bold and successful move which it now seems indispensable for us to make in our own defense is to have recourse to the 'method of immanence' and to apply it to the full, with an inflexible rigour, to the examination of human destiny: nothing else will define the difficult and nothing else will resolve it; and then the solution, like the problem itself, becomes possible only by forcing us to be equally faithful to philosophy and to orthodoxy, or rather by forcing philosophy, like orthodoxy, to remain faithful to itself. ...

[157] ... The method of immanence, then, can consist in nothing else than in trying to equate, in our own consciousness, what we appear to think and to will and to do with what we do and will and think in actual fact–so that behind factitious negations and ends which are not genuinely willed may be discovered our innermost affirmations and the implacable needs which they

imply.

If the meaning of modern philosophy escapes so many who have not lived the life of their own age but in the past, if so many current doctrines seem to them vague or enigmatic, this is doubtless because they have quite failed to grasp the principle of this method, which has become and will be more and more the soul of philosophy. ... [Philosophy's] special business is to criticize all the phenomena which make up our inner life, each one in light of the others, to adjust them, to study the connections between them, to show all their implications, to discover what principles are presupposed by thought and action, to define on what conditions we may ascribe reality to objects or the means of salvation which are inevitably conceived by us, to study (for example) our idea of God, not just as God, but in so far as it is our necessary and effective thought of God, or again to analyse the conception which we are led to form of revealed beliefs and practices, not just as religious and redemptive Revelation, but in so far as we can see them as answering to our needs—in short, without attempting to add to this conception what it cannot give us.

Thus the immanent affirmation of the transcendent, even of the supernatural, does not prejudge in any way the transcendent reality of the immanent affirmations—a radical distinction which no one, perhaps, has preserved in complete consistency, and which enables us to construct in a scientific manner, without distracting preoccupations or fruitless or premature discussions, the entire phenomenology [158] of thought and action. It is the only distinction which is capable of securing the mutual independence of the two orders and it is, moreover, in conformity with the very letter of the dogma which maintains the pure liberality of the author of grace together with the obligation laid upon us men. Formally identical with objective faith, subjective faith is entirely at the mercy of rational criticism, while objective faith remains untouched.

It remains to show—perhaps to the surprise of certain philosophers and equally of certain theologians—that the only possible religious philosophy, which is truly religious and truly a philosophy, results from these principles.

For when we study the close-knit system of our thoughts, it becomes apparent that the very notion of immanence is realized in our consciousness only by the effective presence of the notion of the transcendent. The idea of an absolute intellectual and moral [159] autonomy is conceivable only on condition of our conceiving also, and necessarily, of a possible heteronomy. And if the method of immanence is confined to determining the dynamism of our experience, without pronouncing in the first place on its subjective or objective significance, it is simply a matter of analysing this inevitable idea of a dependence of human reason and human will with all the consequences which it implies. Then there would be no longer any ground for saying that the problem of the supernatural, resulting as it does from the hidden workings of thought which I have just indicated, is inconceivable or inadmissible or unphilosophical; on the contrary, it is the very condition of philosophy as it is now presented in its intransigent independence. And this movement of free thought and exclusive rationalism, becoming fully conscious of itself and reaching, so to speak, the very end of its course, was precisely what was required so that there should arise as philosophical hypothesis the religious thesis on which the whole movement logically depends, so that one may see clearly what its very existence implies. It is when it is fully developed that it becomes most clearly incomplete. Thus we are in line with the defenders of the rights of reason and in a state of philosophical grace. And, at the same time, we are on safe ground in regard to theology. ...

[160] ... To sum up, theology cannot allow philosophy to reach the reality of the supernatural order, or to deny its truth or to admit its intrinsic possibility (which would be again both too much and too little), or to declare itself indifferent and alien to it, or to juxtapose itself to it, judgment itself sufficient and satisfied in its enclosed [161] inviolability. There is only one relationship required—that which is determined by the method of immanence, which considers the supernatural not as a historic reality, not as simply possible like an arbitrary hypothesis, not as optional like a gift which is proposed but not imposed, not as appropriate to our nature and belonging to it as its supreme development, not as so ineffable as to lack all foothold in our thought and our life, but (with the precision of the scientific spirit, which is concerned neither with the merely possible nor with the real and should give us nothing more nor less than the necessary) as indispensable and at the same time as inaccessible for man.

2 PHENOMENOLOGY

MAX SCHELER (1874-1928)

Max Scheler was born in Munich, Germany in 1874. Growing up in a mixed-faith family, his mother Jewish and his father Lutheran, Scheler instead became sympathetic to Marxism and Catholicism. Foreshadowing his transitory life, after a year studying medicine at the University of Munich (1894-1895), Scheler transferred to the University of Berlin (1895-1896) where he studied philosophy with Wilhelm Dilthey and sociology with Georg Simmel. One year later he moved on to the University of Jena (1896-1897) where he studied with Rudolf Eucken, receiving his doctorate in philosophy in 1897. The year 1899 was quite a momentous one for Scheler, as it was then that he completed his Habilitation at Jena, converted to Catholicism through the influence of his maid, teacher, and likely his fiancée, Amlie von Dewitz, whom he also married that same year. As Amlie von Dewitz was a Catholic, but also a divorcee, she and Max Scheler could only marry in a civil ceremony.

Scheler began his career teaching philosophy at the University of Jena where he was Associate (1899-1901) and Privatdozent (1901-1906), and fell under the influence of Brentano, Husserl, and their phenomenology. Scheler, though, had to leave Jena after he seemed to have had an affair with the wife of a publisher, whom his own wife publicly confronted at a partly and slapped. Scheler returned to Munich and taught as Privatdozent at the University there from 1907 to 1910, and became part of the Munich Circle of Phenomenologists along with Dietrich von Hildebrand. Scheler's time at Munich, however, was once again marred with controversy. Scheler divorced his first wife in 1910 after growing close to the Lutheran Märit Furtwängler, the former fiancée of Von Hildebrand, and the sister of the conductor Wilhelm Furtwängler. He eventually married Märit Furtwängler in a Catholic ceremony in 1912, after annulling his first marriage and receiving a dispensation. Though Scheler's first wife, Amlie von Dewitz, was partially placated by her receiving the dowry of Märit Furtwängler, she still went to the local socialist newspaper, the *Münchener Post*, and accused Max Scheler of affairs, borrowing money from students, and leaving her penniless. Scheler ended up losing his position at Munich in 1910. Scheler subsequently lectured briefly at the Philosophical Society of Göttingen with the aid of Von Hildebrand, where he taught Edith Stein. Scheler then moved to Berlin in 1912, where he published his major works, and co-founded with Edmund Husserl and others the *Jahrbuch für Philosophie und phänomenologische Forschung*.

Scheler's wife, Märit Furtwängler, converted to Catholicism in 1916, and Scheler entered into a *rapprochement* with the German Government and the Catholic Church. Hence, in 1919 he resurrected his academic career and became professor of philosophy and sociology at the

University of Cologne, where he taught until 1928; he also gave lectures throughout Germany warning of the dangers of National Socialism, hence the Nazis banned the publication of his works in 1933. Scheler's position in Cologne though was becoming precarious due to his divorce from his second wife in 1923, after she refused to allow him a lover on the side per his request, and his civil-marriage to his student Maria Scheu. Scheler also began to distance himself from the Catholic Church in 1922, disappointed with its conservatism, authoritativism, lack of political influence, and presumably its moral teachings on marriages and the fact that the Archbishop of Cologne had forbidden seminarians from studying with Scheler. Scheler, accordingly, moved to Frankfurt in 1928 to work with the Critical Theorists Adorno and Horkheimer at the University of Frankfurt, but he died before assuming his post, inadvertently being given a Catholic funeral ceremony. He is buried in the Suedfriedhof Cemetery, Cologne, along with his third wife.

Scheler's key writings are his *On Ressentiment and Moral Value-Judgment* [*Über Ressentiment und moralisches Werturteil*] (1912 and 1915); *Formalism in Ethics and Non-Formal Ethics of Value* [*Der Formalismus in der Ethik und die materiale Wertethik*], 2 vols. (1913-1916); *On the Eternal in Humans* [*Vom Ewigen im Menschen*] (1921).

Among the many books on Scheler examine: Frings, Manfred S., *Max Scheler* (Pittsburgh: Duquesne University Press, 1964); Deeken, Alfons, *Process and Permanence in Ethics: Max Scheler's Moral Philosophy* (New York: Paulist Press, 1974); Nota, John H., S.J., *Max Scheler: The Man and His Work* (Chicago: Franciscan Herald Press, 1983); Blosser, Phillip, *Scheler's Critique of Kant's Ethic* (Athens: Ohio University Press, 1995); Frings, Manfred S., *The Mind of Max Scheler* (Milwaukee: Marquette University Press, 1997); Kelly, Eugene, *Structure and Diversity: The Phenomenological Philosophy of Max Scheler* (Dordrecht: Kluwer, 1997); Spader, Peter, *Scheler's Ethical Personalism* (New York: Fordham University Press, 2002).

The selection below is from Scheler's work *Formalism in Ethics and Non-Formal Ethics of Values* (Evanston: Northwestern University Press, 1973): I, ii, B, 4-5: 100-110. This work is a critique of Kant's "formal ethics" which reduces ethics to an abstract moral law and distances the moral realm from human life. While Kant rightly separated ethics from hedonism and egoism, Scheler argues that Kant's ethical system needs supplementation with a "non-formal" or "material" ethics—wherein a concrete but *a priori* affective theory of moral values is developed. In this section of his work, Scheler proceeds to describe different moral values phenomenologically and rank them from lower to higher importance: pleasantness, vitality, spirituality (aesthetic, moral, cognitive), and holiness. Accordingly, Scheler notes that lower values, such as vital ones, ought to be sacrificed to higher values, such as spiritual ones (1973: 107). This claim serves as an ironic commentary on the personal life of Scheler, who continually seemed to gravitate to the "lower" hedonistic values and to sacrifice the so-called "higher spiritual" values to them.

Formalism in Ethics and Non-Formal Ethics of Value (1913)[7]

The A Priori Relations between Heights of Values and "Pure" Bearers of Values

[100] We expect an ethics first of all to furnish us with an explicit determination of "higher" and "lower" in the order of values, a determination that is itself based on the contents of the essences of values–insofar as this order is understood to be independent of all possible positive systems of goods and purposes. It is not our aim at this point in the discussion to furnish such a determination. It will be sufficient here to characterize more fully the *kinds* of a priori orders among values.

In this respect we find two orders. One contains the heights of values in their ordered ranks according to their *essential* [*wesenhaften*] *bearers*. The other is a *pure non-formal* order in that it exists only among the ultimate units of the *series of value-qualities*, which we shall call value-modalities.

We shall discuss here the first order mentioned, which can also be called a relatively "*formal*" order when compared with the second. I will first give a brief survey of values with respect to their *essential* bearers.

a. Values of the Person and Values of Things [*Sachwerte*]

The values of the person pertain to the *person* himself, *without any mediation. Values of things* pertain to *things* of value as represented in "goods." Again, goods may be material (goods of enjoyment, of usefulness), vital (all economic goods), or spiritual (science and art, which are also called cultural goods). In contrast to these values there are two kinds of values that belong to the human person: (1) the value of the person "himself," and (2) the values of virtue. In this sense the values of the person are *higher* than those of things. This lies in their *essence*.

b. Values of Oneself [*Eigenwerte*] and Values of the Other [*Fremdwerte*]

The division of values into "*values of oneself*" and "*values of*

---

7 [Max Scheler, *Formalism in Ethics and Non-Formal Ethics of Values: A New Attempt toward the Foundation of an Ethical Personalism*, translated by Manfred S. Frings and Roger L. Funk. Copyright © 1973 by Northwestern University Press. All rights reserved. Used with permission of Northwestern University Press, nupress.northwestern.edu.]

the other" has nothing to do with the former division, values of the person and values of things. For values of oneself and values of the other can be values of persons and values of things, as well [101] as "values of acts," "values of functions," and "values of feeling-states." Values of oneself and values of the other have equal *heights.*[8] It is, however, a valid question (which we shall not discuss here in detail, since we are concerned with *kinds* of a priori relations) whether the very *apprehension* of "values of the other" is of higher value than the apprehension of a value of oneself. It is certain, however, that the act of realizing a value of the other is of *higher* value than the act of realizing a value of oneself.

c. Values of Acts, Values of Functions, and Values of Reactions

Other bearers of values are *acts* (e.g., acts of cognition, love, hate, will), *functions* (e.g., hearing, seeing, feeling), and *responses* and *reactions* (e.g., "to be glad about something"). The last also contain responses to human persons, like cofeeling, revenge, etc., which, in turn, are distinguished from "spontaneous" acts. All of these are subordinated to the values of the person. But they, too, possess a priori relations among their own heights. For instance, the values of acts as such are *higher* than the values of functions, and both are *higher* than the values of mere "responses." Spontaneous manifestations of comportment are of higher value than reactive ones.

d. Values of the Basic Moral Tenor [*Gesinnungswerte*], Values of Deeds, and Values of Success

Values of the basic moral tenor and values of deeds (both are moral values as opposed to "*values of success*") , as well as the bearers of values between them, such as "intention," "resolve," "performance," are bearers of values having a specific order of heights (apart from their own special contents). But this order will not be further discussed here.[9] ...

---

[8] Eduard von Hartmann correctly proves that values of the other can function as higher values (i.e., higher than proper values) only in ontological pessimism, i.e., when *being* itself is a *disvalue* (see *Phänomenologie des sittlichen Bewusstseins*, Berlin, C. Duncker, 1879). If we were to agree to this (false) presupposition, we would give in to this pessimism.

[9] [Section e discusses the values of intentional vs. feeling states; f the values of relations, and g individual vs. collective or communal values.]

h. Self-Values and Consecutive Values

[103] There are values which retain their value-character independent of all other values. There are also values which by essence possess a *phenomenal* (intuitively feelable) relatedness to other values which is necessary for their being "values." The former I call *self-values*; the latter, *consecutive values*.

But we must remember that all things representing themselves as "*means*" for *causal* productions of goods, and all mere *symbols* of values (insofar as they are *only* that), have *no immediate* or *phenomenal* value and are not independent bearers of values. The so-called value of a mere "means" attributed to a thing (in the form of a "judgment")[10] is attributable to it only by virtue of a calculating act of thinking (or an association) through which this thing represents itself as a "means." Symbols *for* values (e.g., paper money) have no phenomenal value. Therefore, we do not call the value of a "means" or a "symbol" a consecutive value. *Consecutive values* are still *phenomenal* value-facts. Any kind of "*tool-value*," for example, is a genuine consecutive value, for there is intuited in this value of the tool a true *value*. Of course, this value always implies a "reference" to the value of the thing produced by this tool, but this former value is phenomenally "given" *prior* to the value of the product. It is not derived from the given value of the product. We must therefore sharply distinguish the value which something "has as a means" or "can have as a means" from the value which pertains to the means *insofar as it is intuitively given* "*as a means*," and which is attached to its bearer no matter whether or not it is, in fact, used as a means, and no matter to what degree it is used.

[104] All specifically "*technical values*" are also, in this sense, genuine, consecutive values. Among them, the "useful" is a (genuine) consecutive value with regard to the *self-value* of the "agreeable." Among higher values, also, there are self-values and technical values; and for every kind of higher value, there exists a special realm of technical values.[11]

A second basic kind of consecutive values (besides "technical" values) consists of "*symbolic values*." These are not the same as pure "symbols of values," which are not (phenomenal) bearers of values. An example of a true symbolic value is a regimental "flag,"

---

[10] But not in the form of an assessment, which presupposes given values.

[11] See chap. 2, sec. 5.

in which the honor and dignity of a regiment are symbolically concentrated. It is precisely for this reason that a flag possesses a *phenomenal value* that has nothing to do with its cloth value, etc.[12] In this sense all "sacramental things" (*res sacrae*) are also genuine symbolic values, not mere symbols of values. Their special *symbolic* function of pointing to something holy (of a special kind) becomes here, again, another *bearer* of a special kind of value (independent of symbolic things). It is this that raises them above mere "symbols for values."

Self-values and consecutive values also have their own a priori relations between their being-*higher* and being-*lower*.

In contrast, symbols of values serve only for (always artificial) *quantifications of values* and for measurements of *larger* and *smaller*, which have nothing to do with the height of a value.[13] But we shall not dwell on the problem of measurements of values or the question of how one can speak of a "sum of happiness" and the like.

A *Priori* Relations of Rank among Value-Modalities

The most important and most fundamental a priori relations obtain as an *order of ranks* among the systems of qualities of non-formal values which we call *value-modalities*. They [105] constitute the *non-formal a priori* proper in the intuition of values and the intuition of preferences. The facts of these modalities present the *strongest* refutation of Kant's formalism. The ultimate divisions of value-qualities that are presupposed for these essential interconnections must be as independent of all factual goods and the special organizations of living beings that feel values as is the order of the ranks of the value-modalities.

Rather than giving a full development and establishment of these systems of qualities and their implicit laws of preferring, the following presents an explanation through examples of the kinds

---

[12] Likewise, a king's colors or a priest's chasuble.

[13] As pure qualities, values are not measurable. In this respect they are like the *pure phenomena of color and sound*, which become indirectly measurable through their *bearers* and their quantities (through the mediations of the phenomena of light and sound and their relations to extension and spatiality). Values of the *same* modality can be made *indirectly* measurable by measuring their bearers in such a way that their magnitude-units, which assume a just-noticeable difference in value, are used as units of measurement and designated with a certain *symbol of value*. By counting and treating such *symbols* numerically, we achieve an indirect value-measurement.

of a priori orders of ranks among values.

1. The values ranging from *the agreeable to the disagreeable* represent a sharply delineated value-modality (Aristotle already mentions them in his division of the ἡδύ [pleasant], the χρήσιμον [useful], and the καλόν [noble]). The function of *sensible feeling* (with its modes of enjoying and suffering) is correlative to this modality. The respective feeling-states, the so-called feelings of sensation, are pleasure and pain. As in all value-modalities, there are values of *things [Sachwerte]*, values of *feeling-functions*, and values of *feeling-states*.

This modality is *"relative"* to beings endowed with sensibility in general. But it is relative *neither* to a specific species, e.g., man, *nor* to specific things or events of the real world that are "agreeable" or "disagreeable" to a being of a particular species. Although one type of event may be agreeable to one man and disagreeable to another (or agreeable and disagreeable to different animals), the difference between the values of agreeable and disagreeable as such is an *absolute* difference, clearly given prior to any cognition of things.

The proposition that the agreeable is preferable to the disagreeable (*ceteris paribus*) is not based on observation and induction. The preference lies in the essential contents of these values as well as in the nature of sensible feelings. If a traveler or a historian or a zoologist were to tell us that this preference is reversed in a certain kind of animal, we would "a priori" disbelieve his story. We would say that this is impossible unless it is only *things* different from ours that this animal feels are disagreeable and agreeable, or unless its preferring the disagreeable to the agreeable is based on a value of a *modality* (perhaps unknown to us) that is "higher" than that of the agreeable and the disagreeable. In the latter case the animal would only "put [106] up with" the disagreeable in preferring the value of the extra modality. There may also be cases of perverted drive in this animal, allowing it to experience as agreeable those things that are *detrimental* to life. The state of affairs in all of these examples, as well as that which our proposition expresses, namely, that the agreeable is preferable to the disagreeable, also serves as a *law of understanding* external expressions of life and concrete (e.g., historical) valuation (even one's *own*, e.g., in remembering); our proposition is a *presupposition* of all observation and induction and it is "a priori" to all ethnological experience.

Nor can this proposition and its respective facts be "explained" by way of evolutionary theories. It is nonsense to say that values (and their laws of preference) developed as *signs* of kinetic combinations that proved purposeful for the individual or its species. Such a theory can explain only the accompanying feeling-*states* that are connected with impulsive actions directed toward things. But *the values themselves* and their *laws of preferring* could *never* be thus explained. For the latter are independent of all specific organizations of living beings.

Certain groups of consecutive values (technical values[14] and symbolic values) correspond to these self-values of the modality of the agreeable and the disagreeable. But they do not concern us here.

2. The essence of values correlated to *vital feeling* differs sharply from the above modality. Its thing-values, insofar as they are self-values, are such qualities as those encompassed by the "*noble*" and the "*vulgar*" (and by the "good" in the pregnant sense of "excellent" [*tüchtig*] as opposed to "bad" rather than "evil").[15] All corresponding consecutive values (technical and symbolic) belong to the sphere denoted by "*weal*," or "*well-being*."[16] They are *subordinated* to the noble and its opposite. The feeling-states of this modality include all modes of the feelings of life (e.g., the feelings of "quickening" and "declining" [107] life, the feelings of health and illness, the feeling of aging and oncoming death, the feelings of "weakness," "strength," etc.). Certain emotional reactions also belong to this modality–(a certain kind of) "being glad about" or "being sad about," drive reactions such as "courage," "anxiety," revengeful impulses, ire, etc. Here we cannot even indicate the tremendous richness of these value-qualities and their correlates.

Vital values form an entirely *original* modality. They cannot be "reduced" to the values of the agreeable and the useful, nor can they be reduced to spiritual values. Previous ethical theories made

---

[14] They are in part technical values concerning, the production of agreeable things and are unified in the concept of the "useful" (values of civilization), and in part values concerning the enjoyment of agreeable things (luxury values).

[15] One also uses "noble" and its opposite with respect to vital values ("noble horse" "noble tree," "noble race," "nobility," etc.).

[16] "Weal" and "well-being" therefore do not coincide with vital values in general; the value of well-being is determined by the extent to which the individual or the community, which can be in a good or a bad state, is *noble* or *base*. On the other hand, "weal" is superior as a vital value to mere "usefulness" (and "agreeableness"), and the well-being of a community is superior to the sum of its interests (as a society).

a *basic mistake* in ignoring this fact. Even Kant tacitly presupposes that these values can be reduced to mere hedonistic ones when he tries to divide all values in terms of good-evil on the one hand and agreeable-disagreeable on the other.[17] This division, however, is not applicable even to values of "well-being," let alone the vital self-value of the noble.

The particular character of this modality lies in the fact that *"life"* is a *genuine essence* and not an "empirical generic conception" that contains only "common properties" of all living organisms. When this fact is misconceived, the uniqueness of vital values is overlooked. We will not go into this in further detail here.

3. The realm of *spiritual values* is distinct from that of vital values as an original modal unity. In the kind of their *givenness*, spiritual values have a peculiar detachment from and in-dependence of the spheres of the lived body and the environment. Their unity reveals itself in the clear evidence that vital values "ought" to be sacrificed for them. The functions and acts in which they are apprehended are functions of *spiritual* feeling and acts of *spiritual* preferring, loving, and hating. They are set off from like-named *vital* functions and acts by pure phenomenological evidence as well as by their *own proper lawfulness* (which *cannot be reduced* to any *"biological"* lawfulness).

The main types of spiritual values are the following: (1) the values of *"beautiful"* and *"ugly,"* together with the whole range of purely aesthetic values; (2) the values of *"right"* and *"wrong"* [*des Rechten und Unrechten*], objects that are "values" and wholly different from what is "correct" and "incorrect" according to a [108] law, which form the ultimate phenomenal basis of the idea of the objective *order of right* [*Rechtsordnung*], an order that is independent of the idea of "law," the idea of the state, and the idea of the life-community on which the state rests (it is especially independent of all positive legislation);[18] (3) the values of the *"pure cognition of truth,"* whose realization is sought in

---

[17] See Kant, *Critique of Practical Reason*, pt. I, bk. II, chap. 2. The hedonists and the utilitarians, like Kant, make the mistake of reducing this value-modality to the agreeable and the useful; the rationalists make the (equally erroneous) mistake of reducing it to spiritual values (especially the rational ones).

[18] "Law" is only a consecutive value for the self-value of the "order of right"; positive law (of a state) is the consecutive value for the (objective) "order of right" which is valid in the state and which law-makers and judges must realize.

philosophy (in contrast to positive "science," which is guided by the aim of controlling natural appearances).[19] Hence "*values of science*" are consecutive values of the values of the cognition of truth. So-called *cultural values* in general are the consecutive (technical and symbolic) values of *spiritual values* and belong to the value-sphere of *goods* (e.g., art treasures, scientific institutions, positive legislation, etc.). The correlative feeling-states of spiritual values–for instance, the feeling-states of spiritual joy and sorrow (as opposed to the vital "being gay" and "not being gay")–possess the phenomenal quality of appearing *without mediation*. That is to say, they do not appear on an "ego" as its states, nor does an antecedent givenness of the lived body of a person serve as a condition of their appearance.[20] Spiritual feeling-states vary *independent* of changes in vital feeling-states (and, of course, sensible feeling-states). Their variations are directly dependent upon the variations of the values of the *objects themselves* and occur according to their own proper laws.

Finally, there are the reactions belonging to this modality, including "pleasing" and "displeasing," "approving" and "disapproving," "respect" and "disrespect," "retributive conation" (as opposed to the vital impulses of revenge) and "spiritual sympathy" (which is the foundation of friendship, for instance).

4. Values of the last modality are those of the *holy* and the *unholy*. This modality differs sharply from the above modalities. It forms a unit of value-qualities not subject to further definition. Nevertheless, these values have *one* very definite condition of their givenness: they appear only in objects that are given in intention as "absolute objects." This expression, however, refers *not* to a specific or definable *class* of objects, but (in principle) to *any* object given in the "absolute sphere." Again, this modality [109] is quite independent of all that has been considered "holy" by different peoples at various times, such as holy things, powers, persons, institutions, and the like (i.e., from ideas of fetishism to the purest conceptions of God). These latter problems do not belong to an *a priori phenomenology of values* [*apriorische Wertlehre*] and the theory of ordered ranks of values.[21] They

---

[19] We speak of the value of "cognition," not of the value of "truth." Truth does not belong among the values.

[20] See chap. 5, esp. sec. 8.

[21] Thus, e.g., an oath is an affirmation and a promise with reference to the value of the holy, no matter what is holy to the man concerned, no matter by what he swears.

concern the *positive representations of goods* within this value-sphere. With regard to the values of the holy, however, *all* other values are at the same time given as symbols for these values.

The feeling-states belonging to this modality range from "blissfulness" to "despair"; they are independent of "'happiness" and "unhappiness," whether it be in occurrence, duration, or change. In a certain sense these feeling-states indicate the "nearness" or the "remoteness" of the divine in experience.

"Faith" and "lack of faith," "awe," "adoration," and analogous attitudes [sic *atttiudes*] are specific reactions in this modality.

However, the act through which we *originally* apprehend the value of the holy is an act of a specific kind of *love* (whose value-direction *precedes* and *determines* all pictorial representations and concepts of holy objects); that is to say, in essence the act is directed toward persons, or toward something of the *form of a personal being, no matter what* content or what "*conception*" of personhood is implied. The self-value in the sphere of the values of the "holy" is therefore, by essential necessity, a "*value of the person.*"

The values of things and forms of worship implicit in cults and sacraments are consecutive values (technical and symbolic) of all holy values of the person. They represent genuine "symbolic values," not mere "symbols of values."

Since we intend to stick to the most elementary points, we shall refrain from showing how these basic values are connected with the ideas of person and community. We shall likewise refrain from showing how one can obtain from these values the "*pure types of persons,*" such as the saint, the genius, the hero, the leading spirit of civilization, and the *bon vivant*, and their respective technical occupations (e.g., the priest), as well as the *pure types of communal forms of togetherness*, such as the community of love (plus its technical form, the church), the community of law, the community of culture, and the life-community [110] (plus its technical form, the state), and the mere forms of so-called society.

As we have stated, these modalities have their own a priori order of ranks that precedes their series of qualities. This order of value-ranks is valid for the *goods* of correlative values because it is valid for the *values* of goods. The order is this: the modality of vital values is *higher* than that of the agreeable and the disagreeable; the modality of spiritual values is *higher* than that of vital values; the modality of the holy is *higher* than that of spiritual values.

DIETRICH VON HILDEBRAND (1889-1977)

Von Hildebrand was born in Florence, Italy in 1889, son of the famous German sculptor Adolf von Hildebrand, and raised in the former Minim convent of San Francesco on the outskirts of Florence. He studied philosophy at the University of Munich from 1906 to 1909 with Theodor Lipps and befriended the phenomenologist Max Scheler there. Von Hildebrand found himself having to defend Scheler from charges in the *Münchener Post* that he improperly borrowed money from a student and was having an affair with the fiancée of Von Hildebrand. Becoming interested in phenomenology himself, Von Hildebrand studied with Edmund Husserl and Adolf Reinach at the University of Göttingen from 1909-1911. Von Hildebrand received his Ph.D. in philosophy in 1912 from Göttingen, and married Margaret Denck that same year: the couple converted to Catholicism in 1914 through the influence of Scheler.

Von Hildebrand become Privatdozent at the University of Munich in 1918 and then associate professor from 1924-1933. With the rise of the Nazi Party in Germany, Von Hildebrand moved back to Florence and then to Vienna, Austria where he founded the anti-fascist periodical *Der Christliche Staendestaat* and joined the faculty of philosophy at the University of Vienna in 1935. In order to escape the Gestapo, Von Hildebrand fled Vienna in 1938 and became a professor of philosophy at the Catholic University of Toulouse. When France too fell to the National Socialists, Von Hildebrand was able to escape France through the assistance of the politician Edmond Michelet and the Rockefeller Foundation, and he was appointed to a position at Fordham University in New York where he taught from 1941-1960. In 1957 his wife died and he married his colleague Alice Jourdain in 1959. Von Hildebrand died in 1977 in New Rochelle, New York.

The key works of Von Hildebrand are: *Die Umgestaltung in Christus* [*Transformation in Christ*] (Köln: Einsiedeln, 1940); *Christian Ethics* (New York: D. McKay, 1953); and *What Is Philosophy?* (Milwaukee: Bruce, 1960).

For more on von Hildebrand see: Von Hildebrand, Alice, *The Soul of a Lion* (San Francisco: Ignatius Press, 2000); Crosby, John, ed., *Selected Papers on the Philosophy of Dietrich Von Hildebrand* (Steubenville: Franciscan University of Steubenville Press, 2012).

The following selection is from Von Hildebrand's *Christian Ethics* (New York: D. McKay, 1953): III, 34-39, XXXVI, 453-463). Von Hildebrand here contrasts the difference between the subjectively satisfying and the important in itself, or something which is sought because it is pleasing vs. something that is a value and intrinsically important. He also argues for a theistic moral realism based on a phenomenology of moral and aesthetic values. Finally, Von Hildebrand notes how the supernatural can enhance the natural virtues and generate unique virtues of its own.

Christian Ethics (1953)[22]

Value and Motivation

The Categories of Importance

[34] Let us begin our analysis of the different categories of importance which can motivate our will and our affective responses, by comparing the two following experiences:

In the first, let us suppose that someone pays us a compliment. We are perhaps aware that we do not fully deserve it, but it is nevertheless an agreeable and pleasurable experience. It is not a matter neutral and indifferent to us as in the case where someone tells us that his name begins with a T. We may have been told many things before this compliment, things which had a neutral and indifferent character, but now in the face of all other statements the compliment is thrown into relief. It presents itself as agreeable and as possessing the character of a *bonum*, in short, as something important.

In the second, let us suppose that we witness a generous action, a man's forgiveness of a grave injury. This again strikes us as distinguishable from the neutral activity of a man dressing himself or lighting a cigarette. Indeed, the act of generous forgiveness shines forth with the mark of importance, with the mark of something noble and precious. It moves us and engenders our admiration. We are not only aware that this act occurs, but that it is *better* that it occurs, *better* that the man acted in this way rather than in another. We are conscious that this act is something which *ought to be*, something *important*.

If we compare these types of importance, we will soon discover the essential difference between them. The first, that is, the compliment, is merely *subjectively* important; while the latter, the act of forgiving, is *important in itself*. We are fully conscious [35] that the compliment possesses a character of importance only insofar as it gives us pleasure. Its importance is solely drawn from its relation to our pleasure—as soon as the compliment is divorced from our pleasure, it sinks back into the anonymity of the neutral and indifferent.

In contrast, the generous act of forgiveness presents itself as something intrinsically important. We are clearly conscious that its importance in no way depends on any effect which it produces

---

[22] [Dietrich von Hildebrand, *Christian Ethics* (New York: D. McKay, 1953). Public Domain.]

in us. Its particular importance is not drawn from any relation to our pleasure and satisfaction. It stands before us intrinsically and autonomously important, in no way dependent on any relation to our reaction.

Our language itself expresses this fundamental distinction. The importance of what is agreeable or satisfying always involves the prepositions "to" or "for": something is agreeable *to* or satisfying *for* someone. The terms "agreeable" and "satisfying" cannot be applied as such to an object, but only insofar as they affect a person or, analogously, an animal. On the other hand, the terms "heroic," "beautiful," "noble," "sublime" do not at all require the prepositions "to" or "for," but in fact obviate them. An act of charity is not sublime *for* someone, nor is the Ninth Symphony of Beethoven, or a glorious sunset, beautiful *for* someone.

The intrinsic importance with which a generous act of forgiveness is endowed is termed "value" as distinguished from the importance of all those goods which motivate our interest merely because they are agreeable or satisfactory to us.

But, although these two types of importance are essentially different, are they not in another respect quite similar? Is it not true that those things which are good, beautiful, noble, or sublime deeply touch us, fill us with joy and delight? Certainly they do not leave us indifferent. Does not the full experience of beauty necessarily bestow delight on us; again, do we not experience delight when the charity or generosity of someone touches our heart? Such delight and joy are indeed essentially different from the pleasure derived from the compliment. Yet does this difference really supersede the fact that in both cases a similar relation m a joyful experience is to be found?

Certainly those things which we term intrinsically important, [36] those things endowed with *value*, do possess a capacity for bestowing delight. Yet an analysis of the specific character of delight will prove still more clearly the essential difference between these two kinds of importance. It will prove that the value possesses its importance independently of its effect on us.

The delight and emotion which we experience in witnessing a noble moral action or in gazing at the beauty of a star-studded sky essentially presupposes the consciousness that the importance of the object is in no way dependent on the delight it may bestow on us. Indeed, this bliss arises from our confrontation with an object having an intrinsic importance; an object standing majestically before us, autonomous in its sublimity and nobility. Our bliss implies in fact that here is an object which depends in no way on our reaction to it, an object whose importance we cannot alter, which we can neither increase nor diminish: for it draws its importance not from its relation to us, but from its own rank; it stands before us, a message, as it were, from on high, elevating us beyond ourselves.

Thus, this difference between the bliss emanating from the sheer existence of a value and the pleasure accruing from the subjectively satisfying is itself not a difference of degree, but a difference of kind: an essential difference. A life which consisted in a continuous stream of pleasures, as derived from what is merely, subjectively satisfying, could never grant us one moment of that blissful happiness engendered by those objects possessing a value.

The difference between the self-centered pleasure propounded by Aristippus as the only true good, and the happiness for which Socrates and Plato strived, is therefore not a difference of mere degree but of kind of essence.[23] Self-centered happiness at length wears itself out and ends in boredom and emptiness. The constant enjoyment of the merely subjectively satisfying finally throws us back upon our own limitedness, imprisoning us within ourselves.

In contrast, our engagement with a value elevates us, liberates us from self-centeredness, reposes us in a transcendent order which is independent of us, of our moods, of our dispositions. This blissful experience presupposes a participation in the intrinsically important; it implies a harmony which is given forth [37] by the intrinsically good, the essentially noble alone; and it displays to us a brightness which is "consubstantial" (congenial) with the intrinsic beauty and splendor of the value. In this priceless contact with the intrinsically and autonomously important, the important in itself, it is the object which shelters and embraces our spirit. ...

It is indeed a deep characteristic of man to desire to be confronted with something beyond self-centeredness, which obligates us and affords us the possibility of transcending the limits of our subjective inclinations, tendencies, urges, and drives rooted *exclusively* in our nature.[24]

In effect, then, we can say that both the value and the subjectively satisfying can delight us. But it is precisely the *nature*

---

[23] Cf. St. Augustine, *Sermo*, 179, 6.

[24] St. Thomas clearly distinguishes the difference between delectability resulting from a value and delectability resulting from the merely subjectively satisfying, although he does not use the concept of value (*Summa Theologica*, I, Q. V, art. vi, ad. 2).

of this delight which clearly reveals the essential difference between the two kinds of goods. The true, profound happiness which the values effect in us necessarily implies an awareness of the object's intrinsic importance. This happiness is essentially an epiphenomenon, for it is in no way the root of this importance, but flows superabundantly out of it. The consciousness that a generous act of forgiveness possesses its importance independently, whether or not I know of its existence, whether or not I rejoice about it, is at the very root of the happiness we experience when confronted with it. This happiness is thus something secondary, notwithstanding the fact that it is an essential mark of the values to be able to bestow delight on us: we even *should* take delight in them. The value is here the *principium* (the determining) and our happiness, the *principiatum* (the [38] determined), whereas in the case of the subjectively satisfying good our pleasure is the *principium* and the importance of the agreeable or satisfying of the object, the *principiatum*.

A further distinguishing mark is to be found in the way in which each type of importance addresses itself to us. Every good possessing a value imposes on us, as it were, an obligation to give to it an adequate response. We are not yet referring to the unique obligation which we call moral obligation and which appeals to our conscience. This obligation issues from certain values only. Here we are thinking of the awareness which we have as soon as we are confronted with something intrinsically important, for instance, with beauty in nature or in art, with the majesty of a great truth, with the splendor of moral values. In all these cases we are clearly aware that the object calls for an adequate response. We grasp that it is not left to our arbitrary decision or to our accidental mood whether we respond or not, and how we respond. On the other hand, goods which are merely subjectively satisfying address no such call to us. They attract us or invite us, but we are clearly aware that no response is due to them, that it is up to us whether we heed their invitation or not. When a delectable dish attracts us, we are quite aware that it is completely up to our mood whether or not we yield to this attraction. We all know how ridiculous it would be for someone to say that he submitted to the obligation of playing bridge, and overcame the temptation to assist a sick person.

The call of an authentic value for an adequate response addresses itself to us in a sovereign but non-intrusive, sober way.

It appeals to our free spiritual center.[25] The attraction of the subjectively satisfying, on the contrary, lulls us into a state where we yield to instinct; it tends to dethrone our free spiritual center. Its appeal is insistent, ofttimes assuming the character of a temptation, trying to sway and silence our conscience, taking hold of us in an obtrusive manner. Far different is the call of values: it has no obtrusive character; it speaks to us from above, and at a [39] sober distance; it speaks with an objective vigor, issuing a majestic call which we cannot alter by our wishes.[26]

Finally, the essential difference between these two categories of importance is clearly reflected in the type of response which we give. Consider the enthusiasm with which we respond to a heroic moral action, and compare this response with our interest in something subjectively satisfying, such as the interest in a profitable business speculation. We clearly see that in the first case our response has the character of an abandoning of ourselves, a transcending of the boundaries of our self-centeredness, a submission of some sort.

Interest in the subjectively satisfying reveals, on the contrary, a self-confinement, a relating of the object to ourselves, using it for our own self-centered satisfaction. Here we do not conform to the good and to its intrinsic importance, as in the case of admiration of the heroic moral action. Interest in the business speculation rather consists in a conforming of the object to ourselves. Our preoccupation may be very intense; we may invest a great deal of energy in the pursuit, abstain from many pleasures for it. But dynamic absorption in the subjectively satisfying still will have nothing of the character of true abandonment, nothing of the character of surrender to the intrinsically important for its own sake.[27] ...

---

[25] Cf. St. Augustine: "I could see the austere beauty of Continence, serene and indeed joyous but not evilly, honourably soliciting me to come to her" (*Confessions of St. Augustine*, VIII, 11, trans. F.J. Sheed (New York: Sheed and Ward, 1943), p. 177).

[26] The neutral necessity to conform our actions for the sake of success to the inner logic of the things with which we deal must not be confounded with the obligation to conform ourselves to the call of the values. This difference will be discussed in detail later on.

[27] The difference between being absorbed by a speculation and being abandoned to a value is obviously not erased by the fact that in both cases the aforementioned conforming to the neutral, immanent logic of a being is to be found.

The Sources of Moral Goodness

Christian Ethics

[453] The title of this book implies a thesis: the existence of Christian ethics. Does this mean that there are several ethics—a pagan, a Mohammedan, a Buddhist ethics—and that Christian ethics is one among others? Obviously not. The entire analysis of ethical problems which we have offered points to the fact that in saying "Christian" ethics, we mean the one, true, valid ethics. If true ethics and Christian ethics are synonymous, why then speak of Christian ethics? Would it not be more correct to say simply "ethics," even if in its content this ethics is Christian?

In order to answer this question we must first make the following remarks: For a pagan also, the notions of moral good and moral evil exist; he too may admire moral goodness in another person and become indignant over moral wickedness. We have seen that a person does not need to know of God's existence in order to grasp the difference between moral good and evil in general, and between certain moral values and disvalues in particular.[28] A fortiori we must admit that a distinction between moral good and evil can be made and that certain moral values and disvalues can be grasped without Revelation. It is impossible to deny that a pagan can also be honest or dishonest, loyal or disloyal, selfish or unselfish. There exists a morality if we prescind from Revelation and a true natural ethics is concerned with the exploration of this morality.[29] An ethics deprived of the [454]

---

[28] We shall come back to this point on page 455.

[29] Theology tells us that man, separated from God by Adam's fall, cannot by his own effort span the abyss separating him from God. The good will, the natural moral goodness of Socrates, could never do away with this stain. Only through Christ's death on the cross can this abyss be bridged: only the one reborn in baptism can glorify God by the morality of the "new creature" in Christ. In our philosophical analysis, we prescind from this fact which is inaccessible to our reason. We only include the given, fundamental difference between the morality of Socrates and the morality of a saint. We also include the mysterious disrupture in man which manifests itself in experience as well as the evident limitations of morality in a noble pagan. Thus in distinguishing between good and evil in a pagan, we in no way pretend that the moral goodness of Socrates, without grace, is able to glorify God, or that it could in any way alter the separation from God which is due to original sin.

Whether or not the grace of God might be necessary for the moral goodness of a pagan is not a question which philosophy can answer. In epithet "Christian" is the philosophical exploration of the morality which is embodied in a morally noble pagan, for instance in Socrates, or, more correctly, of all the moral values which can be embodied in a human person without Revelation.[30]

Christian ethics in our terminology is, on the contrary, the philosophical exploration of the totality of morality, including the natural moral law and all moral and morally relevant values accessible to a noble pagan, as well as the morality embodied in the sacred humanity of Christ and in those men and women who have been transformed into Christ—the saints. We have stressed several times that this latter morality embodies not only a new world of moral values, unknown and inaccessible without Christ, but it also gives a new character to the entire field of natural morality. It is thus not only an incomparably higher morality, but a completely new one. Yet this morality is simultaneously [455] the fulfillment of all natural morality. Once Christian morality has been disclosed to our minds, we understand that all natural morality is a prelude to Christian morality, and that everything which is to be found in natural morality is found on a higher level and in its ultimate meaning only in the light of Christian morality.

Christian ethics is, however, in no way synonymous with moral theology. It is a pure philosophical exploration introducing

---

any case, this natural morality is possible without any consciousness of grace on the part of the agent, and *a fortiori* without knowledge of Christian Revelation.

[30] In opposing here Christian morality to a mere natural morality, we do not mean by natural morality, the morality of a possible man who, although without supernatural union with God, would have an uncorrupted nature. Faith tells us that such a man never actually existed. The man whom we know by experience and who is accessible to a philosophical analysis manifests a mysterious rupture in his nature; in him pride and concupiscence are undeniable realities. What the morality of a man with an uncorrupted nature would be is not a problem we can discuss in philosophy, at least not a philosophy which has its starting point in the given.

Thus in distinguishing Christian morality from natural morality we consider the morality of a saint on the one hand, and the morality of a noble pagan such as Socrates on the other. Both are data to be found in experience and thus accessible to philosophical analysis. It must however be emphasized that the morality of Socrates is before Christ and the Christian era, and thus it has the character of a prelude. Such a morality can no longer exist in the Christian era, and in a world penetrated by Christian ideas. There is an abyss separating an apostate from a pagan of the pre-Christian era.

no arguments which are not accessible through our *lumen naturale* (light of reason), whereas in moral theology faith is presupposed, and revealed truth which surpasses our reason is included in the argumentation. Christian ethics is a strict *philosophical* analysis, starting from the data accessible to our mind through experience. It in no way ignores the essential distinction between faith and reason, revealed knowledge and natural knowledge. But it implies a relation to Revelation insofar as it includes the morality which is only possible through Christian Revelation. It is purely philosophical in its approach and method, but its object is the undeniable reality of Christian morality which is a full datum for our experience as well.

Before turning to the features of Christian morality, we still have to stress one fundamental fact: morality as such essentially presupposes God's existence. This does not mean, however, that we must have a knowledge of God's existence, either by Revelation or by rational demonstration. If we think of the Socratic statement: "It is better to suffer injustice than to commit it," we find an extraordinary awareness of moral goodness and of the obligation to conform to morality, though the notion of God is, to say the least, very vague in Socrates. The natural moral law, morally relevant values as well as moral values, is "given," and in order to grasp these values together with their call and obligation, no knowledge of God's existence, and therefore no explicit reference to God, is required. The Socratic statement necessarily implies the notion of some absolute reality, the notion of a world above us. Time and again we have stressed this intrinsic relation of the moral values to an absolute above us.[31] The experience of moral obligations, the voice of our conscience, cannot be separated from the awareness of some absolute. But the [456] notion of a *personal* God is not indissolubly connected with the *experience* of moral values, nor does the voice of conscience presuppose the knowledge of a personal God.

But as soon as one philosophically contemplates and analyzes the message embodied in moral values, in their unique gravity, in the categorical character of the obligation which can be grasped by us, we discover that only the existence of a personal God who is the Infinite Goodness can fulfill the message of moral values or can ultimately justify the validity of this obligation. We do not mean thereby that this obligation needs other reasons, for instance, the Infinite Lordship of God, or His right as Creator to

---

[31] Cf. Chapter 15, "The Nature of Moral Values."

impose moral obligations upon us. We do not want to reduce all moral obligations to positive divine commandments. But we want to say that moral values only possess the ultimate reality which justifies the gravity of the moral order, of its majestic obligation, if they are ultimately rooted and embodied in the Absolute Person of God.[32]

The drastic reality of the moral law and its unchangeable character would lack their indispensable foundation if, e.g., the ultimate metaphysical basis were merely the Platonic idea of Goodness. As person, man possesses an incomparably higher being than any impersonal entity. Hence it is impossible that any impersonal goodness could impose on him absolute obligations from above. Only an absolute goodness possessing personal reality can do this. In this sense we must say that if there were no God, all moral values, the moral law itself, would be deprived of their indispensable metaphysical basis.

The existence of contingent beings is accessible to our knowledge without any reference to God. But we also grasp that contingent beings necessarily presuppose a *causa prima*, i.e., an absolute Being. Thus we say *quoad se* (in itself) contingent beings presuppose God; *quoad nos* (for our knowledge) contingent beings are grasped first, and lead us by inference to God's [457] existence. The same thing applies analogously to our problem. For our knowledge of moral values, of the moral obligation, of the natural moral law, the knowledge of God is not required. But objectively these data presuppose God. We do not pretend that the type of demonstration leading to God in both cases is the same. But without any doubt God manifests Himself in moral values; He speaks to us in moral obligation. The moral values, the moral law, the moral order, the moral obligation, the voice of our conscience, objectively presuppose God, and are thus for our minds and knowledge hints at God's existence. The undeniable world of values, and especially of moral values, testifies to the existence of

---

[32] It must be emphasized that in no way do we thereby introduce God's existence as a postulate, as Kant did. A postulate is typically something *quoad nos*; and is something *we* have to assume, or else we would have to give up the moral order. A postulate is something which we must assume because of its practical indispensability, though it is inaccessible to our reason. Our thesis, on the contrary, stresses that *quoad se* the moral values presuppose God and that God manifests Himself in them. Morally relevant values are an objective hint at God's existence and support our knowledge of God.

God for the one who has "eyes to see, and ears that may hear." *Dicit insipiens in corde suo: non est Deus*–"The fool hath said in his heart: there is no God" (Ps. 1.3:1). Thus St. Bonaventure says:

> He, therefore, who is not enlightened by all these splendors of created things is blind; he who is not waked by such callings is deaf; he who from all these effects does not praise God is dumb; he who after such intimation does not observe the first principle is foolish.[33]

This fact has a paramount bearing on natural morality. Every value response, but above all every response to a morally relevant value, is an implicit, indirect response to God. Morally relevant values, and above all moral values, are linked to God in such a way that in affirming them and in giving a positive response to a value-endowed good we implicitly conform to God and respond to God. Analogously, in our disrespect for a morally relevant value we implicitly show disrespect toward God.[34] If this immanent objective relation of every morally relevant value to God, source and sum of all values, did not exist, the value response to this morally relevant value would be deprived of moral value. So long as a man does not know God, this implicit submission and conforming to God will be found in every true, morally good value response which he accomplishes. But as soon as someone, in doing something that objectively is in conformity with [458] the moral law expressly denies any reference to God and subjectively severs from God the morally relevant value to which he conforms, then his response is perverted and deprived of all true moral value.

We shall conclude this book with a brief glance at the nature of Christian morality. We have stressed time and again that many responses and virtues are only possible in the frame of Christian Revelation.[35] Theology tells us that these virtues are "fruits of the Holy Ghost" and only possible in the "new creature." The mysterious relation between sanctifying grace and these virtues is inaccessible to our reason and to philosophical analysis. Yet, as we

---

[33] *Itinerarium mentis in Deum*, quoted from *The Soul's Progress in God*; Selections from the World's Devotional Classics, vol. 3 (New York: Funk and Wagnall, 1916), Chap. I, p. 18.

[34] In this sense St. Thomas says: "To disparage the dictate of reason is equivalent to contemning the command of God" (*Summa Theologica*, 1a2ae, xix, 5 ad).

[35] Cf. Chapter 15, "The Nature of Moral Values"; and "The Sphere of Virtues," p. 357.

have seen, these virtues also presuppose the Revelation of Christ insofar as they are only possible as responses to the God of Christian Revelation as well as to man seen in the light of Christian Revelation. And this relation to Revelation is accessible to the eyes of our mind and can be the subject of philosophical analysis.

In my work *Transformation in Christ* I have tried to elaborate many features of the "new creature," the one reborn in Christ. The unlimited readiness to be changed, true contrition, true self-knowledge, true simplicity, humility, true freedom, patience, meekness, peacefulness, mercifulness, these are only possible as responses to the God of Christian Revelation and to a universe seen in the light of Christ.[36] The same can be said of the love of neighbor. Charity, in contradistinction to a humanitarian sympathy with other persons, responds to the beauty of a human being created after the image of God, destined for eternal communion with God, loved and redeemed by Christ. Patently there can be no love of neighbor, ardent love in the full sense, such as it shines forth in St. Paul's words, *amor Christi urget nos* [The love of Christ impels us], which is not rooted in the love of God. Whereas justice, veracity, honesty, temperance, can also be found in Socrates, that is, [459] without Christian Revelation; whereas these virtues can constitute themselves as responses in the frame of the world known to us without Revelation, there are many virtues which presuppose as their object the notion of God as revealed in Christ, the sacred humanity of Christ, the Christian vision of man.

It is precisely in these virtues that is to be found a moral goodness completely new and beyond compare, a transfigured, holy goodness, reflection of the sacred humanity of Christ. These virtues are the core of Christian morality. But notwithstanding their absolutely new quality, they are also fulfillments of all natural moral goodness. While surpassing it so completely, they yet contain *per eminentiam* every moral value found in a merely natural morality. Whatever is a real moral value is, as we have seen, a special reflection of God and finds its crowning in the

---

36 Christian Revelation is here understood in its entirety including also the elements already present in the Old Testament, elements which find their fulfillment and completion in the Gospel. By Christian morality, we mean the ethos of the saints of the new covenant, reflecting the sacred humanity of Christ, without raising the question what elements in their ethos can already be found in the old covenant.

similitudo Dei [likeness to God] of the saint.

This relation of natural morality to Christian morality will become still clearer if we concentrate on the transfiguration within a saint of virtues which, as such, can be acquired by a pagan. Let us think of the difference between the justice of Socrates and that of St. Ambrose, of the difference between the veracity of Plato and that of St. Paul. The justice and veracity of the saints are filled with a new splendor, a completely new depth and inner freedom. They exhale a new fragrance, they are transfigured by the *lumen Christi*. The same can be said of the reverence, the temperance, the fortitude, the faithfulness, the reliability of the saint.

> As to virtue leading us to a happy life, I hold virtue to be nothing else than perfect love of God. For the fourfold division of virtue, I regard as taken from four forms of love. For these four virtues (would that all felt their influence in their minds as they have their names in their mouths) I should have no hesitation in defining them; that temperance is love giving itself entirely to that which is loved; fortitude is love readily bearing all things for the sake of the loved object; justice is love serving only the loved object, and therefore ruling rightly; prudence is love distinguishing with sagacity between what hinders it and what helps it. The object of this love is not anything, but only God, the chief good, the highest wisdom, the perfect harmony. So we may express the definition thus: that temperance is love keeping itself entire and incorrupt for God; fortitude is love bearing everything readily for the sake of God; justice is love [460] serving God only, and therefore ruling well all else, as subject to man; prudence is love making a right distinction between what helps it towards God and what might hinder it.[37]

All morally relevant values assume a completely new significance against the background of Christian Revelation. A new seriousness, a new realistic character, a breath of eternity pervades the moral order in which the great drama of human existence displays itself *coram Deo*, in the confrontation with God. The voice of the living God is heard in the Decalogue, it is the law of the living God and not a mere abstract law; it is the infinite Holy Lord whom immorality offends and whom moral goodness glorifies. The entire morality of the saints, whether of St. Mary

---

[37] St. Augustine, *The Morals of the Catholic Church*, quoted from *Basic Writings of St. Augustine*, trans. Richard Stothert (New York: Random House), Chap. XV, pp. 331-332.

Magdalen, St. Paul, St. John, St. Francis of Assisi, St. Catherine of Siena, St. Ignatius of Loyola, St. John Bosco, reveal a completely new ethos.

The first decisive mark of the Christian ethos is the indispensable and all-important role of humility. No greater revolution in the field of morality could be imagined than the parable of the Pharisee and the Publican. The ridiculousness and ugliness of vanity would certainly be grasped by Socrates. But the mysterious beauty of the man "who humbles himself," who places himself beneath the level on which he actually stands, who desires to throw away all honors and to accept joyfully all humiliations, which moves St. Teresa of Avila to say on her deathbed that she is one of the greatest sinners that ever lived, is a scandal and foolishness for natural morality. The importance of humility is such that it changes the whole of morality. It pervades every other virtue and gives to each a new and matchless value. It is only on the basis of humility that all other moral values unfold in their full beauty. Humility conveys to the entire ethos of the person a completely new note. It exalts him mysteriously, endows him with a sublime inner freedom and razes the walls in which man has imprisoned himself:

> In humility therefore there is this to be wondered at, that it elevates the heart; and in pride this, that it dejects it. This seems strangely contrary, that elevation should be below, and dejection [461] aloft. But godly humility subjects one to his superior, and God is above all; therefore humility exalts one, in making him God's subject.[38]

A second fundamental aspect of Christian morality is the interpenetration of attitudes which seem to exclude each other on the level of mere natural morality.[39] In a good pagan a great zeal for justice, for moral ideals, does not coexist with gentleness and kindness. A great and powerful personality, a leader possessing an unshakeable courage, will not be modest and meek. It is only in a saint that we find holy courage, hunger and thirst for justice, interpenetrated with humility and meekness. Here we find this *coincidentia oppositorum* [unity of opposites],[40] which is

---

[38] St. Augustine, *De Civitate Dei*, XIV, 13 (*The City of God*, trans. John Healey (New York: E. P. Dutton and Co., 1947), vol. 2).

[39] The exclusiveness in question implies no antithesis, but belongs to the type of friendly polarity mentioned in Chapter 11, "Unity of Values."

[40] Cf. *Transformation in Christ* (San Francisco: Ignatius Press,

embodied in a saint and is possible in Christian morality alone. It is indeed only *holy* zeal which can be interpenetrated with *holy* meekness. It is not simply a synthesis of the same perfections and virtues which exclude each other in a pagan. The two different virtues which interpenetrate each other in the saint are themselves already something completely new and incomparably higher, but they also contain all moral values present in the two perfections which can be found separately in the pagan.

Christian morality is characterized by a holy inner freedom, an elevation above ourselves, a standing in the full light of truth, an unlimitedness which manifests itself in this boundless, irresistible charity, at the sight of which have been heard the words, *qui sunt isti et illi* [these and those are the ones], throughout the centuries since the advent of Christ, and which was the fundamental datum at which Henri Bergson "wondered," and which is according to him the source of a higher morality.

A third mark of Christian morality is the fact that here this specific goodness of charity is its very core, whereas in natural morality rectitude, uprightness, and justice are its very core. For instance, Socrates' personality emanates a spirit of veracity, sobriety, rectitude, justice. But St. Stephen's prayer for his murderers exhales the superabundant goodness of charity. And in St. Francis of Assisi's embrace of the leper there shines forth the [462] same luminous, irresistible charity. But above all this holy goodness of charity is embodied in the words of our Lord: "Love your enemies: do good to them that hate you" (Matt. 5:44). In this morality everything is pervaded by the spirit of mercy. The saint knows that he lives from God's mercy, that all his hope is based on this mercy; the words of the Our Father, "Forgive us our trespasses as we forgive those who trespass against us," are present to his mind. He hears the voice of Christ: *Misericordiam volo et non sacrificium*–"I will have mercy and not sacrifice." Christian morality is imbued with the spirit embodied in the parable of the prodigal son and with the message of the parable of the unmerciful servant.

Finally, the radically new character of Christian morality is disclosed in the fact that all virtues and moral attitudes, whatever their object may be, originate in a response to God; the backbone of all moral attitudes is the love of God, through Christ, with Christ, and in Christ. The most sublime of all value responses is here the basis of all value responses; every response to a morally

2001).

relevant good is rooted in this love and has the character of organically issuing from this love.

> Love, and do what thou wilt; whether thou hold thy peace, of love hold thy peace; whether thou cry out, of love cry out; whether thou correct, of love correct; whether thou spare, through love do thou spare; let the root of love be within, of this root can nothing spring but what is good.[41]

It is easy to realize the sublimity of a morality in which the ultimate basic response is not only directed to morally relevant values, but to the Absolute Person who is infinite Goodness Itself– a morality in which the love of God and God's love in us pervades and forms every act of will and is the first and last word in man.

A detailed philosophical analysis of the specific features of Christian morality will be presented in a later work which we have found it necessary to mention several times. In the present work we have been concerned mainly with the general philosophical features of morality. The same kinds of human acts which are an expression of natural morality are also in evidence [463] in the display of "supernatural" morality. The nature of the value response, of the freedom of the person, of value in general and of moral values in particular, had to be elaborated in order to understand the specific nature of Christian morality. It is true that at times we had to anticipate the analysis of several features of Christian morality for reasons which can now readily be understood. This applies especially to the analysis of the "reverent, humble, loving center" and its incompatibility with pride and concupiscence. This center is indeed only to be found in its full domination in the saint. And not only is the complete victory of this center to be found exclusively in the saint, but only in Christian morality does it have, in its quality, the character of a loving, humble center. Thus in the pagan the morally good center can only be termed the value-responding center, and this in an analogous sense. ...

---

[41] St. Augustine, *In Epist. Joannis ad Parthos*, Tr. vii, 8.

EDITH STEIN (1891-1942)

Stein was born into a Jewish family in Breslau, Germany (now Wrocław, Poland) in 1891. She studied psychology at the University of Breslau from 1911-1913, and then philosophy with Husserl at the Universities of Göttingen and Freiburg from 1913-1916. She received her Ph.D. in philosophy from the University of Freiburg in 1916 and served as Husserl's assistant there for the next two years. In 1921, while on summer vacation in Bad Bergzabern, Stein discovered the work of St. Teresa of Ávila, and converted to Catholicism a year later. Stein acquired a job teaching classical languages and history at the Mädchen-Lyzeum, a school for girls run by Dominican nuns, in Speyer from 1923-1931. In 1932 she began teaching at the German Institute for Scientific Pedagogy in Münster. Stein was forced to resign, however, within a year, when the National Socialists took over Germany and passed laws banning Jews from civil service. Accordingly, Stein followed through with her long-held desire to become a nun and joined the Discalced Carmelites in Cologne in 1934, followed shortly thereafter by her sister. Fearing for their safety, Edith Stein and her sister Rosa were sent to the Carmelite monastery in Echt, Netherlands in 1938. They were arrested in 1942, after the Dutch bishops issued a pastoral letter critical of the Nazis, and put to death in Birkenau, Auschwitz on August 9, 1942.

For more on the life and thought of Stein see Baseheart, Mary Catherine, *Person in the World: Introduction to the Philosophy of Edith Stein* (Dordrecht: Kluwer, 1997); Borden, Sarah, *Edith Stein* (London: Continuum, 2003); MacIntyre, Alasdair, *Edith Stein* (Lanham: Rowman & Littlefield, 2006); Calcagno, Antonio, *The Philosophy of Edith Stein* (Pittsburgh: Duquesne University Press, 2007); Lebech, Mette, *The Philosophy of Edith Stein* (Frankfurt: Peter Lang, 2015). Stein's key works are her 1922 works in phenomenology *Psychological Causality* [*Psychische Kausalität*] and *Individual and Community* [*Individuum und Gemeinschaft*]; and her later *Finite and Eternal Being* [*Endliches und ewiges Sein*] (written in 1936-1937; published in 1950).

The following selection is from Stein's *Philosophy of Psychology and the Humanities* [translation of *Psychical Causality* and *Individual and Community*] (Washington: ICS Publications, 2000): 55-58, 61-64, 75-77, 81-82, and 84-85. Stein investigates the nature of the human person, in particular the person's experience of willing. Stein defends the idea that in free action motives incline but do not determine and so there is a *fiat* or act of free-choice that contravenes any attempt at predicting human behavior. Stein also advances the idea that humans are subject to the sway of lifepower [*Lebenskraft*], a spiritual energy and joy, that can enliven one's experiences and provide energy for action. Indeed motivations coming from the love of others or inspiring words can supply much more energy than they cost. All of which is to say humans possess different levels of being and are tied in to the physical realm, the sentient realm, the mental realm, and the spiritual realm.

Psychical Causality (1922)[42]

Mental Living and Motivation

Free Acts

[Now] dealing with free acts that the ego [55] accomplishes from out of its depths, but that it can just as well abstain from ... the availability of motives does not *compel* the ego to accomplish the acts in question. ... The ego can have and acknowledge the motives and it can abstain from the acts in spite of that. For example, suppose I know that I can cheer up someone who's sick with the reassurance of his imminent recovery and that he expects it from me. I would also like to help him; thus, the motive is present–and in spite of that I abstain from the reassurance. An objection suggests itself: The abstention also requires a motive; accordingly, a countermotive against the execution presents itself. Perhaps the reassurance contradicts my maxim to say nothing of which I am not convinced. Certainly that is often the case: but if I'm stuck in the struggle of conflicting motives, if I'm placed before a decision, still *I* am the one to whom the decision falls. The decision does not impose itself automatically, as the tipping of the scales toward the side of the "weightier" motive indicates. Rather, I make up my mind in its favor *because* it is weightier. Even if more can be said for the doing than for the abstaining, the doing still requires my *"fiat!"* I can grant it according to the "weightiness," but I can also grant it without carrying out any weighing of motives or, finally, when the motives look equally weighty to me. Thus, free acts presuppose a motive. But besides that, they require an impulse that is not motivated itself.

With these arguments we've already approached the sphere of willing and acting. However, it is still quite necessary to delimit willing and acting in the proper sense, from our free or–as we can also say–"deliberate" acts (which encompass it, too). At the same time we can tie into it [sic *the*] the analysis of volition that D. von Hildebrand gave in his article "The Idea of Moral Action."[43] He

---

[43] Dietrich von Hildebrand, "Die Idee der sittlichen Handlung," *Jahrbuch für Philosophie und phänomenologische Forschung* 3 (1916): 126-251.

first distinguished different concepts of volition that frequently get mixed up in conventional speech: (1) aspiring (I "want" to be good or I "want to" forgive—a "wanting to" that is entirely compatible with a not-being-able-to; (2) resolving to do something (for [56] example, to go for a walk—a volition that has the being-able-to as a necessary presupposition); (3) desiring the realization of a state of affairs (which, just like action—that is, the realizing of a state of affairs—is distinguished from a wanting-to that is oriented toward a mere doing in which only the subject's own behavior is realized). It divides again into the stance of will, the resolve of will, and the proper inception of action.

Thus we see that volition in the first sense has a to do with the fact that it is indeed a free act, but a special kind of free act that clearly stands out from others—as affirmation does, for example. Here we merely note that it always pertains to a "willing" subject's own stance, which is not the case throughout with all free acts. We note that it differs even from those acts—decision-making, determination, and such—which likewise have to do with a subject's own stance: it differs from them in that it applies regardless of whether the subject is capable of the attitude in question or not.

Now if we consider planning (of a proper doing), we see that it obviously has more to do with the free acts than the fact that it itself is a free act. Admittedly we can't say that every free act *is* a resolve, nor would it be correct if we wanted to affirm that every free act presupposes a resolve. Yet each of the free acts *can* arise out of a resolve, and they define the realm of subjective behavior to which a plan can be directed. They are the "doing" of the subject for which the planning is meant. (We do not concur with Hildebrand where he regards it as essential to doing that it engages a behavior of the body.[44] We consider it entirely necessary to speak of purely mental doing, too; and incidentally we also would prefer not to restrict action to a realization of states of affairs in the external world.) While information and attitude certainly cost me some effort even though they cannot predispose me, with free acts I never need to strain; rather they can take charge of me, without further ado. You can designate the free acts as "voluntary" precisely with reference to this concept of volition.

In contrast to resolve, the stance of will—as a genuine attitude—is not a free act. You can aspire to adopt it (perhaps "to will correctly" [57] a good deed), but you can't clinch a resolving to

---

44 Von Hildebrand, "Idee der sittlichen Handlung," p. 152.

do so. Conversely, you can propose the resolve as a free act once more. On the other hand, it must be stressed that every resolve, like any free act at all, presupposes a stance–though not always an unequivocally determinate one. A mere image, a notion, or even some information about what the free act is directed toward does not suffice to enable it to be accomplished. In order to be able to affirm something, as we saw, I must be convinced of it. In order to make reassurances about something, I certainly don't need to be convinced of the content of the reassurance, but I have to be somehow "interested" in the reassurance itself. If I'm going to make a resolve, then there has to be present within me a stance of will toward what I have in mind: either toward the specific doing or toward the state of affairs that I want to realize. But it should be stressed that the stance required as foundation for the free act need not be an "alive" stance currently present. It's enough if I acknowledge and "adopt" a stance as rationally required; it need not really impose itself.

Finally, if we take a look at the inception of action (or, of a mere doing), the *"fiat!"* with which the action is set into motion, we see that it belongs necessarily to each genuine doing - even if it be a purely mental doing - as an inner jolt. Going out from the jolt, the doing starts to run its course. ... For example, suppose I have made up my mind to make an important communication to someone at an opportune moment. I get together with him, and in the course of the conversation the "favorable moment" presents itself. As soon as that becomes clear to me, I say to myself "now!" and start my communication. Saying *now* is not the renewal of a resolve with which I was "brimming over" the whole time; rather, it's the *"fiat!"* that leads from the resolve to the performance.

How the *"fiat!"* stands out as a characteristic moment of the incipient doing (instead of as an act in its own right) is something that we can perhaps best see in the case in which an action arises immediately out of the stance of will without the circularity of a resolve. Perhaps I see someone haul off to take a punch at someone else, and I seize him by the arm. The action is produced out of the stance "that shouldn't be!" without any further ado. There isn't any hint of a resolve, and even the inner self-preparation that inheres in the "now" is lacking. Yet you can still detect a jolt the action initiates. We even find it with "coerced" [58] acts (as Reinach has termed them), where both resolve and stance of will alike are missing. If someone uses threats to force me to promise to stop doing something, then I don't positively *want* to stop (in the sense of the stance) and I even inwardly refuse. I entertain no resolve to keep the promise (this is certainly possible as a form of being-coerced), and nevertheless I make it and I commence the making with that inner jolt.

We must distinguish various possible cases here: (1) There is no stance of will present within me with regard to swearing off, but there is indeed a negative) stance with regard to what I'm threatened with. I recognize the swearing off as a means toward averting that, I make up my mind, and I go on and do it. Here we're still dealing with a free act and no genuine compulsion. (2). I am entirely filled with fear and consequently ready to do anything that is demanded of me. Here it's no longer a question of stance of will and resolve at all. We've got a peculiar surrender of my own spontaneity. We've got subjugation under the spontaneity of someone else, which still is to be understood as such and is to be regarded as motivated. Within the subjugation, however, the doing is no longer carried out through motives.

Apart from that, there are relationships whose clarification must be left for a special analysis of intersubjective connections. In our context we wish to mention only this. Insofar as the ego comes into consideration at all as a radiation point of required acts and does not degenerate into the blind tool of someone else's will, you can still detect the jolt that initiates any doing; otherwise we've got no doing at all. Free acts for us are synonymous with the "doing" of the ego, and we can define the realm of free acts by the fact that they, and they alone, *can* emerge out of a resolve and must be initiated by a "*fiat!*" ...

Impulse and Inclination

Inclinations and Attitudes

[61] In order to understand where the lines of demarcation fall between inclining and willing and between the motivatedness or unmotivatedness of inclination, we must first of all consider them from the points of view that were guiding us up until now. Obviously, inclinations are not free acts. They originate in me without my doing anything myself, and they cannot be the result of a plan. To be sure, it makes a kind of sense to say: I wish or I plan to strive for knowledge. That striving then signifies a doing that is initiated in order to attain knowledge. But don't confuse it with the inclining that we have in view here, which should be delimited from willing. Don't confuse deliberate striving with the impulse to jump up and run out into the open air, or even with curiosity, the mysterious urge to break open some path that leads

to knowledge; or with inclining toward the kinds of doing that were designated above as "striving" in an equivocal use of the term. Inclining, in the sense of the impulsive, can only be awakened in me; it cannot be willed or freely executed. Inclining is not a deed of mine; it just happens to me.

This seems to line up with attitude, which we just receive as well and don't furnish ourselves with. This is also supported by the fact that with inclinations–just as with attitudes–we have to distinguish between voluntariness, and the freedom to accept them or refuse them, to allow them to become operative within us or to renounce them. Suppose I accept an inclination. That means I give myself over to it, I allow it to take possession of me. That is not yet to say that the inclining leads to a doing, or that it converts into a willing. For example, the wish awakens in me to make a recreational trip. I accept it as a wish, I don't shut it [62] out, I give it room, and it develops into an intense desire for relaxation for the beauty of the countryside, for fresh air and sunshine. However, alongside of this desire there exists in me the firm resolve to deal first with the work that I've begun, and the desire is not allowed to arrive at its natural consequence. I do not will the trip, and I do not carry it out.

Now if we investigate what it means to renounce an inclination, we notice that there exists yet another possibility here besides those we came to know with the attitudes. If I don't plant my feet on a belief, I make it inoperative but I don't make it go away. An inclination cannot be made merely inoperative, but I can get rid of it altogether if I withdraw myself from it. Instead of giving myself over to every wish that arises, I distract myself from them, I busy myself, completely absorbed in the work that I have before me–and it succeeds. It's not just that the inclination doesn't turn into a doing; rather, it dies away without having taken hold. That doesn't mean only that I have withdrawn my attention from it and in doing so have shoved it into the background. For it's also possible that I make up my mind not to think about the trip any more, and carry through with that resolve. As long as the thought remains outside the scope of my vision, the inclining is dormant, too. (At least, it can be; but it doesn't absolutely have to be dormant. It would also be possible for the inclination to linger as a mysterious and indeterminately directed urge.) But as soon as I grant it admittance again, the inclining wakes up again too. In a similar way, a belief remains "latent" as long as I compel myself not to think about the fact in question; but it revives as soon as I turn to it again.

It's entirely otherwise if you suppress not just the thought of what you're inclining toward, but the inclining itself. I can once again accept the thought of the yearned-for trip after work is done; but now, nothing more of the yearning is to be detected. The yearning is extinguished. In order to understand this "extinction," we must pursue the structure of inclinations from another direction. As they make their appearance, inclinations are conditioned–purely phenomenally–by various features. Sometimes (just like attitudes) they are stirred up by the objectivities to which they are directed, and to be sure, by the objectivities precisely with the determinate character with which they appear–in our example, by the "enticing" trip. On the other hand, they have their "source" (as Pfänder says) partly in an attitude of the ego, perhaps delight over the attractiveness of the trip that I anticipate; and partly in a certain purely [63] egoic condition like fatigue that allows relaxation during the trip to appear so enticing for me. If I turn my gaze away from what I'm inclining toward, then I deprive the inclination (and the attitude presently founding it, respectively) of their objective support; however, I don't choke off their source. As long as that is present, the inclining comes back as soon as its basis is restored.

Considered more exactly now, our case looks like this: in a state of fatigue with exhausting work, the thought of the vacation dawns upon me. Out of the fatigued state, the urge for liberation from the exhausting activity bubbles up, and it "attaches" itself to the vacation. While I am representing it to myself intuitively, tendencies emerge that appear significant for me, and they lend it the character of "tempting," and now desire for it sets in within me. The indeterminate urge has become a goal-directed inclination. Alternatively, suppose that out of love for somebody I develop the inclination to show him some proof of love. This starts out as an indeterminate urge too. Then it strikes me that a gift would please him, and now my inclining directs itself toward procuring the gift and sending it off.

The inclining can also be grounded purely objectively. Because I was considering a beautiful picture and am filled with delight over it, the desire to purchase it seizes hold of me. (Basically that's also the case with the previous example–even if indirectly–since the attitude from which the inclining develops is objectively grounded itself.) In such circumstances, the inclining will become more or less repressed, or will surface again, if you turn your attention away, or turn back again. If inclining arises from an attitude, then it can also be neutralized by my not "accepting" that attitude and by my making it inoperative; for example, the delight over the picture, or the love for the human being whom I'm inclined to please.

It's different when the inclining has its source in a living condition *as well*. Then the resurgence of the inclining depends upon whether or not that source is still itself present with the new turning of the attention toward the goal. If it is no longer present, then the striving doesn't set in again, [64] in spite of the renewal of the objective basis. But multiple possibilities exist here. The fatigue–in our first example–can have developed into utter exhaustion that no longer is able either to produce or to sustain inclining on its own. Then we might turn ourselves with total attention toward the trip that tempted us before, and also recognize its significance for us; yet the trip leaves us cold and arouses no inclination. The suppressing of the inclining has then consisted only in the withdrawal of attention. The total extinction of the inclining is an event that happens within me and that I had absolutely nothing to do with: a *causal* process, in our sense. Yet it's also possible that although the condition of fatigue persists, its corresponding inclining is deliberately held at bay, perhaps even while I advert to the goal. The inclining would like to activate itself, but I don't allow it to get established. And finally, its possible that the condition's effect hasn't just been counteracted, but rather, the condition itself is "conquered."

Thus we see: inclining is (1) objectively grounded; (2) causally dependent; and (3) dependent upon the influence of the will, in a threefold way: (a) the objective basis can be withdrawn from the inclining by turning the attention away, which is itself "free"; (b) the influences of causal factors can be voluntarily counteracted; (c) the causal factors themselves are submitted to the influence of the will. ...

The Intermeshing of Causality and Motivation

Influencing of the Sensate Mechanism by the Contents of Experience

[75] To advance further in understanding, we must now propose distinctions among the acts themselves. Perceptions and recollections of what was perceived, acts of thinking–in short, all acts in which 'matters are given'–are carried out in a manner determined by the distinctive character of life feelings at the time, without exercising any reciprocal effect upon the life feeling itself, regardless of the fact that in the process the acts "consume" as it

were the power necessary to their inception. Besides that, there are other experiences that share life feelings in a distinctive manner and impinge upon its status: the so-called "emotions" or feelings (as to what corresponds to them from a more objective angle, we can also say the value attitudes). Suppose that while I am hearing a report, and thus while this objectivity, "report," is developing for me into a series in the current of self-generating intellective acts, a joy at this report is beginning to fill me up. "Joy," this unity of experience, is oriented toward something "external" to the current. Indeed it is joy "at" the report, therefore an "act." And something on the objective side corresponds to it: the joyousness of the report, which attaches to it by virtue of its positive value. Like all experiences, the joy is causally determined: it is duller or more lively according to the condition of the prevailing life feeling. And it's also possible that the life feeling doesn't even let the joy in, that in its place a feeble phantom enters, in which I very well apprehend the joyousness without being able to "really rejoice."

And this brings us to something entirely new. The joy is not merely joy at the report, but at the same time it fills "me" up, it impinges upon the status of my life feeling. The joy is a new current, as it were, that gushes into the lifestream from elsewhere, "churns it up," influences its subsequent flow, and colors it in a determinate manner. Therefore the kind of impact can vary according to the kind of feeling. To begin with, it seems that when any feeling sets in with a certain strength, it slows down the current. This must be overcome before the feeling makes itself operative in its specific effect. The feeling either impels the rest of the flowing current forward more rapidly or paralyzes it, and colors it either 'brighter' or 'gloomier.' The way in which the life feeling is "colored in" depends—as was said—upon the specific character of whatever the operative experiences may be. This is an "intentional" character that has for its correlate the object toward which the feeling is oriented.

[76] The feeling is *motivated* by the object that it's turned toward. The "depth" of feeling is dependent upon the height of the felt value, and so is the strength of the feeling. The specific coloring of the feeling is dependent upon the particular kind of value. The feeling is insightfully and rationally motivated only insofar as it corresponds in all its dimensions to the value. Accordingly, whatever there is about the feeling that is not "owing" to the value (its greater or lesser strength, perhaps) is unmotivated, uninsightful, and to be explained as merely the effect

of the present life feeling. Now you can designated the impact itself as motivated, inasmuch as the effect that the arising emotional experience exerts upon the life feeling depends upon its specific character, its strength and depth, which are rationally motivated; however, its not possible to construe this effect as motivation. For its not that I accomplish an alteration in the current of my total former experiencing on the grounds of the feeling that's filling me up; rather, this alteration accomplishes itself in me as a blind occurrence.

This is clearly shown if we compare this blind efficacy with the "moving power" that otherwise inheres in the feeling. What the feeling pushes toward is that an action be called into life, for example an act of willing, which I now carry out on the basis of the feeling, and which therefore is rationally motivated. So the joy that someone has given me motivates the resolve on my part to please him. In this, causal occurrences and occurrences of motivation steadily play into one another. A feeling that suddenly "overwhelms" me can be so severely paralyzing that it's just about impossible for the act of the will to arise, the act which the feeling would have had to motivate "insightfully" and "in a rational manner" (the act, which we plainly say, *is* objectively motivated by it).

If we wish to understand the effect of these powers flowing in from without, then we have to make use of the distinctions that we came across in the varieties of experience considered earlier. In the investigation of impulses, we already found that not only the experiencing of impulses, but also the content of the impulses feeds off the lifesphere, and that on the other hand, there is such a thing as a current feeding in to the lifesphere.[45] Obviously that's also the case with the new varieties of experience that we just brought up: that their *contents* either contribute new impelling power to the lifesphere or feed off of it.

To start with, we're seeking to probe more closely how the "influx" of powers is to be understood. Suppose that in a state of fatigue in which [77] I feel "lifeless" or inwardly numb, I reach for a book, for a literary work that I love, and suppose that delight over its beauty takes hold of me. Perhaps it's hard for me at first to summon up this delight–the available power scarcely suffices for the experiencing of this content–but as the content begins to course through me, fills me more and more, and finally inundates me entirely, the fatigue goes away and I feel myself to be "as

---

45 See pp. 65ff.

though newborn," refreshed and lively and full of incentive for new life activity. Thanks to the causal connections in which it is entwined, the delight manifests to me a sentient conditionality–just like the experiences considered earlier. The real sentient subject is constituted on the basis of causal relationships. And in that fact, what appears now is the total experiencing, which we can consider in its purity, regardless of all reality, in altered apprehensions: the current of consciousness turns into a series of states of the real subject; it enters fully and completely into reality. Everything that we can establish in pure reflection upon the experiences therefore transfers without further ado onto the sensate conditionalities that now are designated as "experiences" in the usual manner of speaking. ...

The Co-Operation of Causality and Motivation: Sensate and Mental Lifepower

[81] Yet even without regard to the "influx," it seems that you have to separate a "sensory" and a "mental" stratum, and correspondingly a sensory and a mental lifepower, as different roots of the psyche. With sensory lifepower, the *psyche* appears to be sunk into the *physis*: into bodiliness and, moreover, by means of bodiliness [sic *bodiless*] into material nature. To show this, it would take a thorough investigation of the body and of its dependence on material nature, on one hand, and its relationships to the psyche, on the other hand. But here we are taking under consideration only the fact that sensory life states are experienced at the same time as bodily life states are experienced. Vigor or fatigue appears as something that runs through the body and all of its members, something that, in its own way, colors any activities that are given as bodily. Clearly, this can be set apart from the mental vigor or weariness that, although perhaps consistent with the bodily-sensory conditionality, is something else. Nevertheless, if we are trying to talk about *one* lifesphere and *one* lifepower, this implies that the two aren't existing side by side and unconnected. Mental lifepower appears to be determined by sensory lifepower: as a rule, mental vigor also fades along with bodily vigor. Yet aside from that, mental lifepower remains open to influxes from the object world and through them can become capable of achievements which don't accord with the state of sensory lifepower. Conversely, sensory lifepower does not undergo any enhancement by [82] means of mental lifepower. The mental vigor produced by an influx from without can perhaps merely camouflage a bodily-sensory tiredness and deceive us in that way

concerning the true state of sensory lifepower. Furthermore, it should be noted that all mental life implies a consumption of sensory lifepower, even that whose contents bring with them an increment in mental impulse powers. For when a content has a certain weightiness its impulse power rises, but at the same time this weightiness requires a greater exertion of power so that it can be experienced. So you have to say straight out that the more sensory lifepower you lose, the more mental lifepower you deliver. ... Furthermore, it's possible that the impulse power flowing in from the contents exceeds that necessary for the experiencing of these contents. Then the mental lifepower is enriched and restored, so that the mental life is supplied for a long time *without* a further requisition of sensory lifepower. ...

[84] Beyond these influxes of impulse power, which presuppose a certain amount of lifepower already–namely, that required for the experiencing of power-giving contents–there is obviously still another that isn't tied to that presupposition. There is a state of resting in God, of complete relaxation of all mental activity, in which you make no plans at all, reach no decision, much less take action, but rather leave everything that's future to the divine will, "consigning yourself entirely to fate." This state might have befallen me after an experience that exceeded my power, and that has completely consumed my mental lifepower and deprived me of all activeness. Compared to the cessation of activeness from the lack of lifepower, resting in God is something completely new and unique. The former was dead silence. Now its place is taken by the feeling of being safe, of being exempted from all anxiety and responsibility and [85] duty to act. And as I surrender myself to this feeling, new life begins to fill me up, little by little, and impel me–without any voluntary exertion–toward new activation. This reviving infusion appears as an emanation of a functionality and a power which is not my emanation and which becomes operative within me without my asking for it. The sole prerequisite for such a mental rebirth seems to be a certain receptivity, like the receptivity supporting the structure of the person, a structure exempted from the sensate mechanism.

Something similar may be possible in the communications of one person with another. The love with which I embrace a human being may be sufficient to fill him with new lifepower if his own breaks down. Indeed, the mere contact with human beings of more intense aliveness may exert an enlivening effect upon those who are jaded or exhausted, who have no activeness as a presupposition on their side.

MICHEL HENRY (1922-2002)

Henry was born in 1922 in Haïphong, Vietnam where his father was serving in the French military. His father, however, died when he was a baby, and the family eventually relocated to Lille, France in 1929. Henry studied philosophy at the University of Lille from 1941-1945 and at the École Normale Supérieure from 1942-1943. During the Second World War Henry was active in the French Resistance, serving in the Maquis of the Haut-Jura under the code name of the philosopher Kant. Subsequently, Henry attended the Sorbonne for several years, receiving his doctorate in philosophy in 1963 under Ferdinand Alquié, Henri Gouhier, Jean Hyppolite, Jean Wahl, and Paul Ricoeur. Henry worked at the Centre National de la Recherche Scientifique from 1947-1950, married in 1958, and taught philosophy at the Université Paul-Valéry in Montpellier from 1960-1982. He died in 2002 in Albi, France.

The key works of Henry are his: *L'Essence de la manifestation* (1963), *Philosophie et Phénoménologie du corps* (1965), and his later Christian trilogy, *C'est moi la Vérité: Pour une philosophie du christianisme* (1996), *Incarnation: Une philosophie de la chair* (2000), *Paroles du Christ* (2002). Henry also wrote prize-winning novels.

For more on the thought of Michel Henry see: O'Sullivan, Michael. *Michel Henry* (Frankfurt: Peter Lang, 2006); Kahn, Rolf, and Jad Hatem. *Michel Henry's Radical Phenomenology* (Buthatest: Humanitas, 2009); Hanson, Jeffrey, and Michael R. Kelly, eds. *Michel Henry: The Affects of Thought* (London: Bloomsbury, 2012); Rebidoux, Michelle. *The Philosophy of Michel Henry* (Lewiston: Edwin Mellen Press, 2012); De Rivera, Joseph. *The Contemplative Self after Michel Henry* (Notre Dame: University of Notre Dame Press, 2015).

The selections are from Henry's *I Am the Truth* (Stanford: Stanford University Press, 2003), 101-5 in part, and "Speech and Religion: The Word of God," in D. Janicaud, et al., eds., *Phenomenology and the "Theological Turn"* (New York: Fordham University Press, 2000), 222-9.

Henry undertakes a phenomenology of life. In contrast with visible being which appears in its exteriority, in humans (and God) there is an interior and invisible reality that never manifests itself in the external world and is not discoverable by excavation. Henry is thus opposed to philosophies that reduce being to merely exterior manifestations, an illegitimate form of ontological monism. For human life manifests itself via auto-affection, a radical immanence and interiority in which one experiences oneself, one's happenings, and one's tonalities of joy or suffering. Life then occurs as a passive state of auto-affection wherein what affects is the same as what is affected. Such a life, in fact, is reminiscent of that of the Trinity. Indeed in the end pure auto-affection is only found in the Trinity, as human auto-affection is dependent upon divine auto-affection.

I Am the Truth: Toward a Philosophy of Christianity (1996)[46]

Man as "Son of God"

[101] Far from understanding Christ (or even just a part of his being) on the basis of man and his condition, it is man who must be understood on the basis of Christ, and can be so only in this way.

To understand man on the basis of Christ, who is himself understood on the basis of God, in turn rests on the crucial intuition of a radical phenomenology of Life, which is precisely that of Christianity: namely, that *Life has the same meaning for God, for Christ, and for man.* This is so because there is but a single and selfsame essence of Life, and, more radically, a single and selfsame Life. This Life–that self-generates itself in God and that, in its self-generation, generates the transcendental Arch-Son as the essential Ipseity in which this self-generation comes about– is the Life from which man himself takes his transcendental birth, precisely since he is Life and is explicitly defined as such within Christianity. He is the Son of this unique and absolute Life, and thus the Son of God. ... It is the essence of divine life–that which makes [man] one of the living, and that alone.

The thesis of man as the "son of God" thus has a dual significance, part negative and part positive. In a negative sense, it prevents man from being understood as a natural Being, as do common sense and the sciences. But it also prevents him from being understood, from the transcendental viewpoint, as a Being for whom the world would constitute the horizon of all experiences, or the mode of appearing common to each of these experiences. Thus it is Christ's sweeping assertion about himself that must be reconsidered with regard to man and his true essence: "They are not of the world any more than I am" (John 17:14). Just like Christ, as a man I am not of the world in the radical phenomenological sense that the appearing out of which my phenomenological flesh is made, and which constitutes my true essence, is not the appearing of the world. This is not due to the effect of some supposed credo, philosophical or theological; it is rather because the world has no flesh, because in the "outside-itself" of the world no flesh and no living are possible–they cannot take shape anywhere other than in Life's *pathētik* and a-cosmic

---

embrace. ...

[103] This is the meaning of the thesis that "God created man in his image": that he gave man his own essence. He did not give it to him as one gives an object to someone, like a gift passing from one hand to another. He gave him his own essence in the sense that, his own essence being the self-engendering of Life in which is engendered the Ipseity of all the living, then in giving his own essence God gave man the living condition, the happiness of experiencing himself in this experiencing of self that is Life and in the radical immanence of this experiencing, where there is neither "outside" nor "world." ...

To make sense of man's essence, the phenomenology of the world must be dismissed, as it was for Christ–and through him. Or, if you prefer, it is the idea of man in the usual sense that must be renounced. We think there is something like a man because we are looking at the world. It is within this gaze, formed by it, that the silhouette of a man is traced, against the horizon of visibility that is the world's truth. Because the man one sees takes his appearance from the world's appearance, the laws of this appearance also apply to him: space, time, causality, the multiple determinations woven each day by the natural sciences and the so-called sciences of man, in whose web he is caught. This man is brother [104] to the automata that can be constructed according to the same laws–and will be. What this specter lacks in order to be similar to what we are is to be living–not the kind of living foreign to life of which biology speaks but the living that carries within itself absolute phenomenological Life, the man we do not see, any more than we see Christ, the man who was born into Life and takes from his transcendental birth all its *pathētik* characteristics, the transcendental man of Christianity, the Son of God. ...

I myself am this singular Self engendered in the self-engendering of absolute Life, and only that. *Life self-engenders itself as me.* If, along with Meister Eckhart–and with Christianity–we call Life God, we might say: "God engenders himself as me."[47] The generation of this singular Self that I myself am–the living transcendental Me, in the self-generation of absolute Life: this is my transcendental birth, the one that makes me a true man, the transcendental Christian man. ...

[105] Here let me introduce a crucial concept that perhaps

47 Meister Eckhart, *The Essential Sermons, Commentaries, Treatises, and Defenses*, Bernard McGunn and Edmund Colledge, O.S.A., eds. (New York: Paulist Press, 1981). Sermon 6, p. 187.

ought to have been introduced earlier, since it governs the philosophical understanding of life's essence: the concept of *self-affection*.[48] What is specific to life is, in effect, that it affects itself. This self-affection defines its living, the "experiencing-itself" of which it consists. Affection generally implies a manifestation. If a being of the world affects me, it makes itself felt by me, shows itself to me, gives itself to me, enters into my experience in some way or other. And this is valid for the world itself, which affects me because it is manifests itself to me–this manifestation of the world being, as we have seen, its "truth." Truth and affection are equivalent terms. The concept of affection, designating any affection whatever and thus any manifestation (that affects me via a sound that I hear, an object that I see, an odor I smell, or else that affects my mind via an image or any other representation), contrasts sharply with the concept of self-affection. In self-affection, what affects me is no longer anything foreign or external to me who am affected, and consequently no object belonging to the world or the world itself. What affects in the case of self-affection is the same as what is affected. But this extraordinary situation in which what affects is the same as what is affected occurs nowhere except within life. And such a situation occurs there absolutely, such that it defines the essence of this life. Life is that which itself affects itself in the radical and decisive sense that this life that is affection, and that is affected, is not affected by anything other than itself, by no kind of externality and by nothing exterior to it. In this way, life constitutes the content of its affection. The concept of self-affection as life's essence implies its acosmic character, the face that being affected by nothing other, nothing external or radically foreign to the world, it comes about in itself in the absolute sufficiency of its radical interiority–experiencing only itself, being affected only by itself, prior to any possible world and independently of it.

---

[48] It was in the light of this concept [*auto-affection*] that I explored the concept of life in *L'Essence de la manifestation* (Paris: Presses Universitaires de France, 1963; 2d ed., 1990, esp. pp. 31ff.

"Speech and Religion: The Word of God" (1992)[49]

[222] We arrive now at our question: What do the Gospels say about the *ego*, what do they say about us? They say that we are the Sons. Now Sons and filiation are found only in Life. In the world, by contrast, no such thing as birth is possible. Things are not born, and, for this reason, they do not die, except metaphorically. In the world, things appear and disappear without anything living ever being able to arrive in their appearance or being able to disappear in their disappearance.

Only Sons have a birth; they are born in Life, begotten by it, being one of the living only as such, as Sons. Life is the Word of God. To understand Life as the very Word of God is possible, however, only if by this term "word" we refrain from understanding something that might resemble the words that men speak. The Word of God no doubt has one characteristic in common with the Word of the World: it is phenomenological through and through. This is why the saying of the divine word is a revelation. But how does the divine word reveal, what sort of appearing does it deliver, and what does it say to us? This is the crucial question; it is that of phenomenology–of a phenomenology that grasps itself–and perhaps also that of theology, a theology that grasps itself–not as discourse on God but as the Word of God himself. The Word of God reveals, speaks, as Life. Life, that is to say, the original word, is the Archi-Revelation as self-revelation, as auto-affection. This is to say that life reveals in such [223] a way that what it reveals is itself and nothing other. It affects in such a way that the content of its affection is itself and nothing other. In distinction from the Word of the World, which points away from itself and always speaks of something else, of something else that in this Word is carried outside itself, thrown out of line, deprived of its own reality, reduced to an image, to a content without content, at once opaque and nonetheless empty the Word of Life gives life. It is called the Word of Life because its Logos is Life, namely, self-givenness, self-enjoyment.

Giving in this way, speaking this Logos, Life begets its Sons in it. The transcendental birth of Sons, of those who, in the Word of the World, will be called *ego*, self, men, individuals, persons, and

---

so on, is a birth intelligible in life and in it alone. And this is because there is no other way to come into life except through life itself. In the process of its incessant coming into itself, which is that of its eternal auto-affection, life undergoes itself in such a way that a Self results each time from this ordeal as identical to its pure "undergoing itself." Such an ordeal is singular on principle, undergoing what it undergoes, phenomenologically defined by the content of this ordeal. Life is the essence of ipseity; it is carried out by giving birth to the latter, by giving birth to it in it and without ever departing from itself. But all ipseity, as living, is a singular Self.

Thus life is begotten, carried out, undergone as a singular Self, as this Self that I myself am. Life auto-affects itself as myself. If with Eckhart, one calls life "God," then one will say with him: "God is begotten as myself." But this Self begotten in Life, holding the singularity of its Self only from ipseity and holding its ipseity only from the eternal auto-affection of life, bears the latter in it, inasmuch as it is borne by it and arrives in each instant in life only through it. Thus life communicates itself to each of the Sons by penetrating him as a whole, such that there is nothing in him that would not be living, and moreover nothing inasmuch as its Self arrives only in the auto-affection of life itself–that would not contain in itself this eternal essence of life. "God gives birth to me as himself."[50]

The mystery of the transcendental birth of Sons in Life stems [224] from the fact that in this birth two passivities collapse into each other: the radical passivity of life vis-à-vis the Self in its eternal auto-affection (in theological language, the eternal *jouissance* [enjoyment] of God) and, on the other hand, the passivity of the singular Self begotten in this auto-begetting of absolute life. For, this Self is passive with regard to itself only within the auto-affection of Life that begets it and the passivity proper to this life. Life throws the Self into itself inasmuch as it is thrown into itself, in its eternal auto-affection and thus through it. The phenomenality of these two passivities–that of Life, that of the Self–is the same. It is a non-ecstatic pathos, which is why neither of them can be said to be even the least bit passive in relation to something exterior in the phenomenological sense and thus visible.

---

[50] Meister Eckhart, Sermon 6; English translation from *Meister Eckhart: Teacher and Preacher*, ed. Bernard McGinn (New York: Paulist Press, 1986), p. 187.

The fact that the Self can subsist only in the eternal auto-affection of Life in it invites us to make a more precise distinction between two concepts of this auto-affection. The auto-affection that expresses the essence of absolute life signifies that the latter affects itself in the twofold sense that it is carried out as productive of its own affection and at the same time as the content of this affection. Life is what affects and what is affected. This life can be called absolute because it needs nothing other than itself to exist. Phenomenologically, there is after all nothing else to it. This is why this life can still be called infinite, because the finitude of the ecstatic horizon of a world is totally foreign to it. It can be called eternal because the temporality that deploys this ecstatic horizon has no place in it either. The phenomenological passivity that characterizes all life inasmuch as it is pure self-enjoyment even in sorrow–can just as well be thought as a pure Act since in the case of this absolute life, it is it itself that produces the affection constitutive of its essence, which is self-begotten.

In the case of the auto-affection of the singular Self that I am, auto-affection has changed its meaning. The Self auto-affects itself; it is the identity of the affector and the affected, but in such a way that it has not itself posited this identity. The Self auto-affects itself only insofar as absolute life auto-affects itself in it. Passive, it is so not just in regard to itself and each of the determinations of its life, in the way that each suffering is passive vis-à-vis itself and is possible only as such, getting its affective tenor only from this passivity whose pure phenomenological tenor is affectivity as [225] such. The Self is passive first in regard to the eternal process of the auto-affection of the life that begets it and is forever begetting it. This passivity of the Self in life is not a metaphysical determination posited by thought; it is a phenomenological determination constitutive of the Self's life and which, as such, is forever being lived by it. This determination is so essential, the ordeal that is undergone so unrelenting, that our life is nothing other than this feeling of being lived. If one sticks to the experience proper to it, the Self therefore should not be called what auto-affects itself, but what is found unrelentingly auto-affected. How is it that the specific mode of the singular Self's passivity as auto-affected in the eternal auto-affection of Life does not define simply a general characteristic of its own life? How is it that this particular mode of passivity begets in this life all its essential modalities, which are as such pathetic–for example, the anxiety or the drive that originates directly in the phenomenological structure of the Self and is identical to it? Here is not the place to show this. For us, the problem is rather to understand the relation between these two passivities collapsed each into the other in the transcendental birth of the Self as the birth of a Son in Life. In sum, the issue is this: by pushing phenomenology to its limit, as radical phenomenology, as material phenomenology, to understand man's relation to God, to at least circumscribe what, as phenomenology, it can say about this relation.

What this phenomenology has established, at the point we have arrived at in our analysis, is the quasi-identity of the essence of man and that of God, namely, Life. Such an essence is not merely phenomenological; it is that of an Archi-phenomenality. It is this Archi-phenomenality of life which makes it a Word, an Archiword that speaks of nothing else but itself, at once the how and the content of what it says, of what it says *to us*, inasmuch as in its saying a singular self is built up. If we are in the word and speak only in its wake, if this word is addressed to us[51] and enjoins us in such a way that no one can evade it, this is simply because, as Word of Life finding its essence in Life, it is first in itself, in an absolute immanence that nothing can break. Next, it is because [226] in the immanence of its auto-affection, a singular Self is begotten each time, to which it is addressed henceforth and to which it can address itself and address itself inevitably—in this auto-affection that has become no longer the auto-affection of Life but that of the Self.

This phenomenological essence common to man and God grounds their phenomenological relation, begets man as a man who knows God—"*ein Gott wissender Mensch*"[52]—"we worship what we know"[53]—while, begetting man in the auto-affection of his own auto-begetting, God knows man, reads the depths of his heart in the very act by which he begets him. This commonality of a phenomenological essence could be expressed metaphorically by saying: the Eye with which I see God and the Eye with which God sees me is but one and the same Eye—it being understood that phenomenologically speaking, here there is neither Eye nor vision nor world, nor anything like that.

---

51 Above, cf. Martin Heidegger, *Unterwegs zur Sprache* (Stuttgart: Neske Pfüllingen, 1959), particularly pp. 241, 179, 258, 180; English translation from *On the Way to Language*, translated by Peter D. Hertz (New York: Harper and Row, 1971), pp. 111-112, 75, 126, 76.

52 Eckhart, Sermon 10.

53 John 4:23.

That man knows God is an outrageous proposition, one barely heard today. What is it other than the inevitable response to the most simple question: Is it conceivable that the living know nothing of life? Where and how, why, what formidable hatred for life has gathered in the world where we live that the innermost certainty that life has of living has been hidden, not simply hidden, but to speak truly, denied, thus committing in this long series of murders that is the history whose horror Voltaire saw, a quite particular murder, a theoretical murder in some ways, general, putting to death no one in particular, but stripping each living thing of its living quality and doing so by stripping life of what makes it life. But let us leave aside these questions that pertain to modernity and return to our own question, which belongs to no time and now stands out in its simplicity: What do the living know about life?

In a certain sense, nothing, if it is a matter of that knowing that guides the modern world and modern thought. And this is because such a knowing is excluded from the internal structure of life. In another sense, inasmuch as the essence of the living stems from the Archi-revelation of life, doesn't it know all there is to [227] know about it? Let us try to glimpse this extraordinary knowing, without anything held back or left over, where in the absolute immanence of a pathetic autoaffection, the living has already laid hold of all that which, in this taking possession, is henceforth under its power, one of its powers. For it is but the most humble drive, the most elementary act that presupposes—in order to be carried out without thought, without representation, without imagination, without perception, without conception, without being preceded in any way, and without wanting, without showing itself in any world—nothing but the auto-affection of the living contemporaneous with its transcendental birth and identical to it.

Isn't it significant that Heidegger, when he wanted to think life, taking his inspiration from the biologists of his time, was compelled to turn to the immanence of an original being-in-possession-of-itself belonging to the drive and its specific phenomenality, thought negatively as fascination (*Benommenheit*), or else in categories totally foreign to the analytic of *Dasein* [Human Existence], as Didier Franck has shown.[54] And if in other texts Heidegger believed he could

---

[54] Cf. "L'Être et le Vivant," *Philosophie* 7 (1987): 73-92; English translation, "Being and the Living," in *Who Comes after the Subject?*, ed.

radically separate philosophy and theology and affirm that "faith does not arise from *Dasein*,"[55] isn't this simply because the analytic of *Dasein*, like the later thought of Being, was entirely ignorant of life? For Faith is not some sort of lesser knowledge deprived of its own position and thus of all possible justification. It is simply a name for the unshakeable certainty that life has of living and for its hyperknowing. Faith does not come from the fact that we believe, it comes from the fact that we are the living in life. It is our condition as Sons that makes us believe what we believe, namely, that we are Sons; and it is for this reason alone that Faith can befall us.

Does the living know everything about life? Haven't we said that the auto-affection of the living differs from the auto-affection of life insofar as only the second produces itself in the sense of an absolute auto-affection. If the singular Self is auto-affected in its [228] transcendental birth–that is to say, begotten as a Self–only in the auto-affection of life, doesn't the latter precede it as an already to which it will never be able to return, as a past that it will never be able to rejoin and that will remain forever closed to it an absolute past? In his magnificent work *L'inoubliable et l'inespéré*,[56] Jean-Louis Chrétien reintroduced the concept of the Immemorial. I will take it up here to designate the antecedence of life to all the living.

That there is no memory of the Immemorial means first that we cannot represent it, form a memory of it, relate to it by any thought whatsoever. The Archi-ancient never turns toward thought. In this sense the Immemorial is struck by an insurmountable Oblivion. This Oblivion is not something like the correlate or flip side of a possible memory; it is not the forgetting into which memory changes when we no longer think of it. In their mutual correlation, forgetting and memory each proceed from a single place, from that place that is freed by the Word of the World, from "that clearing that every appearance must seek out

---

Eduardo Cadava, Peter Connor, and Jean-Luc Nancy (New York: Routledge, 1991), pp. 135-147.

55 Martin Heidegger, "*Phänomenologie und Theologie*," from *Wegmarken*, in *Gesamtausgabe* (Frankfurt am Main: Vittorio Klostermann, 1979), vol. 9, p. 52; English translation from "Phenomenology and Theology," in *The Piety of Thinking*, translated by James G. Hart and John C. Maraldo (Bloomington: Indiana University Press, 1976), p. 9 (modified).

56 (Paris: Desclée de Brouwer, 1991).

and every disappearance must leave behind."[57] In the Immemorial of the antecedence of Life no clearing of this sort is ever given out, and this is so simply because there is no possible memory or forgetting of it, no conversion of the one into the other. Now the absolute Oblivion that banishes all memory and all forgetting, that never goes out to meet thought—does this forgetting bar all access to the Immemorial or does it constitute this access as such?

That thought does not have to remember, that the clearing where all appears appears and all that disappears disappears, does not open the path to the Immemorial but forbids access to it this is what renders untenable the claim to submit God to the priority of Being, and this is what justifies the problematic of Jean-Luc Marion.[58] For one can well say "God is," but as Being itself is subordinated to the priority of the givenness of appearing, the meaning of Being is decided only in the latter. From now on, submitting God to the priority of Being implies at least two [229] absurdities. The first is the presupposition that God is in himself foreign to Revelation and consequently obliged to ask an exterior revelation for the right to show himself in it, in the place that it assigns to him and in the way that it prescribes. But the second presupposition is even more mistaken because it has already identified the light to which God would owe his shing for us with that which is deployed in the Difference of the world and things—thus reserving, it is true, a small corner for God in the Fourfold. One must therefore reverse Heidegger's propositions, according to which "the experience of God and of his manifestedness, to the extent that the latter can indeed meet man, flashes in the dimension of Being"[59]; "the sacred ... comes into the light of appearing only when Being has been clarified beforehand."[60] For it is only when this light of appearing is extinguished, outside the clearing of Being, that access to the Immemorial is Possible—in Oblivion.

---

[57] Heidegger, *Unterwegs zur Sprache*, p. 257; English translation, p. 126.

[58] *Dieu sans l'Être* (Paris: Fayard, 1982; rev. ed., P.U.F., 1991); English translation, *God without Being* (Chicago: University of Chicago Press, 1991).

[59] Seminar at Zurich. Cited and commented on by Jean-Luc Marion in Dieu sand L'Être, p. 92 and p. 93, n. 15; English trans., p. 61 and p. 211, n. 16. See also Jean Greisch in *Heidegger et le question de Dieu*, ed. Jean Beaufret (Paris: Grasset, 1980), p. 334.

[60] *Questions III* (Paris: Gallimard, 1966), p. 114.

ROBERT SPAEMANN (1927-2018)

Spaemann was born in Berlin, Germany in 1927 to parents who were to convert to Catholicism from atheism three years later. He lost his mother when he was still a youth and his father afterwards became a Catholic priest in 1942. Spaemann attended the University of Münster starting in 1948 where he came under the influence of Joachim Ritter and received a doctorate in philosophy in 1952 writing on the traditionalist de Bonald. After working as an editor for the Kohlhammer Verlag for four years to support his family, Spaemann had married the author Cordelia Steiner in 1950), he returned to the University of Münster where he acquired his Habilitation in 1962 after writing on the thought of the semi-quietist Fénelon. Spaemann subsequently taught at the University of Stuttgart (1962-1968), the University of Heidelberg (1968-1972) where he succeeded Gadamer, and the University of Munich (172-1992). He died in 2018 in Stuttgart.

Among other honors Spaemann received the Premio Roncesvalles and the Karl Jaspers Prize in 2001 and the Aquinas Medal in 2012, and was honored with nomination to the European Academy of the Sciences and Arts in 1990, the Bavarian Order of Merit in 1994, and the Maximilian Order for Science and Art in 2002.

Spaemann's key works are his *Moralische Grundbegriffe* (Munich: Beck, 1982), translated as *Basic Moral Concepts* (London: Routledge, 1990); *Glück und Wohlwollen: Versuch über Ethik* (Stuttgart: Klett-Cotta, 1989), translated as *Happiness and Benevolence* (Edinburgh: T & T Clark, 2000); *Personen: Versuche über den Unterschied zwischen 'etwas' und 'jemand'* (Stuttgart: Klett-Cotta, 1996), translated as *Persons: The Difference between 'Someone' and 'Something'* (Oxford: Oxford University Press, 2006); and *Love and the Dignity of Human Life: On Nature and Natural Law* (Grand Rapids: William Eerdmans, 2012). He has also written several works on politics. His works are being collected in the *Gesammelten Schriften* (Stuttgart: Klett-Cotta, 2019-).

For more on Spaemann see: Zaborowski, Holger, *Robert Spaemann's Philosophy of the Human Person: Nature, Freedom, and the Critique of Modernity* (Oxford: Oxford University Press, 2010); Schindler, David C. *A Robert Spaemann Reader: Philosophical Essays on Nature, God, and the Human Person* (Oxford: Oxford University Press, 2015).

The translation below is from Spaemann's *Persons: The Difference between 'Someone' and 'Something,'* trans. Oliver O'Donovan (Oxford: Oxford University Press, 2006), pp. 232-235 on Spaemann's phenomenology and analysis of forgiveness. Forgiveness is a key aspect that defines persons for Spaemann for in forgiveness we grasp that a person is more than his or her attributes or actions and has the potential to grow and change. That is to say forgiveness highlights one of the key features of human persons, their freedom.

Persons: The Difference between 'Someone' and 'Something'
(1996)[61]

Promise and Forgiveness

[232] Forgiveness presupposes guilt–which implies the exercise of personal freedom. It is the personal 'self,' not some state in which the self finds itself, that underlies the behaviour in question. But there is another side to it: forgiveness presupposes that the wrong decision has not placed the person in a state that is definitely settled. Of course, *I* am the person who did *this*, and will always be so. My personal identity is not something apart from my innate or acquired attributes; it is the whole of which my attributes are qualifications. Yet the meaning of these qualifications for the whole–for the Being of the person–is not settled once and for all. The person is always more than the sum of the attributes. The person cannot make what has happened not to have happened, and must reckon with what he or she has become. But it makes a difference how this reckoning is done. Disowning a deed in repentance is a way of reintegrating what has happened by re-evaluating it.

Self-transcendence in regard for other persons is, as we have seen, how persons realize themselves. Rising above the egocentricity of our vital instincts is possible for us because as human beings we have the experience of recognition by others. Persons exist only in the plural. That applies also to when it is a question of finding their way back to resume their life-journey when it has been interrupted by the guilty *curvatio in se ipsum*. If the interruption is to be put behind them, it requires the help of others. And what the help consists in is their readiness, and especially the readiness of the injured party, not to identify the offender with what he has become in fact, but to permit him to redefine himself in relation to his deeds. This permission we call 'forgiving,' and it has to be asked for. Here there is a peculiar asymmetry: a duty to forgive corresponds to no right to be forgiven. The guilty party has no claim on forgiveness, and can only plead for it; yet the 'creditor' very definitely has a duty to respond to the plea. If he should fail in this, he too would fall into *curvatio*, his own personality would vanish from sight. For to

---

identify someone definitively with any of his predicates means to refuse him recognition as a person, which is to say, a subject free in respect of all its predicates. The guilty person needs the permission of others to exercise this [233] freedom–and that is his punishment. But one who refuses it, excludes himself, too; for the community of persons is in principle all-inclusive.

Forgiveness may be qualified by conditions, e.g. that the harm intended should be made good. Where the political community is involved, making good may even consist in accepting punishment, since punishment serves as a deterrent, preventing other similar offences. Yet punishment, as Hegel said, is 'the honouring of the offender,' i.e. as a person.[62] Having served his penalty he is restored to equal membership of the civil community as of right. The guilt is 'erased.' Even life imprisonment can be understood in principle as the effacement of guilt, an address to the person as a person, not merely a measure for dealing with him or with the situation. His place as a subject is not eliminated. On antique executioners' swords are engraved the words: 'When'er the blade I lift on high, I pray the sinner heavenward fly.' Naturally, an institution cannot offer forgiveness in the full sense of the word. It can only shape its procedures to make the possibility of forgiveness evident–which means that the procedures must permit and encourage the individual to achieve a distance on his own deed.

The question remains, which comes first, the permission or the inner distance? Both are plausible. Someone who finds himself permanently cast in other people's view as the one who did this thing or that, has no alternative but to make it a point of honour to define himself that way, 'to stand by what he did' as the phrase goes. He cannot go on for ever beginning to be recognized as what he would like to be, while having no claim to be recognized. He really is the one who did what he did; he cannot require anyone to look at him in a new light, as he would look at himself if he were permitted to. On the other hand, how can anyone look at him in a new light if he does not do so himself? How can I forgive an injury if it is persisted in? How can I forgive someone who does not ask for forgiveness?

Can we escape the stalemate of each side waiting for the other to go first? We saw in our discussion of evil that though it does not arise from innocent ignorance (for nothing from that source could

---

[62] *Philosophy of Right*, 100, trans. T.M. Knox (Oxford: Clarendon Press, 1952), 71.

be evil in the true sense), evil is, nevertheless, shrouded in a kind of [234] ignorance, depriving the agent of clarity. This is what makes conversion possible, because conversion is a return to clarity and there is a natural undertow pulling towards clarity. This, too, is what makes possible the first softening of the heart towards forgiveness, even the first step towards forgiveness itself. 'Forgive them, for they know not what they do!'[63] The Socratic intellectualist has nothing to forgive, since he takes evil to be no more than a mistake. But neither can someone who demonizes evil forgive, since evil willed as evil is unforgiveable, and conversion form it is impossible. But that guilty blindness which is evil's mode of appearing in the world of time and history always involved a moment of entanglement. To be set free from entanglement is a possibility, provided it is 'permitted,' provided the victim is prepared to view the offender as someone other than the perpetrator of the offence, which is to say, to forgive him. One who forgives abandons the right to take the offender as he found him, and gives the offender the opportunity to take himself differently, too. Until this opportunity is seized, forgiveness is no more than an exploratory probe. For if we say, 'I know you are not like that!,' we may be beaten back by the response, 'I am like that, and I will go on being so!' Forgiveness is then brought to a stand.

That forgiveness may anticipate a change of attitude and smooth the way for it, turns on what I have elsewhere called 'ontological forgiveness'.[64] We are finite and natural creatures, and we fail to live up to the promise our personhood presents. Which means we cannot treat everyone as they deserve to the same degree. That was why we had to make a promise in the first place, so that someone could rely on us in this or that instance, our sheer existence did not give reason enough for reliance. The 'ontological promise' of our existence is no more than a ground for relying on promises that we actually make. 'Ontological forgiveness' is the acknowledgement that the other person, being finite, cannot really put himself in the right with us. Simply as the finite and natural beings they are, persons stand in need of forbearance. Moral forgiveness offered 'on account' takes a step further, out of the transcendental sphere and into the categorial, out [235] of the ontological into the moral. Forgiveness teaches its goal in reconciliation, and in arriving at that point, makes itself

---

[63] Luke 23:34.

[64] Robert Spaemann, *Happiness and Benevolence*, trans. Jeremiah Alberg (Notre Dame: Notre Dame University Press, 2000), 189.

redundant by bringing to an end the moral asymmetry on which it stands and re-establishing equality of mutual recognition.

Equality, however, can only be re-established because it was never completely destroyed. Nobody, however bad his conduct, can finally annihilate himself as a person while still alive. Nobody can become an 'un-person,' the difference between personal identity and attributes reduced to zero. While someone lives, there is someone there to forgive. No one, on the other hand, is absolute freedom or pure subjectivity, rising above natural and finite perspectives. No one really knows what he does when he does wrong. That is why one cannot wait to forgive until the divergent perspectives have been merged, and the difference in how we see things is overcome. Since everyone is caught in his own perspective, irreconcilability is a sin in itself in that it refuses transcendence. It means locking oneself up in the person of one's own finitude, putting oneself out of reach of others' forgiveness. It is profoundly significant, therefore, that the petition for forgiveness in the Lord's Prayer is immediately expanded with a profession of readiness to forgive.

So forgiveness is the mark of personality, complementary to promising. Both confirm the difference between personal identity and the attributes and qualities that we display in real time. Promise underwrites the independence of personal identity from absorption in actuality. Forgiveness evokes this independence in the teeth of actuality. It is, in an eminent degree, an act of creation.

ENRIQUE DUSSEL (1934-)

Dussel was born in 1934 in La Paz, Argentina. After studying at the Universidad Nacional de Cuyo in Mendoza from 1953 to 1957, Dussel left for Europe to pursue advanced degrees in diverse fields. He received a doctorate in philosophy from the Complutense University of Madrid in 1959, a licentiate in theology from the Catholic Institute of Paris in 1965, and a doctorate in history from the Sorbonne in Paris in 1967. Dussel returned to Argentina in 1966 where he taught philosophy at the Universidad Nacional de Resistencia in Chaco and then at the Universidad Nacional de Cuyo starting in 1968, but, on account of his Marxist political leanings, was targeted during the Argentinian Revolution of 1966 to 1973, receiving death threats, having his house bombed in 1973, and was eventually dismissed from the University in 1976. Dussel fled to Mexico in 1975 where he joined the philosophy department at the Iztapalapa campus of the Universidad Autónoma Metropolitana (UAM) in Iztapalapa and the Universidad Nacional Autónoma de México (UNAM) in Mexico City, where he has taught ever since. Dussel served as rector of UNAM from 2013 to 2014. He received the Aristotle Medal from UNESCO in 2012 for his philosophical reflection on Latin-American politics and society.

Dussel's key writings are his *Para una ética de la liberación latinoamericana*, 2 vols. (Buenos Aires: Cambeiro, 1973); *History and the Theology of Liberation: A Latin American Perspective* (New York: Orbis Books, 1976); *Filosofía de la liberación* (México: Edicol, 1977), translated as *Philosophy of Liberation* (Eugene: Wipf and Stock, 2003); *Teología de la liberación y ética* (Buenos Aires: Latinoamérica, 1977), translated as *Ethics and the Theology of Liberation* (New York: Orbis Books, 1978); and *Ethics of Liberation: In the Age of Globalization and Exclusion* (Durham: Duke University Press, Durham, 2013);

For more on Dussel consult: *Michael Barber, Ethical Hermeneutics: Rationalism in Enrique Dussel's Philosophy of Liberation* (New York: Fordham University Press, 1998) and Linda Alcoff and Eduardo Mendieta, *Thinking from the Underside of History: Enrique Dussel's Philosophy of Liberation* (Lanham: Rowman and Littlefield, 2000); Alan Vincelette, *Recent Catholic Philosophy: The Twentieth Century*, 2nd edn (St. Louis: En Route, 2020), pp. 70-72.

The selection below is from Dussel's *Ethics and the Theology of Liberation* (New York: Orbis Books, 1978), pp. 46-48, in which Dussel combines the philosophy of Levinas with a philosophy of liberation. In this way he hopes to rescue the excluded 'other' from marginalization by the dominant society (the totality). In order to do so he advocates reframing the traditional theological virtues (faith (trust), hope, charity) as well as the cardinal virtues (wisdom (prudence), justice, courage (fortitude), and temperance) in light of a theory of liberation.

Ethics and the Theology of Liberation (1977)[65]

Theological Anthropology II: Ethics as Liberation Criticism:

[46] Only the great saints are capable of displaying clearly their opposition to the system even though they know they will be ground up by it. We stand in awe of their sanctity, their heroism, their spiritual struggles; but we tend to overlook the meaning of their challenge to their times. When Don Bosco rounded up all those orphans and gave them an education, the industrialists of Turin and northern Italy tipped their hand when they said, "This priest is going too far; he's becoming a bother." He was giving dignity to a poor people; but when those technical schools were taken over by influential urban groups, their prophetic contribution came to an end.

The Ethos of Liberation

In the praxis of liberation there are liberating virtues. First among them is the love of justice; it is the love of the Other *as other—charity*. Justice means giving to all people what is due them. But to give to the Other what is due them as other, and not as part of an unjust system, I must love them as other. Thus only in loving the Other as other will I go on to give them their due as persons and not as part of the system.

I cannot love people effectively as other if I do not *trust* their word. They cry out to me, "I'm hungry!" I answer, "Bums, you're hungry because you won't work." Since they shall make no further appeal to me, I have denied them as other. To trust is to have faith in the other; it means accepting their word out of a concrete praxis of commitment—this is the meaning of St. Thomas's *ex voluntate*. My intellect accepts what they say because they say it, even though I do not understand what they say.

The third position is *hope*. Hope means desiring that those who have appealed to me and told me of their hunger achieve their liberation, because I love them as [47] other, that is, I "hope" they will no longer be hungry. These three fundamental positions—to love the Other as other, to believe their word, and to hope for their liberation, their salvation—these are the three alterative or theological virtues. The rest are subordinate.

Prudence knows how to listen to the voice of the Other; it

---

[65] [Enrique Dussel, *Ethics and the Theology of Liberation*. Copyright © 1977 by Orbis Books. All rights reserved. Used with permission of Orbis Books, https://www.orbisbooks.com.]

knows how to orchestrate tactically its service. *Justice* is not merely the offer of bread but of more just laws; it could mean risking one's life so that one day there might be a more just order. Prudence and justice come into play in planning for the liberation of the poor. Anger, too, is involved, which is a manifestation of the virtue of *fortitude*. Being valiant is the capacity to commit oneself to the point of death, and this is the most difficult of all. To do so one must be poor. *Poverty* is an attitude. Poverty is not a question of having nothing but of a willingness to give up one's life for the poor. If I give up all my goods and join twenty people who have nothing, I will frequently have more than I had before: This is wealth and not poverty. The individual poverty of the monk many times comes to be wealth among many; it is security for the future. The strength of Jesus evidenced itself when he pardoned those who were torturing him. He looked upon them as persons. He who did the nailing looked upon him as a mere thing, and not a person. But Jesus looked at him as a person, face-to-face, and forgave his torturer-the noblest act a person is capable of. A school teacher in Argentina just a few years ago was able to forgive the police who were torturing her with electric shock treatments. When we know that the torturer is not sin but only the instrument of sin, we win out over death by treating him or her as a person.

But bravery and fortitude are not enough; we need *temperance* also. Today the opposite of temperance is [48] comfort, or socially acceptable pleasure. People today sell their lives in order not to lose their comfort. They watch what they say or do for fear of losing their jobs, and herefore no one is afraid of them. But those who have no fear of losing all they have bear watching. There is no point in telling Jesus that "we are going to take everything from you" when he had not even a place to lay his head. Jesus was unencumbered by things; he was poor and had no fear of losing anything. So there was no way to shut him up. He was a man to be feared. The only way to shut him up was to kill him. And this is precisely what they did.

Thus the *ethos* of liberation is all the virtues put to the service of liberation.

More about Violence

The violence that killed Jesus was the violence of the conquistador, repressive violence designed to nullify the authentic gesture of liberation. There is, on the other hand, the liberating violence of the liberator, for example, San Martin and his army of the Andes. Furthermore, there is the pedagogical violence of the prophet, the kind we see in Jesus. He organized a church and not a state. The function of the church will always be that of pedagogue and prophet, and not one of armed violence, not even in the cause of liberation. As a prophetic institution its function is eschatological-preaching what is to come. It takes a critical look at the fixation and anti-historicity of the totalized system, which is sin. The system would have wished that the Word of God had never come to this world. Nothing arouses greater anger in it than that God would have become man and placed himself *within* the system. Jesus Christ is now present until the end of time, continuously supplying Christians with the [49] vocation of commitment to the poor. Having done away with the old order, these Christians work toward a new order. But they will have to do this over and over again. The function of the Christian is to deinstitutionalize the institutions of sin and, like Jesus in his identification with the poor, turn history toward eschatology.

Being-in-the-Money

At one point in their history people said that being rich was all that mattered. Then the Christians came along and said that people have a natural right to private property. And this is true if we are talking about what a person needs according to individual human nature: a car, a house, clothing, food. But a piece of land measuring a thousand square miles cannot be *natural* private property, but only juridically so. That kind of property has a social function. If I am able to make institutions work for the good of the poor, I am complying with the demands of the gospel. Excessive private property leads to an economic system of subjugation. ... It frequently happens also that the church aligns itself with the subjugators, and this is its sin. Only by identifying itself with the poor can the church liberate the world from an unjust system. *Natural* private property is not contrary to socialistic principles because I have a natural right to whatever I need to live-things like calories, protein, clothing, housing, etc. There is no socialist system that quarrels with this. But the excessive and unjust accumulation of [50] juridical private property is an offshoot of original sin ... It is at the root of the subjugation of peoples in Latin America. If Jesus had respected the law, the Jewish "constitution" of the Sanhedrin, the reigning order and the socially acceptable virtues, he would have died an old man within the confines of the city. But he died *outside* the city—crucified.

JEAN-LOUIS CHRÉTIEN (1952-2019)

Chrétien was born in Paris (in the Eleventh Arrondissement) in 1952 and he died there as well in 2019. Though raised in an agnostic and Marxist household (his father had been a doctor in the International Brigades in the Spanish Civil War, Jean-Louis Chrétien converted to Catholicism around 1980. He attended the École Normale Supérieure from 1971 to 1974 and received an agrégation in philosophy. After teaching at the lycées of Mâcon and Vire (Calvados), and working for the Fondation Thiers from 1977 to 1980, Chrétien went on to acquire a doctorate in philosophy from the Sorbonne in 1983 under Pierre Aubenque and Vladimir Jankélévitch. Chrétien additionally came under the influence of the philosophers Henri Maldiney, Martin Heidegger, and Augustine. Chrétien taught initially at the University of Créteil (Paris XII) beginning in 1985 and then joined the faculty of the Sorbonne as professor of the history of medieval philosophy in 2007 where he taught until 2017. In 2012 Chrétien was awarded the Cardinal Lustiger Prize.

Besides being a poet, Chrétien composed such philosophical works as: *L'Appel et la réponse* (Paris: Minuit, 1992); *L'Arche de la parole* (Paris: Presses Universitaires de France, 1998); and *Sous le regard de la Bible* (Paris: Bayard-Centurion, 2008).

For more on Chrétien see: Benson, Bruce Ellis, and Norman Wirzba, eds., *Words of Life* (New York: Fordham University Press, 2010); Gschwandtner, Christina M., *Postmodern Apologetics?* (New York: Fordham University Press, 2012), pp. 143-162; Prevot, Andrew L., *Thinking Prayer* (Notre Dame: University of Notre Dame Press, 2015); Alvis, Jason W., *The Inconspicuous God* (Bloomington: Indiana University Press, 2018), pp. 179-193; Aspray, Silvianne, "An Augustinian Response to Jean-Louis Chrétien's Phenomenology of Prayer," *International Journal of Philosophy and Theology* 79, no. 3 (2018), pp. 311-322; DeLay, Steven, *Phenomenology in France* (London: Routledge, 2019), pp. 120-144.

The selection below is from Chrétien's *L'Arche de la parole* (Paris: Presses Universitaires de France, 1998), translated by Andrew Brown as *The Ark of Speech* (London: Routledge, 2003), ch. 2, pp. 18-19, 21-22, 25-26. Chrétien's oeuvre involves a phenomenological examination of fundamental human encounters that involve excess and fragility, transcendence and finitude, call and response, and speech and silence, as with encountering being, prayer, beauty, and art. For example, in the *Ark of Speech* (2003) Chrétien examines how prayer is a form of speech that bears various wounds as is a placing ourselves before an invisible God in silence, a God who has gifted us with the gifts of speech and creation in advance. Still though speech can never fully express what the divine is or render adequate praise and thanks, prayer is our only way of presenting ourselves to the unknown Thou who created us.

The Ark of Speech (1998)[66]

Wounded Speech: A Phenomenology of Prayer

[18] This fundamental phenomenon [of prayer], irreducible to any other, is difficult to describe, so varied are the forms that it can assume and the definitions that have been given of it. The most commonly accepted and most traditional typologies and classifications can be phenomenologically impure and conceal the phenomenon instead of patterning themselves on it. The same is true of the distinction between vocal prayer and mental prayer. It appears clear when we separate silent acts from acts in which prayer is uttered or pronounced. But it becomes much less clear as soon as we note, as did St. Teresa of Ávila, that for prayer to be mental, it is not a question of keeping your mouth shut (*tener cerrada la boca*), it is not a Christian prayer, even though certain practices involving the recitation of a formula or the repetition of a word, to the point of intoxication, occur in various religions; but, if authentic vocal prayer is always accompanied by mental prayer, as St. Teresa claims, this distinction can no longer be claimed to describe rigorously the phenomenon of prayer.[67]

On the other hand, and here we encounter another and no less challenging difficulty for our description, in the constitution of the meaning of prayer its addressee is absolutely essential. But even if, as a phenomenologist, one does not posit the existence or non-existence of the latter, the fact remains that the way we address him, name him, speak to him, the nature of what we ask from him and feel able to ask from him, the fear or the trust with which the person praying turns to him, all depend on the being of this addressee as he appears to the believer. Prayer cannot be described unless the power to which it is addressed is also described. But in that case, does not the attempt to describe prayer relapse into a presentation of the various real and possible theologies, without regard for their existence of non-existence? Does not a phenomenology of prayer then dissolve into the cataloguing of the various possible modes in which the divine can

---

[66] [Jean-Louis Chrétien, *The Ark of Speech*. Copyright © 2003 by Routledge. All rights reserved. Used with permission of Routledge, https://www.routledge.com/.]

[67] St. Teresa of Ávila, *Way of Perfection*, ch. 23, tr. E. Allison Peers (London: Sheed and Ward, 1977), ch. 24-25, pp. 100-105; original text in *Obras completas*, ed. Efrén de la Madre de Dios (Madrid: Biblioteca de Autores Cristianos, 1972), pp. 264-265.

appear, as for every prayer there is a face of the divine, and *vice versa*? Furthermore, every established religion has its *lex orandi*; its prayer has a norm that the phenomenologist cannot ignore, since it is a part of the phenomenon, any more than he can simply adopt it and make it his own.

In order to find a way through these difficulties, the best thing is to limit our study, which could, taken in itself, be indefinitely prolonged. We will examine only prayer as an *act of speech*, even if the history of religion naturally describes all sorts of prayers that are not in the slightest, at least at first sight, [19] acts of speech, and our guiding question will be that of the role played, in this act, by the *voice*. How and why, in prayer, do we come out with our voice, do we give voice, our voice? What is the meaning, within it, of the diverse means of utterance? This is not a matter of an arbitrary or purely opportunistic limitation, as these questions include one on the essence of prayer; is vocal prayer merely one form of prayer among others, or is it the form of prayer *par excellence*, in relation to which alone all others can be defined and constituted, by derivation or antithetically? Is it true that, as Feuerbach puts it, "audible prayer is only prayer revealing its nature?"[68]

While still being incomplete, a first description of prayer can show how it inhabits an act of presence to the invisible. Prayer is the act by which the person praying stands in the presence of a being in whom he believes, but whom he cannot see, and makes himself manifest to that being. If prayer is the response to a theophany, it is first and foremost an anthropophany, a manifestation of man. The invisible to which man shows himself may at one extreme be the radical invisibility of Spirit and at the other the inner sacredness or power of a being that is in itself visible, such as a mountain, a star or a statue. This act of presence brings the whole of man into play, in all the dimensions of his being; it exposes him in every sense of the term, and unreservedly. It concerns our body, its bearing, its posture, its range of gestures, and it can include certain requirements for preliminary bodily purification, such as ablutions, requirements as to clothing, such as covering or uncovering certain parts of our body, certain positions, such as holding up the hands or kneeing, and certain directions in which one must face. All these practices, whether they are obligatory or left to the choice of the person praying,

---

[68] Ludwig Feuerbach, *The Essence of Christianity*, tr. George Eliot (New York: Harper and Brothers, 1957), p. 123.

come together in an appearance (as in the juridical sense) that incarnates an act of presence. Even the person who turns towards the incorporeal does so with his body, with his whole body. This is a *sine qua non*, for to say, as does St. Augustine, that one can prayer in any 'bodily position' at all does not mean that the body is, in prayer, bracketed, or that it has no role and no importance, but that in his view everyone must take up the position most appropriate and most likely to favour his prayer.[69] With its dances and its capers, the Hasidic movement has demonstrated, in this domain, a vital and indeed uncanny freedom.[70] Written into the body, this presence to the invisible and this appearance before it comprise, essentially, acts by which the person praying declares to God or the gods his desires, his thoughts, his needs, his love, his repentance, in accordance with the various possibilities of speech, from crying out to soundlessly moving his lips, via speaking aloud and murmuring. The person praying before God is in his very being an active manifestation of himself to God. All modes of prayer are forms of this self-manifestation, whether individual or collective. ...

[20] That a God for whom everything is clear has no need of anyone telling him anything whatsoever, that an omniscient God has nothing to learn from us, not even our most secret desires: this was the objection repeatedly raised [21] against monotheistic prayer. This objection aims, if not to suppress prayer, at least to suppress it as an act of speech. But this objection is in its own way judicious, in that it includes its own solution within itself, namely the fact that the function of speech is not in this case to communicate a piece of information or to transmit something we know to our invisible interlocutor. At the beginning of his dialogue *De magistro*, St. Augustine supposes that speech has two functions, *docere* and *discere*, teaching and learning, to which his son Adeodatus comes up with the counter-example of song, which we can sing all by ourselves. St. Augustine then distinguishes properly musical pleasure from the very words of the song which, addressed to ourselves, are a *commemoratio*, in which we remind ourselves of something. Then Adeodatus raises a new objection:

---

[69] St. Augustine, *De diversis quaestionibus ad Simplicianum*, ed. A. Muztenbecher (Turnholt: Corpus Christianorum Series Latina, 1970), vol. 44, book 2, qu. 4 (*Que situ corporis orandum*).

[70] Louis Jacobs, *Hasidic Prayer* (London: Routledge and Kegan Paul, 1972), ch. 5, "Gestures and Melody in Prayer," pp. 54 ff. I am grateful to Catherine Chalier for bringing this study to my attention.

'When we pray, we certainly do speak; and–there is the rub–it is not right to think that God should be taught by us or that we should remind Him of anything.' St. Augustine's reply is complex, but it essentially comes down to making a distinction within prayer between an act, the 'sacrifice of justice,' which is not in itself directly an act of speech, and a linguistic dimension, whether internal and silent or external and audible; the latter is assimilated to the commemorative function of speech, to the act of recalling something to oneself or others, to the meditative ingathering of our thought.[71]

How should this be understood? We speak when we address another, and turn towards him, but it is we ourselves we are taught by this speech, and it is on us that it acts. The words of our speech affect and modify the addresser, and not the addressee. We affect ourselves as we stand before the other, in a movement towards him. This is the first wound of speech in prayer: the gap introduced by the addressee has broken the closed circle of speech, opened within it a fault that alters its nature. Another has silently introduced himself into my dialogue with myself, and has radically transformed and broken it. My speech rebounds on to myself and affects me, as indeed would, any speech of mine of the kind I always hear, but it affects me much more in so far as it is not aimed at me, and has a completely different addressee from me. It is precisely because I am not talking to myself, because I am not talking for myself, that my own speech, altered at its very origin, and perhaps even before that, turns back on me with such singular force.

St. Thomas Aquinas puts it very well: "We must pray, not in order to inform God of our needs and desires, but in order to remind ourselves that in these matters we need divine assistance."[72] To ask God, to accomplish in speech an act of question and request, means that, as we speak to him, we at one and the same time say something about him and something about ourselves, inseparably. We make ourselves manifest to ourselves,

---

[71] Augustine, *De magistro*, I, 1 and 2; English translation in *The Greatness of the Soul, and The Teacher*, tr. Joseph M. Colleran (Westminster: Newman Press, 1950, p. 130.

[72] St. Thomas Aquinas, *Summa Theologiae*, vol. 39, *Religion and Worship*, ed. Kevin D. O'Rourke (Cambridge: Cambridge University Press, 1964), IIa IIae, q. 83, art. 2, ad 1um, p. 53; cr. Art 9, ad 5um: "Prayer is not offered to God in order to change his mind, but in order to excite confidence in us" (p. 75).

we are through speech made manifest to ourselves as we manifest ourselves to him. To ask is actively to acknowledge that we are not the origin of every good and every gift, and [22] it is actively to acknowledge that the one whom we address is what he is. All prayer confesses God as giver, by dispossessing us of our self-centredness, in a speech that at every instance the addressee alone, in our eyes, makes possible. By returning to me, prayer does not speak to me of myself alone.

Prayer, says St. Bonaventure, needs the fervour of attention, the concentration of thought, the firmness of patience. This is why God wished us "not only to pray mentally but also to pray verbally to recollect our thoughts through words (*ad recollectionem cogitationum*)."[73] We are far from the mute spiritualism that sees in vocal expression, a mere movement of effusion and dispersal into outwardness, one that is, furthermore, vain and superfluous in the sight of God. The movement of speech is like that of air breathed out and in again. It brings me together before the other, it gives me a being for him, since it paradoxically gives me what it presupposes if it is to take place. One has to be recollected in order to pray, but that is the point: prayer itself, in so far as it is speech, is alone capable of really gathering me and recollecting me. Does this mean that we are turning speech into a mere means, the instrument, so to speak, of a technique of concentration? This may, of course, in some cases be true. But St. Bonaventure does not separate the gift of our voice from the meaning of what we have to say. It is around what it says that the voice gathers and gathers us, just as what it says gathers around the person it addresses. The first function of speech in prayer is thus a self-manifestation to the invisible other, a manifestation that becomes a manifestation of oneself to oneself through the other, in which the presence of self to other and that of other to self cannot be separated, as in the invisible poem of breathing evoked by Rilke.[74] This manifestation does not merely bring to light what was there before it, it has its own light, that of an event, the event in which what is invisible to me illuminates me, in a way that is phenomenologically different from a conversation with oneself or an examination of conscience.

---

[73] St. Bonaventure, *Breviloquium*, V, 10, tr. Erwin Esser Nemmers (St. Louis: B. Herder Book Co., 1946), p. 170 (translation modified).

[74] Rainer Maria Rilke, "Breath, Invisible Poem," *Sonnets to Orpheus*, tr. Claude Neuman (Middletown: Wesleyan University Press, 1987), Part One, IV, p. 31.

The speech of prayer has its tenor of meaning, and the question arises as to its relationship with truth. Aristotle, in the famous words of his *De interpretatione*, states that "a prayer is a sentence but is neither true nor false," it is not a *logos apophantikos*.[75] A question or request, a supplication, a complaint are not, after all, capable of being true in the same way that a predicative proposition is. But prayer still has its norms of correctness, which also involve the truth, including that of the *logos apophantikos*. It cannot avoid including a theology, explicit or implicit, which can be true or false—so that one might describe the way that the divine is thought of in a particular religion simply by examining the way people of that religion pray. The mere linguistic form of petitionary prayer is not enough to bracket the question of truth. Thus, Proclus makes a knowledge of the gods the first stage of prayer,[76] and in all religions the correctness of the divine names is something that is always being questioned: is God (or a god) being named as he should be named and as he [23] wants to be named. ...

[25] Prayer appears, in its own eyes, as always forestalled and always preceded by the person it addresses. It does not begin, it responds, and this is the only thing which, in the very uncertainty it harbours about its rightness, gives it confidence. The circle is not absolutely circular: it leads us to the event of an encounter. This act of speech takes its assurance not from itself, but it is assured of standing in the only place where it can in truth struggle for truth and become upright. For the stumbles of speech are overcome in speech alone, just as lovers' quarrels are resolved in love alone, and thus by keeping on going, together—not by separating and waiting for those difficulties to disappear spontaneously. This completes our first description of prayer: this manifestation of self to other through speech is agonistic and transformative, as it is a dialogue and conversation with the other in an encounter in which our truth is at stake. The person before God is drawn into involvement only in and through prayer.

The Christian tradition has particularly insisted on this agonistic dimension. A very fine discourse by Kierkegaard is called

---

75 Aristotle, *De Interpretatione*, 17a4-5, tr. J.L. Ackrill, in *The Complete Works of Aristotle*, The Revised Oxford Translation, ed. Jonathan Barnes, 2 vols. (Princeton: Princeton University Press, 1984), p. 26.

76 Proclus, *Commentaire sur le Timée*, tr. A. J. Festugière (Paris: J. Vrin, 1967), vol. II, pp. 32-33.

"One Who Prays Aright Struggles in Prayer and Is Victorious–in that God is Victorious."[77] Many centuries earlier, we find St. Macarius's powerful commentary on the phrase in the gospel, which says that the violent are taking the kingdom of heaven by force. He invites man, still a prisoner to his hardness of heart, to "force himself to charity when he has no charity–force himself to meekness when he has no meekness." And he continues that a man must "force himself to prayer, when he has not spiritual prayer; and thus God, beholding him thus striving, and compelling himself by force, in spite of an unwilling heart, gives him the true prayer of the Spirit."[78] And what would gentleness be without the fire of this inner violence of which it becomes the clarity, what would prayer be without this intimate combat against the muteness within us? This violent prayer, at first uttered only with reluctance–who will say whether it is authentic or inauthentic? Does not the mere possibility that it raises exclude such a distinction, which aims at ensuring a clear boundary between the proper and the improper, the clean and the unclean?

Before describing in greater detail these welcome wounds in speech, we have to ponder what is it that makes them possible: address, allocution, familiar speech (saying 'thou'). Feuerbach notes, indeed, "In prayer, man addresses God with the word of intimate affection–Thou," before interpreting this familiar form of address tendentiously by claiming, "He thus declares articulately that God is his *alter ego*."[79] For a philosopher who, like Karl Jaspers, makes of disenchantment a virtue, this second person singular already constitutes a slide towards a misunderstanding of God:

> [26] When man addresses the divinity *in prayer*, this divinity becomes for him a Thou with whom, lost as he is in his own solitude, he would like to enter into communication. It is thus for him a *personal figure*. ... However, an authentic awareness of transcendence refrains from thinking of the absolute God as a person. I resist the impulse to make a Thou of the divinity the

---

[77] This is one of Kierkegaard's *Four Upbuilding Discourses* of 1844, in *Eighteen Upbuilding Discourses*, ed. and tr. Howard V. Hong and Edna H. Hong (Princeton: Princeton University Press, 1990), pp. 377-401.

[78] *Fifty Spiritual Homilies of St. Macarius the Egyptian*, tr. A.J. Mason (London: SPCK, 1921), 19, 3, pp. 158-159.

[79] Feuerbach, *Essence*, p. 256.

minute I sense that I am thereby infringing transcendence.[80]

To be on terms of easy familiarity with the absolute would mean improperly bringing its distance closer, so that this proximity is no longer its own and it is replaced by a mythic image that I have forged for myself.

Thus dialogue with God, far from being the very place where I find him in finding myself, would on the contrary be the place where I lose him by covering over and concealing "the abyss of transcendence" that lies beyond all address. To this, a historical objection can be made first of all: the freedom, the trust, the heartfelt intimacy in the speech addressed to God, what Christians call *parrhesia*, instead of diminishing and weaking with the acknowledgement of its absolute transcendence, on the contrary always accompany it. This is clear if we compare Jewish and Christian prayer with the Greek and Roman prayer of antiquity. Kerenyi points out that the word 'god', *theos*, in the vocative, is introduced only by the Jews and Christians. And a formula of appropriation such as *my God* does not mean that God is degraded into a thing or into a property of man, but, on the contrary, puts its seal on the fact that in speech the one who speaks belongs, without reserve, to the one who is addressed. In any case, it must be a very strange and narrow conception of the other, of speech, and of the familiar form of address (saying 'thou') that decrees that address can only be an excessive familiarity. For it is only in familiar address that objectification comes up against an uncrossable limit, it is only in the hymn in which we sing for the one we sing that "the abyss of transcendence" can be really recognized and confessed. Indeed, even silence as a mark of respect and adoration, the *favete linguis* of the Romans or the *euphemia* of the Greeks, is a silence with an addressee, a silence before, and for, the other. It is silence before You, and it forms a possibility proper to speech, which alone can *fall silent*, transforming, by the act of standing in silence, silence into an act of presence and not into a privation. Silence is still an allocution.

---

[80] Karl Jaspers, *Philosophy*, tr. E.B. Ashton, 3 vols. (Chicago: University of Chicago Press, 1969-1971), vol. I, p. 546.

EMMANUEL FALQUE (1963-)

Falque was born in 1963 in Neuilly-sur-Seine, outside of Paris. He undertook preparatory classes at Sainte-Marie and then attended the University of Paris, Nanterre from 1986 to 1990. He then turned his interests to theology and acquired a licentiate from the Centre Sèvres in Paris in 1993. Returning to philosophy and studying with Jean-Luc Marion at the Sorbonne, Falque received his doctorate in 1998. Falque has taught at the Catholic Institute of Paris since 1998, and also teaches some courses at the Australian Catholic University.

His "triduum" consists of *Le Passeur de Gethsémani: Angoisse, souffrance, et mort* (Paris: Cerf, 1999), *Métamorphose de la Finitude: Essai philosophique sur la naissance et la resurrection* (Paris: Cerf, 2004), and *Les Noces de l'Agneau: Essai philosophique sur le corps et l'Eucharistie* (Paris: Cerf, 2011). These have been translated as *The Guide to Gethsemane: Anxiety, Suffering, Death* (New York: Fordham University Press, 2018), *The Metamorphosis of Finitude: An Essay on Birth and Resurrection* (New York: Fordham University Press, 2012), and *The Wedding Feast of the Lamb: Eros, the Body, and the Eucharist* (New York: Fordham University Press, 2016). Falque has also written *Crossing the Rubicon: The Borderlands of Philosophy and Theology* (New York: Fordham University Press, 2016), and *God, the Flesh, and the Other: From Irenaeus to Duns Scotus* (Evanston: Northwestern University Press, 2014).

Falque undertakes a phenomenology of the human that seeks to show how humans are neither beasts nor angels. They are fleshly animals, albeit ensouled ones. If forgotten angelism whereby humans are conceived as pure spirits results. The following selection is from chapter four of Falque's *The Wedding Feast of the Lamb: Eros, the Body, and the Eucharist* (New York: Fordham University Press, 2016), pp. 70-78.

The Wedding Feast of the Lamb (2011)[81]

The Animal That I Therefore Am

The Other Side of the Angel
[70] Philosophy and theology, throughout their long history, have concerned themselves precisely and at length with the question of a consciousness without a body. Aquinas, discussing the innate self-consciousness of the angel, anticipates the immediate consciousness of the self in the Cartesian cogito.[82] In both cases, as so often where it is a question of "ab-straction," there is no need for the medium of the body to access the self, and thus philosophy leans in the direction of angelism, valuing the *cogitatio* over *affectio, agape* over *eros,* and *nous* over *pathos.*[83] The hypothesis of a mind without body, or the temptation of angelism, is a feature of theology (surpassing human limits) as it is of philosophy (denial of the body in the name of the totality of consciousness). The *mind without body* of the angel is the other side of the coin of the *body without mind* of the animal. One can certainly discuss the possible consciousness of animals at length, and there is much debate on the subject in both philosophy and literature (Epicurus, Rabelais, Montaigne). But it is still the case that the question here is not simply a matter of being-ness, nor of differences of nature or [71] degree, but rather a matter of the metaphysical access of humankind to our own animality.

Whether or not we are animal remains an oppositional discourse that has no counterpart in a propositional discourse today, particularly in the context of phenomenology (Husserl, Heidegger, Deleuze, Derrida, Henry, Jonas, Agamben). The only thing that really matters here is our access to the animal and to our own animality (see §16), where the "animal world" and the

---

[81] [Emmanuel Falque, *The Wedding Feast of the Lamb: Eros, the Body, and the Eucharist,* translated by George Hughes. Copyright © 2016 by Fordham University Press. All rights reserved. Used with permission of Fordham University Press, https://www.fordhampress.com.]

[82] Thomas Aquinas, *Summa Theologia,* l, 56, 1; Rene Descartes, *Meditations on First Philosophy,* Meditation II, in *The Philosophical Works of Descartes,* trans. Elizabeth S. Haldane (1911), accessed 3 November 2015, http://selfpace.uconn.edu/class/percep/
DescartesMeditations.pdf.

[83] On this point, see Falque, *God, the Flesh, and the Other,* trans. W. C. Hackett (Evanston, IL: Northwestern University Press, 2015).

"human world" meet on the same philosophical ground. The work of the biologist and naturalist Jakob von Uexküll has been available for some time to feed the totality of our thought on this subject. Von Uexküll writes,

> Whoever wants to hold on to the conviction that all living things are only machines should abandon all hope of glimpsing their environments. ... [Here we shall] not see in animals simply a mechanical assemblage; [but] ... will also discover the *machine operator* who is built into the organs just as we are into our body. [We shall] address [ourselves] to animals not merely as objects but also as subjects, whose essential activities consist in perception and production of effects. But then, one has discovered the gateways to the life-world, for everything a subject perceives belongs to its *perception world* [*Merkwelt*], and everything it produces, to its *effect world* [*Werkwelt*].[84]

We are concerned with a *limit hypothesis—one* not of existence as difference, but rather of experience in a lived world. Certainly nobody could really say that they had definitely encountered a *mind without body* (the angel), any more than we encounter a *body without mind* (the animal). In both cases, it is not that we have really encountered them—at most it is that our paths have crossed and we haven't understood what it is to be like them (something that would be true for the animal and, of course, rather hypothetical in the case of the angel). Since we are mind *and* body, we are neither all one nor all the other; so, it becomes troublesome to try and believe ourselves simply one or the other. However, the impossible reduction of the mind to a blank sheet (*tabula rasa*), simply to its significations, aimed precisely at introducing this dimension. It also relied on the hypothesis of a pure corporality without mind, a quasi-animal access to the world through the body (*Körper*), or the organic flesh (*Fleisch*), without subsuming it into a signifying flesh (*Leib*); in other words, this is

---

[84] Jacob von Uexküll, *A Foray into the Worlds of Animals and Humans: With a Theory of Meaning* (1930), trans. Joseph D. O'Neil (Minneapolis: University of Minnesota Press, 2010), 41-42. Von Uexküll is notable particularly for having brought together phenomenology and the conception of the "lifeworld" (*Lebenswelt*) with the world of the environment (*Umwelt*). He was frequently cited by Husserl and Heidegger, then brought into prominence in Merleau Ponty's "Le concept de la nature ...," in *Notes de cours: La nature* (Paris: Editions du Seuil, 1995), 220-34. See the celebrated example of the tick.

Kant's "mass of sensations," or the "region of what can no longer be said" in Heidegger, or the "fact that there is [*il y a*]" and "existing without existents" in Levinas [72] (see §3). There the Chaos and the Tohu-Bohu of our own existence open up, reaching to the *Urgrund* or the *original basis* of our life, made up of our instincts, passions, and drives (§4). This is a long way away from psycho-analytic considerations, though no doubt they have their own validity (Part I). But we see here that the existential is universal. It does not need the support of the psychological or the pathological. It expresses itself in a language in which nothing indicates that orientation toward mind is the last word. It doesn't rely upon a psychic process otherwise directed elsewhere. The "unconscious of the body" (Nietzsche), as we shall see (§17), is not attached to the mind or simply enclosed in the unconscious (Freud).

It comes down simply to recognizing that "I am my body," or "There is a body." All the rest, including the mind, depends first of all upon the benchmark (*repère*) of original corporality. "I exist," Gabriel Marcel emphasizes;

> that is to say I have something that makes me known or recognized whether by others or by myself ... and all that is inseparable from the fact that there is my body. ... My body is the benchmark through which what is existent for me is placed. ...There is between the existence of others (including, for example, that of Caesar, who existed in the past) and my own existence, that is to say my organo-psychical presence to myself, an objectively determinable temporal continuity. ... All existence can be brought back to this benchmark (of the body) and cannot be thought of outside this reference except in terms of pure abstraction.[85]

As Pascal says, we are neither angels nor beasts, and thus, "anyone trying to act the angel acts the beast." We can add now, also from Pascal, that the "further one falls, the more wretched one is." Knowing both angels and beasts, in fact, we fear the one (beasts) more than we search for the other (angels).[86] What is said here in philosophical terms—in other words, viewing the

---

[85] Gabriel Marcel, "L'Être incarné repère central de la réflexion mètaphysique," in *Essai de philosophie concrète* (*Du refus à l'invocation*) (Paris: Gallimard, 1967), 3-31.

[86] Blaise Pascal, *Pensées*, trans. A. J. Krailsheimer (London: Penguin, 1966), 242, 61, 60.

temptations of angelism as a form of bestiality, or as a similar way of going beyond frontiers–was actually expressed right from the start in theology. Incarnation made it necessary! This problem was anticipated by Tertullian, and afterwards in the first Christian writings (third century after Christ), when they expressed opposition to an important Gnostic tendency that has in fact come back into contemporary docetism: "Both in Christ's case and that of the angels ... they came in the flesh. Never did any angel descend for the purpose of being crucified, or tasting death, and of rising from the dead. Now, since there never was such a reason for angels becoming embodied, you have the cause why they assumed [73] flesh without undergoing birth."[87] What is substantial in the body of Christ, and is perhaps his most profound aspiration, is not that he resembles the angels (the theme of *Christos angelos*), nor even that he leads us to take up a form of angelism (the addition of the theme of making man divine in a certain interpretation of Dionysius, for example). The Son, in becoming incarnate, has in reality no other wish, no other aim, than to resemble us, or rather to be *like us*–not angel but human, not through pure spirit but made into a body that is first of all material and inhabited also by the spiritual. "He was looked on as man, for no other reason whatever than because He existed in the corporeal substance of a man," Tertullian writes. He goes on to speak "of the muscles as clods; of the bones as stones; the mammillary glands as a kind of pebbles. Look upon the close junctions of the nerves as propagations of roots, and the branching courses of the veins as winding rivulets, and the down (which covers us) as moss, and the hair as grass, and the very treasures of marrow within our bones as ores of flesh."[88]

Our perspective then leads us back to the first origins of the Fathers of the Church. It is not the animal, or our animality, that is to be feared most, but the angel, or rather the Gnostic tendency, which always leads to distancing us from our materiality as well as from our humanity. The *body without consciousness* (the animal) is not the other side of the *consciousness without body* (the angel), except insofar as the hypothesis at the limits we associate with the second (the angel) also sends us back to the reality in ourselves of

---

[87] Tertullian, *On the Flesh of Christ*, chap. 6, in *Ante-Nicene Fathers*, vol. 3, trans. Peter Holmes, rev. and ed. Kevin Knight (1885; New Advent, 2009), http://www.newadvent.org/fathers/0315.htm.

[88] Ibid., chap. 9. See, in connection with this point, my analysis of "On the Flesh of Christ" in Falque, *God, the Flesh, and the Other*, chap. 5.

the first (the animal). We are left with an open question--at the limit of the thinkable, perhaps, but nonetheless central–as to the borders and thresholds of bestiality. Because if there is nothing to fear in our animality–in that, as we have seen, the sum total of our passions and drives, as of our Chaos, is offered and transformed by God in the act of the eucharist (Chapter 2)–there is, on the other hand, everything to fear in bestiality. Because the beast is not the animal, and bestiality marks precisely the descent of animality below the animal–a descent of which, paradoxically, only human beings show themselves capable. Only the human being is in fact "beast," or capable of becoming so, in all senses of the term: the imbecile as well as the brutal beast.

Knowing that human beings can raise themselves–not to the ranks of angels, but to a true spiritual assumption of the incarnate body–humankind can also fall. They can fall not into the animality of which they are already constituted, but into bestiality, where it is uniquely possible to veer off course from nature itself, and to founder below one's own nature. Nothing is beastly except that which humankind describes in such a way–in reality describing ourselves: namely, an animality that human beings come [74] to reject, going so far as to indict it completely. This is where the symbolic dimension of the Beast as a measure of sin comes from. It has no need of the animal as such and gives another meaning, necessary and complementary to the act of the eucharist.

At the start, as at the end, of the biblical narrative–as I have already stressed but not fully developed (§5)–the Beast takes on the shape of the figurehead of sin and will make the redemption (from bestiality to human), not simply one of solidarity (with the animality of humankind). From the "sin at the door like a crouching beast hungering for you" (Gen. 4:7 [JB]), according to God's words to Cain in Genesis, to the "scarlet Beast that was full of blasphemous names, and ... had seven head and ten horns" (Rev. 17:3), the Beast (*therion*) sends us back to the savage and fearful world that menaces the human and could well make him fall below a humanity rooted in the model of the Earth and in a certain form of animality. Like the animality in us, the Beast also has to "ascend from the bottomless pit" (Rev. 17:8), but it is to "go to destruction"–unlike the Lamb, who "will conquer them" (Rev. 17:14) and who will sum up in itself the totality of humanity (Eph. 1:10). A double opposition marks the difference between animality and bestiality.

(1) First is the opposition of the Beast and the Lamb. On the one side bestiality is the image of sin, and on the other, we find the

symbolism of a divinity that can take on all our humanity. In fact, we never leave the basis of a certain animality, being liable either to drop into bestiality (sin) or to raise ourselves into a humanity that awaits its filiation (salvation). To be and to remain human in the recognition of our created being remains the aim of the act of the eucharist, not simply in taking on and transforming our particular animality (Part I), but also in preserving us from the danger of sin and from our own bestiality.

(2) Thus we arrive at the second opposition, or rather, distinction: salvation by *solidarity* that is so much a part of the eucharistic act–"here is the Lamb of God" (John 1:36)–simply as the image of a divinity capable of taking on our animality and transforming it (Chaos, passions, drives; see Part I). This gives way to salvation by *redemption,* classically and correctly required for us in order to undo our falling away and our sin: "Here is the Lamb of God *who takes away the sin of the world*" (John 1:29) (see Part II). The "blood of the Lamb" (Rev. 7:14) that flows from the side of the animal in the Ghent altarpiece, as we have seen (Preface), redeems the whole of humanity in the form of the blood poured onto the cross (John 19:34). So the problem is less that of recognizing in ourselves a certain form of animality than of falling into a bestiality that may go so far as to ruin the aspect of the animal in ourselves.

[75] Neither angel nor beast, the question then is not, or is no longer, how to know what this "Animal That Therefore I Am" (Derrida) is; rather, we must ask ourselves what becomes of animality that is necessarily taken on once there is humanity–either falling into bestiality (human behavior mimicking an animal world that in reality it has never shared: pornography, prostitution, perversion of the self, and so on) or going beyond our humanity (the temptation of angelism, this time denying animality as though we were totally disincarnate, without passions or drives, without darkness or Chaos). The mystery of the Word incarnate (salvation through solidarity) stands as it were in front of the constitutive animality of our humanity, as the mystery of the blood that is spilt (salvation through redemption) stands before the potential fall of humankind into bestiality. In both cases the Beast threatens, but not the animal. We leave the *anima* or the breath that constitutes us (*psuchê*) as we wait for the *animus* or the spirit (*pneuma*), the "supplement of the soul" that permits us not to fall.

The animal in fact is *anima* rather than *animus*–thus we have the term "anima-lity." And it is this anima-lity that is taken on and transformed in the act of the eucharist, and rescued, where there has been a fall into bestiality. As the etymologist R. B. Onians famously shows in *The Origins of European Thought,* "Animus ... was overwhelmingly, throughout Latin literature, not the vital principle but the principle of consciousness As the early tragedian Accius tersely says, *sapimus animo, fruimur anima* [We discern with the rational mind, enjoy with the soul]; introducing which several centuries later the grammarian Nonius says, *animus est quo sapimus, anima qua vivimus* [It is the rational mind by which we know, the soul by which we live]."[89] We can distinguish, not especially to place them in opposition, but at least to point out their distinctive characters, the *anima* as breath and "life-soul" from the *animus* as "consciousness with all the variation of emotion and thought," or "the breath that was consciousness in the chest," or breath in words. Accius, a near-contemporary of Christ (first century before Christ), thus sees in the *animus* an essence of life (breath) in the same way that the Jewish tradition sees in Adam the figure of an "earthly one" (*adâmah*) in which the breath of life (*neshama*) is blown through the nostrils. "The Lord God formed man from the dust of the ground, and breathed into his nostrils the breath of life; and the man became a living being" (Gen. 2:7). The "rite of breath" makes life, as Marcel Jousse tells us, and restores us to life. The theology of the breath (life) responds to the anthropology of the dust (body)–instead of the substance of thought (soul) responding to the extension of a machine (body).

[76] There is not, then, a soul separated from the body in the Greek conception of origins, or in the Jewish world, but rather a living breath (*anima-nèfèsh*) through which Adam becomes alive. The loss of this breath is precisely what indicates death, or a dismantling, rather than the disappearance of thought, or the stopping of the heart, or a flat encephalogram. The narrative of the "mystery of death," as recounted by the anthropologist Jousse, is

---

[89] Richard B. Onians, *The Origins of European Thought: About the Body, the Mind, the Soul, the World, and Fate* (1951) (Cambridge: Cambridge University Press, 2000) 168-69, 171. The distinction between *animus* and *anima* is confirmed and commented upon at the same time by Heidegger, in *Qu'appelle-t-on penser?* [*What Is Called Thinking?*] (Paris: PUF, 1983), 150-51: "*Anima* signifies the fundamental determination of all living beings, including that of man ... The Latin word *animus* can also be translated by our German word *Seele* (soul). Soul does not signify the life-principle, but the presence of the spirit, the spirit of the spirit, the spark of the soul according to Master Eckhart."

so poignant that it deserves to be cited here at length. It helps us see that what *this is my body* offers in the act of the eucharist cannot be reduced to material terms. It is the offering of a body eaten and a life breathed into an earthly Adam waiting to be renewed:

> Country people are so accustomed to be tight-lipped that they cannot conceive how all of life and all of the understanding of life can be irradiated and manifest through the breath that goes in and out of the nostrils. Before the mystery of death you may be confronted by a spectacle—or it might be better to call it a kind of mime-show—that I have witnessed very often in the countryside. Death enters the farm. The farmer takes down the sole mirror in his poor house. He balances it on his mother's bed. She lies there totally immobile, having become cold as earth. He will delicately, religiously, liturgically, place the mirror against the cold nostrils of the one who has worked so hard and who is now lying there, inert. He waits several seconds to complete, for himself, the primordial ritual that I would call the "rite of breath." And with the suffering that comes from inexplicable things, perhaps because these things are inexplicable to us, he will turn the mirror around and will look at it to see if the clouding breath has passed onto it or died away.[90]

The *anima* as "respiratory breath" in the occidental tradition (Onians), or the "breath of life" animating a being made of Earth and dust in the Semitic tradition (Jousse), are what consecrated man, or Adam, as "living": "And the man became a living being [*hâyâh*]" (Gen. 2:7). Nonetheless, we must be careful here. To say of *anthropos,* or the *Adâmâ,* that he becomes a living being does not subtract from his animality; on the contrary, it inscribes him in it. We can point to how, even before Adam names the animals, the author of Genesis is careful to note that "whatever the man called each *living creature,* that was its name" (Gen. 2:19). The living creature who is man, in the insufflation or the breathing of the breath starting off "from the dust" (Gen. 2:7), joins here other living creatures, those animals who also await their names or their welcome into the ark [77] of speech (Gen. 2:19). "The animal is qualified as *living creature* (literally breath of life) like man. ... The Yahwist author, before showing the superiority of man over

---

[90] Marcel Jousse, *La Manducation de la parole* (Paris: Gallimard, 1975), 154-55.

the animals wishes to recall that they have respiration in common."[91] Or, as we have already seen (§5), if the breath is the same as the breath that gives life to all living creatures, and thus inscribes us biblically in the great sphere of animality, the dust or clay is of a similar nature, or of the same texture: the clay with which "the Lord God formed man from the dust of the ground" (Gen. 2:7). The identity of the breath and of the clay does not take us beyond animality, as though Adam and Eve (Semitic tradition), or the rational human being (Greek tradition), had first been thought of independently from animals and their own animality. On the contrary, it brings us back to a common base, something we may see differently and from which we may eventually depart, but without ever denying this community of the *psuché*.

This common texture of the clay and the breath, or of the body and the soul in Graeco-Latin terms (*sôma-psuché–corpus-anima*), thus precedes and makes possible the inspiration of the spiritual breath of God. God breathes his strength into matter that has been created by him, taking account of the density of the matter as well as difference. Irenaeus tells us, "our substance, that is, the union of flesh and spirit [*animae et carnis*], receiving the Spirit of God [*spiritus Dei*], makes up the spiritual man."[92] The trilogy of the Epistle to the Thessalonians cannot really be read in any other way: "May the God of peace himself sanctify you entirely; and may your spirit and soul and body [*pneuma, psuché, sôma*] be kept sound and blameless at the coming of our Lord Jesus Christ" (1 Thes. 5:23). I can only repeat here what I have said elsewhere with regard to the correct interpretation of Irenaeus: "The mixture 'soul-body' [*psuché-sôma*] of the Old Testament (Gen. 2:7) receives the 'spirit-breath' [*pneuma*] of the New Testament (1 Thes. 5:23). This takes the form of a *prefiguration* in the Old Testament, after the initial mixture forms a properly constituted whole, capable of receiving such power from God."[93] The *anima*-lity in us is not an accident of our constitution that can be forgotten or that is simply overcome. We find this from the start in Indo-European culture (*anima* and

---

[91] See note in *Traduction oecuménique de la Bible* on Gen. 2:19 (p. 47).

[92] Irenaeus, *Against Heresies* 5.8.2, in *Ante-Nicene Fathers*, vol. 1, trans. Alexander Roberts and William Rambaut, rev. and ed. Kevin Knight (1885; New Advent, 2009), www.newadvent.org/fathers/0103.htm.

[93] Falque, *God, the Flesh, and the Other*.

animus), as at the origin of Semitic culture (the clay and the breath). It is also constitutive of our humanity, and it is in this respect that the eucharistic tradition also cannot hide it, in the ambivalence of the sacrificial lamb (the animal first of all in taking charge of our humanity and the deliverance from bestiality through the blood that frees us from sin).[94]

Certainly, Adam was not fully satisfied by his kinship with the animal, and thus it is also his belonging to Chaos and Tohu-Bohu that keeps him [78] under the command of the *anima* (see §21). When he is called on to name the animals, in the eyes of God he has to confront his own animality as well as the strong passions and drives that he alone could not control. The difficulty he encounters in naming the animals is, as we shall see, a quite extraordinary indication in the biblical narrative of his human incapacity to live through interior Chaos until another—a female other—is given to him.

Eve shows us a limit for humanity and for man. She will help Adam to love his own limits as well as carry with him the Chaos and the animality by which she also is constituted (§22). It is in discovering Eve as "bone of my bones and flesh of my flesh" (Gen. 2:23) that Adam becomes other than his animality—in calling her "woman" (*ishah*) and not "female." And it is in differentiating herself from Adam and in recognizing him as "man" (*ish*), and not as "male," that Eve also comes to belong to his community of a differentiated humanity that cannot be reduced to a simple animality (Gen. 2:23) (§23). The *anima*-lity is thus preserved, not simply in biblical terms, but also as it becomes metaphysically constitutive of our humanity and of our belonging to the created world—even though that world will come to be, if not surpassed, at least seen in other ways.

However, and it is the least one can say, this question of animality and thus also of Chaos, of passions and drives, will be forgotten. Or rather, the process of history and philosophy as well as that of theology does everything not simply to detach us from the question, but also to make us think that nothing like that can,

---

[94] Apart from the numerous films that have recently shown this ... we find an excellent graph illustration of the original parentage of human and animal in Jean-Christophe Camus, Michel Duffranne, and Damir Zitko, *La Bible: L'Ancien Testament, La Gènese I*re *partie* (Tournai: Delacourt, 2008). See the image of Adam "crouching in the steppe," like an animal, at the time of his face-to-face confrontation with animality (here, the lion) and then with humanity (Eve) (p. 7).

or ever could, happen to us. The difference in nature between human and animal (e.g., reason, liberty, work, laughter) or, even more, the constant spiritualization, at least in artworks, of Adam and Eve before the Fall (without passions, without emotions, almost without heart or body, apart from the paintings of Michelangelo on the ceiling of the Sistine Chapel)–all of that has not simply taken humankind away from our basic animality, but hidden what is suggested in the Bible of our human origins (identity of the same breath and the same clay), and this has been done to the extent of suggesting that those origins do not belong to the created being. How has this come about? And how has such neglect been maintained? What basic shared history has determined this? These questions are all the more meaningful because the *this is my body,* as I have emphasized throughout this book, comes in the form of the consecrated Host, to take on and to transform, in particular, the unspoken of the animal in us, that "disembodied consciousness" (Chaos, passion, drives ...) that we of course do everything to forget and stoically try to master

3 NEO-THOMISM

RÉGINALD GARRIGOU-LAGRANGE, O.P. (1877-1964)

Garrigou-Lagrange was born in Auch, Midi-Pyrénées, France in 1877. He started in medicine at the University of Bordeaux from 1896-1897, but, after reading a book by Ernest Hello, he had a profound religious experience and decided to become a priest. He subsequently decided to enter the Dominican Order at Amiens in 1897. He studied with Ambroise Gardeil at the Dominican House of Studies in Flavigny, France from 1898-1904, and was ordained in 1902. He also studied at the Sorbonne from 1904-1905 with Bergson, Brochard, Durkheim, and Loïsy. Garrigou-Lagrange began teaching philosophy and theology at Le Saulchoir, Kain, Belgium, from 1905 to 1909. He then spent a long career teaching fundamental, dogmatic, and spiritual theology at the Pontifical University of St. Thomas (i.e. the Angelicum) in Rome from 1909 until 1960. In the 1940s and 1950s Garrigou-Lagrange served as a consulter to the Holy Office where he likely influenced the drafting of the encyclical *Humani generis* (1950) against Neo-Modernism and *Munificentissimus Deus* (1950) on the Assumption of Mary. He died in 1964 in Rome.

Garrigou-Lagrange strove to transmit the system of Thomas Aquinas—under the influence of fellow Dominicans Cajetan, Báñez, John of St. Thomas, Billuart, Arintero, and Gardeil—in such works as his *Dieu, son existence et sa nature* (Paris: Gabriel Beauchesne, 1915); *L'amour de Dieu et la croix de Jésus* (Juvisy: Cerf, 1929); and *La Synthesèse thomiste* (Paris: Desclée de Brouwer, 1946). His main theological works was *De revelatione per ecclesiam Catholicam proposita*, 2 vols. (Romae: F. Ferrari, 1918; 2nd ed. 1932), as well as several works on spirituality influenced by John of the Cross that advanced the ideas of a universal call to holiness and abandoning the soul to God, which later influenced the drafting of *Lumen gentium* (1964), nn. 39-42 of Vatican II.

For more on Garrigou-Lagrange see: Peddicord, Richard, *The Sacred Monster of Thomism: An Introduction to the Life and Legacy of Reginald Garrigou-Lagrange* (South Bend: St. Augustine's Press, 2005); Nichols, Aidan, *Reason with Piety: Garrigou-Lagrange in the Service of Catholic Thought* (Naples: Sapientia Press, 2008).

The following selections are from Garrigou-Lagrange's *God, His Existence and His Nature*, trans. Bede Rose, 2 vols. (St. Louis: Herder, 1934-1936): vol. I, III:38, pp. 293-300, then, out of order, 1:6, pp. 40, 54-60; and Walshe, Thomas Joseph, ed., *The Principles of Catholic Apologetics* (London: Sands, 1926): I, pp. 26-31; XVI, pp. 179-189; XX, pp. 235-238; XXV, pp. 328-336. In these works Garrigou-Lagrange tried to stay true to the principles of Aquinas, hence the somewhat misleading moniker applied to him of "Strict-Observance Thomism," and so adopts and defends, in light of modern critiques, the five ways of Aquinas as well as the credibility of the faith.

God, His Existence and His Nature (1915)[95]

Exposé of the Proofs for the Existence of God

Proof Based on Contingency

[293] We have just shown that the source of *becoming* and of *being* must be self-existent; but the existence of a necessary being can be proved *a posteriori* by starting with the principle, not of the dependence of *becoming* or of *being* on its causes, but of being considered in itself as contingent.

We observe that some beings are contingent, that is to say, do not exist forever, but, on the contrary, are born and die. Of such a nature are the minerals which decompose or form a constituent part of fresh matter, such as plants, animals, and human beings. This we know to be a fact. From it we proceed to deduce the existence of a necessary being, of one which always existed a se and cannot cease to exist. It is only a self-existent being that can explain the existence of beings which can either exist or not exist. The principle upon which this proof is based is the metaphysical principle of causality in its most general form. It may be stated as follows: That which has not a sufficient reason for its existence in itself, must have this reason in something else. And this other being, in the final analysis, must exist of and by itself, for if it were of the same nature as contingent beings, far from explaining the others, it would not be able to explain itself. And—we say it again— it does not matter whether the series of contingent beings is eternal or not; if it is eternal, it is eternally insufficient, and always demands a necessary *being*.

St. Thomas develops this proof more fully by taking into consideration the time element. After having established the existence in the world of beings which begin to exist, and then [294] cease to exist—that is to say, of *contingent beings*—he remarks that if there were none but contingent beings, it would be impossible for them to have existed always. To exist without a beginning cannot properly be said of any but self-existent beings, and this could not apply to a series of contingent beings, unless they received their existence from a self-existent, or, in other words, from a necessary, Being. Hence, if there were in existence only contingent beings, there must have been a time when nothing at all existed. Now, "if at any particular moment nothing actually

---

95 [Réginald Garrigou-Lagrange, *God, His Existence and His Nature*, vol. 1, translated by Bede Rose (St. Louis: Herder, 1949). Public Domain.]

exists, then nothing can ever come into existence." Therefore, some necessary being must exist, that is to say, one which cannot not exist; if this being has not its necessity from itself, it derives its necessity from something else. But we cannot continue to proceed indefinitely in this process of dependence of being upon being, and hence we must conclude that there exists a Being which is necessary of and by itself, and which explains the being and continuance of everything else.

The objection is often raised that this demonstration makes scarcely any advance towards the solution of the problem, because it fails to establish conclusively that the necessary being is distinct from the world and infinitely perfect, but merely proves that there is some thing which is necessary. Cajetan replies that this proof may be considered as sufficient in the strictest sense, as the two preceding proofs established conclusively that the prime mover and the first cause are distinct from the world (because the world is subject to *becoming*, which the prime mover and the first cause is not), and the succeeding proof will demonstrate *a posteriori* the unity, simplicity, and absolute perfection of the necessary being.

It is now easy to demonstrate *a priori* that the necessary being, whose existence has just been proved, is not: (a) either an aggregation of contingent beings; or (b) the law governing such beings; or (c) a *becoming* underneath the phenomena, or a [295] substance common to them; but (d) it is *Being itself*, pure being, absolute perfection.

a) The necessary being is not an *aggregation* of contingent beings. A series of contingent and relative beings, even if it were without a beginning, i.e., eternal, could no more result in an absolutely necessary being, than could a numberless series of idiots result in an intelligent man. "But," it may be objected, "how can it be proved that a being is really and truly contingent? Is it not a semblance of reality, which is the result of our having abstracted it from the continuous whole?"[96] The kind of being here referred to, such as plants and animals, is at least a part of the continuous whole, but not the whole; moreover, it is a part which comes into existence and ceases to exist, and, therefore, is contingent. An aggregation of similar parts, even though infinite in time and space, could not constitute a necessary being. For a thing to have a semblance of reality, it would be necessary to add to these parts a dominating principle, be it either the law which

---

96 Édouard Le Roy, "Comment se pose le problème de Dieu," *Revue de Métaphysique et de Morale* 15:2 (March, 1907): 129–178.

governs them, or the process of *becoming* through which they must pass (creative evolution), or the substance common to all the parts.

b) The necessary being cannot be *the law* which unites contingent and transitory elements. For this law, in order to be the necessary being, would have to have its sufficient reason within itself and also contain the sufficient reason for all the phenomena that it has controlled, now controls, and will control in future. Now, a law is nothing but a constant relation between various phenomena or beings, and as every relation presupposes the extremes upon which it is based, the existence of a law presupposes the existence of the phenomena which it unites, instead of being presupposed by them. It exists only if they exist. Heat expands iron on condition that there are heat and iron. Energy conserves itself if there is energy.

[296] It is objected that while the application of a law indeed presupposes the existence of phenomena which it unites, the existence of a law is independent of its application. We answer that what is independent of this application is the ideal existence of the law, its existence in a mind, to which there corresponds a hypothetically objective truth (for instance, if there are heat and iron, the heat will expand the iron). But it cannot be claimed that the *actual* existence of a law is independent of its application and of the existence of the phenomena which it controls. Now, it is the actual existence which the Pantheists have in mind when they say that the necessary being, *actually* existing, is nothing else but the law of phenomena. Eliminate the contingent existence of phenomena, and this necessary being, which is the law, is no more than a hypothetical truth, which demands an existing Absolute for its foundation (proof based on the eternal verities), but which cannot itself be that Absolute. We have previously shown (n. 10) why heat in itself cannot exist in a state separated from the subject which it affects; its very concept implies a common matter, which cannot be realized without at the same time being individualized.

But the Positivists insist that it is a law which produces the phenomena that explain its presence, namely, the law of the conservation of energy, which is a primordial and universal necessity explaining everything else. If "nothing is lost and nothing is created," as this law affirms, then the necessary being is the material world itself, governed by this law. We have already quoted (see n. 35, towards the end) Boutroux's answer to this objection, as given in his thesis entitled, *La Contingence des Lois de la Nature.*[97] First of all, to repeat briefly, this law, far from being a primordial necessity, is itself contingent; it does not contain its own sufficient reason within itself, and because of this, it demands an extrinsic sufficient reason, or a cause. If this law were necessary, like the principle of identity, it would not [297] actually exist by itself, but, like every other law, would presuppose the existence of beings in which it is realized–in this case the existence of energy. Secondly, this law, far from being universal, is not even susceptible of strict verification in the inorganic world; biology cannot prove its existence, nor, *a fortiori*, can psychology. Thirdly, the laws which govern living beings, such as the sentient and the intelligent, cannot be deduced from this law. The combination of elements which produces life and sensation appears as contingent and demands a sufficient reason, which the law of the conservation of energy cannot furnish. ...

d) The necessary being is being itself, pure being, absolute perfection. Kant[98] maintains that we cannot argue from the existence of a necessary being that it is sovereign perfection, *ens realissimum*, except by unconsciously reverting to the ontological proof. He believes that he has proved this point by the simple conversion of a proposition. Let us, he writes, according to the rules of formal logic, convert the proposition, "Every necessary being is perfect," and it becomes: "Some perfect being is necessary." But in that case we should have no means of distinguishing between perfect beings, since each of them is *ens realissimum*. The converted proposition is, therefore, equivalent to the universal one that "Every perfect being is necessary," which is identical with the thesis of the ontological argument. As the transition from the first proposition to the second is effected by a process which is purely logical and according to rule, the truth or falsehood of the one is dependent upon the truth or falsehood of the [300] other. Such is Kant's principal objection against the classical proofs for the existence of God, considered not according to their basic principle, which is that of causality, but according to that step in reasoning by which they proceed from the first cause to the existence of the perfect Being.

This objection is answered sufficiently by stating that St. Anselm was wrong in concluding that *"the perfect being*

---

[97] Émile Boutroux, *De la contingence des lois de la nature* (Paris: Germer Baillière, 1874).

[98] Immanuel Kant, *Critique of Pure Reason*, "Transcendental Dialectic," ch. III, section 5.

necessarily and actually exists." He ought to have been satisfied with affirming that "the perfect being is self-existent, *if it exists.*" He could just as easily have proved *a priori* the hypothetical contrary, namely, "if a self-existent being exists, it is sovereign perfection." To establish the truth of this proposition is precisely what remains for us to do, having demonstrated by the argument from contingency that a necessary being *actually exists.* That the two concepts (necessary and perfect), the very definition of which reveals that they are essentially linked together by their very definition, are equivalent, is a legitimate assumption for those who, unlike Kant, admit that necessary realities correspond to necessary concepts of the mind, and that the *unthinkable* and the *impossible* are correlative terms.

What the Catholic Church Teaches about God's Existence and His Nature, and the Knowledge Which We Can Have of Him by Means of the Natural Light of Reason

[40] The new apologetic spoken of so highly by Blondel and Laberthonnière, though repudiating immanence as a doctrine, admits it to be indispensable as a method and asserts that this method is the *only* one that can succeed in coordinating the various arguments offered by the other methods in such a way that there results from it a valid demonstration; and that this method, therefore, holds the first place, because without it the other methods would be inadequate and ineffective. ...

It seems that this apologetic by the method of immanence, thus understood, cannot be reconciled with the definition of the Vatican Council and it unconsciously revives the error of Baius and Jansenius.

As a matter of fact, in proportion as this method denies the validity of the proofs for the existence of God as given by the schools and traditional theodicy from Plato to Leibniz, it accepts the Kantian and Positivist thesis of the inability of speculative reason to know God with certainty. ...

[54] We see that, for M. Laberthonnière, the affirmation that God exists is a free affirmation. We might view in the same way, as Fr. Chossat, S.J., remarks, our belief in a sense of duty, and say that it also is a matter of free choice. The will imposes the obligation.[99] That we are absolutely in need of supernatural

---

[99] Marcel Chossat, "Dieu," *Dictionnaire de Théologie Catholique*, ed. Alfred Vacant (Paris: Letouzey et Ané, 1910), vol. 4:1, cols. 756–948.

assistance before we can be certain of God's existence, must not, therefore, surprise us.[100] On this point Blondel writes: "It is not because we positively stand in need of the supernatural, and because it is a necessity arising from our human nature, but it is because nature [55] demands this as a necessity and because it is an exigency that is felt within us."[101] Such statements are in agreement with the immanent method, which may be summed up in the sentence that nothing is imposed upon us from without.

Concerning this method, the Encyclical "*Pascendi*" says: "We cannot refrain from once more and very strongly deploring the fact that there are Catholics who, while repudiating immanence as a doctrine, nevertheless employ it as a system of apologetics; they do so, we may say, with such a lack of discretion, that they seem to admit in human nature not only a capacity and fittingness for the supernatural order–both of which Catholic apologists have always been careful to emphasize–but assert that it truly and rigorously demands the same" (Denz., 2103).

The sort of demonstration of the existence of God admitted by those who adopt the method of immanence–since they hold that the Scholastic proofs are inadequate–is practically a defense of the theory that, in our present condition, in order to be sure of God's existence (since human nature left to itself is incapable of this), we have an *absolute claim* upon the necessary help in the supernatural order. P. Chossat, S.J. points out that if some theologians admitted that, in our present condition, we cannot be certain of the existence of God without supernatural help, they were considering only the *actual fact*, or the conditions under which this natural potency operates, by which we acquire a knowledge of God; they did not deny this potency, nor in any way restrict its specification.[102] They distinguished carefully between essence and existence, specification and operation, right and fact. What these theologians meant is that, in our present state, due to original sin, a supernatural help is required for the will to *apply* (operative order) the intellect to the consideration of God in preference to any other object, and also to eliminate (*removens, prohibens*, a purely negative process), the [56] moral dispositions which prevent us from perceiving the cogency of the proofs; but they did not maintain the necessity of this help for the will in the

---

[100] Lucien Laberthonnière, *Essais de philosophie religieuse* (Paris: P. Lethielleux, 1903), p. 317.

[101] Quoted by Laberthonnière, op. cit.

[102] *Loc. cit.*, cols. 864-870.

order of specification, so that it might contribute in some particular way to modify the proofs for the existence of God. They considered these proofs sufficient *just as they are*.

The distinction between specification and operation, between right and fact, can find no place in this new system of apologetics. The reason for this is that the defenders of this system have discarded the classical proofs for the existence of God as unconvincing, and have chosen to adopt the Kantian view, that reason *of itself*, by its very nature, cannot prove the existence of God with a certainty that is objectively sufficient. From this it follows that the supernatural–no matter what Blondel may say–not only makes its demands felt, but is also absolutely required by us. It seems, therefore, that this teaching of the modern school of apologists can no more be reconciled with the definition of the Vatican Council than could the views held by the Traditionalists of Louvain and the Fideists of Bautain's school. These apologists, though starting from different points, arrive at the same conclusions as those who held that the supernatural gifts belonged by right to the first man in a state of innocence, and who exaggerated the fall from original justice so as to admit with Luther, Calvin, Baius, Jansenius, and Quesnel, that reason is incapable of proving the existence of God.[103] The 41st proposition of Quesnel reads as follows: "All knowledge of God, even natural knowledge, even in pagan philosophers, can come only from God; and without grace produces only presumption, vanity, and opposition to God, instead of fostering acts of adoration, gratitude, and [57] love" (Denz., n. 1391). Abbé Laberthonnière expresses himself in almost the same way when, besides what he calls "the faith of love," he admits in certain others who reject God, "a faith of fear." "But to believe solely out of fear," he says, "is to believe and deny at the same time. Such faith is like that of an enemy believing in the existence of his enemy whilst hoping to crush him. Faith actuated entirely by fear, therefore, is not a sincere faith, because it contains within itself the desire not to believe. With it and by it, one plunges into darkness."[104] "They speak and write," justly observes P. Chossat, S.J., "as if all the theories evolved on

---

[103] See *Immanence: Essai critique sur la doctrine de Maurice Blondel*, by Joseph de Tonquédec (Paris: G. Beauchesne, 1913), pp. 149-166, where the author shows that Blondel cannot avoid the error of Baianism except by falling into the more serious error of denying the ontological scope of reason.

[104] Laberthonnière, *Essais de philosophie religieuse*, 1903), p. 80.

these questions by Protestants, Jansenists, and even by otherwise orthodox theologians, were tenable at the present day. We ought not to forget, however, that the notion of the supernatural, and especially the question of the possibility of acquiring certain knowledge about God by the natural light of reason, are not discussed from the same point of view to-day as they were forty or 400 years ago. ... This fact fully explains why the *Essais* of Abbé Laberthonnière were put on the Index."[105] In 1913, all the volumes of *Les Annales de Philosophie Chrétienne*, from 1905 to 1913, were likewise placed on the Index for ventilating the same ideas as the *Essais*.

To present Blondel's views[106] in a more favorable light, Abbé Rousselot proposed the following interpretation: "In the most primitive and spontaneous operation of reason, analysis promptly discloses to us the certain assurance that it is possible for reason to form a clear notion of being, and also that one can get into such a frame of mind as to be satisfied with [58] oneself, with the world, and with life in general. This presumption (I use the word in no disparaging sense) is natural, essential to the intellect, an *a priori* condition of its existence, and, as it were, the vital principle of each of its particular intentions. Now, in addition to this, in the present state of our fallen nature, transmitted by Adam to all his descendants, this presumption, without a special grace of illumination for the intellect, is unjustified. ... Without a revelation from above, without a cure in no wise due to human nature, the intellect cannot come into possession of the truth concerning its real destiny. There follows a deordination of the cognitive powers of the soul, which interferes with the proper functioning of these powers, and which, without rendering each of them false or 'spurious,' separates them from what ought to be their means of full development and for which they are truly intended. ... Viewing things this way, we can understand how supernatural faith alone, considered as a perfection of the intellect, comes to the aid of natural reason, and gives to the knowledge that one may have of

---

[105] Marcel Chossat, "Dieu," *Dictionnaire de Théologie Catholique*, 1910), vol. 4:1, cols. 869-871.

[106] Especially this proposition: "To believe that one can finally arrive at the idea of being, and legitimately affirm whatever reality there may be to it, without having gone through the whole process which originates from an intuitive perception of the necessity of God and of religious experience, means that one remains under an illusion."

any object, its full right to such a claim."[107]

This interpretation recalls that of the older theologians refuted by St. Thomas in the Second Book of the *Sentences*, dist. 28, q. 1, a. 5, and also that of Vasquez, generally combated by the Thomists,[108] and may be summed up in this statement: "Supernatural faith alone gives to the knowledge that one may have of any object, its full right to such a claim."

It seems scarcely possible to reconcile this proposition with that to which Abbé Bautain had to subscribe, to wit: "However feeble and obscure the light of reason may have become through original sin, it still retains sufficient clarity and power to lead us with certainty to the existence of God and to the [59] revelation given to the Jews through Moses and to the Christians through our adorable God-Man" (Denz., n. 1627). In 1844, the Abbé Bautain had to promise "never to teach that reason cannot acquire a true and complete certitude concerning the motives of credibility, especially such as miracles, prophecies, and most particularly the Resurrection of Jesus Christ" (Denz., n. 434). In discussing the definition of the Vatican Council concerning the power of reason to acquire a certain knowledge of the existence of God, we pointed out that it was precisely human nature in its fallen state that was meant.[109] This knowledge, therefore, appears to be fully accounted for without grace.

If one wishes to adopt the method of immanence, one must not view it as an *exclusive* or *indispensable* method, so superior to all the others as to deserve first consideration. The classical arguments have demonstrative force without it, though we may say that it disposes one to consider them and it confirms them.[110]

---

[107] Pierre Rousselot, *Dictionnaire apologétique de la foi catholique*, ed. Adhémar d'Alès (Paris: G. Beauchesne, 1909), art. "Intellectualisme," col. 1074.

[108] See Jean-Baptiste Gonet, O.P., *Clypeus theologiae thomisticae*, *De gratia*, disp. I, I, § 2.

[109] See Alfred Vacant, *Études sur le Concile du Vatican* (Paris: Delhomme et Briguet 1895), vol. 1, pp. 289 and 673. See also Denz., n. 1670.

[110] In so far as it prepares or disposes one to consider the arguments set forth by the other methods, the method of immanence enjoys a priority of time, but not of perfection or validity. It is natural for it to confirm afterwards what it has helped to establish. In the same way, we clearly express our ideas by means of mental images which always precede, and likewise emotion precedes the operation of the will, and then becomes the means by which we attain the desired end. ...

On Revelation (1921)[111]

First Principles

Catholic Apologetics

[26] "Catholic Apologetics" may be simply defined as "the rational defence of Divine Revelation." This defence is made by reason "under the direction of Divine Faith." Not indeed that a Catholic Apologist, may use Faith to enforce reason and reason to establish Faith, but he chooses under the direction of Faith the special rational arguments put forward to defend Revelation, and develops their probative force wholly by means of the light of reason. Regarding the necessity of such a treatise, as the fact of Revelation is not immediately evident to us, we need the establishment of its truths because of their intrinsic value, and because of the momentous consequences for time and eternity which follow therefrom.

The division of the subject matter usually followed by Catholic Apologists is as follows :–

I. Theoretical Part (against Philosophical Rationalism).

(a) Possibility of Revelation.

(b) Congruity and necessity of Revelation.

(c) Cognoscibility of Revelation from certain signs.

II. [27] Positive Part (against Biblical Rationalism).

(a) Historical testimony of Christ regarding His Divine mission and regarding the institution of the Church.

(b) Confirmation of this testimony drawn from

(1) Satisfaction of human aspirations afforded by the teaching of Divine Revelation.

(2) Sublimity of the doctrine revealed.

(3) Marvellous life of the Church.

(c) Confirmation of this testimony by miracles and prophecy.

(d) Comparison of Christianity with Mosaic and other religions.

(e) Consequent obligation of accepting Divine Revelation. ...

[30] The science of Catholic Apologetics is based upon the true scientific method. There is in the first place a searching

---

[111] [Walshe, Thomas Joseph, ed., *The Principles of Catholic Apologetics: A Study of Modernism Based Chiefly on the Lectures of Père Garrigou-Lagrange "De revelatione per ecclesiam catholicam proposita" Adapted and Re-arranged* (London: Sands, 1926). Public Domain.]

analysis of:
    (1) The true notion of Mystery and Revelation,
    (2) The exact idea of Credibility,
    (3) The validity of the Motives of Credibility. ...

The synthetic part of Apologetics sets out from the existence of Divine Revelation proposed by Christ and by the Church, and shows that such Revelation exhibits true notions of mystery, has legitimate claims on human credibility because supported by valid rational motives; that in fact the truths proposed for belief realise, and more than realise, the ideals which previous analytic examination desiderated.

Thus the method of proof adopted by approved Catholic Apologists is analytico-synthetic and corresponds, as far [31] as difference of the subject matter allows, with the method which has been so fruitful in the advancement of physical science.

In physical science, experience is the supreme test, the supreme motive of credibility. It is essential for the enumeration of instances; it is likewise essential for the verification or otherwise of results which follow from hypothetical inference. In Apologetics, motives of credibility are both external and internal. Here too experience is necessary, whether it be the experience of the senses or the mental experience of various emotions. The following table gives an enumeration of the motives of credibility:

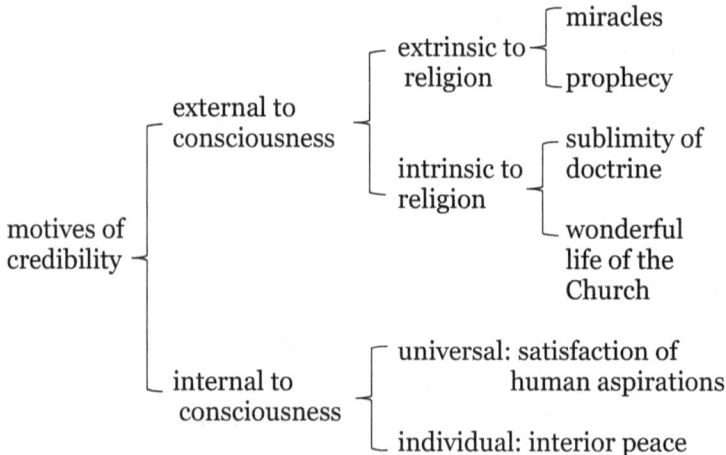

			miracles
		extrinsic to religion	prophecy
	external to consciousness		
motives of credibility		intrinsic to religion	sublimity of doctrine
			wonderful life of the Church
	internal to consciousness	universal: satisfaction of human aspirations	
		individual: interior peace	

Motives of Credibility

Motives Internal and External-Intrinsic

Art. I.–Motives of Credibility in General

[179] I.–For the collective Faith of the Church there is a moral necessity that the fact of Revelation should be proved. Certitude based on universal opinion is in the strict sense sufficient. But scientific proof founded (1) metaphysically, on the probative force of motives of Credibility, and (2) historically, on the existence of such motives, is morally necessary, i.e., such proof is highly suitable and useful. The suitability is shown a posteriori from the fact that objections drawn from philosophical and historical sciences should be answered, and a priori from the consequence that if the signs of Revelation are irrefragable, then the Church should be able to defend irrefragably the cogency of such signs.

II.–Existence and Character of the Proof.

(a) The Vatican Council declares that the proof is not only possible but exists (Denz. 1813, 1799, 1624, 1637).

(b) Scientific proof, in the strict sense, is drawn *a priori* from cause, or *a posteriori* from effect. Inasmuch as in the case of Revelation both cause and effects are supernatural, scientific proof, in its strictest sense, cannot be given. But in a wider and more indirect sense, scientific proof, drawn from extrinsic signs wrought in confirmation of Revelation, exists. It is a proof known, as "*reductio ad absurdum*," the absurdity being the supposition that God would work miracles in confirmation of false doctrine. Even in mathematics the cogency of the "*reductio ad absurdum*" is frequently recognised and invoked.

III.–Motives of Credibility, Credentity, and Faith.

Motives of Credibility are signs or marks whereby Revealed Religion is made evidently credible for Divine Faith. The judgment of Credibility is founded on these signs.

Motive of Credentity signifies the Divine right constituting the obligation of belief.

[180] *Motive of Faith* is the authority of God revealing.

Hence a motive of Credibility must possess three qualities :

(1) Certainty in itself.

(2) Certainty as due to the special intervention of God

(3) Certainty as to its function of confirming Revelation.

IV.–Different kinds of Motives of Credibility.

(A) The Church's teaching.

The Church appeals (1) to external signs of Divine Revelation, viz., miracles and prophecy (Denz. 1790), (2) to the wonderful life of the church (Denz. 1794) and (3) to internal motives (Denz. 1790). But the church has condemned the view that internal motives *alone* can be the basis of Divine Faith (Denz. 1812). ...

Art. II.–Value of Internal Motives.

I.–Those who adopt the method of Immanence do not make right use of the internal motives.

(A) Some Rationalists invoke them to show that the doctrines of Christianity correspond to human aspirations. They do not admit the supernatural origin of Christianity. Kant and Hegel reject all supernatural dogmas, or interpret them in a symbolic sense.

(B) Liberal Protestants and Modernists also make use of internal motives. They regard Christianity as a higher form of religious evolution and consequently changeable. They too regard dogma as only of symbolic value.

(C) Certain Catholic writers, who favour the method of immanence (Blondel, Laberthonnière) hold of course that [181] the Catholic Faith is supernatural. They go on to assert that because Catholicism alone satisfies the internal desire for religion, the practical necessity of embracing Catholicism follows. They give only a symbolic, not an ontological, value to miracles. In their estimation a miracle is an extraordinary sensible symbol attracting the attention of the unbeliever, so that he should examine the Catholic religion, and find therein conformity with the aspirations and exigencies of nature. A development of this mental attitude is their definition of truth, viz., conformity of the intellect with life, with the exigencies of nature.

Critique

(1) Divine Faith is reduced to religious experience.

(2) The method of Immanence diminishes the probative force of miracles.

(3) This method exaggerates the natural desire of supernatural life. It sees in human, nature not only a capacity and suitability for the supernatural order, but a real exigency.

(4) The method fails to show the Credibility and Divine origin of Christianity.

II.–Individual internal motives may produce probability, but not certitude in regard to Credibility.

(a) They may produce probability: A man seeking Faith and reading: "My peace I leave you, my peace I give you: not as the world gives do I give unto you" (John 14:27) may find peace so deeply in conformity with his higher aspirations, and so gratuitously offered as to seem to come from God alone. Similarly in regard to the sublimity of Our Lord's teaching: "When Jesus had finished his discourse, the multitudes were in admiration of his doctrine" (Matt 6:28). Hence in individual cases internal motives may manifest the credibility of the mysteries of Faith, and without doubt they help when joined with external motives.

(b) Ordinarily, internal motives are not sufficient. Internal peace and joy are not necessarily a supernatural effect; they may be merely natural. Three qualities are required so that a fact should be a sufficient motive of Credibility; internal motives fail to show these qualities. [182] Accidentally and in extraordinary cases, internal motives may suffice, in which cases grace supplies the function of the external motives.

III.–The universal internal motives taken together can produce moral certitude regarding Credibility. These motives arise from the satisfaction of the moral and religious aspirations of humanity. To these universal internal motives correspond objectively the external motives drawn from sublimity of doctrine and the wonderful life of the Church.

The Universal internal motives produce *per se* moral certitude of the fact of Revelation. Men cannot quickly and without error acquire a knowledge of all the truths of Natural Religion. Hence if all legitimate aspirations, even the higher aspirations of our nature, are satisfied by a system of religious belief, this fact is a sign of the Divine origin of the religion. But for the possibility of this moral certitude three conditions are required:

1° The ontological validity of first principles (e.g. of efficient and final causes) must be acknowledged, otherwise there is no valid inference from effect to cause.

2° The conformity must be so extraordinary–a moral miracle– as to seem to come from God.

3° The argument must be drawn from all aspirations–negative and positive–taken together.

(a) Aspirations to know, hope in, and love God, to give Him internal and external worship.

(b) Aspirations regarding prudence, justice, temperance, fortitude.

(c) Aspirations towards eternal happiness and desire, conditional and inefficacious, of seeing God essentially.

In Christian teaching the knowledge given of God and of His

intimate life satisfies the aspiration of Faith. The mysteries of the Incarnation and Redemption increase the aspiration of Hope, the Eucharist exceeds the highest aspirations of Charity, etc. Lacordaire, using his marvellous gift of oratory, argued for the divinity of the Christian Faith from the Christian ideals of Charity, Humility, and Virginity.

It is well to note that the internal experience of peace which characterised the Saints differs from the peace which the world gives: (1) Peace which the Saints enjoy is [183] directed to eternal goods, peace of the world to the undisturbed enjoyment of temporal goods; (2) Peace which comes from God is internal and external; peace which the world gives is merely external.

These motives give moral certitude, but must not be separated from correlative external motives intrinsic to religion, joined with which, they constitute an irrefragable argument. ...

Art. III–Value of the external motives intrinsic to Religion ...

[188] III.–Relations of motives inter se: Unity of Apologetics.

(A) Those who favour the method of Immanence claim that the internal, motives come first not only in time, but in value.[112] They reject the ontological value of miracles.

(B) In traditional Apologetics:

(1) Internal motives are subordinated to external:

(2) External motives, extrinsic to Religion, i.e., miracles and prophecy, are more easily recognised by us, but the external motives, intrinsic to Religion, are higher in themselves.

(3) Strongest of all are the great miracles, intrinsic to Religion, in which prophecy is fulfilled, and future happiness announced. For example, the Resurrection of Christ is:

(a) A Mystery of Faith (Resurrection of the Word).

(b) Sensible miracle of the first order.

(c) Fulfilment of several prophecies.

(d) Victory of Christ over sin.

(e) Example of strength gained through persecution.

(f) Pledge of our future happiness.

As regards the first statement–the subordination of internal to external motives–the supreme criterion of truth must be objective not subjective. Moreover internal [189] motives divorced from external give rise to illusions. It is true that internal motives often dispose an enquirer to consider other motives; in which

---

[112] Maurice Blondel, *L'Action* (Paris: F. Alcan, 1893), pp. 425-492.

cases they have priority of time. Again they confirm other motives.

With reference to the second statement, the wonderful life of the Church is higher than a physical miracle but not so easily recognised. Aristotle wrote: "Truths most intelligible in themselves are difficult to be known by us because our intellectual knowledge proceeds from sensible truths." From our standpoint the external-extrinsic criteria are easier and safer to recognise. But the life of the Church, being a moral, is higher than a physical miracle

As far as we now living are concerned, the perpetuity and wonderful life of the Church are of the highest apologetic value. In these qualities the effects of the Resurrection are manifest: *Christus vivit, Christus regnat, Christus imperat.*

Corollary: Unity of Apologetics

By unity in the science of Apologetics is meant the organic unity of the motives of credibility. The true order of arguments is determined by the end to which the science tends, i.e., to the evident credibility of the Mysteries of Faith as revealed by God. Hence priority of value belongs to the method which approaches nearest to the end, i.e., the external method. It is quite possible however that in many cases it would be advisable to begin by the use of the internal method which would thus be given priority of time. Hence the following order:

(1) Internal motives drawn from human aspirations.

(2) Excellence of Christian doctrine and the wonderful life of the Church (External-Intrinsic).

(3) Miracles and prophecy (External-Extrinsic).

(4) All motives are confirmed by experience of the gifts of the Holy Ghost (Internal peace and joy, etc.).

Christ's Testimony Is Conformed by His Miracles
Art. I–The Miracles of Christ.

[328] ... III. The miracles of Christ are historically certain.

1. The witnesses who relate the miracles of Christ relate other facts which are not called in question, and they were willing to suffer death, and actually did so suffer in testimony of the truthfulness of their narrative.

2. The miracles recorded were facts which appealed to the senses, and therefore could be judged by those who witnessed them.

3. The principal miracles of Christ were public. They were seen by such men as Nicodemus, Jairus, the Centurion, Zaccheus, Lazarus, Scribes and Pharisees, Priests and members of the

Sanhedrin.

4. Regarding some miracles a juridical enquiry was held by the enemies of Christ (Cf. John 5:10-16; 9:1-34; 12:9-10; Acts 4:16).

5. The simplicity of the Gospel narrative bears witness to its sincerity.

6. The miraculous facts are intimately connected with other facts of the life of Christ which cannot be denied. They are connected with His life, preaching, passion and death, so that if the miracles be denied, the Gospel narrative is destroyed not partially, but wholly. ...

8. The Apostles and the Fathers could not have so confidently appealed to the miracles of Christ if there were any doubt of their reality.

[329] 9. Jewish contemporaries and adversaries of Christ did not call into question His miracles, but attributed them to magic arts.

IV.–The Miracles of Christ are Supernatural

Rationalists allow that raising from the dead is beyond the powers of nature, and accordingly they deny the historical truth of such miracles. Other miracles they assert to be purely natural effects, regarded as wonderful owing to ignorance of physical, or chemical, or biological or psychological laws. To these assumptions the following replies may be made.

1. The Pharisees, their hostility notwithstanding, could not deny the resurrection of Lazarus.

2. Scribes and Pharisees attributed Christ's miraculous power to some superhuman agency, e.g., Beelzebub (Cf. Mark 3:22 sq.).

3. Instantaneous restoration of sight to one born blind, cure of leprosy, sudden change of water into wine, multiplication of loaves, resurrection of Lazarus–these achievements are clearly beyond the power of created agents.

4. The Divine origin of these miracles is confirmed by reflection upon the circumstances and results. Christ worked miracles solely for the glory of God, and the salvation of souls.

5. Confirmation also comes from the absurd hypotheses adopted to explain them away. It is well known that the power of mental suggestion by hypnotism or otherwise is effective only in cases of functional disorder, and that suggestion works gradually, whereas Christ wrought His miracles of healing, etc., instantaneously. Again suggestion does not work on those who are absent. Christ healed the Centurion's servant.

ÉTIENNE GILSON (1884-1978)

Gilson was born in Paris in 1884. He attended a minor seminary there, Notre-Dame-des-Champs, from 1895-1902, but ultimately decided against joining the priesthood. Instead he went on to study philosophy at the Sorbonne from 1904 to 1907 under Victor Delbos, Émile Durkheim, and Lucien Lévy-Bruhl, while simultaneously attending the lectures of Henri Bergson at the Collège de France. Upon acquiring his *agrégation*, Gilson married his cousin Thérèse Ravisé in 1908 and taught at various lycées throughout France over the next few years. He further successfully defended his dissertation on Descartes at the Sorbonne in 1913.

Gilson, however, found his academic career interrupted by the two world wars. He had just started a position at the University of Lille when he was drafted into the French army in 1914. He participated in the battle of Verdun as a second lieutenant and was captured by German forces in 1916, spending two years in a military prison. Gilson was later on awarded the Croix de Guerre medal for the heroism displayed in the war.

Upon being released from German military prison, and after a short stint back at the University of Lille, Gilson transferred to the University of Strasbourg where he taught from 1919-1921. He triumphantly returned to the Sorbonne in 1921 to become professor of medieval philosophy and taught there until 1932 as well as at the École Pratique des Hautes Études. Always interested in North American Institutions, Gilson lectured at Harvard from 1926-1928 and helped set up the Pontifical Institute of Medieval Studies [PIMS] through St. Michael's College at the University of Toronto in 1929. By now, very much in demand, Gilson delivered the Gifford Lectures at the University of Aberdeen from 1931-1932 and the William James Lectures at Harvard in 1936. Gilson was elected to the prestigious chair of medieval philosophy at the Collège de France where he served from 1932 to 1951 in addition to teaching at the PIMS. He then taught solely at the Pontifical Institute of Medieval Studies until 1968. In part this move was precipitated by the so-called l'Affaire Gilson, where *Commonweal* (December 12, 1950) published an article by Waldemar Gurian of Notre Dame entitled "Europe and the United States" highly critical of Gilson, accusing him of spreading a "Gospel of defeatism" and abandoning Europe to Communism. This piece was picked up by the French newspapers *Figaro* and *Le monde* which accused Gilson of being a traitor, to which Gilson replied in February of 1951. Gilson died in 1978 in Auxerre and is buried in a cemetery in Melun.

Gilson spent the bulk of his time writing on the history of medieval philosophy. Especially notable are his works *Le Thomisme* (Paris: Vrin, 1919), *L'esprit de la philosophie médiévale* (Paris: Vrin, 1932), and *History of Christian Philosophy in the Middle Ages* (London: Sheed and Ward, 1955). Gilson also is known for his original studies in epistemology, metaphysics, and the philosophy of art. Notable in epistemology are his works *Le réalisme méthodique* (Paris: Téqui, 1935),

The Unity of Philosophical Experience (New York: Charles Scribner's Sons, 1937), and *Réalisme thomiste et critique de la connaissance* (Paris: Vrin, 1939). Equally notable are his metaphysical works *God and Philosophy* (New Haven: Yale University Press, 1941), *Being and Some Philosophers* (Toronto: Pontifical Institute of Medieval Studies, 1949), and *L'atheisme difficile* (Paris: Vrin, 1979).

Some of the books that can be consulted for more on the life and thought of Gilson are: Savaria, Madeleine Gabrielle, *Étienne Gilson's Concept of the Nature and Scope of Philosophy* (Washington: Catholic University of America Press, 1951); Casey, Joseph, *The Notion of Being in Recent Works of Etienne Gilson* (Rome: Gregorian University Press, 1953); Quinn, John, *The Thomism of Étienne Gilson: A Critical Study* (Villanova: Villanova University Press, 1971); Shook, Laurence, *Étienne Gilson* (Toronto: Pontificial Institute of Medieval Studies, 1984); Schmitz, Kenneth, *What has Clio to Do with Athena?: Etienne Gilson, Historian and Philosopher* (Toronto: Pontifical Institute of Medieval Studies, 1987); Bloomer, Matthew, *Judeo-Christian Revelation as a Source of Philosophical Reflection according to Étienne Gilson* (Rome: Apollinare Studi, 2001); Murphy, Francesca Aran, *Art and Intellect in the Philosophy of Étienne Gilson* (Columbia: University of Missouri Press, 2004).

The selections below are from Gilson's *Methodical Realism* (Front Royal: Christendom Press, 1990): c. V, 127-140 and *The Spirit of Mediaeval Philosophy* (New York: Charles Scribner's Sons, 1936): c. II, 34-41. In the former Gilson defends a realism in epistemology and in the latter Gilson defends the idea of a "Christian philosophy." He argues that philosophy is best thought of as the handmaid of theology as it can only really flourish when it takes theological doctrines into account. For theology can suggest new ideas to philosophy which can then be developed in all their logical rigor by philosophical methods. Hence as he later puts it "true scholastic philosophers will always be theologians" (*Philosophical Essays*, Eugene: Cascade, 2011, p. 8). There is also an additional selection from Gilson's *Elements of Christian Philosophy* (New York: Doubleday, 1960), 108-111, wherein Gilson, in opposition to Maritain and Garrigou-Lagrange, greatly stresses negative theology and controversially upholds a doctrine of divine ignorance in Thomas Aquinas. Hence we do not really know *what* God is but only *that* God is, or that God is cause of the effects we observe. And though Gilson asserts that we know by analogy that the divine cause resembles its effects, such as wisdom and goodness, insofar as they preexist in God; Gilson also claims that God possesses these attributes to a perfect degree and as such in a manner that is metaphorical and unknowable to finite human beings (ibid., 137-145).

Methodical Realism (1935)[113]

[127] The Realist Beginner's Handbook

1. The first step on the realist path is to recognize that one has always been a realist; the second is to recognize that, however hard one tries to think differently, one will never manage to; the third is to realize that those who claim they think differently, think as realists as soon as they forget to act a part. If one then asks oneself why, one's conversion to realism is all but complete.

2. Most people who say and think they are idealists would like, if they could, not to be, but believe that is impossible. They are told they will never get outside their thought and that a something beyond thought is unthinkable. If they listen to this objection and look for an answer to it, they are lost from the start, because all idealist objections to the realist position are formulated in idealist terms. So it is hardly surprising that the idealist always wins. His questions invariably imply [128] an idealist solution to problems. The realist, therefore, when invited to take part in discussion on what is not his own ground, should first of all accustom himself to saying No, and not imagine himself in difficulties because he is unable to answer questions which are in fact insoluble, but which for him do not arise.

3. We must begin by distrusting the term "thought"; for the greatest difference between the realist and the idealist is that the idealist thinks, whereas the realist knows. For the realist, thinking simply means organizing knowledge or reflecting on its content. It would never occur to him to make thought the starting point of his reflections, because for him a thought is only possible where there is first of all knowledge. The idealist, however, because he goes from thought to things, cannot know whether what he starts from corresponds with an object or not. When, therefore, he asks the realist how, starting from thought, one can rejoin the object, the latter should instantly reply that it is impossible, and also that this is the principal reason for not being an idealist. Since realism starts with knowledge, that is, with an act of the intellect which consists essentially in grasping an object, for the realist the question does not present an insoluble problem, but a pseudo-problem, which is something quite different.

---

[113] [Étienne Gilson, *Methodical Realism*, translated by Philip Trower. Copyright © 1990 by Christendom Press. Now in Public Domain with reversion of rights to translator and death of translator. Last published by Christendom Press, www.christendom.edu/news/christendom-press.]

[129] 4. Every time the idealist calls on us to reply to the questions raised by thought, one can be sure that he is speaking in terms of the Mind. For him, Mind is what thinks, just as for us the intellect is what knows. One should therefore, in so far as one can, have as little as possible to do with the term. This is not always easy, because it has a legitimate meaning, but we are living at a time when it has become absolutely necessary to retranslate into realist language all the terms which idealism has borrowed form us and corrupted. An idealist term is generally a realist term denoting one of the spiritual antecedents to knowledge, now considered as generating its own content.

5. The knowledge the realist is talking about is the lived and experienced unity of an intellect with an apprehended reality. This is why a realist philosophy has to do with the thing itself that is apprehended, and without which there would be no knowledge. Idealist philosophers, on the other hand, since they start from thought, quickly reach the point of choosing science or philosophy as their object. When an idealist genuinely thinks as an idealist, he perfectly embodies the essence of a "professor of philosophy"; whereas the realist, when he genuinely thinks as a realist, conforms himself to the authentic essence of a philosopher; for a philosopher talks about things, while a professor of philosophy talks about philosophy.

[130] 6. Just as we do not have to go from thought to things (knowing that the enterprise is impossible), neither do we have to ask ourselves whether something beyond thought is thinkable. A something beyond *thought* may well be unthinkable, but it is certain that all *knowledge* implies a something beyond thought. The fact that this something-beyond-thought is given us by knowledge only in thought, does not prevent it being a something beyond. But the idealist always confuses "being which is given in thought" with "being which is given by thought." For anyone who starts from knowledge, a something beyond thought is so obviously thinkable that this is the only kind of thought for which there can be a beyond.

7. The realist is committing an error of the same kind if he asks himself how, starting from the self, he can prove the existence of a non-self. For the idealist, who starts from the self, this is the normal and, indeed, the only possible way of putting the question. The realist should be doubly distrustful; first, because he does not start from the self; secondly, because for him the world is not a non-self (which is a nothing), but an in-itself. A thing-in-itself can be given through an act of knowledge. A non-self is what reality is

reduced to by the idealist, and can neither be grasped by knowledge nor proved by thought.

[131] 8. Equally, one should not let oneself be troubled by the classic idealist objection to the possibility of reaching a thing-in-itself, and above all to having true knowledge about it. You define true knowledge, the idealist says, as an adequate copy of reality. But how can you know that the copy reproduces the thing as it is in itself, seeing that the thing is only given to you in thought. The objection has no meaning except for idealism, which posits thought before being, and finding itself no longer able to compare the former with the latter, wonders how anyone else can. The realist, on the contrary, does not have to ask himself whether things do or do not conform to his knowledge of them, because for him knowledge consists in his assimilating his knowledge to things. In a system where the bringing of the intellect into accord with the things, which the judgment formulates, presupposes the concrete and lived accord of the intellect with its objects, it would be absurd to expect knowledge to guarantee a conformity without which it would not even exist.

9. We must always remember that the impossibilities in which idealism tries to entangle realism are the inventions of idealism. When it challenges us to compare the thing known with the thing in itself, it merely manifests the internal sickness which consumes it. For the realist there is no "noumenon" as the realist [132] understands the term. Since knowledge presupposes the presence to the intellect of the thing itself, there is no reason to assume, behind the thing in thought, the presence of a mysterious and unknowable duplicate, which would be the thing of the thing in thought. Knowing is not apprehending a thing as it is in thought, but, in and thought, apprehending the thing as it is.

10. To be able to conclude that we must necessarily go from thought to things, and cannot proceed otherwise, it is not enough to assert that everything is given in thought. The fact is, we do proceed otherwise. The awakening of the intelligence coincides with the apprehension of things, which, as soon as they are perceived, are classified according to their most evident similarities. This fact, which has nothing to do with any theory, is something that theory has to take account of. Realism does precisely that, and in this respect is following common sense. That is why every form of realism is a philosophy of common sense.

11. It does not follow from this that common sense is a philosophy; but all sound philosophy presupposes common sense and trusts it, granted of course that, whenever necessary, appeal

will be made from ill-informed to better-informed common sense. This is how science goes about things; science is not a critique of [133] common sense but of the successive approximations to reality made by common sense. The history of science and philosophy witness to the fact that common sense, thanks to the methodical use it makes of its resources, is quite capable of invention. We should, therefore, ask it to keep criticizing its conclusions, which means asking it to remain itself, not to renounce itself.

12. The word "invention," like many others, has been contaminated by idealism. To invent means to find, not to create. The inventor resembles the creator only in the practical order, and especially in the production of artifacts, whether utilitarian or artistic. Like the scientist, the philosopher only invents by finding, by discovering what up to that point had been hidden. The activity of his intelligence, therefore, consists exclusively in the exercise of his speculative powers in regard to reality. If it creates anything, what it creates is never an object, but a way of explaining the object from within that object.

13. This is also why the realist never expects his knowledge to engender an object without which his knowledge would not exist. Like the idealist, he uses his power of reflection, but keeping it within the limits of a reality given from without. Therefore the starting point of his reflections has to be being, which in effect is for us the beginning of knowledge: *res sunt*. If we go deeper [134] into the nature of the object given us, we direct ourselves towards one of the sciences, which will be completed by a metaphysical of nature. If we go deeper into the conditions under which the object is given us, we shall be turning towards a psychology, which will reach completion in a metaphysics of knowledge. The two methods are not only compatible, they are complementary, because they rest on the primitive unity of the subject and object in the act of knowledge, and any complete philosophy implies an awareness of their unity.

14. There is nothing, therefore, to stop the realist going, by way of reflective analysis, from the object as given in knowledge to the intellect and the knowing subject. Quite the contrary, this is the only way he has of assuring himself of the existence and nature of the knowing subject. *Res sunt, ergo cognosco, ergo sum res cognoscens* [Things exist, therefore I know, therefore I am a knowing subject]. What distinguishes the realist from the idealist is not that one refuses to undertake this analysis whereas the other is willing to, but that the realist refuses to take the final term of his

analysis for a principle generating the thing being analyzed. Because the analysis of knowledge leads us to the conclusion "I think," it does not follow that this "I think" is the first principle of knowledge. Because every representation [135] is, in fact, a thought, it does not follow that it is only a thought, or that an "I think" conditions all my representations.

15. Idealism derives its whole strength from the consistency with which it develops the consequences of its initial error. One is, therefore, mistaken in trying to refute it by accusing it of not being logical enough. On the contrary, it is a doctrine which lives by logic, and only by logic, because in it the order and connection of ideas replaces the order and connection between things. The fatal leap (*saltus mortalis*) which catapults the doctrine into its consequences precedes the doctrine. Idealism can justify everything with its method except idealism itself, for the cause of idealism is not of idealist stamp; it does not even have anything to do with the theory of knowledge; it belongs to the moral order.

16. Preceding any philosophical attempt to explain knowledge is the fact, not only of knowledge itself, but of men's burning desire to understand. If reason is too often content with summary and incomplete explanations, if it sometimes does violence to the facts by distorting them or passing them over in silence when they are inconvenient, it is precisely because its passion to understand is stronger than its desire to know, or because the means of acquiring knowledge at its disposal are not powerful enough to satisfy it. The [136] realist is just as much exposed to these temptations as the idealist, and yields to them just as frequently. The difference is that he yields to them against his principles, whereas the idealist makes it a principle that he can lawfully yield to them. Realism, therefore, starts with an acknowledgement by the intellect that it will remain dependent on a reality which causes its knowledge. Idealism owes its origin to the impatience of a reason which wants to reduce reality to knowledge so as to be sure that its knowledge lets none of reality escape.

17. The reason idealism has so often been in alliance with mathematics is that this science, whose object is quantity, extends its jurisdiction over the whole of material nature, in so far as material nature has to do with quantity. But while idealism may imagine that the triumphs of mathematics in some way justify it, those triumphs owe nothing to idealism, they are in no way bound up with it, and they justify it all the less, seeing that the most mathematically oriented physics conducts all its calculations within the ambit of the experimental facts which those

calculations interpret. Someone discovers a new fact and what happens? After vain attempts to make it assimilable, all mathematical physics will reform itself so as to be able to assimilate it. The idealist is rarely a scientist, more rarely still a research scientist in a laboratory, and yet it is the laboratory that [137] provides the material which tomorrow's mathematical physics will have to explain.

18. The realist, therefore, does not have to be afraid that the idealist may represent him as opposed to scientific thought, since every scientist, even if philosophically he thinks himself an idealist, in his capacity as a scientist thinks as a realist. A scientist never begins by defining the method of the science he is about to initiate. Indeed, the surest way of recognizing false sciences is by the fact that they make the method come first. The method, however, should derive from the science, not the science from the method. That is why no realist has ever written a *Discourse on the Method*. He cannot know how things are known before he knows them, nor discover how to know each order of things except in knowing it.

19. The most dangerous of all the different methods is the "reflective method"; the realist is content with "reflection." When reflection becomes a method, it is no longer just an intelligently directed reflection, which it should be, but a reflection which substitutes itself for reality in that its principles and system become those of reality itself. When the "reflective method" remains faithful to its essence, it always assumes that the final term of its reflection is at the same time the first principle of our knowledge; as a natural consequence of [138] this it follows that the last step in the analysis must contain virtually the whole of what is being analyzed; and, finally that whatever cannot be discovered in the end point of the reflection, either does not exist, or can legitimately be treated as not existing. This is how people are led into excluding from knowledge, and even from reality, what is necessary for the very existence of knowledge.

20. There is a second way of recognizing the false sciences generated by idealism; in starting from what they call thought, they are compelled to define truth as a special case of error. Taine did a great service for good sense when he defined sensation as a true hallucination, because he showed, as a result, where logic necessarily lands idealism. Sensation becomes what a hallucination is when this hallucination is not one. So we must not let ourselves be impressed by the famous "errors of the senses," nor startled by the tremendous business idealists make about

them. Idealists are people for whom the normal can only be a particular instance of the pathological. When Descartes states triumphantly that even a madman cannot deny his first principle "I think, therefore I am", he helps us enormously to see what happens to reason when reduced to this first principle.

[139] 21. We must, therefore, regard the arguments about dreams, illusions, and madness, borrowed by idealists from skeptics, as errors of the same kind. The fact that there are visual illusions chiefly proves that all our visual perceptions are not illusions. A man who is dreaming feels no different from a man who is awake, but anyone who is awake knows that he is altogether different from someone who is dreaming; he also knows it is because he has had sensations, that he afterwards has what are called hallucinations, just as he knows he would never dream about anything if he had not been awake first. The fact that certain madmen deny the existence of the outside world, or even (with all due respect to Descartes) their own, is no grounds for considering the certainty of our own existence as a special case of "true delirium." The idealist only finds these illusions so upsetting because he does not know how to prove they are illusions. The realist has no reason to be upset by them, since for him they really are illusions.

22. Certain idealists say that our theory of knowledge puts us in the position of claiming to be infallible. We should not take this objection seriously. We are simply philosophers for whom truth is normal and error abnormal; this does not mean it is any easier for us to reach the truth than it is to achieve and conserve perfect health. The realist differs from the idealist, not in being [140] unable to make mistakes, but principally in that, when he does make mistakes, the cause of the error is not a thought which has been unfaithful to itself, but an act of knowledge which has been unfaithful to its object. But above all, the realist only makes mistakes when he is unfaithful to his principles, whereas the idealist is in the right only in so far as he is unfaithful to his.

23. When we say that all knowledge consists in grasping the thing as it is, we are by no means saying that the intellect infallibly so grasps it, but that only when it does grasp it as it is will there be knowledge. Still less do we mean that knowledge exhausts the content of its object in a single act. What knowledge grasps in the object is something real, but reality is inexhaustible, and even if the intellect had discerned all its details, it would still be confronted by the mystery of its very existence. ... The virtue proper to the realists is modesty about his knowledge ...

The Spirit of Mediaeval Philosophy (1932)[114]

The Concept of Christian Philosophy

[34] St. Justin, Lactantius, St. Augustine and St. Anselm, four witnesses only—but then, what witnesses! Their high authority, and the perfect accord or their several experience will permit me to dispense, I trust, with the numerous others that might be added. ... It is a fact, then, that for the Christian, reason alone does not satisfy reason and it was not merely in the second century that philosophers became Christian in the interests of their philosophy. To the *fides quaerens intellectum* [faith seeking understanding] of St. Anselm and St. Augustine, corresponds the *intellectus quaerens intellectum per fidem* [understanding seeking understanding through faith] of Maine de Biran. *Optavi et datus est mihi sensus, invocavi et venit in me spiritus sapientiae* [Therefore I prayed, and prudence was given me; I pleaded and the spirit of Wisdom came to me]; this effort of truth believed to transform itself [35] into truth known, is truly the life of Christian wisdom, and the body of rational truths resulting from the effort is Christian philosophy itself. Thus the content of Christian philosophy is that of rational truths discovered, explored or simply safeguarded, thanks to the help that receives from revelation. Whether this philosophy ever really existed or whether it is nothing but a myth, is a question of fact on which we shall have to turn to history for a decision; but before entering on this I would dissipate a misunderstanding which, by obscuring the meaning of the *fides quaerens intellectum* [faith seeking understanding] would make the very concept of Christian philosophy unintelligible.

Unless the expression is to be emptied of all content it must be frankly admitted that nothing less than an intrinsic relation between revelation and reason will suffice to give it meaning. And it is important that this meaning should be exactly defined. There is no question of maintaining—no one has ever maintained—that faith is a kind of cognition superior to rational cognition. It is quite clear, on the contrary, that belief is a succedaneum of knowledge, and that to substitute science for belief, wherever possible, is always a positive gain for the understanding. For Christian

---

[114] [Étienne Gilson, *The Spirit of Mediaeval Philosophy*, translated by Alfred Howard Campbell Downes. Copyright © 1936 Charles Scribner's Sons. All rights reserved. Used with permission of Pontifical Institute of Medieval Studies Press, https://pims.ca/article/publications.]

thinkers the traditional hierarchy of the modes of cognition is always faith, understanding, and vision of God face to face: *Inter fidem et speciem*, wrote St. Anselm, *intellectum quem in hac vita capimus esse medium intelligo* [I understand that the understanding that we grasp in this life is midway between faith and sight].[115]

Nor is there any question of maintaining the absurdity that you can accept the major premiss of a syllogism by faith and know the conclusion as science. If you start from belief and deduce its content you can never get anything more than belief. When those who define the method of Christian philosophy by the *fides quaerens intellectum* [faith seeking understanding] are accused of confusing philosophy with theology the accuser merely shows how little he understands their position, and [36] gives us reason to suspect, besides, that he has no very clear notion of the nature of theology. For although theology is a science, it does not propose as its end the transformation of the belief by which it adheres to its principles into understanding; to do that would be to destroy its proper object. Nor will the Christian philosopher on the other hand, any more than the theologian, attempt to transform faith into science, as if by some queer chemistry you could combine contradictory essences. What he asks himself is simply this; whether, among those propositions which by faith he believes to be true, there are not a certain number which reason may know to be true. In so far as the believer bases his affirmations on the intimate conviction gained from faith he remains purely and simply a believer, he has not yet entered the gates of philosophy; but when amongst his beliefs he finds some that are capable of becoming objects of science then he becomes a philosopher, and if it is to the Christian faith that he owes this new philosophical insight, he a Christian philosopher.

The present discord between philosophers as to the meaning of this expression thus becomes easier to explain. Some are considering philosophy in itself, in its formal essence as philosophy, abstraction being made from the conditions which rule either its constitution or its intelligibility. In this sense it is clear that a philosophy cannot be Christian, nor, for that matter, Jewish or Mussulman, and that the idea of Christian philosophy has no more meaning than "Christian physics" or "Christian mathematics."[116]

---

[115] St. Anselm, *De fide Trinitatis*, Praef.

[116] It serves no purpose to object that a reason which allows itself to

Others, taking account of the evident fact that, for a Christian, faith plays the part of an extrinsic regulative principle, admit the possibility of a Christian philosophy ; but, anxious to safeguard the formal purity of its essence as philosophy, they consider as Christian any philosophy that is true, any philosophy which presents "a conception [37] of nature and reason open to the supernatural."[117] And that, undoubtedly, is one of the characters of Christian philosophy, but by no means the only one nor, perhaps, the deepest. A philosophy open to the supernatural would certainly be compatible With Christianity, but it would not necessarily be a Christian philosophy. If it is to deserve that name the supernatural must descend as a constitutive element not, of course, into its texture which would be a contradiction, but into the work of its construction. Thus I call Christian, *every philosophy which, although keeping the two orders formally distinct, nevertheless considers the Christian revelation as an indispensable auxiliary to reason.* For whoever understands it thus, the concept does not correspond to any simple essence susceptible of abstract definition; but corresponds much rather to a concrete historical reality as something calling for description. It is but one of the species of the genus and includes in its extension

---

be taken in tow by faith is voluntarily blinded, and that it is only too easy to imagine that one has proved what one believes. If the believer's demonstrations make no impression on the unbeliever, he will not hold himself authorized to appeal to a faith that his opponent does not accept. All that the believer can do, as far as regards himself, is to make sure that he is not the victim of illusion and to criticize himself severely. As regards his opponent, he will not fail to wish him the grace of faith, and all the enlightenment of the intelligence that accompanies it. This point cannot honestly be overlooked. The problem of Christian philosophy is not confined to the question of its constitution, but embraces also that of its understanding. The contemporary paradox of a Christian philosophy evidently true for its defenders, and of no value in the eyes of their opponents, does not necessarily imply that its defenders are blinded by their faith; it may perhaps be explained by the fact that absence of the light of faith in the opponent leaves truth opaque where it might be transparent. This in no way authorizes the Christian philosopher to argue in the name of faith, but rather to redouble his purely rational efforts until the light thus gained leads other minds also to turn to its source and draw the same enlightenment.

[117] Marie-Domenique Chenu, O.P., "Étienne Gilson, Le Thomisme," in *Bulletin Thomiste* 2 (January, 1928): 244. Cf. the well-balanced remarks of Jacques Maritain, "De la sagesse augustinienne," in *Revue de Philosophie* 30 (1930): 739-741, to which we wholeheartedly subscribe.

all the philosophical systems which were in fact what they were only because a Christian religion existed and because they were ready to submit to its influence. As concrete historical realities these systems are distinguished from each other by individual differences; as forming a species they present common characteristics, and thus may be grouped together under the same denomination.

In the first place, and it is perhaps his most obvious trait, the Christian philosopher is one who effects a choice between philosophic problems. Like any other philosopher, he has a perfect right to interest himself in the whole circle of these problems; but in fact he is interested uniquely or above all in those which affect the conduct of his religious life. The rest, indifferent in themselves, become the objects of what St. Augustine, St. Bernard and St. Bonaventure stigmatize as curiosity: *vana curiositas, turpis curiositas.* Even Christian philosophers like St. Thomas, whose interest [38] extended to the whole of philosophy, did their creative work only in a relatively restricted sphere. And nothing could be more natural. Since the Christian revelation teaches us only truths which are necessary to salvation, its influence could extend only to those parts of philosophy that concern the existence and nature of God, and the origin, nature, and destiny of the soul. In the very title and in the first lines of his treatise *De la connaissance de Dieu et de soi-même* [On the Knowledge of God and of Oneself], Bossuet held to the teaching of sixteen centuries of tradition: "Wisdom consists in knowing God and in knowing oneself. From the knowledge of self we rise to the knowledge of God." Everyone will recognize in these formulae the *noverim me, noverim te* [Let me know myself, and let me know You] of St. Augustine, and although St. Thomas did not expressly make them his own he put them into practice. There is no question of minimizing his merits as a commentator interpreter of Aristotle; it not in that field, however, that he is greatest, but rather in those views in which he prolonged and surpassed the philosophic effort of Aristotle. And these views are almost always to be found when he is speaking of God and of the soul and of the relations between God and the soul. The deepest of them have often to disentangled from the theological contexts in which they are embedded, for it is there, in the bosom of theology, that they effectively come to birth. In a word, faith has a simplifying influence on all Christian philosophers worthy of the name, and their originality shines forth especially in the sphere directly influenced by faith, that is to say in the doctrine concerning God and man, and man's relations with

God.

From the very fact that faith eliminates vain curiosity, the influence of revelation on philosophy facilitates the work of its constitution. From any Christian point of view the merely curious man is engaged on an interminable enterprise. He takes all knowledge for his province, every [39] reality falls within it, and of none is he entitled to say that, if he knew it, it would not transform his knowledge of all the rest. Reality is inexhaustible and the attempt to synthetize it under principles is consequently impracticable. It may even be, as Comte was later on to suggest, that natural reality is not synthetic, and that it can be unified only by considering it from the point of view a subject. Choosing man in relation to God as his central theme, the Christian philosopher acquires a fixed centre of reference which helps him to bring order and unity into his thought. That is why the tendency to systematization is always so strong in a Christian philosophy: it has less to systematize than any other and it has the necessary centre the system as well.

It has also the necessary material for its completion, and this, in the first place, even in the field of natural philosophy. It seems to be sometimes supposed that only the Augustinians were convinced of this. In fact, in the *Contra Gentiles* (Book 1, Chapter IV) St. Thomas has left a luminous *résumé* of the whole teaching of the Fathers of the Church on this fundamental question. He asks: is fitting that God should reveal philosophical truths which are in fact accessible to reason?–and he answers: yes!–provided that the knowledge of these truths is necessary to salvation. Were it otherwise, both these truths, and the salvation that depends on them, would be the exclusive prerogative or a very few; the bulk of mankind would have to go without them, either for lack of intellectual light, or of leisure for research, or of a taste for study. He adds that even those capable of attaining them would do so only with a great deal of labour, after long thought, and would be running, moreover, all the risks of ignorance for the greater part of their lives. What, he asks, would be the state of mankind, if all our knowledge of God depended [39] only on human reason? *In maximis ignorantiae tenebris* [In the greatest shadows of ignorance]. And this he confirms with a third consideration of no less weight than the other two. The weakness of the human intellect, in its present state, is such, that without the aid of faith what to many would seem to clearly demonstrated would to others be exceedingly dubious; and the spectacle of the philosophic conflicts thus arising would contribute not a little to breed scepticism in the generality of mankind, who, for the most part, would view the discussion from outside.[118] To overcome this *debilitas rationis* [debility of reason] man has therefore need of divine aid; and this is what faith offers him. Like St. Augustine and St. Anselm him, St. Thomas situates the reason of the Christian philosopher in an intermediate position between the faith which guides his first footsteps, and the full knowledge which the beatific vision will bring hereafter; like Athenagoras he thinks that man can aspire to no perfect knowledge of God without putting himself to school with God, *qui est sui perfectus cognitor* [who is a perfect knower of Himself]. Faith, taking him so to speak by the hand, puts him on the right road and goes along with him as long as he needs protection from error.[119]

This, as will be seen, is no very bright picture of the results attainable by human reason alone in the field of natural theology– yet it is the picture drawn by the most thoroughly intellectualist of all Christian philosophers. Why then should we hesitate to follow where so many concordant indications point the way, especially if it is possible to do so without losing sight of the necessary distinctions, the fruit of so many years of laborious reflection, and which reason, moreover, clearly demands? A true philosophy, taken absolutely and in itself, owes all its truth to its rationality and to nothing other than its rationality: that is indisputable, and St. Anselm and even St. Augustine would be the first to admit it. But the constitution or this true philosophy could not in fact be achieved without the aid of revelation, acting as an [41] indispensable moral support to reason; that is equally certain from the standpoint of the Christian philosophers, and, as we have just seen, St. Thomas himself asserts it. Now if he was right, or if we merely admit that he may have been right, the problem of Christian philosophy acquires a meaning. Doubtless in the abstract philosophy professes no religion, but we may very well ask whether it is altogether a matter of indifference that a philosopher should profess one. We may ask especially whether it is indifferent to the history of philosophy as such that there have been philosophers who were Christians, and whether, in spite of the purely rational texture of their systems, we cannot still to-day discern the mark of the influence of their faith on ... their thought.

---

[118] See Fr. Paul Synave's remarkable study, "La revelation des vérités divines naturelles d'après saint Thomas d'Aquin," in Pierre Mandonnet, *Mélanges Mandonnet* (Paris: J. Vrin, 1930), vol. 1, pp. 327-365.

[119] St. Thomas Aquinas, *De Veritate*, q. 14, a. 10, Resp.

Elements of Christian Philosophy (1960)[120]

The Essence of God

[108] The natural knowledge of God cannot exceed what can be known of Him from the quiddities of material things that are the objects proportioned to our own cognitive powers. In Thomas' own words, "in this life, our intellect has a determinate relationship to the forms that are abstracted from sensations."[121] Such objects are finite. Consequently, no natural knowledge thus formed by the human mind can represent God; His immaterial essence cannot be attained by means of abstraction from material things. Generally speaking, there are no material data from which the knowledge of a purely immaterial object can possibly be abstracted. Moreover, since all objects naturally knowable to man are finite, no knowledge of them obtainable by means of abstraction from sense can possibly represent an infinite being, such as the essence of God. In other words, the twofold fact that human knowledge has to be abstracted from sense, and that it deals only with finite objects, makes it impossible for us to grasp the very essence of God, such as it is known by the blessed.

Since to know God *by His essence* is not naturally possible for man, the only knowledge of God still accessible to us is the kind of knowledge that is obtained when a certain form is known from its effects. Even in this case, two ways of knowing have to be distinguished, because there are two kinds of effects. Some belong in the same order as the causal power by which they are produced; they are its equals. By knowing effects of this sort, it is possible to know fully the powers [109] and the quiddities of their causes. But there is another class of effects; namely, those that lack this equality with the power of their causes. By starting from such effects, the human mind can comprehend neither the power of their efficient cause nor, consequently, its essence. The only thing that can be known of such a cause, starting from such effects, is that it is. Now this precisely is what happens in the case of our knowledge of God. Since all the effects of God are unequal to their cause, the only thing we can know about Him is that He is. Neither His power nor His essence is naturally knowable to us.

This position has been an eminently traditional one. The

---

[120] [Étienne Gilson, *Elements of Christian Philosophy*. Copyright © 1960 by Doubleday. Public Domain.]

[121] *Expositio super Boethii de Trinitate*, q. 1, a. 2, ed. Bruno Decker (Leiden: E.J. Brill, 1955), p. 65.

surprise it causes today in the minds of some modern theologians is due mainly to the difficulty they find in grasping its true meaning.

One of the obstacles to be overcome is the illusion that, if the only thing we know of God is that He is, there is for us no way left to progress in the knowledge of the divinity. But it is not so. In the case of effects unequal to their causes, our knowledge of the cause improves according as the true relationship of the effect to the cause becomes better known.

This improvement occurs in three different ways. First, it occurs according as we know better the efficacy of the cause in producing its effects. In the case of God, to know Him as the creator of His effects certainly is to know Him much better than to see Him only as the moving or the final cause of the world. A second improvement takes place if we investigate God as the cause of the higher and higher effects. For instance, to know God as the cause of intellectual substances is to know Him better than to see Him only as the cause of material substances. How far this can make us progress in our knowledge of God has been seen in the preceding chapter. If we know God only as the orderer of material beings, we know that He is a supreme mind; if we know He causes all substances as their Prime Mover, we know that God is a substance, the prime and supreme entity; but if we know God as the prime cause of all existents, then we know that He Himself is the prime and supreme Existent. All this, however, does not tell us *what* God is; it still tells us only *that* He is. We now know of Him that He is the cause of existence; but the very nature of such a cause, that is what we do not know. The third way in which the human understanding can progress in its knowledge of God as a cause is the progressive elimination of our illusion on the true nature of such knowledge. It consists in knowing God as more and more removed from all that which appears in His effects. This is what Dionysius says in his [110] *Divine Names*: that God is known, as the cause of all things, by transcending them and by being removed from them.[122]

Such is the Thomistic form of the traditional doctrine of the "learned ignorance." It has nothing in common with the passive inertia of an understanding giving up all hope of grasping its object. On the contrary, knowing as it does both its own nature

---

[122] Pseudo-Dionysius, *De divinis nominibus*, VII, 4; see *In Librum Dionysii De Divinis nominibus*, ed. C. Pera (Rome: Marietti, 1950), nn. 727-733.

and that of its proper object, the negative theology of Thomas Aquinas is an energetic and eminently positive effort of the mind against the self-deception that it knows the essence of its highest object. Negative theology is a fight relentlessly carried on by the human intellect against the always recurring illusion that, despite all that is said to the contrary, man has a certain positive notion, limited though it may be, of *what* the essence of God really is. Everything in man's intellect rebels against such an attitude. It is not natural to man to busy himself about its objects in order to make sure that he does *not* know them. Even if it knows that it cannot trust images in conceiving immaterial objects, the intellect at least hopes that these images will direct its inquiry toward a deeper truth; we do not usually consider our mental representations as enemies to be defeated but rather as helpful co-workers in our quest of truth.

Not so here. In deep agreement with the most radically imageless mysticism there ever existed, that of Saint Bernard of Clairvaux, Thomas Aquinas invites us to transcend all representation and figurative description of God. If we can imagine what something is, then God is beyond it; if we can grasp the definition of a certain thing, then that thing is not yet God. Nor is it enough to have said this only once; the aim of the doctrine of Thomas Aquinas on this crucial point is to invite us to a sort of intellectual asceticism calculated to rid our intellect of the delusion that we know *what* God is. This requires such an effort on our part that the grace of God and the gifts of the Holy Ghost are here required to help our intellects in this, their highest undertaking. Not that we should expect from God the revelation of any new notion; the grace of God is required here, not to add anything to our knowledge, but rather to give us the strength to acquire nescience and to keep it after acquiring it, instead of continually relapsing into deceptive images of the infinite Being.[123]

---

[123] *Expositio super Boethii de Trinitate*, q. 1, a. 2, ed. Bruno Decker (Leiden: E.J. Brill, 1955), pp. 66-67: "Third, in that God is known more and more as removed from the things that are found in His effects. Hence Dionysius says, in the book *The Divine Names*, that the cause of all things is known both by excess and by remotion. In this progress in knowledge, the human mind is especially aided when its natural light is strengthened by a new illumination: for example, the light of faith, and the gifts of wisdom and understanding, through which illumination the mind is said to be raised in contemplation above itself in so far as it knows God to be above everything that it naturally grasps. But because the mind does not have the power to reach the vision of the divine

The meaning of this doctrine is something everyone has to learn for himself. There is no point in endlessly repeating something that Thomas himself has so often repeated without in any way changing our natural attitude with respect to the problem of our knowledge of God. Nor will anything ever change it. When all is said and done, we shall [111] continue to teach others what God is, what we do know (after all!) of the essence of God. Perhaps we shall ourselves find it hard to realize fully that the summit of the human knowledge of God is to know that we do not know. Then is for us the time to go back to Thomas Aquinas and to meditate at length upon the meaning of formulas he could not have written without first having given the problem the full attention it deserves. Here at least is one of them, the more deserving of our attention as it says absolutely everything Thomas wanted us to understand on this point:

> They say that, on reaching the term of our knowledge, we know God as unknown, because our mind is found to have made its supreme progress in knowledge when it knows that the essence of God is above all that which it can apprehend in this life; and thus although what God is remains unknown, that He is, nevertheless, is known.[124]

This is the spirit in which one should approach the impressive series of chapters devoted by the two *Summae* to the progressive determination of what a metaphysician must say concerning the nature of God. Such as they are, these chapters constitute the most perfect demonstration of negative theology ever given by any scholastic theologian; but what should be particularly noted is the eminently positive nature of this intellectual effort which, by progressively leading us to the conclusion that God is *not* like any being given in human experience, finally raises Him infinitely above anything that can be seen, imagined, or quidditatively conceived.

---

essence, it is said to be in a manner thrown back upon itself by the excelling light. And this is what we read in the *Gloss* of Gregory on *Genesis 32:30* ('I have seen God face to face'): 'When the gaze of the soul is directed toward God, it is beaten back by the dazzling light of His immensity'."

[124] *Expositio super Boethii de Trinitate*, q. 1, a. 2, ad 1, ed. Decker, p. 67.

ALAN VINCELETTE

JACQUES MARITAIN (1882-1973)

Maritain was born in Paris in 1973. He was raised in a liberal Protestant environment, not surprising given that his mother was the daughter of the liberal politician Jules Favre. He studied philosophy and natural science at the Sorbonne from 1900-1906 where, after first embracing the scientism of his biology instructor Félix Le Dantec and the philosophy of Spinoza, he began to feel that science alone could not address all the issues of life. Indeed he met a Jewish student there, Raïssa Oumançoff, and they made a suicide pact to end their lives if they could not discover a deeper meaning to life in a few years' time. Fortunately, they attended the lectures of Henri Bergson at the Collège de France, on the recommendation of the poet Charles Péguy, embraced theism and married in 1904. After receiving his agrégé in philosophy in 1905 from the Sorbonne, Maritain studied biology at the University of Heidelberg, under Hans Driesch, from 1906-1908. Two other major influences on Maritain were the Catholic novelist Léon Bloy, who led him to convert to Catholicism in 1906, and Humbert Clérissac, O.P., who led him to embrace the thought of Thomas Aquinas.

As academic positions for Catholics were limited in France during the Third Republic, Maritain taught at the Collège Stanislas from 1912 to 1914 and the Institut Catholique de Paris from 1914 to 1940. With the fall of France to the Vichy Regime, Maritain moved to North America and taught at the Pontifical Institute of Medieval Studies in Toronto (1940-1941), Princeton University (1941-1942), and Columbia University (1941-1944), and helped to found the École Libre des Hautes Études for French émigrés. Maritain involved himself in French politics, following the liberation of France, serving as French Ambassador to the Vatican from 1945 to 1948 and president of the French delegation to UNESCO in 1947, and assisting in the drafting of the United Nations Declaration on Human Rights in 1948. He returned to the United States and found an academic home at Princeton University where he was professor from 1948-1960. After his wife died in 1960, Maritain lived with the Little Brothers of Jesus in Toulouse, himself becoming a member of the order in 1970. He is buried with his wife in the town of Kolbsheim, Alsace, a former summer retreat for his family.

Maritain was incredibly prolific writing over 70 books and over 700 articles, the key ones being *Distinguer pour unir ou Les degrés du savoir* (Paris: Desclée de Brouwer, 1932); *La philosophie de la nature* (Paris: P. Téqui, 1935); *Les Droits de l'Homme et la loi naturelle* (New York: Éditions de la Maison française, 1942); *Man and State* (Chicago: University of Chicago Press, 1951); and *Approaches to God* (New York: Harper, 1954).

For more on Maritain see: Phelan, Gerald, *Jacques Maritain* (London: Sheed & Ward, 1937); Maritain, Raïssa, *We Have Been Friends Together* (New York: Longmans, Green, and Company, 1942); Fecher, Charles, *The Philosophy of Jacques Maritain* (Westminster: Newman Press, 1953); Knasas, John, *Jacques Maritain: The Man and His Metaphysics* (Notre Dame: American Maritain Association, 1988); Ollivant, Douglas A., ed., *Jacques Maritain and the Many Ways of Knowing* (Washington: Catholic University of America Press, 2002); Dougherty, Jude, *Jacques Maritain* (Washington: Catholic University of America Press, 2003); Morawiec, Edward, *Intellectual Intuition in the General Metaphysics of Jacques Maritain* (Frankfurt: Peter Lang, 2013).

The excerpts are from Maritain's *The Range of Reason* (New York: Charles Scribner's Sons, 1952), VIII, 103-117, and *The Degrees of Knowledge* (London: Geoffrey Bles, 1937): I:i, pp. 58-71, 83-85, distinguishing various kinds of atheism (real, pseudo, practical) and knowledge (perinoetic, dianoetic, ananoetic).

The Range of Reason (1948)[125]

The Meaning of Contemporary Atheism

I. Various Kinds of Atheism

[103] Let us try, first, to establish in a more systematic way the distinction, indicated in the two previous chapters, between the diverse forms of atheism. This distinction can be made from either of two points of view: from the point of view of the attitude of the human being who professes himself to be an atheist; or from the point of view of the logical content of various atheistic philosophies.

From the first point of view, or with regard to the manner in which atheism is professed, I have already remarked that there are, in the first place, *practical atheists*, who believe that they believe in God but who in actual fact deny His existence by their deeds and the testimony of their behavior. Then there are *pseudo-atheists*, who believe that they do not believe in God but who in actual fact unconsciously believe in Him, because the God whose existence they deny is not God but something else. Finally there are *absolute atheists*, who really do deny the existence of the very God in Whom the believers believe—God the Creator, Savior and Father, Whose name is infinitely over and above any name we can utter. Those absolute atheists stand committed to change their entire system of values and to destroy in themselves everything that could possibly suggest the name they have rejected; they have chosen to stake [104] their all against divine Transcendence and any vestige of Transcendence whatsoever.

From the second point of view, that is, with regard to the logical content of various atheistic philosophies, I would divide atheism into negative and positive atheism.

By *negative atheism* I mean a merely negative or destructive process of casting aside the idea of God, which is replaced only by a void. Such a negative atheism can be shallow and empirical, like the atheism of the *libertins* in the XVIIth century—then it digs a hollow in the center of the universe of thought which has taken shape through the centuries around the idea of God, but it does not bother about changing that universe; it is merely concerned with making us live a comfortable life, enjoying the freedom of doing exactly as we please. On the other hand, negative atheism

---

[125] [Jacques Maritain, *The Range of Reason* (New York: Charles Scribner's Sons, 1952). Public Domain.]

can be lived at a profound and metaphysical level: in which case the hollow it creates at the heart of things extends to and lays waste our whole universe of thought; the freedom it claims for the human Self is absolute independence, a kind of divine independence that this Self, like Dostoyevsky's Kirilov, has no better way of affirming than by suicide and voluntary annihilation.

By *positive atheism* I mean an active struggle against everything that reminds us of God–that is to say, antitheism rather than atheism–and at the same time a desperate, I would say heroic, effort to recast and reconstruct the whole human universe of thought and the whole human scale of values in accordance with that state of war against God. Such positive atheism was the tragic, solitary atheism of a Nietzsche; such is today the literary, fashionable atheism of existentialism; such is the revolutionary atheism of dialectical materialism. The latter is of special interest to us, because it has succeeded in getting a considerable number of men to accept whole-heartedly this new kind of faith, and to give themselves to it with unquestionable sincerity.

Now when I speak of contemporary atheism, I have in mind atheism seen under the last aspect I have just mentioned; I consider it the most significant form of atheism, one which spells a new and unheard of historic event because it is an atheism at once *absolute and positive*. Human history has been confronted, for almost a century now, with the stormy bursting forth of an atheism which is both *absolute* (making man actually deny God Himself) and *positive* (anti- theism, demanding to be lived in full by man and to change the face of the earth). I have outlined in the [105] preceding chapter[126] the ideological process which terminated in this atheism which is both absolute and positive.

II. The Two-Fold Inconsistency of Contemporary Atheism

An Act of Faith in Reverse Gear

After these preliminary signposts I should like to point out that today's absolute-positive atheism involves a dual inconsistency.

How does absolute-positive atheism come to birth in the mind of a man? At this point we are faced with a remarkable fact. A man does not become an absolute atheist as a result of some inquiry into the problem of God carried on by speculative reason. No doubt he takes into account the negative conclusions afforded in

---

[126] See pp. 96-97.

this connection by the most radical forms of rationalist or positivist philosophy; he does not neglect, either, the old platitude which will have it that the scientific explanation of the universe purely and simply got clear of the existence of God. But all that is for him a second-hand means of defense, not the prime propelling and determining incentive. Neither those philosophical conclusions nor that nonsensical commonplace does he submit to any critical examination. He takes them for granted. He believes in them. And why? By virtue of an inner act of freedom, in the production of which he commits his whole personality. The starting point of absolute atheism is, in my opinion, a basic act of moral choice, a crucial free determination. If at the moment when he takes stock of himself and decides upon the whole direction of his life, a man confuses the transition from youth to manhood with the refusal not only of childhood's subordinations but of any subordination whatsoever; if he thus considers the rejection of any transcendent law as an act of moral maturity and emancipation; and if he decides to confront good and evil in a totally and absolutely free experience, in which any ultimate end and any rule coming from above are cast aside forever–such a free moral determination, dealing with the primary values of existence, will mean that this man has entirely excluded God from his own universe of life and thought. Here is, in my opinion, the point at which absolute atheism begins in the depths of a man's spiritual activity.

But what is this I have just been describing if not a kind of act of faith, an act of faith in reverse gear, whose content is not an [106] adherence to the transcendent God but, on the contrary, a rejection of Him?

Thus it is that absolute atheism is positive atheism. As I stated above,[127] and this must be stressed once again: "It is in no way a mere absence of belief in God. It is rather a refusal of God, a fight against God, a challenge to God." The absolute atheist is delivered over "to an inner dialectic which obliges him ceaselessly to destroy any resurgence in himself of what he has buried. ... In proportion as the dialectic of atheism develops in his mind–each time he is confronted with the natural notion of and tendency to an ultimate End, or with the natural notion of and natural interest in absolute values or unconditioned standards, or with some metaphysical anxiety–he will discover in himself vestiges of Transcendence which have not yet been abolished. He must get rid of them. God is

---

[127] Chapter VII, p. 98.

a perpetual threat to him. His case is not a case of practical forgetting, but a case of deeper and deeper commitment to refusal and fight." He is bound to struggle against God without pause or respite, and to change, to recast everything in himself and in the world on the base of that anti-theism.

Now what does all this mean? Absolute atheism starts in an act of faith in reverse gear and is a full-blown religious commitment. Here we have the first internal inconsistency of contemporary atheism: it proclaims that all religion must necessarily vanish away, and it is itself a religious phenomenon.

An Abortive Protest and Rupture

The second inconsistency is very like the first one. Absolute atheism starts as a claim of man to become the sole master of his own destiny, totally freed from any "alienation" and heteronomy, made totally and decisively independent of any ultimate end as well as of any eternal law imposed upon him by any transcendent God. According to atheistic theorists, does not the idea of God originate in an alienation of human nature separated from its true subject, and transmuted into an ideal and sublimated image whose very transcendence and sovereign attributes ensure man's submission to an enslaved state of existence? Is it not by getting rid of that sublimated image and of any transcendence, that human nature will achieve the fullness of its own stature and freedom and bring about the final "reconciliation between essence and existence?"

But what is the actual end-all of the philosophy of absolute immanence which is all one with absolute [107] Immanence which is all one with absolute atheism? Everything which was formerly considered superior to time and participating in some transcendent quality–either ideal value or spiritual reality–is now absorbed in the movement of temporal existence and the all-engulfing ocean of Becoming and of History. Truth and justice, good and evil, faithfulness, all the standards of conscience, henceforth perfectly relativized, become radically contingent: they are but changing shapes of the process of History, just as for Descartes they were but contingent creations of divine Freedom. The truth, at any given moment, is that which conforms with the requirements of History's begettings. As a result truth changes as time goes on. An act of mine which was meritorious today will be criminal tomorrow. And that is the way my conscience must pass judgment on it. The human intellect and moral conscience have to become heroically tractable.

And what of the Self, the person, the problem of human destiny? A total rejection of Transcendence logically entails a total adherence to Immanence. There is nothing eternal in man; he will die in the totality of his being; there is nothing to be saved in him. But he can give himself, and give himself entirely, to the Whole of which he is a part, to the boundless flux which alone is real and which bears the fate of mankind. By virtue of his decisive moral experience itself, and of that primary moral choice—against any ultimate End—which I have tried to describe, and which commits the human personality far more profoundly than individualistic egoism or epicureanism can do, the absolute or positive atheist hands himself over, body and soul, to the ever-changing and all-engulfing Whole—be it the social or the cosmic totality. It is not only that he is satisfied to die in it, as a blade of grass in the loam, and to make it more fertile by dissolving in it. He is also willing to make of his own total being, with all its values and standards and beliefs, an offering given, as I said above, to that great Minotaur that is History. Duty and virtue mean nothing else to him than a total submission and immolation of himself to the sacred voracity of Becoming.

Here we are confronted with a new variety of mystical "pure love"—giving up every hope for personal redemption—a real unselfishness, self-denial and self-sacrifice, a total and absolute disinterestedness—but a monstrous one, paid for at the price of the very Self, and the existence and dignity of the human Person: at the price of that which, in each one of us, is an end in itself and [108] the image of God. Christ had said: "He who loses his own soul for Me, shall find it,"[128] because losing one's own soul for God is delivering it over to absolute Truth and Goodness and Love, to the eternal Law itself which transcends all the contingency and mutability of Becoming. The positive atheist delivers over his own soul—and not in order to save it—to a worldly demiurge crazy for human minds to bend and bow and yield at the event's sweet will.

I am not belittling the spiritual significance of the moral attitude of the absolute atheist. On the contrary, I am emphasizing the kind of mystical disinterestedness, and the elements of greatness and generosity which are implied in it. But I say that this moral attitude also involves a basic inconsistency, and that the whole process is in the end a failure. That rupture with God began as a claim to total independence and emancipation, as a proud revolutionary break with everything that submits man to

---

[128] Matthew 10:39.

alienation and heteronomy. It ends up in obeisance and prostrate submission to the all-powerful movement of History, in a kind of sacred surrender of the human soul to the blind god of History.

III. The Atheist and the Saint

The Initial Act of Rupture Brought About by the Saint

The failure I have just mentioned reveals to us a fact which has, to my mind, a deep significance: I mean the fact that absolute atheism has a revolutionary power which materially speaking is exceedingly strong, but spiritually speaking is very weak indeed, minute, and deceptive; I mean the fact that its radicalism is an inevitably self-deluded radicalism, for a genuinely revolutionary spirit does not kneel before History, it presumes to make history; I mean the fact that absolute atheism falls short of that uncompromising protest, of that absolute non-compliance the semblance–and the expectation–of which make it seductive for many people.

Thus, we arrive at the point I should like especially to discuss. Which of these two, the Atheist or the Saint, is the more uncompromising and thorough-going, the harder, the more intractable; which has his axe more deeply embedded in the root of the tree? Which brings about the more complete and far-reaching, the cleaner and more radical break?

Let us try to imagine what takes place in the soul of a saint at the crucial moment when he makes his first irrevocable decision. [109] Let us consider St. Francis of Assisi when he threw away his raiment and appeared naked before his bishop, out of love for poverty; or St. Benedict Labre when he decided to. become a verminous beggar wandering along the roads. At the root of such an act there was something so deep in the soul that it hardly can be expressed, I would say a simple refusal–not a movement of revolt which is temporary, or of despair, which is passive–rather a simple refusal, a total, stable, supremely active refusal to accept things as they are: here it is not a question of knowing whether things and nature and the face of this world are good in their essence–to be sure they are good; being is good insofar as it is being; grace perfects nature and does not destroy it–but these truths have nothing to do with the inner act of rupture, of break, that we are now contemplating. This act is concerned with a fact, an existential fact: Things as they are are not tolerable, positively, definitely not tolerable. In actual existence the world is infected with lies and injustice and wickedness and distress and misery; the creation has been so marred by sin that in the nethermost depths of his soul the saint refuses to accept it as it is. Evil—I mean the power of sin, and the universal suffering it entails, the rot of nothingness that gnaws everywhere—evil is such, that the only thing at hand which can remedy it, and which inebriates the saint with freedom and exultation and love, is to give up everything, the sweetness of the world, and what is good, and what is better, and what is pleasurable and permissible, in order to be free to be with God; it is to be totally stripped and to give himself totally in order to lay hold of the power of the Cross; it is to die for those he loves. That is a flash of intuition and of will over and above the whole order of human morality. Once a human soul has been touched by such a burning wing, it becomes a stranger everywhere. It may fall in love with things, it will never rest in them. To redeem creation the saint wages war on the entire fabric of creation, with the bare weapons of truth and love. This war begins in the most hidden recesses of his own soul and the most secret stirrings of his desire: it will come to an end with the advent of a new earth and new heaven, when all that is powerful in this world will have been humiliated and all that is despised will have been exalted. The saint is alone in treading the winepress, and of the peoples there is no man with him.[129]

And I would say that in that war of which I have just spoken his God has given him the example. For, in calling the intellectual [110] creatures to share in His own uncreated life, God uproots them from the very life of which they are possessed as rooted in nature. And Jews know that God is a hidden God, Who conceals His name and manifests Himself to mankind in prodigies and in the stormy visions of the prophets, in order to renew the face of the earth, and Who has separated for Himself His people from all the nations of the world. And Christians know that God is both so dissatisfied with that lost world which He had made good and which evil has ruined—and at the same time so carried away by love—that He has given His Son and delivered Him over to men, in order to suffer and to die, and in this way redeem the world.

The Great God of Idolaters

To this true God the saint is entirely given. But there are false gods; even, as I shall shortly say, there is a spurious and distorted image of God that can be called the King or Jove of all false gods, the great god of the idolaters. With regard to *this* god, the saint is a

---

[129] Isaiah 63:3.

thorough atheist, the most atheistic of men—just because he adores *only* God.

Let us dwell a moment on this point. And let us consider the merely rational, merely philosophical concept of God. This concept is twofold: there is the true God of the philosophers, and there is the false god of the philosophers. The true God of the philosophers is but the true God Himself, the God of the saints, the God of Abraham, Isaac and Jacob—imperfectly and inchoatively known, known in those attributes only which can be reached by our natural forces: Such a merely rational notion of God is in actual fact open to the supernatural.

But now suppose for yourselves a merely rational notion of God which would know the existence of the Supreme Being, but would disregard at the same time what St. Paul called His glory, deny the abyss of freedom which is meant by His transcendence, and chain Him to the very world He has made. Suppose for yourselves a merely rational—and warped—notion of God which is closed against the supernatural, and makes impossible the mysteries that are hidden in God's love and freedom and incommunicable life. Here we would have the false god of the philosophers, the Jove of all false gods. Imagine a god bound to the order of nature who is no more than a supreme warrant and justification of that order, a god who is responsible for this world without the power of redeeming it, a god whose inflexible will, that no prayer can reach, [111] is pleased with and hallows all the evil as well as all the good of the universe, all the trickery, wickedness and cruelty together with all the generosity which are at play in nature, a god who blesses iniquity and slavery and misery, and who sacrifices man to the cosmos, and makes the tears of the children and the agony of the innocents a stark ingredient of, and a tribute offered without any compensation to the sacred necessities of eternal cycles or of evolution. Such a god would be the unique supreme Being but made into an idol, the naturalistic god of nature, the Jupiter of the world, the great god of the idolaters and of the powerful on their thrones and of the rich in their earthly glory, the god of success which knows no law, and of mere fact set up as law.

I am afraid that such was the God of our modern rationalistic philosophy, the God perhaps of Leibniz and Spinoza, surely the God of Hegel.

Such was also, in quite another mood, not rationalistic, but magical, the God of Pagan antiquity, or rather one of the countenances of that double-faced God. For the pagan God was ambiguous; on the one hand he was the true God of nature and reason, the unknown God of Whom St. Paul spoke to the Athenians; and on the other hand he was the false god of naturalism, the self-contradictory god I have just described, and who does get on very well with the Prince of this world.

It could be added that among Christian sects, some wild Gnostics, especially the followers of Marcion, who regarded the God of the Old Covenant as an evil world-maker in conflict with the Redeemer, mistook for the Creator the same false god I have been discussing, the same absurd Emperor of the world.

And this brings me to the point I want to drive home. The saint, when he brings about the great act of rupture which I stressed earlier, rejects by the same stroke, breaks and annihilates, with an irresistible violence, this spurious Emperor of the world, this false god of naturalism, this great god of the idolaters, the powerful and the rich, who is an absurd counterfeit of God, but who is also the imaginary focus whence the adoration of the cosmos radiates, and to whom we pay tribute each time we bow down before the world. With regard to this god the saint is a perfect atheist. Well, were not the Jews and the first Christians often called atheists by the pagans at the time of the Roman Empire? There was a hidden meaning in this slander.[130]

[112] *The Case of the Absolute Atheist*

But let us turn at present to our modern atheists, our true and actual atheists—what can we say about them? I would suggest that, in the sense I have just emphasized, the absolute atheist is *not atheist enough*. He, too, is indignant against the Jupiter of this world, against the god of the idolaters, the powerful and the rich; he too decides to get rid of him. But instead of hurling against that false god the strength of the true God, and of giving himself to the work of the true God, as the saint does, the atheist, because he rejects the true God, can only struggle against the Jupiter of this world by calling on the strength of the immanent god of History, and by dedicating himself to the work of that immanent god.

It is indeed because he believes in the revolutionary disruptive power of the impetus of History, and because he expects from it the final emancipation of man, that the atheist delivers over his own soul to the blind god of History. Yet he is caught in a trap. Wait a while, and the blind god of History will appear just as he

---

[130] St. Justin Martyr said "We are called atheists. And yes we confess it, we are atheists of those so-called gods" (*First Apology*, ch. VI, n. 1).

is—yes, the very same Jupiter of this world, the great god of the idolaters and the powerful on their thrones and the rich in their earthly glory, and of success which knows no law, and of mere fact set up as law. He will reveal himself as this same false god in a new disguise and crowned by new idolaters, and meting out a new brand of power and success. And it is too late for the atheist. As we saw at the beginning, he is possessed by this god. He is on his knees before History. With respect to a god who is not God, he is the most tractable and obedient of the devotees.

And so his break with this world of injustice and oppression was but a shallow and temporary break. More than ever he is subservient to the world. In comparison with the saint, who consummates in his own flesh his initial rupture with the world, and every day dies unto himself, and is blessed with the beatitudes of the poor and the persecuted and all the other friends of God, and who enjoys the perfect freedom of those who are led by the Spirit, the atheist is, it seems to me, a very poor replica of the liberated mind and the heroic insurgent. Nevertheless, as I have tried to point out, it is by an ill-directed longing for inner freedom and for non-acceptance of things as they are that he has been led astray. A somewhat paradoxical, yet, in my opinion, true statement about absolute atheism would be to say that it deprives God and mankind of some potential saints, in bringing to bankruptcy their attempt at heroic [113] freedom, and turning their effort to break with the world into a total and servile subservience to the world. With all his sincerity and devotion, the authentic, absolute atheist is after all only an abortive saint, and, at the same time, a mistaken revolutionist.

IV. The Saint and Temporal History

A Lost Opportunity

There is now another paradox, this time in an opposite direction. If we look at the saint, it seems that the inner act through which he achieves his total break with the world and total liberation from the world, making him free from everything but God, will inevitably overflow from the realm of spiritual life onto the realm of temporal life. Thus, if he is not dedicated solely to a contemplative state of existence, he will be led to act as a ferment of renewal in the structures of the world, as a stimulating and transforming energy in social matters and in the field of the activities of civilization.

And this is true, of course. As a matter of fact, it is what has been taking place for centuries. The Fathers of the Church were great revolutionaries. Thomas Aquinas in the order of culture, St. Vincent de Paul in the social field, were eminent examples of genuine radicals, whose initiative brought about decisive changes in the history of civilization. For centuries temporal progress in the world has been furthered by the saints.

Yet, here is the paradox that I just mentioned–the day when, in the course of modern history, a particularly inhuman structure of society, caused by the Industrial Revolution, made the problem of social justice manifestly crucial; when, at the same time, the human mind became aware of the *social* as a specific object of knowledge and activity, and when the first attempts to create workers' organizations provided the beginnings of a historical force capable of acting upon social structures–then was it not the moment for the saints to take the lead in the protest of the poor and us the movement of labor toward its historical coming of age? In actual fact, except for a few men of faith, like Ozanam in France and Toniolo in Italy (they are not yet canonized, but some day they might be), the task, as we know, was not conducted by saints. It even happened that atheists, instead of saints, took the lead in social matters, much to the misfortune of all.

Why such a tragic vacancy? It seems difficult not to see in it a [114] kind of punishment of the Christian world, which for a long period has more or less failed Christianity in its practical behavior, and despised the lessons of the saints, and abandoned to their fate, here below, that great flock which also belongs to Christ, that immense herd of men whom destitution and unlivable conditions of existence kept chained to hell on earth. Let us not be mistaken. During the time of which I am speaking, the saints were not lacking on the earth; there was a considerable flowering of saints in the last century. But they did not pass beyond the field of spiritual, apostolic or charitable activities: they did not cross the threshold of temporal, social, secular activity. And thus the gap was not filled, because in the historical age which is ours, the indirect repercussion of the inner renewal of conscience upon the external structures of society is definitely not enough, although it answers a basic need and has made progressively more possible such social changes as the abolition of slavery. A specifically social activity, an activity which directly aims at improving and recasting the structures of temporal life, is also needed.

Why has this kind of activity been neglected by a great many Christians in the past? Is it on account of their supposed contempt for the world, as people say? Nonsense! The saints break with the world, but they have no contempt for creation; that they leave to apprentices. As for the general run of Christians, one need but look at them–at ourselves–(as François Mauriac reminded us rather bluntly in the second *Semaine des Intellectuels Catholiques*)[131] to be assured that we do not despise the world in the least and that we are "of the earth," as it is said in the new devotional jargon. No; the reason for which activities directly aiming at the structural changes required by social justice have been lacking for so many centuries, is quite simple: the means of exercising such activities were non-existent. In the seventeenth century Saint Vincent de Paul could found hospitals but he could not found trade unions. It was only after the Industrial Revolution and the way in which it developed that the possibility of directly social activity could enter people's imaginations, and that such a directly social, and not only spiritual or charitable, activity has become a crying need.

Perhaps a concrete example will help to make clear the difference between the two kinds of activity I have mentioned. A poor priest named Cottolengo, who was a saint (though his name is not to be found in the *Encyclopaedia Britannica*) founded in Turin, in [115] the first half of the past century, a hospital that rapidly grew into a sort of huge city of all kinds of infirmity and human misery; hundreds of the poor were fed and cared for every day. But Cottolengo had established the rule that none of the money contributed for the support of his Institute should ever be saved and invested. Money each day received from the Providence of God should be spent each day, for "sufficient unto the day is the evil thereof."[132] There is even a story that one evening, as he saw that his assistants had set aside a certain amount of money for the morrow, Cottolengo threw that money out of the window–which in our modern world is the height of insanity, and perhaps of sacrilege. This course of action was in itself perfectly revolutionary, and all the more revolutionary in that it succeeded (Cottolengo's work has thrived in an astounding manner; it is now one of the most important institutions in Turin). Yet such a course of action, for all its spiritual significance, remained of no social consequence. It transcended the social problem. The social problem must be managed and solved in its own order. For half a century men of good will have realized better and better that the

---

[131] See Emmanuel Célestin Suhard, ed., *Foi en Jésus-Christ et Monde d'aujourd'hui* (Paris: Éditions de Flore, 1949).

[132] Matthew 6:34.

temporal mission of those who believe in God is to take over the job. Still, we must not forget that, even in the simple perspective of the temporal community, Christian social action is not enough; political action is even less so, however necessary both of them may be. What is required of those who believe in God is a witness of God; and what the world demands and expects of the Christian is first and foremost to see the love of truth and brotherly love made genuinely present in and through man's personal life–to see a gleam of the Gospel shining in the one place where the crucial test and crucial proof are to be found, namely the obscure context of relations from person to person. ...

[117] Here it seems well to stress one of the deepest meanings of absolute atheism. In so doing we shall but be brought back to the conclusion of the preceding chapter. As I put it, absolute atheism is "a translation into crude and inescapable terms, a ruthless counterpart, an avenging mirror, of the practical atheism of too many believers who do not actually believe." It is both the fruit and the condemnation of practical atheism, its image reflected in the mirror of divine wrath. If this diagnosis is true, then we must go on to say that it is impossible to get rid of absolute atheism without first getting rid of practical atheism. Furthermore this has become clear to everyone that from now onwards a decorative Christianity is not enough, even for our existence in this world. The faith must be an actual faith, practical and living. To believe in God must mean to live in such a manner that life could not possibly be lived if God did not exist. Then the earthly hope in the Gospel can become the quickening force of temporal history.

The Degrees of Knowledge (1932)[133]

Science and Philosophy

[58] Though it is true that the *material object* of philosophy and of science can be the same—e.g. the world of bodies—the *formal object*, that which determines, is in the two cases essentially different. In the world of bodies, the scientist studies the laws of phenomena, linking one observed instance to another, and if he seeks for the structure of matter it is by representing to himself—molecules, ions, atoms, etc.—in what way and according to what laws, the ultimate particles (or the mathematically conceived entities which take their place) from which the edifice is constructed, act within the framework of time and space.

The philosopher, on the other hand, seeks for *what in fact that matter is* which is so figured, what, as a function of intelligible being, is the nature of corporeal substance (whether it be split up and reconstructed into a spatial or spacio-temporal construction of molecules, ions, atoms, etc., or into protons and electrons associated or unassorted into a series of waves, his problem remains exactly the same)

The one goes from the visible to the visible, from the observable to the observable (i.e. observable at least indirectly—I do not way it is always [59] imaginatively figurable or representable: for the imagination presents things they appear in our scale of major dimensions, as possible subjects for a complete and continued observation; and when the scientist enters into a region, e.g. the atomic, where even the possibility of a complete and continuous observation of phenomena is out of the question,[134] he so passes from a world of imaginatively representable objects to a world of things without imaginable features. We could say that such a world is indescribable by fault or 'by privation').

The other proceeds from the visible to the invisible, to what is *in itself* outside the bounds of all sensory observation, for the principles which are the aim of the philosopher are pure objects of intellection, not of sensible apprehension or imaginative representation.[135] This is a world naturally indescribable or 'by negation.'

---

133 [Jacques Maritain, *The Degrees of Knowledge*, translated by Bernard Waal. Copyright © 1937 by Geoffrey Bles. Public Domain.]

134 See *infra*, ch. III, pp. 183-4 and 226-8.

135 Ibid., pp. 179-80.

Having totally different formal objects, entirely different principles of explanation and conceptual technique, and in the subject himself requiring fundamentally different intellectual virtues or qualities of discriminating illumination, the proper domains of philosophy and science are not translatable. An explanation of a scientific order can never be displaced or replaced by a philosophic one or *vice versa*. It requires an over-great dose of simplicity to imagine that the recognition of an immaterial soul in man and the study of the glycogenic functions of the liver or the relations between the idea and the image are two explanations which pursue the same lines and that either can be an obstacle to the other.

What is true is that the explanations of science, since they do not bring us into intimate contact with the being of things, and are only explanatory of proximate causes or even simply of that kind of formal cause which is represented by the mathematico-legal system of phenomena (and the entities more or less arbitrarily constructed in support of that system), cannot suffice for the mind, which by necessity, and always, asks questions of a higher order and seeks to enter into regions of intelligibility.

From this point of view we can say that the sciences have a certain dependence on philosophy. The sciences themselves, because they seek for the *raison d'être* and can only proffer it very imperfectly, inspire the mind with philosophical desire, and require the support of a higher [60] form of knowledge. Nothing is more curious than to measure the force with which, after the positivism of the nineteenth century, this need is exemplified in all the domains of science and that in the most disorderly fashion, philosophical competence being inevitably lacking with the lack of philosophical technique even in scientists of genius like Henri Poincaré.

The sciences have, however, no dependence whatever on philosophy with regard to their own intrinsic development. They are only dependent *in principle* (not in the sense that they are dependent on philosophy for their principles and their use, but in the sense in which the explication and justification of the latter belong to philosophy). Perhaps it is precisely because scientists have no need of an immediate recourse to philosophy for the exercise of their own rightful activities that they are so given to misunderstanding the nature of this dependence of which I have spoken. But if they were to reflect rather more attentively on the nature of the very activity which they exercise (which would indeed be already a form of philosophising) how could they fail to observe that it involves in itself a complete order of philosophical activity, wrapped up, so to speak, in practical terms?

All employment of the methods of experimental criticism, like the determination of the degree of approximation of the acquired results, constitutes a form of applied or livingly formed logic (*logica utens*), which only becomes pure logic and the object of a speculative art explicitly studied for its own sake (*logica docens*) under the reflective gaze of the logician, but which in itself is nothing other than that logic, a truly philosophical discipline, in practice.

On the other hand, whatever may be the conscious or unconscious metaphysical opinions from which he draws his conception of the world and which he follows out in his life as a human being, every scientist in fact, in the operations of his own science, when thinking as a scientist—we owe a debt of gratitude to M. Meyerson for having so forcibly stressed this point—practically affirms (*in actu exercito*) and with a dogmatism which is the more fearless in the very degree to which it is unconsidered, a number of eminently metaphysical propositions, whether it be a question of the reality of the physical world, of the existence of things as apart from the mind, of stable ontologies [61] nuclei, or of a substantial x at the base of phenomena:[136] not only these, but the very

---

[136] "The habit of calling a spade a spade keeps scientists from numerous vain causes of quarrel. It is fine to listen to their agreement about words and the things they represent. This remarkable accord creates among scientists an atmosphere of confidence, a unison whence they draw a certitude which is none other than a robust faith. There is probably not a chemist who does not confound the reality of sulphate of baryta with the idea which he has of it. I had the curiosity to ask such a question of several of them. To all it appeared exceedingly odd. I could see, by the dubious glances with which they looked at me, that they doubted whether I were not mad to ask such a thing. What happens in actual fact is that a chemist makes the absolute substratum of bodies from their properties, and knows no preoccupation with the highly hypothetical character of this conception" (Georges Urbain, "Essai de discipline scientifique," *La Grande Revue* 24 (March 1920): 60). Formulated as it is in language which suggests entirely different philosophic opinions, this comment by a scientist of unquestioned authority, as M. Émile Meyerson observes (*op. cit.* II, p. 235) is evidence of all the more value since "the scientist in question himself professes, in theory, a sufficiently orthodox positivism and evidently finds the whole way of thought, which he describes with so much accuracy, definitely blameworthy."

question of the possibility of the apprehension of things in our faculties of knowledge—a difficult thing no doubt and done in a way which demands all sorts of more or less obscurely felt restrictions, but which is also surrounded with a sense of incontestable certitudes—in other words, that of the intelligibility of the world, which, though doubtless in an undefined way and with a sense of imperfect definition, nevertheless in the meanwhile no one hesitates to posit in advance. Or again the question may be that of the values of the principles of the reason, most of all, the principle of causality,[137] in regard to the world of experience, i.e. in other terms, the insufficiency of changes to explain themselves by themselves. ...

[62] In short, there is no science without the first principles on which the whole train of our reasonings must be fixed, an infinite regression in this order evidently rendering all demonstration impossible: and every scientist, by the very fact that he applies himself to no matter what form of demonstration, has already given his adherence, very positively however undeclared, to an important number of philosophical propositions. It very evidently follows from this that all these things which live latently and vitally in the mind of the scientist could advantageously be brought to light and looked at face to face as objects of knowledge, in other words, be dealt with by philosophy. Then we should see explicitly the objective links between the sciences and philosophy. Their axioms are determinations of the principles of metaphysics: for example, the mathematical axiom, two masses equal to a third are themselves

---

[137] My claim is that the scientist affirms *in acta exercito* in the exercise of his own scientific activity, the value of the principle of causality (without waiting for any philosophical reflection on its meaning, its bearing, the various methods of its verification or still less, its critical justification). If he were not practically persuaded that everything which happens has a cause, he would not give himself up to the work of research, he would not even begin it. In the course of its progress along the lines of what I shall later call its empiriological autonomy, science itself may need to refound or transpose the concept of cause, and even perhaps admit, in the picture of the world which it constructs, lacunas which make holes in the field of what for it is 'causality.' (Cp. chap, III, pp. 182-6 and 231-5). Here, between the scientific vision of the world and the springs of mental work from which it emanates, there is an analogous disparity to that between the scientific universe perceived by the physicist as a physicist and the familiar universe which he knows as an ordinary man.

equal, is a particularisation of the metaphysical axiom: two things identical with a third are themselves identical. It is philosophy which justifies and defends their principles, which determines the first objects towards which they work, and as a result, their nature, their value, their limits as sciences. ...

[63] Superior, therefore independent, at least by its own formal constitution: philosophy is, as such, independent with regard to the sciences.

It should be understood: there is no *formal* dependence of philosophy with regard to the sciences. No scientific result, no scientific theory, in short, no science in the exercise of its own proper means, can ever adequately cut the knot of a philosophical problem, for those problems depend both in their origin and their solution on a light which is not in the reach of science.

There is, most certainly, a strong *material* dependence of philosophy on the sciences. To begin with, philosophy is like the culminating point of the hierarchy of knowledge, and as a result comes pedagogically last; and the philosopher, since he judges of the value, the limits and subordinations of the sciences, must evidently know them as they are and the stuff of their proper life; more, scientific data are like illustrations which normally serve the philosopher in the exemplification and embodiment of his ideas; finally and above all, the progress of science, at least in regard to the facts discovered if not the theories, should normally, above all in what is concerned with natural philosophy, renew and enrich the matter offered for philosophical explication. Thus, for example, modern discoveries concerning the organic structure of the cell, in particular the embryo and the sexual elements, artificial parthenogenesis, etc., should give a new precision and a greater quality to the way in which the problem of the eduction of the vegetative soul is posed. The new developments in geometry begun by Lobatchevski and Bolyai equally oblige the philosopher to clear up and re-order his notions concerning quantity.

But such dependence remains material, and the changes which it induces primarily affect the nature of that imagery whose importance is so great in his vocabulary, and the halo of associations which have gathered about the actual didactic terms: to imagine that philosophical doctrines need to be radically transformed to fit in with scientific revolutions is as absurd as to suggest that our souls are vitally affected and altered by a variation in the elements of our dietary.

Some Elucidations on the Notion of Fact

[64] A question arises here which must be briefly treated: that of the part played by experience and experimental fact with regard to philosophy.

The latter, according to St. Thomas, rests on facts; it must accept the facts, begin by an act of humility before the real already made known by the senses, attained by our physical contact with the universe. And the philosophy of nature, differing in this from metaphysics, has not only its origin but the end where it must verify its conclusions in the experience of the senses: although in a way other than that of the experimental sciences.

What then is a fact? It is a well-founded existential truth: in existence a certain group of conceptual objects is posited beside the thing; and this in itself implies that this existence is face to face with a mind, a spirit which can lay hold on its objects. A fact which interests human observation is not created by the human mind, it is given. But it is given *to someone*; if it is given, it is because it is received, a stone is not given to a stone: a fact is given to a mind. That is to say, the mind discerns and judges it. To wish to make of this a sure and simple transcription of external reality without any discrimination is a deceptive simplification due to the unconscious materialism of the imagination.

Even in the order of the external senses, there is, as St. Thomas said, a judgment by the senses; sensible perception is itself induced by and presupposes the bringing into action, instinctively or otherwise, of the internal senses or *ratio particularis*. The discernment of any fact presupposes a judgment either of the senses or of the intellect. On that point the idealists are certainly right. But they are wrong in thinking that the activity of the mind cannot ask or draw from things information which is at once enunciated by and given to it; their error is to believe—a gratuitous postulate and in fact quite absurd—that every interpretation, or more exactly every judgment, by our faculties for knowledge is either a deformation or a creation, not a more or less pure and profound assimilating of oneself to the object, a conformation to what it rightly is.

[65] Their other error is a rejection of the primordial values of sensible intuition. It is from this intuition, in one way or another— and even when the fact in question transcends the whole order of the empiric and the sensible—that all existential apprehension originates (it is the same for our experience of our own existence, which is spiritual and non-empiric, but which supposes reflection upon our acts, as for the knowledge of the existence of God, which

is established apart from sensible things). In the physical order or in that of the knowledge of bodily-nature, it is by the senses, through a discriminating and critical judgment of the intellect, that the facts are given. To distinguish, in that order and in the use made of them in the natural sciences, the category of fact from that of theory, we should not say that the one belongs to the intellect and the other to the senses, which would be far too summary a view; but that the intervention of the intellect, with its natural or artificial resources, we might even say with its knowing devices and most delicate refinements of theory, remains in the former case ordinated to the discernment and formulation of what is furnished to it by the intuition of the senses,[138] while in the latter, with the same resources, to discovering essences and laws, and their underlying reasons.

Into the complex of things attained by the perception of the senses the activity of the mind so intervenes, not in order to create, but to discern what interests the observation. And in so much as the moment a science is born, the rightful point of view which characterises it emerges at the same time as the first facts on which it is based—whether before advancing into a scientific region and there unearthing new facts the mind has already begun to enter and acquired the habit of such science, or whether before crossing the threshold of some particular scientific region it has already begun to philosophise, already in some measure disengaged the notion of being as such from the principles to which it is attached—in that degree the discernment of which we are speaking will take place at a certain level of abstraction and in the light of certain principles in regard to winch the fact holds its value, a value, that is to say, [66] of knowledge and truth. We may conclude from this that all facts are not of the same *rank*, that they do not constitute an indistinct crowd without hierarchical arrangement, piled pell-mell in the field of sensible experience for each of the various sciences to come and pick out the particular wares of their desire. Facts in themselves belong to hierarchies of knowledge: there are facts of common sense, scientific facts (i.e. facts which occupy the natural sciences), mathematical facts[139]

---

[138] In the orders superior to those of physics which will be in question at a later stage, this work of the intellect, characteristic of the 'registration of facts,' is ordinated to make clear an existential position which we conceive *by analogy* with that furnished by the intuition of the senses.

[139] Cp. Pierre Boutroux, *L'idéal scientifique des mathematiciens dans*

(e.g. the (ideal) existence of continuous functions without derivatives), logical facts, philosophical facts.

Materially speaking, one can say from this that philosophy is 'experimental' and founded on facts. This is true in the sense that experience is not for philosophy, as it is for mathematics, entirely pre-scientific, infra-scientific, mathematical science being entirely deductive and axiomatic and apart from imaginative intuition and those notions which experience alone allows abstraction to form and reconstruct. The method of philosophy, on the contrary, is analytico-synthetic; and, just because it deals with real being, rightly capable of existing outside the mind, experimental affirmations form an integral part of philosophic observation as such.

But for philosophy, in contradiction to the natural sciences, this is only the material foundation from which it rises to the consideration of essences and the necessities which they imply, by a formal resolution into the first truths in themselves intelligibly known: it only returns to experience—in natural philosophy to verify deduced conclusions and seek for ever fresh material—in metaphysics to take up new points of departure, new analogical material, not to verify conclusions which belong to an entirely immaterial order. For, formally speaking, metaphysics is in no degree an experimental science, but a form of knowledge far more purely rational than mathematics.

The Structures and Method of the Principal Kinds of Knowledge

The foregoing conclusions imply several important consequences in epistemology.

[67] Here I can only briefly indicate some of these, most of all in the endeavour to exhibit how rare an instrument of epistemological analysis is offered by the principles of St. Thomas, and to draw attention to one of the characteristic features of his noetic: the order and organic differentiations which it establishes among the sciences, and the care which it takes (unlike many modern systems which exhibit them as all on the same plane) to recognise and respect the structure and particular procedure of each.[140]

---

l'antiquité et les temps modernes (Paris: Félix Alcan, 1920), ch. IV.

[140] Here I follow the ideas which St. Thomas develops in his *Commentary on the Posterior Analytics* (book II) and *On the De Trinitate* of Boethius (q. 5 and 6). Let mc recall here the fundamental text from the latter:

Let it be remembered that every science is a response to two questions: first the question *an est*, if a thing exists: second, the question *quid est*, of what nature is it.

For mathematics, experience has only a pre-scientific function, in the sense that if we had never seen a ball or a stick we could not have formed the notion of a circle or of a straight line; if we had never counted on our fingers the parts of a concrete whole we should never have formed the idea of number. But once in possession of these notions, thanks to the abstracting power of the intellect, they present in themselves objects of thought independent of experience, so independent of experience, that we can generalise analogically from them, de-ballasting them of that very intuitive scheme in which they were first made manifest. If mathematical entities could only—when they are capable of existing outside the mind—so exist in matter, they could not exist mathematically: the straight line, the circle, the whole number are realised in sensible things, but lose thereby the conditions of ideal purity which are imposed by the mathematical mode of existence.

In the mathematical order the question AN EST bears on the *ideal* (*possible* [68] or *rational*)[141] existence of the entity under consideration; and starting from the notion of this entity once so posited as capable of mathematical existence, the truths which concern it (*quid est*) are deductively established, by means of constructive operations which may apparently play the principal part, but which in fact remain only material: formally it is by

---

"ln qualibet cognitione duo est considerare, scilicet principium, et finem sive terminum. Principium quidem ad apprehensionem pertinet, terminus autem ad judicium, ibi enim cognitio perficitur. Principium igitur cujuslibet nostrae cognitionis est in sensu. ... Sed terminus cognitionis non semper est uniformiter: quandoque enim est in sensu, quandoque in imaginatione, quandoque in solo intellectu ... ."

"Deduci autem ad aliquid est ad illud terminari: et ideo in divinis neque ad sensum, neque ad imaginationem debemus deduci; in mathematicis autem ad imaginationem, et non ad sensum; in naturalibus autem etiam ad sensum. Et propter hoc peccant qui uniformiter in tribus his speculativae partibus procedure nituntur."

[141] The sense of the words "ideal existence" is fixed according to the following division:

actual

real being { *possible*

being of } *ideal being*
reason

virtue of the intelligible connections which proceed from mathematical deduction, whether these connections are themselves guided and determined all the time by constructive operations, or are established and justified once for all by the rules of an architecture of signs where the art so determined has only need to be applied. The ancients held that in mathematics the judgment—by which knowledge is achieved—resulted not in the sensible, but in the imaginable. This should not be understood as meaning that each of the established [69] conclusions needs to be directly verified by imaginative intuition: but that they need to be verified by it either *directly* or *analogically*, i.e. according to whether they are constructed by intuition, or whether they belong to a system of notions (as for example Non-Euclidian or Archimedian geometrical entities), itself issuing from a system of constructable notions in the intuition (like the Euclidian entities) and which can find in this system an analogical interpretation.[142]

MATHEMATICS

Intelligible Plane   An Est ⟶ Quid Est
      SCIENCE
                                    (knowledge issuing
                                    directly or analogically
                                    in the sensible)

Plane of Sensible   Sensible Fact
Existence

In the experimental sciences experience is in itself essential and *entirely* rules. The question AN EST bears directly on the facts experimentally criticised. Science does not arrive at seeing the essence in itself or *dianoetically*[143] as it lies embedded in facts, it only grasps it blindly: not in its constituting signs but in those of *perinoetic*[144] intellection which it contents itself with in their place (above all the constancy of a well-verified relation), and that substitute which is scientific *law*—the judgment, by which knowledge is achieved, issuing in experience itself, or in other words, every newly acquired conclusion needing to be verified by sensible fact.

---

[142] *Vide infra*, ch. III, pp. 201-2.
[143] Ibid., pp. 251-2.
[144] *Vide infra*, ch. IV, pp. 248-9.

EXPERIMENTAL SCIENCE

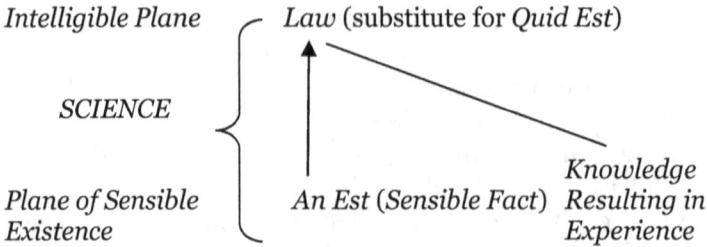

Intelligible Plane — Law (substitute for *Quid Est*)

SCIENCE

Plane of Sensible Existence   An Est (Sensible Fact)   *Knowledge Resulting in Experience*

When it is a question of the physico-mathematical sciences, the deductive theory and the system of notions elaborated by it come face to face with experimental results to find there their verification, although [70] apt to translate them in a somewhat rigorous fashion by means of an adopted vocabulary; and it is a mathematical *quid est*, not an inductively established law, but an algorithm of the physically real, which is then substituted for the ontological *quid est*.

In the philosophy of nature, sensible fact forms the material part of observation, which thus essentially depends on experience, but it does not constitute the formal medium of demonstration. The question AN EST bears on the *real existence* of a nature which abstraction has been able to raise to a point where it can be considered in itself, e.g. the vegetative soul; and starting from this so posited nature, reason establishes its properties by an inductive-deductive alternation, all the while issuing in experience and verifying by sensible facts the conclusions so obtained.

PHILOSOPHY OF NATURE

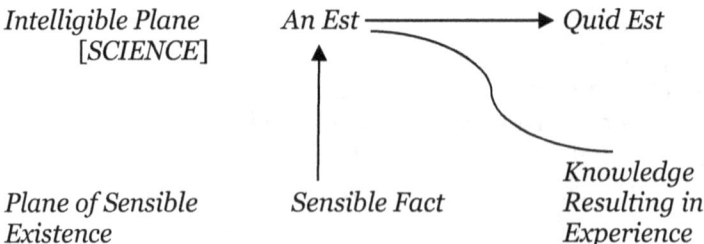

Intelligible Plane [SCIENCE]   An Est ⟶ *Quid Est*

Plane of Sensible Existence   Sensible Fact   *Knowledge Resulting in Experience*

Finally, in metaphysics sensible fact also forms the material part of knowledge, because we only rise to the invisible from the visible, but it does not formally constitute its medium, *neither are its conclusions verified by it*. The judgment, by which knowledge is achieved, issues in pure intelligibility. For it is not because, like the philosophy of nature, it essentially depends on sensible experience, but because of its transcendence that metaphysics (as mathematics does not do) descends to the world of sensible existence. It also ascends to the world of supra-sensible existence. Thus in natural theology the question AN EST bears on the real [71] *existence* of an immaterial object to which knowledge is able to rise by analogy (ananoetic intellection).[145] And from the recognition of such an object reason, by the triple path of causality, eminence and negation, without verification either from the sensible or the imaginable, since it is a case of the purely immaterial, establishes conclusions concerned with nature (analogically known) and the perfections of the Pure Act. ...

NATURAL THEOLOGY

Intelligible Plane   *An Est*   *Quid Non Est (Substituting Quid Est)*
     SCIENCE $\longrightarrow$

           (Knowledge Issuing in the Supra-Sensible)

      $\uparrow$

     (Ananoetic Intellection)

Plane of Sensible   *Sensible Fact*
Existence

Conclusion

[83] We have the right to hold that Thomist philosophy rather than any other is in the position to supply the sciences with the metaphysical framework where they can follow out at ease the necessities of their own proper development and which will do them no violence: not only because it is essentially realist and critically justifies the extra-mental reality of things and the value of our faculties of knowledge, which all science implicitly presupposes, but because it guarantees the autonomy, the specific quality of each, and its metaphysical elucidations of the real imply in consequence no necessary systematic deformation despotically imposed upon experience.

In fact the reproach addressed by the misinformed to Scholastic philosophy recoils on the modern systems. For it is these systems which derive from systematic prejudices like

---

[145] *Vide infra*, ch. IV, pp. 268-71.

mechanism or monism, psycho-physical parallelism, the Cartesian theory of knowledge, universal evolutionism, etc., which necessarily and as such impose on science such exasperating metaphysical fetters.

It is not a question of finding between the Aristotelian-Thomist philosophy and the sciences that concordance of detail which we have just rejected: but of affirming rather a concord in general, a good understanding, a natural friendship, of which the very liberty of science, the ease with which it spreads its wings, is the best indication. This is explicitly affirmed by several representatives of the natural sciences, while elsewhere a remarkable renaissance of themes proper to the moral philosophy of St. Thomas is visible among the juridical and moral sciences, which I have not had the space to speak of in this essay.

If there is no lack of labourers, if unreasonable prejudices—due most of all, it seems, to a morbid fear of ontological research, and of all philosophy directed towards the knowledge of things (as if a philosophy of being could not also be a philosophy of the spirit)—do not turn them back from the study of the sole philosophy which claims to confront the universality of extra-mental reality without claiming in the same stroke to absorb all knowledge into itself, we may hope to see the dawn of a great new scientific period, which will put an end to the misunderstandings engendered in the field of experimental research by the quarrel [84] between Aristotle and Descartes, and where the phenomenological sciences will at last achieve their normative organisation, some, especially physics, subject to the attraction of mathematics and following out on those lines the path of their splendid progress, others, especially biology and psychology, subject to the attraction of philosophy, and finding there that organic order of which they have such need, and the conditions of a development which will be not only material, but rightly worthy of the human mind. A general redistribution which comes from the natural growth of phenomenological science, but which also presupposes, that is clear, the supreme regulative power of metaphysical wisdom.

This would be the restitution to the human soul of that divine blessing of intellectual unity, which for three centuries has been broken.

Kant denied to metaphysics the character of a science, because for him experience was both the product and the end of science, which creates it by applying to sensible data those necessities which are purely mental forms; but St. Thomas recognised in metaphysics the supreme science of the natural order, because for him experience is the point of departure for the science, which, reading in sensible data those intelligible necessities which surpass them, can transcend it in following out those necessities and so come to a supra-experimental knowledge which is absolutely certain.

Being is in fact the proper object of the intellect; it is enracinated in all its concepts, it is towards it, in so far as it is absorbed in what is given through the senses, that it is first of all directed.

When the intellect disengages this conceptual object to consider it in itself, in the degree to which it is being, it perceives that it is not exhausted by the sensible realities in which it is at first discovered; it has a supra-experimental value and so also have the principles founded upon it. Thus the mind, if I may say so, 'loops the loop,' returning in order to grasp it metaphysically and transcendently to that same *being* which it was given first of all in its primary intellection of the sensible.

And so, because it has in its metaphysical concepts the intellectual perception of objects, such as being and the transcendentals, which can be realised otherwise than in the matter where it perceived them, it also attain to these objects— without, this time, directly perceiving [85] them, and as if in the mirror of sensible things—there, where they are realised immaterially, as the facts asserted by the world of experience compel us to infer. The supra-sensible cannot be, at least in the natural order, the object of an experimental science; it is nevertheless the object of a science rightfully so called, the science *par excellence*; for if the universe of being as such, disengaged by the mind when it delivers its objects from all materiality, does not fall under the ken of the senses, on the other hand, intelligible necessities are there seen in such a degree of perfection that the knowledge ordinated in regard to such a world of intelligibility is in itself of the highest certainty, though we Indeed may have difficulty in acknowledging it. For we are an ungrateful and mediocre species, who only ask the right to fail to achieve the heights of which we are capable, and who in ourselves, even when the highest gifts have fortified our eyes, have always a preference for the dark.

ALAN VINCELETTE

JOSEF PIEPER (1904-1997)

Pieper was born in 1904 in the town of Elte, near Rheine, Germany. He studied philosophy and sociology at the Universities of Berlin (1926-1927) and Münster (1923-1926, 1927-1928), receiving a Ph.D. from the latter in 1928. Pieper married in 1935 and, though not fully trusted by the National Socialists, served as a psychologist in the German military during World War II from 1940 to 1945. He became a lecturer in philosophy at the Pedagogical College of Essen in 1946 where he taught until 1972. In 1950 Pieper became professor of philosophy at his alma mater, the University of Münster, until his retirement in 1972. He died in 1997 in Münster, Germany. Among his honors, he was appointed to the Pontifical Academy of St. Thomas of Aquinas in 1980, and he received the Aquinas Medal in 1968. Additionally, there are several items named in his honor including the Josef-Pieper-Stiftung in Münster (1991) and the Josef Pieper Arbeitsstelle at the University of Paderborn (2008).

Pieper was influenced by the thought of Erich Przywara, S.J., Romano Guardini, C.S. Lewis, and most especially of Thomas Aquinas, which he applied to the various domains of life, including leisure and festivals, in his *Über das christliche Menschenbild* [*On the Christian View of Man*] (Leipzig: Hegner, 1936); *Muße und Kult* [*Leisure and Culture*] (Munich: Kösel, 1948); *Glück und Kontemplation* [*Happiness and Contemplation*] (Munich: Kösel, 1957); and *Zustimmung zur Welt: Eine Theorie des Festes* [*In Tune with the World: A Theory of Festivity*] (Munich: Kösel, 1963), all of which have been translated into English.

Perhaps his lasting achievement, however, is his project on the cardinal and theological virtues encompassing *Vom Sinn der Tapferkeit* [*On the Sense of Valor*] (Leipzig: Hegner, 1934); *Über die Hoffnung* [*On Hope*] (Leipzig: Hegner, 1935); *Traktat über die Klugheit* [*Treatise on Wisdom*] (Leipzig: Hegner, 1937); *Zucht und Maß: Über die vierte Kardinaltugend* [*Discipline and Moderation: On the Fourth Cardinal Virtue*] (Leipzig: Hegner, 1939); *Über die Gerechtigkeit* [*On Justice*] (Munich: Kösel, 1953); *Über den Glauben: Ein philosophischer Traktat* [*On Belief*] (Munich: Kösel, 1962); and *Über die Liebe* [*On Love*] (Munich: Kösel, 1972). These works have been translated as *The Four Cardinal Virtues* (Notre Dame: Notre Dame University Press, 1966) and *Faith, Hope, Love* (San Francisco: Ignatius Press, 1997).

For more on Pieper see his autobiography, *Autobiographische Aufzeichnungen* (Munich: Kösel, 1976-1988), as well as Schumacher, Bernard N., *A Philosophy of Hope: Josef Pieper and the Contemporary Debate on Hope* (New York: Fordham University Press, 2003); Schumacher, Bernard N., ed. *A Cosmopolitan Hermit* (Washington: Catholic University of America Press, 2009).

The selection below, a defense of the usefulness and validity of philosophy, is from Pieper's book *Verteidigungsrede für die Philosophie* (Munich: Kösel, 1966), VII, 91-105, translated as *In Defense of Philosophy* (San Francisco: Ignatius Press, 1992), VII, 83-94.

In Defense of Philosophy (1966)[146]

[83] Karl Jaspers, in an academic address in 1960, made the statement that philosophy "has become an embarrassment for everybody."[147] He did not mean philosophy's natural outsider status in relation to a world where usefulness and practicality reign supreme, but rather the situation of philosophy within the realm of the contemporary university. To eliminate this embarrassment, it seems to me, you would have to eliminate at the same time philosophy itself. We are faced here, put in provisional terms, with an equally natural incommensurability, namely, that between scientific and philosophical thinking. What else should we expect, other than an ever more pronounced incommensurability, the more exclusively our universities submit to the standards of the exact sciences? The tendency toward such an exclusive attitude, evident to everybody, has of course its good reasons; it is all but inevitable. Philosophy, in contrast, proceeds in a way that is indeed, by scientific standards, offensive, even impossible—provided we mean by "philosophy" the same that Plato, Aristotle, and the great philosophical tradition up to Karl Jaspers meant.

Nevertheless, scientific research and philosophy in [84] themselves have never been one another's real enemies. A closer look shows it is not they that are the two sides in the dispute going on, true, for quite some time and for everybody to see. The vocal participants in this controversy are rather those who declare the exact sciences to be the one and only and obligatory standard and norm for all serious consideration of reality and truth. In this, however, they advance a thesis obviously not of the specifically scientific domain but pertaining to the theory of science, and therefore a philosophical thesis. In fact, this is the widespread explicit claim, for example, by the proponents of a "scientific philosophy." And on the other side? The one so attacked does not, of course, deny the sovereignty of the scientific domain. Yet he insists that there are other forms of cognitive quest, certainly correlated to science in various ways, even dependent on it, and nonetheless distinct and equally indispensable—for example: philosophy.

Such controversies are usually not the results of irrelevant or

---

[146] *In Defense of Philosophy*, translated by Lothar Krauth. Copyright © 1992 by Ignatius Press. All rights reserved. Used with permission of Ignatius Press, https://www.ignatius.com].

[147] Karl Jaspers, *Wahrheit und Wissenschaft* (Basel: Piper, 1960), 20.

irresponsible whims. We should rather expect them to be connected with certain changes in the total historical structure of human existence. This necessitates from time to time a revision and redefinition of the respective positions. In no way does it mean that such conflicts would basically be nothing more than misunderstandings solvable through better explanations. Definitely not! On the contrary, some disagreements will stand out all the more sharply after more detailed clarification. It is, of course, impossible to specify here the principles of scientific research and, on the other hand, spell out in detail what it means to philosophize. Still, to draw up some kind of inventory concerning the main grievances shall nonetheless be attempted here, at least [85] a brief identification of the "differences" (in a double sense) that quite regularly and predictably trigger the polemic.

First and foremost, we have to recall the image of the unending trail that I have employed, quite tentatively, to characterize the internal situation of the philosopher. This analogy applies much more specifically than may have appeared at first. Above all, it points to the fundamental difference separating philosophy from scientific research. True, science has on occasion also been described as "reaching out to ever new horizons," but this is not the same.

The physicist, tackling a problem confronting him, does not at all set out on an infinite journey. There comes the moment, though perhaps only after a very long time, when he reaches the goal. At that point, the question is answered, the hope held out is fulfilled, the aim is realized. There may arise immediately further questions; but this will then present a new task. He who endeavors to reflect on the totality of world and existence, that is, to philosophize, sets foot on a path that in this life will never come to an end. He will always remain "on the way," the question will never receive an answer once and for all, the hope will never find fulfillment. He may perhaps succeed in explaining to someone, more or less convincingly, that in this way, through the living pursuit of the question and the hope, at least an openness for the infinite object, the whole of reality, is sustained. This object is thus constantly chased after and aimed at, as otherwise its existence might simply be forgotten. Still, this constitutes an exceedingly upsetting and unbearable manner of speaking, not so much for the scientist as rather for the "scientific [86] world view": we do "not acknowledge any unsolvable riddles";[148] "all our knowledge of reality is gained through the techniques of the different scientific disciplines; any other 'ontology' is so much empty talk."[149] In short, making precision and perfection into absolutes on the other hand, and accepting a preliminary "not-yet" on the other—these two approaches are mutually exclusive; nothing could be clearer than that.

There is now, as is well known, the "ancient utterance" that describes man himself, all in all, as ever unfinished and "on his way," the *viator*, the wanderer—no matter how many particular journeys he may complete and how much else he may accomplish in terms of knowledge and practical or creative activity. Existence would therefore be structured on hope—in the same way as philosophy. Indeed, I wonder whether you first have to acknowledge and to accept this admittedly quite vague connection between the intrinsic structure of existence and the philosophical act before you can at all conceive of this philosophical act as the mind's attention, in search and hope, to the mystery of the world— not merely as something "quite possible" but as something that man cannot ignore nor do without.

One other persistent controversy between philosophy and science centers on the radically different concept of what constitutes a greater or lesser perfection in human knowledge. The position taken by science will probably be: knowledge is in the same measure perfect as it succeeds in capturing an instance of reality, no matter what kind, through clear concepts and precise [87] description. The philosopher, in contrast, regardless of how deeply he may be impressed by the formal perfection of scientific thinking, remains for his part quite unable to acknowledge in this quality the perfection of knowledge as such.

Let me relate an event that for me is not only a touching testimony but also a telling fact bearing on our topic here. Alfred North Whitehead, whose career had begun under the auspices of the *Principia Mathematica*,[150] a work of such extremely formalized exactness that it might be fully comprehended and

---

[148] The Vienna Circle, *Wissenschaftliche Weltauffassung* (Wien: Institut Wiener Kreis, Universität Wien, 1929), p. 15.

[149] Moritz Schlick, "Erleben, Erkennen, Metaphysik," *Kant-Studien* 31 (1926): 146.

[150] This is the title of a three-volume work, with Bertrand Russell as coauthor, which has become a standard text of modern mathematical logic; it appeared 1910-1913 (Cambridge: Cambridge University Press).

grasped by only a few, toward the end of his life had come to philosophize with the breadth and depth of the great Western tradition. He could therefore claim greater legitimacy than anybody else when toward the end he declared, "The exactness is a fake," an illusion, a phantom. This is the closing sentence of his farewell lecture at age eighty (on the topic of "immortality"), given at Harvard University in the spring of 1941.[151] Nathaniel Lawrence, who authored a fundamental study on Whitehead's philosophical development,[152] was present at this memorable in lecture; he told me how Whitehead spoke this, his last public statement, "with all the energy that his high-pitched, raspy voice would yield, and with such radiant kindness as to suggest he was about to say, 'The Lord is my Shepherd'; and maybe this is what indeed was [88] on his mind." There can be not even the shadow of a suspicion that this statement would have been intended to advocate or merely acknowledge any form of irrationalism. What it reveals, on the contrary, is a transformed concept of perfection in human cognition, a concept no longer dictated by science; in brief: the philosophical concept.

It has already been mentioned that being "critical," for the philosopher, means diligently taking care not to ignore anything. Yet the whole of reality, which is the object of such care, is not the same as the sum total resulting from adding up each and every thing. Rather it means the *totum*, the ordered structure of the world, containing a hierarchy, greater and lesser actualizations of *being*, and above all a highest reality that at the same time is the most profound foundation and origin of everything, of every single thing and of the whole as well. I am well aware that this, so far, is no more than my assertion, and a rather audacious and "unsecured" assertion at that, standing in dire need of some justification. Still, this is not the place to discuss it further, much less to prove its validity. Here I wanted only to show why he who reflects on reality as such, the philosopher, will necessarily have a concept of "perfect knowledge" different from that held by the individual sciences, and also that for him knowledge is perfect inasmuch as reality is contemplated in its totality and in its foremost manifestations. Decisive in this is the ontological rank of

---

[151] "Immortality," Ingersoll Lecture at Harvard Divinity School, given on April 22, 1941, and printed in *The Philosophy of Alfred N. Whitehead*, ed. Paul Arthur Schilpp (New York: Tudor Publishing, 1951), 700.

[152] Nathaniel Lawrence, *Whitehead's Philosophical Development* (Berkeley: University of California Press, 1956).

what is perceived, not the *modus* of how it is perceived.

The principle of scientific exactness, in turn, by itself does not enable us to distinguish between things on an ontologically "higher" or "lower" level, not even between knowledge more beneficial for us or less. It [89] does not allow such distinction, it rather prevents it. Still, this is entirely as it should be; it should not be held against it. The situation becomes deplorable only when those distinctions, judged from a position that grants the principle of scientific exactness absolute status, are generally declared impossible or simply meaningless. T.S. Eliot relates how the beginnings of his philosophical studies had been overshadowed by a feeling of inferiority with regard to the exact sciences, and he mentions, incidentally, also the *Principia Mathematica*. Since then, he adds, he looks at this overemphasis on formal exactness in philosophy and finds an analogy in certain contemporary approaches to the fine arts: the latter offer the possibility of producing "works of art without imagination," while the former provides "a method of philosophizing" in which "insight and wisdom" seem equally dispensable.[153]

Only out of the soil of "loving pursuit of wisdom," indeed of true *philosophia*, could this be said: "The smallest amount of knowledge about the most sublime realities is more desirable than the most perfect knowledge about the lowest things"; "though we may hardly touch the things supreme and divine, their knowledge is nonetheless more important to us than all the things of this our world together; just as it is so much sweeter to catch but a glimpse, however fleeting, of the beloved than to have exact knowledge of many other, even important things." The first of these quotations is found in the *Summa theologica* of Thomas Aquinas.[154] The author of the second statement is Aristotle[155] whose usually [90] dispassionate prose may not have led you to expect such courtly language from him.

"Philosophy does not result in 'philosophical propositions,' but rather in the clarification of propositions."[156] This thesis, found in Ludwig Wittgenstein's *Tractatus Logico-Philosophicus*, also intends to define one of the fundamental differences between

---

[153] T.S. Eliot, preface to Josef Pieper, *Leisure, the Basis of Culture*, 7th edn., trans. Alexander Dru (London: Faber and Faber, 1964).

[154] Thomas Aquinas, *Summa theologica*, I, q. 1, a. 5, ad 1.

[155] Aristotle, *De partibus animalium*, I, 5, 644b ff.

[156] Ludwig Wittgenstein, *Tractatus Logico-Philosophicus*, 5th edn. (London: Routledge and Kegan Paul, 1951), 4, 112.

philosophy and science. It shall be left open here whether or not Wittgenstein meant to say, as seems likely, that the task of philosophy consists mainly, or even exclusively, in the logical clarification of those statements through which science expresses its findings. All the same, the assertion as formulated expresses indeed, perhaps even beyond the intention of its author, an essential characteristic of philosophy, a characteristic that is bound to appear, when measured with the principle of scientific exactness, once again as implausible and even as somewhat scandalous.

All achievements of science are basically discoveries, that is, they bring into the open what until then has been hidden and unknown. In this sense to explore the world—this is the glory of the sciences! Such glory can obviously not be claimed by the philosopher, and thus the verdict seems rendered already. The remarkable thing here is, however, that in philosophy this very "defect" is specifically singled out and made into an element of philosophy's self-understanding. Philosophy, as we say, is in fact aiming at something totally other than the increase of our knowledge of the world. What else might this be? A tentative answer could be: it is the re-calling of knowledge already present yet forgotten, which must not remain forgotten.

[91] He who reflects as a philosopher, that is, under every possible aspect, on realities such as guilt, freedom, or death; or he who considers the fundamental question as to the structure of *being* ("What does it mean for something to be real?"), will certainly experience a progressively more profound insight into all that is, in the same measure as his cognitive analysis penetrates ever deeper, and as his mind opens up ever more in dispassionate and receptive readiness. More profound insight, of course, is the philosopher's aim. Still, properly speaking, we cannot maintain that the philosopher, through this approach, would discover things totally unknown thus far, totally unthought thus far, things altogether new and original. What happens is rather a process resembling the illumination of something already vaguely and darkly known, the conquest of something almost lost in oblivion, indeed the regaining of what had been forgotten, which is called "remembrance." Even the truly "new" achievements of the masters—say, Aristotle's discovery that contrary to Parmenides' opinion there does exist between *being* and *nothing* a third level, the level of possibilities and becoming, the level of readiness for actualization, called *potentia* (*dynamis*)—even such an insight, never before explicitly conceived and expressed, could be accepted

and acknowledged as valid not as a result of a comparison with empirical and verifiable facts, but only because of a renewed cognition *in remembrance*. This is the rule in the philosophical endeavor: something already known, "by nature and implicitly," is transformed through a "secondary effort"—secondary with respect to this primary awareness—into reflective and explicit cognition.[157]

[92] This is perforce quite unimpressive when compared to the triumphs of the sciences, which every day present something new in terms of facts, structures, and interconnections—bringing all this before people's eyes, and even more so into people's hands: first of all ever more perfect means, scientifically tested, of domination over nature. The philosopher and philosophy, in contrast—do they not deal with the same topics all the time? Do they not discuss perpetually the same problems? Objections of this kind have been raised already against Socrates; Alcibiades mentions this is Plato's *Symposium*.[158] And how is it with progress in philosophy? Does it exist at all? Such questions can without doubt be construed in a context of complete contempt, a contempt that indeed is heaped, every so often, on those who engage in philosophy; a contempt that is justified if the rule of scientific exactness by right possesses or demands absolute authority.

But then, it shall be conceded right away: "progress" in the philosophical realm is assuredly a problematic category—insofar as it means an ever growing collective accumulation of knowledge, growing in the same measure as time passes. There exists, under this aspect, an analogy to poetry. Has Goethe "progressed" farther than Homer?—one cannot ask such a question. Philosophical progress undeniably occurs, yet not so much in the succession of generations as rather in the personal and dynamic existence of the philosopher himself, indeed to the extent to which he is able to behold, in silence and openness, the full depth and extension of his proper object, which is ever new and at the same time so very ancient.

How little opposition there is in principle between [93] the sciences themselves in their own domain and the philosophical quest has rarely been more evident than in our own time. The scientific exploration of reality nowadays seems to have reached, in certain fields at any rate, such an advanced frontier as to be almost identical with the approach of the philosopher. And as long

---

[157] Caspar Nink, *Ontologie: Versuch einer Grundlegung* (Freiburg im Breisgau: Herder, 1952), 6f.

[158] Plato, *Symposium*, 221e

as the interest remains fixed, without bias, on all that can be perceived, this approach is usually adopted without hesitation. Thus it may happen that the *nuclear physicist*, for instance, in his search for the elementary structure of matter and remaining strictly within the domain of physics, comes finally so close to the philosophical question, "What is, after all and in its core, the reality of matter?," that the dividing line between physics and philosophy seems to have vanished. ... To come face to face with the mind-boggling power given into man's hands seems to force as well the contemplation of "what this is all about." To witness this, one has only to read the documentation on the first nuclear explosion in the desert of Alamogordo. "Even the staunchest atheists were so shaken that they could describe their feelings [94] only in religious images.[159] [Or take] Robert J. Oppenheimer's remark that science at last has come face to face with sin ... And the first session of the Atomic Energy Commission was opened by its chairman with the concluding words of the traditional oath, as having for him, he said, a meaning like never before: "So help me God!"[160] Even should one see in all this nothing but helpless romanticism if not sentimentality, one thing cannot be denied: from one moment to the next, you are no longer dealing with the specific "sector" that is the customary and exclusive domain of science and technology. Most clearly, you are all of a sudden dealing with the totality of the world and existence!

The moment a scientist—be he a nuclear physicist, a psychoanalyst, or whatever—steps beyond these boundaries, all that has been said of the philosopher will then obviously apply to him as well. The questions then faced cannot be answered any more with the same exactitude that just a moment earlier, when the specialized expert was speaking, would have been expected unreservedly. And any potential insight thus achieved, unlike scientific results, does not become our property entirely at our disposal; suddenly we realize why the ancients spoke of "a gift on loan"[161] instead. Maybe, if the quest is honest and fortunate, and since the connection between these now all-encompassing questions and one's own existence cannot be ignored any more, it may just be that a new awareness arises: that philosophy and human existence itself, both, are structured in the pattern of hope.

---

[159] Margret Boveri, *Der Verrat im 20. Jahrhundert*, vol. 4 (Hamburg: Rowohlt, 1960), 205.

[160] Ibid., 206.

[161] Aquinas, *In duodecim libros*, 1, 3, no. 64.

KAROL WOJTYŁA [POPE JOHN PAUL II] (1920-2005)

Wojtyła was born in Wadowice, Poland in 1920, losing his mother when only eight years old. In 1938 he attended Jagiellonian University in Kraków, where he studied languages and was active in the drama department. After only a year there, the Germans occupied Kraków, closed down the University, and forced Wojtyła and other young men into manual labor. Wojtyła decided to enter the underground seminary in 1942, hiding in the Archbishop's Palace from 1944 until the Germans left in 1945, to avoid deportation after the Black Sunday uprising.

Wojtyła was ordained as a priest in 1946 and continued his studies at the Angelicum in Rome under Réginald Garrigou-Lagrange, earning a doctorate in theology in 1948, writing on John of the Cross. He went on to study philosophy at Jagiellonian University from 1951-1954, and had just completed a habilitation on the ethics of Scheler when the University was shut down by the Communists. Hence his academic career was launched instead at the Catholic University of Lublin, where Wojtyła taught ethics from 1954-1958. He was appointed Auxiliary Bishop of Kraków in 1958 and took part in the Second Vatican Council where he helped draft the 1965 documents *Dignitatis humanae* and *Gaudium et spes*. Wojtyła became the Archbishop of Kraków in 1964 and a Cardinal in 1967, with his titular parish being San Cesareo in Palatio. In 1978 he became Pope John Paul II. He died in 2005, after surviving a 1981 assassination attempt, and is buried in the Vatican Grottos beneath St. Peter's Basilica in Rome. John Paul II was canonized in 2014 (his feast day is October 22nd) and has been given the unofficial title "the Great" by popular acclaim.

Among his achievements as Pope are the authoring of fourteen encyclicals including *Laborem exercens* (1981), *Sollicitudo rei socialis* (1987), and *Centesiums annus* (1991) on Catholic social doctrine, *Veritatis splendor* (1993) and *Evangelium vitae* (1995) on moral theology, and *Fides et ratio* (1998) on the relation of philosophy and theology; the revised *Code of Canon Law* (1983) and *Catechism of the Catholic Church* (1994; 1997); and the *Joint Declaration on the Doctrine of Justification* (1999) with the Lutheran World Federation.

The key philosophical works of Wojtyła are his *Love and Responsibility* [*Miłość i odpowiedzialność*] (Lublin: Naukowe Katolickiego Uniwersytetu Lubelskiego, 1960), 2nd ed. 2001, and *The Acting Person* [*Osoba i czyn*] (Kraków: Polskie Towarzystwo Teologiczne, 1969). These works have been translated as *Love and Responsibility* (San Francisco: Ignatius Press, 1993) and *Love and Responsibility* (Boston: Pauline Books, 2013) and *The Acting Person* (Reidel: Dordrecht, 1979), the latter translated by his close friend, the Polish-American philosopher Anna-Teresa Tymieniecka. One can also mention his 1979-1984 lecture series published as *Theology of the Body* (Boston: Pauline Books, 1997) and his collection of essays *Person and Community* (New York: Peter Lang, 1993).

For more on the life and thought of John Paul II one can consult: Schmitz, Kenneth, *At the Center of the Human Drama: The Philosophical Anthropology of Karol Wojtyła* (Washington: Catholic University of America, 1993); Buttiglione, Rocco, *Karol Wojtyła: The Thought of the Man Who Became John Paul II* (Grand Rapids: Eerdmans, 1997); Curran, Charles, and Richard McCormick, eds., *John Paul II and Moral Theology* (Mahwah: Paulist Press, 1998); DiNoia, Joseph, and Romanus Cessario, eds., *Veritatis Splendor and the Renewal of Moral Theology* (Hungington: Our Sunday Visitor, 1999); Kupczak, Jarosaw, *Destined for Liberty: The Human Person in the Philosophy of Karol Wojtyła* (Washington: Catholic University of America Press, 2000); Reimers, Adrian, *An Analysis of the Concepts of Self-Fulfillment and Self-Realization in the Thought of Karol Wojtyła, Pope John Paul II* (Lewiston: Edwin Mellen Press, 2001); Simpson, Peter, *On Karol Wojtyła* (Belmont: Wadsworth, 2001); Foster, David, ed., *The Two Wings of Catholic Thought: Essays on Fides et Ratio* (Washington: The Catholic University of America Press, 2003); McNerney, John, *Footbridge towards the Other: An Introduction to the Philosophical Thought of John Paul II* (Bristol: Continuum, 2003); Curran, Charles, *The Moral Theology of Pope John Paul II* (Washington: Georgetown University Press, 2005); Ong, Andre, *John Paul II's Philosophy of the Acting Person: A Personalistic Approach to Life* (Lewiston: Edward Mellon Press, 2008); Barrett, Edward, *Persons and Liberal Democracy: The Ethical and Political Thought of Karol Wojtyła/John Paul II* (Lanham: Lexington Books, 2010); Spinello, Richard A., *Understanding Love and Responsibility* (Boston: Pauline Books, 2014); Acosta, Miguel, and Adrian J. Reimers, *Karol Wojtyła's Personalist Philosophy: Understanding Person and Act* (Washington: Catholic University of America Press, 2016); Petri, Thomas, *Aquinas and the Theology of the Body: The Thomistic Foundations of John Paul II's Anthropology* (Washington: Catholic University of America Press, 2016).

The translation below is from Wojtyła, *Love and Responsibility* (San Francisco: Ignatius Press, 1993): I, 40-44 and II, 95-100. Wojtyła combines the realist metaphysics of Aristotle and Aquinas, especially their notion of substance [substantia; suppositum], with the modern turn to the subject, especially the ethics of Kant and the phenomenology of self-consciousness of Husserl. In the latter section of the work at hand Wojtyła examines the nature of love, in particular its eight elements of attraction, desire, goodwill, reciprocity, sympathy, friendship, comradeship, and betrothedness. He argues that while love rightly contains each of these elements to some degree, the highest form of love, betrothed love, involves giving one's very self to another person. Or in his words "self-giving, in making one's inalienable and non-transferable I someone else's property" (1993, 97). It should also be pointed out that in this section he is presupposing his earlier characterization of the Kantian-inspired personalistic norm whereby we have to treat other humans as ends and with love and not use them as means.

Love and Responsibility (1960)[162]

The Person and the Sexual Urge

Analysis of the Verb 'To Use'

The Commandment to Love, and the Personalistic Norm

[40] The commandment laid down in the New Testament demands from man love for others, for his neighbors–in the fullest sense, then love for persons. For God, whom the commandment to love names first, is the most perfect personal Being. The whole world of created persons derives its distinctness from and its natural superiority over the world of things (non-persons) from a very particular resemblance to God. The commandment formulated in the New Testament, demanding love towards persons, is implicitly opposed to the principle of utilitarianism, which–as we have shown in the previous analysis–is unable to guarantee the love of one human being, one person for another. The opposition between the commandment in the Gospels and the principle of utilitarianism is *implicit* only in that the commandment does not put in so many words the principle on the basis of which love between persons is to be practiced. Christ's commandment, however, and the utilitarian principle, seem to be on different levels, to be norms of a different order. They do not deal directly with the same thing: the commandment speaks of love for others, while the utilitarian principle points to pleasure not only as the basis on which we act but as the basis for rules of human behavior. We have seen in our critique of utilitarianism that if we start from what utilitarians accept as the basis for the regulation of human behaviour, we shall never arrive at love. The principle of 'utility' itself, of treating persons as a means to an end, and an end moreover which in this case is pleasure, the maximization of pleasure, will always stand in the way of love.

The incompatibility of the utilitarian principle with the commandment to love is then clear: if the utilitarian principle is accepted the commandment simply becomes meaningless. There is also an obvious connection between the utilitarian principle and a particular scale of values: that according to which pleasure is not only the sole, but also the [41] highest, value. This we need not

---

[162] [Karol Wojtyła, *Love and Responsibility*, translated by H.T. Willetts. Copyright © 1993 by Ignatius Press. All rights reserved. Used with permission of Ignatius Press, https://www.ignatius.com.]

analyse here any further. But it becomes obvious that if the commandment to love, and the love which is the object of this commandment, are to have any meaning, we must find a basis for them other than the utilitarian premise and the utilitarian system of values. This can only be the personalistic principle and the personalistic norm. This norm, in its negative aspect, states that the person is the kind of good which does not admit of use and cannot be treated as an object of use and as such the means to an end. In its positive form the personalistic norm confirms this: the person is a good towards which the only proper and adequate attitude is love. This positive content of the personalistic norm is precisely what the commandment to love teaches.

In view of this can it be said that the commandment to love is the personalistic norm? Strictly speaking the commandment to love is only based on the personalistic norm, as a principle with a negative and a positive content, and is not itself the personalistic norm. It only derives from this norm, which, unlike the utilitarian principle, *does* provide an appropriate foundation for the commandment to love. This foundation for the commandment to love should also be sought in a system of values other than the utilitarian system—it must be a personalistic axiology, within whose framework the value of the person is always greater than the value of pleasure (which is why a person cannot be subordinated to this lesser end, cannot be the means to an end, in this case to pleasure). So, while the commandment to love is not, strictly speaking, identical with the personalistic norm but only presupposes it, as it implies also a personalistic system of values, we can, taking a broader view, say that the commandment to love *is* the personalistic norm. Strictly speaking the commandment says: 'Love persons', and the personalistic norm says: 'A person is an entity of the sort to which the only proper and adequate way to relate is love.' The personalistic norm does, as we have seen, provide a justification for the New Testament commandment. And so, if we take the commandment together with the justification, we can say that it is the same as the personalistic norm.

[42] This norm, as a commandment, defines and recommends a certain way of relating to God and to people, a certain attitude towards them. This way of relating, this attitude is in agreement with what the person is, with the value which the person represents, and therefore it is fair. Fairness takes precedence of mere utility (which is all the utilitarian principle has eyes for)— although it does not cancel it but only subordinates it: in dealings with another person everything that is at once of use to oneself

and fair to that person falls within the limits set by the command-ment to love.

In defining and recommending a particular way of relating to the particular beings called persons, a particular attitude to them, the personalistic norm in the form of the commandment to Love assumes that this relation, this attitude, will be not only fair but just. For to be just always means giving others what is rightly due to them. A person's rightful due is to be treated as an object of love, not as an object for use. In a sense it can be said that love is a requirement of justice, just as using a person as a means to an end would conflict with justice. In fact the order of justice is more fundamental than the order of love–and in a sense the first embraces the second inasmuch as love can be a requirement of justice. Surely it is just to love a human being or to love God, to hold a person dear. At the same time love–if we are to consider its very essence–is something beyond and above justice; the essence of love is simply different from the essence of justice. Justice concerns itself with things (material goods or moral goods, as for instance one's good name) in relation to persons, and hence with persons rather indirectly, whereas love is concerned with persons directly and immediately: affirmation of the value of the person as such is of its essence. Although we can correctly say that whoever loves a person is for that very reason just to that person, it would be quite untrue to assert that love for a person consists merely in being just. Later in the book we shall try to analyse separately and more fully what it is that constitutes love for a person. So far, we have elicited one fact–namely that love for a person must consist in affirmation that the person has a value higher than that of an object for consumption or use. He who loves will [43] endeavour to declare this by his whole behaviour. And there can be no doubt that he will, *ipso facto*, be just towards the other person as a person.[163]

This aspect of the question, this interpenetration of love and justice in the personalistic norm is very important to the whole

---

[163] Justice, here, is used in what may be called the strict sense (for in the broad, biblical sense a 'just' man is the same as the 'man of good will'). Justice in the strict sense signifies satisfaction of someone's minimum entitlement to personal or material services. But since love is just only when it is not minimalistic the services which justice in this narrow sense demands can only be the basis and condition of a full interpersonal affirmation. Cf. Aristotle, *Nicomachean Ethics*, VII, 1, 1955a26, and St. Thomas Aquinas, *Summa contra Gentiles*, III, 130.

complex of our enquiries into sexual morality. It is precisely here that the main task is the elaboration of a concept of love which is just to the person, or if you like a love prepared to concede to each human being that which he or she can rightfully claim by virtue of being a person. For in the sexual context what is sometimes characterized as love may very easily be quite unjust to a person. This occurs not because sensuality and sentimentality play a special part in forming this love between persons of different sex (a fact which we shall also analyse separately), but rather because love in the sexual context lends itself to interpretation, sometimes conscious, sometimes unconscious, along utilitarian lines.

In a sense this kind of love is wide open to such an interpretation, which turns to account the natural gravitation of its sensual and sentimental ingredients in the direction of pleasure. It is easy to go on from the experience of pleasure not merely to the quest for pleasure, but to the quest of pleasure for its own sake, to accepting it as a superlative value and the proper basis for a norm of behaviour. This is the very essence of the distortions which occur in the love between man and woman.

Since, then, sexuality is so easily connected with the concept of 'love,' and is at the same time the arena of constant conflict between two fundamentally different value systems, two fundamentally different ways of determining norms of behaviour, the personalistic and the utilitarian—we must, if the subject is to be fully clarified, distinctly state that the love which is the content of the commandment in the Gospels, can be combined only with the personalistic, not with the utilitarian norm. It is therefore within the compass of the personalistic norm that proper solutions to the problems of sexual morality must be sought, if they are to be Christian solutions. They must be based upon the commandment to [44] love. For although man can fully and completely realize the commandment to love in the full sense which the New Testament gives to it through supernatural love for God and his neighbours, this love nevertheless is not a contradiction of personalistic love, and indeed cannot be practiced without it. ...

St. Augustine differentiated in this way between two attitudes. One of them is intent on pleasure for its own sake, with no concern for the object of pleasure, and that is what he calls *uti*. The other finds joy in a totally committed relationship with the object precisely because this is what the nature of the object demands, and this he called *frui*. The commandment to love shows the way to enjoyment in this sense–*frui*–in the association of persons of different sex both within and outside marriage. ...

The Person and Love

Metaphysical Analysis of Love

Betrothed Love
[95] The general analysis of love has a primarily metaphysical character, although we have to refer continually to its psychological and ethical aspects. These various aspects of love interpenetrate, so that we cannot examine any one of them without mentioning the others. In our analysis so far we have tried to clarify what is essential to all forms of love, and manifests itself in a specific way in the love of man and woman. Love in the individual develops by way of attraction, desire and goodwill. Love however finds its full realization not in an individual subject, but in a relationship between subjects, between persons. Hence the problem of friendship, which we have analysed here in our discussion of sympathy, hence too a problem connected with friendship, that of reciprocity. The transition from 'I' to 'we' is no less important for love than the escape from one's own 'I' by way of attraction, desire and goodwill. Love, especially of the kind which concerns us in the present book, is not just an aspiration, but rather a coming together, a unification of persons. This takes place, of course, on the basis of the attraction, desire and goodwill which develop in individual subjects. The individual aspect of love does not disappear from view in its interpersonal aspect–on the contrary, the latter is [96] conditioned by the former. As a result love is always a sort of interpersonal synthesis and synchronization of attraction, desire and goodwill.

Betrothed love [*miłość oblubieńcza*] differs from all the aspects or forms of love analysed hitherto. Its decisive character is the giving of one's own person (to another). The essence of betrothed love is self-giving, the surrender of one's 'I'. This is something different from and more than attraction, desire or even goodwill. These are all ways by which one person goes out towards another, but none of them can take him as far in his quest for the good of the other as does betrothed love. 'To give oneself to another' is something more than merely 'desiring what is good' for another–even if as a result of this another 'I' becomes as it were my own, as it does in friendship. Betrothed love is something different from all and more than the forms of love so far analysed, both as it affects the individual subject, the person who loves, and as it regards the interpersonal union which it creates. When betrothed love enters into this interpersonal relationship something more than friendship results: two people give themselves each to the other.

This matter demands more thorough consideration. First of all, the question arises whether any person can give himself or herself to another person. We said above that the person is always, of its very nature, untransferable, *alteri incommunicabilis*. This means not only that it is its own master (*sui juris*), but that it cannot give itself away, cannot surrender itself. The very nature of the person is incompatible with such a surrender. Indeed, in the natural order it makes no sense to speak of a person giving himself or herself to another, especially if this is meant in the physical sense. That which is personal is on a plane where there can be no giving of the self, and no appropriation in the physical sense. The person as such cannot be someone else's property, as though it were a thing. In consequence, the treatment of a person as an object for use is also excluded, as we have seen in our closer examination of that subject. But what is impossible and illegitimate in the natural order and in a physical sense, can come about in the order of love and in a [97] moral sense. In this sense, one person can give himself or herself, can surrender entirely to another, whether to a human person or to God, and such a giving of the self creates a special form of love which we define as betrothed love.[164] This fact goes to prove that the person has a dynamism of its own, and that specific laws govern its existence and evolution. Christ gave expression to this in a saying which is on the face of it profoundly paradoxical: 'He who would save his soul shall lose it, and he who would lose his soul for my sake shall find it again' (Matthew 10:39).

Indeed, the problem of betrothed love does contain a profound paradox, a very real, and not merely a verbal paradox: the words of the Gospel point to a concrete reality, and the truth which they contain is made manifest in the life of the person.

---

[164] 'It [betrothed love] is realized according to Christ's teaching—in one way if a person gives himself or herself exclusively to God, in another in marriage where two human persons give themselves to each other. ... At the same time it must be emphasized that although God as Creator possesses the *dominium altum*, the supreme right, in relation to all creatures, and hence also over man, who is a person, this decision to give oneself completely, become 'the property of a beloved God' (KK 44), is, according to the will of Christ himself, left to the free choice of man under the influence of Grace ("O znaczeniu miłości oblubieńczej" ["On the Meaning of Betrothed Love"], *Roczniki Filozoficzne* 22:2 (1974), p. 171).

Thus, of its very nature, no person can be transferred or ceded to another. In the natural order, it is oriented towards self-perfection, towards the attainment of an ever greater fullness of existence – which is, of course, always the existence of some concrete 'I'. We have already stated that this self-perfection proceeds side by side and step by step with love. The fullest, the most uncompromising form of love consists precisely in self-giving, in making one's inalienable and non-transferable 'I' someone else's property. This is doubly paradoxical: firstly in that it is possible to step outside one's own 'I' in this way, and secondly in that the 'I' far from being destroyed or impaired as a result is enlarged and enriched–of course in a super-physical, a moral sense. The Gospel stresses this very clearly and unambiguously–'would lose–shall find again' 'would save–shall lose'. You will readily see that we have here not merely the personalistic norm but also bold and explicit words of advice, which make it possible for us to amplify and elaborate on that norm. The world of persons possesses its own laws of existence and of development.

Self-surrender as a form of love is the result of a process within the person, and presupposes a mature vision of values, and a will ready and able to commit itself in this particular way. Betrothed [sic *Bethrothed*] love can never be a fortuitous or imperfect event in the inner life of the person. It always constitutes a [98] special crystallization of the whole human 'I', determined because of its love to dispose of itself in this particular way. In giving ourselves we find clear proof that we possess ourselves. As for the particular manifestations of this form of love, they can, I think, vary greatly. Leaving aside the devotion of a mother to her child, do we not find self-giving in, for instance, the relationship of a doctor with his patient, or in a teacher, who devotes himself with utter dedication to the education of his pupil, or a pastor who devotes himself with equal dedication to a soul entrusted to his care? In the same way great public figures or apostles can devote themselves to many people at once, people for the most part personally unknown to them, whom they serve by serving society as a whole. To determine in any of the cases mentioned, or in others like them, how far genuine dedicated love is involved is no easy matter. For in each of them no more than sincere goodwill and friendliness may be at work. In order, for instance, to 'give oneself entirely' to the vocation of the doctor, teacher, or pastor, it suffices simply to 'desire the good' of those for whom these duties are performed. And even if this form of behaviour comes to resemble a complete surrender of the self and so establishes its claim to be love, it would still be difficult to apply the name 'betrothed love' to it.

The concept of betrothed love implies the giving of the individual person to another chosen person. We speak therefore of love in certain cases when we seek to define the relationship between man and God. (This will be discussed separately in Chapter IV.) We have also the best possible grounds for speaking of betrothed love in connection with matrimony. The love of two persons, man and woman, leads in matrimony to their mutual dedication one to the other. From the point of view of each individual person this is a clear surrender of the self to another person, while in the interpersonal relationship it is surrender of each to the other. 'Self-giving', in the sense in which we are discussing it, should not be identified (confused) with 'giving oneself' in a merely psychological sense, with the sensation of self-surrender, still less with surrender in a merely physical sense. As far as surrender in the first (the psychological) sense is [99] concerned, it is only the woman, or at any rate it is above all the woman, who feels that her role in marriage is to give herself; the man's experience of marriage is different, since, 'giving oneself' has as its psychological correlative 'possession'. However, the psychological approach is insufficient here for if we think the problem through objectively, and that means ontologically, what happens in the marital relationship is that the man simultaneously gives himself, in return for the woman's gift of herself to him, and thus although his conscious experience of it differs from the woman's it must none the less be a real giving of himself to another person. If it is not there is a danger that the man may treat the woman as an object, and indeed an object to be used. If marriage is to satisfy the demands of the personalistic norm it must embody reciprocal self-giving, a mutual betrothed love. The acts of surrender reciprocate each other, that of the man and that of the woman, and though they are psychologically different in kind, ontologically they combine to produce a perfect whole, an act of mutual self-surrender. Hence a special duty devolves upon the man: he must give to 'conquest' or 'possession' its appropriate form and content—which means that he too must give himself, no less than she does.

It is all the more obvious that this giving of oneself of which we speak cannot, in marriage or indeed in any relationship between persons of opposite sex, have a merely sexual significance. Giving oneself only sexually, without the full gift of the person to validate it, must lead to those forms of utilitarianism which we have endeavoured to analyse as thoroughly as we could in Chapter I. We must stress this because there is a more or less pronounced tendency to interpret the 'gift of self' in a purely sexual, or sexual and psychological, sense. A personalistic interpretation is, however, absolutely necessary in this context. Thus, the moral code which has the commandment to love at its centre finds itself in perfect agreement with the identification of marriage with betrothed love, or rather–looking at it from the educational point of view–with the treatment of marriage as the result of this form of love.

There are further consequences of this, to which we shall [100] return in Chapter IV (Part I) where we show the necessity for monogamy. When a woman gives herself to a man as she does in matrimony this–morally speaking–precludes a simultaneous gift of herself to other persons in the same way. The sexual aspect plays a specific part in the development of betrothed love. Sexual intercourse has the effect of limiting that love to a single pair of persons, though at the same time it gains in intensity. Moreover, only when it is so limited can that love open itself fully to the new persons who are the natural result of marital love between man and woman.

The concept of goodwill is crucial to the establishment of norms of sexual morality generally. There certainly exists a very special connection between sex and the person in the objective order, which at the level of consciousness has its counterpart in a special awareness of the right of personal property in one's 'I'. This question will be analysed separately in Chapter III ('The Metaphysics of Shame'). Consequently, there can be no question of a sexual giving of oneself which does not mean a giving of the person–and does not come in one way or another within the orbit of those demands which we have a right to make of betrothed love. These demands derive from the personalistic norm. Betrothed love, though of its nature it differs from all the forms of love previously analysed, can nevertheless not develop in isolation from them. In particular, it is essential that betrothed love should ally itself closely with goodwill and friendship. Without these allies it may find itself in a very dangerous void, and the persons involved in it may feel helpless in face of conditions, internal and external, which they have inadvertently permitted to arise within themselves or between themselves.

JOHN HALDANE (1954-)

An individual of wide interests, the lay Scottish philosopher John Haldane (1954-) grew up in Glasgow. He pursued higher education in London, where he received a B.A. in Fine Art from the Wimbledon School of Art in 1975 and a B.A. in Philosophy from Birbeck College, University of London in 1980. Four years later he attained his Ph.D. in philosophy from Birbeck College, University of London as well. After teaching art for three years at St Joseph's Convent School in London, in 1983 Haldane attained a philosophy position at the University of St. Andrews in Scotland where, since 1988, he has also been Director of the Centre for Ethics, Philosophy and Public Affairs. More recently, Haldane has become the J. Newton Rayzor, Sr., Distinguished Professor in Philosophy, at Baylor University (2015-). He is married with four children. In 2005 he was made a Consultor to the Pontifical Council for Culture and in 2011 the Chairman of the Royal Institute of Philosophy.

Haldane has penned nearly 200 philosophy essays, the main ones being collected in *Faithful Reason: Essays Catholic and Philosophical* (London: Routledge, 2004), *Practical Philosophy: Ethics, Society and Culture* (Exeter: Imprint Academic, 2009), and *Reasonable Faith* (London: Routledge, 2010), as well as his debates with J.J.C. Smart, published as *Atheism and Theism* (London: Blackwell, 1996 and 2003) and with Christopher Hitchens through the Veritas Forum at Oxford in 2010. We can also mention his books *An Intelligent Person's Guide to Religion* (London: Duckworth, 2003) and *Seeking Meaning and Making Sense* (Exeter: Imprint Academic, 2008).

Haldane specialized in the philosophy of the mind, aesthetics, and the philosophy of religion. He is one of the founders of analytical Thomism, which is an attempt to combine the method of analytical philosophy with the content of Thomism. See in this regard Haldane's articles "Analytical Thomism: A Prefatory Note," *Monist* 80:4 (October, 1997): 485-486; "What Future has Catholic Philosophy," *Proceedings of the American Catholic Philosophical Association* 71 (1997): 79-90; "Thomism and the Future of Catholic Philosophy," *New Blackfriars* 80:938 (April, 1999): 158-169; and "Analytical Thomism," in Craig Paterson and Matthew S. Pugh, eds., *Analytical Thomism: Traditions in Dialogue* (London: Ashgate, 2006): 303-310.

The following essay "Finding God in Nature: Beauty, Revulsion and Art," originally appeared in Craig Titus, ed., *Christianity and the West: Interaction and Impact in Art and Culture* (Washington: Catholic University of America Press, 2009): 21-47, though the text below is from the slightly modified version found in Haldane's *Reasonable Faith* (London: Routledge, 2010): 80-94. This essay is representative of Haldane's work both in aesthetics and the philosophy of religion, and it examines whether reductive accounts of the beauty of nature are justifiable or whether natural beauty is best conceived as an objective reality and is evidence for the divine.

"Finding God in Nature: Beauty, Revulsion, and Art" (2009)[165]

"Into every beautiful object, there enters somewhat the immeasurable and divine, and just as much into form bounded by outlines, like mountains of the horizon, as into tones of music, or depths of space" (Ralph Waldo Emerson, *The Conduct of Life*).[166]

Introduction

[80] Certainly there are different conceptions or understandings of the ideas of *God*, of *nature* and of *art*, but there have also been, and perhaps still are, different concepts of these. It strains coherence to say that two people are merely differing in their conception of the nature of God when one allows that deity must have and another denies that it may have a material embodiment. Again, where someone says that nature is the sum total of matter in motion, and another that it is an integrated ecological system of flora and fauna, we should allow, that they are differing over more than the right account of what is otherwise the subject of broad definitional agreement.

Delineating the boundaries within and between concepts, and charting the course of intellectual development from one concept or conception to another, requires analytical acuity and considerable historical knowledge. Here I shall not test my competence or readers' patience by engaging extensively in these forms of conceptual and historical study. Nor for my purposes is it necessary to do so, since whatever the differences it is clear enough that there is a significant tradition within Western culture (and beyond) of finding in the experience of nature, and in the making of art related to nature, intimations of a transcendent creative cause: God. For these purposes I understand *nature* to be the empirically observable material world as it is independent of human construction.[167] I take *art* to be the domain of human production in which objects (broadly construed) are created primarily for aesthetic effect, to be experienced for their

---

[165] [John Haldane, *Reasonable Faith*. Copyright © 1993 by Routledge Press. All rights reserved. Used with permission of Routledge Press, www,routledge.com.]

[166] Ralph Waldo Emerson, *The Conduct of Life* (Boston: James R. Osgood, 1871), ch. 8, "On Beauty."

[167] Empirical observability is of course a relative notion. I have in mind the normal range of human sense-perception, in the first instance unaided but then supplemented tele- and microscopically.

compositional, expressive and/or narrative content. And I take God to be the unique ultimate cause; personal, active and providential; infinitely good, powerful and knowledgeable.

Previously we saw St Paul writing of the cosmos as manifesting divine activity when he noted that 'Ever since the creation of the world, [God's] [81] invisible attributes of eternal power and divinity have been able to be perceived in the things that have been made' (Romans 1:20). Far from suggesting a passing thought, the brevity of this remark indicates Paul's assumption that his readers were already familiar with this idea. Certainly educated people knowledgeable in the speculations of Greek and Roman philosophers and poets would have been used to the notion that nature manifests design. In words echoing Cicero, Paul began his presentation of the case for deities by saying 'What can be so obvious and clear, as we gaze up at the sky and observe the heavenly bodies, as that there is some divine power of surpassing intelligence by which they are ordered?' Then later he adds that the greatest reason for believing in a creator is 'the individuality, usefulness, beauty, and order of the sun and moon and stars'.[168]

One might then suppose that the experience of the beauty and sublimity of nature would complement and enhance this theology of creation. For many it has done. Gerard Manley Hopkins made this a central element of his poetry, sometimes lamenting that human manufacture grossly obscured the order and beauty of nature. His complaint in the latter regard is not just the charge of vandalism, but of self-injury, impairing the power of eye to see and ear to hear the beauty of God's grandeur manifest in the natural world. He writes:

> The world is charged with the grandeur of God.
> It will flame out, like shining from shook foil;
> It gathers to a greatness, like the ooze of oil
> Crushed. Why do men then now not reck his rod?
> Generations have trod, have trod, have trod;
> And all is seared with trade; bleared, smeared with toil;
> And wears man's smudge and shares man's smell: the soil
> Is bare now, nor can foot feel, being shod.
> And for all this, nature is never spent;
> There lives the dearest freshness deep down things;
> And though the last lights off the black West went

---

[168] Cicero, *The Nature of the Gods*, trans. P.G. Walsh (Oxford: Clarendon Press, 1997), pp. 48 and 52.

Oh, morning, at the brown brink eastward, springs–
Because the Holy Ghost over the bent
World broods with warm breast and with ah! bright wings.[169]

Evidently, like many another poet and artist before and since, Hopkins took delight in landscape and in the flora and fauna within it; and he found in this not merely external evidences of creative design in the manner of effects remaining after some activity, but ongoing expressions of divinity. In one interpretation this thought leads in the direction of *pantheism*, identifying God and nature, or *panentheism*, treating nature as part of God. But there is another way of understanding the relationship, and one licensed by orthodox Christian theology, according to which God is present in nature not spatially but actively, continuously causing the natures and existings of things. Conceived of in this way, or in ways that yield similar conclusions about the immanence of God in nature, one [82] would welcome the experience of natural beauty as reinforcing the sense of the world as a place of creation.

Writing in the 1930s the Cambridge philosopher and theologian, F.R. Tennant, having set his face against *a priori* proofs of theism, interestingly developed a cumulative argument for God's existence, drawing upon a range of experienced features. In this he interwove the traditional argument from apparent natural order to design, with an argument to the same conclusion from the human experience of beauty in nature. He writes:

> On the telescopic and on the microscopic scale, from the starry heaven to the siliceous skeleton of the diatom [microscopic algae], in her inward parts (if scientific imagination be veridical) as well as on the surface, in flowers that 'blush unseen' and gems that 'unfathomed caves of ocean bear' [quoting Thomas Gray, 'Elegy in a Country Churchyard'], Nature is sublime or beautiful, and the exceptions do but prove the rule. However, various be the taste for beauty, and however diverse the levels of its education or degrees of its refinement, Nature elicits aesthetic sentiment from men severally and collectively.[170]

The question for Tennant is what is it that explains the

---

[169] *The Poems of Gerard Manley Hopkins*, ed. W.H. Gardner and N.H. MacKenzie (Oxford: Oxford University Press, 1970), p. 66.

[170] F.R. Tennant, *Philosophical Theology*, vol. 2: *The Soul, the World and God* (Cambridge: Cambridge University Press, 1930), p. 91.

ubiquity of natural beauty. We know from our own case that far from being invariably aesthetically pleasing, our works and products are really so, and then generally only when they are the products of aesthetic intention, even if in association with other purposes. A mere aggregation or distribution of objects is not apt to exhibit beauty. Yet in nature everywhere we look we see it 'sublime or beautiful'. This degree of aesthetic value, both in the sense of extent and of intensity, is inexplicable other than as the intended product of design. Given that it exits, however, so too must a creative 'Artist' of nature who, as Aquinas would have added, 'we call God' (*et hoc dicimus Deum*).

A Series of Challenges

Appealing as it may be, Tennant's aesthetic argument faces a series of pertinent questions. First, is it really the case that nature is generally sublime or beautiful? Second, to the extent that it appears so might not these judgements be products of our own sensibility projected onto a reality that in itself is neither beautiful nor ugly? Third, even if beauty is real, might it not be a rare phenomenon only appearing ubiquitous because of our unconscious attention to what pleases us, and our aversion to and avoidance of what is repellent? Fourth, even if beauty is real and perhaps extensive might it not be a product of chance? Fifth, might not the whole thing have an evolutionary explanation?

The issue as to whether nature is really beautiful might be answered by saying that it certainly seems to be so, and that this is the recurrent testimony of human beings over time and across cultures. To this might be added the thought that, other things being equal, one should take it that things are as they generally seem [83] to be. Combined, these two propositions yield the conclusion that, other things being equal, one should take it that nature really is beautiful. This qualified conclusion only serves, however, to direct attention to the possible ways in which other things might not be equal. Might it not be, as the second question envisages, that what we seem to find there is but a reflection of our sensibility? This in turn introduces a version of the familiar question: do we find something good because it is so, or is it good because we find it to be such? Historically, philosophers were inclined to take it that our judging things to be good or bad, and beautiful or ugly, are responses to objective features. So the judgement that this or that is beautiful would be true just in case the object possessed objective beauty. What this attribute might consist in remained open to debate: mathematical ratios, significant form, organic unity, are a few of the candidates; but it was generally agreed that whatever its exact nature beauty is a real feature of the world. Consequent upon this account is the idea that the notion of aesthetic experience is conceptually posterior to that of an aesthetic object: what makes an experience to be of this sort is that it is focused on something possessed of beauty, and more precisely on the beauty of that thing.

From antiquity, however, it was always seen to be a possibility that the order of priority might run in the other direction. It might be that aesthetic objects are those things which, whatever their own character, are the objects of aesthetic experience, where the idea of such an experience is to be explained in terms of a conscious subject adopting a certain kind of attitude. By analogy, consider the claim that the view of a still pond and the sound of a small waterfall are relaxing. Are we to say that being relaxed is induced by a relaxing experience resulting from encountering a relaxing object? It is hard to believe that there are in nature such things as relaxing views or sounds, save in the sense that, having a certain sensibility, we feel various things to be relaxing. Here then we are drawn to the view that something is relaxing because we find it so. This subjectivist orientation seems the best direction of explanation for a variety of other verdicts regarding the quality of objects of sensuous experience, but what of beauty?

Phenomenologically beauty seems to reside *in* things: in their form, structure and texture, in the overall shape, internal arrangement and medium. Certainly we 'feel' the beauty but that feeling is referred towards its object as occasioning the experience. In the case of the relaxing, by contrast, it is more natural to say that we are relaxed by the thing as an effect of it, where it is allowed that others might not be similarly affected. Moreover, in the case of beauty there is the sense that the favourable judgement is *merited* and indeed called for. In identifying something as beautiful one acknowledges its quality as something to be *appreciated*. Furthermore, while judgements of beauty are not governed by rules or sets of criteria they do have *grounds*, and there is such a thing as aesthetic criticism. While these several points do not put the matter beyond dispute they do, I suggest, provide effective support to the idea that beauty is something real in the world and not just a projection on to it of our sensibility.

What of its extent? Tennant writes that 'Nature is sublime or beautiful, and the exceptions do but prove the rule'. *Exceptio probat regulum in casibus non exceptis* [84] (that there are exceptions proves the rule in all other cases) warrants an expectation of near to universal conformity to the principle of natural beauty. Considering this, someone is likely to begin with conspicuous and culturally familiar categories: flowers, sunsets, mountains and so on; and then to start imagining other 'parts' of nature to see whether these also conform. Sortal terms divide a domain by kinds, corresponding either to mass or count nouns that attract, respectively, the questions How much? and How many? 'Water', unlike 'horse', designates a kind that divides into quantities rather than individuals; so that while we may ask 'how *many* horses are there?' we can only ask 'how *much* water is there?' With this simple semantic apparatus in place, we can now ask whether, for the most part, actual states of affairs properly, and primarily describable in terms of natural sortals, exhibit aesthetic qualities. Clouds, mountains, meadows, lakes, rivers, trees, horses, cows, sheep, dogs, cats, fish, algae, can easily be imagined to rest along a scale of the aesthetically pleasing, both in respect of their structure and with regard to their immediately apparent empirical properties. When it comes to quantities of stuffs of various kinds the issue is less clear, but here two things may be said: first, that the thesis of natural beauty holds properly and primarily of things that have some intrinsic principle of unity or organization; and second, that even where something lacks this and is just an aggregation, such as a mound of snow, or a heap of sand, there are other aspects, colour, texture, etc., that provide aesthetic interest. As counter-examples suggest themselves so too does the thought that in saying nature is aesthetic one need not be claiming that all of nature is outstanding, but the deficiencies may be seen as degrees of privation; also where nature is apt to seem repellent that is likely to be because of other non-aesthetic aspects of the situation or of the character of what is contemplated. Again, therefore, I am inclined to think that Tennant's claim stands up.

So we arrive at the two last challenges. Even granting that beauty, or the aesthetic more broadly, is ubiquitous might this not be the product of chance rather than design? A familiar counterpart of that question haunts traditional teleological arguments for the existence of God based on the apparent functional order occurring in nature. For the ancients and medievals there was no doubt that the universe exhibits purposeful order, but attempts to draw theological conclusions from this assumption were shown by David Hume to be problematic,[171] and the assumption itself was called into question

---

[171] See David Hume, *Dialogues Concerning Natural Religion*, in

by Darwin's theory of evolution by natural selection among the products of random variation. Since Hume's challenges are themselves problematic and ambiguous in intent and outcome, and since the Darwinian challenge is directed against the prior claim that nature exhibits purposeful order, and has been the more pressing, here I consider only it.

The first point to be made is that the theory of evolution aims to give a naturalistic explanation of the development of species in terms of the persistence of features that confer advantages on their possessors. It does not exclude the possibility that those features exist by design, but it provides a non-design alternative explanation of them. Strictly this focuses on the adaptive utility of a feature showing how things possessing it are better equipped to survive and hence to [85] reproduce; but the process of natural selection does not account for the origination of the feature itself, that fact is left to be explained as a product of random mutation among offspring.

Here is one place where defenders of design arguments may respond. Since it is inconceivable that a heritable adaptive feature could emerge in a single generation it must be the product of iterative reproduction and cumulative selection. But this presupposes regularities in the mechanisms of replication which themselves can hardly be explained as chance products. Otherwise chance is being multiplied many times over into the far outer-reaches of improbability. There is something here deserving of attention[172] but I pass over it now so as to point out that in any case the attempt to account for the ubiquity of beauty by evolution through natural selection can hardly begin, since in order to be 'selected for', a feature has to play a causal role in the survival of the organism, and this either fails to apply, where the natural object in question is not an organism, or else, though it may be such, its aesthetic properties cannot intelligibly benefit or disadvantage it.

An exception to the latter would be where the chances of survival depend upon the predation or support of other organisms. Logically speaking one could imagine a world where everything natural is beautiful because beautiful things are favoured by other

---

David Hume, *Dialogues and Natural History of Religion*, ed. J.C.A. Gaskin (Oxford: Oxford University Press, 1998).

[172] For some further discussion see John Haldane, 'Further Reflections on Theism', in J.J.C. Smart and J.J. Haldane, eds., *Atheism and Theism*, 2nd edn (Oxford: Blackwell, 2003), pp. 233-237.

creatures, but this is an absurd hypothesis regarding our world, not least because most living things seem indifferent to aesthetic properties, and many of the things whose beauty impresses us, such as mountains and oceans, were formed without significant, if any, contribution from living things. So we are returned to the element of chance without supplement of natural selection, and we have to consider how likely it is that undirected physico-chemical processes could more or less invariably produce aesthetic results. Certainly there is no probability measure by which to determine this (un)likelihood. More to the point, however, it is barely intelligible to think of events and processes whose causes are not themselves aesthetic, systematically yielding aesthetic effects, and not 'surface finishes' but form and compositional structure. One might speculate that perhaps the processes of natural formation are subject to aesthetic causality immanent within nature itself. That would be to countenance a sort of pan-aestheticism, analogous to pan-psychism or pan-vitalism. As a causal hypothesis about the recurrent emergence of beauty this is afflicted with the difficulty that apart from it being quite mysterious how nature could be like that, it remains obscure how any such process could work. If at this point one is moved to posit a productive source of beauty in line with the everyday causes with which we are already familiar, namely a designer or artist, then we are brought closer to Tennant's conclusion. Admittedly such an artist of nature would not yet have been shown to be Divine, but in context and taking account, as Tennant does, of other lines of argument theism might then appear the best explanation.[173]

There remains, however, one further iteration of the Darwinian theme, not in the effort to account for beauty itself but to interpret our experiences as products of a kind of interest that can be explained without recourse to any aesthetic reality. This

---

[173] In addition to the beauty and sublimity of nature Tennant argues (pp. 81-103) from (1) the adaptation of human thought to its object, or the harmony of thought and world; (2) the adaptation of parts to whole in organisms; (3) the adaptation of the inorganic world to the production, maintenance and development of living things; and (4) the existence and content of morality; for details see Tennant, *Philosophical Theology*, vol. 2, pp. 81-103. While (2) seems vulnerable to a Darwinian challenge, as may (4); (1) and (3) deserve attention. For efforts in these directions (not related to Tennant's own) see my contributions (chs. 2, 4 and 6) to Smart and Haldane, *Atheism and Theism*. For further discussion of Tennant's argument from beauty see Mark Wynn, *God and Goodness: A Natural Theological Perspective* (London: Routledge, 1999), ch. 1.

conforms to a pattern of reductionist explanation that is currently widely favoured among philosophical materialists. Take some feature of human thought [86] and experience judged to be intrinsically important and significant of some aspect of the world. Let it be the sense of moral conscience, or relatedly that of objective moral demands and prohibitions, or let it be the idea that human life is subject to providence and judgement, or that nature is beautiful. Of themselves, these seem to be real and enduring features of human experience and reflection not temporary impressions or culturally local phenomena, and they seem to call for an explanation, of which the most direct would they are recognitions of objective fact.

If that were so then they would indicate realities transcendent of the material world described and accounted for by the natural sciences. Over the centuries philosophers and theologians have pointed to just such features to argue for the existence of a transcendent domain. Thanks to Darwin and his followers, however, another explanation is available that confines all of this to the material realm, We have already seen an example of this in the previous chapter in Dennett's treatment of religious consciousness, but now the application is to aesthetic experience.

Assume nothing except life, reproduction, variability and environmental pressures and a fully sufficient explanation of these matters is forthcoming. By virtue of the benefits they confer certain features will be enduringly selected for: psychological stability, cooperative skills, group loyalty, the tendency to internalize advantageous social norms, the propensity to regard the world as well ordered, and the liability to be at ease with one's natural environment. Given, then, that these dispositions and beliefs confer selectional advantages it is no surprise that beings who have emerged from generations of environmental and inter-species struggle are possessed of them. Indeed, how could it be otherwise, for animal species that were cognitively ill-adapted in their dealings with the world would not be around to speculate on the fact?

This looks to be an almost irresistible form of explanation, one that promises to sweep away any alternative, and currently it is everywhere to be found: as a species we think, feel, expect, are attracted to, or are repelled by this that, or hope for or dread such and such, *because* such attitudes either confer selectional advantages or conferred them upon ancestors long enough for them to settle in our nature. So powerfully illuminating can this explanatory device seem that observers are often frozen in its am, unable to look away. Yet it should be clear that in form it is quite like the sort of general explanation offered by Marxists in terms of the unconscious struggle between classes, or by Freud in terms of sexual impulses, and if it has the apparent power of these it also has their real weaknesses. In the present case the claim takes the following form. The appearance to us of beauty and sublimity in nature is to be explained by reference to relationships between our ancestors and the environments in which they evolved, and in the advantages conferred by features of these. So, for example. appreciation of the beauty of hills and wooded landscapes is an ancestral legacy from a time when our forebears hunted in the forests and took advantage of the possibilities of concealment and overview.[174] Creatures sensitive to that sort of terrain fared better, reproduced more extensively, and handed down that sensitivity which somehow along the way transmuted itself into an impression of beauty.

[87] What to say of this? First, in common with many such explanations from evolutionary psychology (as from Marxism and psychoanalysis) it is an untestable after-the-fact speculative construction. Second, even if it provided a sufficient explanation of our experiences (which I am about to dispute) it does not provide a necessary condition for them. This second point might seem an obvious logical one but in fact the purveyors of these sorts of explanations typically speak as if only these could provide an account of our experiences. But of course there is another and simpler reason why, for example, we seem to see beauty in nature: *because there is beauty in nature*. Sophisticated advocates of the reductive alternatives recognize that their position is not logically unique, but they assume that alternative explanations in terms of the reality of the apparent phenomena are excluded because the world could not be such as to contain irreducibly aesthetic properties, or moral ones, or the universe be such as to intimate a creator. Why not? Because that would be incompatible with materialism. In other words the reductive explanations are deemed logically sufficient and *de facto* necessary since their proponents have antecedently excluded reference to values or to a creator. This is somewhat reminiscent of those biblical exegetes who interpret talk of miracles as metaphorical rather than literal, notwithstanding that the literary context appears to be a narrative

---

[174] For further (critical) discussion of this approach see John Haldane, 'Some Recent Work in Environmental Aesthetics," *Environmental Values* 3 (1994): 173-182.

in which actual suspensions or reversals of nature would be relevant to the situation described and to the task of demonstrating the special nature of the agent. Why? Because they are committed in advance to denying preternatural efficacy. The technical legal term for such stances is 'prejudice', and these are no less cases of it for being advanced by academic authors.

A fair-minded reader might grant this point while yet feeling the pull of the claim that the reductive accounts fully explain the experiences of value. So let me say why they do not. First, I am not excluding (which would be prejudicial) the possibility that our relations to the world and to one another are influenced by the environments in which our ancestors lived, or by our sexual natures, or by the economic relations which shaped the past and condition the present; but it is one thing to allow these as framing conditions and another to think that they explain the interior of what is framed. Second, and following on from this, if such factors play a role it is in directing attention not in structuring the detail of what is seen. Third, they do not provide norms of critical assessment. Suppose that our liking for wooded hillsides owes something to our ancestors hunting practices, how does that fact explain the differences in response to a variety of forested landscapes which from the point of view of hunting interest are equivalent? Suppose I say of some river valley scene that it is especially engaging for the way in which the rising skyline of the tree tops establishes a dramatic contrast with the plunging incline of the ground towards the river; or that the olive green of the ground is highlighted by the dark tones of timber and canopy; and that the stability of the earth is accentuated by the ever-changing waters of the river; and so on. How is this detailed critical appreciation informed, let alone explained, by the claim that this sort of landscape was useful to my distant hunter-gatherer ancestors in their efforts to see without being seen? The question is rhetorical and stands as a challenge to the reductionist. Until such time as he or she has an answer we have reason to [88] stand by the initial inference to the conclusion that on the basis of our seeming experience of beauty in nature we should take it that indeed nature is beautiful, and that being the case, other explanations of this appearance having been set aside as wanting, we also have reason to attribute this beauty, as in the case of an artwork, to a creator-designer.

4 TRANSCENDENTAL THOMISM

PIERRE ROUSSELOT, S.J. (1878-1915)

Rousselot was born in Nantes, France in 1878. He joined the Jesuit Order in 1895 and received both a doctorate in philosophy from the Sorbonne and holy orders in 1908. Rousselot began teaching at the Catholic Institute of Paris the following year, but only had completed five years as a professor when, in 1914, he was drafted into the French army during World War I. He commenced duties as a Sergeant and was tasked with relaying orders between French army units as well as communicating with the Germans when necessary, the latter of which cost him his life when he was shot down on the way over to the German trenches at Les Éparges in 1915.

Despite his short life Rousselot produced three works that had immense influence on the French and larger Catholic scene: namely, his work on the epistemology of Aquinas that helped to launch Transcendental Thomism, *L'intellectualisme de saint Thomas* (Orne: Librairie de Montligeon, 1908); his work on the Thomistic doctrine of love, *Pour l'histoire du problème de l'amour au Moyen Âge* (Münster: Aschendorff, 1908); and his essay on how the eyes of faith lets us grasp the rationality of religious belief, "Les yeux de la foi," *Recherches de science religieuse* 1 (1910) 241-259, 444-475. These works were to influence fellow Jesuits Henri Bouillard, Henri de Lubac, Avery Dulles, Karl Rahner, as well as the former Jesuit Hans Urs von Balthasar.

For more on the thought of Rousselot consult: McDermott, John, *Love and Understanding: The Relation of Will and Intellect in Pierre Rousselot's Christological Vision* (Rome: Gregorian University Press, 1983); McCool, Gerald A., *From Unity to Pluralism: The Internal Evolution of Thomism* (New York: Fordham University Press, 1989): 39-58; Boersma, Hans, *Nouvelle théologie and Sacramental Ontology: A Return to Mystery* (Oxford: Oxford University Press, 2009): 67-82; and Nicholas, Aidan, *Conversations of Faith and Reason: Modern Catholic Thought from Hermes to Benedict* XVI (Mundelein: Hillenbrand Books, 2011): 151-171.

The first selection is from Pierre Rousselot's *The Problem of Love in the Middle Ages: A Historical Contribution* (Milwaukee: Marquette University Press, 2001), pp. 76-88. In it Rousselot argues that Aquinas rightly sees love as combining self-interested and disinterested components, *amor concupiscentiae* and *amor amicitiae*. This is because for Aquinas God is our final end and we naturally love God for His own sake, and ourselves for His sake. The second selection is from Pierre Rousselot, *The Eyes of Faith* (New York: Fordham University Press, 1990), pp. 23-35 where Rousselot defends his view that faith is rational and at the same time supernatural as the assent of faith simultaneously gives us new eyes with which to grasp the evidence in support of it.

The Problem of Love in the Middle Ages (1908)[175]

[76] What is here called the "problem of love" could be formulated in abstract terms as follows: Is a love that is not egoistic possible? And if it is possible, what is the relation between this pure love of the other and the love of self that seems to be the basis of all natural tendencies? The problem of love is thus analogous to that of knowledge: regarding the latter we ask ourselves whether and how a being can be conscious of that which is not itself; regarding the former we ask ourselves whether and how the appetite of a being can tend toward that which is not its own good. In both cases an affirmative response seems more and more implausible once the notion of consciousness and the notion of appetite are more thoroughly studied.

In the Middle Ages, the problem of love primarily arose in the following form: *Utrum homo naturaliter diligat Deum plus quam semetipsum?* [Whether humans by nature love God more than themselves?][176] Scholasticism, it seems, could not have focused this question into a more suitable formulation because none would have been both so concrete and so profound. For these people, God was, *par excellence*, the Real, Personal, Living Being and the question of His love was continually pressing and real. Moreover, this God, who is the object of the virtuous love commanded of free creatures, is at the same time the author of the natural appetites and the sole final end, uniting in Himself the totality of the Good. If therefore the reconciliation of self-love and the pure love of the other was possible, it seems that it had to be found in the love of God, and that the analysis of this love would consequently give the principles that would allow for the judging of the other "disinterested" affections.

As can easily be seen, however, the universal willingness to proclaim that God alone is the beatifying end of humans left the problem of love unresolved. Clearly everyone back then thought that the best way for humans to love themselves was to surrender themselves entirely to the love of God. Yet to assert, with respect to the eternal [77] life, the real convergence of the two loves (the

---

[175] [Pierre Rousselot, *The Problem of Love in the Middle Age: A Historical Contribution*, translated by Alan Vincelette. Copyright ©2001 by Marquette University Press. All rights reserved. Reprinted with permission of Marquette University Press, http://www.marquette.edu/mupress.]

[176] For references to the first Scholastics see Appendix 1.

love of personal happiness and pure love, i.e. the love of benevolence or friendship) was not to settle this speculative question: are the two kinds of love irreducible or can they be brought back to a common principle? I add moreover, in order to delimit the question as it then arose, that one of the most radical responses to the problem of love was unanimously rejected–that which would have consisted in making the love of God, purely and simply, a means to the love of self. Tradition said too loudly that one must love God for Himself and more than oneself.[177] And if such a love was commanded, it was therefore possible, and no Scholastic would have considered denying it. That is precisely what made the position difficult of those disciples of Augustine and Aristotle who defined the will of humans through the appetite for happiness. It was necessary for them to reconcile with this first principle the possibility of a love of God such that humans were prepared to sacrifice to this Being, who was distinct from themselves, all of their bodily and spiritual goods, indeed their happiness itself.[178]

---

[177] It suffices to refer to the famous chapter of Saint Augustine on the *fruenda* [*things that are to be enjoyed*] and the *utenda* [*things that are to be used*]; this distinction, as is well-known, provided the Master of the Sentences [Peter Lombard] with the beginning and the division of his work. Note especially the assertion: "sed nec se ipso quisquam frui debet, si liquido advertas; quia nec se ipsum diligere, sed propter illum quo fruendum est ..." [but no one should enjoy oneself, if you take note clearly, because no one should love oneself except for the sake of Him who ought to be enjoyed (i.e. God) ...] (Augustine, *De Doctrina Christiana*, b. I, c. 22, n. 21; PL. 34, 26). Another text often cited is that of Pseudo-Prosper (Julianus Pomerius, *De Vita Contemplativa*, III, c. 25; PL. 59, 508): "si vero propter illa quae praestat amatur, non utique gratis amatur: quia iam illud propter quod diligitur, ei, quod dictu quoque nefas est, antefertur" [If, however, He (God) is loved for the sake of what He bestows, He is not loved gratuitously at all, because then that for the sake of which He is loved is preferred to Him, which is to say something wicked].

[178] The love of God, such as Christianity presented it, necessarily implied a certain contempt of self, a renunciation of oneself. And this habit of Christian thought brought several authors to look upon sacrifice and suffering as the essential elements of all love (see Part 2, Chapter 2, of this work). For those who wanted to reconcile the love of God and the love of self, as long as this only concerned the sacrifice of temporal goods and the mortification of evil appetites, the task was not too difficult. As for the idea of a possible sacrifice of spiritual goods, this was not put forward in the Middle Ages as clearly as it was at a later date.

[78] Confronted with the problem thus defined, two conceptions of love divided the minds of the Middle Ages. We can call them the *physical* [*physique*] conception and the *ecstatic* [*extatique*] conception of love. *Physical*, it goes without saying, does not here signify *corporeal*. Even the most resolute advocates of this way of thinking regard sensible love [*l'amour sensible*] merely as a reflection, a feeble image of spiritual love. *Physical* here signifies *natural* and serves to designate the doctrine of those who base all real or possible loves on the necessary propensity of natural beings to seek their own good. For such authors, although hidden, there is between the love of God and the love of self a fundamental identity. Hence they are the twofold expression of one identical appetite, the deepest and the most natural of all, or better yet, the sole natural appetite. This way of thinking is, for example, that of Hugh of Saint-Victor in his treatise *De Sacramentis* [*On the Sacraments*] and Saint Bernard in the *De Diligendo Deo* [*On Loving God*]: it also finds very strong backing in the Neoplatonic doctrines of Pseudo-Dionysius. Finally, it is made precise and systematized by St. Thomas Aquinas. It is St. Thomas, inspired by Aristotle, who brings out its fundamental principle, showing that *unity* (rather than *individuality*) is the *raison d'être*, measure, and ideal of love. He reestablishes, as a result, the perfect continuity between the love of desire [*l'amour de convoitise*] and the love of friendship [*l'amour d'amitié*].–The *physical* conception of love therefore could equally-well be called the Greco-Thomist conception of love.

[79] The *ecstatic* conception of love, on the contrary, is especially pronounced in authors the more they exercise care in severing all the connections that seem to link the love of the other to egoistic inclinations. Love, for the supporters of this school, is all the more perfect, is all the more *love*, the more thoroughly it

---

Nevertheless, the most famous of these "impossible suppositions" that were debated during the period of Quietism, the one which consisted in offering to God the sacrifice of one's personal beatitude, could not be completely ignored. This "impossible supposition" was in fact suggested by two passages of the Bible: Exodus 32:32 "Aut dimitte eis hanc noxam, aut dele me de libro tuo, quem scripsisti" [Either forgive them this sin, or erase me from Your book that You have written] and Romans 9:3 "Optabam ... ego anathema esse a Christo pro fratribus meis" [I wished ... that I was anathema to Christ for my brethren]. We see how it could appear difficult to reconcile the expressions of Moses and Saint Paul with the classical doctrine of the beatitude.

places the subject "outside of itself."[179] It follows that a love that is perfect and truly worthy of the name calls for a real *duality* of terms [*termes*]. The paradigm of true love is no longer, as it was for the previous authors, the one that every natural being necessarily bears for itself. Rather here love is both extremely violent and extremely free. It is free because no reason can be found for it other than itself, independent as it is from the natural appetites. It is violent because it runs counter to these appetites and tyrannizes them. Indeed it seems it could only be satisfied by the destruction of the loving subject, by its absorption in the object loved. Being such, love has no other aim than itself and everything in the human being is sacrificed for its sake, including happiness and reason. This ecstatic conception of love has been set forth with infinite artistry, fervor, and subtlety by some of those mystics who had a passion for dialectics and who were the most original figures of the twelfth century. It is encountered in the school of Saint-Victor, in the Order of Citeaux [the Cistercian monks], in the school of Abelard, and traces of it are recognizable in the Scholasticism of the Franciscans.

The texts that we will cite and the logical connections that we will try to highlight are sufficient, we believe, to legitimize our classification of the medieval theories of love. It is clear, however, that this division into two groups, or according to two directions of thought, must not be looked upon as corresponding to an absolute partition. Still on the whole it is a true distinction, and one that can be a useful guide when studying individual thoughts so infinitely nuanced. Furthermore, we will find the same authors (Hugh of Saint-Victor and St. Bernard, for example), cited in succession as proponents of the *physical* [80] conception and the *ecstatic* conception of love. Such a procedure is necessary when one studies the history of ideas in the twelfth century. In those times, when speculation was still entirely academic [*scolaire*], the defined concepts readily found themselves in disagreement with some profound intuitions. These intuitions, while missing from the systematic treatises that were then initiated, did manifest themselves in powerful locutions in the very numerous sermons, meditations, confessions, and lyrical outpourings that this century

---

[179] It is in this sense that the Pseudo-Areopagite [Pseudo-Dionysius] calls love "ecstatic" (*Noms Divins*, c. 4, n. 13; PG. 3, 712). This expression moreover was accepted by writers from all of the schools; its originator himself in actuality conceives of love in the manner of the Neoplatonists [that is to say as physical] (see pp. 118-19 [herein]).

has bequeathed to us. And the historian finds traces of them in later elaborated systems. It is therefore the historian's right to seek for them in these poems taking the form of passionate prose, where they preexisted perhaps merely in a metaphorical and sentimental state. Only the obscure psychological labor of the contemplatives can explain (since this alone has rendered it possible) the clear conflict of ideas that is to follow.[180]

Besides, our ambition here was never to write a history of the two conceptions of love even if this only concerned the twelfth and thirteenth centuries, the period to which the present work is restricted. Our intention was simply to assemble some material for those who [81] would attempt such a study, and to shed some light on certain points involving the hidden logical relations that made these ideas converge or clash with each other. The results of our research have been divided up into two sections.

The first part is dedicated to the *physical* conception of love. Here above all, we intend to clearly bring out what is original in the solution of St. Thomas. For this reason, after some brief observations on the elements of this solution found in antiquity and in the Middle Ages, we examine the sketches of the *physical* conception made by Hugh of St. Victor and St. Bernard in the twelfth century. After such an investigation, we can better

---

[180] If one wanted, for example, to write a *Philosophy of Saint Bernard*, this study would naturally be divided into two parts: *explicit Philosophy* and *implicit Philosophy*. The first would be brief, dry, and in short, of little interest. It is the second that would allow St. Bernard to be assigned his true place in the history of Christian thought by isolating his original contribution. We further on cite several passages from the *Sermons on the Song of Songs*. The oratorical exaltation of these pieces is precisely what allows the metaphysics latent in the interior life of the author to find its expression in formulations of unexpected precision. These sermons have all the freedom of a solitary outpouring, while the presence of an audience stimulates the boldness of expression: consequently, the imparted, the conventional, the traditional, drops out insofar as it is not incorporated into the sermon. Here one speaks as one sees fit.—It is admittedly a difficult and delicate task to extract a "metaphysics" from all this lyricism, but it is a task necessary to the history of ideas. Thus, to take an example from the systematic conceptions of the following century, the idea of the *real possession* by love, so completely foreign to antiquity but which plays such a large role in the Franciscan theories of the will, has been rendered possible only through the continual usage of certain metaphors in the twelfth century (see Part 2, Chapter 4 of this work).

comprehend the role of the new principles taken from Aristotle in allowing St. Thomas to conceive of a love that is in perfect continuity with self-love, and yet in spite of that is truly disinterested.

In the second part, with the aid of texts that we hold to be particularly significant, we highlight the principal characteristics of the "ecstatic" conception of love, and relate to them certain systematic speculations stemming from them in the philosophical or theological domain.

The Physical or Greco-Thomist Conception of Love

Thomist Solution to the Problem of Love

Theory of the Whole and the Part

[82] *Amicabilia quae sunt ad alterum venerunt ex amicabilibus quae sunt ad seipsum* [The friendly feelings that we bear for another have arisen from the friendly feelings that we bear for ourselves.] This statement of the Philosopher [Aristotle] in Book 9 of the *Nicomachean Ethics*,[181] which could serve as the common motto of all the proponents of the "physical" conception of love, is open to two different interpretations. One can take the words in their immediate and superficial [83] sense, and say that self-love is only a necessary starting point, an occasional moving cause, that gives in all humans the first impetus to the power of love. Or, by digging deeper and searching not only for the first occasion, but also for the *formal reason* of love, one can maintain that an appetition[182] is conceivable only as a seeking of oneself.

---

[181] τὰ φιλικὰ δὲ τὰ πρὸς τοὺς φίλους [πέλας] ... ἔοικεν ἐκ τῶν πρὸς ἑαυτὸν ἐληλυθέναι [And the friendly feelings that we bear for our friends ... seem to have proceeded from the friendly feelings that we bear for ourselves] (*Eth. Nic.*, IX, 4, 1166a1-2, ed. of Berlin). I cite, of course, the text of the *Nicomachean Ethics* that the Scholastics were acquainted with, that is to say the translation of Hermann the German [Hermann of Carinthia].

[182] It is perhaps not without merit to recall that according to the common doctrine of the Middle Ages love is included and presupposed in every appetition. Aelred of Rievaulx distinguishes three things in the soul: memory, knowledge, "et amorem sive voluntatem" [and love or rather will] (*Speculum Caritatis*, PL. 195, 507). See William of St. Thierry: "Quantum enim ad animum, amore movemur, quocunque movemur" [For with respect to the soul, we are moved by love wherever we are moved] (*Exp. in Cantica*, c. I, PL. 180, 492). St. Thomas, *In Div.*

This not only makes the altruistic inclinations derive from self-love, but also reduces them to it, in a manner that remains to be clarified. If the first option is adopted, it is not too difficult to side [84] with the proponents of "ecstatic" love. If the second is chosen, the altruistic affections, it seems, must be looked upon only as imitations or participations of the egoistic inclination. The love that a singular substance bears for itself then becomes the measure, model, and ground of all the other loves that can be found in it. And it is here that it becomes difficult to explain the facts that experience establishes or that dogma presupposes. It seems that the love of friendship [*l'amour d'amitié*] and the love of longing [*l'amour de désir*] or desire [*convoitise*] can be distinguished only as words.

St. Thomas teaches that the tendency toward the final end specifies the will. Wherever the will is turned, it is the appetite for the final end that impels it to act. Now, this final end, this perfect good, this universal and necessary driving force [*moteur*] of the will, is happiness. In asserting this, St. Thomas only makes precise

---

Nom., c. 4, l. 9: "Est autem amor prima et communis radix omnium appetitivarum operationum, quod patet inspicienti per singula" [Now love is the first and universal foundation of all appetitive operations, which is evident upon inspecting each case] (Fretté, v. XXIX, p. 451). See, ibid., p. 452, and 1a 2ae q. 28 a. 6: "Omne agens agit propter finem aliquem ... Finis autem est bonum desideratum et amatum unicuique. Unde manifestum est quod omne agens, quodcunque sit, agit quamcunque actionem ex aliquo amore" [Every agent acts for the sake of some end ... Now an end is the good that is desired and loved by each agent. Therefore it is clear that every agent whatsoever performs every action out of a love of some sort]. See also 2^a 2^{ae} q. 125 a. 2. Love, taken in this broad sense, consists of even these transitory "*predilections*" [*benevolences*] which are distinct from love taken in the strict sense of a habitual and strong *passion* (stabilimentum voluntatis in bono volito [the fixation of the will in the good that is willed], St. Thomas, *Pot.* q. 9 a. 9; see 2a 2ae q. 27 a. 2, and col. 213 and 216 in the first editions of the *Summa Contra Gentiles* published by Uccelli, Paris, Migne, 1858). Love in the strict sense is, according to this doctrine, a special case wherein conditions favorable to amplification allow love in the broad sense to be more effectively studied.–It is love in the sense of a deep-seated passion in the soul that is the subject matter of the famous treatise of Andrew the Chaplain [Andreas Capellanus], as his definition shows: "Amor est passio quaedam innata procedens ex visione et *immoderata cogitatione* formae alterius sexus ..." [Love is a certain innate passion arising from the sight of and *uncontrolled thinking about* the form of the other sex ...] (*De Amore Libri*, III, ed. Trojel, Hauniae, 1892, b. I, c. 1, p. 3).

the Augustinian doctrine of beatitude, which fits quite naturally into his Peripatetic philosophy.

> It is necessary that all that humans long for, they would long for for the sake of the final end ... In this way the final end in relation to the moving appetite is like the prime mover in relation to other movements. Now it is evident that secondary moving causes do not move except insofar as they are moved by the prime mover. Likewise secondary objects of the appetite do not move the appetite except as ordered to the primary object of the appetite, which is the final end (1a 2ae [85] q. 1 a. 6). The final end is happiness, which all desire according to Augustine (1a 2ae q. 1 a. 8 Sed Contra). The perfect good ... is the final end] (ibid., a. 6). Now the ground of the common happiness is that it is the perfect good as has been said. For since the good is the object of the will, the perfect good is that thing that wholly satisfies this will. Likewise to desire happiness is nothing other than to desire that the will be satisfied, which everyone wants (1a 2ae q. 5 a. 8). (See, in addition the first questions of 1a 2ae, articles 1 and 2 of q. 10, and 1 q. 82 a. 1 and 2; *Ver.* q. 22 a. 5 and 6; *Mal.* q. 6 a. 4.)

It seems merely to be drawing the legitimate conclusion of the texts just cited, to assert, as the author does elsewhere, that the love of self is the measure of all the other loves and surpasses them all.

> The final end of any maker as a maker, is itself. For we use things made by us for our own sakes, and, if ever a human makes something for another, this has reference to his or her [86] own good, either as useful, as delightful, or as good in itself (3 *CG.* 17, 8). All other things being equal, each individual loves him or herself more than someone else, a sign of which is that the closer a thing is to someone the more naturally it is loved] (1 *CG.* 102, 3). [And that which is highest in any kind is the measure of all those of that kind, as is made clear by the Philosopher in *Metaphysics* X. Now the highest in the kind of human love is the love by which one loves oneself. And so it is necessary to take from this love the measure of every love by which one loves another. Whence in *Nicomachean Ethics* IX the Philosopher says that "The friendly feelings that we have toward others ..." etc. (*Quodl.* 5 a. 6; see *In 9 Eth.*, l. 4). Properly speaking, friendship is not had for oneself; rather friendship is something greater, because friendship implies a union with another. For Dionysius says in the *Divine Names*, c. 4, that love is a unifying power. But with respect to itself, each

228

individual is a unity, which is something superior to union. Accordingly, as unity is the foundation of union, so too the love by which one loves oneself is the form and root of friendship. For we have friendship toward others insofar as we are related to them as we are to ourselves. For in *Nicomachean Ethics* IX it is said that the friendly feelings ... etc. (2a 2ae q. 25 a. 4). Likewise 3 d. 28 q. 1 a. 6.[183]

It is in accordance with these notions that St. Thomas defines love:

[87] On account of this ... something is said to be loved to the extent that the appetite of the lover is related toward it as it is toward its own good. Thus the very relation or adaptation of the appetite toward something as toward its own good is called love ... We love each thing insofar as it is our good (*In Div. Nom.*, c. 4, l. 9, Fretté, v. XXIX, pp. 451-52).

For St. Thomas, accordingly, it is the *coaptatio appetitus* [adaptation of the appetite], *connaturalitas* [connaturality], or the *sicut ad se* [as to oneself] that is the true definition of love. If he sometimes appears (3 *CG*. 90, 6, ibid., 153, 2; 4 *CG*. 21, 8; 1 q. 20 a. 1 ad 3) to place the last word on love in the *velle bonum* [willing of the good] (see Aristotle, *Rhetoric*, II, c. 4), this is only to assert the same thing in different words, since "the good" can be described in no other way than as the object of natural desires: *id quod omnia desiderant* [that which all desire]. (The discussion of the relation between love and the *velle bonum* [willing of the good] in 2a 2ae q. 27 a. 2 sheds great light on this point, even though this discussion does not concern love in the broad sense).

Now given all of this, how is it that humans can love God more than themselves? One response is simply that humans recognize in God a good more excellent than themselves, since their own being is only an imitation of the being of God and a gift of divine goodness. Yet to respond in this manner is to display a difference

---

[183] St. Thomas also maintains that one can no more hate oneself (1a 2ae q. 29 a. 4) than one can hate the good or the beatitude (ibid.; see 1a 2ae q. 5 a. 8, q. 10 a. 2, etc.). The supernatural precepts are in agreement with the natural inclinations: humans *must* love themselves more than they love others (*Quodl.* 8, a. 8: Peccaret in ordine caritatis magis alium quam se diligens) [One would have sinned in the order of charity by loving another more than one loves oneself]. See *Sermones Dominicales*, Serm. 25), where one should love oneself more even than one's spouse (2a 2ae q. 26 a.11 ad 2).

of intellectual assessment that can leave intact the primacy of the love of self. For if indeed we love this more excellent good for ourselves, friendship still remains reduced to desire.[184] In order to avoid this reduction, one would need to find a principle that would bring humans to tend to the good of God just as spontaneously, just as naturally, just as *directly*, as they tend to their own good. Now, as has already been said, there is no other principle of direct and true love besides unity.

It is precisely this concept of unity that St. Thomas utilizes in order to resolve this difficulty. Here is then how he responds to the decisive question: *Does the created soul naturally love God more than itself?*

> To love God above all things and more than oneself is natural not only for an angel and humans but also for any creature, according as it can love either sensibly or naturally. In fact natural inclinations can especially be discerned in these things that are done naturally, without deliberation. For in this way each thing acts in nature as it is naturally fitted to do. Now we see that each part by a certain natural inclination operates for the good of the whole, even with risk or damage to itself, as is clear when someone exposes a hand to a sword to protect the head, upon which the welfare of the whole body is dependent. Hence it is natural that each part in its own way should love the whole more than itself. Hence, both in accordance with this natural inclination and in accordance with political virtue, the good citizen exposes him or herself to the risk of death on behalf of the common good. Now it is clear that God is the common good of the whole universe and of all its parts. Hence each creature in its own way naturally loves God more than itself: insensible beings, for instance, naturally, irrational animals sensitively, and the creature of reason through the intellectual love that is called *dilectio* (*Quodl.* 1, a. 8).

---

[184] *Quodl.* 1, a. 8. The solution mentioned is that of William of Auxerre (see Appendix 1).

"The Eyes of Faith" (1910)[185]

[23] Since the problem has been framed in this fashion, many modern theologians look for a middle term to use as a kind of "schematism" in order to explain the meaning of infused faith (supernatural power of knowing) with dogmatic faith (the ensemble of objects known). They admit that there may or even must be present in the believer a "scientific faith" or, to use a more general expression and one that also corresponds better to their thought, a faith that is naturally acquired and legitimately certain.[186] They hold that reason can discover the specification of

---

[185] [Pierre Rousselot, *The Eyes of Faith: With Rousselot's Answer to Two Attacks*, translated by John M. McDermott and Avery Dulles. Copyright © 1990 by Fordham University Press. All rights reserved. Used with permission of Fordham University Press, www.fordhampress.com.]

[186] The theologians of the most diverse schools agree on this opinion. Mr. Alfred Vacant writes, "It is generally admitted that it is not impossible for man to adhere to the revealed truths because of the authority of God who reveals, through natural assents that would not constitute supernatural faith, although they would in several days resemble it" (*Études théologiques sur les constitutions du Concile de Vatican* (Paris: Delhomme et Briguet, 1895), volume 2, p. 74. Mr. Jean Vincent Bainvel says, "Although theologians admit and common sense teaches that there may exist a purely natural faith in God's word ..., it will possess an absolute assurance, acquiescence, and certitude" (*La foi et l'acte de foi*, 2nd ed (Paris: P. Lethielleux, 1908), p. 159; cf. p. 172). Likewise Father Ambroise Gardeil: "That is why all theologians admit that a natural belief, a 'scientific faith' in the revealed truth, is the normal result, possible in itself, of the search for credibility" (*La crédibilité et l'apologétique* (Paris: Lecoffre, 1908), p. 23). Likewise Father Hilaire de Barenton, a follower of the Franciscan School ("Les derniers travaux d'apologétique," *Études Franciscaines* 20 (September, 1908): 239); likewise Father Louis Billot, whose affirmations are particularly clear (*De virtutibus infusis*, 2nd edn (Rome: J. Martin, 1905), volume 1, pp. 76-77), and so on. They speak also, quite logically, of a purely rational demonstration of credibility, by which they mean *either* the possibility of demonstrating the very fact of divine revelation *or* the possibility of demonstrating the legitimacy of the act of faith (performed in virtue of a reflex principle even though the fact of divine attestation is not rigorously demonstrated. See the many authors quoted by Father Étienne Hugueny in "L'évidence de crédibilité," *Revue Thomiste* 17 (May-June, 1909): 275-298. The demonstration of credibility (in the wide or strict sense) and the possibility of a natural faith that is certain go together. For all admit that revealed statements offer an intelligible meaning to natural reason; hence it seems to me that one cannot attribute to this reason the power of

the truths of faith by itself, without grace, through a demonstration of credibility that shows with certitude that we must adhere to the Church of Jesus Christ as God's messenger on earth. In this way, reason presents its object to supernatural faith ready-made.

The doctrine of these modern theologians is by no means Hermesianism. They know that dead faith is a grace. They may, like Hermes, think that reason can by means of demonstrable credibility, discover the *material* of faith's object. They may even acknowledge the possibility of a natural faith that not only is certain but, *psychologically speaking, perfectly resembles supernatural faith*.[187] But they do not thereby reduce the knowledge of faith to this [semblance]. They accept, as it were, "twin" faiths, one supernatural, the other natural, the latter lesser in value, solidity, and certitude than the former but nevertheless co-extensive with it, either actually or potentially, with respect to its object.

[24] These theologians do not claim to force the Holy Spirit to adapt Himself to their approach. Having explained—almost always with great dialectical finesse, often with exceptional analytical skill—how they envisage the mechanism of the act of faith, they rarely fail to add that their system does not exhaust the wealth of the divine ingenuity. If natural certitude turns out to be impossible for some souls, grace can find its own path and make up for that weakness.[188] Some say this only in passing, after exerting

---

holding fast to the *fact* of revelation and deny it the power of giving to its *content* a proportionate adhesion.

In order to know the philosophical roots of this concept of a natural faith it is worthwhile to outline its historical origins. We will try to do so in a separate note. Let us remark here that this conception has, in its most rigorous form, penetrated into current teaching: among the faithful who have some cultural background, among intelligent youngsters, in Catholic high schools, etc., many conceive of the act of faith as including an act of natural knowledge. "I am a Catholic, because the divinity of the Church is *scientifically* demonstrated by the prophets, the miracles, the monuments both of the Old and of the New Testament" (from a latter of the father of a family, quoted in *La Croix* of December 2, 1909, page 1, last column; italics in the original).

[187] Thus Father Louis Billot, in the passage cited in note 5.

[188] In the address delivered, on June 11, 1870, before twenty-four delegates of the Council, Johann Baptist Franzelin said about the Scheme of the theologians: "We must also hold that God's inner grace supplies what is lacking for *such kinds of people* (the illiterate), in the external

themselves fully to make their explanation of natural certitude fit every case imaginable.[189] Others develop an explicit theory of what they call gratuitous *surrogates of credibility* [*suppléances de la crédabilité*].[190] But almost all of them continue to reduce the normal act of faith to one of these types: either the supernatural act of faith virtually *contains* and elevates a natural act of faith[191] or it has been at least preceded by a natural authentication of the fact of revelation.

It is obvious that such a doctrine makes it difficult to explain the faith of children and of the unlearned. For in the case of the learned a number of authors see no difficulty.[192] The documents of the Church are there; they require that faith be not blind but reasonable, and all theologians accept the principle that St. Thomas formulated as follows: *non crederemus, nisi videremus esse credendum* ["we would not believe if we did not see that we ought to believe"]. But in the case of the young villager brought up on the catechism, how can we claim that he possesses either a scientific faith or a rational demonstration, or in any event the perfect certitude of credibility based on reasons that are absolutely valid? And how could any such thing be claimed of the native whose belief relies on the word of a missionary? We need more

---

presentation of the faith" (*Acta*, col. 1623A). The words that I have italicized show that to his mind this help is accidental. This is shown even more clearly by the way he speaks elsewhere (*De traditione et scriptura*, 2nd edn (Romae: De Propaganda Fide, 1875), p. 684).

189 Everyone admits most willingly that *in practice* it is difficult or morally impossible to believe in Christianity with a purely natural faith (Franzelin, *De traditione et scriptura* , p. 688; Billot, *De virtutibus infusis*, volume 1, pp. 77-78). So one might wonder why we should argue about an abstract possibility when we agree about what really happens. Why insist so much that we should speak of a *physical impossibility* and not only of a *moral impossibility*? The discussion may not matter much for the individual apostate; it matters a great deal for the theory of religious knowledge that looks wholly different according to which opinion one accepts.

190 See Father Ambroise Gardeil in his clear and impressive book *La crédibilité et l'apologétique* (Paris: Lecoffre, 1908), pp. 97ff.

191 I borrow this formula that perfectly characterizes the theory of scientific faith from Mr. Jean de Séguier, "L'acte de foi," *Annales de Philosophie Chrétienne* 37 (December, 1897): 276.

192 "Nulla difficultas quoad doctors" ["No difficulty insofar as the learned are concerned"] (Camillus Mazzella, *De virtutibus infusis*, 3rd edn (Romae: De Propoganda Fide, 1884), p. 794; cf. p. 394); Santo Schiffini, *De virtutibus infusis* (Freiburg: Herder, 1904), p. 262.

than a *psychological* explanation purporting to show how belief or credulity operates, for any such explanation [25] would apply to the Moslem's faith as well as to the Christian's. If the young Catholic is right in believing his mother or his pastor, is the young Protestant wrong in believing his minister or his mother?

Hence, when the answer is given by appealing to "respective certitudes," based when necessary upon "reflex practical principles,"[193] the difficulty does not seem to vanish. Buddhists and Shintoists have "respective certitudes," and Socrates appealed to a "reflex principle" in order to conclude that everyone ought to worship the gods of his city. An absolute speculative assent, even of the natural order, requires a perfect objective certitude as its foundation. I would fear that translating it might weaken the following proposition of St. Thomas': "The proper motive of the intellect is the true that possesses infallible truth. Hence, whenever the intellect is moved by some fallible sign, there is some disorder in it, whether it be moved perfectly or imperfectly."[194] Is it fitting that faith be based upon or make its entry by way of a disorder?

Hence it seems necessary to appeal to the light of grace. What could be more natural in this sort of question? Some explicitly claim that they will explain credibility without grace. Others, like Suarez, for example, believe that they cannot do without grace, at least in explaining the belief of the unlearned and of children.

[26] One might wonder why all theological writers have not adopted this approach and why they persist in multiplying all manner of subtle investigations and hypotheses to explain how the reasons for believing can be perceived in a purely natural way. It looks as though the reason may be that those who appealed to

---

[193] "As for me," writes Domenico Viva, "I share the opinion of [Juan de] Lugo and others that there is no need to appeal to a supernatural illumination by the Holy Spirit to explain the presence in the young and the ignorant of a sufficient evidence of credibility as distinguished from a mere probability. ... Thus everyone argues within himself ...: I who know nothing about some things, especially in the field of religion, must follow the judgment of those who are wise and pious. But the pastor is wise and pious. So I must follow his judgment and I am bound to believe what he tells me to believe ..." (*Damnatae theses*, prop. XXI of Innocent XI, n. 10). Such is the usual explanation taken over by an infinite number of authors. What a shaky foundation for supernatural faith! Where is the difference from the unbeliever? What if the youngster prefers the schoolteacher to the pastor?

[194] *De veritate*, q. 18, a. 6.

grace did not show clearly enough how it can create perfect certitude without upsetting the psychological context, without injecting, along with grace, new notions or new objects.

To my mind it is a prejudice, philosophical in nature, that has blocked their path. They had a feeling for the difficulty. They paid attention to the facts. How often admirable, in their ponderings, is that supple argumentative agility, along with that feel for concrete psychology, that Balzac so prized in members of the Catholic clergy. But we must not fail to notice something else. Most of these writers restrict themselves to *analyzing* the believer's conscious states: they take account only of the elements of representation and overlook the synthetic activity of the intelligence, whether natural or supernaturalized. In Scholastic language we would say that they consider exclusively *id quod repraesentatur* ["that which is represented"] and never mention the *lumen* ["light"], *id quad inclinat ad assensum* ["that which moves us to assent"]. Some ochers, it is true, do consider this aspect. But when, following St. Thomas, they speak of an assent that is given by virtue of an attraction, they regard it too much as something needed to *supplement*[195] external motives rather than something that illuminates them. It would seem, for these writers, as though we were dealing with attractions that are consciously experienced, satisfactions grasped reflexively, lines of coherence qua *represented*.[196] Some, as a result, deploy all their inventive ingenuity to discover objective elements in the *representative* consciousness of the Catholic child that would be [27] lacking in the Protestant youngster, while others incur the charge of reducing the proofs of faith to a mixture of probabilities and subjective preferences, and of depicting the unlearned as believing only by virtue of a blissful superficiality. It seems as if no one saw clearly enough how a supernatural illumination could combine with the genuine efficacy of external signs, in such fashion that both elements would be integrated into *one* selfsame *certitude*. For both groups true intellectual certitude was still being modeled as the mind's possession of representative concepts that could be

---

[195] Some authors, however, such as Suárez, *De fide*, disp. 4, sect. 5, nn. 9-10, understand the influence of grace as intrinsic, as complementary to the motives.

[196] John of St. Thomas, *Cursus theologicus in 2am 2ae, De fide*, disp. 3, a. 1, s. 2, n. 3: *"From the side of the object it adds a certain representation* by penetrating not into the truth, but into the fitness of the object to move us to assent." Emphasis added.

equated by *substituting equivalent concepts.*[197]

But even if we limit our consideration to natural knowledge, we know that such a conception does not sufficiently account for the facts. The real movement of the intelligence remains unexplained unless we view it, above all, as an active power of synthesis.

Let us stay with the clearest, most ordinary facts. Take the case of two scientists, both looking for the exact law that explains a set of obscure phenomena and both directed in their search by the thought of the same hypothesis. Or consider two detectives, both examining the scene of a crime and both inclined to suspect a certain individual. Let us assume that the same phenomenon comes to the attention of both scientists, or that the identical detail is simultaneously noticed by both detectives. It does not follow that both will necessarily arrive at identical conclusions.

---

[197] A recent discussion has pitted against each other, about the question mentioned here, two theologians of great authority, Mr. Jean Bainvel and Father Ambroise Gardeil (*Revue Pratique d'Apologétique* 6 (May, June, August, November, 1908). I am not trying to summarize their suggestive and nuanced explanations. May I be allowed nevertheless to say that the impression produced by these debates seems to me clearly to confirm what I am saying in the text. To my mind Mr. Bainvel grounds perfectly the proposition which he states in this way: "The unlearned possess really sufficient reasons for believing, although they are unable to systematize them. ... We should speak not so much ... of 'subjective surrogates' to explain credibility as of some help that makes us directly and spontaneously perceive motives that are really valid" ("Un essai de systematization apologétique," *Revue Pratique d'Apologétique* 6 (May 1, 1908): 178). It is evident, moreover, from the arguments of his adversary that without grace this perception is not certain (which Mr. Bainvel would not deny, at least as far as the question of *fact* is concerned). So the point is to see how grace can cause someone to perceive, with an objective and true certitude, reasons that would only be probable for natural intelligence left to its own resources, to indicate for grace a role between the two roles which are often the only ones that are considered: *objective instruction* or revelation (opposed to experience), *subjective* or affective *impulsion* (impossible to prove). The first part of this study tries to state precisely wherein this middle role consists; the next part will consider the Thomistic theory of knowledge by way of attraction, to which Father Gardeil so rightly draws our attention. We shall try to determine the conditions on which these attractions can fulfill the role that is defined here, that role being not exactly to *supply for*, but rather to *effect*, knowledge, to *make us see* and not to *exempt us from seeing*.

One of them may immediately leap to certainty, while the other remains in the dark. Yet materially–that is, in its individuality–the new fact is represented in like fashion in both minds. But one man has perceived it, not as a raw and isolated phenomenon, but *as a clue* pointing to the law or conclusion both were seeking. He has perceived that fact in its connection with the law, made the synthesis of fact with law, and [28] instantly affirmed that connection as real. Not so the other. He "does not see." He has the same representations of both the hypothesis and the new fact, and with the same material accuracy as his colleague; he may even *think* of their relation if his partner explains it to him. Yet the connection escapes him; the synthesis remains unmade. So the difference between the one who sees and the one who does not does not consist in any difference in the notes of the representation, but in the greater or lesser power of their intellectual activity. But, it may be objected, could not the difference reside in the knowledge one of them has acquired, or the experience he has accumulated? Not necessarily, for it may derive uniquely from inborn talent. But even were the difference to derive from experience, our explanation would remain true in principle. For in our example the one who sees does not, at the instant of seeing, have the whole of his knowledge or experience before his mind's eye; his knowledge is present as *perceiving*, not as *perceived*.[198] And so we are once more driven back to some difference in the intellectual faculty itself.

The same thing for faith, for the *lumen fidei* ["the light of faith"], when we perceive something as credible. Short of a miracle this light does not provide us with new objects for knowing; *determinatio fidei est exauditu* ["faith is specified by what we hear"]. But it accounts for our perceiving the connection, making the synthesis, giving the assent. The sufficient reason for these three operations, which, we shall presently show, really come down to one, is not located in the *representations* entertained. Imagine two nearly identical psychological contexts: to explain the luminous certitude of one person and the persisting obscurity of the other, the presence or absence of a new faculty of perception is sufficient. From a different angle, consider two children who [29] only know the "faith of their fathers"; their respective assents *when analyzed* may disclose no difference between them, and yet those assents need not be equally valid. The one may possess

---

[198] If knowledge is ἕξις [habit], it should be considered here, not as *having*, but as what Scholasticism understands by *habitus*.

legitimate certitude; the other, false opinion. To come back to the first case, observe that the unbeliever may have an exact representation of each one of the propositions in terms of which the one who *sees* endeavors to explain to him in detail the connection between them, to make it intelligible for him, even to reduce it, as far as such a reduction is possible, by substituting equivalent terms. The exact representation does not yet amount to assent. One of the characters in *Loss and Gain* [by John Henry Newman] tells Charles Reding: "I enter into your reasons; I cannot, for the life of me, see how you come to your conclusion." And the convert answers, "To me, on the other hand, Carlton, it is like two and two make four."[199] It should not constitute a real theological difficulty *that the affirmation can differ although the represented notes are alike*, since theology conceives of faith as a supernatural cognitive activity.

There is more to extract from the simple example that we have been using. We should also consider the *reciprocal priority between the affirmation of the law and the perception of the fact that serves as a clue*. Recent theorists of the logic of discovery have highlighted this peculiarity. We do not first perceive a proof as such. and only then what has been proved. Rather, we sec both conjointly, grasping the general law as it subsumes the particular case. Depending on one's point of view, the particular is both cause and effect, proof and application, clue to and consequence of the law. The law is seen through the clue, but it is only *in* seeing the law that the clue is seen as clue. [30] The fact cannot be known *as a* clue unless we affirm the law.

If the idea of such a reciprocal causality puzzles some readers, I would ask them to consider a case in which we are no longer looking for an explanation or trying to verify a hypothesis, but trying, rather, to *enter into a mind*, so to speak, to grasp the inner harmony of a psychological makeup. I may have read *Hamlet* ten times, without understanding Hamlet. I take up the play again and, lo and behold, an utterance that I had hitherto read without really grasping it all at once awakens me to the intuition of the character as an intelligible whole, of a reality that makes sense. "I've got it! That's it!" I exclaim. The perception of that utterance *as a clue, as meaningful*, is simultaneous in time with the perception of the character as a whole. Logically, it comes first, as truly causing my act of understanding; it is the clue that

---

[199] John Henry Newman, *Loss and Gain* (London: James Burns, 1848), p. 324.

introduces me into Hamlet, *makes* me understand Hamlet. But just as logically, from another point of view, it follows upon the understanding; perceiving an utterance as disclosing a character trait makes sense only if the character is already known.

One might perhaps object that in this instance we are called upon not to affirm or to deny, but only to understand. To which we reply that it is a mistake to consider our assent as a more or less voluntary act, as distinguished from the synthesis of the terms. Let us go back to the example of affirming a natural law; *perceiving the connection and giving one's assent* are one and the same thing.[200] To perceive the connection is to perceive the clue as clue. But the clue cannot be perceived as clue without at the same time perceiving, by necessary correlation and with the same epistemic stringency,[201] that to which it is the clue.

[31] In the theory of faith this last point is of real importance. It compels us to understand, in fact, that in the cases of supernatural knowledge we have been discussing, we must not imagine a "judgment of credibility" that constitutes a distinct act. *Perception of credibility and belief in truth are identically the same act.*[202]

But if the perception of credibility coincides with the act of faith, just as the perceiving of the connection coincides with the accepting of the hypothesis, then clearly nothing stands in the way of our affirming, with St. Thomas, that it is the light of faith that shows that we must believe.[203] A vicious circle? Only if we claim to demonstrate a proposition as certain by means of another that is as yet undemonstrated and that depends in turn on the former. But there is no trace of a vicious circle if we say that affirming some proposition requires that we possess the spiritual faculty that makes the connection of its terms clear, the synthetic activity that unites those terms, or, to speak as older authors did, the light

---

[200] In Scholastic language: the *esse quod significant compositionem et divisionem intellectus* ["the being that means affirmation and negation by the intellect"] is not, like predicamental being, a represented note, a note belonging to the *essence*.

[201] This means that if the clue is perceived as probable, the hypothesis confirmed by it is affirmed only as probable, etc.

[202] Hence the credibility perceived in the light of grace is not *objectum quod*, i.e., the term of knowledge, a thought object, it is *quo*, or *sub quo*, i.e., a condition of the object. Earlier authors conceive its role in this way, but only in some instances. (See, for instance, John of St. Thomas, *Cursus theologicus in 2am 2ae, De fide*, disp. 2, art. 3, nn. 12ff.)

[203] 2a2ae, q. 1, a. 5, ad 1; cf. ibid., a. 4, ad 3.

that illuminates them. This applies to the *Credendum est* ["we should believe"] if one makes it a condition for affirming a supernatural truth or, what comes down to the same thing, if one makes of it a proposition that is explicitly uttered, yet *believed*, not simply affirmed by natural reason.

Theologians will readily grant, supposing faith to be present, that its light can make credibility manifest. But there is no reason for explaining the *first* act of faith any differently, and refusing to say that the supernatural light illuminates the very act through which we acquire that initial faith. The clue is really the cause of the assent we give to the conclusion, yet it is the perceived conclusion that sheds light on the clue, that endows it with meaning. The same is true when we come to believe: insofar as it makes the assent reasonable, the perceived clue [32] precedes the assent; insofar as it is supernatural, it follows upon the assent. There are two orders, of rationality and of supernaturality, and we can construct some abstract scheme along the lines of either order. One may say "I see the virtue of a Christian; I conclude to the divine holiness of the Church; I make my profession of faith." Or one may say "I acquire from above a new power of seeing;[204] I confess to the holiness of the Church, and I recognize the holiness of this man as an effect, an application, of the Church's holiness." These two logical sequences represent only aspects of the real, both of them true and both incomplete. Their truths are united and reconciled in the living unity of the affirmation. And there is no vicious circle. There would be a vicious circle–or a leap into the dark, an arbitrary and unjustified affirmation–only if the affirmed truth were absolutely prior to the condition of its affirmation, without in any way bringing it about through reciprocal causality. The same applies in the case of Hamlet or of the scientific law. The instantaneously acquired habit, call it *perceptive knowledge*, both precedes and follows its counterpart, *perceived knowledge*.

"My Lord and my God!" "Truly this man was the Son of God!" Tradition has always seen in these exclamations of the converted centurion and of the apostle who recovered his faith both the

---

[204] This power is acquired only through an act of the will, the *oboeditio fidei*, the *pius affectus credenda* ["the obedience of faith, the pious will to believe"], as we shall show in the second part of our investigation. Therefore the joining of the two objects indicated here by no means exhausts the complex reality of the act of faith, which unites in its living *unity* what is too often scattered into a great number of "judgments" and "commandments."

beginning and the manifestation of faith. There is no room here for a "judgment of credibility" as distinct act. But these words of the Gospel also exemplify very well another feature of the rapid and supernatural induction that, to our mind, explains belief better than what is generally meant by "demonstration of credibility." Consider now what we mean by this last feature.

[33] The external signs that make us see are surprising in their variety: the holiness of a good priest, the healing of a sick person, the impression produced by a religious feast, and so on. But such a sign is always known both as a real fact, interwoven with the entire fabric of human experience, and as a clue pertaining to the same order as the truth to which it points. So it is known under a new aspect, as constituting part of another world, the supernatural world. This is why many theologians say that the *formal object*[205] of this knowledge is new. The formal object of natural intelligence is natural being, accommodated to our natural end; the formal object of the knowledge of faith is supernatural being, pertaining to the order of grace, a means to lead us to intuitive vision.

The selfsame being may, therefore, belong to the natural order of our experience and to the supernatural order of grace, and, as we have repeatedly said, inner grace does not present us with new objects of knowledge, but illuminates a new aspect of some object already known. Thus through illumination by grace the gentle disposition of divine Providence *prolongs*, without any bump or break in conscious life, smoothly and with no violent irruption, what natural knowledge makes clear to us; it makes us see, within the very ambit of objects we were already attending to, clues to the higher world. Discerning a new nature in them is the same as penetrating more clearly and more thoroughly into their reality. The apostle Thomas "saw the man and believed in the God," as the Fathers quite aptly put it. But the God and the man were the same Christ Jesus. Many in our time have *seen Rome*, i.e., a marvelously human, surpassingly reasonable, and civilizing institution, and have *believed in the Church*,[206] i.e., the mother of the children of God, the spouse of Christ, the teacher of salvation. The two kinds of knowledge are very different, and the former [34] often occurs without the latter. And yet, Rome is the Church, and the Church is Rome.

---

[205] *Ratio sub qua* ["the aspect under which"].

[206] See, for instance, Paul Löwengard, *La splendeur catholique: Du Judaïsme à l'Église* (Paris: Perrin et Cie, 1910), pp. 163ff.

Such a continuity of the two kinds of knowledge is possible only on one condition; that the two formal objects, the natural and the supernatural, be neither *opposed* nor *disparate*. The one must encompass and transcend the other, deepening and perfecting it *from within*. Otherwise the new faculty of seeing would be as experientially perceptible as the sudden acquisition of a sixth sense or the infusion of mystical contemplation in its higher degrees. Experience shows that such is not the case with faith. Hence the supernatural being we are speaking about is natural being, but elevated. In the final analysis the essence of natural being consists in its essential aptitude to served as a means for created spirits to ascend to God, their final end; the essence of supernatural being, in its aptitude to lead them to God, object of the beatific vision. The two "formal objects" are no more opposed or disparate than the two ends are.[207]

Natural intelligence, which may err about notes that are more comprehensive than being, never errs concerning the notion of *being* itself, which constitutes its formal object, because only this notion can *move* it. Likewise and much more so, the light of faith is infallible in making supernatural being manifest.[208] The reasons for believing, perceived under the influence of grace, are good reasons for believing, and necessarily so.[209]

The solidity of these reasons is absolutely independent of the power that discursive reason may have of establishing a series of syllogistic arguments between the fact acting as clue and the credibility of this Christian faith. The Holy Spirit can manifest this credibility to the soul just as well by illuminating the bond that exists between the holiness of the pastor of his or her parish[210] and

---

[207] "The supernatural end and the natural end are not disparate ends and do differ not as two opposites, but only as that which exceeds and that which is exceeded" (Louis Billot, *De gratia Christi* (Rome: Universitatis Gregorianae, 1908), p. 46). No modern theologian has emphasized more strongly this essential ideal than the author of this remarkable little book. It seems to me that all those who are interested in the question of nature and the supernatural would read it with pleasure and profit, even if they have not received a Scholastic formation. ...

[208] Cf. St. Thomas, *In Boetium de Trinitate*, q. 3, a. 1, ad 4.

[209] When we say that somebody believes for a reason that is only probable "in itself," either this expression has no meaning, or it means: a reason that is capable of lawfully engendering only a probability in the human mind, as it is too weak to perceive fully the reality of the phenomenon in question.

[210] The impossibility of expressing this connection in words and

the divine holiness of the Church as by illuminating the connection [35] existing between the Church's entire history and her direction by God's providence. For that to happen, it is enough that the connection be a real one.

We must take an even further step. In natural knowledge, the quicker and more penetrating the mind is, the more effectively a slight clue suffices to lead it to a certain conclusion. The same happens in the case of supernatural knowledge. The more responsive the mind is to the promptings of the Holy Spirit, the more easily it will come to assent to the Christian faith by means of signs that are ordinary, everyday signs, in no way "extraordinary" or "miraculous."[211] That is why an incontrovertible tradition, going back to the Gospel itself, praises those who have no need of wonders. They are not praised for having believed without reasons; that would only be reprehensible. But we see in them truly illuminated souls, capable of grasping a vast truth through a tiny clue. Does not experience show that, when the Holy Spirit visits the soul with His consolation, the soul is no longer capable of doubting, as it were, and glimpses manifest signs of the truth in everything. "Think of anything you wish," says the author of *L'Aiguillon d'amour*, "and you will find in it many reasons for loving your Creator." Some saints went into ecstasy on viewing a blade of grass. So, too, when it comes to faith. When responding to the divine light, the believer sees all of world history as proving the Church's mission: the most commonplace word or fact floods the soul with certitude and peace. Experiences of this sort cannot be expressed in words. But in defining that there are motives drawn from outward signs, the Church never defined thar there exist only motives susceptible of expression. The motives we are talking about, if given expression, might well seem contemptible to those bereft of the Spirit. But the lover recognizes the Spouse "by a single hair of her neck."

---

concepts by no means prevents its being certain and intellectual. There are many examples of such an inability even in the natural exercise of the intellect as an illative sense.

[211] We should not believe that the sign of the Church mentioned by the Vatican Council must necessarily assume the form of a consideration of the whole of ecclesiastical history or even of the total action of the Church in the world in our time. The "holiness of an outstanding Christian woman" or the "marvelous effects of Holy Communion"–all this enters into the "proof based upon the Church."

ALAN VINCELETTE

JOSEPH MARÉCHAL (1878-1944)

Maréchal was born in Charleroi Belgium in 1878. He joined the Jesuits in 1895 and after initial studies in philosophy and theology, he decided to take up the natural sciences. He took up the study of biology and psychology, studying biology at the Catholic University of Louvain from 1901 to 1905, acquiring a doctorate in biology in 1905. He was ordained in 1908 and in 1911 went to study psychology with Wilhelm Wundt in Munich, Germany. He taught philosophy and psychology from then on at St. Albert's Philosophical and Theological College in Louvain from 1919 to 1935. Maréchal passed away in 1944 in Louvain, Belgium.

Maréchal major opus is his *Le point de départ de la métaphysique*, 5 vols (Louvain: Museum Lessianum, 1922-1947). Sections of this work have been translated in *A Maréchal Reader* (New York: Herder & Herder, 1970). This work helped initiate the tradition of Transcendental Thomism as it seeks to combine the insights of Kant with those of Thomas Aquinas. Maréchal asserts that knowledge involves both empirical and *a priori* elements, and indeed a dynamism of the human mind to the infinite which allows for a realistic grasp of nature. For the mind is actively seeking God in each and every act of knowing, no matter how humble, and it is this finality and dynamism that allows it to acquire a true knowledge of reality. Maréchal is also known for his work *Études sur le psychologie des mystiques*, 2 vols. (Bruxelles: L'Édition universelle, 1926-1937), translated by Algar Thorold as *The Psychology of the Mystics* (New York: Dover, 2004).

For more on Maréchal see: Van Riet, Georges, *Thomistic Epistemology* (St. Louis: Herder, 1963), vol. 1, pp. 236-271; John, Helen J., *The Thomist Spectrum* (New York: Fordham University Press, 1966), pp 139-149; McCool, Gerald A., *From Unity to Pluralism* (New York: Fordham University Press, 1989), pp. 87-113; Matteo, Anthony, *Quest for the Absolute: The Philosophical Vision of Joseph Maréchal* (De Kalb: Northern Illinois University Press, 1992); McCamy, Ronald, *Out of a Kantian Chrysalis?* (New York: Peter Lang, 1998).

The following section is from the fifth volume of Maréchal's *The Point of Departure of Metaphysics* (1947), as found in *A Maréchal Reader* (1970), pp. 174-191.

The Point of Departure of Metaphysics (1947)[212]

Intellectual Dynamism and Supernatural End

The Supernatural Factor of Our Destiny
[174] With St. Thomas we shall conclude that the natural impulsion of our intellectual faculties drives them towards the immediate intuition of the absolute Being. It is true that this intuition exceeds the power and the exigencies of every finite intelligence, left to its sole natural resources. Yet the radical [175] impulsion which drives it to this intuition is not conceivable without the objective, at least remote, possibility of reaching it.

But this objective, even remote, possibility implies two necessary conditions: *the existence of an absolute Being*, which is capable of communicating itself, and the *capability of our intelligence* for receiving this communication.

But if this is the case, if the "vision of the divine essence" is not a utopian perspective, but something which is "possible in itself," we know now to what "absolutely last end" our intellectual representations refer during the dynamic and implicit stage of objective knowledge.

Thomistic Exemplarism
We have already said that the "natural form" which is logically previous to every elicited act of the intellect—hence the form of the intellectual "first act"—is the universal and abstract form of *being*.

At this primary stage it does not yet represent an "object," not even a virtual object, but only the form of an assimilating virtuality, an "*a priori* formal condition," the previous rule of our apprehension of eventual objects. It can objectivate itself in our consciousness only after first meeting, in some matter presented by the senses, an "intelligible in potency."

Whence comes to the intellective subject this "formal principle" which rules all its particular intellections?

As in corporeal movement that is called *the mover which gives the form that is the principle of movement*, so that is said to move the intellect which is the *cause of the form that is the*

---

212 [Joseph Maréchal, *A Maréchal Reader*, translated by Joseph Donceel. Copyright © 1970 Herder and Herder. All rights reserved. Used with permission of Crossroad Publishing, crossroadpublishing.com/ crossroad/publishers/herder-herder.]

principle of the intellectual operation called the movement of the intellect. Now there is a twofold principle of intellectual operation in the intelligent being: one is *the intellectual power itself*, which principle exists also in the one who understands in potentiality; while the other is *the principle of actual understanding*, namely, the likeness of the thing understood. So a thing is said to move the intellect, whether it gives to him who understands the power of understanding, or impresses on him the likeness of the thing understood. *Now God moves the created intellect in both ways* (Aquinas, *Summa theologiae*, I, q. 105, a. 3, c). ...

[176] The "uncreated light" designates the purely intuitive intelligence which creates its external objects. According to St. Thomas, like the pure spirits we receive something of this intuitive power which creates its object. That is, our intelligence itself, although extrinsically dependent on the senses, introduces into the immanent object, into the "mental word," a higher, metempirical element, which it possessed by itself, virtually. Of the "intelligible in potency" it makes an "intelligible in act." ...

If anything represents, in our intellect, a participation in the intuitive power of the absolute intelligence, it must be the virtual possession of the "first principles," of the "principles of being." ... Hence sense experience by no means brings to us from without the "first principles of being," it only embodies them in objective representations. They themselves surge from the very bottom of our intellectual nature and this surge is divine in its primordial origin. They are at once a *subjective virtuality* and a *virtual objective principle*, and they constitute in us something remotely analogous to the "first truth." ...

Thus we understand in what sense it is correct to compare Thomism with ontologistic or Platonic exemplarism.

Both sides profess that man receives some participation of the divine Truth, of the divine Ideas. But unlike Platonic ontologism, Thomism admits only a participation restricted to the "first intelligible principles"–to the transcendental attributes of being– and by no means a participation according to the generic and specific types.

Moreover, this participation which, in the ontologistic language, would mean that ready-made, although latent, ideas are inborn, designates here a natural disposition of a dynamic nature, which demands a material complement. The "first intelligibles" are first imprinted in our Ego as the lived form of [177] a natural tendency. Next, they are objectivated in the way in which for us the form of such a tendency can be objectivated, that is, by revealing themselves, through connaturality, in the very objects met by the concrete exercise of this tendency.

In short: *Thomistic exemplarism is a dynamic exemplarism restricted exclusively to the "first intelligible principles."*

Objectivation in Finality: Deduction of the Ontological Affirmation

The act of intellection occurs in a "becoming" whose universal *form*, original *principle* and last *end* we have defined in the line of St. Thomas. We shall now use these analytic results to finish bringing out the conditions which necessarily rule in our consciousness the "apprehension" of the object as *object*. ...

What kind of relation is capable of disjoining from a subjective activity some of the conditions inherent in it? How is it possible for a subject to represent, as separated from itself and extraposed in an outside absolute (*en soi*) the very form of its immanent activity? This is the heart of the problem of the constitution of the object *in* consciousness and *for* consciousness.

Internal Finality as the Basis of the Opposition Between Object and Subject in Consciousness

Can the intentional "form" of our intellection—the species of the scholastics—become, in its immanence, the term of some [178] ontological relation which implies the opposition of subject to object?

First it would seem that, through its empirical elements (or through its "representational" content) the form should be, in the subject, the term of a relation of receptivity, of passivity, of a *passio*, which refers it to an outside agent, to a non-Ego, a thing-in-itself, as to its efficient cause. Would this not constitute a possible foundation for the conscious opposition of subject and object?

This is doubtful, or at least, it is doubtful that this foundation is sufficient. For the intellect in its second act, the only one of which we are aware, is not directly passive with respect to sense objects. Such an immediate passivity belongs properly to the senses. It is true that the intellect models itself after the form of the sensation. Yet, ontologically speaking, there is passivity in the intellect only with respect to itself, of the possible intellect to the agent intellect (guiding the phantasm). Such a passivity introduces an *immediate* relative opposition only within the intellect, between its active and its passive function.

Let us even suppose that this intra-intellectual relation should become conscious in the direct act of intellection—which is not the case. It would project neither of its two terms into some absolute (*en soi*) outside the intellect, hence it would not provide us *directly* with an objective knowledge.

It would do even less to confuse, like the empiricists and the semi-empiricists, the objectivity of the intellect with the imperfect objectivity of the senses, as if the former were only an intellectual transposition of the latter. The senses give us merely *spatial extraposition, not intelligible reality*. Even were one to suppose— as might be done without incoherence—that the intellect, associated with the senses, should somehow perceive intelligibly the passivity of the latter, one would at the utmost have to admit with Kant that the intellect, in its collaboration with the senses, refers their phenomenal contribution to a *thing-in-itself*, which is absolute, but wholly undetermined, a mere logical counterpart of the sense phenomenon. Such a solution would not sufficiently justify the "relation to the object," which is essential in each direct act of the understanding. Moreover, it would be unable to extend its "objective value" beyond the [179] material realities manifested in the phenomena. It would never lead us, even indirectly, to a transcendent object. We might as well admit it: if the natural objective function of our intellect is measured by the undetermined "thing-in-itself," by a reality which is nothing but *the limit and the counterpart* of the phenomenon, Kant has correctly set down the boundaries of our knowledge. All the constructions of our reason, in search of a *transcendent* absolute beyond experience, are "*a priori* syntheses" in the pejorative sense, lacking any objective guarantee. They may be useful in many respects but, speculatively speaking, they remain empty. In that case we cannot escape theoretical agnosticism.

Let us add this rather abstract remark, which we consider decisive for a Thomist: the subject's passivity before the outside object can, at any rate, not appear to consciousness as a total passively, but only as the *limitation of an activity* of the subject itself. For, as demonstrated by Cajetan interpreting St. Thomas, although knowledge may—on account of the imperfection of the knowing subject—require the previous reception of a form in matter, of an accident in a substance, it does not take place according to this very relation of matter to form or of accident to substance, but according to the identity *of an act*. Hence, in any event, if the sense passively contributes something to the awareness of the object as object, this can only derive from the perceivable repercussion of this passivity in the very exercise of the subjective activity. But this steers our problem in a quite different direction. We are no longer inquiring whether a *potency* perceives itself *as potency* in the very actuation which it undergoes (an absurd supposition), but whether an act may perceive the terminal limitation by which it is affected (which does not seem wholly impossible).

Besides the relation of a patient to an outside agent, we meet in the process of objective knowledge another kind of relation which, unlike the former, intrinsically affects the specifying form (*species*) of the intellectual act itself, and, moreover, extends beyond the restricted limits of the phenomenon. We mean the *relation of finality*. Without wholly overlooking the function of finality in knowledge, Kant limits it to the "reflecting judgments"; he excludes the "tendency" from any intrinsic [180] participation in the structure of the "determining judgment," that is, of the judgment through which we exercise our natural, primary power of objectivation. In this respect the Thomistic thesis, as understood here, is radically opposed to the Kantian thesis.

A form may refer to an end in two ways: first, as the *exemplary type* (*idea, forma factiva*) of a reality which is to be produced. Such is the ideal design which directs the artist's hand, such are the eternal ideas of creative intelligence. Since such a form can belong only to an intellectual subject, who is aware of himself, the latter intuitively knows in it the real or possible effect which it outlines or projects. The knowledge of the object (as real or as possible) coincides here with the awareness of the exemplary form as a productive actuality or virtuality. We are outside the critical hypothesis; an intuition stands in no need of a rational justification of its proper object. On the other hand, the finality which we meet in our intellectual dynamism is that of an immanent action through which the subject *acquires and assimilates* new determinations.

We have shown several times ... that the specifying form of our intellection, the *species*, is not a mere static ornament of it, but, at every moment, the actual form of a movement, of a tendency striving towards its end. Caught up in the natural desire which draws our intellect from empty potency to integral act, every acquired *species* assumes clearly a dynamic value. Since it constitutes at least a temporary term of the intellectual activity, it possesses the attractiveness of an *end* with respect to this activity. On the other hand, since it does not exhaust the active potency of the intellect which, having assimilated it, looks out for more knowledge, it cannot be the intellect's ultimate end. Now, when an end is not an ultimate end, it refers to the latter as *a subordinate end*, as a means or as a stage.

Our problem is then to find out how this relation of finality, which intrinsically affects the successive forms of our intellectual activity, might be the very basis of their "objectivation."

The first condition required for the "objectivation" of an immanent form is, of course, that it be somehow separated from the subject as such, and that, as so separated, it should acquire a value in itself (*un "en soi"*) and qualify "a thing."

[181] We wish to insist upon the exact terms of our problem: the subject to whom the immanent form should be opposed, if it is to be perceived objectively, is the "subject as such" or the knowing function in exercise (*cognoscens in actu*), not the subject in its full ontological reality. Before this kind of limited subject the extraposed form must, in order to possess the character of an intelligible *object*, refer, at least in general, to some absolute (*un "en soi"*), to a subsistence. This first degree of objectivity does not at once imply that the "in itself" of the objectivated form be distinct from the ontological reality of the subject itself. The metaphysical opposition of two subsistences, that of the subject and that of the object, presents a more complex problem than that of the objective apprehension (*sub ratione entis*) of the content of the representation. In the present case it is enough that the subject as *function* be opposed to the object as *in itself*.

Hence we set up the following thesis: in a discursive intelligence, the assimilated form is opposed to the subject and acquires an "in itself" insofar as it constitutes, for the subject, a *dynamic value*, a *moment of an active becoming*.

We say: an *active* becoming. In every becoming, whether active or passive, every moment, by its very definition, saturates something in an antecedent tendency, and gives rise to a consequent tendency.

But when an immanent form is experienced as an end both retrospectively and prospectively, in that fleeting moment when aspiration turns into possession, and a still imperfect possession is overtaken by further desire, is it not then immanent in the subject according to a relation which distinguishes it from the latter? A value is distinct from the need which takes hold of it as well as from the need which still craves it. And since this relation is posited in the order of ends—the absolute order of the noumenon— the immanent form refers also *ipso facto* to a subsistence, to an "in itself" and takes on in our mind the essential features of an ontological object.

Thus the enigma of objective knowledge can be solved, if we can show that the *ad extra* (outward) relations of the immanent form are not only *in us* real attributes of this form, but also *for us* attributes which we can know.

[182] Yet, should we stop here, we would have solved only a *psychological* problem. Our real problem, which is a problem of epistemology, a problem of *logical* value, would only be halfway to its solution. In the natural impulsion itself, which projects the immanent form outside of our self, as an end, we should be able to discover not only a dynamic exigency, but also a *logical implication* of the "in itself" reality of the end. ... the tendency's rational coherence and the ontological possibility of the end depend on each other, so that, should the logical incoherence of the tendency be unacceptable, the ontological possibility of the end must be accepted. ...

To facilitate the reader's task, we shall once more summarize *our whole argumentation.*

(a) In virtue of the "first principle" every content of thought is ontologically *affirmable* (critical *preambulum*).

(b) The content of a non-intuitive (discursive) mind may be affirmed only *objectively*, that is, in opposition to the subjective function exercised upon it (relation of "logical truth").

(c) This "objectivity" in immanence, the necessary condition of the exercise of a non-intuitive thought, is itself logically and psychologically possible only if the content of this thought is inserted in an *assimilating movement* which tends towards an absolutely final end.

(d) This finality, without which there can be no non-intuitive thought, dynamically posits the "reality in themselves" of the (objective) ends intended by it. But, from the strictly critical point of view, a dynamic exigency, however ineluctable, establishes only, by itself alone, a *subjective* certitude.

(e) Therefore, we must still show that the "reality in themselves" of these ends, which are necessarily intended in the very exercise of every discursive thought, is for the knowing subject not only a dynamic exigency, but a *logical necessity.*

[183] When this point has been established, our task will be ended. For, through critical reflection, we would have rediscovered the indissoluble vital unity which exists between the intellect as speculative faculty (as formally knowing) and the intellect as an assimilating dynamism (as some reality, whose good or end is the true itself).

Towards Objective Affirmation

Let us therefore consider even more attentively, so as to bring out its logical implications, the intellectual operation in which an immanent intelligible form is referred to the domain of ends. We know that the basic tendency which carries the intellectual becoming exists before any objective apperception, as a "natural tendency" (natural appetite). It is finalized towards act and starts moving as soon as the senses provide the indispensable "matter." It is precisely in this elicited activity, where the "natural form" of the tendency and the determination coming from outside meet for the first time, that, for the first time too, are realized the immanent conditions of objective knowledge.

Let us restrict ourselves to this first elicited act of our intellectual faculty ... It combines, as mentioned above, a natural dynamism and empirical determinations. But, in order to be grasped by the original dynamism, these determinations must be subordinated to the proper end of this dynamism. A tendency, even a "natural tendency," intends only its own end or that which leads to it. Hence the native dynamism of the intellect grasps the empirical determinations as a beginning or a participation of this end, and the dim volition by which it assimilates them is but the very volition of this end itself. Thus the "empirical determination" of the first intellectual act enters into the mind's dynamism not only as *assimilated to the natural form*, but also as *referred to the proper end* of this dynamism.

The whole secret of objective knowledge lies in the logical necessities implied in this respective situation of the "form" and the "end."

[184] The adequate subjective end of our intellectual dynamism—perfect happiness, the possession of the perfect Good—consists in a saturating "assimilation" of the form of *being*, in other words, in the possession of God. Although this end is supernatural, it must, *in itself*, be possible. Else the basic tendency of our intellectual nature turns into a logical absurdity, the appetite for nothingness.

But the *possibility* of the *subjective* end (*finis quo*) presupposes the *reality* of the objective end (*finis cujus*). The first condition for the possibility of the assimilation of the absolute Being is the *existence* of this Being.

Moreover, the knowing subject guarantees, of logical necessity, the existence of this being. To posit any intellectual act whatsoever in virtue of the natural tendency towards the subjective ultimate end of the intellect is tantamount to implicitly or explicitly willing this end, hence to adopting it *as at least possible*. Strictly speaking one may intend an end without being certain of reaching it, even with the certitude of never reaching it. But it would be contradictory to strive towards an end which one considers *absolutely and in every respect* unattainable. This would mean to will nothingness. This logical incompatibility, in the subject himself, between willing some end and affirming its total emptiness, applies as well to the implicit as to the explicit domain of reason.

Hence, even if one rejects the immediate metaphysical value of the "natural" tendencies, a value which is admitted by the scholastics, it would still be true that to posit any intellectual act whatsoever means to affirm *implicitly* not only the possibility but the reality of the "objective end," of the *finis qui, vel cujus*, as the logical condition of the possibility of the "subjective end."

When the "objective end" is a *finite object*, its mode of reality is not totally determined by the sole fact that it objectively "terminates" a tendency. A subjective end may be intended, without logical incoherence, even should the object whose possession one desires be actually nonexistent. It is enough that this object *may* exist when and in the conditions in which the subjective end would be reached. Nothing prevents us from desiring to acquire a thing which is not, but which will be [185] (which exists in its causes). I may even, without contradiction, although rather whimsically, desire to possess an object which is merely possible, provided, of course, that I suppose it to be really existing when my subjective end is hypothetically achieved. The degree of reality, logically postulated in the object of a tendency in virtue of this very tendency, does not, by itself, go beyond the pre-existence of the object "in its causes," or its reality as "possible."

But when this object is God, when the objective end is identified with the Being which is *necessary by itself* (the pure Act), which has no other mode of reality than absolute existence, the dialectical exigency implied by the desire assumes a new scope, not merely on account of the natural desire, but on account of the nature of the desire's object. To affirm of God that he is possible is the same as to affirm that he exists, since his existence is the condition of every possibility.

Hence we may state, in strictest logic, that the *possibility* of our subjective last end presupposes logically the *existence* of our objective last end, God. Thus, in every intellectual act, we affirm implicitly the existence of an absolute Being. "All knowing beings implicitly know God in everything they know" (Aquinas, *De veritate*, q. 22, a. 2, ad 1; to be interpreted according to *Summa theologiae*, I, q. 84, a. 5 and q. 88, a. 3).

But it is not enough to discover the logical implications of every contingent *fact* of knowledge. In the present instance the *fact* implies a radical necessity, which does not depend on the fact which reveals it to us. Our implicit affirmation of the absolute Being was *necessary a priori*. For the "objective end" is affirmed exactly to the extent that the "subjective end" is explicitly or implicitly willed. If we willed the subjective end contingently, we would only *in fact* adopt the possibility of this end, hence *in fact* affirm the (necessary) existence of the objective end. But when the subjective end is the ultimate end, it is necessarily intended, in virtue of an *a priori* disposition, of a natural volition which precedes logically every contingent activity. But if we necessarily and *a priori* will the subjective end, we necessarily and *a priori* admit its possibility, hence we affirm *necessarily and a priori* the (necessary) existence of the objective end. Therefore our implicit affirmation of the absolute Being is *a priori* necessary. This is exactly what we had to demonstrate.

[186] Of course, the presuppositions which we have made explicit are not immediately known by us; they are at first implicit. Yet, as such, they provide the assimilated object with its *logical* characteristics.

What exactly is their influence upon our original awareness of the object? At the first moment of the direct intellection, nothing is "in act" in consciousness, hence nothing is directly known but an *empirical content* which provides the assimilating movement of our spirit with an actual specification. Hence we are not aware of the general form of our intellectual power (potency is not directly knowable as potency), but we know the form of the mental becoming insofar as it is right now "actuated" from the outside, we know the totality of the determinations actively assimilated by the intellect at this particular stage of its progression towards the ultimate end.

Hence we are aware of the "form of an active movement." It is important to realize what this means for a consciousness which is not, like sense consciousness, totally obstructed by the form which it receives, but which remains capable of penetrating, beyond the given form, to the vital activity which animates this form.

We should remember that, at every moment, the form of the intellectual becoming is at once the form of a *fieri* [becoming], of a *factum esse* [existing fact] and of a new *fieri* [becoming]. It is the point of transition of a dim desire which finds in it a temporary rest, only to surge forward again towards the infinite. This dynamic state, with its bilateral orientation, is present here in *proximate potency* of distinct consciousness. All its active and formal elements are "cognoscible" elements which are already immanent, they are virtually known; only a glance of reflexive consciousness is required to make them fully conscious.

Objective knowledge, in its first moment, is the total and complex expression, both implicit and explicit, of this state of affairs:

(1) The qualitative content which is actually assimilated (the "representative" content of the direct concept), insofar as it is the form of an "*operari*" (activity), realizes all the conditions required for distinct consciousness. Hence it can be explicitly known *according to its proper diversity.*

(2) [187] But this content can be assimilated only if the intellectual faculty has assumed and keeps before it the dynamic attitude of an agent before a partial end, projected in the perspective of an ultimate end, that is, an actively and actually *objectivating* attitude. Thus the represented form stands really before the intellectual subject *in the situation of an object.*

It does not follow that the subject is at once aware of the two terms of this opposition. Psychological experience shows us and reason confirms that the orientation of consciousness is always ruled by the impulsion of its appetite (whether natural or elicited), which St. Thomas calls the "*intentio.*" This "*intentio*" varies with the agent's interest. For an assimilating faculty, which has to look outside itself for that which fills its need, the first interest lies in the good which fills this need. Hence the first *known object* can only be the assimilated object, not yet formally the activity itself of the assimilating subject.

Thus the content which is represented in the direct act of knowledge is at once known *objectively* (although not necessarily formally known as an object), because, impelled by his nature, the subject assumes first before this content a dynamic attitude, which, logically and psychologically, implies *objectivation.* ...

The undeniable property of extroversion in immanence—so hard to explain by nominalistic logic—is no longer a worrisome paradox, if one admits that every intellectual knowledge of objects is carried by some dynamism, whether creative or assimilating. Both a *creative* will and the *tendency* towards an end, more generally a finality *diffusive* of the good and one which *strives towards* the good, introduce into the subject the principle of an immanent disjunction of subject from object. Lacking such a finality, there is no *possible* psychological foundation for the objectivating function of the knower in act.

We should remember here that the *judicative affirmation,* which we have analyzed above, constitutes in objective consciousness the bilateral dynamic moment according to which the intellectual assimilation of the data takes place, according to which they are introduced into the absolute domain of ends. Thus the dynamic function of affirmation coincides with the imperfect *objective function* which belongs to discursive intelligences.

[188] In what order does a dynamic explanation of knowledge bring the representations up to clear consciousness?

(1) In line with the natural finality of an immaterial power, which looks for being and intelligibility, it is first the new acquisition, the actual content of the intellect, that is aimed at by the "*intentio*" and focused in consciousness, not as a form of the subject, but as something opposed to him. From this first stage on we know objectively, we possess an objective representation. This is the classical stage of the "direct concept": a universal, objective concept whose universality and objectivity are not yet explicitly grasped. The initial moment of intellectual knowledge presents only the formal diversity of the phantasm, the "intelligible in potency" as illuminated before us by the objectivating light of the abstractive understanding.

Is this direct concept a "simple apprehension" or is it already an "apprehensive judgment"? We answer with a venerable scholastic distinction, which keeps all its value: the direct concept is not an apprehensive judgment (a judgment of reality) *signate* or *representative,* but *exercite* [implicit]. It is not an explicit judgment, but a "lived" one. In other words, at the very moment when the conceptual content lights up in our consciousness, the activity exercised by us contains all the logical and psychological elements of a judgment of reality. Hence that which penetrates first and at once into our explicit consciousness is an objectivated content, a "something," object or being. *Primo ens*: first being.

(2) But the immanent form is objectivated as being (*ens*) only in virtue of the objectivating attitude of the subject. His natural inclination pushed him towards the object. But afterwards, he may reflect, and know himself as an objectivating activity molded on the object and opposing himself to it. Starting with this first step in reflection, there emerges in consciousness the *relation* of the intellectual subject to the represented object. The intellect recognizes itself, albeit dimly, in "something of its own" (*quoddam proprium*), as St. Thomas put it. In other words, the relation of

"logical truth" itself, which was first dimly exercised, suddenly becomes luminous. *Secundo verum*; in the second place, the true.

[189] Then, as reflection goes on, there emerges before consciousness not only the mere relation of logical truth, as an opposition of subject and object, but also the *dynamic value* of this relation. The objectivated form is seen as the term of the subject's inclination. It stands out, explicitly, in the wide open perspective of desire, as an end which stands in itself, as the term of a possible action, as a good (in the transcendental sense in which every being necessarily is good). *Tertio bonum*: in the third place the good. ...

Deduction of the Ontological Affirmation

If we have reasoned correctly thus far, we would really have made the "objective deduction" of the metaphysical affirmation according to the very principles of St. Thomas.

Let us present this deduction in a different and shorter way, so as to put in better light its necessary connections:

(1) For a non-intuitive intelligence, which receives formal determinations (*species*) from outside, these immanent determinations will have the immediate value of *objects* only if the [190] very mode of their immanence to the subject *opposes* them to the latter (principle of the necessary immanence of all the determinations of knowledge).

(2) Opposition in immanence is possible only according to a *relation* which inheres in the subject. And this opposition can affect consciousness only if the relation inherent to the subject is implicitly or explicitly knowable by him. But only that is knowable for a subject which is immanent to him according to his *ultimate actuality*.

(3) The only immanent relations which fulfill the above conditions are the relation of *cause to effect* and the relation of *tendency to end*. Both of them and no other put in the creative or appetitive activity of a subject an immanent principle of disjunction. To know oneself as a cause means to distinguish oneself ontologically from the effect. To know oneself implicitly or explicitly as a tendency means to know oneself implicitly or explicitly as really distinct from an objective end. The former relation is the foundation of creative intuition, which does not concern us here. The secret of *our* objective knowledge lies in the dynamic relation of *finality*.

(4) If it is to extrapose immediately, before the intellect, an object corresponding to the immanent determinations, the

dynamic relation of finality must affect the *very act* by which they are assimilated, so that the act which assimilates is identically the act which opposes. Hence the assimilation itself must project and keep the immanent form opposed to the subject, in the domain of ends. This is possible only if the assimilation occurs under the initial and permanent influence of a wider end, with respect to which the assimilated form is grasped and held as a *subordinated end*, as a beginning of possession, as an eventual means or possible approach. And this already introduces the immanent form within the ontological order, since the ends are noumenal.

But once they are posited, subordinated ends possess exactly the same necessity as the higher, superordinated ends on which they depend. Hence we must demonstrate—and we may do so either *a priori* or psychologically—that the primordial motion which causes the intellectual dynamism is the motion of the [191] absolutely ultimate objective end, of the *Good in itself.* The articular forms, immanent to our intellect, derive their objective value from their final subordination to an absolute necessity. They are contingent in their existence and through their differential features, but they receive from this subordination the "hypothetical" necessity which is the share of absolute possessed by all things under God. The absolute end introduces them virtually into the rigorous concatenations of *Metaphysics.*

(5) Let us call "affirmation," in the widest sense of the word, the active referring of a conceptual content to reality (*ad rem*). Then the above remarks lead us to assert that the representations which are immanent to our thought possess in it the value of objects only in virtue of an *implicit affirmation*; not of any affirmation, however, but in virtue of a *metaphysical affirmation* which connects the object with the absolute realm of being. Hence the metaphysical affirmation, as a dynamic attitude, is really the condition of the possibility of the object in our mind, that is, in a discursive mind. This is precisely the point which we promised to demonstrate. ...

(6) The ontological conditions postulated by the objective affirmation are *really implicit* in it, are objectively "constitutive" of it. ... (... implicit in the Kantian sense), that is, the totality of the *a priori* conditions, of the functional exigencies of the intellect as such, actuated in objective knowledge, whose subjective conditions of possibility they constitute. They may be discovered by the subject through self-reflection and introduced into a rational deduction which renders them *objectively* necessary.

HENRI DE LUBAC, S.J. (1896-1991)

De Lubac was born in 1896 in Cambrai, in the North of France. His family moved shortly thereafter to Lyon where de Lubac was educated by the Jesuits. He joined the Jesuits himself in 1913 at their St. Leonard's-on-Sea Novitiate in East Sussex, England. De Lubac was drafted into the French army in 1914 and was wounded in the battle of Les Éparges in 1917, the same battlefield on which Rousselot died. With the cessation of World War I in 1919, de Lubac studied philosophy at the Maison Saint-Louis Scholasticate in St. Helier, on the island of Jersey, followed by theological studies at Ore Place in Hastings, East Sussex (1924-1926) and Fourvière in Lyons (1926 to 1927). He was ordained a Jesuit priest in 1927 and received an honorary doctorate from the Gregorian University.

De Lubac taught fundamental theology at the Catholic Institute of Lyons from 1929-1940, and additionally at the Fourvière theologate from 1935 to 1940. During the Second World War, de Lubac initially became part of the Vichy Regime, teaching at its School of Uriages, near Grenoble, from 1940-1941. He later on, however, distanced himself from the Vichy Regime, joined the French Resistance, and assisted in the publication of the Resistance journal *Témoignage chrétien* from 1942-1943. In 1944, de Lubac returned to the Catholic Institute of Lyons and taught there until 1950. In 1950, because of questions of orthodoxy surrounding his theory of grace, the Jesuits removed de Lubac's teaching faculties, terminated his editorship of the journal *Recherches de science religieuse* which he had assumed in 1947, and banished several of his books from Jesuit libraries. That same year the encyclical *Humani generis* was issued by Pius XII, and some speculate that de Lubac was among those accused in section 26 of "destroy[ing] the gratuity of the supernatural order, since God, they say, cannot create intellectual beings without ordering and calling them to the beatific vision."

In any case, De Lubac had become part of the Nouvelle théologie movement, along with Henri Bouillard, Pierre Teilhard de Chardin, Yves Congar, Marie-Dominique Chenu, Louis Bouyer, Jean Daniélou, and Jean Mouroux, advocating a return to the teachings of the Church Fathers [*ressourcement*], a need to reformulate key doctrines in light of contemporary concerns and ecumenical considerations, and a renewal of the Church. One of the major achievements of the Nouvelle théologie movement was the publication, beginning in 1940, of critical editions of the Church Fathers in the series *Sources Chrétiennes*, under the editorship of Daniélou and de Lubac. Only in 1958 was de Lubac allowed to resume teaching at the Catholic Institute of Lyons, where he taught until 1961. Finding himself now favored by the Magisterium, De Lubac was made a *peritus* at the Second Vatican Council, where his ecclesiology influenced the drafting of the documents *Lumen gentium* and *Gaudium et spes*, a member of the International Theological Commission (1969-1974), and Consultor to the Pontifical Secretariats for Non-Christians and Non-Believers. In 1972 de Lubac, along with Joseph Ratzinger

[Benedict XVI], Hans Urs von Balthasar, Walter Kasper, and Karl Lehmann, founded the journal *Communio*. De Lubac was appointed a Cardinal by John Paul II in 1983, with his titular church being Santa Maria in Domnica. He died in 1991 in Paris.

The key philosophical works of de Lubac are his *Le drame de l'humanisme athée* (Paris: Spes, 1944); *De la connaissance de Dieu* (Paris: Seuil, 1945); *Surnaturel* (Paris: Aubier, 1946); *Augustinisme et théologie moderne* (Paris: Aubier, 1965); *Le mystère du surnaturel* (Paris: Aubier, 1965); *Athéisme et sense de l'homme* (Paris: Cerf, 1968). His major theological works are *Catholicisme: Les aspects sociaux du dogme* (Paris: Cerf, 1938); *Corpus Mysticum: Essai sur l'Eucharistie et l'Église au moyen âge* (Paris: Aubier, 1944); as well as books on Buddhism, Scriptural Exegesis, Ecclesiology, and Teilhard de Chardin.

For more on the work of de Lubac, see Feingold, Lawrence, *The Natural Desire to See God According to St. Thomas and His Interpreters* (Washington: Catholic University of America Press, 2004); Milbank, John, *The Suspended Middle: Henri de Lubac and the Debate concerning the Supernatural* (Grand Rapids: William B. Eerdmans, 2005); Bonino, Serge-Thomas, O.P., ed. *Surnatural: A Controversy at the Heart of Twentieth-Century Thomistic Thought* (Washington: Catholic University of America Press, 2007); Grumett, David, *De Lubac: A Guide for the Perplexed* (Edinburgh: T&T Clark, 2007); Braine, David. "The Debate between Henri de Lubac and His Critics." *Nova et Vetera* 6 (2008): 543-590; Long, Steven A., *Natura Pura: On the Recovery of Nature in the Doctrine of Grace* (New York: Fordham University Press, 2010); Malloy, Christopher J., "De Lubac on Natural Desire: Difficulties and Antitheses," *Nova et Vetera* 9:3 (Summer, 2011): 567-624; Mulcahy, Bernard, O.P., *Aquinas's Notion of Pure Nature and the Christian Integralism of Henri de Lubac: Not Everything is Grace* (New York: Peter Lang, 2011); Nichols, Aidan, O.P., "Henri de Lubac: Panorama and Proposal." *New Blackfriars* 93:1043 (January, 2012): 3-33; Swafford, Andrew Dean, *Nature and Grace: A New Approach to Thomistic Ressourcement* (Eugene: Pickwick Publications, 2014); Oakes, Edward, *A Theology of Grace in Six Controversies* (Grand Rapids: William B. Eerdmans Publishing, 2016): 1-46; Hillebert, Jordan, ed., *T&T Clark Companion to Henri de Lubac* (London: Bloomsbury, 2017).

The text of de Lubac found below is from his *The Mystery of the Supernatural* (New York: Crossroad, 1998): IV, 54-62, 68-74. In it de Lubac argues that the Neo-Scholastic concept of a "state of pure nature," stemming from Cajetan and others, wherein humans have or could have had a purely natural finality as well as a supernatural finality, is a corruption of the thought of Aquinas and in any case theologically inapposite. It makes grace wholly extrinsic to human nature. As opposed to this view, Aquinas held that humans have a natural desire for the beatific vision, one constitutive of and affecting their very being. Hence the desire for the vision of God is inscribed upon the concrete nature of humans and is their only proper end.

The Mystery of the Supernatural (1965)[213]

Towards a Real Gratuitousness

[54] It is said that a universe might have existed in which man, though without necessarily excluding any other desire, would have his rational ambitions limited to some lowly purely human, beatitude. Certainly I do not deny it. But having said that, one is obliged to admit—indeed one is automatically affirming—that in our world as it is this is not the case: in fact the "ambitions" of man as he is cannot be limited in this way. Further, the word "ambitions" is no longer the right one, nor as one must see even more clearly, is the word "limits." In me, a real and personal human being, in my concrete nature—that nature I have in common with all real men, to judge by what my faith teaches me, and regardless of what is or is not revealed to me either by reflective analysis or by reasoning—the "desire to see God" cannot be permanently frustrated without an essential suffering. To deny this is to undermine my entire Credo. For is not this, in effect, the definition of the "pain of the damned"? And consequently—at least in appearance—a good and just God could hardly frustrate me, unless I, through my own fault, turn away from him by choice. The infinite importance of the desire implanted in me by my Creator is what constitutes the infinite importance of the drama of human existence. It matters little that, in the actual circumstances of that existence, immersed as I am in material things, and unaware of myself, this desire is not objectively recognized in its full reality and force: It will inevitably be so the day I at last see my nature as what it fundamentally is—if it is ever to appear to me in this way. "Certainly it is not now that reason dissimulates truth, or that the soul declines the view of reason, disconnected from corporeal limbs and drawn into itself."[214] For this desire is not some "accident" in me. It does not result from some peculiarity, possibly alterable, of my individual being, or from some historical contingency whose effects are more or [55] less transitory. *A fortiori* it does not in any sense depend upon my deliberate will. It

---

[214] St. Bernard, *De consideratione*, bk. 5, c. 72, n. 26 (Leclercq, Jean, ed. Bernard of Clairvaux, *Opera* (Romae: Editiones Cistercienses, 1964), vol. 3, p. 489).

is in me as a result of my belonging to humanly as it is, that humanity which is, as we say, "called." For God's call is constitutive. My finality, which is expressed by this desire, is inscribed upon my very being as it has been put into this universe by God. And, by God's will, I now have no other genuine end, no end really assigned to my nature or presented for my free acceptance under any guise, except that of "seeing God."

It remains necessary therefore to show how the supernatural is a free gift not only in relation to a given hypothetical human nature, or in relation to a given hypothetical state of human nature, or even in relation to human nature in general as it may be abstracted from the observation of its concrete realization; but how it is so precisely in relation to the concrete human beings we are, in relation to all those who make up mankind as it is, mankind created by God to see him, or, as we sometimes say, "historic nature." It remains to be shown that the supernatural is absolutely freely given *to me*, it my condition now. Otherwise nothing at all has been said. For my situation in relation to my final end is no longer exactly the same as the situation of nature from which we first reasoned (whatever may be the link or absence of link which we It thought we saw between that nature and its supernatural end). For instance when St. Irenaeus declared: "God makes himself seen by men when he wishes, to whom he wishes, and how he wishes," we can only understand his words (which are the expression of his faith) if we apply them directly to the human beings we are now, to all the people in the world, and first of all to our first father, in the concrete. In other words, the real problem, if problem it is, involves the being whose finality is "already," if one can say so, wholly supernatural–for such is the case with us. It involves the creature whose "vision of God" marks not only a possible, or futurable, or "most fitting" end, but the end which, as far as it can be humanly judged, seems to have to be–since it is, by hypothesis, the end God assigns to that creature. As soon as I exist, in fact, all indetermination vanishes, and whatever might have been the case "before," or whatever might have been in any other existence, no other finality now seems possible for me than that which is now really inscribed in the depths of my nature;[215]

---

[215] This was seen very clearly by Père Edmund Brisbois in the article quoted supra, p. 10, n. 51 ["Le désir de voir Dieu et la métaphysique du vouloir selon Saint Thomas," *Nouvelle Revue Théologique* 63 (1936): 983-984]. It is what Karl Rahner today calls "an abiding supernatural existential foreordained to grace" ("Relationship between Nature and

there is only one end, and [56] therefore I bear within me, consciously or otherwise, a "natural desire" for it.

Whatever may be said of desire being "elicited" by, or following upon, a knowledge of the object, however indeterminate that object in fact remains, this "natural desire" is not only just as "necessary" but just as "determinate" as its correlative end. "To each thing a single end is naturally appropriate, which it seeks by a natural necessity, for nature always tends to one thing," says St. Thomas, and he says further: "the natural appetite is determined to one thing." He is definitely concerned here with the end and the desire of a rational being, possessing free will, whose acts are not "determined to one thing" in the same way as those of things lacking cognition."[216] In terms reminiscent of the Scotists, Gregory of Valencia gives a similar explanation:

> To seek in this way [=naturally] beatitude in general and in particular is nothing other than to have some measure of, and capacity to, nature. This objectively truly limits the common concept of beatitude, and even the particular [concept of beatitude] to the enjoyment of God, which is known to be true beatitude. But it is placed in the freedom of no man to have or not to have this capacity of nature, since all men naturally, and to this extent necessarily, have it. Therefore naturally and necessarily all men seek beatitude in general and in particular by an appetite that is natural and not elicited.[217]

And it is this same fundamental reason that makes St. Thomas conclude so certainly, regardless of the contradictory evidence that common experience seems to suggest: "Every intellect naturally desires the vision of divine substance."[218]

Grace," in *Theological Investigations* (New York: Crossroad, 1974), vol. 1, p. 312, n. 1.

[216] *De Malo*, q. 16, art. 5; *De Veritate*, q. 22, art. 3, ad 5um. Cf. Peter of Tarantaise, *In 4 Sent.*, dist. 49, q. 1, art. 2 (Doucet, Victorin, *Commentaires sur les Sentences: Supplément au répertoire de M. Frédéric Stegmüller* (Florentiae: Quaracchi, 1954), p. 184).

[217] *Commentaria theologica*, vol. 2 (3rd edn, Lyon, 1963), col. 99 B.

[218] *Summa Contra Gentiles*, III, c. 57, etc. 57, etc. I wonder whether it is enough to speak of an "indeterminate disposition," or "indeterminate tendency," which the author of an *Essai sur la problème de la destinée* (1933) considers "essential to the natural desire of the mind." It is an idea similar to that found in John of St. Thomas, *Cursus theologicus*, disp. 12, n. 23: "Man by reason of his own nature, does not have a final end determined materially and in particular but only vaguely and in general,

[57] That is why, if I fail to achieve this which is my end, it may be said that I have failed in everything; if I lose it, I am "damned"; and to be aware of such a situation is for me the "pain of damnation." This *poena damni*, as I have said, can be explained in no other way: for, as Karl Rahner observes, "the loss of a good which is possible but not the object of an ontological ordination prior to free endeavor (*voluntas ut res*), can only be felt as a painful evil when the loser wills it *freely*."[219] Hence the statement of the Venerable Mary of the Incarnation: "I contemplated the court of heaven itself, that abode of the blessed, with all the happiness that scripture tells us is felt there; and all that happiness without God seemed to me nothing but misery and grief of heart."[220] This is what Augustine expressed so magnificently in the *Confessions*; "This only I know, that I am wretched apart from you, not only without, but also within myself, and all plenty that is not God is indigence."[221]

---

and according to the reason of beatitude, i.e. the good" (Solesmes edn, vol. 2, p. 145). Cf. Dom Georges Frénaud, who speaks of a certain natural capacity "open in itself to a whole gamut of possible finalities with no strictly determined orientation to any one of them" ("La gratuité des dons surnaturels," *La Pensée Catholique* 6 (1948): 4). The element of truth that we can recognize here is that in fact the nature of a spiritual, intelligent, and free being is not "determined towards one thing [*determinata ad unum*]" as is that of "natural being" [see *infra*, chapter 7]. Further, that the last end actually assigned to human nature is only known naturally "vaguely and in common [*vage et in communi*]," this I understand and would allow (*infra*, chapter 9); but that it is in itself, in man as he actually exists, as God wills, envisages and sees it, "vague and common" [*vaga et communis*]," this I find harder to understand. Cf. Petrus Trigosus, "An in nobis sit natural desiderium ..." (in Julien Eymard d'Angers, "De visionis beatificae naturali desiderio apud Petrum Trigoso a Catalayud, O.F.M. Cap (1533-1593)," *Antonianum* 32 (1957): 9).

[219] *Loc cit.*

[220] *Relations d'oraison*, First Relation, 2, n. 2 (Jamet, Paul, ed., *Marie de l'Incarnation: Écrits spirituels et historiques* (Paris: Desclée de Brouwer, 1929), vol. 2, p. 30). Cf. St. Catherine of Genoa, *Vita e dottrina*, chapter 7: "She said: A Soul which truly loves God, if it is drawn to the perfection of love, as it sees itself imprisoned in the world and the body, if God does not support it by his providence, then bodily life will be a hell for it, because it prevents it from attaining the end for which it has been created" (Debongnie, Pierre, ed., *Sainte Catherine de Gênes* [Études Carmélitaines] (Paris: Desclée de Brouwer, 1960), p. 30).

[221] St. Augustine, *Confessions*, bk. 13, c. 8, n. 9 (*Bibliotheque*

This is the human situation resulting from the free will of God, as Christian tradition has expressed it over and over again. Bérulle, as magnificent as he is severe wrote:

> Let us bless God who has given us being, and a being which has a relationship and a movement towards him. That movement is impressed by the Creator's power in the depths of his creature, deep within it from the very moment of its creation. And it is a movement so deep and so powerful that the will cannot affect it except to fight against it, that no sin we commit can hold it back, that hell itself cannot obliterate it. That movement [58] will last as long as the creature itself, and is inseparable from it. And the struggle that will take place in hell between the movement naturally imprinted upon the creature by the Creator, and the movement of will whereby the creature turns away from him, will be one of the chief and everlasting torments of the damned. That inclination, which is natural to the soul, is hidden in this life, just as the soul is hidden from itself as long as it is buried within the body. It sees neither its own being, nor what lies at the depths of its being. When it leaves the body, it will see itself and will then also feel the powerful weight of that inclination, but without the power or freedom to make any good use of it.[222]

Such a being, then, has more than simply a "natural desire" [*desiderium naturale*] to see God, a desire which might be interpreted vaguely and widely, which might, as a later commentator on St. Thomas has said, simply be "a desire conform to nature," or as another says, "in proportion to nature" [*juxta naturam*].[223] St. Thomas is most clear that such is not the case. The desire to see God is, for him, a "desire of nature" in man; better, it is "the desire of his nature," *naturae desiderium:*[224] this

---

Augustinienne (Paris: Desclée de Brouwer, 1992), vol. 14, p. 438): *De Civitate Dei*, bk. 12, c. 1, n. 2: "the creature is blessed in possessing that which, by its absence, leaves it miserable" (*Bibliotheque Augustinienne* (Paris: Desclée de Brouwer, 1993), vol. 35, p. 150).

[222] *Opuscules de piéte*, 27, on man's obligation, in nature and in grace, to refer himself wholly to God, n. 10 (Rotureau, Gaston, ed., *Le Cardinal de Bérulle: Opuscules de piété* (Paris: J. Galy, 1943), p. 134).

[223] T. Richard, O.P., "À propos d'une célèbre controverse," *Revue Thomiste* 41 (1936): 229: "The true formula is this: I would like to see. The desire is neither so urgent nor so universal as some writers seem to think."

[224] "Natural desire" [*desiderium naturale*] can be translated in

expression, which he uses on several occasions, should be enough in itself to do away with any tendency to fancy interpretation. It therefore remains necessary to show how, even for a being animated with such a desire, there still is not and cannot be any question of such an end being "owed"–in the same sense in which the word rightly gives offense. It remains to show how it is always by grace–even apart from the additional question of sin and its forgiveness–that God "shows himself to him."[225] Whether or not [59] the hypothesis of a purely natural universe, involving a "purely natural end," and the various conclusions that may be drawn from such a hypothesis, do in fact date from a much earlier age, we certainly cannot dispense ourselves from envisaging this new aspect of the problem now. Whatever suppositions we may accumulate, this aspect will constantly reappear, "demanding" to be envisaged. We may re-echo the words of a great Thomist who died in 1351:

> No created intellect, human or angelic, is able by its natural powers to attain the vision of the divine essence in which perfect beatitude consists; [it is able to] out of divine grace. ... God cannot be seen in his essence unless by the grace of God. ... No one arrives to it of himself but one to whom it is given from the gift of God. It is not in our power to see God, but in his power to appear ..., to be seen is in his will: the will of God is to be seen. For if he wills it, he is seen; if he does not will it, he is not seen. Now he appeared to Abraham, because he willed to;

---

various senses, but "desire of nature" [desiderium naturae] has only one, far more pregnant, meaning, Prima, q. 12, a. 1: "the desire of nature will remain vain [remanebit inane naturae desiderium]." Summa contra Gentiles, III, c. 48: "It is impossible for natural desire [naturale desiderium] to be vain ... the desire of nature [naturae desiderium] would be vain, if it could never be fulfilled." These texts can be compared with De Malo, q. 5, a. 2. My intention here does not include any deeper study of this "desire," either in itself, or in Thomist thinking. Yet I do wonder how anyone could believe, as Père Ambroise Gardeil has recently claimed (La structure de l'âme et l'expérience mystique (Paris: J. Gabalda, 1927), vol. 1, pp. 305-306), that the desire St. Thomas speaks of is no more than a desire of mere "complacence," solely stimulated from without, and free, optional and uncertain in its exercise. Cf. Stanislas Dockx, O.P., "Du désir naturel de voir l'essence divine d'après saint Thomas," Archives de philosophie 27 (1964): 49-96.

[225] Cf. St. Thomas, Summa contra Gentiles, III, c. 52, quoting John 14:21.

to others he did not appear: because he did not will to.[226]

For in effect, to maintain the gratuitousness of the supernatural simply by referring to another possible end, it is not enough to say, as we have just seen, that the same human nature might, in a different order of things, have been constituted with that other finality. This does not bring us sufficiently to grips with the question. One would have to be able further to affirm it of the same humanity, of the same human being, and ultimately of myself as I am. And this, if one considers it, makes no sense. For by putting forward the hypothesis of another order of things, one cannot help by that very fact supposing another humanity, a different human being, and thus a different "me." In this "purely natural" universe which some have imagined, or have at least declared to be possible, "my nature," they say, would be included. We may perhaps agree–though it cannot be as certain as they think, except in the most abstract sense, since it must be said at the same time that this nature would be "materially" different. But even then it would not be [60] the same "me." You may put into this hypothetical world a man as like me as you can, but you cannot put me into it. Between that man who, by hypothesis, is not destined to see God, and the man I am in fact, between that futurable and this existing being, there remains only a theoretical, abstract identity, without the one really becoming the other at all. For the difference between them is not merely one of individuation, but one of nature itself. What can possibly be learnt from the situation of the first, the hypothetical man, in regard to the gratuitousness of the gift given to the second, the man that I am in reality? I can only repeat that ultimately it is solely in relation to me, in relation to us all, to our nature as it is, this actual mankind to which we belong, that this question of gratuitousness can be asked and answered.[227]

---

[226] Raynerius de Pisis, *Pantheologia, Beatitudo*, c. 11 (Brescia, 1580), vol. 2, 1, p. 242. And the nominalist Gabriel Biel, *Collectorium*, bk. 1, dist. 17, q. 1, F: "Whenever God beatifies, he does so merely contingently, freely and mercifully, from his grace. ... No form is needed for eternal life, not even a supernatural one; but, just as he pours out grace from his goodness freely and contingently, so also, granted whatever form, does he grant eternal life freely and mercifully from his grace, and always would be able not to confer it [without injustice to himself]."

[227] The objection will have particular force against the thesis that denies all "natural desire" properly so called in the state of pure nature. If, indeed, the vision of God in himself does not inspire "any curiosity" in

In other words, put in terms which, though not those used by St. Thomas, express his ideas faithfully, if it is true that "the power to see the divine essence is the specific obediential power (*potentia obedientalis*) of man as an intellectual creature,"[228] it is important to demonstrate [61] that in the world as it actually is, this power still remains in that sense wholly "obediential."

Put in yet another way, if I should be able to declare unequivocally that God gives himself to me, and makes himself to be seen by me freely, and quite independently, then that supernatural gift must be clearly seen to be free not merely in relation to some generic nature, abstract and theoretical, but actually in relation to the concrete nature in which I, here and

---

the created spirit, then either an effective ordering to that vision, supervening upon another state, is not felt by it as a blessing (and it reacts as does a man who is not hungry to even the finest of meals); or, in order that hunger may come with that ordering, the spirit in question will have to be very profoundly transformed. And if so (apart from the dangerous empiricism which such a conception of spirit must suppose), if it was already clear that there was no identity of subject between one and the other, it now becomes clear that there is no identity of "nature" either. How can the hypothesis of "pure nature" help to resolve the problem in these circumstances?

[228] A. Raineri, O.P., "De possibilitate viendi Deum per essentiam" in *Divus Thomas* 39 (1937), "The power to see the divine essence is the specific obediential power of man as an intellectual creature [*potentia visionis divinae essentiae est potentia obedientalis specifica hominis, prout est creatura intellectualis ut sic*] (p. 4); "Only in the actuation of its specific obediential power or only in the vision of the divine essence according as it is in itself [*in se*], does the perfect beatitude of man consist, which however by no means establishes its own natural or due end" (p. 113). "Despite the contrary opinion of certain theologians, the texts of St. Thomas show that he considers the desire for the vision as distinct from the obediential power," (Bernard Fraigneau-Julian, P.S.S., in the French edition of Scheeben's *Natur und Gnade* (French translation (Paris: Desclée de Brouwer, 1957), p. 74, note); and ibid., p. 34: According to St. Thomas, "natural desire" is distinguished from mere obediential power by four characteristics: by its particular object, which is the vision of God, and not the infinite mass of actuations of which a creature can be the object; by its subject: only the intellectual creature is capable of that desire, and this is one of its proper characteristics; by him who brings it about: it belongs only to God to actuate that power, not as creator, but as directly superior agent; finally, by its nature: it brings to the intellectual creature not some random achievement, but its own final perfection, in other words its perfect happiness."

now, share. Just as "it is the gratuitousness of God's plan now and not of some hypothetical plan, that we need to know," so too it is "God's plan now that is the theologian's true object of contemplation."229 We must be grateful to Père Le Guillou for reminding us of this; it was thus that the great scholastics understood it. One may point out that they did not deny the hypotheses of the moderns; nor would I dream of doing so. But it remains true that they did not put them forward, and when they spoke of the gratuitousness of the supernatural they did not mean it in terms of some abstract human nature as envisaged in those hypotheses. They would have found such an approach most unsatisfactory. St. Thomas, for instance, says: "That God wishes to give to someone [*alicui*] grace and glory proceeds from his sheer generosity." *Alicui*: to someone, to some person at whom we can point.230 To someone, to you, to me, this very day. God can be no more bound by our nature as it is than by the nature of some humanity that might have been. I do not believe that it keeps the truth of the dogma intact to suggest, as Palmieri (among others) does in his great *Tractatus de ordine supernaturali*, that human desire can *claim* the vision of God from the moment of its being no longer the desire of "pure nature," but of nature "raised up" or "called."231 This would hardly allow for the liberty of God [62] in

---

229 Marie-Joseph Le Guillou, O.P., "Surnaturel," *Revue des Sciences Philosophiques et Théologiques* 34 (1950), p. 242.

230 *De Veritate*, q. 6, a. 2. Similarly, when speaking of knowledge, St. Thomas says: "Here the individual man understands." I would say here: "Here the individual man has a gratuitous end."

231 Domenico Palmieri, *Tractatus de ordine supernaturali et de lapsu angelorum*, 2nd edn. (Prati: Giachetti, 1910), p. 109: "The desire of which Augustine speaks ... is the elicited desire, but of raised up nature, which consequently demands the acquisition of the vision of God through supernatural powers." Such a requirement seems to me as unacceptable in itself as it is contrary to the teaching of, for instance, St. Augustine, or of St. Thomas as set out perfectly clearly in *De Veritate*, q. 6, a. 2. Similarly, Brisbois, *art. cit.*, p. 1104: "There must then be, in human nature as called to supernatural beatitude, a new subjective disposition, a new demand, prior to any deliberate choice of the will, prior even to faith and sanctifying grace which directs human nature to its supernatural destiny in the guise of a necessary, unreflecting need for the final absolute good." That same word "demand" (*exigence*) occurs again in a note. When Fr. Philip Donnelly wrote in "The Gratuity of the Beatific Vision and the Possibility of a Natural Destiny" (*Theological Studies* 11 (1950): 392): "God cannot refuse to fulfill this supernatural destiny which is inscribed in the very essence of finite spirits," he intended it is a

distributing his gifts; it would make supernatural beatitude no longer "truly a grace", but as Fénelon pointed out, "a debt given the title of grace."[232]

Then there is the hypothesis that seeks to posit a "purely natural" universe, in which man could claim "natural" happiness from God. Now, alongside this another universe is imagined–our own in fact–in which man still requires happiness from God, this time "supernatural." Whether we add the two together or set them up against each other, we can hardly hope to find in them the gratuitousness we are looking for.

It is always within the real world, within a world whose supernatural finality is not hypothetical but a fact, and not by following any supposition that takes us out of the world, that we must seek an explanation of the gratuitousness of the supernatural–in so far as the human mind can do so. But this is precisely what the modern hypothesis we are concerned with fails to do. I do not say that it is false, but I do say that it is insufficient. For it completely fails to show, as people seem to think and as by the logic of the theory it should, that I could have had another, more humble, wholly "natural" destiny. It only demonstrates–presuming it to be well-founded–that in another universe I might really have had this humbler destiny–humbler, but note, also less onerous–you need only show it to me, even momentarily, as something really imprinted upon me, in my nature as it is. Most people would agree that this is precisely what is, by hypothesis, impossible. My destiny is something ontological, and not something I can change as anything else changes its destination. We must therefore seek along some other path for a more real certainty of the gratuitousness we need to find. ...

[68] Sought along this path of a different finality, the solution to the problem of the gratuitousness of the supernatural could only really be found in the following way. It would have to be possible to note in the actual course of every real and personal

---

formulation of my position, but was in fact stating the precise opposite of what I have clearly said. But that is what Palmieri seems to think, and with him many others, and it is that which in fact fits in with the logic of one theory of "pure nature," at least when being used as an ultimate explanation.

[232] Cf. François Fénelon, *Réponse à la Relation sur le Quiétisme*, forward. Cf. id., *Première letter à M. de Chartres* (*Oeuvres* (Paris: Firmin Didot, 1882), vol. 3, pp. 128-29). Also *Troisième letter en réponse à celle de Mgr l'évêque de Meaux* (*Oeuvres*, vol. 2, pp. 654, 664).

existence–or, at least, if one envisages not so much individuals in themselves as the humanly of which they are a part and which unites them by the assignation of a single destiny, in the actual course of our race's concrete, historic existence–a definite moment when God intervenes either to assign an end which till then had been in doubt, or to change the end previously assigned to me. Either hypothesis would be absurd, if one considers it. In either case, one would be supposing a radical extrinsicism which must destroy either the idea of nature or that of finality, or possibly both. Neither the epic of the universe, nor the acting out of my personal destiny could include such a second start. Such a supposition is in any case–at least apparently and in principle–excluded by the axiom, which everyone admits, that the so-called state of "pure nature" can only be posited as a "futurable," as something which has never actually existed, even for a moment. However, it becomes impossible to escape from it once one has produced the theory that an end cannot be given freely for a definite being, existing here and now, unless there had first of all been a different end for him that was objectively, concretely realizable–in other words, once one has made "pure nature" in the modern sense the indispensable and sole guarantee of the gratuitousness of the supernatural.

In fact, this modern theory of a spiritual nature–whether angelic or human–with a "purely natural" finality, was born and developed in the intellectual context of a watered-down idea of what finality is. What it assumed at its beginnings, though not always very explicitly, was something very different from what most of those who hold it today would assume. This was that every man, in our world as it is, before having received the grace of baptism or any other enabling grace, was in that state of "pure nature" (at least if one excludes original sin and its consequences).[233] Finality was therefore considered as something fairly extrinsic; not a destiny inscribed in a man's very nature, directing him [69] from within, and which he could not ontologically escape, but a mere destination given him from

---

[233] Though this restriction does not apply to the teaching of all of them. "Suarez considered temerarious and to be mistrusted the opinion of those who dared to affirm that, in the state of fallen nature, man as he actually is is intrinsically wounded, weakened or unbalanced" (Blaise Romeyer, "La théorie suarézienne d'un état de nature pure," *Archives de Philosophie* 18 (1949): 44-45).

outside when he was already in existence.[234] This is certainly what Suarez supposes, for example; for him, the punishment of Adam's sin was essentially the withdrawal of the supernatural finality which God had bestowed upon human nature as one gift, among others, added over and above nature.[235] According to this idea–put forward again in so many words in modern times by Fr. Philip Donnelly[236]–if God had not then envisaged and determined upon the plan of redemption, Adam and all his descendants, all those people whose names and histories we know, all existing mankind to which we ourselves belong, all these people, *ipsissimi*, would have had to merit, in a nature left essentially intact by sin, by the use of a free will left to itself but keeping all its original strength, "a certain state of happiness in its own order and level" [*in suo ordine et gradu*], or as some express it, a certain "natural possession" of God, as the only end to which they were called by anything actually inscribed within them.[237] "Had God not redeemed us," comments Blaise Romeyer, "we should be born *viatores* journeying towards a possession to be won by the right use of our free will."[238] In short, fallen man, brought back by this fall to his natural state, was no longer "called." In the framework of ideas which this theory presupposes, there would be no obstacle to a "supernatural" beatitude reaching a stage where, at any given moment, by God's decision, it is given in addition to the essential, wholly natural, happiness that is desired, postulated, required, and won by nature. This seems indeed a most simple and satisfactory explanation of the whole thing.

---

[234] And even that was only made possible, it seems, because of an initial ambiguity: the expression "pura natura" (or earlier such similar expressions as "pura naturalia") having for a long time meant no more than a certain state of nature as yet unprovided with supernatural gifts, without reference to its finality or later history one can see thus how the transition took place between the older teaching and the new.

[235] See also, in regard to the supernatural gifts bestowed on the first man, gifts which he compares to that of eternal beatitude, his naïve way of saying: "The question needs to be enlarged to all time. ... More, or less, does not change its form" (*De gratia*, prolog. 4, c. 1, n. 5: *Opera omnia* (Paris: Vivès, 1857), vol. 7, p. 180).

[236] "The Gratuity of the Beatific Vision," *Theological Studies* 11 (1950): 401-403. It is rare for anyone today to take up Suarez's teaching as literally as this.

[237] Suarez, *De Gratia* (Paris: Vivès, 1857), vol. 7, pp. 206ff., 216-221).

[238] "La théorie suarézienne d'un état de nature pure," *loc. cit.* One may note in passing this "conquest" of the possession of God.

This theory had begun to take shape well before Suarez. Cajetan was not properly speaking its inventor, for it was not produced all of a piece [70] in a day, but he was one of its chief initiators.[239] He certainly would seem to have been the first to claim the patronage of St. Thomas for it, in his commentary on the *Summa Theologica*. As I noted earlier, it is usual now to speak in this context of "historic nature." Now, we must not forget that this "historic nature," with the desire to see God which goes with it and marks it out in contrast with "pure nature," involves according to Cajetan both positive revelation and the objective knowledge of certain supernatural effects observed in the world.[240] It was far from being that nature first established in another state, and belonging to all those who make up the human race now. It could only be taken to be so if the theory of "pure nature" were explicitly stated, and in Cajetan's day that had not yet been done. In other words, according to this notion, which Père Gardeil rightly judges to be "singular"[241] and which is the earliest notion to be formulated

---

[239] Cf. Suarez, *De Gratia*, prolog. 4, c. 1, n. 2: "Cajetan, and more recent theologians, considered a third state, which they called purely natural ..." (Paris: Vivès, 1857), vol. 7, p. 179). See *infra*, chapter 8; also my *Augustinisme et théologie moderne* (Paris: Aubier, 1965), chapter 5, Eng. trans., *Augustinianism and Modern Theology* (London: Chapman; New York: Herder & Herder, 1969); Juan Alfaro, S.J., *Lo natural y lo sobrenatural* (Madrid: Consejo Superior de Investigaciones Científicas, 1952), is very instructive on the antecedents of Cajetan's teaching.

[240] *In Primam*, q. 72, a. 1: "He knew certain effects, say of grace and glory whose cause is God as God is in himself absolutely [*ut Deus est in se absolute*], not as a universal agent. Now since the effects are known, it is natural for the individual intellect to desire acquaintance with the cause. Therefore the desire for the divine vision, although it is not natural to the intellect absolutely created, is nevertheless natural to it granted the revelation of such effects"–what a contrast with the simple and pregnant "desire of nature [*desiderium naturae*]" of St. Thomas! In *Secundam Secundae*, q. 3, a. 8: "The author deals with man as a theologian. ... And so, although there is no such natural desire in man in the absolute, it is nevertheless natural to man ordered to heaven by Divine Providence ..., for it has been naturally evidenced that, once the effect has been seen, we desire to know what is the cause, whatever it be." Cf. John of St. Thomas, *Cursus theologicus*, Disput. 12, a. 3, n. 6: "Cajetan explains this concerning man with some knowledge of faith or of supernatural things being granted, not considering him from a strictly natural point of view" (vol. 2, p. 140).

[241] Ambroise Gardeil, *La structure de l'âme et l'expérience mystique* (Paris: J. Gabalda, 1927), vol. 1, p. 183: "it is clear that St. Thomas

---

of "historic nature," there is no room for what Maurice Blondel was to call "the transnatural state."[242]

[71] Since then, various theologians have taken up this "singular opinion." They still understand "historic nature" in Cajetan's sense–which is also that of Suarez. Even among those who appear nowadays to give it the greatest depth and consistency, there are a certain number who, basically, mean nothing else by it. When they say with the rest that the state of "pure nature" has not in fact ever existed, or that "historic man" has been in fact created in a supernatural order, it becomes clear in what an attenuated, or perhaps rather extenuated, transformed sense, one must understand their statement. For them, the ultimate destination of the universe has been changed in the course of time, without this fact making any change in the structure of that universe or the essence of the beings who constitute it; supposing that God had not willed to make himself seen, or even that to see him were utterly impossible, everything that goes to make up the universe and man would still be exactly the same.

This paradox has been upheld by various commentators of St. Thomas, for instance Billuart[243] and Gotti. Yet one informed historian of Thomist thought, Père A. Motte, has written: "One could dream of no more categorical reverse inflicted by

---

envisaged no such restriction" which takes away from his effort "all real interest."

[242] When Père Rousselot, *L'intellectualisme de saint Thomas*, 2nd edn. (Paris: Beauchesne, 1921), p. 183, Eng. trans. *The Intellectualism of St. Thomas* (London: Sheed and Ward, 1935), p. 179, wrote of "those who see man's whole orientation towards the Beatific Vision as due to some secret transformation of man brought about historically by grace. It was in this sense that Cajetan interpreted the view of St. Thomas," the interpretation which he himself put forward of Cajetan was, to say the least, incomplete; it was indeed incorrect too, if what it was saying was that the "inner transformation" was to be understood as affecting the nature of every man coming into this world.

[243] "[The intuitive vision of God] has no connection with natural cause or effect from the understanding of which the mind may ascend to its investigation or demonstration. As a result, if this vision did not exist or were impossible, all natural things would nevertheless have the same existence as that which they have now" (Quoted with approval by Père Réginald Garrigou-Lagrange, *Le sens du mystère* (Paris: Desclée de Brouwer, 1934) part 2, chapter 2, pp. 191-192).

commentators on the idea of the Master."²⁴⁴ We know how firmly
St. Thomas held that finality is something intrinsic, affecting the
depths of the being. We know too what reality he attached to what
he called the "order of the universe" [*ordo universi*] or "order of
the parts of the universe in relation to each other"²⁴⁵–so much so
that for him a single change in the natures making up the universe
would be enough to mean that one was really dealing with a
different universe.²⁴⁶ Duns Scotus here joins with St. Thomas in a
general reproof of those who, by distending the organic bonds of
reality too much, "make the substance of the universe
discontinuous [72] [*inconnexam*]."²⁴⁷ To both these men,
"everything in the real world is linked together."²⁴⁸ "Creation is
homogeneous."²⁴⁹

Here I will rest content for the moment with pointing out that,
if the conception inherited from Cajetan and completed by Suarez
is all that really follows from the premises I have been criticizing,

---

²⁴⁴ Antonin Motte, O.P., "La possibilité de la vision béatifique," in
Bulletin Thomiste 4 (1935): 577.

²⁴⁵ *Summa contra Gentiles*, I, c. 78. *De Potentia*, q. 3, a. 16, ad 1um;
etc.

²⁴⁶ *Prima*, q. 25, a. 6, ad 3um: "... God however could make things
differently or add others to those things already made, *and there would
be a different* better *universe.*"

²⁴⁷ *In 2 Sent.*, d. 1, 4, 11: following Aristotle, *XII Metaph.* A general
principle recalled in regard to those who deny "that relation is a thing
outside of the act of the intellect."

²⁴⁸ Testis (= Maurice Blondel), *La semaine sociale de Bordeaux*
(Paris: Bloud, 1910): "The lower degrees, though not ceasing to be lower
and to be powerless of themselves to initiate any ascent, are none the less
degrees, in other words stepping-stones, springboards. ... The higher
degrees are really the final cause of this world, which is not just a
patchwork of coinciding episodes, but an order filled with the unity of the
divine plan. ... Through the condescending action of the higher, the lower
is, as it were, pregnant with a higher cooperation."

²⁴⁹ Cf. Paul Claudel, "La théologie du coeur" in *Le coeur* [Etudes
Carmélitaines] (Paris: Desclée de Brouwer, 1950): 396: "If we firmly
accept this idea that God created all things together (Ecclus. 18:1), that
creation is homogeneous. ..." People will argue similarly (and indeed
some have done so) in relation to sin; this was expressed naïvely by
Alexander Neckam, *De naturis rerum*, bk. 2, c. 156: "Bear in mind that
because of the sin of original prevarication, the brilliance of planets and
stars was diminished ..." (Wright, Thomas, ed., *Alexandri Neckham: De
naturis rerum* (London: Longman, Green, Longman, Roberts, and
Green, 1863), p. 251).

in itself it appears to have little meaning. One can of course readily admit that the supernatural finality of our universe has no direct relationship with, for instance, the laws of physics or chemistry; and that therefore if *per impossibile* this universe should be suddenly deprived of any supernatural finality, those laws would remain unchanged. But can anyone reasonably say that the same would be true of man, of the foundations of his intellectual and moral life? And even supposing such a radical change had no repercussion on the material universe or the knowledge man can have of it, would it not be change enough that man himself was not exactly the same?[250] And finally, on the other hand, how could one allow that the Creator would so recast his work? What possible acceptable meaning could there be in such "repetitions of the creative act"?[251] If God really destines man to see him, one can understand his not actually admitting him to that vision from the first, but there can be no understanding [73] the idea that he only destines him to it from a given moment of his life or of world history.

Either the idea of "pure nature" must be conceived as being actually in our world now, as its protagonists see it; in that case, if we are not to be led into absurdity, we must return to its earlier significance which never questioned the supernatural character of the last end, but only described "the structure proper to created spirit in our world."[252] Or this idea of "pure nature" must be related to a different universe, since a purely natural order has never in fact existed, as the great majorly of theologians would hold nowadays;[253] in that case, being quite abstract, though there

---

[250] Then too, if I can thus be given a new finality at will, we must allow that the arbitrary is the rule, and give up any consistent idea of nature or of reason.

[251] Cf. Ambroise Gardeil, O.P., "Le désir naturel de voir Dieu," *Revue Thomiste* 9 (1926): 409-410: "... the existence in rational nature of a capacity for the divine vision, of the same order as the capacity of every being dependent upon God to be subject to renewals of his creative action, in any way that does not contradict what has gone before."

[252] When, for instance, Père Le Guillou writes (loc. cit., p. 242): "Pure nature is not a nature wholly foreign to us ...; it indicates the structure proper to created spirit in our world," I find myself in complete agreement with him provided always that he is concerned, as is St. Thomas himself, with our world and the structure of our being, and is not tacitly introducing a different kind of finality from that spoken of by St. Thomas.

[253] Cf. François Taymans, S.J., "L'encyclique Humani generis et la

is nothing to criticize in it of itself, it does not appear wholly suitable for the service expected of it. However, whether one adopts or rejects it, if one succeeds in making clear—as at all costs we must—that the supernatural end can *in no case* be the object of any requirement or debt, even by a being who here and now has no other end, then there will no longer be any need to refer to this indirect consideration of an order that is purely natural even as to its finality. We have seen that it is not an adequate consideration. Perhaps we may now go so far as to admit that it is not a necessary one either.[254] By trying, without seeking any fiction to take us beyond the limits of our world as God has made it, the only world we know, to show that the gift God offers of himself is and can only be totally free, and that one could never imagine any loftier or purer gratuitousness, I think we are embarking upon a really effective way, a way along which others may happily advance further. It seems to me, too, that this is the chief way opened to [74] us by tradition. If I succeed in this, without totally rejecting or obliging anyone else to reject every idea of "pure nature," then I shall have reinforced this all too fragile rampart of a fortress which defends for us all a truth older and loftier than all our reasonings and theories,[255] a Truth which the Church's magisterium has recalled to us many times in the most explicit terms, and reiterated quite recently, without ever having allowed any one explanatory theory to become tied to it. And if there are those who feel that it is impossible to preserve that divine truth except by reference to the system of "pure nature," I would be the first to tell them that not merely have they every right to maintain it, but that they would be wrong to reject it.

---

théologie," *Nouvelle Revue Théologique* 73 (1951): 17: "It is thus the common opinion of the weightiest doctors that the purely natural order has never in fact existed." See also Edmund Brisbois, O.P., "Le désir de voir Dieu et la métaphysique du vouloir selon saint Thomas," *Nouvelle Revue Théologique* 63 (1936): 1103-1105.

[254] It was right to allow for it at first, in order to avoid any conception of "nature" which did not fully preserve the gratuitousness of the supernatural. But it would not be legitimate; it would be reversing the roles, and taking the means for the end, to think only of avoiding every conception which would not appeal exclusively to "pure nature," for one would in that case be treating it as an absolute.

[255] Cf. Jules Lebreton, "Dogme et critique," in *Revue Pratique d'Apologétique* 4 (1907): 197: "The revealed dogmas are not to be treated as theorems to be inserted into the working-out of our human systems; they are the facts which must govern them."

BERNARD LONERGAN, S.J. (1904-1984)

Lonergan was born in 1904 in Buckingham, Quebec, Canada. He attended Jesuit-run Loyola College in Montreal from 1918-1922, and, attracted to the life of the Society of Jesus himself, joined the Order in 1922. Lonergan attended Heythrop College, London from 1926-1930 where he studied philosophy, classics, and mathematics. Upon completion of his bachelor's degree in philosophy, he returned to Canada and taught at his alma mater of Loyola College from 1930-1933. Lonergan then studied theology at the Gregorian University in Rome from 1933-1940. Though he was ordained in 1936 and had completed his classes, his theological studies were interrupted by the Second World War, and Lonergan did not acquire his doctorate in theology until 1946. In the meantime Lonergan again returned to Canada and taught at the Lycée de l'Immaculée-Conception from 1940-1947. After finally attaining his doctorate, Lonergan taught theology first at Regis College, University of Toronto, from 1947-1953, and next at the Gregorian University in Rome from 1953-1964. Lonergan returned to North America at the end of his life, teaching at Regis College from 1965 to 1975, Harvard University from 1971-1972, and Boston College from 1975-1983. He died in 1984 in Pickering, Ontario.

Lonergan's key works are his *Insight: A Study of Human Understanding* (London: Longmans, Green, and Company, 1957) and *Method in Theology* (New York: Herder and Herder, 1972). Also important are his two studies on the thought of Thomas Aquinas: *Verbum: Word and Idea in Aquinas* (Notre Dame: University of Notre Dame Press, 1946); *Grace and Freedom: Operative Grace in the Thought of Thomas Aquinas* (New York: Herder and Herder, 1971).

For more on Lonergan consult: Vertin, Joseph, *Critical Realism: Cognitional Approach and Ontological Achievement according to Bernard Lonergan* (Washington: Theological College Publications, 1970); Tyrell, Bernard, *Bernard Lonergan's Philosophy of God* (Notre Dame: University of Notre Dame Press, 1974); Meynell, Hugo, *An Introduction to the Philosophy of Bernard Lonergan* (New York: Barnes & Noble, 1976); Falcao, Nelson, *Knowing according to Bernard Lonergan* (Rome: Urbaniana University Press, 1987); Crowe, Frederick, *Appropriating the Lonergan Idea* (Washington; Catholic University of America Press, 1989); Oko, Dariusz, *The Transcendental Way to God according to Bernard Lonergan* (Frankfurt: Peter Lang, 1991); Rende, Michael, *Lonergan on Conversion* (Lanham: University Press of America, 1991); Crowe, Frederick, *Lonergan* (Collegeville: The Liturgical Press, 1992); Kinberger, Mary, *Lonergan on Conversion* (Frankfurt: Peter Lang, 1992); Stewart, William, *Introduction to Lonergan's Insight* (Lewiston: Edward Mellen Press, 1996); Tekippe, Terry, *What is Lonergan Up to in Insight?* (Collegeville: Liturgical Press, 1996); Flanagan, Joseph, *Quest for Self-Knowledge: An Essay in Lonergan's Philosophy* (Toronto: University of Toronto Press, 1997); Jonsson, Ulf,

Foundations for Knowing God: Bernard Lonergan's Foundations for Knowledge of God and the Challenge from Antifoundationalism (Frankfurt: Peter Lang, 1999); McPartland, Thomas, *Lonergan and the Philosophy of Historical Existence* (Columbia: University of Missouri Press, 2001); Kanaris, Jim, *Bernard Lonergan's Philosophy of Religion* (Albany: State University of New York Press, 2002); Tekippe, Terry, *Bernard Lonergan: An Introductory Guide to Insight* (New York: Paulist Press, 2003); Tekippe, Terry, *Bernard Lonergan's Insight: A Comprehensive Commentary* (Lanham: University Press of America, 2003); Fitzpatrick, Joseph, *Philosophical Encounters: Lonergan and the Analytic Tradition* (Toronto: University of Toronto Press, 2005); Mathew, William, *Lonergan's Quest: A Study of Desire in the Authoring of Insight* (Toronto: University of Toronto Press, 2005); Liddy, Richard, *Startling Strangeness: Reading Lonergan's Insight* (Lanham: University Press of America, 2007); Walmsley, Gerard, *Lonergan on Philosophic Pluralism* (Toronto: University of Toronto Press, 2008); Beer, Peter, *An Introduction to Bernard Lonergan* (Glen Waverley: Sid Harta Publishers, 2009); Beards, Andrew, *Insight and Analysis: Essays in Applying Lonergan's Thought* (New York: Continuum, 2010); Halse, Scott Andrew, *Bernard Lonergan's Methodology and the Philosophy of Religion: Functional Specialization and Religious Diversity* (Lewiston: Edward Mellen Press, 2010); Lambert, Pierrot, *Bernard Lonergan: His Life and Leading Ideas* (Vancouver: Axial, 2010); Ormerod, Neil, et al., eds., *Fifty Years of Insight* (Hindmarsh: ATF, 2011); Miller, Mark, *The Quest for God and the Good Life: Lonergan's Theological Anthropology* (Washington: Catholic University of America Press, 2013); Piscitelli, Emile J., *A Passion for God: The Religious Philosophy of Bernard Lonergan, S.J.* (Baltimore: Publish America, 2013); McCarthy, Michael H., *Authenticity as Self-Transcendence: The Enduring Insights of Bernard Lonergan* (Notre Dame: University of Notre Dame Press, 2015); Roy, Louis, *Engaging the Thought of Bernard Lonergan* (Montreal: McGill-Queen's University Press, 2016).

The text below is from: Lonergan, Bernard, *Insight: A Study of Human Understanding* (Toronto: University of Toronto Press, 1992): I, pp. 27-35; IX, pp. 298-303. In it Lonergan presents his epistemological version of Transcendental Thomism wherein knowledge occurs in the threefold process of making observations through the senses, formulating an insight by grasping patterns in the data with the understanding, and testing the insight by judgment to determine if it is valid or not and to what degree. If we grasp that this is our process of understanding then we see how both radical empiricists like Hume and idealists like Kant have misconstrued how we acquire knowledge, and we see that knowledge cannot be limited to the empirical plane. As Lonergan writes: "Thoroughly understand what it is to understand, and not only will you possess the broad lines of all there is to be understood but also you will possess a fixed base, an invariant pattern, opening upon all further developments of understanding" (Introduction, p. 22).

ALAN VINCELETTE

Insight: A Study of Human Understanding (1957)[256]

Insight as Activity

Elements

[27] In the midst of that vast and profound stirring of human minds which we name the Renaissance, Descartes was convinced that too many people felt it beneath them to direct their efforts to apparently trifling problems. Again and again in his *Regulae ad directionem ingenii*, he reverts to this theme. Intellectual mastery of mathematics, of the departments of science, of philosophy is the fruit of a slow and steady accumulation of little insights. Great problems are solved by being broken down into little problems. The strokes of genius are but the outcome of a continuous habit of inquiry that grasps clearly and distinctly all that is involved in the simple things that anyone can understand.

I thought it well to begin by recalling this conviction of a famous mathematician and philosopher, for our first task will be to attain familiarity with what is meant by insight, and the only way to achieve this end is, it seems, to attend very closely to a series of instances all of which are rather remarkable for their banality.

A Dramatic Instance

Our first illustrative instance of insight will be the story of Archimedes rushing naked from the baths of Syracuse with the cryptic cry 'Eureka!' King Hiero, it seems, had had a votive crown fashioned by a smith of rare skill and doubtful honesty. He wished to know whether or not baser metals had been added to the gold. Archimedes was set the problem and in the bath had hit upon the solution. Weigh the crown in water! [28] Implicit in this directive were the principles of displacement and of specific gravity.

With those principles of hydrostatics we are not directly concerned. For our objective is an insight into insight. Archimedes had his insight by thinking about the crown; we shall have ours by thinking about Archimedes. What we have to grasp is that insight (1) comes as a release to the tension of inquiry, (2) comes suddenly and unexpectedly, (3) is a function not of outer circumstances but

---

of inner conditions, (4) pivots between the concrete and the abstract, and (5) passes into the habitual texture of one's mind.

First, then, insight comes as a release to the tension of inquiry. This feature is dramatized in the story by Archimedes' peculiarly uninhibited exultation. But the point I would make does not lie in this outburst of delight but in the antecedent desire and effort that it betrays. For if the typical scientist's satisfaction in success is more sedate, his earnestness in inquiry can still exceed that of Archimedes. Deep within us all, emergent when the noise of other appetites is stilled, there is a drive to know, to understand, to see why, to discover the reason, to find the cause, to explain.

Just what is wanted has many names. In what precisely it consists is a matter of dispute. But the fact of inquiry is beyond all doubt. It can absorb a man. It can keep him for hours, day after day, year after year, in the narrow prison of his study or his laboratory. It can send him on dangerous voyages of exploration. It can withdraw him from other interests, other pursuits, other pleasures, other achievements. It can fill his waking thoughts, hide from him the world of ordinary affairs, invade the very fabric of his dreams. It can demand endless sacrifices that are made without regret though there is only the hope, never a certain promise, of [29] success. What better symbol could one find for this obscure, exigent, imperious drive, than a man, naked, running, excitedly crying, 'I've got it'?

Secondly, insight comes suddenly and unexpectedly. It did not occur when Archimedes was in the mood and posture that a sculptor would select to portray 'The Thinker.' It came in a flash, on a trivial occasion, in a moment of relaxation. Once more there is dramatized a universal aspect of insight. For it is reached, in the last analysis, not by learning rules, not by following precepts, not by studying any methodology. Discovery is a new beginning. It is the origin of new rules that supplement or even supplant the old. Genius is creative. It is genius precisely because it disregards established routines, because it originates the novelties that will be the routines of the future. Were there rules for discovery, then discoveries would be mere conclusions. Were there precepts for genius, then men of genius would be hacks. Indeed, what is true of discovery also holds for the transmission of discoveries by teaching. For a teacher cannot undertake to make a pupil understand. All he can do is present the sensible elements in the issue in a suggestive order and with a proper distribution of emphasis. It is up to the pupils themselves to reach understanding, and they do so in varying measures of ease and rapidity. Some get the point before the teacher can finish his exposition. Others just manage to keep pace with him. Others see the light only when they go over the matter by themselves. Some, finally, never catch on at all; for a while they follow the classes, but sooner or later they drop by the way.

Thirdly, insight is a function, not of outer circumstances, but of inner conditions. Many frequented the baths of Syracuse without coming to grasp the principles of hydrostatics. But who bathed there without feeling the water, or without finding it hot or cold or tepid? There is, then, a strange difference between insight and sensation. Unless one is deaf, one cannot avoid hearing. Unless one is blind, one has only to open one's eyes to see. The occurrence and the content of sensation stand in some immediate correlation with outer circumstance. But with insight internal conditions are paramount. Thus, insight depends upon native endowment, and so with fair accuracy one can say that insight is the act that occurs frequently in the intelligent and rarely in the stupid. Again, insight depends upon a habitual orientation, upon a perpetual alertness ever asking the little question, Why? Finally, insight depends on the accurate presentation of definite problems. Had Hiero not put his problem to Archimedes, had Archimedes not thought earnestly, perhaps [30] desperately, upon it, the baths of Syracuse would have been no more famous than any others.

Fourthly, insight pivots between the concrete and the abstract. Archimedes' problem was concrete. He had to settle whether a particular crown was made of pure gold. Archimedes' solution was concrete. It was to weigh the crown in water. Yet if we ask what was the point to that procedure, we have to have recourse to the abstract formulations of the principles of displacement and of specific gravity. Without that point, weighing the crown in water would be mere eccentricity. Once the point is grasped, King Hiero and his golden crown become minor historical details of no scientific importance. Again the story dramatizes a universal aspect of insight. For if insights arise from concrete problems, if they reveal their value in concrete applications, nonetheless they possess a significance greater than their origins and a relevance wider than their original applications. Because insights arise with reference to the concrete, geometers use diagrams, mathematicians need pen and paper, teachers need blackboards, pupils have to perform experiments for themselves, doctors have to see their patients, troubleshooters have to travel to the spot, people with a mechanical bent take things apart to see how they work. But because the significance and relevance of insight goes beyond any concrete problem or application, men formulate abstract sciences with their numbers and symbols, their technical terms and formulae, their definitions, postulates, and deductions. Thus by its very nature insight is the mediator, the hinge, the pivot. It is insight *into* the concrete world of sense and imagination. Yet what is known by insight, what insight adds to sensible and imagined presentations, finds its adequate expression only in the abstract and recondite formulations of the sciences.

Fifthly, insight passes into the habitual texture of one's mind. Before Archimedes could solve his problem, he needed an instant of inspiration. But he needed no further inspiration when he went to offer the king his solution. Once one has understood, one has crossed a divide. What a moment ago was an insoluble problem now becomes incredibly simple and obvious. Moreover, it tends to remain simple and obvious. However laborious the first occurrence of an insight may be, subsequent repetitions occur almost at will. This, too, is a universal characteristic of insight, and indeed it constitutes the possibility of learning. For we can learn inasmuch as we can add insight to insight, inasmuch as the new does not extrude the old but complements and combines [31] with it. Inversely, inasmuch as the subject to be learnt involves the acquisition of a whole series of insights, the process of learning is marked by an initial period of darkness in which one gropes about insecurely, in which one cannot see where one is going, in which one cannot grasp what all the fuss is about; and only gradually, as one begins to catch on, does the initial darkness yield to a subsequent period of increasing light, confidence, interest, absorption. Then the infinitesimal calculus or theoretical physics or the issues of philosophy cease to be the mysterious and foggy realms they had seemed. Imperceptibly we shift from the helpless infancy of the beginner to the modest self-confidence of the advanced student. Eventually we become capable of taking over the teacher's role and complaining of the remarkable obtuseness of pupils that fail to see what, of course, is perfectly simple and obvious to those that understand.

Definition

As every schoolboy knows, a circle is a locus of coplanar points equidistant from a center. What every schoolboy does not know is the difference between repeating that definition as a parrot might and uttering it intelligently. So, with a sidelong bow to Descartes's insistence on the importance of understanding very simple things, Let us inquire into the genesis of the definition of the circle.

The Clue

Imagine a cartwheel with its bulky hub, its stout spokes, its solid rim. Ask a question. Why is it round? Limit the question. What is wanted is the immanent reason or ground of the roundness of the wheel. Hence a correct answer will not introduce new data such as carts, carting, transportation, wheelwrights, or their tools. It will refer simply to the wheel. Consider a suggestion. The wheel is round because its spokes are equal. Clearly, that will not do. The spokes could be equal yet sunk unequally into the hub and rim. Again, the rim could be flat between successive spokes. Still, we have a clue. Let the hub decrease to a point; let the rim and spokes thin out into lines; then, if there were an infinity of spokes and all were exactly equal, the rim would have to be perfectly round; [32] inversely were any of the spokes unequal, the rim could not avoid bumps or dents. Hence we can say that the wheel necessarily is round inasmuch as the distance from the center of the hub to the outside of the rim is always the same.

A number of observations are now in order. The foregoing brings us close enough to the definition of the circle. But our purpose is to attain insight, not into the circle, but into the act illustrated by insight into the circle.

The first observation, then, is that points and lines cannot be imagined. One can imagine an extremely small dot. But no matter how small a dot may be, still it has magnitude. To reach a point, all magnitude must vanish, and with all magnitude there vanishes the dot as well. One can imagine an extremely fine thread. But no matter how fine a thread may be, still it has breadth and depth as well as length. Remove from the image all breadth and depth, and there vanishes all length as well.

Concepts

The second observation is that points and lines are concepts.

Just as imagination is the playground of our desires and our fears, so conception is the playground of our intelligence. Just as imagination can create objects never seen or heard or felt, so too conception can create objects that cannot even be imagined. How? By supposing. The imagined dot has magnitude as well as position, but the geometer says, 'Let us suppose it has only position.' The imagined line has breadth as well as length, but the geometer says, 'Let us suppose it has only length.'

Still, there is method in this madness. Our images and especially our dreams seem very random affairs, yet psychologists offer to explain them. Similarly, the suppositions underlying concepts may appear very fanciful, yet they too can be explained. Why did we require the hub to decrease to a point and the spokes and rim to mere lines? Because we had a clue–the equality of the spokes–and we were pushing it for all it was worth. As long as the hub had any magnitude, the spokes could be sunk into it unequally. As long as the spokes had any thickness, the wheel could be flat at their ends. So we supposed a point without magnitude and lines without thickness, to obtain a curve that would be perfectly, necessarily round.

Note, then, two properties of concepts. In the first place, they are [33] constituted by the mere activity of supposing, thinking, considering, formulating, defining. They may or may not be more than that. But if they are more, then they are not merely concepts. And if they are no more than supposed or considered or thought about, still that is enough to constitute them as concepts. In the second place, concepts do not occur at random; they emerge in thinking, supposing, considering, defining, formulating; and that many-named activity occurs, not at random, but in conjunction with an act of insight.

The Image
The third observation is that the image is necessary for the insight.

Points and lines cannot be imagined. But neither can necessity or impossibility be imagined. Yet in approaching the definition of the circle there occurred some apprehension of necessity and of impossibility. As we remarked, if all the radii are equal the curve must be perfectly round, and if any radii are unequal the curve cannot avoid bumps or dents.

Further, the necessity in question was not necessity in general but a necessity of roundness resulting from these equal radii. Similarly, the impossibility in question was not impossibility in the abstract but an impossibility of roundness resulting from these unequal radii. Eliminate the image of the center, the radii, the curve, and by the same stroke there vanishes all grasp of necessary or of impossible roundness.

But it is that grasp that constitutes the insight. It is the occurrence of that grasp that makes the difference between repeating the definition of a circle as a parrot might and uttering it intelligently, uttering it with the ability to make up a new definition for oneself.

It follows that the image is necessary for the insight. Inversely, it follows that the insight is the act of catching on to a connection between imagined equal radii and, on the other hand, a curve that is bound to look perfectly round.

The Question

The fourth observation adverts to the question.

There is the question as expressed in words. Why is the wheel round?

Behind the words there may be conceptual acts of meaning, such as 'wheel,' 'round,' etc.

[34] Behind these concepts there may be insights in which one grasps how to use such words as 'wheel,' 'round,' etc.

But what we are trying to get at is something different. Where does the 'Why?' come from? What does it reveal or represent? Already we had occasion to speak of the psychological tension that had its release in the joy of discovery. It is that tension, that drive, that desire to understand, that constitutes the primordial 'Why?' Name it what you please—alertness of mind, intellectual curiosity, the spirit of inquiry, active intelligence, the drive to know. Under any name, it remains the same, and is, I trust, very familiar to you.

This primordial drive, then, is the pure question. It is prior to any insights, any concepts, any words; for insights, concepts, words have to do with answers, and before we look for answers we want them; such wanting is the pure question.

On the other hand, though the pure question is prior to insights, concepts, and words, it presupposes experiences and images. Just as insight is into the concretely given or imagined, so the pure question is about the concretely given or imagined. It is the wonder which Aristotle claimed to be the beginning of all science and philosophy. But no one just wonders. We wonder about something.

Genesis

A fifth observation distinguishes moments in the genesis of a definition.

When an animal has nothing to do it goes to sleep. When a man has nothing to do he may ask questions. The first moment is an awakening to one's intelligence. It is release from the dominance of biological drive and from the routines of everyday living. It is the effective emergence of wonder, of the desire to understand.

The second moment is the hint, the suggestion, the clue. Insight has begun. We have got hold of something. There is a chance that we are on the right track. Let's see.

The third moment is the process. Imagination has been released from other cares. It is free to cooperate with intellectual effort, and its cooperation consists in endeavoring to run parallel to intelligent suppositions, while at the same time restraining supposition within some limits of approximation to the imaginable field.

The fourth moment is achievement. By their cooperation, by successive adjustments, question and insight, image and concept present a solid [35] front. The answer is a patterned set of concepts. The image strains to approximate to the concepts. The concepts, by added conceptual determinations, can express their differences from the merely approximate image. The pivot between images and concepts is the insight. And setting the standard which insight, images, and concepts must meet is the question, the desire to know, that could have kept the process in motion by further queries had its requirements not been satisfied.

The Notion of Judgment

[297] ... On the basis of the foregoing determinations we next attempt to relate [298] judgment to the general structure of our cognitional process. We distinguish a direct and an introspective process, and in both of these we distinguish three levels: a level of presentations, a level of intelligence, and a level of reflection.

Hitherto, our inquiry has centered on the level of intelligence. It consists in acts of inquiry, understanding, and formulation. Thus, the question, What is it? leads to a grasp and formulation of an intelligible unity-identity-whole in data as individual. The question, Why? leads to a grasp and formulation of a law, a correlation, a system. The question, How often? leads to a grasp and formulation of an ideal frequency from which actual frequencies nonsystematically diverge.

Our account of the classical and statistical phases of empirical method, of the notion of the thing, of explanatory abstraction and system has been concerned with the level of intelligence in cognitional process.

However, this level of intelligence presupposes and complements another level. Inquiry presupposes elements in knowledge about which inquiry is made. Understanding presupposes presentations to be understood. Formulation expresses not only what is grasped by understanding but also what is essential to the understanding in the understood. This prior level was described in the chapter on common sense. It is the level of presentations. Its defining characteristic is the fact that it is presupposed and complemented by the level of intelligence, that it supplies, as it were, the raw materials on which intelligence operates, that, in a word, it is empirical, given indeed but merely given, open to understanding and formulation but by itself not understood and in itself ineffable.

Thirdly, the level of intelligence, besides presupposing and complementing an initial level, is itself presupposed and complemented by a further level of reflection.

The formulations of understanding yield concepts, definitions, objects of thought, suppositions, considerations. But man demands more. Every answer to a question for intelligence raises a further question for reflection. There is an ulterior motive to conceiving and defining, thinking and considering, forming suppositions, hypotheses, theories, systems. That motive appears when such activities are followed by the question, Is it so? We conceive in order to judge. As questions for intelligence, What? and Why? and How often? stand to insights and formulations, so questions for reflection stand to a further kind of insight and to judgment. It is on this third level that there emerge the notions of truth and falsity, of certitude and the probability that is not a frequency but a [299] quality of judgment. It is within this third level that there is involved the personal commitment that makes one responsible for one's judgments.

It is from this third level that come utterances to express one's affirming or denying, assenting or dissenting, agreeing or disagreeing.

It will be useful to represent schematically the three levels of cognitional process.

I. Data. Perceptual Images. Free Images.	Utterances.
II. Questions for Intelligence. Insights.	Formulations.
III. Questions for Reflection. Reflection.	Judgment.

The second level presupposes and complements the first. The third level presupposes and complements the second. The exception lies in free images and utterances, which commonly are under the influence of the higher levels before they provide a basis for inquiry and reflection. Further, by questions for intelligence and reflection are not meant utterances or even conceptual formulations; by the question is meant the attitude of the inquiring mind that effects the transition from the first level to the second, and again the attitude of the critical mind that effects the transition from the second level to the third. Finally, the scheme is anticipatory inasmuch as the nature of reflection comes up for discussion only in the next chapter.

Now, as has been remarked, the three levels of the cognitional process operate in two modes. Data include data of sense and data of consciousness. Data of sense include colors, shapes, sounds, odors, tastes, the hard and soft, rough and smooth, hot and cold, wet and dry, and so forth. The direct mode of cognitional process begins from data of sense, advances through insights and formulations to reach reflection and judgment. Thus, empirical science pertains to the direct mode of cognitional process. On the other hand, the data of consciousness consist of acts of seeing, hearing, tasting, smelling, touching, perceiving, imagining, inquiring, understanding, formulating, reflecting, judging, and so forth. As data, such acts are experienced; but as experienced, they are not described, distinguished, compared, related, defined, for all such activities are the work of inquiry, insight, and formulation. Finally, such formulations are, of themselves, just hypotheses; they may be accurate or inaccurate, correct or mistaken; and to pronounce upon them is the work of reflection and judgment. Thus the three levels of the direct mode of cognitional process provide the data for the introspective mode; and as the direct mode, so also the introspective unfolds on the three [300] levels: an initial level of data, a second level of understanding and formulation, and a third level of reflection and judgment.

The foregoing offers an analysis of cognitional process. A whole is divided into different levels; on each level different kinds of operation are distinguished and related; each level is related to the others; and two modes of the whole process are contrasted. But analysis prepares the way for synthesis. Accordingly, we have now to ask how the various elements come together to constitute knowing. As yet, we are unprepared to answer the Kantian question that regards the constitution of the relation of knowing subject and known object. Our concern is the more elementary question of the unification of the contents of several acts into a single known content.

To this the general answer has already been indicated. Contents of different acts come together inasmuch as the earlier are incomplete without the later while the later have nothing to complete without the earlier. Questions for intelligence presuppose something to be understood, and that something is supplied by the initial level. Understanding grasps in given or imagined presentations an intelligible form emergent in the presentations. Conception formulates the grasped idea along with what is essential to the idea in the presentations. Reflection asks whether such understanding and formulation are correct. Judgment answers that they are or are not.

The cognitional process is thus a cumulative process: later steps presuppose earlier contributions and add to them. However, not all additions have the same significance. Some are merely provisional, as are free images. Some put together in a new mode the contributions of previous acts; thus, abstract formulation puts generally what insight grasps in a particular presentation. Finally, some constitute, as it were, the addition of new dimensions in the construction of the full cognitional content; and it is this addition of a new dimension that forms the basis of the distinction between the three levels of presentation, intelligence, and reflection.

From this viewpoint one may distinguish between the proper and the borrowed content of judgment.

The proper content of a judgment is its specific contribution to cognitional process. This consists in the answers yes or no.

The borrowed content of a judgment is twofold. There is the direct borrowed content that is found in the question to which one answers yes or no; and there is the indirect borrowed content that emerges in the [301] reflective act linking question and answer, that claims the yes or no to be true and, indeed, either certainly or only probably true.

Thus, the direct borrowed content of the judgment, I am writing, is the question, Am I writing? The proper content of that judgment is the answer, Yes, I am. The indirect borrowed content of the same judgment is the implicit meaning 'It certainly is true that I am writing.'

Again, from the same viewpoint, the judgment may be described as the total increment in cognitional process.

Every element in that process is at least a partial increment. It makes some contribution to knowing. But the judgment is the last act in the series that begins from presentations and advances through understanding and formulation ultimately to reach reflection and affirmation or denial. Thus, the proper content of judgment, the yes or no, is the final partial increment in the process. But this proper content is meaningless apart from the question it answers. With the question it forms an integrated whole. But the question takes over a formulation from the level of intelligence, and that formulation draws upon both insight and presentation.

It follows that the judgment as a whole is a total increment in cognitional process, that it brings to a close one whole step in the development of knowledge.

Finally, there is the contextual aspect of judgment. Though single judgments bring single steps in inquiries to their conclusion, still the single steps are related to one another in a highly complex fashion.

The most general aspects of cognitional context are represented by logic and dialectic. Logic is the effort of knowledge to attain the coherence and organization proper to any stage of its development. Dialectic, on the other hand, rests on the breakdown of efforts to attain coherence and organization at a given stage, and consists in bringing to birth a new stage in which logic again will endeavor to attain coherence and organization.

From the viewpoint of the logical ideal, every term has one and only one precise meaning, every relation of every term to every other term is set down in an unequivocal proposition, the totality of propositions is neatly divided into primitive and derived, the derived may all be obtained by the rules of inference from a minimum number of primitive propositions, no proposition contradicts any other, and finally the employment of the principle of excluded middle does not introduce undefined or false suppositions, as does the question, Have you or have you not stopped beating your wife?

[302] Now the pursuit of the logical ideal, so far from favoring a static immobility, serves to reveal the inadequacy of any intermediate stage in the development of knowledge. The more deeply it probes, the more effectively it forces the cognitional process to undergo a radical revision of its terms and postulates and so to pursue the logical ideal from a new base of operations. However, such revision has its limits, for there is no revision of revisers themselves. They are subject to the general conditions of beginning from presentations, advancing through insights and formulations, to terminate with reflections and judgments. Their insights are acts of grasping concrete unities, systematic regularities, or ideal frequencies. Their judgments are personal commitments to a yes or no; both answers cannot be given to the same question; and under ideal conditions either one of the two answers has to be given. The simple fact of the uniformity of

nature in revisers provides both logic and dialectic with an immutable ultimacy.

Within the general schemes of logic and dialectic, the contextual aspect of judgment appears in three manners.

There is the relation of the present to the past. Thus, past judgments remain with us. They form a habitual orientation, present and operative, but only from behind the scenes. They govern the direction of attention, evaluate insights; guide formulations, and influence the acceptance or rejection of new judgments. Previous insights remain with us. They facilitate the occurrence of fresh insights, exert their influence on new formulations, provide presuppositions that underlie new judgments whether in the same or in connected or in merely analogous fields of inquiry. Hence, when a new judgment is made, there is within us a habitual context of insights and other judgments, and it stands ready to elucidate the judgment just made, to complement it, to balance it, to draw distinctions, to add qualifications, to provide defence, to offer evidence or proof, to attempt persuasion.

Secondly, there are the relations within the present. Existing judgments may be found to conflict, and so they release the dialectical process. Again, though they do not conflict, they may not be completely independent of each other, and so they stimulate the logical effort for organized coherence.

Thirdly, there are the relations of the present to the future. The questions we answer are few compared to the questions that await an answer. Knowing is a dynamic structure. If each judgment is a total increment consisting of many parts, still it is only a minute contribution [303] towards the whole of knowledge. But further, our knowing is dynamic in another sense. It is irretrievably habitual. For we can make but one judgment at a time, and one judgment cannot bring all we know into the full light of actual knowing. A judgment may be very comprehensive and so bear witness to the depth and breadth of our perspectives. It may be very concrete and so reveal our grasp of nuance and detail. But it cannot be both comprehensive and concrete. All we know is somehow with us; it is present and operative within our knowing; but it lurks behind the scenes, and it reveals itself only in the exactitude with which each minor increment to our knowing is effected. The business of the human mind in this life seems to be, not contemplation of what we know, but relentless devotion to the task of adding increments to a merely habitual knowledge.

5 EXISTENTIALISM

LOUIS LAVELLE (1883-1951)

Lavelle was born in 1883 in the rural French town of Saint-Martin-de-Villeréal. While attending the University of Lyon from 1906-1909, and studying with Arthur Hannequin, Lavelle became a follower of Nietzsche and participated in anarchist demonstrations. After receiving his agrégé he taught at various lycées throughout France. From 1909-1914 Lavelle attended the lectures of Léon Brunschvicg and Octave Hamelin at the Sorbonne and Henri Bergson at the Collège de France and his thought became idealist in orientation. In 1913 Lavelle married Julie Bernard and in 1915 volunteered to join the French army, whence he was subsequently captured at Verdun, and interred in the prisoner-of-war-camp of Giessen for two years. Lavelle received a doctorate from the Sorbonne in 1921 under Léon Brunschvicg, André Lalande, Léon Robin, and Étienne Gilson. After again teaching at lycées in Strasbourg and Paris, in 1932 Lavelle became a professor of philosophy at the Sorbonne where he taught until 1941. During the early Vichy Regime Lavelle was appointed Inspector General for Public Education (1941) and in 1941 he was elected a professor at the prestigious Collège de France (1941-1951). He died in Parranquet in 1951.

Lavelle's key work is his 4-volume La Dialectique de l'éternel present, consisting of De l'Être (Paris: Alcan, 1928), De l'Acte (Paris: Aubier, 1937), Du Temps et de l'Éternité (Ibid., 1945) et De l'Âme humaine (Ibid., 1951). In addition he is known for his moral works Le Moi et son destin (Paris: Aubier, 1936), L'Erreur de Narcisse (Paris: Grasset, 1939), Le Mal et la souffrance (Paris: Plon, 1940), Quatre saints (Paris: Albin Michel, 1951), and the two-volume Traité des valeurs (Paris: Presses Universitaires de France, 1951-1955).

For more on Lavelle see: D'Ainval, Christiane, Une doctrine de la présence spirituelle: La philosophie de Louis Lavelle (Paris: Nauwelaerts, 1967); Hardy, Gilbert, La Vocation de la liberté chez Louis Lavelle (Paris: Nauwelaerts, 1968); École, Jean, Louis Lavelle et le renouveau de la métaphysique de l'Être au XXe siècle (Hildesheim, Georg Olms, 1997); and Robert, Sébastien, La philosophie de Louis Lavelle: Liberté et participation (Paris, L'Harmattan, 2007).

The following selection is from Lavelle's The Dilemma of Narcissus (1939) (London: George, Allen, and Unwin, 1973): III, 1-13, pp. 55-66; IX, 7-13, pp. 141-146. In this work Lavelle develops his existential themes that human beings are what they make of themselves, ideally forging their manifest self in light of their real self, or the vocation to align oneself with the divine. In so doing they are called to be sincere in revealing who they are, and being gentle and present to others.

The Error of Narcissus (1939)[257]

On Being Oneself

Polyphony of Consciousness

[55] The drama of consciousness consists in this: in order to constitute itself, it must break the unity of the self. After that, it starts an interminable struggle to reconquer this lost unity, but were it ever to succeed it would destroy itself.

It follows that consciousness, which is a dialogue with others and with the world, begins with a dialogue with oneself. We need two eyes to see and two ears to hear, as though we could not perceive anything except through the interplay of two images at once similar and different. Furthermore, neither sight nor hearing ever operates alone but only with reference to each other, or else to one of the other senses, which they stimulate, and which then contributes new information. Thus a sort of polyphony comes into being, wherein all the voices of the soul match all the voices of nature.

But we can go further: sense perception never stands alone; it always brings to birth an idea, a memory, an emotion, an intention, which in turn react upon it, and set up within us new dialogues–between present and past, past and future, universe and spirit, what we think and what we feel, what we feel and what we will. Moreover, in our consciousness there is always a gap between what we are and what we have, what we have and what we desire, a gap which we are ever seeking to close without ever quite succeeding. When I question myself with total sincerity, I find that the goal of my desire is too mobile to satisfy me, and too complex for me to be able to express it without debasing and mutilating it.

The difficulty one has in being sincere is the difficulty of being present in what one says and does, with the whole of oneself; for we divide ourselves, and show certain aspects of ourselves, none of which is the true self. But a wholly honest conscience, when deciding on a course of action, does not forget or cast away the rejected alternatives. Without wasting its strength on futile regrets on their account, it will try to introduce their positive essence and their original flavor into the chosen one.

---

257 [Louis Lavelle, *The Dilemma of Narcissus*, translated by William T. Gairdner. Copyright © 1973 by George, Allen, and Unwin. Public Domain with reversion of rights and death of translator.]

Logic and morality have accustomed us to think and to act according to alternatives, as though one always had to say yes or no, as though there were no third possibility. But this method of proceeding [56] suits only somewhat rigid souls, those who do not know that the third alternative does not lie between the yes and the no, but in a higher yes, one which always combines the yes and the no.

Cynicism

Each of us is an object of scandal for himself when, cynically comparing what he is and what he shows, he reflects that there is no man living to whom he would dare to show all the ideas which pass through his consciousness, even though they flicker and are gone. He feels indeed that he himself could not consider them too closely without shame.

The reason is that all humanity dwells in each man, the best and the worst. True sincerity does not consist in considering as real and our own all the obscure impulses, the unformed desires, the vague temptations which flit across our minds. They are not ours until we have begun to dwell upon them and to give them some consistency. True sincerity is to pass through them, to descend into the depths of ourselves, there to discover what we want to be. There is an apparent sincerity which consists in laying bare to our horrified gaze all that we think we are, which in fact is nothing but what we might become if we were suddenly to relax our vigilance.

Consciousness contains within itself the ambiguity of every possibility. It becomes the source of discouragement and frustration if one conceives of it as a fully-fledged reality rather than the power which constructs this reality. And so, to be sincere is not to be content to become conscious of one's inchoate desires, and to body them forth in words before ever performing the inner act which alone makes them ours. It is only when we consent to them that we can be judged.

And so it is that sincerity often appears like a conversion, when we recognize that our life is bad, but are already beginning to show that it is good. That is why it is said that he who makes a confession which changes him triumphs over the shame of the confession. If the light in which we bathe and purify our past reconciles us to our past, it is because it compels our past actions to conjure up in our minds a potentiality of which we intend to make better use in the future. And we should not be surprised that the man for whom we feel the keenest and the most passionate interest should not be he who is exempt from all the vices, but he who, though continuing to feel their stab, sharpens against them the cutting edge of his whole spiritual life.

Play-Acting for One's Own Benefit

[57] It is the man who thinks who is in most danger of play-acting before an audience consisting of himself. He is never satisfied with what he finds in himself. He spoils it by constantly thinking about it. His true being is always, for him, somewhere other than in his present being; he never manages to distinguish what he imagines from what he feels. He can make out scores of different characters in himself. He images scores of possibilities, stretching out in every direction beyond the reality which has been given him. He must needs resolutely turn his face towards the latter and concentrate his attention upon it, though often all that is required is a touch of simplicity and a little love; with these he would make contact with it, almost without trying.

All this is not difficult to explain. When I look at myself, another is there, and he is the spectator to whom I am exhibiting myself; further, this spectator always resembles a stranger, for whom I can never be anything but a mere appearance: I have ceased to be a person; I am a thing, an "image" which I deliberately compose.

The dialogue in which Narcissus engages inevitably contains an element of duplicity: to be double is the very nature of consciousness. And the difference between what I am and what I show is the product of reflection and of my effort to be sincere. And so I have the impression that I never am. Sincerity is always a problem; no one can rightly estimate another's or his own.

Deception Is Impossible

In a man's relationships with other men, an apparently real being springs up, and always takes the place of the real one. This is an abdication and a humiliation of the self which often passes unnoticed; we use a dishonorable subterfuge to disguise what has happened. For our real being seeks every to take advantage of the high opinion in which our apparent being is held.

But can I really hope that men will take the appearance that I show for the reality that I am? In every one of my words and acts the hallmark of self-love can be observed, unmistakable to all, though people sometimes allow one to think the contrary; or else I betray a sense of guilt, which, indeed, everyone is expecting, waiting for, and yet it serves no useful purpose; but the others pounce on it, some to bring me help, and others to crush me.

Dissimulation is more difficult than people think. One's body, one's voice, one's eyes, one's face do not merely bear witness to what one is; they are one's very being, and to a fairly perspicacious observer [58] they reveal our most secret intention, even the intention to reveal nothing, which recalls the legend of the Nordic maiden, the jewel in whose ring would change color every time she told a lie. So it is with the boldest, the most brazen countenance. And if the face were to remain immobile, the eyes, which are subtler, would change; or failing the eyes, there would be a disturbance in that almost imperceptible harmony of all the features, which is the stamp of a man's perfect naturalness.

People are forever talking of refusing to exhibit their inner feelings, of reserve, of reticence. But in reality they are equally incapable of doing this and of not doing it. For sincerity is ambiguous, and it is true that the two most difficult things in the world are showing oneself and hiding oneself. Often there is nothing harder than to show another the very thing I want him to see. The degree of sincerity I can achieve depends on him as much as on me. Over and beyond the sincerity which the individual may consciously strive for, there is another sincerity, which only friends can recognize and experience.

Inversely, dissimulation also presupposes the complicity of two people, each of whom is prepared to accept as more real what the other shows than what he is hiding, and each of whom refuses to admit to himself that his real concern is with what he is trying to hide, but which always comes to the surface in one way or another, together with the desire to hide it.

But again, it sometimes happens that a man deceives himself before he sets about deceiving others. Self-love gets the better of him before he begins betting the better of other people. He experiments first on himself, measuring the success he can hope for with others by the success he has with himself. Even when he fails, he keeps up the same desperate enterprise. For men have agreed to live in a world of appearance and pretense. It is in this world that their words echo back and forth, although truth in its entirety is there before their eyes, nor do they fail to recognize it. They are fully conscious of this inconsistency; it may even give them a cruel delight.

Gyges' Ring

How is it possible, it may be asked, not to be sincere, if my being coincides with my acts even more closely than with my thoughts? If my acts perfectly express what all men see, what difference could there be between what I appear and what I am?

[59] Let us leave aside the insincerity which is a deliberate intention to put people on the wrong scent: it deceives none but the obtuse; and it never deceives the deceiver. It is nothing but a trick which I adopt on the spur of the moment to achieve a certain effect; but the intention to produce this effect leaves an impression on him who uses it, and this will not be effaced.

Men know perfectly well that they cannot hide any part of what they are, and if they possessed Gyges' ring, that is precisely what they would wish it to accomplish for them. This ring would make our bodies invisible, thus enabling us to achieve in the world of visible things an effect whose cause was invisible, and not of this world: this would certainly be the first miracle. But the miracle would only be complete if the ring, while making us invisible to others, made us also perfectly interior and perfectly transparent to ourselves; if, in short, it made the myth of Narcissus at the fountain come true.

Fortunately the ring has not been vouchsafed us. It would be the supreme temptation. The anguish of existence and the secret of responsibility reside at that precise point at which, before the eyes of the world, we convert into an act which leaves an indelible trace upon the world, a possibility which previously had no existence except for us. But since they do not possess the ring, most men struggle desperately to produce an image of themselves, by means of their words, their silence and their works–an image which represents not what they are, nor even what they would like to be, but what they wish people to believe they are.

Sim ut sum aut non sim [*Let Me Be What I Am or Let Me Not Be*]

The highest duty, the most subtle difficulty, the gravest responsibility is to be all that one is, to assume full responsibility for it, and for all the consequences. Frankness sets me free and gives me the courage I need. It is falsehood which binds me.

The function of consciousness is to force me to take possession of myself. And this taking possession resembles a creation, since it consists in giving reality to a potential being which has, so to say, been put at our disposal. But to remain as a potentiality is not to be. I can then, if I choose, not be; I can refuse to accept the existence which is ceaselessly offered me. But what I cannot do is become other than what I am. It is inconceivable that I should become other than I am without my self being annihilated. Falsehood is the self's refusal of its being.

[60] To be what one is—nothing is more difficult than this for the man who has begun to think, to reflect, and to distinguish, however imperfectly, between his nature and his liberty. Will he follow nothing but his nature, while disapproving of it, suffering under it oftentimes, and occasionally condemning it outright? Or on the other hand will he put his trust in his judgement and in the freedom of his will, as though he had no nature? But one's nature will not be forgotten: merely to ignore it is not to reduce it to silence. Nature it is who puts at our disposal every potentiality we have; sincerity first recognizes them, then sets them to work.

To be sincere is to descend into the depths of our selves, and there to find the gifts which are ours, and yet which are nothing except by the virtue of the use we make of them. It is refusing to let them lie unused. It is preventing them remaining buried within us, in the darkness of the realm of possibility. It is bringing them forth into the light of day, so that, in the view of all, they increase the wealth of the world, by being, as it were, a revelation which continually enriches it. Sincerity is the act by which, at one and the same time, a man knows himself and makes himself. It is the act by which he shows himself to be what he is, and consents to contribute, according to the measure of his strength to the work of creation.

Discovering What I Am

In our relationships with others, sincerity is an attempt to abolish all the distinction between our real and our manifest selves; but the ultimate sincerity in our relationship with ourselves. It consists not so much in showing oneself as one is as in discovering what one is. It demands of us that we should penetrate below and beyond all the superficial layers of consciousness, the domain of fleeting impressions, into that mysterious region where are born those deep desires which we acknowledge as our own, and which are our life's contact with the absolute. Introspection produces the best effects or the worst, according to where we look, and the intention which motivates our looking. Either we dwell upon our passing impressions (in which we are always unduly interested); or else we penetrate to their place of origin, and, in so doing, we free ourselves from our slavery to them.

Real sincerity is to compel myself to be myself; to become what I am. It is to search for my essence, which begins to lose its purity the moment I look outside myself for the motives of my actions. For this essence is not an object which I can observe, but a creation which I am bringing into being; it is the act whereby I give effect [61] to certain potentialities which are in me, and which wither away if I cease to exercise them.

Sincerity is an act involving, indivisibly, entering into oneself and going out from oneself, a quest which is from the first a discovery; a commitment which is from the first a self-transcendence; a waiting for a voice which from the first was calling; an opening of the heart which from the first was an act of faith in a revelation as yet undisclosed, but ever on the point of breaking forth. Sincerity is the link between what I am and what I intend to be.

It may be said that it is a virtue of the heart and not of the intelligence. "For where your heart is, there is your true treasure" (Luke 12:34). Which suffices to explain why sincerity brings with it infinitely more reward than the most glittering sham.

A Sword Through the Heart

A sword must go through one's heart (Luke 2:35), says Saint Luke, if one is to pierce through to one's deepest thoughts; but only innocence can wield this sword. It is quite wrong to say that innocence sees no evil; it discerns, and then tears away, all the veils with which self-love convers our naked being. But this is the way of virtue which, as Plato says, knows virtue and vice, whereas vice knows vice only.

Sincerity consists in that tranquil courage which enables us to enter into existence as we truly are. But a double fear nearly always holds one back, fear of the very power one has at one's disposal, and fear of being exposed to public opinion. It is the passage from the hidden into the manifest world which creates our perplexity.

But we are too concerned with appearances. If I am what I ought to be within, I will also be so without. It is true that a capacity for stripping one's soul bare is called for, a capacity which I do not possess at all times. Sometimes I am not granted enough light. Sometimes I am not sufficiently present to myself. I am not always as read to speak or to act. Often I must be content to wait. Sincerity calls for much discretion and much silence.

The mere thought of another man watching has a paralyzing effect upon us. It can make us ashamed of that very quality wherein lies our superiority, if he questions it, or fails to recognize its worth. But when we are alone, we should act as though the eyes of the world were upon us; and when they are, we should act as though we were alone. Indeed, vanity itself, if only it were great enough, could not [62] be satisfied with appearance, which, however, almost always is all that it feeds on: it should dissolve itself in the ocean of its own exacting demands, seeking no satisfaction other than that which perfect sincerity would afford it. It is a weak and miserable kind of vanity which imagines that appearance can go one better than being; and yet, it is within the power of vanity to transcend itself continually, and even to become its exact opposite, when a man refuses to allow his being ever to fall short of his manifested appearance.

There are two sorts of men: those whose ears are turned to self-love, and whose eyes are fixed upon the image of themselves they offer to the world; and those who cannot imagine that such an image exists, or, if it exists, that it can differ from what they are.

Beyond Myself

Sincerity lays an obligation upon me to withhold everything in me which belongs to me and me alone, and to manifest everything in me which resembles a revelation whose interpreter I am. It follows that, if I am sincere, I can express only what is indeed within me, but always as though it were not of me. Sincerity expresses at one and the same time what is most interior to ourselves, and what is farthest removed from ourselves, namely the truth with which we are entrusted.

You say, "I am sincere," and you think that you have thereby justified what you say and what you do. But what does your sincerity mean to me if it is the sincerity of nothing, if it communicates nothing but the reactions of your self-love, and the pathetic expressions of your weakness and your wretchedness? And yet you present this sincerity of yours as an excuse and as a matter of pride. "This is what I am. I am frank about myself. And this being that I offer to your gaze has, like you, its place in the world, and the same shun shines upon it with the same light."

But this flaunted sincerity of yours is often nothing but a sham, of no interest either to yourself or to anybody else: it awakens no echo in me if it communicates nothing more than a fact which neither you nor I can grasp and hold firm. The sincerity which I am looking for, and the only one I need, the only one which brings my eyes to bear on a destiny, in yourself and in myself, which is private to each of us and which is yet common to us both, is not the attempt, however, genuine, to describe yourself as a thing; it is rather a resolve to seek yourself, to affirm yourself, and to begin even now to commit yourself, the determination to penetrate to the very essence of the real wherein [63] each of us is rooted, and to recognize by unmistakable signs what is required of you, namely the task which you have to accomplish, and to which you are even now beginning to put your hand.

Sincerity and Truth

It is common belief that there is nothing in the world easier than being sincere, and that all that is required is not to alter to the smallest degree reality such as it has been given to us. To lie or to dissimulate, in this view, is to intervene, to bring one's will into play, to substitute for my real self a false self which is entirely different. Is it not true, it will be said, that to be sincere is to be content to let things be what they are?

But the problem is not so easy. The moment I begin to speak or to act, the moment my eyes open to the light, I add something to the real, and modify it. This modification is nothing less than the creation of a spectacle without which the real would not exist for me. It is when I look out upon the world that it comes to birth before my eyes, like a view which takes its contours from the perspective in which it is seen, and from the constant play of lights and shadows upon it. And yet no one would content that the real world is created by myself, by my act which apprehends it. It has certain characteristics which I must accept whether I like it or not, and which I can check against the experience of other men. Thus it is that I can distinguish error from truth.

But sincerity is not truth. For example, the painter translates by his art, with varying degrees of sincerity, his entirely personal vision of the universe, and it is only this vision that one can qualify as true. And yet no one would agree that to be sincere is to reproduce my own vision of things, just as it is, while on the other hand that to be true is to reproduce, within this vision itself, things just as they are. For it is in the *quality* of the vision that my sincerity consists. It lies in my effort to make it every more delicate, more penetrating, and more profound.

Truth is a light which bathes everything, that is, and which enlightens me provided I open my eyes. One may say that sincerity is nothing more than simply consent to this light, provided one adds that the truth which is in question here is the very truth of what I am, and further that it is not enough that I should contemplate this truth, but I must first of all bring it into being.

The commonly accepted view is that truth is the coincidence of thought and reality. But how could such a coincidence be possible [64] so long as the real is something other than myself? If, on the other hand, sincerity is the coincidence of ourselves with ourselves, how is it possible to miss it? Nevertheless self-love achieves just this. The essence of sincerity is to conquer self-love. And one may say that, unlike truth, the search for which is the attempt to make the act of my consciousness conform to the spectacle presented by things, sincerity is the attempt to make the spectacle which I offer to the world conform to the act of my consciousness.

It would thus seem that sincerity alone is capable of resolving the duality of object and subject which philosophers have made the supreme condition of all knowledge. If Narcissus went down to destruction, it was because he actually tried to create this duality in his very being. For he thought he could see himself and enjoy himself before he had acted and before he had made himself. He lacked the courage to engage upon the splendid and unique venture wherein action precedes being and determines it–that creative activity of which mathematics offers us a model in the realm of pure knowledge, and inner sincerity a dramatic application to ourselves.

Sincerity in Action

To be sincere is to show oneself, but at the same time as one is making oneself. It is not to talk but to act. Unfortunately, one is always inclined to water down the meaning of the word "sincerity," reducing it to the idea of speaking about oneself truthfully. But how can one speak truthfully about a being who is still in the making, whose every word and every action adds something to what he is? And who can claim to be able to tell the truth about himself without a tremor, or without the blush which both perverts the truth and debases the self?

But sincerity must reach out, beyond all speech, to an invisible inner life, which speech may always betray, for it can only trace its shadow. Sincerity appears only when this inner life begins to be incarnated in acts which determine both our being and our destiny.

Sincerity does not consist in reproducing a good likeness of a pre-existent reality. It is itself creative. It is a virtue shown forth in action, not merely in the act of expression. Our self is nothing more than a bundle of virtualities: it is for us to realize them. True sincerity is an accomplishment. And it is quite conceivable that one should miss it, whether through laziness or through fear, or because one finds it easier or more expedient to yield to public opinion and to [65] renounce oneself, letting oneself be dragged unresistingly down the slope of social conformity.

In sincerity, the act by which we find ourselves and the act by which we make ourselves are one and the same. Sincerity is at once the attention which arouses our potentialities, and the courage which gives them form, without which they would be nothing. Potentiality is the voice within us; our courage is our response. Sincerity consists not merely, as is imagined, of examining with pitiless lucidity one's own secret thoughts; it compels this same inner being to cross its own frontiers, to take its place in the world, and there to manifest what it is.

The Return to the Source

From the moment I begin to act, my life is imprisoned in a situation. It bears the weight of its past; countless forces begin to sweep it along; it is caught up in a movement; and I cannot tell whether I am carried by this movement or whether I am producing it. But sincerity challenges all the voices which call to me from without, and commands me to descend into my heart's heart. It is always a return to the source. It makes me a being perpetually being born.

Sincerity liberates us from every preoccupation with public opinion or with the effect we are producing. It brings us back to our own origin, showing us to ourselves as we were when we left the Creator's hands, when life first flashed forth, and before outer appearances had begun to seduce us, or we had learned the art of pretending.

It shows us to ourselves as we are, and not in a portrait which would necessarily be something outside ourselves. It needs no oaths or promises to carry conviction. It is a perfect transparency in the eyes which casts no shadow between you and me; nor does the remembrance of things past or the desire of things to come cast any shadows between us; again it is rectitude of a will which admits no duplicity, no evasion, and no dissembling, between a man and other men.

Sincerity is a spiritual nobility. For the sincere man seeks to live under the open sky. He alone has enough self-respect to hide nothing from himself, and to expect nothing except from the truth; he alone is not content merely to appear, but establishes himself so firmly in being that for him being is indistinguishable from appearance.

Under the Eye of God

Sincerity is the act by which I put myself under the eye of God; there is no other sincerity. For of God alone may it be said that outward appearance is as though it were not. He is himself the pure [66] presence of everything that is. When I turn to Him, everything in me but what I am ceases to count.

For God is not only the ever-open eye, from whom I can hide nothing of what I know about myself; but He is also the light which pierces the darkness, revealing me to myself as I have always been without knowing it. Self-love which hid me from myself is a garment which suddenly drops off. Another love folds about me, one which makes my soul itself transparent.

As long as life remains in us, we nurse the hope that we can change what we are, or conceal it. But once it is threatened or near its end, nothing counts but what we are. One is only perfectly sincere in the presence of death, because death is irrevocable, and, by terminating our existence confers upon it the character of the absolute. That is what is expressed in the picture of the judge whose eye misses nothing, and who, at the moment of our death, sees into the remotest corners of our soul. What is the truth behind this idea of the Divine Eye? Is it not that it is now impossible for us to add anything to what we have made, to escape from ourselves into any future, and to continue to make a distinction between our real and manifested being? And since this is the moment when the will loses its power, it is now impossible to avoid confronting the spectacle of our being in its finished state, our being, which, up to this moment, had been nothing more than a rough sketch, susceptible of endless additions and corrections?

To be sincere, we must not merely think of God as a witness: we must take Him as a model. For sincerity does not consist merely in seeing ourselves in His light, but in making ourselves in conformity with His will. What am I but what He wishes me to be? And yet, there immediately appears before me an infinite disparity between what I do and this power within me, which, in spite of everything, it is my one aspiration to exercise. And indeed I constantly fail, and in exact proportion to my failure I become, for myself and for others, a mere appearance, dissipated by a puff of wind, and finally annihilated by death.

This is the sense in which we should take the words: "Whoever disowns me in this world, I will disown him before my Father; whoever acknowledges me in this world, I will acknowledge him before my Father. I came into the world to bear witness to the truth" (Matt. 10:32-3; John 18:37). ...

Communion

The Light of Charity
[141] Of all the attitudes of the soul, charity is at once the simplest, and the most difficult to achieve. It is pure attention to the existence of another person. But charity is love, and love is never, as is too often believed, a rush of passion which blinds the spirit instead of bringing it light. When perfect spiritual communion exists between two persons, we say that there is an understanding between them; this is a summit beyond which it is impossible to go, and which love alone is capable of attaining. This state may not be recognized as such by those who have attained it; for there are no shadows there, it is pure light.

I cannot free myself from the desire to advise others, to change their ideas and improve their behavior, to make them agree with me; I cannot help desiring to make them feel and think as I do. And this is in part, doubtless, because I want to dominate them, and to make them the confirmation and extension of myself. But it is also [142] because I know that all individuals are really one, struggling to find the same truth and the same good.

And yet in every man there is also a desire for independence and separateness from all others, a refusal both to impose the law of his being upon them and to submit to theirs, a determination to defend the original quality of his vocation, rather than to enter with them into a common uniformity. However these two aspirations are really one. For no man discovers his own genius except by discovering the source of inspiration whence proceeds the proper genius of every other. Consequently, each will draw closer to others to the exact extent that he is faithful to himself.

Bear Ye One Another's Burdens
Is it possible for a man to do the least good to another? Does not each man live in a solitary retreat, where no one ever enters? On the other hand, when he responds to another's initiative, can one truthfully say that his solitude has been broken down, or is it rather that a surface contact has been made, leaving the ultimate depths of their lives still separate? But even if it is only thus far that we can penetrate, is the effect not comforting or cruel, as the case may be? Is despair made keener for being discovered, or alleviated when shared?

"Bear ye one another's burdens, and so fulfill the law of Christ" (Galatians, 6:2). But, you will reply, are not my own burdens enough for me? Moreover, is it possible to bear another's?

How could they ever become mine? Is not the desire to do so a mark of indiscretion rather than of generosity, of presumption rather than of consideration for the other? And yet, just as the knowing mind can only know the world and not itself, the responsibility which everyone thinks he assumes for himself is in reality the responsibility which he assumes, in himself, for the world. My own misfortunes I merely suffer of necessity; egoism is sufficient to ensure that I will do so. But for the misfortunes of another, I need an act of liberty and an act of love if I am ever to take them upon myself.

It has been said that the verb "to serve" is the noblest word in the language, and this is because it emphasizes the fact that each of us is subordinated to a good whose essential quality is ever to transcend the individual. And when we serve another, we force ourselves to go beyond our own frontiers and seek the goal of our action outside them. Then we co-operate with the work of creation, instead of [143] remaining in the world of created things, or merely turning things already created to our own use.

Giving and Receiving

It is said that no one can receive anything that he is not capable of giving, and that in order to be able to receive a gift, one must be capable of giving it.

And yet the honor we pay God does not consist of giving anything to Him, but of showing ourselves worthy of receiving His gifts. And if the good man is not honored by the evil man, it is because he is incapable of receiving anything from him.

Now the greatest good that we can do to other men is not the gift of a treasure of our own, but the revelation of something which was theirs already. For no one can receive any good thing which is not of his nature. It follows that he can only receive himself as a gift. Every gift one receives is the discovery of a power one already possessed without suspecting it. But as soon as it is revealed to us, it appears as more intimately our own than everything we previously thought we had.

And if the function of consciousness is to enable us to penetrate into a presence which transcends us, it is understandable that the one who is conscious of the good must be the one who receives it, not the one who does it. For he who does it needs only to act according to what he is already, while he who receives it finds his life enriched by a potentiality which he bore within himself, but which he did not exercise before he met the other man. That being so, if there is nothing more sterile than a gift rejected, it may be said that he who receives a gift is the giver, for it is who he gives it its efficacy and its virtue.

Recognition of Greatness

It is certain that no man can create his own genius; he is doing his all when he discovers it, and remains faithful to it. And he cannot achieve this alone. The greatest men need the reassurance that comes from the response or the secret sympathy of certain quite simple people whom destiny places in their path, and who are sufficient to console them for the ignorance and contempt of the majority.

For the value of a man never resides in what he is, but in a truth whose presence he recognizes in himself, and whose interpreter he is. And if he is not to feel threatened by doubt or despair, he needs must have the experience, if only for a brief moment, that the light [144] he has received can be shared. The mark of greatness is a man's ability to have created an inner void within himself, the perfect silence of the individual, when self-love and the body are stilled, a silence in which all men hear the same voice bringing them a common revelation. And events of great moment also never fail to produce this silence.

The purest conscience is always the most transparent. It is in an abdication of oneself in which all his potentialities appear to melt away that the individual realizes himself, and that there is born in him the inner confidence which enables him to grow and to become fully himself. And it is when the attention to the object is the most docile and the most faithful that our acts are most efficacious and most our own.

There is therefore no such thing as the greatness of an individual as such; at least, his greatness can always be contested. One can even say that in one sense there is no other greatness than that which is recognized, or which may be so, and this often leads men to mistake it, or to judge it by popular applause. But we find within ourselves other, secret, intimations of greatness, inklings which kindle our aspirations and fulfill them at one and the same time; which sow our hearts with the best and most fruitful seeds; which break through the frontiers of our solitude and make us for a moment co-extensive with the universe.

Thus it is true to say that the greatest men are great not by virtue of what they give us, but in virtue of the way we respond to their gifts. In a sense they owe their greatness to us. It comprises nothing more than that those same riches which we receive from them as soon as we become capable of recognizing their origin, or, in other words, of giving them back to them.

Spiritual Affinities

The most elusive center of our vocation does not lie in the choice of a task for which we seem specially made, for this will merely determine the influence we may have on things. It lies in the choice of our friends, those whose company gives savor to life, those who understand us and help us, with whom we can live in uninterrupted familiarity, those who never cramp our genius by suspicion or hostility, but support it and enable it to unfold.

The ability to recognize kindred spirits without sacrificing one's integrity to them, is the secret of strength, success, and happiness. The writer no less than other men needs a sympathetic circle of readers, [145] if he is to develop confidence in himself and his work grow to maturity. Some writers may have missed their destiny because they failed to find, or to be able to create or to recognize such a circle, or again, because they had been mistaken about it. Just as the author needs a public which understands him and supports him (and often if his field of vision is narrow, their devotion will be particularly intense), just so every seed can bear fruit. But it would be a mistake to think that this milieu is given to us, and that our part is merely to accept it. Like every other event in our lives, it is a meeting-place of chance and free-will.

But we must be prudent; for all those about us, all those we meet along the way are, for us, opportunities and challenges. We have no right to reject them. And so what we are left with is less the choice of people among whom we live, than the discovery of the precise point of contact between their destiny and ours which will lead us to mutual enrichment rather than to separation or enmity.

Predestined Friendships

There is no one who does not yearn to find another soul, similar to his own, with whom he will feel united in thought and in the pursuit of the same goals. Reflection shows that it is in this community of desire that the true foundation of love resides, much more than in the mutual search for self with which it is too often confused, and which is in fact the perversion of love. Love always reaches out beyond the lovers toward an object to which they both aspire, and in which they find communion. Although this object is universal, and it is for this reason that we are obliged to love all created beings (just as intelligence is universal also, whence our obligation to think everything that is), it is understandable that for each man there should be one soul set apart to whom it is right that he should turn, just as his mind dwells with special love on some favorite idea, which is for him the gateway to the whole of truth.

There dwells in me a capacity for friendship which is ever ready to be realized, and until experience disillusions me, I cannot understand why every human face should not be the face of a friend. But this capacity can only be exercised by being bestowed on some individual. For I am myself a unique and individual being; my presence to myself is an experience which always occurs in time, in space, and in the flesh, and my capacity for friendship is the same. It is still a mere possibility so long as it is moving freely from one to another: [146] sooner or later it must come to rest. I need some one who, like myself, has a name, who is alone as I myself am alone, and whose inner being goes from him to me alone: it would be contrary to his nature too if he bestowed it on all alike.

Every man thinks that one day he will find another man capable of understanding him, or in other words of being one with him in desire. Now identical desires seem fated to alienate men in the animal part of their nature, they become enemies who would tear each other to pieces and slay each other; and yet it draws them together so closely in the spiritual part that they become friends, which is to say no less than that each one becomes indeed the soul of the other.

A friend is he in whose presence we hold nothing back; we show ourselves as we are; there is no difference between what we are and the impression we wish to create. And in him also there is abolished the difference, characteristic of our relations with all other men, between the within, which is only real for us, and the without, which is the appearance we offer to the world.

But a friend is also he in whose presence we cease to be anything at all, and we can, without fear of humiliation, leave the question both of what we want, and what we are worth, in total indetermination. A friend is he in whose presence we can tryout unashamed all the potentialities of our inner life.

A Glimpse of Paradise

There is a moment when a spiritual communion begins with another person, which changes all the feelings we have had for him till then; then we forget that they could ever have existed without him. This spiritual communion only comes into being with the discovery of a world in which each shows the other what he was already on the point of seeing unaided; here every truth is bathed in an inner light which converts it into beauty; here everything that is seems to melt into a desire which is no sooner born than fulfilled.

Nothing is rarer than this communion; most often it only appears in flashes, either with those whom we are seeing for the first time, or with those whom we know best. Almost always it comes as a fleeting impression; we cannot hold it fast, or recapture it at will. For it carries us out of the material world where the will is powerless to lay a hand upon it or to bid it stay. It is a spiritual paradise, whose door never opens more than a chink.

All those relationships we have with others—based on justice, for instance, or confidence, or sympathy—all these have meaning only if [147] they prefigure it, herald it, and begin to lead us in this direction. They should make us seek it, even though success is not assured. So long as they fail to develop into this deeper thing, they remain exposed to every peril. For when two people first meet, it is as strangers who, as soon as they begin to know each other, are amazed at finding each other so different. When individuality asserts itself, its first effect is always to divide us. It is only later that a certain understanding is born, together with consideration for each other, the sense of certain limits to be observed—limits whose purpose is to protect in each an inviolable retreat—sometimes a mutual complicity between the two which increases their separation from everyone else; and finally, in the most fortunate cases, a mysterious union which adds a new dimension to the life of each, strengthening it and increasing its substance.

Although there exists in all human relationships a reflection and indeed a foretaste of true spiritual communion, they are all poor substitutes, and sometimes they even prevent it from coming to be. For true communion is far removed from the kind of attachment which chance or common desires create between two individuals, and which may be more or less strong and more or less satisfying. It begins only when two people become conscious of a presence which they are content to explore, and into which they enter by a mutual mediation.

Two souls can draw together only if they inhabit a single spiritual country. To discover another spirit is to discover other eyes meeting our own in one and the same light. Then it may be that we find a communion so pure that it seems purged of all matter, and as soon as the analytic mind discovers some, it becomes slightly less perfect.

GABRIEL MARCEL (1889-1973)

Marcel was born in Paris in 1889, and raised by his aunt and father, after his mother died when he was a toddler. After receiving his agrégation in philosophy in 1910, from the Sorbonne, Marcel taught at various French lycées, including the well-known Louis-le-Grand in Paris, and worked as a playwright and drama critic. During the First World War Marcel served in the Red Cross where he assisting in conveying the news of injured and deceased soldiers to their families, and his experience there of assigning numbers to soldiers was instrumental in the formulation of his philosophical concept of brokenness. He married shortly after the war ended. In 1929 Marcel converted to Catholicism from the agnosticism of his father. He hosted a famous weekly discussion group attended by other notable thinkers such as Simone de Beauvoir, Nicolas Berdyaev, Louis Lavelle, Emmanuel Levinas, Paul Ricœur, Jean-Paul Sartre, and Jean Wahl. Marcel also was involved in the Moral Re-Armament movement during World War II. He died in Paris in 1973.

In addition to penning over thirty plays, Marcel's key philosophical works are his *Journal métaphysique* (Paris: Gallimard, 1927); *Être et avoir* [*Being and Having*] (Paris: Aubier, 1935); and *Le Mystère de l'être* [*The Mystery of Being*], 2 vols. (Paris: Aubier, 1951).

For more on Marcel's life and thought see his autobiography *Awakenings* (Milwaukee: Marquette University Press, 2002), as well as: Randall, Albert B., *The Mystery of Hope in the Philosophy of Gabriel Marcel* (Lewiston: Edwin Mellen Press, 1992); Cain, Seymour, *Gabriel Marcel's Theory of Religious Experience* (Frankfurt: Peter Lang, 1995); Sweetman, Brendan, *The Vision of Gabriel Marcel* (New York: Rodopi Press, 2008); Hernandez, Jill Graper, *Gabriel Marcel's Ethics of Hope: Evil, God and Virtue* (London: Continuum, 2013).

The following except is from Marcel's essay "Position et approches concrètes du mystère ontologique," published as a postscript to his key philosophical play *Le monde cassé* [*The Broken World*] (Paris, Desclée de Brouwer, 1933). It has been translated into English as "On the Ontological Mystery" in *The Philosophy of Existentialism*, trans. Manya Harari (Secaucus: Citadel Press, 1956): 10-46. In this selection Marcel describes the modern condition of the human in a "broken world," wherein people are functionalized, depersonalized, and associated with the functions they perform. He argues that this is to conceive a human in the same way we conceive a technical "problem," something that can be analyzed, delimited, broken into elements, and its explanation isolated, such as why a machine is not working. Instead we must treat humans as mysteries wherein we must look at things holistically and cannot fully remove ourselves and our hopes from the equation, and wherein elements of encounter with transcendence are found. By doing so we will find ourselves engaging in acts of charity, or being present to others with the whole of ourselves, and grasping that ultimately we exist immersed in a Being which is in turn present to us, or on our side, as it were.

"On the Ontological Mystery" (1933)[258]

[10] The characteristic feature of our age seems to me to be what might be called the misplacement of the idea of function, taking function in its current sense which includes both the vital and the social functions.

The individual tends to appear both to himself and to others as an agglomeration of functions. As a result of deep historical causes, which can as yet be understood only in part, he has been led to see himself more and more as a mere assemblage of functions, the hierarchical interrelation of which seems to him questionable or at least subject to conflicting interpretations.

To take the vital functions first. It is hardly necessary to point out the role which historical materialism on the one hand, and Freudian doctrines on the other, have played in restricting the concept of man.

Then there are the social functions—those of the consumer, the producer, the citizen, etc.

Between these two there is, in theory, room for the psychological functions as well; but it is easy to see how these will tend to be interpreted in relation either to the social or the vital functions, so that their independence will be threatened and their specific character put in doubt. In this sense, Comte, served by his total incomprehension of psychical reality, displayed an almost prophetic instinct when he excluded psychology from his classification of sciences.

So far we are still dealing only with abstractions, but [11] nothing is easier than to find concrete illustrations in this field.

Traveling on the Underground, I often wonder with a kind of dread what can be the inward reality of the life of this or that man employed on the railway—the man who opens the doors, for instance, or the one who punches the tickets. Surely everything both within and outside him conspires to identify this man with his functions—meaning not only with his function as worker, as trade union member or as voter, but with his vital functions as well. The rather horrible expression "time table" perfectly describes his life. So many hours for each function. Sleep too is a function which must be discharged so that the other functions may be exercised in their turn. The same with pleasure, with relaxation;

---

[258] [Gabriel Marcel, "On the Ontological Mystery," *The Philosophy of Existentialism*, translated by Manya Harari. Copyright © 1956 by Citadel Press. Public Domain.]

it is logical that the weekly allowance of recreation should be determined by an expert on hygiene; recreation is a psycho-organic function which must not be neglected any more than, for instance, the function of sex. We need go no further; this sketch is sufficient to suggest the emergence of a kind of vital schedule; the details will vary with the country, the climate, the profession, etc., but what matters is that there is a schedule.

It is true that certain disorderly elements—sickness, accidents of every sort—will break in on the smooth working of the system. It is therefore natural that the individual should be overhauled at regular intervals like a watch (this is often done in America). The hospital plays the part of the inspection bench or the repair shop. And it is from this same standpoint of function that such essential problems as birth control will be examined.

As for death, it becomes, objectively and functionally, the [12] scrapping of what has ceased to be of use and must be written off as a total loss.

I need hardly insist on the stifling impression of sadness produced by this functionalized world. It is sufficient to recall the dreary image of the retired official, or those urban Sundays when the passers-by look like people who have retired from life. In such a world, there is something mocking and sinister even in the tolerance awarded to the man who has retired from his work.

But besides the sadness felt by the onlooker, there is the full, intolerable unease of the actor himself who is reduced to living as though he were in fact submerged by his functions. This uneasiness is enough to show that there is in all this some appalling mistake, some ghastly misinterpretation, implanted in defenseless minds by an increasingly inhuman social order and an equally inhuman philosophy (for if the philosophy has prepared the way for the order, the order has also shaped the philosophy).

I have written on another occasion that, provided it is taken in its metaphysical and not its physical sense, the distinction between the *full* and the *empty* seems to me more fundamental than that between the *one* and the *many*. This is particularly applicable to the case in point. Life in a world centered on function is liable to despair because in reality this world is *empty*, it rings hollow; and if it resists this temptation it is only to the extent that there come into play from within it and in its favour certain hidden forces which are beyond its power to conceive or to recognise.

It should be noted that this world is, on the one hand, riddled with problems and, on the other, determined to allow no room for mystery. I shall come back to this distinction between problem and mystery which I believe to be fundamental. [13] For the moment I shall only point out that to eliminate or to try to eliminate mystery is (in this functionalist world) to bring into play in the face of events which break in on the course of existence– such as birth, love and death–that psychological and pseudo-scientific category of the "purely natural" which deserves a study to itself. In reality, this is nothing more than the remains of a degraded rationalism from whose standpoint cause explains effect and accounts for it exhaustively. There exists in such a world, nevertheless, an infinity of problems, since the causes are not known to us in detail and thus leave room for unlimited research. And in addition to these theoretical puzzles there are innumerable technical problems, bound up with the difficulty of knowing how the various functions, once they have been inventoried and labelled, can be made to work together without doing one another harm. These theoretical and technical questions are interdependent, for the theoretical problems arise out of the different techniques while the technical problems cannot be solved without a measure of pre-established theoretical knowledge.

In such a world the ontological need, the need of being, is exhausted in exact proportion to the breaking up of personality on the one hand and, on the other, to the triumph of the category of the "purely natural" and the consequent atrophy of the faculty of *wonder*.

But to come at last to the ontological need itself; can we not approach it directly and attempt to define it? In reality this can only be done to a limited extent. For reasons which I shall develop later, I suspect that the characteristic of this need is that it can never be wholly clear to itself.

To try to describe it without distorting it we shall have to say something like this:

[14] Being is–or should be–necessary. It is impossible that everything should be reduced to a play of successive appearances which are inconsistent with each other ("inconsistent" is essential), or, in the words of Shakespeare, to "a tale told by an idiot." I aspire to participate in this being, in this reality–and perhaps this aspiration is already a degree of participation, however rudimentary.

Such a need, it may be noted, is to be found at the heart of the most inveterate pessimism. Pessimism has no meaning unless it signifies: it would surely be well if there were being, but there is no being, and I, who observe this fact, am therefore nothing.

As for defining the word "being," let us admit that it is

315

extremely difficult. I would merely suggest this method of approach: being is what withstands–or what would withstand–an exhaustive analysis bearing on the data of experience and aiming to reduce them step by step to elements increasingly devoid of intrinsic or significant value. (An analysis of this kind is attempted in the theoretical works of Freud.) When the pessimist Besme says in [Paul Claudel's] *La Ville* (Paris: Mercure de France, 1914) that nothing is, he means precisely this, that there is no experience that withstands this analytical test. And it is always towards death regarded as the manifestation, the proof of this ultimate nothingness that the kind of inverted apologetic which arises out of absolute pessimism will inevitably gravitate.

A philosophy which refuses to endorse the ontological need is, nevertheless, possible; indeed, generally speaking, contemporary thought tends towards this abstention. But at this point a distinction must be made between two different attitudes which are sometimes confused: one which consists in a systematic reserve (it is that of agnosticism in [15] in all its forms), and the other, bolder and more coherent, which regards the ontological need as the expression of an outworn body of dogma liquidated once and for all by the Idealist critique.

The former appears to me to be purely negative: it is merely the expression of an intellectual policy of "not raising the question."

The latter, on the contrary, claims to be based on a positive theory of thought. This is not the place for a detailed critical study of this philosophy. I shall only note that it seems to me to tend towards an unconscious relativism, or else towards a monism which ignores the personal in all its form, ignores the tragic and denies the transcendent, seeking to reduce it to its caricatural expressions which distort its essential character. I shall also point out that, just because this philosophy continually stresses the activity of verification, it ends by ignoring *presence*–that inward realisation of presence through love which infinitely transcends all possible verification because it exists in an immediacy beyond all conceivable mediation. This will be clearer to some extent from what follows.

Thus I believe for my part that the ontological need cannot be silenced by an arbitrary dictatorial act which mutilates the life of the spirit at its roots. It remains true, nevertheless, that such an act is possible, and the conditions of our life are such that we can well believe that we are carrying it out; this must never be forgotten.

[18] At this point we can begin to define the distinction between [19] mystery and problem. A mystery is a problem which encroaches upon its own data, invading them, as it were, and thereby transcending itself as a simple problem. A set of examples will help us to grasp the content of this definition.

It is evident that there exists a mystery of the union of the body and the soul. The indivisible unity always in· adequately expressed by such phrases as *I have a body, I make use of my body, I feel my body*, etc., can be neither analysed nor reconstituted out of precedent elements. It is not only data, I would say that it is the basis of data, in the sense of being my own presence to myself, a presence of which the act of self-consciousness is, in the last analysis, only an inadequate symbol.

It will be seen at once that there is no hope of establishing an exact frontier between problem and mystery. For in reflecting on a mystery we tend inevitably to degrade it to the level of a problem.

[20] ... This brings out how the distinction between what is *in me* and what is only *before me* can break down. This distinction falls under the blow of a certain kind of thought: thought at one remove.

But it is, of course, in love that the obliteration of this frontier can best be seen. It might perhaps even be shown that the domain of the meta-problematical coincides with that of love, and that love is the only starting point for the understanding of such mysteries as that of body and soul, which, in some manner, is its expression.

Actually, it is inevitable that, in being brought to bear on love, thought which has not thought itself—unreflected reflection—should tend to dissolve its meta-problematical character and interpret it in terms of abstract concepts, such as the will to live, the will to power, the *libido*, etc. On the other hand, since the domain of the problematical is that of the objectively valid, it will be extremely difficult—if not impossible—to refute these interpretations without changing to a new ground: a ground on which, to tell the truth, they lose their meaning. Yet I have the assurance, the certainty—and it envelops me like a protective cloak—that for as much as I really love I must not be concerned with these attempts at devaluation.

It will be asked: What is the criterion of true love? It must be answered that there is no criteriology except in the order of the objective and the problematical; but we can already see at a distance the eminent ontological value to be assigned to fidelity.

Let us take another illustration, more immediate and more [21] particular, which may shed some light on the distinction between problem and mystery.

Say that I have made an encounter which has left a deep and lasting trace on all my life. It may happen to anyone to experience the deep spiritual significance of such a meeting–yet this is something which philosophers have commonly ignored or disdained, doubtless because it effects only the particular person as person–it cannot be universalised, it does not concern rational being in general.

It is clear that such a meeting raises, if you will, a problem; but it is equally clear that the solution of this problem will always fall short of the only question that matters. Suppose that I am told, for instance: "The reason you have met this person in this place is that you both like the same kind of scenery or that you both need the same kind of treatment for your health"–the explanation means nothing. Crowds of people who apparently share my tastes were in the Engadine or in Florence at the time I was there; and there are always numbers of patients suffering from the same disease as myself at the health resort I frequent. But neither this supposed identity of tastes nor this common affliction has brought us together in any real sense; it has nothing to do with that intimate and unique affinity with which we are dealing. At the same time, it would be transgression of this valid reasoning to treat this affinity as if it were itself the cause and to say: "It is precisely this which has determined our meeting."

Hence I am in the presence of a mystery. That is to say, of a reality rooted in what is beyond the domain of the problematical properly so called. Shall we avoid the difficulty by saving that it was after all nothing but a coincidence, a lucky chance? But the whole of me immediately protests [22] against this empty formula, this vain negation of what I apprehend with the deepest of my being. Once again we are brought back to our first definition of a mystery as a problem which encroaches upon its own data: I who inquire into the meaning and the possibility of this meeting, I cannot place myself outside it or before it; I am engaged in this encounter, I depend upon it, I am inside it in a certain sense, it envelops me and it comprehends me–even if it is not comprehended by me. Thus it is only by a kind of betrayal or denial that I can say: "After all, it might not have happened, I would still have been what I was, and what I am to-day." Nor must it be said: I have been changed by it as by an outward cause. No, it has developed me from within, it has acted in me as an inward principle.

But this is very difficult to grasp without distortion. I shall be inevitably tempted to react against this sense of the inwardness of the encounter, tempted by my probity itself, by what from a certain standpoint I must judge to be the best—or at least the safest—of myself. ...

[26] Let us recall what we said earlier on: that the ontological need, the need of being, can deny itself. In a different context we said that being and life do not coincide; my life, and by reflection all life, may appear to me as forever inadequate to something which I carry within me, which in a sense I am, but which reality rejects and excludes. Despair is possible in any form, at any moment and to any degree, and this betrayal may seem to be counselled, if not forced upon us, by the very structure of the world we live in. ...

[27] Let us take despair. I have in mind the act by which one despairs of reality as a whole, as one might despair of a person. This appears to be the result, or the immediate translation into other terms, of a kind of balance sheet. Inasmuch as I am able to evaluate the world of reality (and, when all is said and done, what I am unable to evaluate is for me as if it were not) I can find nothing in it that withstands that process of dissolution at the heart of things which I have discovered and traced. I believe that at the root of despair there is always this affirmation: "There is nothing in the realm of reality to which I can give credit—no security, no guarantee." It is a statement of complete insolvency.

As against this, hope is what implies credit. Contrary to what was thought by Spinoza, who seems to me to have confused two quite distinct notions, fear is correlated to desire and not to hope, whereas what is negatively correlated to hope is the act which consists in putting things at their worst—an act which is strikingly illustrated by what is [28] known as defeatism, and which is ever in danger of being degraded into the desire of the worst. Hope consists in asserting that there is at the heart of being, beyond all data beyond all inventories and all calculations, a mysterious principle which is in connivance with me, which cannot but will that which I will, if what I will deserves to be willed and is, in fact, willed by the whole of my being.

We have now come to the centre of what I have called the ontological mystery, and the simplest illustrations will be the best. To hope against all hope that a person whom I love will recover from a disease which is said to be incurable is to say: It is impossible that I should be alone in willing this cure; it is impossible that reality in its inward depth should be hostile or so much as indifferent to what I assert is in itself a good. It is quite useless to tell me of discouraging *cases* or *examples*: beyond all experience, all probability, all statistics, I assert that a given order shall be re-established, that reality is on my side in willing it to be so. I do not wish: I assert; such is the prophetic tone of true hope.

No doubt I shall be told: "In the immense majority of cases this is an illusion. But it is of the essence of hope to exclude the consideration of cases; moreover, it can be shown that there exists an ascending dialectic of hope, whereby hope rises to a plane which transcends the level of all possible empirical disproof–the plane of salvation as opposed to that of success in whatever form.

It remains true, nevertheless, that the correlation of hope and despair subsists until the end; they seem to me inseparable. I mean that while the structure of the world we live in permits–and may even seem to counsel–absolute despair, yet it is only such a world that can give rise to an unconquerable hope. If only for this reason, we cannot be sufficiently [29] thankful to the great pessimists in the history of thought; they have carried through an inward experience which needed to be made and of which the radical possibility no apologetics should disguise; they have prepared our minds to understand that despair can be what it was for Nietzsche (though on an infra-ontological level and in a domain fraught with mortal dangers) the springboard to the loftiest affirmation.

At the same time, it remains certain that, for as much as hope is a mystery, its mystery can be ignored or converted into a problem. Hope is then regarded as a desire which wraps itself up in illusory judgments to distort an objective reality which it is interested in disguising from itself. What happens in this case is what we have already observed in connection with encounter and with love; it is because mystery can–and, in a sense, logically must–be degraded into a problem that an interpretation such as that of Spinoza, with all the confusion it implies, had to be put forward sooner or later. It is important and must be stressed that this attitude has nothing against it so long as our standpoint is on the hither-side of the realm of the ontological. Just as long as my attitude towards reality is that of someone who is not involved in it, but who judges it his duty to draw up its minutes as exactly as possible (and this is by definition the attitude of the scientist), I am justified in maintaining in regard to it a sort of principle of mistrust, which in theory is unlimited in its application; such is the legitimate standpoint of the workman in the laboratory, who must in no way prejudge the result of his analysis, and who can all the better envisage *the worst*, because at this level the very notion of worst is empty of meaning. But an investigation of this sort, which is just like that of an accountant [30] going through the books, takes place on the hither-side of the order of mystery, an order in which the problem encroaches upon its own data.

It would indeed be a profound illusion to believe that I can still maintain this same attitude when I undertake an inquiry, say, into the value of life; it would be a paralogism to suppose that I can pursue such an inquiry as though my own life were not at issue.

Hence, between hope—the reality of hope in the heart of the one whom it inhabits—and the judgment brought to bear upon it by a mind chained to objectivity there exists the same barrier as that which separates a pure mystery from a pure problem. ...

[36] I must insist once again: A presence to which we are faithful is not at all the same thing as the carefully preserved effigy of an object which has vanished; an effigy is, when all is said and done, nothing but a likeness; metaphysically it is *less* than the object, it is a diminution of the object. Whereas presence, on the contrary, is *more* than the [37] object, it exceeds the object on every side. We are here at the opening of a vista at whose term death will appear as the *test of presence*. This is an essential point and we must consider it carefully.

It will no doubt be said: What a strange way of defining death! Death *is* a phenomenon definable in biological terms; it *is not* a test.

It must be answered: It is what it signifies and, moreover, what it signifies to a being who rises to the highest spiritual level to which it is possible for us to attain. It is evident that if I read in the newspaper of the death of Mr. So-and-so, who is for me nothing but a name, this event is for me nothing more than the subject of an announcement. But it is quite another thing in the case of a being who has been granted to me as a presence. In this case, everything depends on me, on my inward attitude of maintaining this presence which could be debased into an effigy.

It will be objected: This is nothing more than a description in recondite and unnecessarily metaphysical terms of a common psychological fact. It is evident that it depends upon us in a certain measure to enable the dead to survive in our memory, but this existence is no more than subjective.

I believe that the truth is altogether different and infinitely more mysterious. In saying, "It depends upon us that the dead should live on in our memory," we are still thinking of the idea in terms of a diminution or an effigy. We admit that the object has disappeared, but that there remains a likeness which it is in our power to keep, as a daily woman "keeps" a flat or a set of furniture. It is all too evident that this manner of keeping can have no ontological value whatsoever. But it is altogether different in the case where fidelity is creative in the sense which I have tried to define. A [38] presence is a reality; it is a kind of influx; it depends upon us to be permeable to this influx, but not, to tell the truth, to call it forth. Creative fidelity consists in maintaining our lives actively in a permeable state; and there is a mysterious interchange between this free act and the gift granted in response to it.

An objection which is the converse of the preceding one may be expected at this point. I will be told: "All right. You have now ceased to decorate a psychological platitude with metaphysical ornaments, but only to make a gratuitous assertion which is unproved and which is beyond all possible experimental proof; this was inevitable as soon as you replaced the ambiguous and neutral term 'presence' by the much more compromising term 'influx.'"

To reply to this objection, we must refer again to what I have already said of mystery and of recollection. Indeed, it is only on the meta-problematical level that the notion of influx can possibly be accepted. If it were taken in its objective sense, as an accretion of strength, we would indeed be faced with a thesis, not of metaphysics but of physics which would be open to every possible objection. When I say that a being is granted to me as a presence or as a being (it comes to the same, for he is not a being for me unless he is a presence), this means that I am unable to treat him as if he were merely placed in front of me; between him and me there arises a relationship which, in a sense, surpasses my awareness of him; he is not only before me, he is also within me— or, rather, these categories are transcended, they have no longer any meaning. The word influx conveys, though in a manner which is far too physical and spacial; the kind of interior accretion, of accretion from within which comes into being as soon as presence is effective. [39] Great and almost invincible is the temptation to think that such effective presence can be only that of an object; but if we believed this we would fall back to the level of the problematical and remain on the hither-side of mystery; and against this belief fidelity raises up its voice: "Even if I cannot see you, if I cannot touch you, I feel that you are with me; it would be a denial of you not to be assured of this." *With* me: note the metaphysical value of this word, so rarely recognised by philosophers, which corresponds neither to a relationship of inherence or immanence nor to a relationship of exteriority. It is of the essence of genuine *coesse*–I must use the Latin word–that is to say, of genuine intimacy, to lend itself to the decomposition to which it is subjected by critical thought; but we already know that there exists another kind of thought, a thought which bears upon that thought itself, and is related to a bottled up yet efficacious underlying intuition, of which it suffers the attraction.

It must be added (and this brings us to the verge of another sphere) that the value of such intimacy, particularly in regard to the relation between the living and the dead, will be the higher and the more assured the more this intimacy is grounded in the realm of total spiritual availability (*disponibilité*)–that is to say, of pure charity; and I should note in passing that an ascending dialectic of creative fidelity corresponds to the dialectic of hope to which I have already referred.

The notion of availability is no less important for our subject than that of presence, with which it is bound up.

It is an undeniable fact, though it is hard to describe in intelligible terms, that there are some people who reveal themselves as "present"–that is to say, at our disposal–when we are in pain or in need to confide in someone, while there [40] are other people who do not give us this feeling, however great is their goodwill. It should be noted at once that the distinction between presence and absence is not at all the same as that between attention and distraction. The most attentive and the most conscientious listener may give me the impression of not being present; he gives me nothing, he cannot make room for me in himself, whatever the material favours which he is prepared to grant me. The truth is that there is a way of listening which is a way of giving, and another way of listening which is a way of refusing, of refusing *oneself*; the material gift, the visible action, do not necessarily witness to presence. We must not speak of proof in this connection; the word would be out of place. Presence is something which reveals itself immediately and unmistakably in a look, a smile, an intonation or a hand shake.

It will perhaps make it clearer if I say that the person who is at my disposal is the one who is capable of being with me with the whole of himself when I am in need; while the one who is not at my disposal seems merely to offer me a temporary loan raised on his resources. For the one I am a presence; for the other I am an object. Presence involves a reciprocity which is excluded from any relation of subject to object or of subject to subject-object. A concrete analysis of unavailability (*indisponibilité*) is no less necessary for our purpose than that of betrayal, denial or despair.

Unavailability is invariably rooted in some measure of alienation. Say, for instance, that I am told of some misfortune with which I am asked to sympathise: I understand what I am told; I admit in theory that the sufferers deserve my sympathy; I see that it is a case where it would be logical [41] and just for me to respond with sympathy; I even offer my sympathy, but only with my mind; because, when all is said and done, I am obliged to admit that I feel absolutely nothing. Indeed, I am sorry that this should be so; the contradiction between the indifference which I feel in fact and the sympathy which I know I ought to feel is humiliating and annoying; it diminishes me in my own eyes. But it is no use; what remains in me is the rather embarrassing awareness that, after all, these are people I do not know—if one had to be touched by every human misfortune life would not be possible, it would indeed be too short. The moment I think: After all, this is only a case, No. 75,627, it is no good, I can feel nothing.

But the characteristic of the soul which is present and at the disposal of others is that it cannot think in terms of *cases*; in its eyes there are *no cases at all*.

And yet it is clear that the normal development of a human being implies an increasingly precise and, as it were, automatic division between what concerns him and what does not, between things for which he is responsible and those for which he is not. Each one of us becomes the centre of a sort of mental space arranged in concentric zones of decreasing interest and participation. It is as though each one of us secreted a kind of shell which gradually hardened and imprisoned him; and this sclerosis is bound up with the hardening of the categories in accordance with which we conceive and evaluate the world.

Fortunately, it can happen to anyone to make an encounter which breaks down the framework of this egocentric topography; I know by my own experience how, from a stranger met by chance, there may come an irresistible appeal which overturns the habitual perspectives just as a gust [42] of wind might tumble down the panels of a stage set—what had seemed near becomes infinitely remote and what had seemed distant seems to be close. Such cracks are repaired almost at once. But it is an experience which leaves us with a bitter taste, an impression of sadness and almost of anguish; yet I think it is beneficial, for it shows us as in a flash all that is contingent and—yes—artificial in the crystallised pattern of our personal system.

But it is, above all, the sanctity realised in certain beings which reveals to us that what we call the normal order is, from a higher point of view, from the standpoint of a soul rooted in ontological mystery, merely the subversion of an order which is its opposite. In this connection, the study of sanctity with all its concrete attributes seems to me to offer an immense speculative value; indeed, I am not far from saying that it is the true introduction to ontology.

Once again a comparison with the soul which is not at the disposal of others will throw light on our subject.

To be incapable of presence is to be in some manner not only occupied but encumbered with one's own self. I have said in some manner; the immediate object of the preoccupation may be one of any number; I may be preoccupied with my health, my fortune, or even with *my inward perfection*. This shows that to be occupied with oneself is not so much to be occupied with *a particular object* as to be occupied in *a particular manner*. It must be noted that the contrary of this state is not a state of emptiness or indifference. The real contrast is rather between the being who is opaque and the being who is transparent. But this inward opacity remains to be analysed. I believe that it consists in a kind of obduracy or fixation; and I wonder if, by generalising and adapting certain psychoanalytical data, we would not find that it is [43] the fixation in a given zone or in a given key of a certain disquiet which, in itself, is something quite different. But what is remarkable is that the disquiet persists within this fixation and gives it that character of constriction which I mentioned in connection with the degradation of the will. There is every reason to believe that this indefinite disquiet should be identified with the anguish of temporality and with that aspiration of man not towards, but by death, which is at the heart of pessimism.

Pessimism is rooted in the same soil as the inability to be at the disposal of others. If the latter grows in us as we grow old, it is only too often because, as we draw near to what we regard as the term of our life, anxiety grows in us almost to the point of choking us; to protect itself, it sets up an increasingly heavy, exacting and, I would add, vulnerable mechanism of self-defence. The capacity to hope diminishes in proportion as the soul becomes increasingly chained to its experience and to the categories which arise from it, and as it is given over more completely and more desperately to the world of the problematical.

Here at last can be brought together the various motifs and thematic elements which I have had to bring out one by one. In contrast to the captive soul we have described, the soul which is at the disposal of others is consecrated and inwardly dedicated; it is protected against suicide and despair, which are interrelated and alike, because it knows that it is not its own, and that the most legitimate use it can make of its freedom is precisely to recognise that it does not belong to itself; this recognition is the starting point of its activity and creativeness.

The difficulties of a philosophy of this sort must not be disguised. It is inevitably faced by a disquietening alternative [44]: Either it will try to solve these difficulties—to give all the answers; in that case it will fall into the excesses of a dogmatism which ignores its vital principles and, I would add, into those of a sacrilegious theodicy, or else it will allow these difficulties to subsist, labelling them as mysteries.

Between these two I believe that there exists a middle way—a narrow, difficult and dangerous path which I have tried to discover. But, like Karl Jaspers in his *Philosophy of Existence* [*Existenzphilosophie* (Berlin: Walter de Gruyter, 1938)] I can only proceed in this kind of country by calling out to other travellers. If, as it occasionally happened, certain minds respond—not the generality, but this being and that other—then there is a way. But, as I believe Plato perceived with incomparable clarity, it is a way which is undiscoverable except through love, to which alone it is visible, and this brings us to what is perhaps the deepest characteristic of that realm of the meta-problematical of which I have tried to explore certain regions.

A serious objection remains to be mentioned. It will perhaps be said: All that you have said implies an unformulated reference to the data of Christianity and can only be understood in the light of these data. Thus we understand what you mean by presence if we think of the Eucharist and what you mean by creative fidelity if we think of the Church. But what can be the value of such a philosophy for those who are a Christian—for those who ignore Christianity or who do not accept it? I would answer: it is quite possible that the existence of the fundamental Christian data may be necessary *in fact* to enable the mind to conceive some of the notions which I have attempted to analyse; but these notions cannot be said to depend on the data of Christianity, and *they do not presuppose it*. On the other hand, should I be told that the intellect must leave out of account anything which is not a universal data of thinking as [45] such, I would say that this claim is exaggerated and in the last analysis, illusory. Now, as at any other time, the philosopher is placed in a given historical situation from which he is most unlikely to abstract himself completely; he would deceive himself if he thought that he could create a complete void both within and around himself. Now this historical situation implies as one of its essential data the existence of the Christian fact–quite independently of whether the Christian religion is accepted and its fundamental assertions are regarded as true or false. What appears to me evident is that we cannot reason to-day as though there were not behind us centuries of Christianity, just as, in the domain of the theory of knowledge, we cannot pretend that there have not been centuries of positive science. But neither the existence of Christianity nor that of positive science plays in this connection more than the role of a fertilising principle. It favours the development of certain ideas which we might not have conceived without it. This development may take place in what I would call para-Christian zones; for myself, I have experienced it more than twenty years before I had the remotest thought of becoming a Catholic.

Speaking more particularly to Catholics, I should like to note that from my own standpoint the distinction between the natural and the supernatural must be rigorously maintained. It will perhaps be objected that there is a danger that the word "mystery" might confuse this very issue. I would reply that there is no question of confusing those mysteries which are enveloped in human experience as such with those mysteries which are revealed, such as the Incarnation or Redemption, and to which no effort of thought bearing on experience can enable us to attain.

It will be asked: why then do you use the same word for [46] two such distinct notions? But I would point out that no revelation is, after all, conceivable unless it is addressed to a being who is *involved–committed*–in the sense which I have tried to define– that is to say, to a being who participates in a reality which is non-problematical and which provides him with his foundation as subject. Supernatural life *must*, when all is said and done, find a hold in the natural–which is not to say that it is the flowering of the natural. On the contrary it seems to me that any study of the notion of *created Nature*, which is fundamental for the Christian, leads to the conclusion that there is in the depth of Nature, as of reason which is governed by it, a fundamental principle of inadequacy to itself which is, as it were, a restless anticipation of a different order.

To sum up my position on this difficult and important point, I would say that the recognition of the ontological mystery, in which I perceive as it were the central redoubt of metaphysics, is, no doubt, only possible through a sort of radiation which proceeds from revelation itself and which is perfectly well able to affect souls who are strangers to all positive religion of whatever kind; that this recognition, which takes place through certain higher modes of human experience, in no way involves the adherence to any given religion; but it enables those who have attained to it to perceive the possibility of a revelation in a way which is not open to those who have never ventured beyond the frontiers of the realm of the problematical and who have therefore never reached the point from which the mystery of being can be seen and recognised. Thus, a philosophy of this sort is carried by an irresistible movement towards the light which it perceives from afar and of which it suffers the secret attraction.

FERDINAND ULRICH (1931-)

Ferdinand Ulrich was born in 1931 in Odry, Czech Republic. He studied at the University of Munich, receiving a doctorate in 1956, and completed his Habilitation at the University of Salzburg in 1959. He went on to teach at the Jesuit Scholasticate in Pullach-Munich beginning in 1964 and the University of Regensburg from 1967 until retiring in 1996.

For more on Ulrich see Pitschl, Florian, "'Unless You Become Like Children': Ferdinand Ulrich's Philosophical Anthropology of Childhood," *Communio* 22 (Spring, 1995): 56-64; Bieler, Martin, "'Analogia entis' as an Expression of Love according to Ferdinand Ulrich," in White, Thomas., ed., *The Analogy of Being: Invention of the Antichrist or the Wisdom of God?* (Grand Rapids: William B. Eerdmans, 2010): 314-339; Oster, Stefan, "Thinking of Love at the Heart of Things: The Metaphysics of Being as Love in the Work of Ferdinand Ulrich." *Communio* 37:4 (Winter, 2010): 660-700; Schindler, David, "The Grace of Being: Ferdinand Ulrich and the Task of a Faithful Metaphysics in the Face of Modernity," in Oakes, Kenneth, ed., *Christian Wisdom Meets Modernity* (London: Bloomsbury, 2016): 149-163 and *A Companion to Homo Abyssus* (Washington: Humanum Academic Press, 2019).

Besides *Homo Abyssus* (Einsiedeln: Johannes Verlag, 1961) discussed below, the other key works of Ulrich are his *Der Mensch als Anfang: Zur philosophischen Anthropologie der Kindheit* (Einsiedeln: Johannes Verlag, 1970); *Gebet als geschöpflicher Grundakt* (Einsiedeln: Johannes Verlag, 1973), of which pages 9-19 have been translated as "A Dangerous Reflection on the Fundamental Act of the Creature," *Communio* 23 (Spring, 1996): 36-46; and *Gabe und Vergebung: Ein Beitrag zur biblischen Ontologie* (Einsiedeln: Johannes Verlag, 2006) on the parable of the prodigal son, from which pages 458-461 have been translated as "Giving Time: The Trinitarian Origin of Created Spatio-Temporality," *Communio* 43:3 (Fall, 2016): 484-487.

The following short excerpts are from Ulrich's *Homo Abyssus: Das Wagnis der Seinsfrage*, 3.1-5 and 4.2-5, translated as *Homo Abyssus: The Drama of the Question of Being* (Washington: Humanum Academic Press, 2018), pages 28-30 and 49-51. *Homo Abyssus* is a deeply metaphysical work that combines Aquinas with Heidegger and had a major influence on Hans Urs von Balthasar. It defends the idea that being is a gift of God to creatures which displays the key characteristics of wealth and poverty. For beings (*ens*) with their essence (*essentia*) receive being from outside and without the gift of being would not be. Yet they receive being as their own and it only occurs in union with their own essence. Hence being is a gift only insofar as God gives it away to another and separates it from Himself in poverty. Yet in that very act it becomes the wealth possessed and usable by a creature. Humans are called to be free receptors of the gift of being as well and echo this finitization of being by giving their love away to other human thous.

Homo Abyssus: The Drama of the Question of Being (1961)[259]

Being and "Nothing"

Esse as Completum et Simplex, sed non Subsistens: The 'Convertibility' of Being and 'Nothing'

[28] ... To being, "nothing can be added other than non-being, *quod non potest esse nec forma nec materia.*"[260] Being, as the "first effect of God' is in its infinite actuality the "likeness of God." But being does not remain stuck in itself in this actuality; to put it metaphorically, being is not caught up in and captivated by its own glory. ... Thus being is nothing other than self-diffusing actuality. But it does not subsist as a thing between God and the creature. Thomas therefore says, "'*Esse*' signifies something complete and simple, *but non-subsistent.*"[261] As pure mediation, to be "is" not an existing thing, an *ens [kein Seiendes].*

[29] But what does *ens* mean? "An *ens* is, as it were, a thing that has *esse*; it is the *ens* alone that is a substance, which subsists."[262] The *ens* is a thing that has being. ... Now, if Thomas goes on to say that the substance is most properly called *ens*, then, with respect to being, which does not subsist, we can affirm that it "is" a *non ens* in a particular sense.

To say that "to be" is not a "being," however, is not to turn it into a "pure potentiality." Ontologically speaking, it is rather the case that "act is always more perfect than potency."[263] Moreover, it becomes evident that neither form nor matter is extrinsic to *esse*. It is never legitimate to think of *esse* in its non-subsistence as potency and to call it "nothing" in this particular sense. Not only should we say that to be is a nonbeing, but we should say that it is "nothing"! There is therefore no contradiction in calling *esse* as a

---

260 *De potentia Dei,* q. 7, a. 2, n. 9.
261 *De potentia Dei,* q. 1, a. 1.
262 *In metaphysica* 12.1.
263 *De potentia Dei,* q. 7, a. 2, n. 9.

completum et simplex, "nothing' if we are thus simply bringing to expression its "non-subsistent" character. ...

[30] The more we conceive being as fullness *given away* the more its non-subsistence comes to light. The absolute intimacy of being in the creature—as God's highest 'gift' precisely excludes its clinging-to-itself in an ideal ontological vacillation. Here it is once again revealed that depotentiating God the Creator into an absolute essence-block, closed up in itself, implies the impossibility of perceiving being as "gift." Indifferentiating being's kenosis in this way also forces its non-subsistence from our speculative view.

Precisely *because* nothing can be external to being as fullness other than *non ens*,[264] insofar as God presupposes "nothing" in his communication of being as a material (mater!), receptive principle, being is not set off *against* finite (as against something "other" in relation to itself), but is rather a *non subsistens* as a gift and fullness that does not cling to itself. In other words, being is not "something outside the existing thing."[265] ...

The Crisis of Being and Its Exposition in the Difference between Being and Beings

The Crisis of Being and the Decision of the Movement into Subsistence

[49] We call the "beginning" of the speculative unfolding of the difference between being and beings the "crisis of being," insofar as the convertibility of being and "nothing" in the concrete substance, which has always already superseded this movement through God's positive positing, comes to a decision in it.

The movement into subsistence thereby not only circumscribes the ontological difference between being and beings, but also and at the same time it sets this difference forth in *the concrete substance*. ...

[50] [This] "necessary sense of being" ... makes manifest that insofar as the convertibility of being and "nothing" comes to a decision in it, the crisis of being can never be neutralized in the pseudo-subsistence of the *ens indifferens*, and being can never be

---

[264] *De potentia Dei*, q. 7, a. 2, n. 9.
[265] *Summa contra Gentiles*, I, 26.

depotentiated into a potency that is able to receive determination, which means in this context reduced to a mere concept.

The necessary sense of being affirms being both as a *completum et simplex* in the sense of infinite actuality, and as the non-subsistence of the same. It can justly be said, *sit venia verbo*, that the necessary sense of being *transnihilates* being in the ideal vacillation and unveils its *exinanitio* [kenosis]. But being is always what it is on the basis of this nihilation, and, precisely in the apparent impotence of its expropriation into finitude, it reveals its infinite positivity to the thinking of mere understanding that seeks to grasp onto stable fixed quantities. In this "poverty," which is the ultimate seal of its fullness, being calls reason to obedience, in which the wealth of being opens up to it. By contrast, the being that clings to itself and affirms itself in the calculated wealth of the all-comprehensive vacillation collapses into the abject state of the merely rationally posited *ens rationis*. ...

[51] The "crisis of being" stands in the power of the "necessary sense of being. It shows that being is already positively itself as the *similitudo divinae bonitatis*. But the way in which it "arrives at itself" occurs along the "path" upon which speculative reason sublates the contradiction and thus dehypostasizes the ideal vacillation of being. If being is the highest likeness of God in its non-subsistence, then it is on this basis always already transnihilated and positively itself as *completum et simplex* without being handed over to this transnihilation beforehand in a surreptitious cringing to itself: "nam ens simpliciter dicitur id quod in se habet esse, scilicet *substantia*."[266] ...

[52] But because being does not subsist, it has really handed itself over to beings. Because it holds "nothing" back, it enables reason to reach out into it in a radical way precisely on the basis of the finite. Being does not reveal its wealth [53] by clinging to itself, just as the gift that has truly been given to the recipient, as it releases him into his own proper independence, moves the recipient toward the giver as origin and makes the giver's fullness and positivity manifest."

---

[266] *In metaphysica* 11.3.

6 ANALYTICAL PHILOSOPHY

PIERRE DUHEM (1861-1916)

Duhem was born in 1861 in Paris, France. Duhem studied physics at the Collège Stanislas from 1872 to 1882 under Jules Moutier and at the École Normale Supérieure from 1882 to 1887 where he received a doctorate in mathematics under Edmond Bouty, Gaston Darboux, Henri Poincaré, after being denied a doctorate in physics a committee consisting of Gabriel Lippmann, Charles Hermite, and Emile Picard, on account of Duhem's criticisms of the theories of Lippmann's friend Marcellin Berthelot and perhaps his conservative political and religious views. Duhem went on to teach at the University of Lille in 1887 where he married but lost his wife to childbirth. He then taught at the University of Rennes from 1893 to 1894 and then became professor of theoretical physics at the University of Bordeaux where he taught for the rest of his life, becoming famous for the Gibbs-Duhem equation. He turned down a position in the history of science at the Collège de France at the end of his life. Duhem died in 1916 in Cabrespine, France in his family's ancestral house. He was elected into the French Academy of Sciences in 1913.

Among Duhem's major works are his *La Théorie Physique: Son Objet, sa Structure* (Paris: Chevalier et Riviére, 1906); *Sauver les Phénomènes* (Paris: A. Hermann, 1908); and *Le Système du Monde*, 10 vols. (Paris: A. Hermann, 1913-1959). For more on Duhem consult: Sandra G. Harding, ed., *Can Theories be Refuted?: Essays on the Duhem-Quine Thesis* (Dordrecht: D. Reidel, 1976); Jaki, Stanley, *Uneasy Genius: The Life and Work of Pierre Duhem* (Leiden: Martinus Nijhoff, 1987); and R.N.D. Martin, *Pierre Duhem: Philosophy and History in the Work of a Believing Physicist* (La Salle: Open Court, 1991).

What follows is Duhem's "Logical Examination of Physical Theory" (1913) which summarizes his account of the methodology of science, in particular his setting forth of what has come to be known as the Duhem-Quine thesis of the underdetermination of theory by data. Duhem argues that there are rarely crucial experiments in physics as observations are interpreted in light of a robust theoretical framework and it is difficult if not impossible to isolate any single hypothesis for experimental testing. Hence one can always adjust various background assumptions to account for an experimental failure. It is not that science cannot grasp reality but this is only something it continually verges on doing without ever fully attaining, it is its ideal limit.

"Logical Examination of Physical Theory" (1913)[267]

[109] A science can progress pursuing the Newtonian method when its means of knowing are still those of common sense. Induction can no longer be practiced, in the manner this method presupposes, when science no longer directly observes facts but substitutes for them the measure, given by instruments, of magnitudes which are wholly defined by mathematical theory.

"An experiment of physics," we said, "is not [110] simply the observation of a phenomenon. ... An experiment of physics is the precise observation of a group of phenomena, accompanied by the *interpretation* of these phenomena. This interpretation substitutes for the concrete data, actually gathered by observation, abstract and symbolic representations which correspond to them in virtue of physical theories admitted by the observer."[268] From this truth numerous consequences may be deduced, ones sharply opposed to the idea of a science in which each principle is furnished by induction. "The physicist," we said, "can never submit to the control of experiment an isolated hypothesis, but only a whole set of hypotheses. When experiment is in disagreement with its predictions, it teaches him that at least one of the assumptions that make up this set is wrong and must be changed; but it does not point out to him which one should be changed."[269]

"We are here very far from the experimental mechanism such as those foreign to its operation readily imagine it. It is commonly believed that each of the hypotheses which physics makes use of can be taken in isolation, subjected to the control of experiment, then, when diverse and multiple tests have established its value, incorporated in a nearly definitive manner into the body of science. In reality, it is not so. Physics is not a machine that lets itself be disassembled; one cannot test each part in isolation and wait to adjust it after its soundness has been meticulously checked. Physical science is an organism that must be taken as a whole; it is an organism of which one part cannot be made to function without the parts furthest from it coming into play, some more, others less, all to some degree. If any trouble, any frailty is revealed in its

---

[267] [Translated by Alan Vincelette from *Notice sur les titres et travaux scientifiques de Pierre Duhem* (Bordeaux: Gounouilhou, 1913). Public Domain.]

[268] Cf. Pierre Duhem, *La theorie physique, son objet, sa structure* (Paris: Chevalier et Rivière, 1906), pp. 221-222.

[269] Cf. Duhem, *La theorie physique*, 1906, pp. 284-285.

functioning, the physicist will be obliged to guess which organ has need of being rectified or modified, without it being possible for him to isolate this organ and examine it apart. The watchmaker given a watch that does not work, separates all the cogs and examines them one by one until he has found the one that is bent or broken. The doctor to whom a sick patient is presented cannot dissect him in order to establish his diagnosis; he must discern the seat of the malady through the inspection of the effects produced on the whole body alone. It is the latter, not that former, that the physicist charged with correcting a shaky theory resembles."

[111] Physical theory is not an explanation of the inorganic world; is it not an inductive generalization of the teachings of experience either. What is it?[270] Is theory simply, as the pragmatist school wants it, an artifice which makes the truths of empirical knowledge easier to wield for us, which enables us to make a more prompt and profitable use of them in our action on the external world, but which does not teach us anything about this world that we have not already been taught by experience alone? Or instead, on the contrary, does theory, making contact with the real, teach us something that experience has not taught us and that it could not teach us, something which is transcendent to purely empirical knowledge?

If it is necessary to respond affirmatively to this last question, we will be able to say that physical theory is *true*, that it has the merit of *knowing*. If, on the contrary, it is the first question which compels us to say 'yes,' we will also have to say that physical theory is not *true*, but simply *convenient*, that it does not have the merit of knowing, but only *practical value.*–"When the physicist,[271] focusing his attention on the science he constructs, subjects the diverse procedures he has put to work in building it to a rigorous examination, he discovers nothing which can introduce into the structure of the edifice the least particle of truth apart from experimental observation. Of propositions which claim to express the facts of experience, and of these only, can we say: *it is true*, or,

---

[270] Cf. Pierre Duhem, "Physique et métaphysique," *Revue des Questions Scientifiques* 2, no. 34 (1893): 55-83; *La theorie physique, son object et sa structure* (Paris: Chevalier et Rivière, 1906); "Sur un fragment, inconnu jusqu'ici, de l'Opus tertium de Roger Bacon," *Archivium Franciscanum historicum* 1 (1908): 238; "La valeur de la théorie physique, à propos d'un livre récent," *Revue Générale des Sciences Pures et Appliquées* 19, no. 1 (January 15, 1908): 7-19.

[271] Cf. Duhem, "La valeur de la théorie physique," 1908, 7-19.

it is false. Of these alone can we assert that that they are not able to accommodate an illogicality, and that, of two contradictory propositions, one at least must be rejected. In regard to the propositions introduced by the theory, they are neither *true* nor *false*; they are only *convenient* or *inconvenient*, if the physicist considers it convenient to construct two segments of physics by means of hypotheses which contradict each other, he is free to do so. The principle of contradiction can judge without appeal about the true and the false; it has no power to decide about the *useful* and *non-useful.* To oblige physical theory then to maintain a rigorous logical unity in its development would be to exercise an unjust and unsupportable tyranny over the intelligence of the physicist."

"When, after having subjected the science which occupies him to this meticulous examination, the physicist ventures into himself, when he becomes aware of the tendencies which direct the steps of his reason, he immediately recognizes that [112] the most powerful and deepest of all his aspirations are disappointed by the discouraging conclusions of his analysis. No, he cannot bring himself to see in physical theory only an ensemble of practical procedures, a rack filled with tools. No, he cannot believe that it only classifies the knowledge accumulated by empirical science, without transforming in any way the nature of this knowledge, without imprinting on it a character which experience alone would not have engraved there. If there were in physical theory only what his own critical reflection caused him to discover in it, he would cease devoting his time and his efforts to a work of such small importance. *Study of the physical method is powerless to reveal to the physicist the reason which leads him to construct the physical theory.*"

"No physicist, however positivist one supposes him to be, can refuse this admission. But his positivism will have to be very rigorous in order that he not go beyond this admission, in order that he does not assert that his efforts towards an ever more unified and complete physical theory are reasonable, albeit critical reflection on the physical method has not been able to discover the reason for it. It will be very difficult for him not to set forth this reason into the exactitude of the following propositions here below:"

"Physical theory confers on us a certain knowledge of the external world which is irreducible to purely empirical knowledge. This knowledge comes from neither experience nor from the mathematical procedures employed by the theory, so that the purely logical dissection of the theory cannot discover the fissure through which it has entered the edifice of physics. By a path whose reality the physicist cannot deny, any more than he can describe the course, this knowledge derives from a truth other than the truths which our instruments are capable of capturing. The order in which theory arranges the results of observation does not find its full and entire justification in its practical or aesthetic characteristics. We discern, moreover, that it is or tends toward being a *natural classification*; by an analogy, the nature of which escapes the grasp of physics, but the existence of which imposes itself as certain on the mind of the physicist, we discern that it corresponds better and better to a certain supereminent order."

"In a word, the physicist is forced to recognize that *it would be unreasonable to work for the progress of physical theory if this theory were not the reflection, more and more clear and more and more precise, of a metaphysics. The belief in an order transcending physics is the sole reason for being of physical theory.* [113] "The attitude, by turns hostile or favorable, that every physicist takes with regard to this affirmation is summed up in this assertion of Pascal: We have "an inability to prove invincible to all dogmatism"; we have "an idea of the truth invincible to all Pyrrhonism."[272]

Separated from the various pragmatic schools on the subject of the value of physical theory, we would not, under any circumstance, rank ourselves among their disciples. The analysis which we have given of the experiment of physics, by which we have shown, in this experiment, the fact wholly penetrated by theoretical interpretation, to the point that it becomes impossible to present it by isolating it from the theory, this analysis, we say, has found great favor with several pragmatists; they have extended it to the most diverse fields, to history, to exegesis, to theology. We do not deny that this extension is *legitimate to some extent*; however different the problems may be, it is always the same human reason that tries to solve them, so that there is always something common to the many processes it employs. But if it is good to note analogies between our various scientific methods, it is on the condition that we do not forget the differences which separate them. And when one compares the method of physics with other methods, so strangely specialized by the appeal to mathematical theory and by the use of measuring instruments,

---

[272] Cf. Duhem, *La theorie physique*, 1906, pp. 507-509.

there are surely more differences to be noted than analogies to be found.

We admit that physical theory can achieve a certain knowledge of the nature of things; but this purely analogical knowledge appears to us as the term of the theory's progress, as the limit to which it constantly approaches without ever attaining. It is, on the contrary, at the starting point of physical theory that the Cartesian and atomist schools place a hypothetical knowledge of the nature of things. If therefore we have moved away from the Pragmatists, it is not to take our place among the Cartesians or the atomists. The neo-atomist school, whose doctrines center on the notion of the electron, has taken up with a superb confidence the method which we refuse to follow. It thinks that its hypotheses finally reach the intimate structure of matter, that they cause us to see the elements as if some extraordinary ultra-microscope were magnifying them to the point of rendering them perceptible to us.

This confidence, we cannot share. We cannot, in these hypotheses, recognize a divinatory view of what there is beyond [114] sensible things; we regard them only as models. Of these models, dear to the physicists of the English School,[273] we have never denied the usefulness; they lend, we believe, an indispensable aid to minds more extensive than deep, more apt to imagine the concrete than to conceive the abstract. But the time will undoubtedly come when, by their increasing complication, these representations, these models will cease to be auxiliaries for the physicist, where he will regard them rather as embarrassments and obstacles. Leaving these hypothetical mechanisms behind, he will carefully extract from them the experimental laws that they helped to discover; without claiming to explain these laws, he will seek to classify them according to the method we have just analyzed ... .

---

[273] Cf. Pierre Duhem, "L'École anglaise et les theories physiques," *Revue des Questions Scientifiques* 2, no. 34 (1893): 345-378; *La theorie physique*, 1906.

PETER GEACH (1916-2013)

Geach was born in Chelsea, London in 1916 and introduced to philosophy at a young age by his father, who taught philosophy at the University of Lahore in Pakistan. He attended Balliol College, Oxford from 1934 to 1938, and converted to Catholicism and met his future wife Elizabeth Anscombe his last year there. Geach and Anscombe were married in 1941 in Brompton Oratory. Geach acquired his first major academic position in 1951 at the University of Birmingham where he taught logic and was influenced by his conversations with Wittgenstein and Quine. He transferred to the University of Leeds in 1966 and taught there until 1981. He and his wife were also active in the Catholic Spode House conferences in Staffordshire. Geach died in 2013 in Cambridge.

Among his honors, Geach was elected Fellow of the British Academy in 1965, awarded the Alexander von Humboldt Stiftung Prize in 1983, the Pro Ecclesia et Pontifice medal in 1999, and the Aquinas Medal in 2000.

Geach's key works are his *Mental Acts* (London: Routledge and Kegan Paul, 1957), *Reference and Generality* (Ithaca: Cornell University Press, 1962), *God and the Soul* (London: Routledge and Kegan Paul, 1969), and *Logic Matters* (Berkeley, University of California Press, 1972). He also wrote on the philosophy of McTaggart and Frege.

For more on the work of Geach see: Lewis, H.A., ed., *Peter Geach: Philosophical Encounters* (New York: Springer, 1991); Stuart Brown, ed., *Dictionary of Twentieth-Century British Philosophers* (Bristol: Thoemmes Continuum, 2005): vol. II, 314-320; Chapman, Siobham, and Christopher Routledge, eds., *Key Thinkers in Linguistics and the Philosophy of Language* (Oxford: Oxford University Press, 2005): 99-101; Alexander, David E., *Goodness, God, and Evil* (London: Bloomsbury Academic, 2014); Todd, Patrick, "Geachianism," *Oxford Studies in Philosophy of Religion* 3 (2011): 222-251; Kenny, Anthony, "Peter Thomas Geach," *Biographical Memoirs of Fellows of the British Academy* 14 (2015): 185-203.

The following excerpt is from Geach's "God's Relation to the World," *Sophia* 8:2 (1969): 1-9 [*Logic Matters* (Oxford: Basil Blackwell, 1972): 318-327] which is a classic example of Analytical Thomism. In this essay Geach proceeds analytically to defend and elaborates upon the Thomistic notion of divine immutability, and he introduces the famous notion of Cambridge changes or changes in the relationships between two objects that do not involve real changes in the objects themselves, such as positional or epistemological interrelationships.

"God's Relation to the World" (1969)[274]

[318] It is a well-known thesis of Thomistic theology that the relations of creatures of God are 'real' but the relations of God to creatures are not 'real'. This is a systematically misleading expression, to borrow Gilbert Ryle's term, if ever there was one; for of course we cannot suppose that among the relations that *there are*, only certain ones *are real*. I can see no hope of making the Thomistic thesis intelligible unless we paraphrase it by using language about language: we must take it as a way of saying that some relational *propositions* latch on to reality in a way that others do not. This difference would have to hold between *true* relational propositions, and even between pairs of logically equivalent true propositions; for clearly "God providentially governs the world" is logically equivalent to "The world is providentially governed by God", but by the Thomistic theory only the second of these propositions predicates a 'real' relation, though both are true.

In saying that both are true, I am deliberately flouting a muddled scholastic tradition which, if taken seriously, would mean that not both are true. This tradition, to be found in scholastic manuals, is a misconstruction of Aquinas's sound doctrine that the way our mind works need not be the same as the way things are–that our mind in thinking need not, as Wittgenstein once believed, mirror the structure of the world. The doctrine in the manuals is rather the doctrine that, a thought of things *as being, as if they were*, what they are not, may both be inescapable for minds like ours and *not* be false thought. (For example, our thought may by this doctrine represent nonentities as entities, or attributes as subjects of inherence, without ceasing [319] to be true thought.) In that case our minds could inescapably represent *all* relations as having converses although in reality there are relations without converses. This doctrine is sheer muddle and inconsistency. A thought that represents things *as being* what they are *is* a false thought–that is precisely what falsity is–and to deny this is mere confusion. It seems to me that Aquinas himself clearly saw the distinction between saying that a true thought need not *be* the way that the situation thought of is, and saying that a true thought need not *represent a situation to be* the way that situation is; and that he rejected the second view as erroneous. This is a matter of interpretation; I would ask my readers to look at passages like *Summa theologiae* I, q. 13, a. 12 ad 3 and I, q. 85, a. 1, ad 1 and to judge for themselves. If I am right in my reading of Aquinas, he did not fall into the error of the scholastic manuals; at least sometimes, he saw and avoided it. But even if he could fairly be cited against me on this issue—*magis amica veritas*.

Some philosophers have held, though nobody is likely to ascribe to Aquinas, the view that our way of thinking 'in present experience' is inescapably erroneous in certain fundamental ways; and Bradley in particular held that our thinking is both inescapably relational in character and on that very account inescapably erroneous. I gladly leave to others the defence of such a position; I shall here simply take for granted that our ordinary relational thought is sometimes quite true, and *therefore* represents things as being what they in fact are.

As I have said, the question of 'real' relations is a question of *how* a true relational proposition latches on to reality. I must begin by refuting a false view as to the logical syntax of relational propositions: the view that such propositions do not admit of subject-predicate analysis. This is a narrowly logical point to make; but the acceptance of such a view would prevent us from accepting or even understanding the Thomistic doctrine of 'real' relations. If a relational proposition indeed made no predications about A or B, but only affirmed a relation 'between' them, then it would be quite unintelligible how, if true, the proposition could correspond to a reality in A rather than to a reality in B; and of the two converse relations, alike holding 'between' A and B, one could not very well be more 'real' than the other. So we need to see why the 'between' account of relations is wrong.

[320] The account has been widely accepted because it is believed to follow from modern formal logic; Bertrand Russell himself may very well have given this impression in his more popular and polemical writings, and certainly it has been propagated as a truth of modern logic by some of Russell's epigoni. But in fact the logical system of *Principia Mathematica*, 3 vols. (Cambridge: Cambridge University Press, 1910-1913) positively requires that propositions of the form "Φab" be treated as particular examples of the form "Ψa": that is, that a proposition saying how A is related to B be treated as a particular sort of predication about A.

To make this important matter perfectly clear, I take a concrete example of relational argument (from W.V.O Quine's *Methods of Logic* (New York: Holt, 1950). Given the premises:

> (1)   Edith envies everybody luck[i]er than Edith

> (2)   Herbert is not luckier than anybody who envies Herbert

> to prove:

> Herbert is not luckier than Edith.

One easy proof uses a combination of dilemma and syllogism; we can prove that the addition to the premises of either (3), "Edith envies Herbert", or (4), "Edith does not envy Herbert", yields our conclusion by a valid syllogism. For with (3) and (2) we get Syllogism (A):

> (2)   Herbert is not luckier than anybody who envies Herbert

> (3)   Edith envies Herbert

> *Ergo*: Herbert is not luckier than Edith.

And with (4) and (1) we get Syllogism (B):

> (1) Edith envies everybody luckier than Edith

> (4) Edith does not envy Herbert

> *Ergo*: Herbert is not luckier than Edith.

This method of proof is formally valid by modern logical standards, and indeed must count as valid by any reasonable standards. But now let us notice that in Syllogism (A) we took "envies Herbert" as a term, and in Syllogism (B) we took "luckier than Edith" as a term. This would be quite illegitimate if we took seriously the view that relational propositions do not admit of [321] subject-predicate analysis; for then out of a proposition like "Edith envies Herbert" or "Herbert is (not) luckier than Edith" we could not isolate the end piece as a logical unit, a predicable term; the sense of the binary relative term "envies" or "is luckier than" would be completable only by adding the two names simultaneously, as an 'ordered pair', and it would not combine with *one* of the names to form a predicate. Since this would break the back of even such simple and clearly valid inferences as I have given, the non-predicative view of relations may safely be rejected.

If we may after all regard a relational proposition as making predications about the related things *A* and *B*, then it will make sense (whether it is true or not) to suppose that when we take the proposition as a predication about *A*, there is some actuality in *A* answering to the predication, but that when we take the same (or a logically equivalent) proposition as a predication about *B* there is no actuality in *B* answering to the predication. And in concrete examples we can make it plausible that this is true. Take "Edith envies Herbert", for example: if Edith comes to envy Herbert, it is natural to regard this as a change in Edith rather than a change in Herbert (his 'coming to be envied'); and it is very natural to regard a state of envy as an actual condition of Edith, but very unnatural to regard a 'state of being envied' as an actual condition of Herbert. This gives a plausible content to the statement that, when Edith envies Herbert, this involves a 'real' relation on Edith's side but not on Herbert's.

I have thus tied up 'real' relations with 'real' changes. I have written about the problem of 'real' changes elsewhere (cf. the index to my recent collection *God and the Soul* (London: Routledge and Kegan Paul, 1969); I have urged that we need to distinguish 'real' changes, processes that actually go on in a given individual, from among 'Cambridge' changes. The great Cambridge philosophical works published in the early years of this century, like Bertrand Russell's *The Principles of Mathematics* (Cambridge: Cambridge University Press, 1903) and John McTaggart's *The Nature of Existence*, 2 vols. (Cambridge: Cambridge University Press, 1921-1927) explained change as simply a matter of contradictory attributes' holding good of individuals at different times. Clearly any change logically implies a 'Cambridge' change, but the converse is surely not true; there is a sense of "change", hard to explicate, in which it is *false* to say that Socrates' changes by coming to be shorter than Theaetetus when the boy grows up, or that the butter [322] changes by rising in price, or that Herbert changes by 'becoming an object of envy to Edith'; in these cases, 'Cambridge' change of an object (Socrates, the butter, Herbert) makes no 'real' change in that object. Now the denial that God is 'really' related to creatures is quite traditionally bound up with the denial that God undergoes change. This latter denial can be true only if we are thinking of 'real' change; for all things are subject to 'Cambridge' changes—even a timeless abstract entity like a number is subject to a 'Cambridge' change if it comes to be thought of by A, or ceases to be the number of B's living children.

As with other theses of traditional theology, there has been some 'rethinking' about the changelessness of God; I have heard Catholics defending a 'Biblical' view that God is so far from changeless that he is liable to frustration by men's misdeeds (It reminds me not of the Bible but of the *Iliad*–Zeus futilely lamenting the death of Sarpedon). What I am going to say about the matter will doubtless not impress the sort of reader who will swallow the remark that the theological application of a developed formal logic, and the burning of witches, were two signs of degeneracy in the Church of the late Middle Ages (see the *Dutch Catechism*, English version, p. 220). Anyhow, what makes it necessary to regard God as changeless is that otherwise we cannot consistently regard God as cause of the world.

If God is changeless, then we may dismiss the question "Who made God?"–the question of a cause for A does not arise if A is changeless. But if God is changed by the changes of creatures, then God will only be one more ingredient in that aggregate of changeable beings which we call the world, and will not be the Maker of the world. Even if we could consistently think of such a God as causing *all the rest* of the world (as I do not believe we could, not consistently), even then the causal questions that arise about other changeable beings could rightly be raised about such a changeable God; as Schopenhauer said, you cannot pick up an argument like a cab and pay it off when it has taken you as far as you want to go. So this God would not be God after all, since he, like his so-called creatures, would have to have a cause. So I dismiss any 'rethinking' of God's changelessness; it can lead only to an alien and incoherent view of the Divine.

Those true propositions about God which seem to involve a change in him (and do involve a change in him, if we stick to the [323] Cambridge criterion of change) are traditionally explained away as involving a 'real' change only in creatures, not in God. This is not too difficult to understand if we consider causal propositions; God's 'becoming' Creator or Lord of a new creature involves a 'real' change only in the created world, not in God. But severe difficulties arise as regards the Divine knowledge and will.

(1) If we, who have to speak about God at different times, are to speak the truth about God, we shall certainly have to enunciate different propositions at different times about what God knows or wills. "God wills to bring it about that so-and-so" will no longer be

a true thing to say when so-and-so has already been brought about; nor is it true any longer to say "God knows that Socrates is sitting down" after Socrates has got up. How then can God's mind be 'really' changeless in so far as he is concerned with creatures?

(2) Knowledge and will are, in the old jargon, immanent acts: to know or will is an actuality in the knowing or willing person, and does not consist in an action upon an object like kicking or biting; to be the object of knowledge or will is not something that 'really' happens to an individual. This doubly threatens the Thomistic doctrine: it is hard to see how the object of God's knowledge and will can be 'really' related to him, and equally hard to see how God can fail to be 'really' related to the objects of his knowledge and will.

However, merely to speak of "objects of knowledge and will"– as though *individuals* could be such objects–is to use a misleading expression. A proposition affirming that something is known or willed just does not affirm a binary relation of two individuals, whether or not one of the individuals is God. As regards knowledge, the point was made long ago in the *Theaetetus* (in a theory Socrates feigns to have heard in a dream); what one knows is not nameable, like an individual, but only expressible in a *logos,* a proposition. I can learn or assert *that* Jones is such- and-such; it is nonsense to say "I learned Jones" or "I asserted Jones". With the verb "to know" the matter is not so clear; unfortunately in English we *can* say "I know Jones" as well as "I know that Jones is a rascal". But this only shows that the natural selection of words is not so uniformly beneficent as John Austin perhaps supposed. It is just our bad luck that in current English we do not say "I ken John Peel" and "I wot that John [324] Peel keeps a pack of hounds"; the distinction that used to be marked by a pair of verbs in English still is so marked in many languages (as it was in Greek).

Philosophers have misconstrued knowing-*that* as a binary relation by *inventing* objects of knowing, such as timeless Propositions:[275] "I know that Jones drinks" would be short for "I know the Proposition that Jones drinks", and this Proposition here referred to by a complex phrase "the Proposition that Jones drinks" would be an individual, a nameable entity, which could also be the object of belief, doubt, assertion, etc. But this is nonsense: "I've just asserted Fido" (or "learned Fido") is non-significant if "Fido" is a proper name of *any* individual–that

---

[275] I use the capital letter to distinguish this use of the word from its use to mean a piece of language with a certain logical role.

is the whole point of the 'dream' theory in Plato. (Calling the alleged entity a "fact" or a "situation" instead of a Proposition naturally makes no difference.)

As regards will, the same point can be made, and fortunately is less obscured by philosophical theories. I will *that* so-and-so, e.g. that Jones shall be punished; it would be nonsensical to say "I will Jones".

It is thus a mistake from the outset to treat what is known or willed as one term of a two-term relation, the other term being the person who knows or wills. Following Aristotle, Aquinas often speaks as though we had a two-term relation here; whenever he does so, *pietas* must not hide it from us that his logical apparatus is inadequate and his language misleading.

Another mistake we tend to fall into is to regard God's knowledge of creatures as contemplative. But it is an old doctrine that this knowledge is practical; *scientia Dei, causa rerum;* it is analogous not to our observational knowledge but to our knowledge of our own skilled performances. We could better assimilate this old truth if we worked towards a better understanding of what practical knowledge amounts to in human beings: Miss G.E.M. Anscombe's *Intention* (Oxford: Basil Blackwell, 1957), a pioneering investigation, among other valuable points rightly emphasizes that some of a man's knowledge of his own performances is non-observational. The glib sciolism of our time will say "It's just a matter of feedback"; but 'feedback' does not account for all of our control of our own actions; quite familiar facts show this–when a skilled musician [325] plays a passage with many short notes in rapid succession, 'feedback' certainly cannot account for his skill, because nervous conduction is too slow to give him a 'feedback' of his own playing. And very often the sensations that are supposed to give us observational knowledge of our own performances are merely postulated occurrences. We ought to try harder to understand this non-observational knowledge whereby we control our own actions; for this is the way we are made in God's image, as Aquinas says in the prologue to the Prima Secundae.

Just because man's control of his own actions is an image of God's providential control of the world; because, as Sir Leslie Stephen said, there is a great First Cause and ever so many little first causes; we must avoid representations that would make us into mere puppets of God. A parable I have found useful is this: a chess master, without looking at the board, plays a score of opponents simultaneously; his knowledge of chess is so vastly superior to theirs that he can deal with any moves they are going to make, and he has no need to improvise or deliberate. There is no evident contradiction in supposing that God's changeless knowledge thus governs the whole course of the world, whatever men may choose to do.

As regards will, what we need is a correct account of voluntary causality. The most usual account is that the will is a faculty of the soul with special acts of its own, *actus eliciti;* these are what is primarily voluntary, and whatever else is brought about is a consequence of some *actus elicitus* of the will. This account is the most common one in philosophy books and scholastic manuals; and it is *sometimes* followed by Aquinas. If we try to apply to it the Divine will, it leads to a hopeless puzzle; for happenings in the world are contingent, but they follow infallibly upon the *actus elicitus* of the Divine will; is this act, then, itself contingent or necessary? The familiar answer that this *actus elicitus* is necessary "in its entity but not in its term" is quite useless; for all that this answer tells us is that the Divine act of will is necessary, but its 'term', the happening in the world (which follows infallibly upon God's willing it!), is a contingent event; and that is just the problem, not an answer to the problem.

Fortunately, we can come to see that this puzzle arises not from the mystery of the Divine nature, but from inept philosophizing even about the human will. For there are no mental [326] states identifiable as the *actus eliciti* of the will which regularly precede voluntary actions of the mind or body. There are indeed such acts as trying, setting oneself to do something, formulating an intention, and the like; but a little thought shows that these are not the supposed *actus eliciti* of the will; for many voluntary performances are not preceded by anything like trying or setting oneself to do it or formulating an intention. And as for the 'volitions' of recent philosophy, which are supposed to trigger off the movements of muscles, they are a mere myth, devastatingly exposed by Gilbert Ryle in *The Concept of Mind* (Chicago: University of Chicago Press, 1949). (Scholastically trained readers should notice that in modern philosophy this word is not used equivalently with "volitio" in medieval Latin).

In Aquinas, side by side with the untenable notion of *actus elicitus,* we find a quite different account: that "nature" and "will" signify two ways in which an agent can bring about something. "A brings it about naturally (voluntarily) that so-and-so happens" does not signify that first of all A has a natural (voluntary) kind of event happening within himself, and then, as a result of this event, so-and-so happens; rather, the adverbs "naturally" and "voluntarily" serve to differentiate two ways in which the so-and-so that happens may proceed from the agent A (Cf. e.g. *Summa theologiae*, I, q. 41, a. 2).

With this account many puzzles are removed. For example, if the *actus elicitus* of the will were an actual observable event in its own right, then there would be no obvious reason why such an event could not be 'elicited' from a man by outsiders using some technique; indeed, some people believe that just this can be done by 'brainwashing'. But on the account of voluntariness we are now considering, it is simply self-contradictory to say that some issue *both* is up to A's choice *and* is decided by factors wholly outside A's control; external control of the will is an inconsistent notion (as indeed Aquinas holds–*Summa theologiae*, I-II, q. 6, a. 4). The same consideration removes the deterministic dream that 'in principle' the movements of men's bodies could be predicted independently of any mention of what men intend to do. Sometimes it is said that such a purely physical account is 'complementary' to the familiar account in terms of intentions; but "complementary" is just a way of papering over a logical inconsistency.

This account of will enables us to make sense of certain dark sayings of Aquinas:

> Knowledge relates to things as they are in the knower; will relates to things as they are in themselves. Now all other things exist necessarily as they exist in God, but they have no inherent absolute necessity. So God knows necessarily whatever he knows; but he does not will necessarily whatever he wills (*Summa theologiae*, I, q. 19, a. 3, ad 6)

I have argued that the practical knowledge by which God controls the world may be regarded as eternal and unchangeable. But to say "God brings it about by his will that *p*" is to say "It comes about, voluntarily *ex parte Dei,* that *p*". And as a matter of logic this proposition will be contingently true if "*p*" is contingently true.

ELIZABETH ANSCOMBE (1919-2001)

Anscombe was born in Limerick, Ireland, in 1919, where her father was an English officer dealing with the Irish War of Independence. She studied the classics at St. Hugh's College, Oxford, and converted to Catholicism in 1938 after studies on her own and with the Dominicans at Blackfriars College in Oxford. Anscombe married the fellow convert and philosopher Peter Geach in 1941. Anscombe was greatly influenced by the philosophy of Wittgenstein and transferred to Newnham College, Cambridge, where she obtained a research fellowship from 1942-1945 and studied with Wittgenstein. Anscombe would go on to edit and translate several of Wittgenstein's works. Anscombe returned to Oxford in 1945 and taught at Somerville College until 1970 and was active in the Socratic Club debates and the Spode House discussions. Anscombe once again moved to Cambridge where she was a professor from 1970-1986. Anscombe was buried near Wittgenstein in 2001 at the Ascension Parish cemetery in Cambridge.

Anscombe's most important works include her book *Intention* (Oxford: Basil Blackwell, 1958) and her ethical essays such as "Mr. Truman's Degree" (Oxford: Oxonian Press, 1956), "Does Oxford Moral Philosophy Corrupt the Youth?" (1957), and "Modern Moral Philosophy" *Philosophy* 33:124 (January, 1958): 1-19.

For more on the thought of Anscombe see Richter, Duncan, *Ethics after Anscombe: Post "Modern Moral Philosophy"* (Dordrecht: Kluwer, 2000); Teichmann, Roger, *The Philosophy of Elizabeth Anscombe* (Oxford: Oxford University Press, 2008); Rayappan, Pathiaraj, *Intention in Action: The Philosophy of G. E. M. Anscombe* (Bern: Peter Lang, 2010); Richter, Duncan, *Anscombe's Moral Philosophy* (Lanham: Lexington Books, 2010); Wiseman, Rachael, *Routledge Philosophy Guidebook to Anscombe's Intention* (London: Routledge, 2016).

The selections below are from Anscombe's book *Intention* (Cambridge: Harvard University Press, 2000): nn. 23-27, pp. 37-49, and her essay "Mr. Truman's Degree," in *Ethics, Religion and Politics* [Collected Papers 3] (Oxford: Blackwell, 1981): 64-67, 70-71. The former book on intention launched action theory by distinguishing intentional from non-intentional actions and discussing the different levels at which an action could be described. The latter essay on morality helped institute the modern turn to virtue ethics, as well as serving as a critique of utilitarianism and the awarding of an honorary degree at oxford to the American President Harry Truman who ordered the terror bombing of German cities and atomic bombs to be dropped on Japanese cities. In them Anscombe defends the view that certain actions are intrinsically wrong and ought not to be done, even for the greater good.

Intention (1957)[276]

[37] 23. Let us ask: is there any description which is *the* description of an intentional action, given that an intentional action occurs? And let us consider a concrete situation. A man is pumping water into the cistern which supplies the drinking water of a house. Someone has found a way of systematically contaminating the source with a deadly cumulative poison whose effects are unnoticeable until they can no longer be cured. The house is regularly inhabited by a small group of party chiefs, with their immediate families, who are in control of a great state; they are engaged in exterminating the Jews and perhaps plan a world war.-The man who contaminated the source has calculated that if these people are destroyed some good men will get into power who will govern well, or even institute the Kingdom of Heaven on earth and secure a good life for all the people; and he has revealed the calculation, together with the fact about the poison, to the man who is pumping. The death of the inhabitants of the house will, of course, have all sorts of other effects; e.g., that a number of people unknown to these men will receive legacies, about which they know nothing.

This man's arm is going up and down, up and down. Certain muscles, with Latin names which doctors know, are contracting and relaxing. Certain substances are getting generated in some nerve figures-substances whose generation in the course of voluntary movement interests physiologists. The moving arm is casting a shadow on a rockery where at one place and from one position it produces a curious effect as if a face were looking out of the rockery. Further, the pump makes a series of clicking noises, which are in fact beating out a noticeable rhythm.

Now we ask: What is this man doing? What is *the* description of his action?

First, of course, *any* description of what is going on, with him as subject, which is in fact true. E.g. he is earning wages, he is supporting a family, he is wearing away his shoe-soles, he is making a disturbance in the air. He is sweating, he is generating those substances in his nerve fibres. If in fact good government, or the Kingdom of Heaven on earth and a good life for everyone, comes about by the labours of the good men who get into power

---

because the party chiefs die, then he will have been helping to produce this state of affairs. However, our enquiries into the [38] question 'Why?' enable us to narrow down our consideration of descriptions of what he is doing to a range covering all and only his intentional actions. 'He is X-ing' is a description of an intentional action if (*a*) it is true and (*b*) there is such a thing as an answer in the range I have defined to the question 'Why are you X-ing?' That is to say, the description in 'Why are you contracting those muscles?' is ruled out if the *only* sort of answer to the question 'Why?' displays that the man's knowledge, if any, that he was contracting those muscles is an inference from his knowledge of anatomy. And the description in the question 'Why are you generating those substances in your nerve fibres?' will *in fact* always be ruled out on these lines unless we suppose that the man has a plan of producing these substances (if it were possible, we might suppose he wanted to collect some) and so moves his arm vigorously to generate them. But the descriptions in the questions 'Why are you making that face come and go in the rockery?', 'Why are you beating out that curious rhythm?' will be revealed as descriptions of intentional actions or not by different styles of answer, of which one would contain something signifying that the man *notices* that he does that, while the other would be in the range we have defined. But there are a large number of X's, in the imagined case, for which we can readily suppose that the answer to the question 'Why are you X-ing?' falls within the range. E.g. 'Why are you moving your arm up and down?'-'I'm pumping'. 'Why are you pumping?'-'I'm pumping the water supply for the house'. 'Why are you beating out that curious rhythm?',-'Oh, I found out how to do it, as the pump does click anyway, and I do it just for fun'. 'Why are you pumping the water?'-'Because it's needed up at the house' and (*sotto voce*) 'To polish that lot off'. 'Why are you poisoning these people?'-'If we can get rid of them, the other lot will get in and ...'

Now there is a break in the series of answers that one may get to such a question. Let the answer contain a further description Y, then sometimes it is correct to say not merely: the man is X-ing, but also: 'the man is Y-ing'-if that is, nothing falsifying the statement 'He is Y-ing' can be observed. E.g. 'Why are you pumping?'-'To replenish the water supply'. If this was the answer, then we can say 'He *is* replenishing the water-supply'; [39] unless indeed, he is not. This will appear a tautologous pronouncement; but there *is* more to it. For if after his saying 'To replenish the water-supply' we can say 'He is replenishing the water-supply', then this would, in ordinary circumstances, of itself be enough to characterize *that* as an intentional action. (The qualification is necessary because an intended effect just occasionally comes about by accident). Now that is to say, as we have already determined, that the same question 'Why?' will have application to this action in its turn. This is not an empty conclusion: it means that someone who, having so answered 'To replenish the water-supply', is asked 'Why are you replenishing the water-supply?', must not say e.g. 'Oh, I didn't know I was doing that', or refuse any but a causal sense of the question. Of rather, that if he does, this makes nonsense of his answers.

A man can *be doing* something which he nevertheless does not *do*, if it is some process or enterprise which it takes time to complete and of which therefore, if it is cut short at any time, we may say that he *was doing* it, but *did not do* it. This point however, is in no way peculiar to intentional action; for we can say that something was falling over but did not fall (since something stopped it). Therefore we do not appeal to the presence of intention to justify the description 'He is Y-ing'; though in some cases his own statement that he is Y-ing may, at a certain stage of the proceedings, be needed for anybody else to be able to say he is Y-ing, since not enough has gone on for that to be evident; as when we see a man doing things with an array of wires and plugs and so on.

Sometimes, jokingly, we are pleased to say of a man 'He is doing such-and-such' when he manifestly is not. E.g. 'He is replenishing the water-supply', when this is not happening because, as we can see but he cannot, the water is pouring out of a hole in a pipe on the way to the cistern. And in the same way we may speak of some rather doubtful or remote objective, e.g. 'He is proving Fermat's last theorem'; or again one might say of a madman 'He is leading his victorious armies'. It is easy, however, to exclude these cases from consideration and point out the break between cases where we can say 'He is Y-ing', when he has mentioned Y in answer to the question 'Why are you X-ing?', and ones where we say rather 'He is [40] going to Y'. I do not think it is a quite sharp break. E.g. is there much to choose between 'She is making tea' and 'She is putting on the kettle in order to make tea'- i.e. 'She is going to make tea'? Obviously not. And hence the common use of the present to describe a future action which is by no means just a later stage in activity which has a name as a single whole. E.g. 'I am seeing my dentist', 'He is demonstrating in Trafalgar Square' (either might be said when someone is at the moment 'e.g. travelling in a train). But the less normal it would be to take the achievement of the objective as a matter of course, the more the objective gets expressed *only* by 'in order to'. E.g. 'I am going to London in order to make my uncle change his will'; not 'I am making my uncle change his [sic *is*] will'.

To a certain extent the three divisions of the subject made in #1, are simply equivalent. That is to say, where the answers 'I am going to fetch my camera', 'I am fetching my camera' and 'in order to fetch my camera' are interchangeable as answers to the question 'Why?' asked when I go upstairs.

Now if all this holds, what are we to say about all these many descriptions of an intentional action? Are we to say that there are as many distinct actions as we can generate distinct descriptions, with X as our starting point? I mean: We say 'Why are you X-ing?' and get the answer 'To Y', or 'I'm Y-ing', Y being such that we can say 'he's Y-ing'; and then we can ask 'Why are you Y-ing?' and perhaps get the answer 'To Z', and can still say 'He's Z-ing'. E.g. 'Why are you moving your arms up and down?' 'To operate the pump', and he is operating the pump. 'Why are you pumping?' To replenish the water-supply' and he is replenishing the water-supply; 'Why are you replenishing the water-supply?' 'To poison the inhabitants' and he is poisoning the inhabitants, for they are getting poisoned. And here comes the break; for though in the case we have described there is probably a further answer, other than 'just for fun', all the same this further description (e.g. to save the Jews, to put in the good men, to get the Kingdom of Heaven on earth) is not such that we can now say: he is saving the Jews, he is getting the Kingdom of Heaven, he is putting in the good ones. So let us stop here and say: are there four actions here, because we have found four distinct descriptions satisfying [41] our conditions, namely moving his arm up and down, operating the pump, replenishing the water supply, and poisoning the inhabitants?

24. Before trying to answer this, however, we must raise some difficulties. For someone might raise the objection that pumping can hardly be an act of poisoning. It is of course, as the lawyers would say, an act of laying poison, and one might try to reply by saying the man poisons the inhabitants if he lays poison and they get poisoned. But after all we said it was a cumulative poison; this means that no single act of laying the poison is by itself an act of poisoning; besides, didn't the other man 'lay' the poison? Suppose we ask 'When did our man poison them?' One might answer: all the time they got poisoned. But in that case one might say 'His

poisoning them was not an action; for he was perhaps doing nothing relevant at any of the times they were drinking the poison.' Is the question 'When exactly did he poison them?', to be answered by specifying all the numerous times when he laid the poison? But none of them by itself could be called poisoning them; so how can we call the man's present pumping an intentional act of poisoning? Or must we draw the conclusion that he at no time poisoned them, since he was not engaged in poisoning at the times at which they were being poisoned? We cannot say that since at some time he poisoned them, there *must* be actions which we can label 'poisoning them', and in which we can find what it was to poison them. For in the acts of pumping poisoned water nothing in particular is necessarily going on that might not equally well have been going on if the acts had been acts of pumping non-poisonous water. Even if you imagine that pictures of the inhabitants lying dead occur in the man's head, and please him-such pictures could also occur in the head of a man who was *not* poisoning them, and *need* not occur in this man. The difference appears to be one of circumstance, not of anything that is going on *then*.

25. A further difficulty however arises from the fact that the man's intention might not be to poison them but only to earn his pay. That is to say, if he is being improbably confidential [42] and is asked 'Why did you replenish the house water-supply with poisoned water?', his reply is, not 'To polish them off', but 'I didn't care about that, I wanted my pay and just did my usual job'. In that case, although he knows concerning an intentional act of his-for it, namely replenishing the house water-supply with *poisoned* water, it would be incorrect, by our criteria, to say that his act of replenishing the house supply with poisoned water was intentional. And I do not doubt the correctness of the conclusion; it seems to shew that our criteria are rather good. On the other hand, we really do seem to be in a bit of a difficulty to find the intentional act of poisoning those people, supposing that this is what his intentional act is. It is really not at all to be wondered at that so very many people have thought of intention as a special interior movement; then the thing that marked this man's proceedings as *intentional* poisoning of those people would just be that this interior movement occurred in him. But (quite apart from the objections to this idea which we have already considered) the notion of an interior movement tends to have the most unfortunately absurd consequences. For after all we can *form* intentions; now if intention is an interior movement, it would appear that we can choose to have a certain intention and not

another, just by e.g. saying within ourselves: 'What I *mean* to be doing is earning my living, and *not* poisoning the household'; or 'What I *mean* to be doing is helping those good men into power; I withdraw my intention from the act of poisoning the household, which I prefer to think goes on without my intention being in it'. The idea that one can determine one's intentions by making such a little speech to oneself is obvious bosh. Nevertheless the genuine case of 'I didn't care tuppence one way or the other for the fact that someone had poisoned the water, I just wanted to earn my pay without trouble by doing my usual job-I go with the house, see? And it doesn't matter to me who's in it' does appear to make it very difficult to find anything except a man's thoughts-and these are surely interior-to distinguish the intentional poisoning from poisoning knowingly when this was nevertheless not the man's intention.

Well, one may say, isn't my proposed criterion in a way a [43] criterion by thoughts? If the answer to the question 'Why did you replenish the house supply with poisoned water?' is 'To polish them off', or any answer within the range, like 'I just thought I would', then by my criterion the action under that description is characterized as intentional; otherwise not. But does this not suppose that the answer is or would be *given*? And a man can surely make up the answer that he prefers! So it may appear that I have supplied something just like the interior movement, which a man can make what he likes; but (perhaps out of an attachment to 'verificationism') preferred an external answer (actual or hypothetical) which a man can equally make what he likes-at least within the range of moderately plausible answers. Of course I must mean that the *truthful* answer is, or would be, one or the other; but what sort of control of truthfulness can be established here?

The answer to this has to be: there can be a certain account of control of the truthfulness of the answer. For example, in the case of the man who didn't care tuppence, part of the account we imagined him as giving was that he just went on doing his usual job. It is therefore necessary that it should be his usual job if his answer is to be acceptable; and he must not do anything, out of the usual course of his job, that assists the poisoning and of which he cannot give an acceptable account. E.g. suppose he distracts the attention of one of the inhabitants from something about the water source that might suggest the truth; the question 'Why did you call him from over there?' must have a credible answer other than 'to prevent him from seeing'; and a multiplication of such points needing explanation would cast doubt on his claim not to have done anything with a view to facilitating the poisoning.-And yet here we might encounter the following explanation: he did not want the enormous trouble that would result from the person's noticing; hoped that since the poison was laid it would all go off safely. All along the line he calculated what looked like landing him personally in least trouble, and he reckoned that preventing anything from being suspected would do that. That is quite possible.

Up to a point, then, there is a check on his truthfulness in the account we are thinking he would perhaps give; but still, there is an area in which there is none. The difference between the [44] cases in which he doesn't care whether the people are actually poisoned or not, and in which he is very glad on realizing that they will be poisoned if he co-operates by going on doing his ordinary job, is not one that necessarily carries with it any difference in what he overtly does or how he looks. The difference in his thought on the subject *might* only be the difference between the meanings of the grunt that he gives when he grasps that the water is poisoned. That is to say, when asked 'Why did you replenish the house supply with poisoned water?' he might either reply 'I couldn't care tuppence' or say 'I was glad to help to polish them off', and if capable of saying what had actually occurred in him at the time as the vehicle of either of these thoughts, he might have to say only that he grunted. This is the kind of truth there is in the statement 'Only you can know if you had such-and-such an intention or not'. There is a point at which only what the man himself says is a sign; and here there is room for much dispute and fine diagnosis of his genuineness.

On the other hand, if, say, this was not his normal job, but he was hired by the poisoner to pump the water, knowing it was poisoned, the case is different. He can say he doesn't care tuppence, and that he only wants the money; but the commission by the acceptance and performance of which he gets the money is-however implicit it is allowed to be-to pump poisoned water. Therefore unless he takes steps to cheat his hirer (he might e.g. put what he mistakenly thought was an antidote into the water), it is not an acceptable account if he says 'I wasn't intending to pump poisoned water, only to pump water and get my hire', so that the forms he adopts for refusing to answer the question 'Why did you pump poisoned water?' with an answer in our defined range-e.g. with the answer 'to get the pay'-are unacceptable. So that while we can find cases where [sic] only the man himself can say whether he had a certain intention or not; they are further limited by this: he cannot profess not to have had the intention of doing the thing that was a means to an end of his.

All this, I think, serves to explain what Wittgenstein says at #644 of *Philosophical Investigations*:

'"I am not ashamed of what I did then, but of the intention which I had". And didn't the intention reside [45] *also* in what I did? What justifies the shame? The whole history of the incident.'

And against the background of the qualifications we have introduced, we can epitomize the point by saying 'Roughly speaking, a man intentions to do what he does'. But of course that is *very* roughly speaking. It is right to formulate it, however, as an antidote against the absurd thesis which is sometimes maintained: that a man's intended action is only described by describing his *objective*.

The question arises: what can be the interest of the intention of the man we have described, who was only doing his usual job, etc.? It is certainly not an ethical or legal interest; if what he said was true, *that* will not absolve him from guilt of murder! We just *are* interested in what is true about a man in this kind of way. Here again Wittgenstein says something relevant, in his discussion of 'I was going to':

'Why do I want to tell him about an intention too, as well as telling him what I did? ... because I want to tell him something about *myself*, which goes beyond what happened at that time. I reveal to him something of myself when I tell him what I was going to do.-Not, however, on grounds of self-observation, but by way of a response (it might also be called an intuition).' (*Philosophical Investigations*, # 659). Wittgenstein is presumably thinking of a response, or reaction, to the memory of 'that time'; in the context of *our* interests, we can think of it as a response to our special question 'Why?'.

26. Let us now return to the question with which we ended #23: Are we to say that the man who (intentionally) moves his arm, operates the pump, replenishes the water supply, poisons the inhabitants, is performing *four* actions? Or only one? The answer that we imagined to the question 'Why?' brings it out that the four descriptions form a series, A-B-C-D, in which each description is introduced as dependent on the previous one, though independent of the following one. Then is B *a* description of A, C of B, and so on? Not if that means that we can see that 'he is operating the pump' is another [46] description of what is here also described by 'he is moving his arm up and down'-in such a way that is, that

what verifies the latter, in this case, also verifies the former. On the other hand, if we say there are four actions, we shall find that the only action that B consists in here is A; and so on. Only, more circumstances are required for A to be D, than for A to be B. But these circumstances *need* not include any particularly recent action of the man who is said to do A, B, C and D (although we made it a cumulative poison, for present purposes we can suppose that a single pumping is enough to do the trick). In short, the only distinct action of his that is in question is this one, A. For moving his arm up and down with his fingers round the pump handle *is*, in these circumstances, operating the pump; and, in these circumstances, it *is* replenishing the house water-supply; and, in these circumstances, it *is* poisoning the household.

So there is one action with four descriptions, each dependent on wider circumstances, and each related to the next as description of means to end; which means that we can speak equally well of *four* corresponding intentions, or of *one* intention-the last term that we have brought in in the series. By making it the last term so far brought in, we have given it the character of being the intention (so far discovered) *with* which the act in its other descriptions was done. Thus when we speak of four intentions, we are speaking of the character of being intentional that belongs to the act in each of the four descriptions; but when we speak of one intention, we are speaking of intention *with which*; the last term we give in such a series gives the intention *with* which the act in each of its other descriptions was done, and this intention so to speak swallows up all the preceding intentions *with* which earlier members of the series were done. The mark of this 'swallowing up' is that it is not wrong to give D as the answer to the question 'Why?' about A; A's being done with B as intention does not mean that D is only indirectly the intention of A, as, if I press on something which is pressing on something ... which is pressing against a wall, I am only indirectly pressing against the wall. If D is given as the answer to the question 'Why?' about A, B and C can make an appearance in answer to a question 'How?'. When terms are related in this [47] fashion, they constitute a series of means, the last term of which is, just by being given as the last, so far treated as end.

A term falling outside the series A-D may be a term in another series with some of the members A, B, C in it: for example, if a man is beating out the rhythm of God Save the King in the clicking of the pump. The intention of doing so *with* which he moves his arm up and down is not 'swallowed up' by the intention of D (beating out the rhythm is not *how* he pumps the water); and the mark of this is that if the question 'Why are you moving your arm up and down?' receives as answer 'To click out the rhythm of God Save the King', the answer to 'Why?' asked about *this* action does not lead to D.

Another implication of what I call 'swallowing up' is that nothing definite has to hold about *how many* terms we put between A and D; for example, in the imagined case we did not put in a term 'making the water flow along the pipes', which yet would take its place in the series if anyone thought of asking the question 'Why?' about it.

27. Is there ever a place for an interior act of intention? I suppose that the man I imagined, who said 'I was only doing my usual job', might find this formula and administer it to himself in the present tense at some stage of his activities. However, if he does this, we notice that the question immediately arises: with what intention does he do it? This question would always arise about anything which was deliberately performed as an 'act of intending'. The answer in this case might be 'So that I don't have to consider whose side I am on'. Thus the interior performance has not secured what you might have thought, namely that the man's action in pumping the water *is* just doing his usual job; it is itself a new action, like clicking out the rhythm of God Save the King on the pump. It is in fact only if the thought 'I'm only doing my usual job' is spontaneous rather than deliberate that its occurrence has some face-value relevance to the question what the man's intentions really are. And when spontaneous, it is subject to those tests for truthfulness, which, as we saw, applied to the same form of words given as an explanation after the event; and given that it survives all the same external tests, it comes under the same last determination: [48] '*In the end* only you can know whether that is your intention or not'; that means only: there comes a point where a man can say: 'This is my intention', and no one else can contribute anything to settle the matter. (It does not mean that when he says 'This is my intention', he is evincing a knowledge available only to him. I.e. here 'knows' only means 'can say'. Unless indeed we imagine a case where it could be said: he *thought* this was his intention, but it became clear that he was deceived.) The only new possibility would be one of eliciting some obviously genuine reaction by saying such things as (to give crude examples): 'Well, then you won't be much interested to hear that the poison is old and won't work'; or 'Then you won't be claiming a share in a great sum with which someone wishes to reward the

conspirators'. This sort of thing is of course a stock way of bringing out pretences, often met with in literature-e.g. the deaf man who hears clearly what he ought not to—and in life pretences are no doubt discerned by skilled psychological detectives. But there comes a point at which the skill of psychological detectives has no criteria for its own success. For, after all, probing questions may lead a man to pretend something new, instead of revealing what was there already. So perhaps no concrete inferences as to matters of fact which are quite simply testable can be drawn from the detectives' verdicts. One may *feel* that the verdict is right; that the man who gives it has 'insight'. But, as Wittgenstein puts it (*Philosophical Investigations*, p. 128) the consequences here are of a diffuse kind ... nuances in relationships with others in the plot.

... We can imagine an intention which is a purely interior matter nevertheless changing the whole character of certain things. A contemptuous thought might enter a man's mind so that he meant his polite and affectionate behaviour to someone on a particular occasion only ironically, without there being any outward sign of this (for perhaps he did not venture to give any outward sign). There need not be any specific history, or any consequences, in the light of which an outside observer could see the forms of [49] affection as ironically meant; for as far as concerns history, it is always possible to find things to despise in people without any very special story issuing in contempt on this occasion; and afterwards he might change his mind, think of the episode as an odd aberration, and never turn future occasions into a development of it. Let us suppose that the thought in his mind is 'you silly little twit!' Now here too, it is not enough that these words should occur to him. He has to mean them. This shews once more, that you cannot take any performance (even an interior performance) as itself an act of intention; for if you describe a performance, the fact that it has taken place is not a proof of intention; words for example may occur in somebody's mind without his meaning them. So intention is never a performance in the mind, though in some matters a performance in the mind which is seriously *meant* may make a difference in the correct account of the man's action-e.g. in embracing someone. But the matters in question are necessarily ones in which outward acts are 'significant' in some way.

"Mr. Truman's Degree" (1956)[277]

[64] The Japanese refused the [Potsdam] Declaration. In consequence, the bombs were dropped on Hiroshima and Nagasaki. The decision to use them on people was Mr. Truman's.

For men to choose to kill the innocent as a means to their ends is always murder, and murder is one of the worst of human actions. So the prohibition on deliberately killing prisoners of war or the civilian population is not like the Queensbury Rules: its force does not depend on its promulgation as part of positive law, written down, agreed upon, and adhered to by the parties concerned.

When I say that to choose to kill the innocent as a means to one's ends is murder, I am saying what would generally be accepted as correct. But I shall be asked for my definition of "the innocent." I will give it, but later. Here, it is not necessary; for with Hiroshima and Nagasaki we are not confronted with a borderline case. In the bombing of these cities it was certainly decided to kill the innocent as a means to an end. And a very large number of them, all at once, without warning, without the interstices of escape or the chance to take shelter, which existed even in the "area bombing" of the German cities.

I have long been puzzled by the common cant about President Truman's courage in making this decision. Of course, I know that you can be cowardly without having reason to think you are in danger. But how can you be courageous? Light has come to me lately: the term is an acknowledgement of the truth. Mr. Truman was brave because, and only because, what he did was so bad. But I think the judgement unsound. Given the right circumstances (e.g. that no one whose opinion matters will disapprove), a quite mediocre person can do spectacularly wicked things without thereby becoming impressive.

I determined to oppose the proposal to give Mr. Truman an honorary degree here at Oxford. Now, an honorary degree is not a reward of merit: it is, as it were, a reward for being a very distinguished person, and it would be foolish to enquire whether a candidate deserves to be as distinguished as he is. That is why, in general, the question whether so-and-so should have an honorary

---

[277] [Elizabeth Anscombe, "Mr. Truman's Degree," *Ethics, Religion and Politics.* Copyright © 1981 by Blackwell Publishing. All rights reserved. Used with permission of Blackwell Publishing, www.wiley.com/en-us.]

degree is devoid of interest. A very distinguished person will hardly be also a notorious criminal, and if he should chance to be a non-notorious criminal it would, in my opinion, be improper to bring the matter up. It is only in the rather rare case in which a man is known everywhere for an action, in fact of which it is sycophancy to honor him, that the question can be of the slightest interest.

I have been accused of being "high-minded." I must be saying "You may [65] not do evil that good may come," which is a disagreeably high-minded doctrine. The action was necessary, or at any rate it was thought by competent, expert military opinion to be necessary; it probably saved more lives than it sacrificed; it had a good result, it ended the war. Come now: if you had to choose between boiling one baby and letting some frightful disaster befall a thousand people—or a million people, if a thousand is not enough—what would you do? Are you going to strike an attitude and say "You may not do evil that good may come"? (People who never hear such arguments will hardly believe they take place, and will pass this rapidly by.)

"It pretty certainly saved a huge number of lives." Given the conditions, I agree. That is to say, if those bombs had not been dropped the Allies would have had to invade Japan to achieve their aim, and they would have done so. Very many soldiers on both sides would have been killed; the Japanese, it is said—and it may well be true—would have massacred the prisoners of war; and large numbers of their civilian population would have been killed by "ordinary" bombing.

I do not dispute it. Given the conditions, that was probably what was averted by that action. But what were the conditions? The unlimited objective, the fixation on unconditional surrender. The disregard of the fact that the Japanese were desirous of negotiating peace. The character of the Potsdam Declaration—their "chance." I will not suggest, as some would like to do, that there was an exultant itch to use the new weapons, but it seems plausible to think that the consciousness of the possession of such instruments had its effect on the manner in which the Japanese were offered their "chance."

We can now reformulate the principle of "doing evil that good may come" Every fool can be as much of a knave as suits him.
I recommend this history to undergraduates reading Greats as throwing a glaring light on Aristotle's thesis that you cannot be or do any good where you are stupid.

I informed the Senior Proctor of my intention to oppose Mr.

Truman's degree. He consulted the Registrar to get me informed on procedure. The Vice-Chancellor was informed; I was cautiously asked if I had got up a party. I had not; but a fine House was whipped up to vote for the honour. The dons at St. John's were simply told "The women are up to something in Convocation; we have to go and vote them down." In Worcester, in All Souls, in New College, however, consciences were greatly exercised, as I have heard. A reason was found to satisfy them: *It would be wrong to try to PUNISH Mr. Truman!* I must say I rather like St. John's.

The Censor of St. Catherine's had an odious task. He must make a speech which should pretend to show that a couple of massacres to a man's credit are not exactly a reason for not showing him honour. He had, however, one great advantage: he did not have to persuade his audience, who were already perfectly convinced of that proposition. But at any rate he had to make a show.

The defence, I think, would not have been well received at Nuremberg.

[66] We do not approve the action; no, we think it was a *mistake.* (That is how communists now talk about Stalin's more murderous proceedings.) Further, Mr. Truman did not make the bombs by himself, and decide to drop them without consulting anybody; no, he was only responsible for the decision. Hang it all, you can't make a man responsible just because "his is the signature at the foot of the order." Or was he not even responsible for the decision? It was not quite clear whether Mr. Bullock was saying that or not; but I never heard anyone else seem to give the lie to Mr. Truman's boasts. Finally, an action of this sort is, after all, only one episode: an incident, as it were, in a career. Mr. Truman has done some good.

I know that in one way such a speech does not deserve scrutiny; after all, it was just something to say on its occasion. And he had to say something. One must not suppose that one can glean anything a man actually thinks from what he says in such circumstances. Professor Stebbing exposing the logical fallacies in politicians' speeches is a comic spectacle

II. Choosing to kill the innocent as a means to your ends is always murder. Naturally, killing the innocent as an end in itself is murder too; but that is no more than a possible future development for us: [This will seem a preposterous assertion; but we are certainly on the way, and I can think of no reasons for confidence that it will not happen.] in our part of the globe it is a practice that has so far been confined to the Nazis. I intend my formulation to be taken strictly; each term in it is necessary. For killing the innocent, even if you know as a matter of statistical certainty that the things you do involve it, is not necessarily murder. I mean that if you attack a lot of military targets, such as munitions factories and naval dockyards, as carefully as you can, you will be certain to kill a number of innocent people; but that is not murder. On the other hand, unscrupulousness in considering the possibilities turns it into murder. I here print as a case in point a letter which I received lately from Holland:

> We read in our paper about your opposition to Truman. I do not like him either, but do you know that in the war the English bombed the dykes of our province Zeeland, an island where nobody could escape anywhere to. Where the whole population was drowned, children, women, farmers working in the field, all the cattle, everything, hundreds and hundreds, and we were your allies! Nobody ever speaks about that. Perhaps it were well to know this. Or, to remember.

That was to trap some fleeing German military. I think my correspondent has something.

It may be impossible to take the thing (or people) you want to destroy as your target; it may be possible to attack it only by taking as the object of your attack what includes large numbers of innocent people. Then you cannot very well say they died by accident. Here, your action is murder.

[67] "But where will you draw the line? It is impossible to draw an exact line." This is a common and absurd argument against drawing any line; it may be very difficult, and there are obviously borderline cases. But we have fallen into the way of drawing no line and offering as justifications what an uncaptive mind will find only a bad joke. Wherever the line is, certain things are certainly well to one side or the other of it.

Now who are "the innocent" in war? They are all those who are not fighting and not engaged in supply those who are with the means of fighting. A farmer growing wheat which may be eaten by the troops is not "supplying them with the means of fighting." Over this, too, the line may be difficult to draw. But that does not mean that no line should be drawn, or that, even if one is in doubt just where to draw the line, one cannot be crystal clear that this or that is well over the line.

"But the people fighting are probably just conscripts! In that case they are just as innocent as anyone else." "Innocent" here is not a term referring to personal responsibility at all. It means rather "not harming." But the people fighting are "harming," so they can be attacked; but if they surrender they become in this sense innocent and so may not be maltreated or killed. Nor is there round for trying them on a criminal charge; not, indeed, because a man has no personal responsibility for fighting, but because they were not the subjects of the state whose prisoners they are.

There is an argument which I know from experience it is necessary to forestall at this point, though I think it is visibly captious. It is this: on my theory, would it not follow that a soldier can only be killed when he is actually attacking? Then, e.g., it would be impossible to attack a sleeping camp. The answer is that "what someone is doing" can refer to what he is doing at the moment or to his role in a situation. A soldier under arms is "harming" in the latter sense even if he is asleep. But it is true that the enemy should not be attacked more ferociously than is necessary to put them *hors de combat*.

These conceptions are distinct and intelligible ones; they would formerly have been said to belong to the Law of Nations. Anyone can see that they are good, and we pay tribute to them by our moral indignation when our enemies violate them. But in fact they are going, and only fragments of them are left. General Eisenhower, for example, is reported to have spoken slightingly once of the notion of chivalry towards prisoners—as if that were based on respect for their virtue or for the nation form which they come, and not on the fact that they are now defenceless.

It is characteristic of nowadays to talk with horror of killing rather than of murder, and hence, since in war, since you have committed yourself to killing—i.e. "accepted an evil"—not to mind whom you kill. This seems largely to be the work of the devil; but I also suspect that it is in part an effect of the existence of pacifism, as a doctrine which many people respect though they would not adopt it. This effect would not exist if people had a distinct notion of what makes pacifism a false doctrine. ...

[70] The correct answer to the statement that "war is evil" is that it is bad—i.e., a misfortune—to be at war. And no doubt if two nations are at war at least one is unjust. But that does not show that it is wrong to fight or that if one does fight one can also commit murder.

Naturally my claim that pacifism is a very harmful doctrine is contingent on its being a false one. If it were a true doctrine, its encouragement of this nonsensical "hypocrisy of the ideal standard" would not count against it. But given that it is false, I am inclined to think it is also very bad, unusually so for an idea which seems as it were to err on the noble side.

When I consider the history of the events from 1939 to 1945, I am not surprised that Mr. Truman is made the recipient of honours. But when I consider his actions by themselves, I am surprised again.

Some people actually praise the bombings and commend the stockpiling of atomic weapons on the ground that they are so horrible that nation as will be afraid ever again to make war. "We have made a covenant with death, and with hell we are at an agreement." There does not seem to be good ground for such a hope for any long period of time.

Pacifists have for long made it a point in their propaganda that men must grow more murderous as their techniques of destruction improve, and those who defend murder eagerly seize on this point, so that I imagine by now it is pretty well accepted by the whole world. Of course, it is not true. In Napoleon's time, for example, the means of destruction had much improved since the time of Henry V; but Henry, not Napoleon, was a great massacrer of civilians, saying when he did particularly atrocious things that the French were a sinful nation and that he had a mission from God to punish them. And, of course, really large scale massacre up to now has belonged to times with completely primitive methods of killing. Weapons are now manufactured whose sole point is to be used in massacre of cities. But the people responsible are not murderous because they have these weapons; they have them because they are murderous. Deprived of atomic bombs, they would commit massacres by means of other bombs.

Protests by people who have not power are a waste of time. I was not seizing an opportunity to make a "gesture of protest" at atomic bombs; I vehemently object to *our* action in offering Mr. Truman honours, because one can share in the guilt of a bad action by praise and flattery, as also by defending it. When I puzzle myself over the attitude of the Vice-Chancellor and the Hebdomadal Council, I look round to see if any explanation is available why so many Oxford people should be willing to flatter such a man.

I get some small light on the subject when I consider the productions of Oxford moral philosophy since the First World War, which I have lately had occasion to read. Its character can easily be briefly demonstrated. Up to the Second World War the prevailing moral philosophy in Oxford taught that [71] an action can be "morally good" no matter how objectionable the thing done may be. An instance would be Himmler's efforts at exterminating the Jews: he did it from the "motive of duty" which has "supreme value." In the same philosophy—which has much pretence of moral seriousness, claiming that "rightness" is an objective character in acts, that can be discerned by a moral sense—it is also held that it might be right to kill the innocent for the good of the people, since the "prima facie duty" of securing some advantage might outweigh the "prima facie duty" of not killing the innocent. This sort of philosophy is less prevalent now, and in its place I find another, whose cardinal principle is that "good" is not a "descriptive" term, but one expressive of a favourable attitude on the part of the speaker. Hand in hand with this, though I do not know if there is any logical connection, goes a doctrine that it is impossible to have any quite general moral laws; such laws as "It's wrong to lie" or "Never commit sodomy" are rules of thumb which an experienced person knows when to break. Further, both his selection of these as the rules on which to proceed, and his tactful adjustments of them in particular cases, are based on their fitting together with the "way of life" which is his preference. Both these philosophies, then, contain a repudiation of the idea that any class of actions, such as murder, may be absolutely excluded. I do not know how influential they may have been or be; they are perhaps rather symptomatic. Whether influential or symptomatic, they throw some light on the situation.

It is possible still to withdraw from this shameful business in some slight degree; it is possible not to go to Encaenia; if it should be embarrassing to someone who would normally go to plead other business, he could take to his bed. I, indeed should fear to go, in case God's patience suddenly ends.

MICHAEL DUMMETT (1925-2011)

Dummett was born in London in 1925 and attended Christ Church College of the University of Oxford from 1947-1950, receiving a bachelor's degree in philosophy after serving in military intelligence during the Second World War, and converting to Catholicism from a teenage atheism in 1944. At Christ Church he studied under Austin and Anscombe and was attracted to the thought of first Wittgenstein and then Frege. Dummett became a Fellow of All Soul's College, Oxford in 1950 and remained there until he became Wykeham Professor of Logic at New College, Oxford in 1979, a position he held until he retired in 1992. Dummett, along with his wife, was very involved in the fight against racism throughout his career and joined the National Association for the Advancement of Colored People, helped to found the Committee against Racial Discrimination (1965) and the Joint Council for the Welfare of Immigrants (1967), and he wrote several works on voting procedures, developing the so-called Farquarson–Dummett conjecture.

Dummett's key contribution to philosophy was his 1959 paper "Truth" which was collected in the anthology *Truth and Other Enigmas* (1978). His other major work is *The Logical Basis of Metaphysics* (1991). He is also known for his writings on the philosophy of Frege and on the history of tarot cards. Finally, one can also mention Dummett's *Thought and Reality* (Oxford: Oxford University Press, 2008) [Gifford Lectures].

For more on the thought of Dummett consult: Green, Karen, *Dummett: Philosophy of Language* (Cambridge: Polity, 2001); and Weiss, Bernhard, *Michael Dummett* (Princeton: Princeton University Press, 2002).

The following selection is from Dummett "Bringing about the Past," originally published in the *Philosophical Review* 73 (1964): 338-348 and 357-359, and collected in his *Truth and Other Enigmas* (Harvard: Harvard University Press, 1978): 333-341 and 348-350. Dummett develops and coins the term "anti-realism" in order to describe the view that, for certain classes of propositions, no truth-value is determinable, namely statements about the distant past, the future, arithmetic, and counter-factual conditionals. Dummett also defends a neo-verificationism wherein, for the select areas above, "truth" is merely what can be verified by human epistemic capacities and not what can transcend the evidence available to us due to its external reality. Hence there arises the question as to whether it would make sense to pray for something to have happened or not have happened in the past.

"Bringing about the Past" (1964)[278]

[338] I observe first that there is a genuine sense in which the causal relation has a temporal direction: it is associated with the direction earlier-to-later rather than with the reverse. I shall not pause here to achieve a precise formulation of the sense in which this association holds; I think such a formulation can be given without too much difficulty, but it is not to my present purpose to do this. What I do want to assert is the following: so far as I can see, this association of causality with a particular temporal direction is not merely a matter of the way we speak of causes, but has a genuine basis in the way things happen. There is indeed an asymmetry in respect of past and future in the way in which we describe events when we are considering them as standing in causal relations to one another; but I am maintaining that this reflects an objective asymmetry in nature. I think that this asymmetry would reveal itself to us even if we were not *agents* but mere *observers*. It is indeed true, I believe, that our concept of cause is bound up with our concept of intentional action: if an event is properly said to cause the occurrence of a subsequent or simultaneous event, I think it necessarily follows that, if we can find any way of bringing about the former event (in particular, if it is itself a voluntary human action), then it must make sense to speak of bringing it about *in order* that the subsequent event should occur. Moreover, I believe that this connection between something's being a cause and the possibility of using it in order to bring about its effect plays an essential role in the fundamental account of how we ever come to accept causal laws: that is, that we could arrive at any causal beliefs only by beginning with those in which the cause is a voluntary action of ours. Nevertheless, I am inclined to think that we could have some kind of concept of cause, although one differing from that we now have, even if we were mere observers and not agents at all–a kind of intelligent tree. And I also think that even in this case the asymmetry of cause with respect to temporal direction would reveal itself to us.

[339] To see this, imagine ourselves observing events in a world just like the actual one, except that the order of events is reversed. There are indeed enormous difficulties in describing such a world if we attempt to include human beings in it, or any

---

[278] [Michael Dummett, "Bringing about the Past." Published in the *Philosophical Review* (1964), originally by Cornell University Press and currently by Duke University Press. Public Domain.]

other kind of creature to whom can be ascribed intention and purpose (there would also be a problem about memory). But, so far as I can see, there is no difficulty whatever if we include in this world only plants and inanimate objects. If we imagine ourselves as intelligent trees observing such a world and communicating with one another, but unable to intervene in the course of events, it is clear that we should have great difficulty in arriving at causal explanations that accounted for events in terms of the processes which had *led up* to them. The sapling grows gradually smaller, finally reducing itself to an apple pip; then an apple is gradually constituted around the pip from ingredients found in the soil; at a certain moment the apple rolls along the ground, gradually gaining momentum, bounces a few times, and then suddenly takes off vertically and attaches itself with a snap to the bough of an apple tree. Viewed from the standpoint of gross observation, this process contains many totally unpredictable elements: we cannot, for example, explain, by reference to the conditions obtaining at the moment when the apple started rolling, why it started rolling at that moment or in that direction. Rather, we should have to substitute a system of explanations of events in terms of the processes that led back to them from some subsequent moment. If through some extraordinary chance we, in this world, could consider events from the standpoint of the microscopic, the unpredictability would disappear theoretically ('in principle') although not in practice; but we should be left—so long as we continued to try to give causal explanations on the basis of what leads up to an event—with inexplicable coincidences. 'In principle' we could, by observing the movements of the molecules of the soil, predict that at a certain moment they were going to move in such a way as to combine to give a slight impetus to the apple, and that this impetus would be progressively reinforced by other molecules along a certain path, so as to cause the apple to accelerate in such a way that it would end up attached to the apple tree. But not only could we not make such [340] predictions in practice: the fact that the 'random' movements of the molecules should happen to work out in such a way that all along the path the molecules always happened to be moving in the same direction at just the moment that the apple reached that point, and, above all, that these movements always worked in such a way as to leave the apple attached to an *apple* tree and not to any other tree or any other object—these facts would cry out for explanation, and we should be unable to provide it.

I should say, then, that, so far as the concept of cause possessed by mere observers rather than agents is concerned, the following two theses hold: (i) the world is such as to make appropriate a notion of causality associated with the earlier-to-later temporal direction rather than its reverse; (ii) we can conceive of a world in which a notion of causality associated with the opposite direction would have been more appropriate and, so long as we consider ourselves as mere observers of such a world, there is no particular conceptual difficulty about the conception of such a backwards causation. There are, of course, regions of which we are mere observers, in which we cannot intervene: the heavens, for example. Since Newton, we have learned to apply the same causal laws to events in this realm; but in earlier times it was usually assumed that a quite different system of laws must operate there. It *could* have turned out that this was right; and then it could also have turned out that the system of laws we needed to explain events involving the celestial bodies required a notion of causality associated with the temporal direction from later to earlier.

When, however, we consider ourselves as agents, and consider causal laws governing events in which we can intervene, the notion of backwards causality seems to generate absurdities. If an event C is considered as the cause of a preceding event D, then it would be open to us to bring about C in order that the event D should have occurred. But the conception of doing something in order that something else should have happened appears to be intrinsically absurd: it apparently follows that backwards causation must also be absurd in any realm in which we can operate as agents.

We can affect the future by our actions: so why can we not by [341] our actions affect the past? The answer that springs to mind is this: you cannot *change* the past; if a thing has happened, it has happened, and you cannot make it not to have happened. This is, I am told [by Mr. G. Kreisel], the attitude of orthodox Jewish theologians to retrospective prayer. It is blasphemous to pray that something should *have* happened, for, although there are no limits to God's power, He cannot do what is logically impossible; it is logically impossible to alter the past, so to utter a retrospective prayer is to mock God by asking Him to perform a logical impossibility. Now I think it is helpful to think about this example, because it is the only instance of behavior, on the part of ordinary people whose mental processes we can understand, designed to affect the past and coming quite naturally to us. If one does not think of this case, the idea of doing something in order that

371

something else should previously have happened may seem sheer raving insanity. But suppose I hear on the radio that a ship has gone down in the Atlantic two hours previously, and that there were a few survivors: my son was on that ship, and I at once utter a prayer that he should have been among the survivors, that he should not have drowned; this is the most natural thing in the world. Still, there are things which it is very natural to say which make no sense; there are actions which can naturally be performed with intentions which *could* not be fulfilled. Are the Jewish theologians right in stigmatizing my prayer as blasphemous?

They characterize my prayer as a request that, if my son has drowned, God should make him not have drowned. But why should they view it as asking anything more self-contradictory than a prayer for the future? If, before the ship set sail, I had prayed that my son should make a safe crossing, I should not have been praying that, if my son was going to drown, God should have made him not be going to drown. Here we stumble on a well-known awkwardness of language. There is a use of the future tense to express present tendencies: English newspapers sometimes print announcements of the form 'The marriage that was arranged between X and Y will not now take place.' If someone did not understand the use of the future tense to express present tendencies, he might be amazed by this 'now'; he might say, 'Of course it *will* not take place *now*: either it *is* taking place [342] *now*, or it *will* take place *later*.' The presence of the 'now' indicates a use of the future tense according to which, if anyone had said earlier, 'They are going to get married,' he would have been right, even though their marriage never subsequently occurred. If, on the other hand, someone had offered a bet which he expressed by saying, 'I bet they will not be married on that date,' this 'will' would normally be understood as expressing the *genuine* future tense, the future tense so used that what happens on the future date is the decisive test for truth or falsity, irrespective of how things looked at the time of making the bet, or at any intervening time. The future tense that I was using, and that will be used throughout this paper, is intended to be understood as this genuine future tense.

With this explanation, I will repeat: when, before the ship sails, I pray that my son will make the crossing safely, I am not praying that God should perform the logically impossible feat of making what will happen not happen (that is, not be-going-to happen); I am simply praying that it will not happen. To put it another way: I am not asking God that He should now make what is going to happen not be going to happen; I am asking that He *will* at a future time make something not to happen at that time. And similarly with my retrospective prayer. Assuming that I am not asking for a miracle–asking that if my son has died, he should now be brought to life again–I do not have to be asking for a logical impossibility. I am not asking God that, even if my son has drowned, He should *now* make him not to have drowned; I am asking that, at the time of the disaster, He should then have made my son not to drown at that time. The former interpretation would indeed be required if the list of survivors had been read out over the radio, my son's name had not been on it, and I had not envisaged the possibility of a mistake on the part of the news service: but in my ignorance of whether he was drowned or not, my prayer will bear another interpretation.

But this still involves my trying to affect the past. On this second interpretation, I am trying by my prayer *now* to bring it about that God made something not to happen: and is not this absurd? In this particular case, I can provide a rationale for my [343] action–that is why I picked this example–but the question can be raised whether it is not a bad example, on the ground that it is the only kind for which a rationale *could* be given. The rationale is this. When I pray for the future, my prayer makes sense because I know that, at the time about which I am praying, God will remember my prayer, and may then grant it. But God knows everything, both what has happened and what is going to happen. So my retrospective prayer makes sense, too, because at the time about which I am praying, God knew that I was going to make this prayer, and may then have granted it. So it seems relevant to ask whether foreknowledge of this kind can meaningfully be attributed only to God, in which case the example will be of a quite special kind, from which it would be illegitimate to generalize, or whether it could be attributed to human beings, in which case our example will not be of purely theological interest.

I have heard three opinions expressed on this point. The first, held by Bertrand Russell and Alfred Jules Ayer, is that foreknowledge is simply the mirror image of memory, to be explained in just the same words as memory save that 'future' replaces 'past,' and so forth, and as such is conceptually unproblematic: we do not have the faculty but we perfectly well might. The second is a view held by a school of Dominican theologians. It is that God's knowledge of the future should be compared rather to a man's knowledge of what is going to happen, when this lies in his intention to make it happen. For example,

God knows that I am going to pray that my son may not have drowned because He is going to make me pray so. This leads to the theologically and philosophically disagreeable conclusion that everything that happens is directly effected by God, and that human freedom is therefore confined to wholly interior movements of the will. This is the view adopted by Wittgenstein in the *Tractatus Logico-Philosophicus* (London: Kegan Paul, 1922), and there expressed by the statement, 'The world is independent of my will.' On this view, God's foreknowledge is knowledge of a type that human beings do have; it would, however, be difficult to construct a nontheological example of an action intelligibly designed to affect the past by exploiting this alleged parallelism. The third view is one of which it is difficult to make a clear [344] sense. It is that foreknowledge is something that can be meaningfully ascribed only to God (or perhaps also to those He directly inspires, the prophets; but again perhaps these would be regarded not as themselves possessing this knowledge, but only as the instruments of its expression). The ground for saying this is that the future is not something of which we could, but merely do not happen to, have knowledge; it is not, as it were, *there* to be known. Statements about the future are, indeed, either-true-or-false; but they do not yet have a particular one of these two truth values. They have present truth-or-falsity, but they do not have present truth or present falsity, and so they *cannot* be known: there is not really anything to be known. The nontheological part of this view seems to me to rest on a philosophical confusion; the theological part I cannot interpret, since it appears to involve ascribing to God the performance of a logical impossibility.

We saw that retrospective prayer does not involve asking God to perform the logically impossible feat of changing the past, any more than prayer for the future involves asking Him to change the future in the sense in which that is logically impossible. We saw also that we could provide a rationale for retrospective prayer, a rationale which depended on a belief in God's foreknowledge. This led us to ask if foreknowledge was something which a man could have. If so, then a similar rationale could be provided for actions designed to affect the past, when they consisted in my doing something in order that someone should have known that I was going to do it, and should have been influenced by this knowledge. This inquiry, however, I shall not pursue any further. I turn instead to more general considerations: to consider other arguments designed to show an intrinsic absurdity in the procedure of attempting to affect the past–of doing something in order that something else should have happened. In the present connection I remark only that if there is an intrinsic absurdity in *every* procedure of this kind, then it follows indirectly that there is also an absurdity in the conception of foreknowledge, human or divine.

Suppose someone were to say to me, 'Either your son has drowned or he has not. If he has drowned, then certainly your prayer will not (cannot) be answered. If he has not drowned, [345] your prayer is superfluous. So in either case your prayer is pointless: it cannot make any *difference* to whether he has drowned or not.' This argument may well appear quite persuasive, until we observe that it is the exact analogue of the standard argument for fatalism. I here characterize fatalism as the view that there is an intrinsic absurdity in doing something in order that something else should subsequently happen; that any such action–that is, any action done with a further purpose–is necessarily pointless. The standard form of the fatalist argument was very popular in London during the bombing. The siren sounds, and I set off for the air-raid shelter in order to avoid being killed by a bomb. The fatalist argues, 'Either you are going to be killed by a bomb or you are not going to be. If you are, then any precautions you take will be ineffective. If you are not, all precautions you take are superfluous. Therefore it is pointless to take precautions.' This belief was extended even to particular bombs. If a bomb was going to kill me, then it 'had my number on it,' and there was no point in my attempting to take precautions against being killed by *that* bomb; if it did not have my number on it, then of course precautions were pointless too. I shall take it for granted that no one wants to accept this argument as cogent. But the argument is formally quite parallel to the argument supposed to show that it is pointless to attempt to affect the past; only the tenses are different. Someone may say, 'But it is just the difference in tense that makes the difference between the two arguments. Your son has either *already* been drowned or else *already* been saved; whereas you haven't *yet* been killed in the raid, and you haven't *yet* come through it.' But this is just to reiterate that the one argument is about the past and the other about the future: we want to know what, if anything, there is in this fact which makes the one valid, the other invalid. The best way of asking this question is to ask, 'What refutation is there of the fatalist argument, to which a quite parallel refutation of the argument to show that we cannot affect the past could not be constructed?'

Let us consider the fatalist argument in detail. It opens with a tautology, 'Either you are going to be killed in this raid or you are not.' As is well known, some philosophers have attempted [346] to escape the fatalist conclusion by faulting the argument at this first step, by denying that two-valued logic applies to statements about future contingents. Although this matter is worth investigating in detail, I have no time to go into it here, so I will put the main point very briefly. Those who deny that statements about future contingents need be either true or false are under the necessity to explain the meaning of those statements in some way; they usually attempt to do so by saying something like this: that such a statement is not true or false now, but *becomes* true or false at the time to which it refers. But if this is said, then the fatalist argument can be reconstructed by replacing the opening tautology by the assertion, "Either the statement 'You will be killed in this raid' is going to become true, or it is going to become false." The only way in which it can be consistently maintained not only that the law of excluded middle does not hold for statements about the future, but that there is no other logically necessary statement which will serve the same purpose of getting the fatalist argument off the ground, is to deny that there is, or could be, what I called a 'genuine' future tense at all: to maintain that the only intelligible use of the future tense is to express present tendencies. I think that most people would be prepared to reject this as unacceptable, and here, for lack of space, I shall simply assume that it is. (In fact, it is not quite easy to refute someone who consistently adopts this position; of course, it is always much easier to make out that something is not meaningful than to make out that it is.) Thus, without more ado, I shall set aside the suggestion that the flaw in the fatalist argument lies in the very first step.

The next two steps stand or fall together. They are: 'If you are going to be killed in this raid, you will be killed whatever precautions you take' and 'If you are not going to be killed in this raid, you will not be killed whatever precautions you neglect.' These are both of the form, 'If p, then if q then p'; for example, 'If you *are* going to be killed, you will be killed even if you take precautions.' They are clearly correct on many interpretations of 'if'; and I do not propose to waste time by inquiring whether they are correct on 'the' interpretation of 'if' proper to well-instructed users of the English language. The next two [347] lines are as follows: 'Hence, if you are going to be killed in the raid, any precautions you take will be ineffective' and 'Hence, if you are not going to be killed in the raid, any precautions you take will have been superfluous.' The first of these is indisputable. The second gives an appearance of sophistry. The fatalist argues from 'If you are not going to be killed, then you won't be killed even if you have taken no precautions' to 'If you are not going to be killed, then any precautions you take will have been superfluous'; that is, granted the truth of the statement 'You will not be killed even if you take no precautions,' you will have no motive to take precautions; or, to put it another way, if you would not be killed even if you took no precautions, then any precautions you take cannot be considered as being effective in bringing about your survival–that is, as effecting it. This employs a well-known principle. St. Thomas, for instance, says it is a condition for ignorance to be an excuse for having done wrong that, if the person had not suffered from the ignorance, he would not have committed the wrongful act in question. But we want to object that it may be just the precautions that I am going to take which save me from being killed; so it cannot follow from the mere fact that I am not going to be killed that I should not have been going to be killed even if I had not been going to take precautions. Here it really does seem to be a matter of the way in which 'if' is understood; but, as I have said, I do not wish to call into question the legitimacy of a use of 'if' according to which '(Even) if you do not take precautions, you will not be killed' follows from 'You will not be killed.' It is, however, clear that, on any use of 'if' on which this inference is valid, it is possible that both of the statements 'If you do not take precautions, you will be killed' and 'If you do not take precautions, you will not be killed' should be true. It indeed follows from the truth of these two statements together that their common antecedent is false; that is, that I am in fact going to take precautions. (It may be held that on a, or even the, use of 'if' in English, these two statements cannot both be true; or again, it may be held that they can both be true only when a stronger consequence follows, namely, that not only am I as a matter of fact going to take precautions, but that I could not fail to take them, that it [348] was not in my power to refrain from taking them. But, as I have said, it is not my purpose here to inquire whether there are such uses of 'if' or whether, if so, they are important or typical uses.) Now let us say that it is correct to say of certain precautions that they are capable of being effective in preventing my death in the raid if the two conditional statements are true that, if I take them, I shall not be killed in the raid, and that, if I do not take them, I shall be killed in the raid. Then, since, as we have seen, the truth of these two statements is quite compatible with the truth of the statement that, if I do not take precautions, I shall not be killed, the truth of this latter statement cannot be a ground for saying that my taking precautions will not be effective in preventing my death.

Thus, briefly, my method of rebutting the fatalist is to allow him to infer from 'You will not be killed' to 'If you do not take precautions, you will not be killed'; but to point out that, on any sense of 'if' on which this inference is valid, it is impermissible to pass from 'If you do not take precautions, you will not be killed' to 'Your taking precautions will not be effective in preventing your death.' For this to be permissible, the truth of 'If you do not take precautions, you will not be killed' would have to be incompatible with that of 'If you do not take precautions, you will be killed'; but, on the sense of 'if' on which the first step was justified, these would not be incompatible. ...

[357] Here there is an exact parallel with the case of affecting the future. We *never* combine the beliefs (i) that an action A is positively correlated with the subsequent occurrence of an event B; (ii) that the action A is in my power to perform or not as I choose; and (iii) that I can know whether B is going to take place or not independently of my intention to perform or not to perform the action A. The difference between past and future lies in this: that we think that, of any past event, it is in principle possible for me to know whether or not it took place independently of my present intentions; whereas, for many types of future event, we should admit that we are never going to be in a position to have such knowledge independently of our intentions. (If we had foreknowledge, this might be different.) If we insist on hanging onto this belief, for all types of past event, then we cannot combine the two beliefs that are required to make sense of doing something in order that some event should have previously taken place; but I do not know any reason why, if things were to turn out differently from the way they do now, we could not reasonably abandon the first of these beliefs rather than either of the other two.

My conclusion therefore is this. If anyone were to claim, of some type of action A, (i) that experience gave grounds for holding the performance of A as increasing the probability of the previous occurrence of a type of event E; and (ii) that experience gave no grounds for regarding A as an action which it was ever not in his power to perform—that is, for entertaining the possibility of his trying to perform it and failing—then we could either force him to abandon one or other of these beliefs, or else to abandon the belief (iii) that it was ever possible for him to have knowledge, independent of his intention to perform *A* or not, of whether an [358] event *E* had occurred. Now doubtless most normal human beings would rather abandon either (i) or (ii) than (iii), because we have the prejudice that (iii) must hold good for every type of event: but if someone were, in a particular case, more ready to give up (iii) than (i) or (ii), I cannot see any argument we could use to dissuade him. And so long as he was not dissuaded, he could sensibly speak of performing *A* in order that *E* should have occurred. Of course, he could adopt an intermediate position. It is not really necessary, for him to be able to speak of doing *A* in order that *E* should have occurred, that he deny all possibility of his trying and failing to perform *A*. All that is necessary is that he should not regard his being informed, by ordinary means, of the nonoccurrence of *E* as making it more probable that if he tries to perform *A*, he will fail: for, once he does so regard it, we can claim that he should regard the occurrence of *E* as making possible the performance of *A*, in which case his trying to perform *A* is not a case of trying to bring it about that *E* has happened, but of finding out whether *E* has happened. (Much will here depend on whether there is an ordinary causal explanation for the occurrence of *E* or not.) Now he need not really deny that learning, in the ordinary way, that *E* has not occurred makes it at all more probable that, if he tries to perform *A*, he will fail. He may concede that it makes it to some extent more probable, while at the same time maintaining that, even when he has grounds for thinking that *E* has not occurred, his intention to perform A still makes it more probable than it would otherwise be that *E* has in fact occurred. The attitude of such a man seems paradoxical and unnatural to us, but I cannot see any rational considerations which would force him out of this position. ... My theological example thus proves to have been a bad–that is, untypical–example in a way we did not suspect at the time, for it will never lead to a discounting of our ordinary methods of finding out about the past. I may pray that the announcer has made a mistake in not including my son's name on the list of survivors; but once I am convinced that no mistake has been [359] made, I will not go on praying for him to have survived. I should regard this kind of prayer as something to which it was possible to have recourse only when an ordinary doubt about what had happened could be entertained. But just because this example is untypical in this way, it involves no tampering with our ordinary conceptual apparatus at all: this is why it is such a natural thing to do. On my view, then, orthodox Jewish theology is mistaken on this point.

ALASDAIR MACINTYRE (1929-)

MacIntyre, though born in Glasgow, Scotland in 1929, attended Queen Mary College of the University of London, from which he received a bachelor's degree in classics in 1949. He went on to receive master's degrees in philosophy from the University of Manchester in 1951 and from Nuffield College, Oxford in 1961. MacIntyre has been quite transitory in his academic career, teaching at over a dozen institutions, the primary ones being the University of Manchester (1951-1957), Leeds University (1957-1961), University College, Oxford (1963-1966), Boston University (1972-1980), Vanderbilt University (1982-1988), the University of Notre Dame (1989-1994 and 2000-2010), Duke University (1995-1997), and London Metropolitan University (2010-). MacIntyre's philosophical views have been equally unsettled. MacIntyre came to prominence in England defending a fideistic Protestant Marxist under the influence of Barth and Wittgenstein, then went through an atheist post-Marxist phase in the 60s and 70s, before converting to Catholicism around 1983 as a result of trying to disabuse students of their Thomism.

MacIntyre's fame rests on a defense of virtue ethics and a tradition-constituted rationality in his *After Virtue* (1981; 1984; 2007), *Whose Justice? Which Rationality?* (1988), and *Three Rival Versions of Moral Inquiry* (1990). Also notable is his *God, Philosophy and Universities* (2011). For more on MacIntyre see: Weinstein, Jack, *On MacIntyre* (Belmont: Wadsworth, 2003); D'Andrea, Thomas, *Tradition, Rationality and Virtue* (Burlington: Ashgate, 2006); Lutz, Christopher, *Reading Alasdair MacIntyre's After Virtue* (New York: Continuum, 2012).

There are three short selections below from MacIntyre's *After Virtue*, 3rd edition (Notre Dame: University of Notre Dame Press, 2007): 188, 190-191, and 202-203, as well as a longer one from his *Ethics in the Conflicts of Modernity* (Cambridge: Cambridge University Press, 2016): 214-220. MacIntyre is critical of modern moral philosophy as it has focused on utility, i.e. seeking the greatest good for the greatest number, along with subjective egoistic preferences and means to ends, and has forgotten about the Aristotelian and Thomistic notion of virtues, i.e. "internal goods" or teleological ends to be pursued for their own sakes rather than for external rewards. To reform morality thus requires reembracing the idea of virtues or acquired human qualities whose exercise enables us to achieve goods internal to practices, as well as practices themselves or "coherent and complex form of socially established cooperative human activity through which goods internal to that form of activity are realized in the course of trying to achieve those standards of excellence which are appropriate to, and partially definitive of, that form of activity" (2007: 187).

After Virtue: A Study in Moral Theory (1981)[279]

The Nature of the Virtues

[188] Consider the example of a highly intelligent seven-year-old child whom I wish to teach to play chess ... I therefore tell the child that if the child will play chess with me once a week I will give the child 50 cents worth of candy; moreover I tell the child that I will always play in such a way that it will be difficult, but not impossible, for the child to win and that, if the child wins, the child will receive an extra 50 cents worth of candy. Thus motivated the child plays and plays to win. Notice however that, so long as it is the candy alone which provides the child with a good reason for playing chess, the child has no reason not to cheat and every reason to cheat, provided he or she can do so successfully. But, so we may hope, there will come a time when the child will find in those goods specific to chess, in the achievement of a certain highly particular kind of analytical skill, strategic imagination and competitive intensity, a new set of reasons, reasons now not just for winning on a particular occasion, but for trying to excel in whatever way the game of chess demands. ...

There are thus two kinds of good possibly to be gained by playing chess. On the one hand there are those goods externally and contingently attached to chess-playing and to other practices by the accidents of social circumstance—in the case of the imaginary child candy, in the case of real adults such goods as prestige, status and money. There are always alternative ways for achieving such goods, and their achievement is never to be had only by engaging in some particular kind of practice. On the other hand there are the goods internal to the practice of chess which cannot be had in any way but by playing chess or some other game of that specific kind. ...

[190] ... [Now] a practice involves standards of excellence and obedience to rules as well as the achievement of goods. To enter into a practice is to accept the authority of those standards and the inadequacy of my own performance as judged by them. It is to subject my own attitudes, choices, preferences and tastes to the standards which currently and partially define the practice. Practices of course, as I have just noticed, have a history: games, sciences and arts all have histories. Thus the standards are not

---

themselves immune from criticism, but nonetheless we cannot be initiated into a practice without accepting the authority of the best standards realized so far. ...

[191] But what does all or any of this have to do with the concept of the virtues? It turns out that we are now in a position to formulate a first, even if partial and tentative definition of a virtue: *A virtue is an acquired human quality the possession and exercise of which tends to enable us to achieve those goods which are internal to practices and the lack of which effectively prevents us from achieving any such goods.* ... For it is not difficult to show for a whole range of key virtues that without them the goods internal to practices are barred to us, but not just barred to us generally, barred in a very particular way.

[202] [Moreover] ... without an overriding conception of the *telos* of a whole human life, conceived as a unity, our conception of certain individual virtues has to remain partial and incomplete. ... Justice, on an Aristotelian view, is defined in terms of giving each person his or her due or desert. To deserve well is to have contributed in some substantial way to the achievement of those goods, the sharing of which and the common pursuit of which provide foundations for human community. But the goods internal to practices, including the goods internal to the practice of making and sustaining forms of community, need to be ordered and evaluated in some way if we are to assess relative desert. Thus any substantive application of an Aristotelian concept of justice requires an understanding of goods and of the good that goes beyond the multiplicity of goods which inform practices. As with justice, so also with patience. Patience is the virtue of waiting attentively without complaint, but not of waiting thus for anything at all. To treat patience as a virtue presupposes some adequate answer to the question: waiting for what? Within the context of practices a partial ... answer can be given: the patience of a craftsman with refractory material, of a teacher with a slow pupil, of a politician in negotiations, are all species of patience. But what if the material is just too refractory, the pupil too slow, the negotiations too frustrating? Ought we always at a certain point just to give up in the interests of the practice itself? The medieval exponents of the virtue of patience claimed that there are certain types of situation in which the virtue of patience requires that I do not ever give up on some person or task, situations in which, as they would have put it, I am required to embody in my attitude to that person or task something of the patient attitude of God towards his creation. But this could only be so if patience served

some overriding good, some *telos* which warranted putting other goods in a subordinate place. ...

[203] [So] ... unless there is a *telos* which transcends the limited goods of practices by constituting the good of a whole human life ... it will *both* be the case that a certain subversive arbitrariness will invade the moral life *and* that we shall be unable to specify the context of certain virtues adequately.

Ethics in the Conflict of Modernity (2016)[280]

Neo-Aristotelianism Developed in Contemporary Thomistic Terms: Issues of Relevance and Rational Justification

The Relevance of the Virtues Understood in Aristotelian and Thomistic Terms

[214] That in our society families, schools, and workplaces must be scenes of potential and actual conflict is evident from my earlier description of the two opposing frames of mind that we bring to our common lives in those institutions. Confronted with any situation in which there are alternative possibilities for action, we may ask either 'How and under what constraints should I act in this situation, if I am to maximize the satisfaction of my preferences?' or 'How should we act in this situation in order to achieve our common good?' Those who ask the former question will find themselves on some occasions in conflict with those who ask the latter, but they may also find themselves at odds with other preference maximizers, while those who ask the latter question will sometimes disagree with others concerned about how their common goods are to be attained as well as with preference maximizers. Rational agents therefore badly need a map of those particular conflicts, open or suppressed, within or concerning families, workplaces, and schools, in which they are or ought to be involved, so that they can identify the particular goods that are at stake in each of those conflicts.

[215] What is at stake will of course vary with local cultural,

---

social, and eco-nomic circumstance, with what types of practice and institution structure social relationships. It will make a difference how power, income, and wealth are distributed. It matters what history different groups bring to conflicts and what their members take themselves to have learned from that history. But crucial to all of them, so runs the Aristotelian Thomistic claim, is the question of whether and how far by acting in this way rather than that the protagonists in these conflicts will open up possibilities of shared rational deliberation about the achievement of common goods or will instead frustrate and obstruct such possibilities. In claiming this, Thomistic Aristotelians are also saying to those protagonists that, insofar as they do understand their conflicts in this way, they will be understanding themselves and those with whom they are in conflict in terms that presuppose the truth of the Thomistic Aristotelian account of the human condition. How so?

Everything turns on how and to what extent agents in their every-day practice conceive of themselves and others as having the powers and potentialities of rational agents, as rank ordering goods as rational agents do, and as needing the virtues, if they are to develop and exercise those powers. Much in their cultural, social, and economic environment may stand in the way of their so understanding themselves. But insofar as they are unable or refuse to do so, they will to varying degrees be in conflict with themselves, a conflict the ongoing resolution of which is a condition of their further development as rational agents. They will have grounds for taking Thomistic Aristotelianism as a set of theses about the practical life to be justified if and only if they as rational agents, as they further develop their powers, find themselves with further grounds for assenting to this understanding of themselves and their conflicts, especially with regard to the place of the virtues in their lives. For they have to learn that it is only as they acquire the virtues that they can adequately understand their need of the virtues. How then do such agents justify their decisions and actions?

Invited to give reasons for judging and acting as they do in some particular situation, they will respond by identifying what they did or propose to do as the just or courageous or generous or truthful thing to do in that situation, given the goods and harms at stake. Invited to give reasons for taking *this* to be the just, courageous, generous or truthful thing to do, they will, depending on how articulate they are, give a more or less full account of what it is to be just or courageous or generous or truthful, citing paradigmatic examples. Invited to give reasons for being just, courageous, generous, and truthful, they will, if adequately articulate, explain how [216] if defective in any of these respects and above all in prudence, they will become victims of their own disordered or inadequately ordered desires, so that they will be unable to achieve those common and individual goods toward which they are directed by their nature as rational agents. How far those to whom they address these arguments find them compelling will depend on whether or not they themselves are able to assent to what has been said about justice, courage, generosity, and truthfulness as virtues and that in turn will depend on how far they themselves are just, courageous, generous, and truthful. For having these virtues is a condition of recognizing their range of application. To have these and other virtues, even to some degree, is for one's desires to have been educated and transformed to just that degree. It is not, as the protagonists of Morality argue in respect of moral rules, to impose constraints on one's desires or rather, insofar as it does involve imposing such constraints, this is always a sign that one's desires have not yet been adequately educated, that one is still acting as one desires to desire rather than as one desires.

To have the virtues is to be something quite other than a preference maximizer. We should therefore not expect preference maximizers to find compelling arguments advanced in support of the thesis that rational agents need the virtues. Does this imply that those who act as preference maximizers act are always bound to reject the kind of argumentative justifications that I have described? Certainly they will be apt to do so, since to find those arguments compelling would involve not only a radical change of mind, a withdrawal of assent from a set of theses in politics and ethics to which they have been hitherto committed, but also a change in their attitudes toward themselves and their desires, an acknowledgment of a desire to desire otherwise than as they have hitherto desired. Yet it is also true of them, on the Thomistic Aristotelian account of human nature, that in understanding themselves as preference maximizers they have misunderstood themselves, that there is that in them which has been obscured from their view by the way in which they have understood agency and agents.

Thomistic Aristotelian criticisms of their practical arguments, when well designed, are therefore advanced not only as objections to their concepts, their premises, and their inferences, but as directed to that in them which they cannot account for in their own terms. Aristotle held that those whose understanding and practice of the virtues is defective have suffered from a defective education. Aquinas held that even they have at least a minimal capacity to recognize their potentialities as rational agents, a capacity that may be elicited and even developed at any time. Certainly, however, most [217] practical disagreements between those whose politics and ethics are a politics and ethics of common goods and those who are constrained preference maximizers will not result in a change of mind by either party. Indeed in the political arenas of the present, those who aspire to achieve common goods will often be able to argue effectively only by demonstrating to their preference maximizing critics and opponents that to act as the achievement of the relevant common goods dictates is also on this occasion, on a cost-benefit analysis, to act so as to satisfy the preferences of the relevant contending parties. How in detail such debates proceed will depend, as I have emphasized, on the particularities of the situations of the contending parties and on the argumentative and other resources that each party brings to the encounter.

The range of questions to which such agents may have to give explicit or implicit answers in the course of arriving at a decision on disputed practical questions is very large and so too therefore is the range of possible disagreements and conflicts. 'What resources of time, money skill, and/or power should I/we devote to this project?' 'What kind of risks and what degree of risk are permissible?' 'What weight should be given to long term rather than short term considerations?' 'What predictable reactions of others need to be taken into account?' 'What responsibility do I/we have for possible side-effects of our activities?' 'Is this the right time to do this?' and, prior to all of these, 'With whom do I need to deliberate about this?' Some or all of these questions are relevant, when individuals or groups face decisions as various as whether to continue working the farm or to emigrate to the city or abroad, to take time off from work for the sake of one's education or vice versa, to leave one's job or to organize a trade union branch, to stay in one's job or to borrow money to start one's own small business or to found a cooperative, decisions that are part of the fabric of a great many contemporary lives. Every one of these decisions by the way in which it delivers answers to the kinds of questions that I have catalogued is an expression of the relevant agents' stance with respect to the common goods and the virtues or the constrained maximization of preferences or perhaps in some cases both. What then is it for particular decisions to be shaped by an agent's virtues or by her or his lack of them? What goods will provide an agent with compelling reasons that would not weigh as much or at all if those decisions were not shaped by the virtues?

Of course the common goods of family, workplace, and school will have a foremost place, but only as particularized, as the particular goods needed by *this* family, workplace, or school here and now, given *these* circumstances. So a sensitivity to and a responsiveness to the particularities of [218] both individual and institutional settings and needs will be indispensable virtues. Such sensitivity and responsiveness are aspects of prudence, but of prudence informed by those virtues—or vices—that determine which features of their situation are salient for agents in understanding their situation and deciding what to do. So someone with a strong trait of acquisitiveness, *pleonexia*, may see in a situation what he takes to be immediate opportunities and a good use for his resources, but what others view as distractions from their long-term projects. So someone may perceive the needs of others as affording him an advantage in bargaining with them, while others view those same needs as providing a basis for a future cooperative relationship.

How agents view other agents and themselves in their social settings and relationships will vary similarly. From the standpoint of the virtues, understood in Thomistic Aristotelian terms, every life has or lacks a certain kind of directedness toward that agent's end, and individual acts are to be understood either as so directed or as frustrating movement toward that end. Judgments that seem to lack any such reference to the ongoing narrative of the agent's life are certainly to the point in many contexts, as when we judge some particular action to be simply cowardly or unjust or ungenerous or some particular course of action to be self-defeating. But in such cases we are saying that *any* agent who acts thus would be going astray with regard to her or his end, while in many contexts our judgments require explicit, if often abbreviated reference to the directedness of this or that particular agent, to the relationship between her or his exercise of the virtues in particular situations and the overall direction of her or his life. As with judgments on individuals, so it is analogously with judgments on institutions. For families, schools, productive enterprises, and political societies too are directed toward the achievement of their specific goods, goods that, like those of individuals, may in their particularized forms change over time. How we evaluate them will therefore also involve reference to the relationship between the exercise of the virtues by individuals in their social roles, as family members, as students or teachers or janitors, as workers or managers or whatever, and the overall direction of the institution.

To evaluate in this way is to presuppose a narrative understanding of both individual agents and institutions, to presuppose that it is only in the contexts supplied by background narratives that particular actions and courses of action can be adequately understood and evaluated. One important source of practical disagreements therefore is between those who agree in thinking in narrative terms, but differ as to what they take the [219] relevant form of such narrative to be. Contrast, for example, someone whose evaluative standpoint is informed by Jane Austen's or George Eliot's mode of storytelling–translated of course into contemporary terms–with someone similarly influenced by Virginia Woolf or Iris Murdoch. Another quite as important source of practical disagreement is between neither of these and anyone whose evaluative and normative judgments are independent of and incompatible with any narrative presuppositions whatsoever, as is the case with judgments made from the standpoint of most modern moral philosophers, the standpoint of Morality, philosophers whose work confirms Lawrence's thesis of the loss to both the novel and philosophy when each takes no account of the other. (One test of whether a particular academic course in ethics is or is not being taught in a morally serious way is whether or not its students are taught that a close reading of certain novels is indispensable to their learning what now needs to be learned.)

I laid stress earlier on the importance of, whenever possible, treating disagreements, practical or theoretical, as opportunities for learning from one's critics. It is their positions against which one argues, not them, and the adoption of an adversarial attitude toward those with whom one is in philosophical debate is a hindrance to enquiry. But there are types of disagreement, types of conflict, that have a peculiar importance in our own cultural, social, and economic order where what the virtues require is a very different attitude, where the opponents have defined themselves as enemies of any rationally defensible conception of civil and political order. During the last thirty years, poverty has been recurrently generated and regenerated within advanced capitalism, and welcome technologically based advances in productivity have been accompanied by stagnation or near stagnation in wages. Not only, as I noticed earlier, have the costs of those measures which enable capitalism to recover from its crises been widely inflicted on children, but at the same time those who dominate the economic order have, as I also noticed, appropriated an increasing proportion of the wealth produced, especially in the United States. In the United Kingdom, as I write, the average compensation for the Chief Executive Officer of a corporation is 84 times the average compensation of a worker, while in Sweden the number is 89, in France 104, in Germany 147, and in the United States 275. These numbers are an index of how far, without any sense of their own absurdity, those with the most power and money have been able to immunize themselves from risk, while by their decisions and actions exposing the weakest and most vulnerable to risk and making them pay the costs, when those decisions and actions go [220] astray. They have identified themselves as having an interest that can only be served and a status that can only be preserved if the common goods of family, workplace, and school are not served. Disagreement with them and with those theorists dedicated to the preservation of the economic and political order in which they flourish is therefore of a very different kind from most other theoretical and philosophical disagreements. It is and should be pursued as a prologue to prolonged social conflict.

CHARLES TAYLOR (1931-)

Taylor was born in 1931 in Montreal, Quebec. He attended McGill University there from 1946-1952 and acquired a B.A. in History. He then went overseas and attended Balliol College, Oxford as a Rhodes Scholar, acquiring a B.A. in philosophy and politics in 1955, and later a Ph.D. in philosophy from Balliol College in 1961, where he studied under Isaiah Berlin and Elizabeth Anscombe.

Taylor began teaching philosophy at All Soul's College, Oxford from 1956 to 1961 (coming back to teach there again from 1976-1983). He then returned to Canada and taught philosophy at McGill University from 1961 until he became Emeritus Professor in 2002, and then briefly at Northwestern from 2002-2008. Taylor has also been quite involved in Canadian politics, running, albeit unsuccessfully, for the New Democratic Party in 1962-1968. Taylor has also won nearly all of the major prizes of which a philosopher is capable.

The key works of Charles Taylor are his *The Explanation of Behaviour* (London: Routledge Kegan Paul, 1964), *Sources of the Self: The Making of Modern Identity* (Cambridge: Harvard University Press, 1989), *Varieties of Religion Today: William James Revisited* (Cambridge: Harvard University Press, 2002); *A Secular Age* (Cambridge: Harvard University Press, 2007).

For more on the thought of Charles Taylor see: Abbey, Ruth, *Charles Taylor* (Princeton University Press, 2001); Smith, Nicholas, *Charles Taylor: Meaning, Morals and Modernity* (Cambridge: Cambridge University Press, 2002); Colorado, Carlos D., et al., eds., *Aspiring to Fullness in a Secular Age: Essays on Religion and Theology in the Work of Charles Taylor* (Notre Dame: University of Notre Dame Press, 2014); Smith, James K.A., *How (Not) To Be Secular: Reading Charles Taylor* (Grand Rapids: William B. Eerdmans, 2014).

The following selection is from Charles Taylor, *Sources of the Self: The Making of the Modern Identity* (Cambridge: Harvard University Press, 1989): I, XXV, pp. 4-8, 515-521. In it Taylor argues that humans form part of their personal identity by embracing strong evaluations, or qualitative views wherein some things are considered morally higher than others. For instance, humans embrace the moral demands of benevolence and universal justice. Furthermore, Taylor argues that, in the end, only a moral realism and a personal theism, such as Christianity, can provide the necessary ontology and moral sources to ground and support and explain these strong evaluations.

Sources of the Self: The Making of the Modern Identity (1989)[281]

Identity and the Good

Inescapable Frameworks

[3] What I want to bring out and examine is the richer background languages in which we set the basis and point of the moral obligations we acknowledge. More broadly, I want to explore the background picture of our spiritual nature and predicament which lies behind some of the [4] moral and spiritual intuitions of our contemporaries. In the course of doing so, I shall also be trying to make clearer just what a background picture is, and what role it plays in our lives. Here is where an important element of retrieval comes in, because much contemporary philosophy has ignored this dimension of our moral consciousness and beliefs altogether and has even seemed to dismiss it as confused and irrelevant. I hope to show, contrary to this attitude, how crucial it is.

I spoke in the previous paragraph about our 'moral and spiritual' intuitions. In fact, I want to consider a gamut of views a bit broader than what is normally described as the 'moral.' In addition to our notions and reactions on such issues as justice and the respect of other people's life, well-being, and dignity, I want also to look at our sense of what underlies our own dignity, or questions about what makes our lives meaningful or fulfilling. These might be classed as moral questions on some broad definition, but some are too concerned with the self-regarding, or too much a matter of our ideals, to be classed as moral issues in most people's lexicon. They concern, rather, what makes life worth living.

What they have in common with moral issues, and what deserves the vague term 'spiritual', is that they all involve what I have called elsewhere 'strong evaluation,'[282] that is, they involve discriminations of right or wrong, better or worse, higher or lower,

---

[281] [Charles Taylor, *Sources of the Self*. Copyright © 1989 by Harvard University Press. All rights reserved. Reprinted with permission of Harvard University Press, https://www.hup.harvard.edu.]

[282] See my "What Is Human Agency," in Charles Taylor, *Human Agency and Language* (Cambridge: Cambridge University Press, 1985), pp. 15-44. A good test for whether an evaluation is 'strong' in my sense is whether it can be the basis for attitudes of admiration and contempt.

which are not rendered valid by our own desires, inclinations, or choices, but rather stand independent of these and offer standards by which they can be judged. So while it may not be judged a moral lapse that I am living a life that is not really worthwhile or fulfilling, to describe me in these terms is nevertheless to condemn me in the name of a standard, independent of my own tastes and desires, which I ought to acknowledge.

Perhaps the most urgent and powerful cluster of demands that we recognize as moral concern the respect for the life, integrity, and well-being, even flourishing, of others. These are the ones we infringe when we kill or maim others, steal their property, strike fear into them and rob them of peace, or even refrain from helping them when they are in distress. Virtually everyone feels these demands, and they have been and are acknowledged in all human societies. Of course the scope of the demand notoriously varies: earlier societies, and some present ones, restrict the class of beneficiaries to members of the tribe or race and exclude outsiders, who are fair game, or even condemn the evil to a definitive loss of this status. But they all feel these demands laid on them by some class of persons, and for most contemporaries this class is coterminous with the human race (and for believers in animal rights it may go wider).

We are dealing here with moral intuitions which are uncommonly deep, powerful, and universal. They are so deep that we are tempted to think of [5] them as rooted in instinct, in contrast to other moral reactions which seem very much the consequence of upbringing and education. There seems to be a natural, inborn compunction to inflict death or injury on another, an inclination to come to the help of the injured or endangered. Culture and upbringing may help to define the boundaries of the relevant 'others,' but they don't seem to create the basic reaction itself. That is why eighteenth-century thinkers, notably Rousseau, could believe in a natural susceptibility to feel sympathy for others.

The roots of respect for life and integrity do seem to go as deep as this, and to be connected perhaps with the almost universal tendency among other animals to stop short of the killing of conspecifics. But like so much else in human life, this 'instinct' receives a variable shape in culture, as we have seen. And this shape is inseparable from an account of what it is that commands our respect. The account seems to articulate the intuition. It tells us, for instance, that human beings are creatures of God and made in his image, or that they are immortal souls, or that they are all emanations of divine fire, or that they are all rational agents and thus have a dignity which transcends any other being, or some other such characterization; and that *therefore* we owe them respect. The various cultures which restrict this respect do so by denying the crucial description to those left outside: they are thought to lack souls, or to be not fully rational, or perhaps to be destined by God for some lower station, or something of the sort.

So our moral reactions in this domain have two facets, as it were. On one side, they are almost like instincts, comparable to our love of sweet things, or our aversion to nauseous substances, or our fear of falling; on the other, they seem to involve claims, implicit or explicit, about the nature and status of human beings. From this second side, a moral reaction is an assent to, an affirmation of, a given ontology of the human.

An important strand of modern naturalist consciousness has tried to hive this second side off and declare it dispensable or irrelevant to morality. The motives are multiple: partly distrust of all such ontological accounts because of the use to which some of them have been put, e.g., justifying restrictions or exclusions of heretics or allegedly lower beings. And this distrust is strengthened where a primitivist sense that unspoiled human nature respects life by instinct reigns. But it is partly also the great epistemological cloud under which all such accounts lie for those who have followed empiricist or rationalist theories of knowledge, inspired by the success of modern natural science.

The temptation is great to rest content with the fact that we have such reactions, and to consider the ontology which gives rational articulation to them to be so much froth, nonsense from a bygone age. This stance may go along with a sociobiological explanation for our having such reactions, which [6] can be thought to have obvious evolutionary utility and indeed have analogues among other species, as already mentioned.

But this neat division cannot be carried through. Ontological accounts offer themselves as correct articulations of our 'gut' reactions of respect. In this they treat these reactions as different from other 'gut' responses, such as our taste for sweets or our nausea at certain smells or objects. We don't acknowledge that there is something there to articulate, as we do in the moral case. Is this distinction illegitimate? A metaphysical invention? It seems to turn on this: in either case our response is to an object with a certain property. But in one case the property marks the object as one *meriting* this reaction; in the other the connection between the two is just a brute fact. Thus we argue and reason over what and who is a fit object of moral respect, while this doesn't seem to be even possible for a reaction like nausea. Of course we can reason that it might be useful or convenient to alter the boundaries of what we feel nausea at; and we might succeed, with training, in doing so. But what seems to make no sense here is the supposition that we might articulate a description of the nauseating in terms of its intrinsic properties, and then argue from this that certain things which we in fact react to that way are not really fit objects for it. There seems to be no other criterion for a concept of the nauseating than our in fact reacting with nausea to the things which bear the concept. As against the first kind of response, which relates to a proper object, this one could be called a brute reaction.

Assimilating our moral reactions to these visceral ones would mean considering all our talk about fit objects of moral response to be utterly illusory. The belief that we are discriminating real properties, with criteria independent of our de facto reactions, would be declared unfounded. This is the burden of the so-called 'error theory' of moral values which John Mackie espoused.[283] It can combine easily with a sociobiological standpoint, in which one acknowledges that certain moral reactions had (and have) obvious survival value, and one may even propose to fine-tune and alter our reactions so as to increase that value, as above we imagined changing what we feel nausea at. But this would have nothing to do with a view that certain things and not others, just in virtue of their nature, were fit objects of respect.

Now this sociobiological or external standpoint is utterly different from the way we in fact argue and reason and deliberate in our moral lives. We are all universalists now about respect for life and integrity. But this means not just that we happen to have such reactions or that we have decided in the light of the present predicament of the human race that it is useful to have such reactions (though some people argue in this way, urging that, for instance, it is in our own interest in a shrinking world to take account of Third World poverty). It means rather that we believe it would be utterly wrong and [7] unfounded to draw the boundaries any narrower than around the whole human race.

Should anybody propose to do so, we should immediately ask what distinguished those within from those left out. And we

---

[283] J. L. Mackie, *Ethics: Inventing Right and Wrong* (Harmondsworth: Penguin Books, 1977).

should seize on this distinguishing characteristic in order to show that it has nothing to do with commanding respect. This is what we do with racists. Skin colour or physical traits have nothing to do with that in virtue of which humans command our respect. In fact, no ontological account accords it this. Racists have to claim that certain of the crucial moral properties of human beings are genetically determined: that some races are less intelligent; less capable of high moral consciousness, and the like. The logic of the argument forces them to stake their claim on ground where they are empirically at their weakest. Differences in skin colour are undeniable. But all claims about innate cultural differences are unsustainable in the light of human history. The logic of this whole debate takes intrinsic description seriously, that is, descriptions of the objects of our moral responses whose criteria are independent of our de facto reactions.

Can it be otherwise? We feel the demand to be consistent in our moral reactions. And even those philosophers who propose to ignore ontological accounts nevertheless scrutinize and criticize our moral intuitions for their consistency or lack of it. But the issue of consistency presupposes intrinsic description. How could anyone be accused of being inconsistently nauseated? Some description could always be found covering all the objects he reacts to that way, if only the relative one that they all awake his disgust. The issue of consistency can only arise when the reaction is related to some independent property as its fit object.

The whole way in which we think, reason, argue, and question ourselves about morality supposes that our moral reactions have these two sides: that they are not only 'gut' feelings but also implicit acknowledgements of claims concerning their objects. The various ontological accounts try to articulate these claims. The temptations to deny this, which arise from modern epistemology, are strengthened by the widespread acceptance of a deeply wrong model of practical reasoning,[284] one based on an illegitimate extrapolation from reasoning in natural science.

The various ontological accounts attribute predicates to human beings–like being creatures of God, or emanations of divine fire, or agents of rational choice–which seem rather analogous to theoretical predicates in natural science, in that they (a) are rather remote from our everyday descriptions by which we

---

[284] See the discussion below in section 3.2 and also my "Explanation and Practical Reason," in Ullmann-Margalit, Edna, ed., *The Scientific Enterprise* (Dordrecht: Kluwer, 1992), pp. 179-201.

deal with people around us and ourselves, and (b) make reference to our conception of the universe and the place we occupy in it. In fact, if we go back before the modern period and take the thought of Plato, for example, it is clear that the ontological account underlying the morality of just [8] treatment was identical with his 'scientific' theory of the universe. The theory of Ideas underlay one and the other.

It seems natural to assume that we would have to establish these ontological predicates in ways analogous to our supporting physical explanations: starting from the facts identified independently of our reactions to them, we would try to show that one underlying explanation was better than others. But once we do this, we have lost from view what we're arguing about. Ontological accounts have the status of articulations of our moral instincts. They articulate the claims implicit in our reactions. We can no longer argue about them at all once we assume a neutral stance and try to describe the facts as they are independent of these reactions, as we have done in natural science since the seventeenth century. There is such a thing as moral objectivity, of course. Growth in moral insight often requires that we neutralize some of our reactions. But this is in order that the others may be identified, unmixed and unscreened by petty jealousy, egoism, or other unworthy feelings. It is never a question of prescinding from our reactions altogether.

Moral argument and exploration go on only within a world shaped by our deepest moral responses, like the ones I have been talking about here; just as natural science supposes that we focus on a world where all our responses have been neutralized. If you want to discriminate more finely what it is about human beings that makes them worthy of respect, you have to call to mind what it is to feel the claim of human suffering, or what is repugnant about injustice, or the awe you feel at the fact of human life. No argument can take someone from a neutral stance towards the world, either adopted from the demands of 'science' or fallen into as a consequence of pathology, to insight into moral ontology. But it doesn't follow from this that moral ontology is a pure fiction, as naturalists often assume. Rather we should treat our deepest moral instincts, our ineradicable sense that human life is to be respected, as our mode of access to the world in which ontological claims are discernible and can be rationally argued about and sifted.

I spoke at the outset about exploring the 'background picture' lying behind our moral and spiritual intuitions. I could now rephrase this and say that my target is the moral ontology which articulates these intuitions. What is the picture of our spiritual nature and predicament which makes sense of our responses? 'Making sense' here means articulating what makes these responses appropriate: identifying what makes something a fit object for them and correlatively formulating more fully the nature of the response as well as spelling out what all this presupposes about ourselves and our situation in the [9] world. What is articulated here is the background we assume and draw on in any claim to rightness, part of which we are forced to spell out when we have to defend our responses as the right ones.

Subtler Languages

Conclusion: The Conflicts of Modernity
[515] We agree surprisingly well, across great differences of theological and metaphysical belief, about the demands of justice and benevolence, and their importance. There are differences, including stridently debated one about abortion. But the very rarity of these cases, which contributes to their saliency, is eloquent testimony to the general agreement. To see how much our consensus embraces, we need only compare any strand in our culture with basic beliefs held earlier and outside it: we may think, for instance, of judicial torture, or mutilation for crimes of theft, or even of an openly declared (as against hidden and unavowed) racism.

So why worry that we disagree on the reasons, as long as we're united around the norms? It's not the disagreement which is the problem. Rather the issue is what sources can support our far-reaching moral commitments to benevolence and justice.

In our public debates standards which are unprecedentedly stringent are put forward in respect of these norms and are not openly challenged. We are meant to be concerned for the life and well-being of all humans on the face of the earth; we are called on to further global justice between peoples; we subscribe to universal declarations of rights. Of course, these standards are regularly evaded. Of course, we subscribe to them with a great deal of hypocrisy and mental reservation. It remains that they are the publicly accepted standards. And they do from time to time galvanize people into action–as in the great television-inspired campaigns for famine relief or in movements like Band-Aid.

To the extent that we take these standards seriously (and that varies from person to person), how are they experienced? They can just be felt as peremptory demands, standards that we feel inadequate, bad, or guilty for failing to meet. No doubt many people, probably almost all of us some of the time, experience them this way. Or perhaps we can get a 'high' when we do sometimes meet them, from a sense of our own worth or, more likely, from the momentary relief from the marginal but oppressive sense we usually have of failing to meet them. But it is quite a different thing to be moved by a strong sense that human beings are eminently *worth* helping or treating with justice, a sense of their dignity or value. Here we have come into contact with the moral sources which originally underpin these standards.

The sources are plural, as we saw. But they have in common that they [516] all offer positive underpinning of this kind. The original Christian notion of *agapē* is of a love that God has for humans which is connected with their goodness as creatures (though we don't have to decide whether they are loved because good or good because loved). Human beings participate through grace in this love. There is a divine affirmation of the creature, which is captured in the repeated phrase in Genesis I about each stage of the creation "and God saw that it was good." *Agapē* is inseparable from such a "seeing-good."

The different, more or less secularized successor notions all incorporate something similar. Thus Enlightenment naturalism, as I argued above, is in part motivated by the sense that in rejecting religion it is for the first time doing justice to the innocence of natural desire, that it is countering the calumny implicit in ascetic codes.

High standards need strong sources. This is because there is some morally corrupting, even dangerous, in sustaining the demand simply on feeling of undischarged obligation, on guilt, or its obverse, self-satisfaction. Hypocrisy is not the only negative consequence. Morality as benevolence demand breeds self-condemnation for those who fall short and a depreciation of the impulses to self-fulfillment, seen as so many obstacles raised by egoism to our meeting the standard. Nietzsche has explored this with sufficient force to make embroidery otiose. And indeed, Nietzsche's challenge is based on a deep insight. If morality can only be powered negatively, where there can be no such thing as beneficence powered by an affirmation of the recipient as a being of value, then pity is destructive to the giver and degrading to the receive, and the ethic of benevolence may indeed be indefensible. Nietzsche's challenge is on the deepest level, because he is looking precisely for what can release such an affirmation of being. His unsettling conclusion is that it is the ethic of benevolence which stands in the way of it. Only if there is such a thing as *agapē*, or one of the secular claimants to its succession, is Nietzsche wrong.

There are other consequences of benevolence on demand which Nietzsche didn't explore. The threatened sense of unworthiness can also lead to the projection of evil outward; the bad, the failure is now identified with some other people or group. My conscience is clear because I oppose them, but what can I do? They stand in the way of universal beneficence; they must be liquidated. This becomes particularly virulent on the extremes of the political spectrum, in a way which Dostoyevsky has explored to unparalleled depths.

In our day as in his, many young people are driven to political extremism, sometimes by truly terrible conditions, but also by a need to give meaning to their lives. And since meaninglessness is frequently accompanied by a sense of guilt, they sometimes respond to a strong ideology of polarization, in which one receives a sense of direction as well as a sense of purity by lining up in [517] implacable opposition to the forces of darkness. The more implacable, even violent the opposition, the more the polarity is represented as absolute, and the greater the sense of separation from evil and hence purity. Dostoyevsky's *Devils* is one of the great documents of modern times, because it lays bare the way in which an ideology of universal love and freedom can mask a burning hatred, directed outward onto an unregenerate world and generating destruction and despotism.

The question which arises from all this is whether we are not living beyond our moral means in continuing allegiance to our standards of justice and benevolence. Do we have ways of seeing-good which are still credible to us, which are powerful enough to sustain these standards? If not, it would be both more honest and more prudent to moderate them. And in this connection, the issue I raised briefly in Chapter I recurs. Is the naturalist seeing-good, which turns on the rejection of the calumny of religion against nature, fundamentally parasitic? This it might be in two senses: not only that it derives its affirmation through rejecting an alleged negation, but also that the original model for its universal benevolence is agape. How well could it survive the demise of the religion it strives to abolish? With the 'calumny' gone, could the affirmation continue?

The question might arise in another form, following the discussion in section 23.6: perhaps the original Enlightenment affirmation was indeed confident, based on a highly idealized, immediately post-providential vision of nature. But can this affirmation be sustained in face of our contemporary post-Schopenhauerian understanding of the murkier depths of human motivation? Is there somewhere a transfigurative power to see these as good, without paying Nietzsche's price?

Or must benevolence ultimately come to be conceived as a duty we owe ourselves, somehow required by our dignity as rational, emancipated moderns, regardless of the (un)worth of the recipients? And to the extent that this is so, how close will we have come to the world Dostoyevsky portrays, in which acts of seeming beneficence are in fact expressions of contempt, even hatred?

Perhaps another question might be put here as well. Is the naturalist affirmation conditional on a vision of human nature in the fullness of its health and strength? Does it move us to extend help to the irremediably broken, such as the mentally handicapped, those dying without dignity, fetuses with genetic defects? Perhaps one might judge that it doesn't and that this is a point in favour of naturalism; perhaps effort shouldn't be wasted on these unpromising cases. But the careers of Mother Teresa or Jean Vanier seem to point to a different pattern, emerging from a Christian spirituality.

I am obviously not neutral in posing these questions. Even though I have refrained (partly out of delicacy, but largely out of lack of arguments) from [518] answering them, the reader suspects that my hunch lies towards the affirmative, that I do think naturalist humanism defective in these respects—or, perhaps better put, that great as the power of naturalistic sources might be, the potential of a certain theistic perspective is incomparably greater. Dostoyevsky has framed this perspective better than I ever could.

But I recognize that pointed questions could be put in the other direction as well, directed at theistic views. My aim has been not to score points but to identify this range of questions around the moral sources which might sustain our rather massive professed commitments in benevolence and justice. This entire range is occluded by the dominance of proceduralist meta-ethics, which makes us see these commitments through the prism of moral obligation, thereby making their negative face all the more dominant and obtrusive[285] and pushing the moral sources further

---

[285] Bernard Williams, in his *Ethics and the Limits of Philosophy* (London: Fontana, 1985), chap. 10, pp. 174-196, shows the centrality of the notion of obligation to the dominant meta-ethic. Williams's chapter is

out of sight. But the picture I have been drawing of the modern identity brings this range back into the foreground. ...

And the discussion we have just finished about the sources of benevolence brought us also to a crucial conflict, which has been illuminatingly explored in rather different ways by Nietzsche and Dostoyevsky: the demands of benevolence can exact a high cost in self-love and self-fulfillment, which may in the end require payment in self-destruction or even in violence.

And indeed, there has been some awareness of this for some centuries now in our culture. The naturalist rebellion against the ascetic demands of religion and the earlier quiet rejection of Christianity by discreet individuals in the name of paganism reflect at least in part the recognition that a terribly high cost was being demanded.

In our day, the conflict has been further articulated by writers who have drawn on Nietzsche. One of the important themes one can find in the work of the late Michel Foucault is the understanding of the way in which high ethical and spiritual ideals are often interwoven with exclusions and relations of domination. William Connolly has formulated this aspect of Foucault's [519] thought very aptly.[286] And contemporary feminist critique has also contributed greatly to this understanding, in showing how certain conceptions of the life of the spirit exclude women, accord them a lesser place, or assume their subordination.[287] The sense that in this and other ways hypergoods can stifle or oppress us has been one of the motives for the naturalist revolt against traditional religion and morality, as I argued in part I (sections 3.2-3).

From all these examples, in my view, a general truth emerges, which is that the highest spiritual ideals and aspirations also threaten to lay the most crushing burdens on humankind. The great spiritual visions of human history have also been poisoned chalices, the causes of untold misery and even savagery. From the very beginning of the human story religion, our link with the highest, has been recurrently associated with sacrifice, even

---

entitled "Morality, the Peculiar Institution", and this gives some indication of its bent.

[286] See, e.g., William Connolly, "Taylor, Foucault and Otherness," *Political Theory* 13: 3 (August 1985): 365-376.

[287] See, e.g., the discussion of the tradition of political theory in Jean Bethke Elshtain, *Public Man, Private Woman* (Princeton: Princeton University Press, 1981).

mutilation, as though something of us has to be torn away or immolated if we are to please the gods.

This is an old theme, well explored by Enlightenment thinkers, and particularly by those with what I called the 'neo-Lucretian' outlook (section 19.3). But the sad story doesn't end with religion. The Kharkov famine and the Killing Fields were perpetrated by atheists in an attempt to realize the most lofty ideals of human perfection.

Well, then, one might say, the danger attends religion, or else millenarist ideologies which are somewhat similar to religion in putting moral passion before hard evidence. What we need is a sober, scientific-minded, secular humanism.

But in spite of the richness, as yet not fully explored, of the neo-Lucretian stance, this still seems to me too simple. And the reason lies in the crucial difference between the perspective I have been exploring here and the various naturalist and Nietzschean critiques of self-immolation. Characteristically, these take the self-destructive consequences of a spiritual aspiration as a refutation of this aspiration. They make once again what I believe is the cardinal mistake of believing that a good must be *invalid* if it leads to suffering or destruction.

Thus Enlightenment naturalism thought it was refuting Christianity in showing the cost of asceticism; Nietzsche often gives a picture of 'morality' which shows it to be merely envy, or a device of the weak, or ressentiment, and which thus deprives it of all claim on our allegiance.[288] Foucault in his writings seemed to be claiming (I believe) impossible neutrality, which recognize no claims as binding.

But I have argued that this way of reasoning is deeply mistaken. Not only can some potentially destructive ideals be directed to genuine goods; some of them undoubtedly are. The ethic of Plato and the Stoics can't be written off as mere illusion. And even non-believers, if they don't block it off, will feel a [520] powerful appeal in the gospel, which they will interpret in a secular fashion; just as Christians, unless immured in blinkered self-sufficiency, will recognize the appalling destruction wrought in history in the name of the faith.

That is why adopting a stripped-down secular outlook, without any religious dimension or radical hope in history, is not a

---

[288] But Nietzsche's thought is, as always, more many-sided and complex than this. See the section "Was bedeuten asketische Ideale?" in *Jenseits von Gut und Böse*.

way of *avoiding* the dilemma, although it may be a good way to live with it. It doesn't avoid it, because this too involves its 'mutilation'. It involves stifling the response in us to some of the deepest and most powerful spiritual aspirations that humans have conceived. This, too, is a heavy price to pay.

This is not to say, though, that if we have to pay some price, this may not be the safest. Prudence constantly advises us to scale down our hopes and circumscribe our vision. But we deceive ourselves if we pretend that nothing is denied thereby of our humanity.

Is this the last word? Does something have to be denied? Do we have to choose between various kinds of spiritual lobotomy and self-inflicted wounds? Perhaps. Certainly most of the outlooks which promise us that we will be spared these choices are based on selective blindness. This is perhaps the major point elaborated in this book.

But I didn't undertake it in this downbeat a spirit. The kind of study I have embarked on here can be a work, we might say, of liberation. The intuition which inspired it, which I have recurred to, is simply that we tend in our culture to stifle the spirit. We do this partly out of the prudence I have just invoked, particularly after the terrible experiences of millenarist destruction of our century; partly because of the bent of modern naturalism, one of our dominant creeds; partly because of partisan narrowness all around. We have read so many goods out of our official story, we have buried their power so deep beneath layers of philosophical rationale, that they are in danger of stifling. Or rather, since they are our goods, human goods, *we* are stifling.

The intention of this work was one of retrieval, an attempt to uncover buried goods through rearticulation—and thereby to make these sources again empower, to bring the air back again into the half-collapsed lungs of the spirit.

Some readers may find this overblown (though these will probably have stopped reading long ago). And perhaps I am merely overreacting to a narrowness of the academy which has little effect on the world outside—although I don't think this is so. Others may accuse me with greater apparent justice of inconsistency—or even irresponsibility. If the highest ideals are the most potentially destructive, then maybe the prudent path is the safest, and we shouldn't unconditionally rejoice at the indiscriminate retrieval of empowering goods. A little judicious stifling may be on the part of wisdom.

The prudent strategy makes sense on the assumption that the dilemma is inescapable, that the highest spiritual aspirations must lead to mutilation or [521] destruction. But if I may make one last unsupported assertion, I want to say that I don't accept this as our inevitable lot. The dilemma of mutilation is in a sense our greatest spiritual challenge, not an iron fate.

How can one demonstrate this? I can't do it here (or, to be honest, anywhere at this point). There is a large element of hope. It is a hope that I see implicit in Judaeo-Christian theism (however terrible the record of its rents in history), and in its central promise of a divine affirmation of the human, more total than humans can ever attain unaided.

But to explore this properly would take another book. My aim in this Conclusion has only been to show how my picture of the modern identity can shape our view of the moral predicament of our time.

BAS VAN FRAASSEN (1941-)

The lay convert Van Fraassen was born in Goes, Netherlands, in 1941. His family emigrated to Canada in 1956 where he attended the University of Alberta, earning a B.A. in philosophy in 1963. He then went to the University of Pittsburgh, obtaining a M.A. in philosophy in 1964 and a Ph.D. in philosophy in 1966, under Adolf Grünbaum. Van Fraassen taught philosophy at Yale (1966-1969), the University of Toronto (1969-1982), and the University of Southern California (1976-1981), before becoming a mainstay at Princeton University (1982-2008). In 2008 he transferred to San Francisco State University.

Van Fraassen is most famous for his work in the philosophy of science presented in his book *The Scientific Image* (Oxford: Oxford University Press, 1980), as well later works such as *The Empirical Stance* (New Haven: Yale University Press, 2002) and *Scientific Representation* (Oxford: Oxford University Press, 2008).

For more on the work of Van Fraassen consult Suhm, Christian, *Bas Van Fraassen: The Fortunes of Empiricism* (Berlin: Walter de Gruyter, 2006); Dicken, Paul, *Constructive Empiricism: Epistemology and the Philosophy of Science* (New York: Palgrave-MacMillan, 2010); and Gonzalez, Wenceslao J., *Bas van Fraassen's Approach to Representation and Models in Science* (New York: Springer, 2014).

The following selection is from *The Empirical Stance* (2002): V, 189-196. In this work Van Fraassen continues his defense of "constructive empiricism" or the pragmatically-inspired view that scientific theories are true as long as they are empirically adequate in accounting for the observed data and preserving the classical structural regularities of natural phenomena. In his words from an earlier work "scientific activity is one of construction rather than discovery: construction of models that must be adequate to the phenomena, and not discovery of truth concerning the unobservable" (1980, p. 5)." Indeed, Van Fraassen famously makes a distinction between observable and non-observable entities, and argues that observable entities of scientific theories can exist in a realistic manner, i.e. as we perceive them to be, but this is not the case for non-observable entities, where theories can only be empirically adequate to the phenomena. In any case, Van Fraassen sets forth his view that scientific objectivity is characterized by the study of a limited domain, independently of the views of any particular individual, seeking to account for the relevant parameters in terms of models that one has drawn up. If this is the case science need not walk hand-in-hand with secularism and there is room for religion, or a face-to-face encounter with the divine.

ALAN VINCELETTE

The Empirical Stance (2002)[289]

Persons: Encounter with the Divine

> Dust thou art, and unto dust shalt thou return (*Genesis* 3:19)

[189] Science, whether understood with the scientific realist or with the empiricist, provides us with a world picture, the world picture Fackenheim and Bultmann point to as sufficing for the secular. Accepted in either sense, it can be our entire world picture. But if it is, we ourselves don't seem to fit into our own world picture. This was an acute problem from the very beginning of modern science. It was the problem that engendered Descartes's dualism, Malebranche's mind-body occasionalism, and Leibniz's monads reconciled by preestablished harmony, as well as a panoply of contemporary metaphysical positions on the mind-body problem. If Bultmann or any of the others is to complete the religious response to secularism, this problem must not remain a problem. For if it does, then their response will always be written off as mere capitulation to materialism by one side and as a mixture of mutually incoherent parts by the other.

As I argued in the second lecture, this is a problem area beset by [190] illusions and false philosophical consciousness. There is no factual thesis of materialism to confront. Materialism and naturalism as embraced in contemporary analytic philosophy have nothing to them but a certain attitude, a spirit of deference to the content of physics. That is a sort of deference to science not shared by empiricism in general. (As far as I can see it is also quite foreign to the physicists themselves, who playfully and adventurously alter that content in their explorations of theory and nature.) Nevertheless, we still face the question of how to think about persons, especially because that topic covers the, for religion, all-important subject of personal encounter with the divine, of the presence of God in human history.

We can dispense with mind-body dualism at once, or so it seems to me. There is a mystery about consciousness, a mystery about how it is possible for flesh and bones to think, feel, and communicate. But how could that mystery be dispelled by postulating a special mental substance as bearer of consciousness?

---

[289] [*The Empirical Stance* by Bas Van Fraassen. Copyright © 2002 by Yale University Press. All rights reserved. Used with permission of Yale University Press, https://yalebooks.yale.edu.]

Drop the rhetorically chosen persuasive name of "mental substance," call it "ectoplasm;' say, and you see at once that the mystery remains unchanged. It is just as difficult to understand how ectoplasm can think as how flesh and blood can think.

But neither does it help to postulate that there are special parameters, so far unknown or at least left outside the scope of science until now, that characterize persons among things in the world. That philosophical move may have initially represented a tactical advance; for as we saw, identifying a domain of inquiry takes in general the form of specifying a set of "relevant" parameters instead of things. David Chalmers brought this move into special salience, and as he clearly recognizes, any such newly postulated parameters can then appear in the domain of future science.[290] Despite their present near-total obscurity, such putative parameters already have names such as "qualia."

[191] But no objectifying inquiry can reveal what persons are or who the persons are among things in the world.[291] Consider how that question arises in a concrete setting: the question whether black slaves, descendants of blacks sold on the open market, belong to the domain of discourse of the Constitution of the United States of America. This question arose in the middle of the nineteenth century, when some blacks sued for that status, and was settled in the negative by the Supreme Court of that day. Was this a factual ques-tion concerning the parameters pertaining to these organisms? I imagine that essentially the same question arose in history for other races and ethnic groups. Perversely enough, it arose all over again in recent history for Slavs, Jews, Gypsies, but perhaps the question first arose between Neanderthal and Cro-Magnon, long before Greek and barbarian. We must entertain the possibility that in the future it will arise for other species, whether some already known, such as dolphins, or presently unknown. The question is not a theoretical but a moral

---

[290] David Chalmers, *The Conscious Mind: In Search of a Fundamental Theory* (Oxford: Oxford University Press, 1996).

[291] There are many arguments in the literature against reductionism; see, e.g., the papers in Evandro Agazzi, *The Problem of Reductionism in Science* (Dordrecht: Springer, 1991), and especially that by Patrick Suppes, "Can Psychological Software Be Reduced to Physiological Hardware?," pp. 183-198. But like the above remarks about mind-body dualism and qualia, I mean to note this only as background. The point I wish to make about the concept of a person and objectification is a different point.

and existential question, and it is not settled, unless relative to a prior moral decision, by factual inquiry. What counts as thinking counts as consciousness, and what counts as conscious counts as a person, with the rights of a person–that is the crucial point. In an encounter with a different being, group, or species in which this question arises we are called to decision, called to take a stand. That is also, of course, why the traditional philosophical "problem of other minds" is a pseudo problem.

Were these beings already persons before we accepted them as such? Yes, of course; our opinion that they are persons implies that they were persons all along. Equally, we would have faced the same tribunal before them; we can only hope that we were recognized as persons there. Could we make a mistake in reaching such a judgment? Of course, there are conditions under which we will revise a judgment. That revision would then imply the belief that they were never persons at all. I am not oblivious to the problems in [192] philosophy of language in this neighborhood; for now I merely want to focus on what I see as more important problems.[292] The point here is only that acceptance of something as a person, although it involves an element of decision, does not make that being a person. Nor was it required for that being to be a person; to say so would also involve a conceptual mistake. Nor does our finding about the limits of objectifying inquiry here entail that it is all "just subjective;' and least of all that it is "objectively unimportant."

The question of personhood and the decision it calls for are significant. When I come face to face with you, it is of crucial importance to me whether you are a person. The question whether you are a "you" coincides with the demand that I take a certain attitude toward you. Hegel, Marx, and Sartre speak perhaps all too simplistically of lordship and bondage, Heidegger of more

---

[292] The judgment that some being is a person can be true or false, it can enter as a component in complex statements constructed with sentential connectives and quantifiers, and so on. It does not follow from this that the standard truth-and-reference semantics dear to many philosophers is adequate to dealing with them. I accept that we have difficult tasks in philosophy of language but I don't think that we should hold up our thinking about objectivity until they are solved. What I say is in any case not provocative within analytic philosophy in the way it would have been a few decades ago; although I am grateful for this without being able to accept, say, Simon Blackburn's noncognitivist account or Michael Smith's cognitivist rival, both of which seem to me to be ensnared in the confusions of naturalism.

nuanced forms of care. For much contemporary philosophy this domain of interpersonal knowledge and interaction is simply terra incognita.[293] It is easier to escape into theoretical-sounding, quasi- (if not blatantly pseudo-) scientific questions of fact about "mental states" and evade the element of choice.

We are indeed beings of flesh and blood. This is a simple truism; it is not materialism, and there is no reductionist claim involved (even if any such claim really makes sense at all). It means simply that we persons manifest ourselves in the first instance through our bodies and bodily movements and equally, in a seamlessly woven fabric, by how we choose and arrange our clothes, environments, rooms, houses, the paths we take to work and the work itself, all the incarnate activities and processes into which we enter.

There is one special case of personhood: God. The God of Abraham, Isaac, and Jacob is a person. (If you like, bracket the question whether God exists. What follows will, I hope, be the right thing to say whether or not it has any application in the real world.)[294] I shall not even mention in the same breath such naïve simulacra as [193] Descartes' God, let alone a ruler of the universe located somewhere in space or space outside of space, or some other pseudoscientific miscreant. Encounter with the divine does not mean seeing the ghost in the world machine, nor contemplation of a theoretically postulated hypothesis of which neither science nor we ourselves have any need. The great myth in which we live and breathe and have our being has long since broken our anthropocentric categories.[295]

But an encounter with the divine is a personal encounter. As

---

[293] For a philosophically illuminating dramatization, see Peter Høeg's novel *The Woman and the Ape* (London: Farrar, Straus, and Giroux, 2006).

[294] I add this for the sake of argument. Unfortunately, it invites the hackneyed question of whether God exists or whether God is real, a question which it is impossible to hear today unburdened by the concepts in which philosophers have simulated religion. There is a real question: does it ever really happen that anyone anywhere encounters God? I will leave it as an exercise for the readers to amuse themselves by imagining how this could be chosen as subject for an objectifying inquiry and what could come of that.

[295] See further the discussion of science and myth in my "The World of Empiricism," in "The World of Empiricism" in Hilgevoord, Jan, ed., *Physics and Our View of the World* (Cambridge: Cambridge University Press, 1994), pp. 114-134.

we human persons do, so God too manifests himself to us only through the familiar materials among which we live; how else? There is no similar localizing constraint; God's work goes on everywhere and every-when, throughout history. Sacred places are where we encounter God, or perhaps a sacred place is precisely a place where God was encountered. The sacraments, as we are taught, are but the outward signs of inward grace. An encounter with God does not involve solving a theoretical equation or answering a factual query; its searing question is an existential demand we face in fear and trembling. As with a human person, the encounter coincides with a call to decision: possible stances toward ourselves and to our world come to the fore and ask for choice. The choice is momentous and sometimes, in some ways, inescapable, for it pertains to our ultimate concerns.

We would indeed land in a but slightly disguised materialism if we added that the objectifying inquiry, brought to perfection in the sciences, suffices to understand all there is to understand about persons. If, moreover, we added this about God, the result would be rhetorically embellished pantheism.[296] Then, indeed, persons and God would be best studied as objectified "scientific objects" in the sense we saw displayed by Catherine Wilson in her study of the microscope. Such additions are also, we note, precisely what characterize the typical core of secularism, the salient necessary condition in what it is to be secular. But we make no such addition.

Stranger in a Strange Land

> ... one of the things writing does is wipe things out. Replace them (Marguerite Duras, *Emily L.*)

[194] There is much to fault the three philosophical theologians I discussed. Fackenheim's contrast between the secular and the religious actually goes no further than the objectifying attitude, which is at best typical but certainly not definitive of the secular. Buber falls into the all-too-easy fiction of

---

[296] Theology today offers some surprising variants on such themes; cf. Charley Hardwick, *Events of Grace: Naturalism, Existentialism, and Theology* (Cambridge: Cambridge University Press, 1996). Since physicalism is mainstream opinion in analytic philosophy, Hardwick contends, there is a clear need for a theology compatible with physicalism.

golden ages and ages on feet of d ay. The fact is that each one of us, and every one of the many centuries we have lived through, is an incoherent superposition of alternate realities. Bultmann wanders somewhat negligently, almost blithely, into the modern myth of the stranger and the call to authenticity of existentialism. Yet each of these weaknesses is but the other side of a genuine coin, the blindness that accompanies true insight.

In this lecture, too, as I did earlier, I placed all the weight of change on stance or attitude rather than on theory. If I am right, then what distinguishes the secular from the religious is not the theories they hold, or beliefs about what the world is like, although those too are often found among the differences. The crucial distinction lies in a certain attitude, in how we approach the world and relate to our own experience. We can theorize about that, of course, but having a theory about a stance is no substitute for having it, and rejecting it won't consist in disbelieving a theory. I have argued this now for empiricism, for materialism and naturalism, and finally for the secularism that relegates all religion to subjectivity and illusion.

Each of the "isms" I mention here has at some time appropriated for itself all the credit for the advances of science, in order to claim its liberating power and moral authority. Each has at some point intimated that it consists in nothing more than full-fledged [195] acceptance of what science tells us about the world. Coupled with this, a little paradoxically, comes the insistence that science would die if it weren't for the scientists' conscious or unconscious adherence to this philosophical position. All of this is false; in fact, it is in philosophy that we see the most glaring examples of false consciousness, and they occur precisely at this point.

I am an empiricist, or at least I try to be, while trying to discern what empiricism can be after all we have learned during the demise of modern philosophy. As an empiricist, I see the empirical sciences as a paradigm of rationality in a largely irrational and often anti-rational world. I see objectifying inquiry as the sine qua non of the development of modern science and its incredible, breathtaking achievements in our increasing knowledge of nature. At the same time, while this objectifying inquiry has brought us untold riches, what does it profit us to gain the whole world and lose our own soul? Riches come with a temptation, a tempting fallacy, namely, to have us view them as all there is to be had, when they are so much. This is true of all riches, and it is true of the riches of objective knowledge. Poor are the rich who succumb to this fallacy.

So now, how shall we go on? Philosophy may already have suffered too much from its perennial revolutions for us to ask for yet another revolution. And I certainly do not think we need new theories in philosophy. But I do think that we must change, or change back, the way we do philosophy. Technical work is required; there are many problems to be solved, but this work should be in aid of an authentic, engaged project in the world, self-conscious and conscious of what sort of enterprise it is. That means, in the first place, consciousness of its own limits. ...

7 POSTMODERNISM

MICHEL DE CERTEAU, S.J. (1925-1986)

De Certeau was born in 1925 in Chambéry, Savoie, France and spent the holidays with his family at a Carthusian monastery, the Chartreuse d'Aillon. He studied philosophy at the University of Grenoble and the Catholic Institute of Lyon from 1943-1944 and was also active in the French Resistance with the Maquis des Glières during the Second World War. De Certeau entered the Society of Jesus in 1950 and was ordained in 1956. He later attended the École pratique des hautes études and the Sorbonne in Paris, receiving a doctorate in philosophy from the latter in 1960. De Certeau was very active in the French intellectual scene; he co-founded both the journal *Christus* (1954) and the École Freudienne de Paris (1964) with Jacques Lacan, and he supported the Parisian Student Protests of 1968. De Certeau taught at the Catholic Institute of Paris (1964-1978), the University of Paris-Vincennes [Paris-VIII] (1968-1971), the University of Paris-Diderot [Paris-VII] (1971-1978), the University of California at San Diego (1978-1984), and the *l'École des hautes études en sciences sociales* (1984-1986). He died in Paris in 1986.

De Certeau's key work is his *L'Invention du quotidien*, 2 vols. (Paris: Gallimard, 1980-1990). Other notable works of De Certeau are his: *La Fable Mystique*, 2 vols. (Paris: Gallimard, 1982-2013); and *La Faiblesse de croire* (Paris: Seuil, 1987).

For more on the thought of De Certeau one can consult: Conley, Tom, *Michel de Certeau* (Baltimore: John Hopkins University Press, 1993); Ahearne, Jeremy, *Michel de Certeau: Interpretation and Its Other* (Stanford: Stanford University Press, 1996); Buchanan, Ian, *Michel de Certeau: Cultural Theorist* (London: Sage Press, 2000); Buchanan, Ian, *Michel de Certeau in the Plural* (Durham: Duke University Press, 2002); Highmore, Ben, *Everyday Life and Cultural Theory: An Introduction* (London: Routledge, 2002); Highmore, Ben, *Michel de Certeau: Analysing Culture* (London: Continuum, 2006); Sheringham, Michael, *Everyday Life* (Oxford: Oxford University Press, 2006); Bocken, Iñigo Kristien Marcel, *Spiritual Spaces: History and Mysticism in Michel de Certeau* (Leuven: Peeters, 2013);

The following translation is from De Certeau, Michel, *The Practice of Everyday Life* (Berkeley: The University of California Press, 1984): 94-99, 103-108. De Certeau is influenced by the thought of Martin Heidegger and Michel Foucault. He argues that though Foucault is correct in that daily existence is imbued with power-structures due to governments and corporations that constrain life (strategies), nonetheless, humans can maneuver in free and creative ways all the same (tactics), making use of these very structures to resist them and reappropriate them in innovative ways.

The Invention of Everyday Life (1980)²⁹⁷

Spatial Practices: Walking in the City

From the Concept of the City to Urban Practices

An Operational Concept?
[94] The "city" founded by utopian and urbanistic discourse²⁹⁸ is defined by the possibility of a threefold operation:

1. The production of its *own* space (*un espace propre*): rational organization must thus repress all the physical, mental and political pollutions that would compromise it;

2. The substitution of a nowhen, or of a synchronic system, for the indeterminable and stubborn resistances offered by traditions; univocal scientific strategies, made possible by the flattening out of all the data in a plane projection, must replace the tactics of users who take advantage of "opportunities" and who, through these trap-events, these lapses in visibility, reproduce the opacities of history everywhere;

3. Finally, the creation of a *universal* and *anonymous* subject which is the city itself: it gradually becomes possible to attribute to it, as to its political model, Hobbes' State, all the functions and predicates that were previously scattered and assigned to many different real subjects–groups, associations, or individuals. "The city," like a proper name, thus provides a way of conceiving and constructing space on the basis of a finite number of stable, isolatable, and interconnected properties.

Administration is combined with a process of elimination in this place organized by "speculative" and classificatory operations.²⁹⁹ On the one hand, there is a differentiation and

---

²⁹⁷ [*The Practice of Everyday Life* by Michel Certeau, translated by Steven Rendall. Copyright © 1984 by the University of California Press. All rights reserved. Used with permission of University of California Press, https://www.ucpress.edu.]

²⁹⁸ See Françoise Choay, "Figures d'un discours inconnu," *Critique* 28 (April 1973): 293-317.

²⁹⁹ Urbanistic techniques, which classify things spatially, can be related to the tradition of the "art of memory": see Frances A. Yates, *The Art of Memory* (London: Routledge and Kegan Paul, 1966). The ability to produce a spatial organization of knowledge (with "places" assigned to each type of "figure" or "function") develops its procedures on the basis of this "art." It determines utopias and can be recognized even in Bentham's *Panopticon*. Such a form remains stable in spite of the

redistribution of the parts and functions of the city, as a result of inversions, displacements, accumulations, etc.; on the other there is a rejection of everything that is not capable of being dealt with in this way and so constitutes the "waste products" of a functionalist administration (abnormality, deviance, illness, death, etc.). To be sure, progress allows an increasing number of these waste products [95] to be reintroduced into administrative circuits and transforms even deficiencies (in health, security, etc.) into ways of making the networks of order denser. But in reality, it repeatedly produces effects contrary to those at which it aims: the profit system generates a loss which, in the multiple forms of wretchedness and poverty outside the system and of waste inside it, constantly turns production into "expenditure." Moreover, the rationalization of the city leads to its mythification in strategic discourses, which are calculations based on the hypothesis or the necessity of its destruction in order to arrive at a final decision.[300] Finally, the functionalist organization, by privileging progress (i.e., time), causes the condition of its own possibility–space itself–to be forgotten; space thus becomes the blind spot in a scientific and political technology. This is the way in which the Concept-city functions; a place of transformations and appropriations, the object of various kinds of interference but also a subject that is constantly enriched by new attributes, it is simultaneously the machinery and the hero of modernity.

Today, whatever the avatars of this concept may have been, we have to acknowledge that if in discourse the city serves as a totalizing and almost mythical landmark for socioeconomic and political strategies, urban life increasingly permits the re-emergence of the element that the urbanistic project excluded. The language of power is in itself "urbanizing," but the city is left prey to contradictory movements that counterbalance and combine themselves outside the reach of panoptic power. The city becomes the dominant theme in· political legends, but it is no longer a field of programmed and regulated operations. Beneath the discourses that ideologize the city, the ruses and combinations of powers that have no readable identity proliferate; without points where one can take hold of them, without rational transparency, they are impossible to administer.

---

diversity of its contents (past, future, present) and its projects (conserving or creating) relative to changes in the status of knowledge.

[300] See André Glucksmann, "Le Totalitarisme en effet," *Traverses* 9 (1977): 34-40.

The Return of Practices

The Concept-city is decaying. Does that mean that the illness afflicting both the rationality that founded it and its professionals afflicts the urban populations as well? Perhaps cities are deteriorating along with the procedures that organized them. But we must be careful here. The ministers of knowledge have always assumed that the whole universe [96] was threatened by the very changes that affected their ideologies and their positions. They transmute the misfortune of their theories into theories of misfortune. When they transform their bewilderment into "catastrophes," when they seek to enclose the people in the "panic" of their discourses, are they once more necessarily right?

Rather than remaining within the field of a discourse that upholds its privilege by inverting its content (speaking of catastrophe and no longer of progress), one can try another path: one can analyze the microbe-like, singular and plural practices which an urbanistic system was supposed to administer or suppress, but which have outlived its decay; one can follow the swarming activity of these procedures that, far from being regulated or eliminated by panoptic administration, have reinforced themselves in a proliferating illegitimacy, developed and insinuated themselves into the networks of surveillance, and combined in accord with unreadable but stable tactics to the point of constituting everyday regulations and surreptitious creativities that are merely concealed by the frantic mechanisms and discourses of the observational organization.

This pathway could be inscribed as a consequence, but also as the reciprocal, of Foucault's analysis of the structures of power. He moved it in the direction of mechanisms and technical procedures, "minor instrumentalities" capable, merely by their organization of "details," of transforming a human multiplicity into a "disciplinary" society and of managing, differentiating, classifying, and hierarchizing all deviances concerning apprenticeship, health, justice, the army, or work.[301] "These often miniscule ruses of discipline," these "minor but flawless" mechanisms, draw their efficacy from a relationship between procedures and the space that they redistribute in order to make an "operator" out of it. But what *spatial practices* correspond, in the area where discipline is

---

[301] Michel Foucault, *Surveiller et punir* (Paris: Gallimard, l975), translated by Alan Sheridan as *Discipline and Punish* (New York: Pantheon, 1977).

manipulated, to these apparatuses that produce a disciplinary space? In the present conjuncture, which is marked by a contradiction between the collective mode of administration and an individual mode of reappropriation, this question is no less important, if one admits that spatial practices in fact secretly structure the determining conditions of social life. I would like to follow out a few of these multiform, resistance, tricky and stubborn procedures that elude discipline without being outside the field in which it is exercised, and which should lead us to a theory of everyday practices, of lived space, of the disquieting familiarity of the city.

The Chorus of Idle Footsteps

"The goddess can be recognized by her step" (Virgil, *Aeneid*, I, 405).

[97] Their story begins on ground level, with footsteps. They are myriad, but do not compose a series. They cannot be counted because each unit has a qualitative character: a style of tactile apprehension and kinesthetic appropriation. Their swarming mass is an innumerable collection of singularities. Their intertwined paths give their shape to spaces. They weave places together. In that respect, pedestrian movements form one of these "real systems whose existence in fact makes up the city."[302] They are not localized; it is rather they that spatialize. They are no more inserted within a container than those Chinese characters speakers sketch out on their hands with their fingertips.

It is true that the operations of walking on can be traced on city maps in such a way as to transcribe their paths (here well-trodden, there very faint) and their trajectories (going this way and not that). But these thick or thin curves only refer, like words, to the absence of what has passed by. Surveys of routes miss what was: the act itself of passing by. The operation of walking, wandering, or "window shopping," that is, the activity of passers-by, is transformed into points that draw a totalizing and reversible line on the map. They allow us to grasp only a relic set in the nowhen of a surface of projection. Itself visible, it has the effect of making invisible the operation that made it possible. These fixations constitute procedures for forgetting. The trace left behind

---

[302] Christopher Alexander, "La cité semi-treillis, mais non arbre," *Architecture, Mouvement, Continuité* 1 (1967): 3-11.

is substituted for the practice. It exhibits the (voracious) property that the geographical system has of being able to transform action into legibility, but in doing so it causes a way of being in the world to be forgotten.

Pedestrian Speech Acts

A comparison with the speech act will allow us to go further[303] and not limit ourselves to the critique of graphic representations alone, looking from the shores of legibility toward an inaccessible beyond. The act of walking is to the urban system what the speech act is to language or to the statements uttered.[304] At the most elementary level, it has a triple "enunciative" function: it is a process of *appropriation* of the topographical system on the part of the pedestrian (just as the speaker [98] appropriates and takes on the language); it is a spatial acting-out of the place (just as the speech act is an acoustic acting-out of language); and it implies *relations* among differentiated positions, that is, among pragmatic "contracts" in the form of movements (just as verbal enunciation is an "allocution," "posits another opposite" the speaker and puts contracts between interlocutors into action).[305] It thus seems possible to give a preliminary definition of walking as a space of enunciation.

We could moreover extend this problematic to the relations between the act of writing and the written text, and even transpose it to the relationships between the "hand" (the touch and the tale of the paintbrush [*le et la geste du pinceau*]) and the finished painting (forms, colors, etc.). At first isolated in the area of verbal communication, the speech act turns out to find only one of its applications there, and its linguistic modality is merely the first determination of a much more general distinction between the *forms used* in a system and the *ways of using* this system (i.e., *rules*), that is, between two "different worlds," since "the same things" are considered from two opposite formal viewpoints.

---

303 See Roland Barthes's remarks in *Architecture d'aujourd'hui* 153 (1970-1971): 11-13: "We speak our city ... merely by inhabiting it, walking through it, looking at it." Cf. Claude Soucy, *L'image du centre dans quatre romans contemporains* (Paris: CSU, 1971), pp. 6-15.

304 See the numerous studies devoted to the subject since John Searle's "What is a Speech Act?," in Black, Max, ed., *Philosophy in America* (Ithaca: Cornell University Press, 1965), pp. 221-239.

305 Émile Benveniste, *Problèmes de linguistique générale* (Paris: Gallimard, 1974), II, pp. 79-88, etc.

Considered from this angle, the pedestrian speech act has three characteristics which distinguish it at the outset from the spatial system: the present, the discrete, the "phatic."

First, if it is true that a spatial order organizes an ensemble of possibilities (e.g., by a place in which one can move) and interdictions (e.g., by a wall that prevents one from going further), then the walker actualizes some of these possibilities. In that way, he makes them exist as well as emerge. But he also moves them about and he invents others, since the crossing, drifting away, or improvisation of walking privilege, transform or abandon spatial elements. Thus Charlie Chaplin multiplies the possibilities of his cane: he does other things with the same thing and he goes beyond the limits that the determinants of the object set on its utilization. In the same way, the walker transforms each spatial signifier into something else. And if on the one hand he actualizes only a few of the possibilities fixed by the constructed order (he goes only here and not there), on the other he increases the number of possibilities (for example, by creating shortcuts and detours) and prohibitions (for example, he forbids himself to take paths generally considered accessible or even obligatory). He thus makes a selection. "The user of a city picks out certain fragments of the statement in order to actualize them in secret."[306]

He thus creates a discreteness, whether by making choices among the [99] signifiers of the spatial "language" or by displacing them through the use he makes of them. He condemns certain places to inertia or disappearance and composes with others spatial "turns of phrase" that are "rare," "accidental" or illegitimate. But that already leads into a rhetoric of walking.

In the framework of enunciation, the walker constitutes, in relation to his position, both a near and a far, a *here* and a *there*. To the fact that the adverbs *here* and *there* are the indicators of the locutionary seat in verbal communication[307]—a coincidence that reinforces the parallelism between linguistic and pedestrian enunciation—we must add that this location (*here-there*) (necessarily implied by walking and indicative of a present appropriation of space by an "I") also has the function of

---

[306] Roland Barthes, quoted in Claude Soucy, *L'image du centre dans quatre romans contemporains* (Paris: CSU, 1971), p. 10.

[307] "*Here* and *now* delimit the spatial and temporal instance coextensive and contemporary with the present instance of discourse containing I" (Émile Benveniste, *Problèmes de linguistique générale* (Paris: Gallimard, 1974), I, p. 253.

introducing an other in relation to this "I" and of thus establishing a conjunctive and disjunctive articulation of places. I would stress particularly the "phatic" aspect, by which I mean the function, isolated by Malinowski and Jakobson, of terms that initiate, maintain, or interrupt contact, such as "hello," "well, well," etc.[308] Walking, which alternately follows a path and has followers, creates a mobile organicity in the environment, a sequence of phatic *topoi*. And if it is true that the phatic function, which is an effort to ensure communication, is already characteristic of the language of talking birds, just as it constitutes the "first verbal function acquired by children," it is not surprising that it also gambols, goes on all fours, dances, and walks about, with a light or heavy step, like a series of "hellos" in an echoing labyrinth, anterior or parallel to informative speech.

The modalities of pedestrian enunciation which a plane representation on a map brings out could be analyzed. They include the kind of relationship this enunciation entertains with particular paths (or "statements") by according them a truth value ("alethic" modalities of the necessary, the impossible, the possible, or the contingent), an epistemological value ("epistemic" modalities of the certain, the excluded, the plausible, or the questionable) or finally an ethical or legal value ("deontic" modalities of the obligatory, the forbidden, the permitted, or the optional).[309] Walking affirms, suspects, tries out, transgresses, respects, etc., the trajectories it "speaks." All the modalities sing a part in this chorus, changing from step to step, stepping in through proportions, sequences, and intensities which vary according to the time, the path taken and the walker. These enunciatory operations are of an unlimited diversity. They therefore cannot be reduced to their graphic trail. ...

Myths: What "Makes Things Go"

[103] From this point of view, after having compared pedestrian processes to linguistic formations, we can bring them back down in the direction of oneiric figuration, or at least discover on that other side what, in a spatial practice, is inseparable from the dreamed place. To walk is to lack a place. It is

---

[308] Roman Jakobson, *Essais de linguistique générale* (Paris: Seul Points, 1970), p. 217.

[309] On modalities, see Herman Parret, *La Pragmatique des modalités* (Urbino: Centro di Semiotica, 1975); Alan R. White, *Modal Thinking* (Ithaca: Cornell University Press, 1975).

the indefinite process of being absent and in search of a proper. The moving about that the city multiplies and concentrates makes the city itself an immense social experience of lacking a place—an experience that is, to be sure, broken up into countless tiny deportations (displacements and walks), compensated for by the relationships and intersections of these exoduses that intertwine and create an urban fabric, and placed under the sign of what ought to be, ultimately, the place but is only a name, the City. The identity furnished by this place is all the more symbolic (named) because, in spite of the inequality of its citizens' positions and profits, there is only a pullulation of passer-by, a network of residences temporarily appropriated by pedestrian traffic, a shuffling among pretenses of the proper, a universe of rented spaces haunted by a nowhere or by dreamed-of places.

Names and Symbols

An indication of the relationship that spatial practices entertain with that absence is furnished precisely by their manipulations of and with "proper" names. The relationships between the direction of a walk [le sens de la marche] and the meaning of words [le sens des mots] situate two sorts of apparently contrary movements, one extrovert (to walk is to go outside), the other introvert (a mobility under the stability of the signifier). Walking is in fact determined by semantic tropisms; it is attracted and repelled by nominations whose meaning is not clear, whereas the city, for its part, is transformed for many people into a "desert" in which the meaningless, indeed the terrifying, no longer takes the form of shadows but becomes, as in Genet's plays, an implacable light that produces this urban text without obscurities, which is created by a technocratic power everywhere and which puts the city-dweller under control (under the control of what? No one knows): "The city [104] keeps us under its gaze, which one cannot bear without feeling dizzy," says a resident of Rouen.[310] In the spaces brutally lit by an alien reason, proper names carve out pockets of hidden and familiar meanings. They "make sense"; in other words, they are the impetus of movements, like vocations and calls that turn or divert an itinerary by giving it a meaning (or a direction) (sens) that was previously unforeseen. These names create a nowhere in places; they change them into passages.

A friend who lives in the city of Sevres drifts, when he is in

---

[310] Philippe Dard, Florence Desbons, et al., *La Ville, symbolique en souffrance* (Paris: CEP, 1975), p. 200.

Paris, toward the rue des Saints-*Pères* and the rue de *Sèvres*, even though he is going to see his mother in another part of town: these names articulate a sentence that his steps compose without his knowing it. Numbered streets and street numbers (112th St., or 9 rue Saint-Charles) orient the magnetic field of trajectories just as they can haunt dreams. Another friend unconsciously represses the streets which have names and, by this fact, transmit her—orders or identities in the same way as summonses and classifications; she goes instead along paths that have no name or signature. But her walking is thus still controlled negatively by proper names.

What is it then that they spell out? Disposed in constellations that hierarchize and semantically order the surface of the city, operating chronological arrangements and historical justifications, these words (*Borrégo, Botzaris, Bougainville* ...) slowly lose, like worn coins, the value engraved on them, but their ability to signify outlives its first definition. *Saints-Pères, Corentin Celton, Red Square* ... these names make themselves available to the diverse meanings given them by passers-by; they detach themselves from the places they were supposed to define and serve as imaginary meeting-points on itineraries which, as metaphors, they determine for reasons that are foreign to their original value but may be recognized or not by passers-by. A strange toponymy that is detached from actual places and flies high over the city like a foggy geography of "meanings" held in suspension, directing the physical deambulations below: *Place de l'Étoile, Concorde, Poissonnière* ... These constellations of names provide traffic patterns: they are stars directing itineraries. "The Place de la Concorde does not exist," Malaparte said, "it is an idea."[311] It is much more than an "idea." A whole series of comparisons would be necessary to account for the magical powers proper names enjoy. They seem to be carried as emblems by the travellers they direct and simultaneously decorate.

[105] Linking acts and footsteps, opening meanings and directions, these words operate in the name of an emptying-out and wearing-away of their primary role. They become liberated spaces that can be occupied. A rich indetermination gives them, by means of a semantic rarefaction, the function of articulating a second, poetic geography on top of the geography of the literal, forbidden or permitted meaning. They insinuate other routes into

---

[311] See also, for example, the epigraph in Patrick Modiano, *Place de l'Étoile* (Paris: Gallimard, 1968).

the functionalist and historical order of movement. Walking follows them: "I fill this great empty space with a beautiful name."[312] People are put in motion by the remaining relics of meaning, and sometimes by their waste products, the inverted remainders of great ambitions.[313] Things that amount to nothing, or almost nothing, symbolize and orient walkers' steps: names that have ceased precisely to be "proper."

In these symbolizing kernels three distinct (but connected) functions of the relations between spatial and signifying practices are indicated (and perhaps founded): the believable, the memorable, and the primitive. They designate what "authorizes" (or makes possible or credible) spatial appropriations, what is repeated in them (or is recalled in them) from a silent and withdrawn memory, and what is structured in them and continues to be signed by an in-fantile (in-fans) origin. These three symbolic mechanisms organize the topoi of a discourse on/of the city (legend, memory, and dream) in a way that also eludes urbanistic systematicity. They can already be recognized in the functions of proper names: they make habitable or believable the place that they clothe with a word (by emptying themselves of their classifying power, they acquire that of "permitting" something else); they recall or suggest phantoms (the dead who are supposed to have disappeared) that still move about, concealed in gestures and in bodies in motion; and, by naming, that is, by imposing an injunction proceeding from the other (a story) and by altering functionalist identity by detaching themselves from it, they create in the place itself that erosion or nowhere that the law of the other carves out within it.

Credible Things and Memorable Things: Habitability

By a paradox that is only apparent, the discourse that makes people believe is the one that takes away what it urges them to believe in, or never delivers what it promises. Far from expressing a void or describing [106] a lack, it creates such. It makes room for a void. In that way, it opens up clearings; it "allows" a certain play within a system of defined places. It "authorizes" the production of

---

[312] Joachim du Bellay, *Regrets*, p. 189.

[313] For example, *Sarcelles*, the name of a great urbanistic ambition (near Paris), has taken on a symbolic value for the inhabitants of the town by becoming in the eyes of France as a whole the example of a total failure. This extreme avatar provides its citizens with the "prestige" of an exceptional identity.

an area of free play (*Spielraum*) on a checkerboard that analyzes and classifies identities. It makes places habitable. On these grounds, I call such discourse a "local authority." It is a crack in the system that saturates places with signification and indeed so reduces them to this signification that it is "impossible to breathe in them." It is a symptomatic tendency of functionalist totalitarianism (including its programming of games and celebrations) that it seeks precisely to eliminate these local authorities, because they compromise the univocity of the system. Totalitarianism attacks what it quite correctly calls *superstitions*: supererogatory semantic overlays that insert themselves "over and above" and "in excess,"[314] and annex to a past or poetic realm a part of the land the promoters of technical rationalities and financial profitabilities had reserved for themselves.

Ultimately, since proper names are already "local authorities" or "superstitions," they are replaced by numbers: on the telephone, one no longer dials *Opera*, but 073. The same is true of the stories and legends that haunt urban space like superfluous or additional inhabitants. They are the object of a witch-hunt, by the very logic of the techno-structure. But their extermination (like the extermination of trees, forests, and hidden places in which such legends live)[315] makes the city a "suspended symbolic order."[316] The habitable city is thereby annulled. Thus, as a woman from Rouen put it, no, here "there isn't any place special, except for my own home, that's all. ... There isn't anything." Nothing "special": nothing that is marked, opened up by a memory or a story, signed by something or someone else. Only the cave of the home remains believable, still open for a certain time to legends, still full of shadows. Except for that, according to another city-dweller, there are only "places in which one can no longer believe in anything."[317]

It is through the opportunity they offer to store up rich silences and wordless stories, or rather through their capacity to create cellars and garrets everywhere, that local legends (*legenda*: what is *to be read*, but also what *can be read*) permit exits, ways of going out and coming back in, and thus habitable spaces. Certainly

---

[314] *Superstare*: "to be above," as something in addition or superfluous.

[315] See Françoise Lugassy, *Contibution à une psychosociologie de l'espace urbain: La relation habitat-forêt* (Paris: Recherche Urbaine, 1970).

[316] Dard, Desbons et al., *La Ville, symbolique en souffrance*.

[317] Ibid., pp. 174, 206.

walking about and traveling substitute for exits, for going away and coming back, which were formerly made available by a body of legends that places nowadays lack. Physical moving about has the itinerant function of yesterday's or today's "superstitions." Travel (like walking) is a substitute for the legends that [107] used to open up space to something different. What does travel ultimately produce if it is not, by a sort of reversal, "an exploration of the deserted places of my memory," the return to nearby exoticism by way of a detour through distant places, and the "discovery" of relics and legends: "fleeting visions of the French countryside," "fragments of music and poetry,"[318] in short, something like an "uprooting in one's origins" (Heidegger)? What this walking exile produces is precisely the body of legends that is currently lacking in one's own vicinity; it is a fiction, which moreover has the double characteristic, like dreams or pedestrian rhetoric, of being the effect of displacements and condensations.[319] As a corollary, one can measure the importance of these signifying practices (to tell oneself legends) as practices that invent spaces.

From this point of view, their contents remain revelatory, and still more so is the principle that organizes them. Stories about places are makeshift things. They are composed with the world's debris. Even if the literary form and the actantial schema of "superstitions" correspond to stable models whose structures and combinations have often been analyzed over the past thirty years, the materials (all the rhetorical details of their "manifestation") are furnished by the leftovers from nominations, taxonomies, heroic or comic predicates, etc., that is, by fragments of scattered semantic places. These heterogeneous and even contrary elements fill the homogeneous form of the story. Things *extra* and *other* (details and excesses coming from elsewhere) insert themselves into the accepted framework, the imposed order. One thus has the very relationship between spatial practices and the constructed order. The surface of this order is everywhere punched and torn open by ellipses, drifts, and leaks of meaning: it is a sieve-order.

The verbal relics of which the story is composed, being tied to lost stories and opaque acts, are juxtaposed in a collage where their relations are not thought, and for this reason they form a

---

[318] Claude Lévi-Strauss, *Tristes topiques* (Paris: Plon, 1955), pp. 434-436; translated by John Russell as *Tristes tropiques* (New York: Criterion, 1962).

[319] One could say the same about the photos brought back from trips, substituted for and turned into legends about the starting place.

symbolic whole.[320] They are articulated by lacunae. Within the structured space of the text, they thus produce anti-texts, effects of dissimulation and escape, possibilities of moving into other landscapes, like cellars and bushes: "*ô massifs, ô pluriels.*"[321] Because of the process of dissemination that they open up, stories differ from *rumors* in that the latter are always injunctions, initiators and results of a levelling of space, creators of common movements that reinforce an order by adding an activity of making people believe things to that of making people do things. Stories diversify, rumors totalize. If there is still a certain oscillation between them, it [108] seems that today there is rather a stratification: stories are becoming private and sink into the secluded places in neighborhoods, families, or individuals, while the rumors propagated by the media cover everything and, gathered under the figure of the City, the masterword of an anonymous law, the substitute for all proper names, they wipe out or combat any superstitions guilty of still resisting the figure.

The dispersion of stories points to the dispersion of the memorable as well. And in fact memory is a sort of anti-museum: it is not localizable. Fragments of it come out in legends. Objects and words also have hollow places in which a past sleeps, as in the everyday acts of walking, eating, going to bed, in which ancient revolutions slumber. A memory is only a Prince Charming who stays just long enough to awaken the Sleeping Beauties of our wordless stories. "*Here*, there used to be a bakery." "*That's* where old lady Dupuis used to live." It is striking here that the places people live in are like the presences of diverse absences. What can be seen designates what is no longer there: "you *see*, here there used to be ...," but it can no longer be seen. Demonstratives indicate the invisible identities of the visible: it is the very definition of a place, in fact, that it is composed by these series of displacements and effects among the fragmented strata that form it and that it plays on these moving layers.

"Memories tie us to that place. ... It's personal, not interesting

---

[320] Terms whose relationships are not thought but postulated as necessary can be said to be symbolic. On this definition of symbolism as a cognitive mechanism characterized by a "deficit" of thinking, see Dan Sperber, *Le Symbolisme en general* (Paris: Hermann, 1974), translated by Alice L. Morton as *Rethinking Symbolism* (Cambridge: Cambridge University Press, 1975).

[321] Francis Ponge, *La Promenade dans nos serres* (Paris: Gallimard, 1967).

to anyone else, but after all that's what gives a neighborhood its character."322 There is no place that is not haunted by many different spirits hidden there in silence, spirits one can "invoke" or not. Haunted places are the only ones people can live in–and this inverts the schema of the *Panopticon*. But like the gothic sculptures of kings and queens that once adorned Notre-Dame and have been buried for two centuries in the basement of a building in the rue de la Chaussée-d'Antin,323 these "spirits," themselves broken into pieces in like manner, do not *speak* any more than they *see*. This is a sort of knowledge that remains silent. Only hints of what is known but unrevealed are passed on "just between you and me."

Places are fragmentary and inward-turning histories, pasts that others are not allowed to read, accumulated times that can be unfolded but like stories held in reserve, remaining in an enigmatic state, symbolizations encysted in the pain or pleasure of the body. "I feel good here":324 the well-being under-expressed in the language it appears in like a fleeting glimmer is a spatial practice.

---

322 A woman living in the Croix-Rousse quarter in Lyon (interview by Pierre Mayol): see *L'Invention du quotidien*, II, *Habiter, cuisiner* [10/18] (Paris: UGE, 1980).

323 See *Le Monde* for May 4, 1977.

324 See note 48.

JOHN CAPUTO (1940-)

Caputo was born in 1940 in Philadelphia. After graduating from La Salle University in 1962 he received a Master's Degree from Villanova University in 1964 and his Ph.D. in Philosophy from Bryn Mawr College in 1968. Caputo returned to teach philosophy at his alma mater of Villanova University from 1968 to 2004. He then accepted a post at Syracuse University where he taught from 2004 to 2011.

Caputo has been influenced by the postmodern thinkers Jacques Derrida, Jean-Luc Marion, and Gianni Vattimo, and has developed their thought into what he calls "weak theology" stressing God's kenosis and self-humbling. This construction of God is found in his key work *The Weakness of God: A Theology of the Event* (Bloomington: Indiana University Press, 2006). Other notable works are his *Radical Hermeneutics* (Bloomington: Indiana University Press, 1987); *Against Ethics* (Bloomington: Indiana University Press, 1993); *On Religion* (London: Routledge, 2001); *What Would Jesus Deconstruct?: The Good News of Postmodernism for the Church* (Grand Rapids: Baker Academic, 2007); and *The Insistence of God: A Theology of Perhaps* (Bloomington: Indiana University Press, 2013).

For more on the thought of Caputo see: Dooley, Mark, ed., *A Passion for the Impossible: John D. Caputo in Focus* (Albany: State University of New York Press, 2002); Olthius, James D., ed., *Religion With/Out Religion: The Prayers and Tears of John D. Caputo* (London: Routledge, 2002); Simpson, Christopher Ben. *Religion, Metaphysics, and the Postmodern: William Desmond and John D. Caputo* (Bloomington: Indiana University Press, 2009); Zlomislić, Marko, and Neal DeRoo, eds., *Cross and Khôra: Deconstruction and Christianity in the Work of John D. Caputo* (Eugene: Wipf and Stock, 2010); Trozzo, Eric J., *Rupturing Eschatology: Divine Glory and the Silence of the Cross* (Minneapolis: Fortress Press, 2014).

The following text is from Caputo's *The Weakness of God: A Theology of the Event* (Bloomington: Indiana University Press, 2006): 32-41, where Caputo rejects a God of metaphysical theology and substitutes a God of weak theology, a God not of infinite power or sovereignty but a God who stands with the destitute and marginalized.

The Weakness of God (2006)[325]

God without Sovereignty

[32] Now I turn to God (a lifelong task), to the name of God, and to my hypothesis that the event that this name shelters is a weak force.

Suppose we grant all this business about a kingdom without kingdom, of disturbing the prestige of the present by means of an event—what has any of this to do with God or with a kingdom of God? Does not *différance* spell big trouble for God? Does not *différance's* subversive misspelling spell the end of religion and the death of God? *Différance* steadfastly resists becoming a "master word or master concept" and accordingly "blocks every relationship to theology,"[326] since the discourse on God is a discourse on the master word *par excellence*, the Lord of history and the master of the universe, the royal power omnipotent. Is not God the dream of power aplenty, of omnitude and plenitude and plenipotentiarity, of exnihilatory and annihilatory power, "of being as presence, as parousia, as life without *différance*"? And is not "theology" the very name, the very model, of the logocentric love of presence and the effacement of the trace?[327] Can one imagine a more permanent presence or a more prestigious *ousia* or a more powerful *parousia* than the "God" under whose protection the religious powers that be huddle for protection? Can one imagine any more sovereign power than God's?

Can one imagine anything more supportive of the established order, anything more top-down, more entrenched in the *status quo*, anything more immobilized, actualized, contented, and *nunc stans* than religion and religion's "God"? *Pro deo et patria*: is that not a lethal combination, literally a deadly, ultra-divisive call to arms in whose ungodly name more blood has been spilled than just about anything else we can imagine? What has founded and grounded top-down orders of sovereign power more firmly than such a "God"? Is not the very idea of God as the sovereign lord of the universe the very model after which every terrestrial

---

[325] [John Caputo, *The Weakness of God*. Copyright © 2006 by Indiana University Press. All rights reserved. Used with permission of Indiana University Press, https://iupress.org.]

[326] Jacques Derrida, *Positions*, trans. Alan Bass (Chicago: University of Chicago Press, 1981), p. 40.

[327] Jacques Derrida, *Of Grammatology*, trans. Gayatri Spivak (Baltimore: John Hopkins University Press, 1998), p. 71.

sovereignty is designed? Is not the sovereign Father Almighty, Creator of Heaven and Earth, the very model of every earthly patriarchy? How often has the "reign of God" meant a sovereign [33] reign of theocratic terror? What has been more violent than theocracy? What more patriarchal, more hierarchical? What more authoritarian, inquisitorial, misogynistic, colonialist, militaristic, terroristic?

But suppose all this power mongering is just rouged and powdered theology?

Suppose—and this is the working hypothesis of a theology of the event—as a regular reader of essays like "différance," Kierkegaard's "The Present Age," and St. Paul, we raise the possibility of a "God" who belongs, not to the fixed order of presence, but to the (dis)order of the deconstruction of presence? Suppose we abandon the top-down schema of one Father Almighty, one king to rule the land (another father), in favor of a paradigm where such sovereign power slips out of favor? Suppose we say that the event that is sheltered in the name of God does not belong to the order of power and presence, but rather withdraws from the world in order to station him or herself (Godself is the gender-neutral word, if you can get used to it) with everything that the world despises?[328] Suppose we think of God as someone who prowls the streets (a *voyou*) and disturbs the peace of what Kierkegaard called "Christendom?" Suppose we imagine God as a street person with a definite body odor, like Lord Shiva living as a beggar?[329] Suppose our thought of God is not domesticated by Sunday sermons by His Reverence or co-opted by ecstatic visions of a great military show of arms in a massive square, visions of the

---

[328] Commenting on Hegel, who is commenting on Moses Mendelson, Derrida writes: "Since God does not manifest himself, he is not truth for the Jews, total presence or parousia. He gives orders without appearing." *Glas*, trans. Richard Rand and John Leavey (Lincoln: University of Nebraska Press, 1986), 51a, cited by Kevin Hart, *The Trespass of Sign* (Cambridge: Cambridge University Press, 1989), p. 62. Yahweh then would be what is "essentially other than truth," not Heideggerian *lethe*, which is the very heart of truth, *pace* John Sallis, "Deformatives: Essentially Other than Truth," *Double Truth* (Albany: SUNY Press, 1995).

[329] See Indira Viswanathan Peterson, *Poems to Siva: The Hymns of the Tamil Saints* (Delhi: Motilal Barardsidass Publishers, 1991), "Bhiksatana: The Beggar (Poems 37–39)," pp. 123-126; and the story of Nandanaar in Periya Puranamby Sekkizhaar, condensed English version by G. Vanmikanathan (Mylapore, Madras: Sri Ramakrishna Math, 1985), pp. 558-567. My thanks to my colleague Joanne Waghorne for this tip.

supereminent power of the supreme creator of heaven and earth, of the hyper-eminence of the *arche*? Suppose instead we take our lead in thinking about God from images of the most powerless remnants and marginalized bodies and nobodies, the little *me onta*, the obscure pockets and folds and hovels of the world? Suppose God most especially pitches his tent among the homeless, so that God has no place on which to lay his head?

Suppose, further, that "religion" and "theology," which are human, all too human and not to be confused with God, tend systematically, structurally, regularly to forget this, and to associate themselves with a discourse of power, which is what we mean by strong theology? Suppose that we reverse these gears and thrust theology in the direction of weakness and the disavowal of power? Suppose that the God of religion and theology, which is also our invention, might almost be defined by its prevention of the event that is sheltered by the name of God, by its oblivion of this event, so that the first step that would be required, as Meister Eckhart said, is to pray God to rid us of this God? To which we might add, "I pray God to rid us of religion," since, according to Isaiah (1:11–17), Amos (5:21–24), and Hosea (6:6), God can do *without* religion if religion means only cultic sacrifice and ritual, but not without the event of justice, which is not always what religion means,[330] a point also frequently made by Karl Barth.[331] Suppose we [34] add the prophets to the list that Derrida composes of those who advocate a religion *without* religion and what we called a theology without theology or a weak theology? Suppose, indeed, that the event that is astir within the name of God is stationed, not on the side of the *arche* and the *principium*, or of timeless being and unchanging presence, or of the true, the good, and the beautiful, but on the side of the an-archic and subversive, as the driving force of a divine subversion? Suppose God is the prime mover unmoved not of physical movement but of justice, and that God moves not by force but by attraction, like a call, by drawing us on and luring us? Suppose the name of "God" harbors an event of solicitation, that it solicits us by being situated, not inside the churches on the high altars, but with the beggars

---

[330] Daniel Maguire, *The Moral Core of Judaism and Christianity* (Minneapolis: Fortress Press, 1993), pp. 189-190.

[331] See Karl Barth, *The Epistle to the Romans*, trans. E. C. Hoskyns (London: Oxford University Press, 1933). Throughout this famous book, Barth delimits "all ethical and religious illusions" (p. 68), in favor of the "impossible possibility" (p. 79) of God.

with outstretched hands on the church steps?

Suppose God is not to be conceived as the overarching and sovereign governor of the *ordo universi*, of the *cosmos*, but as what disorders such orders, de-worlds such worlds, and subverts and polyverts such universes, all for the chaosmic ends of justice? Suppose God is not conceived as the rock-solid ground on which the onto-theo-political edifice of sovereignty is erected but is systematically associated with the different, the marginal, the outsider, the left out; with the naked ones, not the long robes in the sanctuary within; with the least among us, the destitute, the *anawim*, those who are plundered and ground under (Amos 8:4), and hence as a subversive and "revolutionary" impulse? Suppose God is to be found hidden in a subversive corner of a revolutionary age, not as the stabilizing center of the present age?

Suppose the event that is sheltered by the name of God is not identified with timeless infinite power invested in an *omnipotens deus*, but with the powerless who suffer the ravages of time? Suppose the sense of "God" is to interrupt and disrupt, to confound, contradict, and confront the established human order, the human, all too human way and sway of doing business, the authority of man over man—and over women, animals, and the earth itself—human possessiveness and dominion—to pose, in short, the contradiction of the "world"? Suppose God has no time for the hierarchical power structures that human beings impose on one another and even less time for the power of God over human beings, which is actually the power that human beings exert "in the name of God"? Suppose the event that simmers in the name of God, if it were to be written out, would read: "No God, No Master?" Suppose that God's power over human beings is limited by love and that God takes up a place beside them in their powerlessness?[332]

Suppose the idea behind the "rule of God" is not to back up human authority with a divine fist but to turn the eye of the law to the widow, the orphan, and the stranger, which is the *Augen-blick* of justice? Suppose the idea [35] behind calling God a father is not to set up an oppressive patriarchal model of sovereign power but the relativization of worldly power: "Do not call any man on earth father, for you have one Father, and he is in heaven ... the greatest among you must be your servant" (Matt. 23:8–12). Then repeat and update that with a sexual difference, and say that you have

---

[332] See Jacques Ellul, *Anarchy and Christianity* (Grand Rapids: William B. Eerdmans, 1992), pp. 32-34.

one mother in heaven, and for the same reason (which should make us worry about some of these mothers here on earth). Then generalize it in terms of parents and human authorities.

Suppose we associate God with disseminating tongues and deconstructing towering edifices, with confusion and profusion, the way God interrupted the plans of the Shemites (Gen. 11:1–9), who wanted to build the tower of Babel, and then disseminated their language into a profusion of mutually unintelligible tongues so that they could no longer build up a consensus, no longer construct an ideal speech community, and no longer build their transcendental tower?[333]

Suppose we stop thinking about God onto-theo-logically as *prima causa,* as some sort of ontological power plant or power source, the first mover of the motions of the firmament, as if we need God to explain why the heavens move, and onto-theo-politically as the foundation of political sovereignty, "one nation under God," the backup for the established order, and begin to think of "God" in terms of what is left out and ground under by the whole economy of causes, orders, and nations, in terms of what groans for freedom in all these establishments. Suppose "God" stands for an event that confounds, confuses, contradicts, and scandalizes this economy, these crusts of power and privilege, this order of presence, *not,* I hasten to add, in order to throw us to the wolves of lawlessness, but in order to let the lamb lie down with the wolf (Isa. 11:6), not in order to level institutions and structures, but precisely in order to open them up, to keep them just, to let justice reign? Suppose, then, the international politics that accompanies the theology of this event is a community of nations without individual sovereignty?

Suppose, when you cross the wires of *différance* with the name of God, the result is to have crossed out the name of God in order to release the event this name contains? That is a move made by Jean-Luc Marion, which he has adapted from Heidegger's crossing out of the name of Being[334] and which here, in these pages, deforms the name of God in conformity with the deforming *a* in *différance.* Suppose we do this just in order to save the name of God, saving the event sheltered by the name of God,

---

[333] See Hart, *The Trespass of the Sign,* 107 ff.; see Jacques Derrida, "Des tours de Babel," trans. Joseph Graham, in *Difference in Translation* (Ithaca, N.Y.: Cornell University Press, 1985), 209 ff.

[334] Jean-Luc Marion, *God without Being: Hors-Texte,* trans. Thomas A. Carlson (Chicago: University of Chicago Press, 1991), 70 ff.

from the God of religion and strong theology, which is an idol, a graven image, an instrument of institutional power, of moral melancholy, of top-down authoritarianism, and confessional and identitarian divisiveness? Suppose we cross out the name of God, not in the spirit of a mystical theology, where [36] God is the *nomen innominabile* of a *hyperousios*, or of Heideggerian *Denken*, where it signifies the mystery of the great power of Being, but in the name of a weak theology, which is composed of graffiti that defaces standard theological writing, like a body that is scratched, scarred, and defaced, marred by lines of hunger or persecution, wounded and bleeding? Suppose we imagine weak theology as a meditation upon God crossed out, cut and bruised, bleeding and bent in pain, like the crucified God of which Moltmann speaks?

Suppose we think of God, not as the *hyperousios* of negative theology, the purity of/from being (*puritas essendi*), the God of eminence and supereminence, who towers tall *beyond* being—negative theology, for all its modesty is very strong; it is the tall, strong, silent type—but as the one who lies down with nullity and insignificance, who clings steadfastly with the nothings of the world, the lowly bodies and nobodies *below* being.[335] Suppose this anarchic God is not to be found high above the seventh heaven in the realm of Neoplatonic *hyperousios*, but down below in the bowels of the earthly khoral kingdom of the *me onta*?

Suppose we imagine God, not as a prime mover unmoved, but as removed from the order of cosmic movements and cosmological explanations, removed from the onto-causal order altogether, from being, presence, power, and causality? Suppose we imagine God otherwise, not really having a seat in being at all, but below being and beings, simmering beneath the ontico-ontological difference, as the heart of a heartless world? Suppose we think of God not so much in terms of everything that we desire, which seems a little acquisitive, but in terms of everything that desires us, everything that draws us out of ourselves and calls upon us, calling from below being to what is beyond, that summons up

---

[335] I agree that the discourse of mystical theology has a role to play, that it is itself a powerful and disruptive discourse in its own right, which I very much love. See my discussion of Derrida and Meister Eckhart in *More Radical Hermeneutics* (Bloomington: Indiana University Press, 2001), pp. 249-264. This raises the daunting problem of the relation between the discourse of mystical theology and the scriptural discourse on the "kingdom of God."

what is best in us, that asks us to go out of our creaturely way of being and live generously, to live and love, to live and let live, to love and let love, to live by loving, unconditionally? Suppose we hold that whatever has being can come to be only under certain conditions, while the unconditional would somehow be free from being, otherwise than being, a kind of demi-being, almost like a ghost, a very holy one, no doubt, and almost nothing?

Suppose, then, in short, and contrary to the expectations of religion, mainstream theology, and the vested interests of His Reverence, the name of God harbors an event that is at best a "weak force" (*force faible*), and that the "weakness of God" is, nonetheless, the only thing that is strong enough to save us, which is why we want to save this name?

What then?

Then the wires of the "kingdom of God" would be crossed with this so-called "kingdom without kingdom" of *différance*, and we would find ourselves with just the short circuit we desired. Then we would have the [37] sparks of anarchy on our hands, sacred sparks and a sacred anarchy. Then, instead of a great onto-theological power supply surging from on high, we would have a short circuit, where the wires of the kingdom of God, which threatens and subverts the "world" (*kosmos*), are crossed with the wires of *différance*, which threatens and subverts the order of presence. This little bit of cross wiring—a transference that is neither an *analogia fidei* nor an *analogia entis*, but at best an *analogia non-entis*—is crucial to my experiment. In the New Testament, the "world" means the holding sway of the real power of this world, the *strong force* of the power of the present age, of the *aion*, to which the weak force of the kingdom is opposed. The "world" is what really exists, whereas the kingdom *calls for* something else. The world stands for the business as usual of the powerful and privileged, the oppressive order of presence that builds wealth on the backs of the poor and the outcast, that builds privilege on the backs of the despised and the different, while the kingdom contradicts the world, which means it calls for something contrary to the world. The kingdom calls the world out, calls it what it is, and calls for something else. The kingdom belongs to a different order, a different plane, than that of being or presence. Make no mistake, there is only one world, in the sense of what Heidegger calls "being-in-the-world," but within it the kingdom and the "world" are its tensions. (We will come back to this kingdom in more detail in the second part of this study.)

The Transcendence of God

But let us not shirk our duty and run from the paradoxes and improbabilities provoked by speaking about the "weakness of God." If God is weak, how can God still be God at all? How, for example, on such anarchical terms, can we still speak of what has always been called the "transcendence" of God?

One quite classic way to explain the transcendence of God in strong theology is to adapt the Platonic way of eminence, of the Good beyond being, the Good for which being is not good enough. God is "without being" where "without" signifies an excess beyond, not a lack, that than which nothing that is can be greater. But that is not good enough for a weak theology, because the Good in the *Republic* is the ultimate sovereign power, a king (*kurios*) in its own kingdom (*basileia*), the very knowledge of which entitles the philosopher to be a king, a real king not an ironic one, because knowledge rules.[336] The Good in the *Republic* is the most powerful and superlative power, which imposes a hierarchical order upon lower being, just in accord with the model of sovereignty, which is not what I mean by the power of powerlessness. The Good is the father of all, the *arche*,[337] the *hyperousios*, [38] the hyper-being beyond being, the Godhead beyond God (*Gottheit über Gott*), not the power of powerlessness, not the weak force of a powerless solicitation or promise or provocation. Strong theology loves the order of the *Republic*, whereas a theology of the event, as we will see, is happy down below with *khora*.

I treat God, not as an eminent omnipotent onto-power capable of leveling tall buildings and reducing his enemies (no need for gender-neutral language here) to ashes, but as the weak force of a call. If pressed by the Lord Cardinal, His Eminence the Grand Inquisitor, to say what then God "is," I would nervously defer because I prefer to say not that God "is" but that God "calls," that God promises, not from beyond being but from below, without being or sovereignty. If I were then pressed further by His Awful Eminence to say what God's transcendence is, I would again defer because I prefer to say, not that God is a transcendent super-essential hyperbeing towering over other beings, but that God's

---

336 Plato, *Republic*, trans. Paul Shorey, in *The Collected Dialogues of Plato*, ed. Edith Hamilton and Huntington Cairns (New York: Random House, 1961), Bk. VI, 509 (d), p. 745.

337 See Jacques Derrida, *Voyous* (Paris: Galilée, 2003), pp. 193-194 (*Roques*, trans. Pascale-Ann Brault and Michael Naas (Stanford: Stanford University Press, 2005), pp. 139-140).

transcendence is that of a call, of an address that, while arising from the hinter regions below being, lays us low. God's transcendence is a matter of the transcendence of the event that transpires in the name of God. God's transcendence means that we are laid low by a call arising from on high, but whose heights are eventful, provocative, and arise from someone who, lacking the wherewithal to lay down his head, pitches his tent among the lowly bodies and nobodies below in the bodily bowels of hypo-being. The transcendence of God is not that of a fist that smashes, but of a Spirit who breathes, who inspires, and whose gentle breath urges us on.

God's transcendence is the power of a spirit, not of the sword. The transcendence of God is not at odds with the weak force of God; it *is* the weak force of God. Otherwise it would not be transcendence of God but the transcendence of the world, which is a strong force, one with a real army and the real power to enforce its word. The word of God, the God of the word. The promise of God, the God of the promise. If it is true that we can hardly resist God's promise, it is not less true that this irresistible force is weak—for on our premise, God can only promise.

The weak force of God is to lay *claim* upon us—*uns in Anspruch nehmen*, as Heidegger would say—but not the way a sovereign power in the domain of being invades and then lays claim to territory, overpowers its native population and plants a foreign flag, but in the way of a summons that calls and provokes, an appeal that incites or invites us, a promise that awakens our love. The name of God harbors an unconditional appeal without the sovereign force to enforce it. God is, without being, of unconditional import and the stuff of unconditional desire.

To say, as is said in strong theology, that God is the judge is to say in weak theology that it is in the *name* of God that we judge that the kingdom [39] is hardly here, has hardly begun, is still to come, even as it is urgently required now and we cannot wait any longer. It is in the name of God that the kingdom is called for; the kingdom of God is the event that is called by the name of God. That is how God can be God. That is how to prevent the event from being trapped by the name of God. Considered in terms of the event, the issue is not so much with what name we are to call God, but what the name of God calls for, what it calls upon us to do. To live "before God" (*coram deo*), as Augustine put it so beautifully, is to live on call, under the call, always already solicited, called upon, pressed by the weak force of the call, called by the call to let the kingdom come, which is what is called *for*. Let the kingdom come, in the name of God.

God's transcendence is not to be taken onto-theo-logically as a *summum ens* towering over finite beings, nor is it to be taken onto-theo-politically as a sovereign master who supplies the paradigm for the human mastery over everything else. That is rouged theology. As Derrida says, the "unavowed theologeme" of the power politics of sovereignty is the sovereignty of God.[338] I do not think of God as some super-being who out-knows, out-wills, out-does, out-powers, and out-exists every entity here below, a higher super-entity, a hyper-presence dwelling in a higher world. I do not think of God as an [*sic* a an] omnipotent onto-theo-cosmo-logical power source for the universe, but as the unconditional demand for beneficence that shocks the world with a promise that is not kept, as the heart of a heartless world, as the call from below being that summons us to rise beyond being, beyond ourselves. I think of the world as addressed by a call, not produced by a cause, as an addressee, not an effect, and of God as a call, not a cause, as a beneficence, not a sovereign power.[339]

Another way to put all this is to say that, in my vocabulary, the world is there, being is there, and there we are, there, in the world, being right there along with the world. By "God," on the other hand, I do not mean a being who is there, an entity trapped in being, even as a super-being *up there*, up above the world, who physically powers and causes it, who made it and occasionally intervenes upon its day-to-day activities to tweak things for the better in response to a steady stream of solicitations from down below (a hurricane averted here, an illness averted there, etc.). That I consider an essentially magical view of the world. I do not mean anything that is *there*, because what is *there* belongs to the order of being and power; to the strong force of the world, where you solve problems by raising money—or an army. I mean a call that solicits and disturbs what is there, an event that adds a level of signification and meaning, of provocation and solicitation to

---

[338] Ibid., p. 155; *Roques*, p. 110.

[339] In the poetry of the Scriptures, as Abraham Heschel has very nicely shown, God is not an unmoved but very much a moved mover, who suffers with the suffering and grieves with the grieving (see "The Theology of Pathos," in *The Prophets* (New York: Harper & Row, 1962), 2:1-11). When metaphysical theology reaches the point where it finds itself hard-pressed to explain how God can suffer, the whole onto-theological tradition ship-wrecks, having drifted out of sight of its biblical shores.

what is there, that makes it impossible for the world, for what is *there*, to settle solidly in place, to consolidate, to close in upon itself. By the name of "God" I mean the event of this solicitation, an event of deconsolidation, an [40] electrifying event-ing disturbance, the solvent of the weak force of this spectral spirit who haunts the world as its bad conscience, or who breathes lightly and prompts its most inspired moments, all the while readily conceding that there are other names than the name of God. I am trying to save the name of God, not absolutize it.

Whether over and beyond what we might call the hermeneutics of the event, the lived experience of the call and of being on call, there is some entitative cause calling, some entity or hyper-entity out there with a proper name, verifiable by a metaphysical argument or certifiable by a divine revelation, is no part of my hypothesis, one way or the other (for or against). I leave that stock to fluctuate on the open market of existence. I leave that question to fluctuate in that domain of undecidability wherein all concrete decisions are made, which has the effect of intensifying this decision, not attenuating it. About that decision I have no inside-trader information to pass along. About God, God alone knows. That is a matter for each poor existing individual to work out, and no part of the trouble we are buying for ourselves with this experiment. No one has authorized us to settle that question. We are not a party to that dispute. Although I have my opinions, I have not the least firsthand information to convey about that. Relative to that sort of strong decision, a theology of the event is but a prolegomenon aimed at keeping that decision out of trouble.

The trouble rouged theology buys for itself is the result of selling the body of theology to power. The very core of the mistake made by onto-theology derives from conceiving God on the horizon of being, power, and causality, as if God were a cosmic power supply. In the weak and colorless theology whose cause I am promoting, it is profane magic, thaumaturgy, to think of God as an omnipotent meteorological onto-power who could stop (or start) hurricanes, landslides, and floods, or as an omni-historical superpower who can stop or start wars or prevent holocausts and put an end to pornography, obesity, junk TV, computer spam, crime in the streets, and the ruining of the environment. When we see an athlete praying for victory in a game, blame the strong theologians, for the athlete simply makes the logic of this onto-theo-cosmo-interventionism embarrassingly visible, right on national TV, as if God were a party to a Final Four office pool.

The thoroughly onto-theological project of "theodicy," of

getting God off the causal hook, whether for the vagaries of natural disasters or for the disasters caused by human vagary and malice, is no less profane. The authentically religious way to think about God, on my slightly heretical hypothesis, which keeps holy the idea of the anarchical, is in terms of the power of powerlessness, which is what I mean by the weak force of God. That is the sense described by St. Paul in First Corinthians 1 even as it picks up on what Levinas means when he says that those who are destitute and [41] laid low come to us from on high and lay claim to us.[340] The voice of God, the Word of God, the Spirit of God, is the call that calls to us without causality, power, or prestige, calling upon what is best in us.[341]

In the end, I am just proposing a theology of the cross. That is what I will now try to show—and in the process, settle an outstanding account or two with an apostle.

---

[340] If one were willing to surrender the deliciously disruptive effect of "sacred anarchy" (*hier-an-arche*), one might, on strictly Levinasian grounds, prefer to speak instead of a "holy" anarchy (which has the advantage, in American English, of sounding a little like "[raising] *holy* hell"). ...

[341] In this view I have enough textual support in the New Testament to hold off the Grand Inquisitor at least long enough to make a clean escape out the back door. I even have a theologian or two who will give me provisional cover ... In *Narratives of a Vulnerable God* (Louisville: John Knox Press, 1994), pp. 3-26, William Placher, for example, argues that the God of the New Testament is to be thought in terms of love not power, and that accordingly the sense of God's power must be ordered (or sub-ordinated) to the preeminence of God's love. The power of God in the New Testament is not to be conceived like the pagan Zeus wielding bolts of thunder at anyone who incurs his wrath. Nor is it to be taken as the arbitrary power of a mad Roman emperor like Caligula, who can destroy anything he will with a single imperial edict. These are blasphemous and pagan images that distort the power of God—our dear Peter Damian, whom I have found a way to love, is a good example of this error—that is revealed in the New Testament, as Placher shows. If, as Roger Haight explains so well in *Jesus: The Symbol of God* (Maryknoll, N.Y.: Orbis, 1999), Jesus is the revelation of God, the *eikon* of the Father, the symbol of God, then the God revealed by Jesus is revealed in powerlessness, in suffering and vulnerability, and this not just docetically, as an appearance God assumes, but quite really. If God is a father, then God is, in all fairness, also a mother, and then God is a father and mother weeping over their suffering children whose sorry fate is out of their control. I also see some signs of life in *The Openness of God*, ed. Clark Pinnock et al. (Downers Grove, Ill.: InterVarsity Press, 1994).

JEAN-LUC MARION (1946-)

Marion was born in 1946 in Meudon, France. He studied philosophy under the Marxist Louis Althusser and the Postmodernists Jacques Derrida and Gilles Deleuze at the École normale supérieure from 1967-1971. He then attended the Sorbonne from which he received a doctorate in philosophy in 1980. Marion began his career as a professor of philosophy at the University of Poitiers (1981-1988), then the University of Paris X-Nanterre (1988-1995), before settling down at the Sorbonne in 1996. Marion has also held positions at the University of Chicago since 2004, succeeding Paul Ricoeur, and the Catholic Institute of Paris.

In addition to works on the philosophy of Descartes, Marion's key philosophical works are his *Dieu sans l'être* (Paris: Arthème Fayard, 1982), *Étant donné: Essai d'une phénoménologie de la donation* (Paris: Presses Universitaires de France, 1997), *De surcroit: Études sur les phénomenes saturés* (Paris: Presses Universitaires de France, 2001), and *Givenness and Revelation* (Oxford: Oxford University Press, 2016).

On Marion consult: Horner, Robyn, *Jean-Luc Marion* (Burlington: Ashgate, 2005); Gschwandtner, Christina, *Reading Jean-Luc Marion* (Bloomsbury: Indiana University Press, 2007), *Degrees of Givenness* (Bloomsbury: Indiana University Press, 2014); MacKinlay, Shane, *Interpreting Excess* (New York: Fordham University Press, 2010); and Jones, Tamsin, *A Genealogy of Marion's Philosophy of Religion* (Bloomsbury: Indiana University Press, 2011).

The first selection is my translation of Marion's *God without Being, Dieu sans l'être* (Paris: Presses Universitaires de France, 2013), 69-75, wherein Marion famously argues that God should be conceived as love rather than as self-subsistent being. For God's nature and even existence are not really knowable via metaphysics, following the tradition of Pseudo-Dionysius and other mystics as well as postmodernism. In order to represent this fact that God is inconceivable and unseekable for human reason, we should thus cross out the name of God whenever we write it: G⊗d. Rather we know God as a saturated phenomenon, as Marion will later say, a phenomenon that overwhelms our intellect and which contains an excessive encounter that cannot be conceptualized. This latter view is represented in the second selection, "The Saturated Phenomenon," in D. Janicaud et al, eds., *Phenomenology and the "Theological Turn"* (New York: Fordham University Press, 2000), 211-216. I have also provided an excerpt of Marion's apologetical "non-apologetics, "Evidence and Bedazzlement," *Prolegomena to Charity*, tr. Stephen Lewis (New York: Fordham University Press, 2002): pp. 53-58, 65-68. Here Marion defends a non-apologetics as opposed to an argumentative apologetical machine, a logic of love instead of a logic of syllogisms, wherein we do not appeal to constraining reasons but rather seek to engender an openness to Revealing Love in the heart of others.

God without Being (1982)[342]

Double Idolatry

The Screen of Being

[69] But does it go without saying that God would have to be, therefore to be as [a] being (supreme, plural, however one wishes) to give Himself as God? Whence does it arise that Being is admitted without question as the temple open (or closed) in advance to any theophany past or to come? And could not one even suspect, conversely, [70] that the temple of Being, by the definition and axiom of the thought of Being as such, could in no sense assist, call for, admit, or promise whatever would *be* concerning what one should not even name–God? And if this suspicion need not be confirmed, can one at least raise it legitimately, and need one be astonished that it does not astonish more both the followers and the readers of Heidegger? Undoubtedly, if "God" is, He is a being; but does God have to be?

In order not to have to avoid this question, and because it seems incontestable to us that the texts of Heidegger texts do avoid it, we will say that it is necessary to speak of a second idolatry in this precise sense. That it bears on the "more divine god"[343] does not invalidate, but confirms this idolatry: for what "God" thus allows that an aim determines his greater or lesser divinity, if not that "God" which results from a gaze both pious and blasphemous? What assurance would permit us to introduce a more legitimate equivalence between God and Being, where He would still play a role of being, than that between God and the *causa sui* "God" of metaphysics? Or again, does not the quest for the "more divine god" impose, more than going beyond onto-theo-logy, also going beyond ontological difference, in short, no longer attempting to think of God in view of a being, because one will have given up, first of all, thinking of Him on the basis of Being? To think of God without any condition, not even that of Being, therefore to think of God without claiming to list or describe Him

---

343 See, amongst other items, *Nietzsche* (Stuttgart: Klett-Cotta, 2008), vol. 1, p. 324 et *Identität und Differenz* (Stuttgart: Klett-Cotta, 2002), p. 65, French translation *Questions* (Paris: Gallimard, 1968), I, p. 306.

as a being.

But what indeed can permit and guarantee the attempt at a thought of God without and outside of ontological difference allow and promise?–The danger that this critical requirement [71] renders, in fact, the whole of thought immediately impossible cannot be minimized. Indeed, to think outside of ontological difference eventually condemns one to not being able to think at all. But precisely no longer being able to think, when it is a question of God, does not indicate either absurdity or impropriety, inasmuch as God Himself, in order to be thought of, must be thought of as "*id quo majus cogitari nequit*," in other words as what goes beyond, confuses, worries all thought, even non-representative. By definition and decree, God, if He has to be thought about, cannot encounter any theoretical space equal to His measure, because His measure exerts itself in our eyes as exceeding measure [*démesure*]. The ontological difference itself and therefore also Being becomes too small (even if they are universals, better yet: because they form a universe for us, because in them the world "worlds") to pretend to offer the dimension, still less the "divine abode," where God would become thinkable. Whence Biblical Revelation seems, in its way, to give a confirmation, or at least an indication, when it mentions, under the same name, what one *can* (but not must) understand as *Sum qui sum*, hence God as Being, and what one *must*, at the same time, understand as a denial of all identity––"I am who I want to be." Being says nothing about God that God cannot immediately contest. Being, even and especially in *Exodus* 3:14, says nothing about God; or does not say anything determinate about him. It is therefore necessary to recognize that the impossibility, or at least the extreme difficulty, of thinking outside of ontological difference, could, in some way, justly suit the impossibility–itself, indisputable and definitive–of thinking of God as such. Ontological difference, *nearly* indispensable to all thought, is thus offered as a negative *propaedeutic* of the unthinkable thought of God. [It is the] ultimate idol, the most dangerous, but also the most educational and, in its [72] way, profitable, since it offers itself as an obstacle which, knocked down and trampled upon, becomes an ultimate scaffolding–*scabellum pedibus tuis*–without entering into the unthinkable, the indispensable unthinkable [*indispensable impensable*]. Because the unthinkable here has no provisional or negative meaning: indispensable, in fact, the unthinkable offers the only face critiqued by the one of whom it is a question of thinking. Let us clearly admit that we can only think of God under the figure of the unthinkable, but of an unthinkable which goes beyond what we cannot think as well as what we can think; for what I cannot think still pertains to *my* thought, and therefore remains thinkable *for me*. The unthinkable, on the contrary, taken as such, pertains to God Himself, and characterizes Him as the *aura* of his advent, the glory of his insistence, the brilliance of his withdrawal. The unthinkable determines God with the seal of his definitive indetermination for a created and finite thought. The unthinkable masks the gap, the rupture ever open, between God and the idol, better yet: between God and the pretension of every possible idolatry. The unthinkable forces us to substitute for the idolatrous quotation strokes surrounding "God," the very God whom no mark of knowledge demarcates; and, to put it otherwise, let us cross out G⊗d with a cross, provisionally of Saint Andrew, which shows the limit of the temptations, conscious or naïve, to blaspheme the unthinkable in an idol. The cross does not indicate that G⊗d should disappear as a concept, or intervene only in function of a hypothesis in the process of validation, but that the unthinkable enters into the field of our thought only by rendering it unthinkable, by excess, that is to say by critiquing it: to cross out G⊗d, in fact, indicates and recalls that G⊗d crosses out our thought because He saturates it; better yet, enters into our thought only by forcing it to critique itself. We only trace the crossing out of G⊗d on his written name because, first of all, He exercises it on our thought about Him as His unthinkableness [*impensable*]. [73] We only cross out the name of G⊗d in order to show ourselves, ourselves of course, that His unthinkableness [*impensable*] saturates our thinking–from its origin and forever.

To think of G⊗d, therefore, outside of ontological difference, outside of the question of Being, at the risk of the unthinkable, indispensable, but unsurpassable as well. What name, what concept and what sign are still feasible? No doubt only one, love, or as we want to say, as Saint John proposes it–"God [is] love [*agapè*]" (1 John 4:8). Why love? Because this term, which Heidegger, like all metaphysics, albeit in another manner, maintains in a derived and secondary state, still remains, paradoxically, sufficiently unthought to, one day at least, free the thought of G⊗d from the second idolatry. This task, immense and, in a sense, still intact, requires elaborating love conceptually (and therefore, in return, elaborating the concept through love), to the point where its full speculative power is deployed. We cannot here, even in outline, undertake to indicate its lineaments. Suffice it to mark two decisive traits of love, and their speculative commitments.

a. Love does not suffer from the unthinkable, nor from the absence of conditions, but is strengthened therein. For the nature of love consists in this, that it gives itself; now the gift, in order to give itself, does not need an interlocutor to receive it, nor an abode to accommodate it, nor a condition to assure or confirm it. Which means, first, that as love, Gᴀd can straightaway transgress idolatrous constraints; for idolatry—especially the second kind—is exercised through the conditions of possibilities (Being, if "God" is a being, the "divine abode," if "God" depends on the divine, etc.), which alone provide "God" with a place worthy of him, and therefore, if the conditions of this dignity cannot be met, assign Him to a residence in escheat, therefore assign Him to [74] marginality. If, on the contrary, God is not because He does not have to be, but loves, then by definition, no condition can any longer restrict His initiative, amplitude, and ecstasy. Love loves unconditionally, from the simple fact that it loves, He also loves without limit or restriction. No refusal rebuffs or limits what, in order to give itself, does not expect the slightest welcome, nor require the least consideration. This means then that, as an interlocutor of love, the human does not first have to claim to provide a "divine abode" for it—assuming that this very claim can be sustained—but purely and simply to accept it. Accept it, or more modestly, not shy away from it. Thus, even the inevitable inability of the human to correspond to the destiny that love freely imposes on him is not enough to disqualify the initiative nor the accomplishment. For in order to accomplish the response to love, it is necessary and sufficient to want it, since only the will can refuse or receive; such that the human cannot impose any condition, *even negative*, on the initiative of Gᴀd. Thus no aim shows up any more to idolatrously determine the possibility or the impossibility of an access to and from "God."

b. There is more: to think of Gᴀd as love [*agapè*] prohibits us just as much from ever fixing the aim on first visible, or freezing it on an invisible mirror. Why? Because, unlike the concept which, by the definition itself of apprehension, gathers up what it comprehends, and which, as a result, almost inevitably ends in an idol, love (even and especially if it comes to make itself thought about, to give itself—by surplus—to thinking) does not claim to understand, since it does not intend to claim at all; it postulates its own donation, a donation wherein the donor coincides strictly with this gift [*don*], without any restriction, restraint, nor regulation. Thus love only gives itself by abandoning itself, ceaselessly transgressing the limits of its own gift, to the point of transplanting itself outside of [75] itself. In consequence: this transferal of love outside of itself, without end or limit, immediately prohibits fixation on a response, a representation, an idol. It belongs to the essence of love–*diffusivum sui*–to submerge, like a tidal wave submerges the wall of a jetty, any delimitation, whether representative or existential, of its flow: love excludes the idol, or better yet, includes it by subverting it. It can even be defined as the movement of a donation which, in order to advance unconditionally, imposes on itself a self-critique without end or restraint. For love retains nothing, neither itself, nor its representation. The transcendence of love signifies, first of all, that it transcends itself in a critical movement where nothing–not even Nothingness/Nothing–can contain the excess of an absolute donation–absolute: the conquering of everything that is not exercised in this abandonment itself.

The second idolatry can therefore be surpassed only by letting God be thought about on the basis of His sole and pure demand [*exigence*]. Such a demand goes beyond the limit of a concept–even that of metaphysics in its onto-theo-logy–but also the limit of any condition whatsoever–even that of being conceived in terms of ontological difference. God can only give Himself to be thought about without idolatry on the basis of Himself: to give Himself to be thought about as love, therefore as gift; to give Himself to be thought about as a thought of the gift. Or better yet, as a gift for thought, as a gift that gives itself for thought. But a gift that gives itself forever, can only be thought about by a thought that gives itself to the gift to be thought about [*à penser*]. A thought which gives itself [*se donne*] can alone give itself over [*s'adonner*] to a gift for thought [*pour la pensée*]. But what is it for thought to give itself, if not to love?

"The Saturated Phenomenon" (1992)[344]

[211] In order to introduce the concept of the saturated phenomenon in phenomenology, we have just described it as *invisable* (unforeseeable) according to quantity, *unbearable* according to quality, but also *unconditioned* (absolved from any horizon) according to relation, and *irreducible* to the I (incapable of being looked at) according to modality. These four characteristics imply the term-for-term reversal of all the rubrics under which Kant classifies the [212] principles and thus the phenomena that these determine. However, in relation to Husserl, these new characteristics are organized in a more complex way; the first two—the *invisable* and the *unbearable*—offer no difficulty de jure for the "principle of all principles," for what intuition gives can quantitatively and qualitatively exceed the scope of the gaze; it is sufficient that intuition actually give it. The case is not the same for the last two characteristics: the "principle of all principles" presupposes the horizon and the constituting *I* as two unquestioned presuppositions of anything that would be constituted in general as a phenomenon; but the saturated phenomenon, inasmuch as it is unconditioned by a horizon and irreducible to an *I*, pretends to a possibility that is freed from these two conditions; it therefore contradicts and exceeds the "principle of all principles." Husserl, who nonetheless surpassed the Kantian metaphysics of the phenomenon, must himself be surpassed in order to reach the possibility of the saturated phenomenon. Even and especially with the "principle of all principles" Husserl maintains a twofold reserve toward possibility. Nevertheless, that reserve of Husserl *toward* possibility can prove to be a reserve *of* phenomenology itself—which still maintains a reserve of possibility, in order itself to be surpassed toward a possibility without reserve. Because it gives itself without condition or restraint, the saturated phenomenon offers the paradigm of the phenomenon without reserve. Thus, in the guiding thread of the saturated phenomenon, phenomenology finds its ultimate possibility: not only the possibility that surpasses actuality, but the possibility that surpasses the very conditions of possibility, the

[344] ["The Saturated Phenomenon," in Dominique Janicaud, et al., eds., *Phenomenology and the "Theological Turn": The French Debate*, translated by Thomas A. Carlson. Copyright © 2000 by Fordham University Press. All rights reserved. Reprinted with permission of Fordham University Press, https://www.fordhampress.com.]

possibility of unconditioned possibility—in other words, the possibility of the impossible, the saturated phenomenon.

The saturated phenomenon must not be understood as a limit case, an exceptional, vaguely irrational, in short, a "mystical," case of phenomenality. On the contrary, it indicates the coherent and conceptual completion of the most operative definition of the phenomenon: it alone truly appears as itself, of itself, and starting from itself, since it alone appears without the limits of a [213] horizon and without the reduction to an *I*. We will therefore call this appearance that is purely of itself and starting from itself,[345] this phenomenon that does not subject its possibility to any preliminary determination, a *revelation*. And we insist on this— here it is purely and simply a matter of the phenomenon taken in its fullest meaning.

Moreover, the history of philosophy has a long-standing knowledge of such saturated phenomena. One could go so far as to maintain that none of the most important metaphysicians has avoided the description of one or more saturated phenomena, even at the price of a head-on contradiction of his own presuppositions. Among many fairly obvious examples, let us simply call to mind Descartes and Kant.

(a) Descartes, who everywhere else reduces the phenomenon to the idea and the idea to the object, nevertheless thinks the idea of infinity as a saturated phenomenon. According to quantity, the idea of infinity is not obtained by summation or successive synthesis, but "tota simul"; thus, the gaze [*intueri*] becomes the surprise of admiration [*admirari*]. According to quality, it admits no finite degree, but a *maximum*: "maxime Clara et distincta," "maxime vera." According to relation, it maintains no analogy with any idea at all: "nihil univoce"; indeed, it exceeds every horizon since it remains incomprehensible, capable only of being touched by thought: "attingam quomodolibet cogitatione." According to modality, far from letting itself be led back to a constituting *I*, it comprehends the *I* without letting itself be comprehended by it: "non tam capere quam a ipsa capi," such that

---

345 [That is], "das Sich-an-ihm-selbst-zeigende," Heidegger, *Sein und Zeit*, 10th ed. (Tübingen: Niemeyer, 1963), n. 7, p. 31, 12. See "das an ihm selbst Offenbare von ihm selbst her sehen lassen," *Prolegomena zur Geschichte des Zeitbegriffs*, n. 2, *Gesamtausgabe* (Frankfurt am Main: Vittorio Klostermann, 1979), vol. 20, p. 117. The "von ihm selbst her" indeed indicates an appearance "of itself" in the strict sense of "starting from itself."

perhaps even the ego could also be interpreted at times as one who is called [*un interpellé*]. But furthermore, would it not suffice to translate "idea of infinity" word for word by "saturated phenomenon" in order to establish our conclusion?

(b) Kant furnishes an example of the saturated phenomenon that is all the more significant insofar as it does not concern, as does [214] Descartes's, rational theology: in fact, it is a question of the sublime. We relied above on the "aesthetic idea" to challenge the principle of the shortage of intuition and to introduce the possibility of a saturation. In fact, already with the doctrine of the sublime we are dealing with a saturated phenomenon. Indeed, according to quantity, the sublime has neither form nor order, since it is great "beyond all comparison," absolutely and not comparatively (*absolute, schlechthin, bloss*)[346] According to quality, it contradicts taste as a "negative pleasure" and it provokes a "feeling of inadequacy," a feeling of "monstrosity."[347] According to relation, it very clearly escapes any analogy and any horizon since it literally represents "unlimitedness [*Unbegrenztheit*].[348] According to modality, finally, far from agreeing with our power of knowing, "it can seem [*erscheinen mag*] in its form to contradict the purpose [*zweckwidrig*] of our faculty of judgment"; the relation of our faculty of judgment to the phenomenon is therefore reversed, to the point that it is the phenomenon that hereafter "looks at" the *I* in "respect."[349] The Kantian example of the sublime would thus permit us to widen the field of application for the concept of the saturated phenomenon.

From now on we can recapitulate. Phenomena can be classified, according to their increasing intuitive content, in three fundamental domains. (a) The phenomena that are deprived of intuition or that are poor in intuitions: for example, formal languages (endowed with categorial intuition by Husserl) or

---

[346] *Kritik der Urteilskraft*, respectively n. 25, *Gesammelte Schriften* (Berlin: Walter de Gruyter, 1962), vol. 5, p. 248; *Formlosigkeit*, n. 24, p. 247; *Unordnung*, n. 23, p. 246; "über alle Vergleichung," and *schlechthin* n. 25, p. 248 (and n. 26, p. 251).

[347] *Kritik der Urteilskraft*, respectively n. 23, op. cit., p. 245; *Gefühl der Unangemessenheit*, n. 26, p. 252; *Ungeheuer*, n. 26, p. 253.

[348] *Kritik der Urteilskraft*, respectively *Unbegränzheit*, n. 23, p. 244. See "keine angemessene Darstellung," p. 245.

[349] *Kritik der Urteilskraft*, n. 23, p. 245. See *subjektive Unzweckmässigkeit*, n. 26, p. 252; *Widerstreit* of the subjective end, n. 27, p. 258. Respect (*Achtung*) comes in n. 27, p. 257. Here we follow Philippe Lacoue-Labarthe in *Du sublime* (Paris: Belin, 1988).

mathematical idealities (whose pure intuition is established by Kant). (b) The common law phenomena, whose signification (aimed at by intention) can ideally receive an adequate intuitive fulfillment, but that, right at the start and most of the time, do not reach such [215] fulfillment. In these first two domains, the constitution of objects is rendered possible precisely because the shortage of intuition authorizes comprehension, foresight, and reproduction. (c) There remain, finally, the saturated phenomena, which the excess of intuition shields from objective constitution.

Conveniently, we can distinguish two types. (i) First, pure historical events: by definition nonrepeatable, they occur most often without having been foreseen; since through a surfeit of intuitive given they escape objectivation, their intelligibility excludes comprehension and demands that one move on to hermeneutics;[350] intuitive saturation surpasses a single horizon and imposes multiple hermeneutics within several horizons; finally, the pure historical event not only occurs to its witness (the nonconstituting *I*) without the latter comprehending it, but itself, in return, comprehends the *I* (the constituted *I*): the *I* is comprehended on the basis of the event that occurs to it in the very measure that the *I* itself does not comprehend the event. Pure events offer a type of saturated phenomenon that is historical and thus communal and in principle communicable. (ii) Such is not always the case for the second type: the phenomena of revelation. Let us repeat that by *revelation* we here intend a strictly phenomenological concept: an appearance that is purely of itself and starting from itself, that does not subject its possibility to any preliminary determination. Such revealed phenomena occur principally in three domains. First, the picture as a spectacle that, due to excess of intuition, cannot be constituted but still can be looked at (the idol). Next, a particular face that I love, which has become invisible not only because it dazzles me, but above all because in it I want to look and can look only at its invisible gaze weighing on mine (the icon). Finally, the theophany, where the surfeit of intuition leads to the paradox that an invisible gaze visibly envisages me and loves me. And it is here that the question of the possibility of a phenomenology of religion would be posed in terms that are not new (for it is only a matter of pushing the phenomenological intention to its end), but simple.

---

[350] Such is the objective of Paul Ricoeur, particularly with *Temps et récit, vol. 3: Le temps raconté* (Paris: Éditions Points, 1985). Our analyses quite obviously owe much to his decisive works.

"Evidence and Bedazzlement" (1986)

[53] When a simple-minded and recurrent criticism sets itself against the discourse put forth under the name of apologetics, at what does it aim its apparent indictment? Usually, the criticism stigmatizes the claim, supposedly held by the ecclesial intelligentsia, to rigorous proof of the truth of Christianity by means of a compelling conceptual system—an insupportable claim, incidentally, first and above all because it supposes that Christian, and namely Catholic, thought has at its disposal a sufficient conceptual system, thus marking itself with a "triumphalism" worthy of condemnation. The Christian faith would of course have nothing to win by advancing itself with such a train of reasons or arguments, because "poverty" and "self-denial" befit its fundamental humility. Let us put aside the question of whether, historically, the Church might have practiced an apologetics that was triumphal to the point of excess,[351] and whether the humility of charity [54] necessitates the cultivation of intellectual wretchedness; let us instead ask if such an attitude does not lead, with regard to apologetics, to a surreptitious recuperation, and also to a theological misunderstanding.

Nonapologetics

A recuperation: ostensibly renounce all preparation or rational confirmation of faith, and thus assure the non-Christian or "atheistic" (as we think we can say) interlocutor that we will not

---

[351] For the most part, it is legitimate to doubt this. Indeed, in the most significant case, Roman authority spoke plainly: Georg Hermes (1775-1831) held (among others, in *Einleitung in die christkatholische Theologie* (Münster: Coppenrath, 1819) that each point of revelation could and should be the object of a rational demonstration, and that, while awaiting such demonstration, the employment of a positive doubt was legitimate. This position, tending to collapse the "content" of faith into the "means" of believing, was expressly condemned by Gregory XVI (*Dum acerbissomas*, 1835; Denzinger, *Enchiridion Symbolorum*, n. 1619; etc.). This condemnation obviously does not contradict in any way the affirmation of Vatican I that God *certo cognosci posse* (Denziger 1785, 1806), inasmuch as this certainty concerns God as *rerum omnium principium et finem*, as *creatorem et Dominum nostrum*, that is to say, God as manifested by the *visibilia*, and not in the definitive figure of Christ. The argumentation remains strictly rational, because the revelation of God as Love has not yet entered in. But a finally Christic apologetics must go all the way to this last point.

deploy against him any argumentative machine (because we lack one), and that his identity will thereby be perfectly respected (even if the obliging Christian risks losing his own)—such an approach has at least one consequence. The Christian, clearly having withdrawn from all intellectual imperialism, no longer disturbs the "conflict of ideas" (even if, in another sense, he can become bothersome by dint of his smiling pusillanimity); he stands there in his place, and nowhere but his place. The renunciation of all apologetics can also facilitate the Christian's warm welcome into his cultural surroundings and permit him to be accepted. But how then does nonapologetics differ, as to its result, from apologetics? Certainly, such good will must come at the price of a certain weakness: it is an already almost anonymous Christian, because without theology, if not without Church, that those who tolerate being called "anonymous Christians" will admit into their circle, because their benevolent commiseration knows perfectly his inoffensive and childish impoliteness. Nevertheless, a difference remains: apologetics, with its reasons, attempts to gain Christ's admittance (at the risk of the Christian's being poorly received), while nonapologetics, free of reasons, tries to gain the "Christian's" reception (at the price, sometimes, of Christ's not being admitted). The aim of convincing, or at least of trying to please, is the same for both; the point of application has simply been displaced. One might surmise, then, that the change in attitude toward apologetics reflects a conceptual displacement in dogmatics, [55] and that the renunciation of constructed apologetic discourse should be recognized according to decidedly conceptual themes: to a dogmatics that is suffering from mounting difficulties (at least in France) in defining both its epistemological status and, above all, the irreducible and specific primacy of the "Christianity" of the Christic fact, there can obviously correspond only a nonapologetics, which perhaps no longer has at its disposal even the means to sustain a dialogue with anyone at all. Such continuity between dogmatics and apologetics stands out, then, all the better because the same negative index, at times, seems to affect them; in what we are considering here, this point says much, for it signals a new status for apologetics. The aim would no longer be (but has this ever been the goal?) to develop an argumentative machine, which would claim, like well-executed propaganda, to force an intimate conviction by force of reasons, or rather of popular slogans, an approach that testifies more to a will to dominate and strengthen an apparatus, than to a gesture of love revealing Love. Rather, the aim would be the external expansion of what shapes, lifts, and incites dogmatics from the depths of itself, or rather from the depths of what convokes and institutes it: the tremendous and incompressible δύναμις τοῦ Θεοῦ [power of God] that exposes its explosion in liturgy, contemplation, and dogmatic theology, in order to be carried on naturally in apologetics, supposing of course that a perfect, humble, and poor availability toward the Spirit of God poured out in our hearts is natural. Apologetics does not so much constitute a discipline other than dogmatics, nor even its prolongation or its pastoral transcription, as it offers the index of the impregnation by the power of God of theological meditation as a whole. For a thought's power of conviction rests not so much in the energy of the zealot ... as it does in the power of the thought. How much more so if this thought comes to us from He who "sustains all things by the power of his word" (Hebrews 1:3).

Necessary Failure

[56] We have risked a theological misunderstanding, and for a reason. The spiritual relation of expansion between dogmatics and apologetics becomes unrecognizable as soon as one believes that one can fix as the goal of apologetics to convince, necessarily and by reasons. From this first hypothesis, two choices appear. Either (and this is at present the most widespread case) apologetics appears useless, because its goal–to convince, or at least to "open a dialogue"–can be reached by other means than reasons; the confiding exchange of opinions, the silent community of experiences the sharing of hopes and struggles in a word the irrational of "lived experience," would allow much more efficiently for the convincing of those who are not Christian of the truth of the God who is revealed in Jesus Christ or at least for the admittance of oneself as a Christian among them. But such silence, in its refusal to speak, already says too much: it implies that faith, in order to transmit itself, requires neither speech nor listening (in opposition to Romans 10:14-18), and thus that, finally and quite logically, faith does not transmit itself at all. With this assertion, an "invention of faith" must be supposed the speaking of which does not happen without an uproar, and implies once again one or several discourses in dogmatic theology. Dogmatic theology will have to justify the apologetic silence, whose taciturnity will often appear gregarious, by dint of explanations. Thus we find ourselves brought to the other possibility: apologetics can hold the sense of being able to convince necessarily through demonstrations; this temptation certainly does not have priority among the threats menacing us at this time, but its current disappearance perhaps

reflects our situation all the better, because such was for a long time its aim, and this aim no doubt remains operative in the sharpest current criticisms of apologetics. Let us suppose–in what is an extreme and unthinkable case–that an apologetic discourse were to attain such a degree of rigor that it could claim to convince necessarily a normally rational mind. What result would in [57] fact have been gained? The voluntary moment of adherence would come up only as a simple consequence of the evidence, by a sort of moral necessity, following the principle that from a great light in the understanding there follows a great inclination in the will. What is called "conversion" is played out precisely in this consequence, which ought to be self-evident, and which, most of the time, seems all the less self-evident, exactly because the proofs claim to have established their result. Who has not come across these minds who, fine connoisseurs of dogmatics and Christian spirituality, intellectually disposed to expound them and justify them, never cease their whole life long to avoid the consequences and to dodge, by the inky cloud of a limitless sympathy, the adversity of a faith decision? So long as the will does not freely will to love, apologetics has gained nothing. Consequently, in not recognizing the most decisive factor, an apologetics that means to be absolutely demonstrative would, by its very success, be condemned to the most patent failure. What can be demonstrated has no value, Nietzsche claimed; for in saying it all and even too much, we say infinitely too little. Renouncing apologetics, like succeeding in it, leads to failure. Why?

Because apologetics does not correctly understand its office insofar as it claims to convince necessarily and through reasons, where it should claim only to constrain (unless it aims to constrain where it should instead hope to convince). Let us be more precise: a constraint is legitimately tolerable only where its exercise does not introduce any heteronomy. In such a case, the reasons that an argument assembles can constrain reason because reason in such a case still follows only its own necessity. If, then, apologetics laid claim only to rational evidence, it could, supposing it had the means, be content with constraint, that is to say, with leading a mind, necessarily, to the end of a demonstration. But apologetics is concerned with something wholly other: to convince. To convince supposes a new factor, the will (or whatever one wants to call the ultimate compelling cause of existential decision), which decides–that is to say, decides for itself on the [58] basis of itself alone, such that all other causal authority appears exterior and therefore ineffectual, whether it claims to be threatening or helpful. Only the will can allow itself to be convinced, and all constraint of reason by reasons remains totally heterogeneous to it, remains on the threshold and decides nothing. Apologetics, in using reasons alone, can, in the best of cases, constrain reason; but even in this event, it will not for all that convince the will, and will fail in its duty at the precise moment when it believes it is fulfilling it. As for confusing everything, and hoping to constrain the will, because reasons cannot do it, one can aspire to do so only by having recourse to force; but force, no matter how subtle it might be, emphasizes and confirms all the more the exteriority of its violence, which it never tops extending. If it wants to leave nothing outside rational constraint, apologetics loses any adherence of the will, which alone can allow itself to be convinced. In short, it is only by admitting the irreducible gap between constraint (of reason by reasons) and conviction (of the will by itself) that apologetics recognizes its proper task, which begins beyond any demonstration. Not only when demonstration reveals itself to be impossible, but also when it seems fully established. For it is then up to the will to let itself be convinced, in its heart of hearts. Thus, because it accedes to its proper task, apologetics finds itself destitute: without reasons, for by right all the sufficient reasons in the world do not suffice to convince a will. In clearly distinguishing constraint from conviction, apologetics runs up against its originality and its destitution: it becomes possible as such only in admitting the impossibility of a necessary success. Its identity coincides with its failure. ...

Bedazzlement

[65] Still, when defined thus, apologetics would appear to lead from evidence to obscurity, and to rely on the irrational. But apart from the fact that the domain of the will, being here radically foreign to the order of reasons, remains thus also unharmed by any irrationality, the nature of the obscurity at issue here still must be correctly understood. On this condition alone, this obscurity will be able to enter upon another clarity. If "God does not manifest himself to men as obviously as he might" (*Pensées*, §556/449), no doubt this is in order to indicate to the will its particular and fitting task, but especially it is because, just as "first principles have much too [66] much evidence for us" (*Pensées*, §72/199), so too what Jesus Christ reveals of God shows much too much evidence for our gaze. For if God opts for "the presence of a hidden God" (*Pensées*, §449/156), this is because no other presence would remain bearable: no mortal can see him without

dying, no eye can fix on his shining forth without blinding itself in such a bedazzling sight. What blindness interprets as a simple obscurity must be understood at base as a bedazzlement, in which, in the revelatory figure of Jesus Christ, the Father enters into an absolute epiphany, though filtered through finitude. If blindness sees nothing there and does not even suspect bedazzlement, the fault lies not with revelation, but with the gaze that cannot bear the evidence. In effect, if what reveals itself is always summed up in Love, then only the gaze that believes, and thus only the will that loves, can welcome it.[352] Thus only the conversion of the gaze can render the eye apt to recognize the blinding evidence of love in what bedazzles it. Standing before Christ on the Cross, who contains in Himself all the prophecies, and who a placard identifies—in three languages!—as the King of the Jews, those who do not accept to love him see nothing, except the confirmation of their denial; those who do love him (the "good thief," Mary, John, the soldier of Mark 15:34) see, with a clarity that is variable to be sure but always indisputable, the highest figure of God, royal in his *kenosis*. The same single figure thus provokes this ambivalence, not because it is itself weighted with the least ambiguity, but because each mind uses its own measure to interpret it. This measure is [67] defined by what the gaze can bear; for simply in order to see a figure (that is, to let a figure constitute itself in the realm of the visible), it behooves us first to bear its brilliance, to support the sight of it. As when confronted with the obscene (the menacing as well as the forbidden), the divine, and above all the *kenosis of the Son*, our gaze cannot remain fixed; it blinks and closes. It finds too much to see there, too much to envisage and look at squarely, and, thus, too much to interpret and to allow to interpret us, and so it flees; our furtive gaze turns away from and deserts the visible whose effrontery threatens us. In short, our gaze deserts, and closes. Only love, "which bears all" (1 Corinthians 13:7), can bear with its gaze Love's excess. In proportion to our love, our gaze can open, be it only by blinking, to

---

[352] See Pascal, *Pensées*, §564/835: "There is enough evidence to condemn and not enough to convince, so that it should be apparent that those who follow it are prompted to do so by grace and lot by reason, and those who evade it are prompted by concupiscence and not by reason"; see also *Lettre IV aux Rouannez*, ... (*Oeuvres Complètes*, ed. Louis Lafuma (Paris: Éditions du Seuil, 1963), p. 267; translated by Émile Caillat and John C. Blankenagel, *Great Shorter Works of Pascal* (Philadelphia: Westminster Press, 1948), p. 146).

the evidence of Love. In this proportion also, bedazzlements can become evidence, by the simple fact that we can envisage upholding them. But once again, only love can bear certain sights without flinching: the suffering of a mind that is in bodily agony, the nakedness of a body rendered spiritual by its fullness of pleasure, God's abandon in the manifested form of a humanity.

This indeed is why one always begins in apologetics with the weakest evidence possible, which requires a small investment of love to be seen and thus interpreted; one begins, at the threshold, with arguments based on fact (Jesus historically lived; he claimed divinity, and was put to death for it; a community believed in his resurrection to the point of likewise risking its life; for twenty centuries, his disciples have remained)–the weakest possible evidence precisely because it "calls upon" each and every one without demanding a choice or an answer. Then apologetics proposes other arguments that, in demanding a growing degree of interpretation, enjoin a greater effort from the gaze (for instance, the completion of the prophecies, the meaningful succession of historical events, and so on), until, at its limit, it culminates in the ultimate bedazzlement, before which any human gaze, as loving as it may be, will never stop blinking until the Holy Spirit qualifies it absolutely and permits it to receive bedazzlement as an unsurpassable [68] evidence, that is, as a proof (in the English sense of the word): the Resurrection, absolute theophany. In this sense only, then, does faith have proofs at its disposal, yet these are proofs upon which faith does not rest, for only faith can see them; a fact by which these proofs escape radically from any suspicion of "subjectivism."

JEAN-YVES LACOSTE (1953-)

Lacoste was born in 1953 and entered the École Normale Supérieure in 1972 where he studied with Jacques Derrida and received an aggregation in 1976. He was ordained in 1981 then attended the Catholic Institute of Toulouse from 1981 to 1983 acquiring a doctorate in theology. He followed this up with studies at the University of Poitiers from 1985 to 1988 with Jean-Luc Marion where Lacoste received his doctorate in philosophy. He has taught at Clare Hall, Cambridge since 1990 and the Catholic Institute of Paris since 2001. He received the Prix Cardinal-Grente in 2019.

Lacoste's key work is his *Expérience et absolu: Questions disputées sur l'humanité de l'homme* (Paris: Presses Universitaires de France, 1994), translated as *Experience and the Absolute: Disputed Questions on the Humanity of Man*, trans. Mark Raftery-Skehan (New York: Fordham University Press, 2004). Also noticeable are his *La phénoménalité de Dieu: Neuf études* (Paris: Cerf, 2008), translated as *The Appearing of God*, trans. Oliver O'Donovan (Oxford: Oxford University Press, 2018) and *From Theology to Theological Thinking* (Charlottesville: University of Virginia Press, 2014).

For more on Lacoste consult Gschwandtner, Christina M., *Postmodern Apologetics?: Arguments for God in Contemporary Philosophy* (New York: Fordham University Press, 2012), pp. 163-183; Schrijvers, Joeri, *An Introduction to Jean-Yves Lacoste* (London: Routledge, 2016); Wardley, Kenneth Jason, *Praying to a French God: The Theology of Jean-Yves Lacoste* (London: Routledge, 2014); DeLay, Steven, *Phenomenology in France* (London: Routledge, 2018), pp. 165-199.

The following selection is from Lacoste's *Experience and the Absolute*, trans. Mark Raftery-Skehan (New York: Fordham University Press, 2004), pp. 41-49, 90-93, wherein Lacoste engages in a phenomenology of the liturgy and describes how liturgy is more of a non-experience of God and a patient waiting for the God who will come in the Parousia.

Experience and the Absolute (1994)[353]

Nonexperience and Nonevent

Opening and Exposition

[41] It is a primary truth to state that, if the Absolute is a free subject, if man owes to it what he is, and if this debt should not pass by unacknowledged (or, at least, may not pass by unnoticed), then the elementary structures of experience do not destine us to atheism, paganism, or both. It would, however, be untrue to suppose that a relation to the absolute natively structures experience. Dasein exists in the world without God–this does not presume the nonexistence of God but teaches only that the world, as world, draws a veil between Dasein and God. ... Our inherence in the world, or the shelter given to us by the earth, can suffice to quality what we are: we can choose to exist solely in the mode of Dasein or in that of the "mortal." But just as we are free to affirm the existence of an Absolute who is someone with whom a relation has been promised, so we can choose to exist in his presence: to expose ourselves to him. In so doing, we refuse to exist under any ultimate claim world and earth might make on us. Ex-position declares itself indifferent to our opening onto the world. This of course, means that liturgy, if we take the risk (for risk there is since we thereby lose every verifiable measure of our being), may redistribute all the terms in which the question of our identify is posed.

Dwelling at the Limit

[42] Who, then, am I and where am I when I pray? To the second part of this question, a response has already been provided–we said that [43] what was involved there was primary in our investigations. This does not, however, exempt us from a more precise questioning of those who refuse to identify themselves other than by respectfully invoking the figures of the humanity of man that are Dasein and the "mortal." Liturgy is a worldly and historical work: it is also necessary to interpret the link that it maintains with the grounds of a worldly logic of existence furnished by the topological. It is, furthermore, a work that

---

[353] [Jean-Yves Lacoste, *Experience and the Absolute*, translated by Mark Raftery-Skehan. Copyright © 2004 by Fordham University Press. All rights reserved. Used with permission of Fordham University Press, https://www.fordhampress.com.]

constantly reminds us of the distance that history establishes between man and the Absolute. We pray, of course, in order to praise—it is in praise that the prayer manifests its essence in its purity—and praise can pass for the historical image or inchoation of an eschatological practice. But we always pray in the knowledge of the inescapable reality of the world and in the knowledge that it interposes itself between us and a God (whose existence and presence it maintains in the realm of the chiaroscuro) who grants us both our existence and the chiaroscuro presence. It nevertheless remains, and this is the point we must bear in mind, that liturgy, though no experience can fail to recognize it, does not simply sanction this interposition. We pray here or there, but always while submitting our relation to place to a subversion. We must perhaps take another step forward in our inquiry. The liturgical subversion of the topological is still—paradoxically—a mode of inherence. It has neither the theoretical ambition nor the power to create a theophanic space out of world or earth. On the other hand, and as we have already seen in § 9, that it calls into question both our usage of place and, more radically, the reality of our inherence is an essential characteristic of liturgy: the world actually appears in the mode of closure, but of a closure that can be broken through.

To the world, or to the earth, which are not themselves beings but conditions presiding over the presencing of beings, we cannot attribute a closure, as we can, for example, to the cosmos; this would amount to a confusion of categories. But it is by no means absurd to affirm that, in liturgical experience, experience lived within the horizon of the world lets itself be interpreted as a figure enclosed by experience, and that liturgy enables us to break free from this closure. By giving itself, from within the world, a horizon not of the world, liturgy proves that the world is not intranscendable. Although it claims to represent a beyond only under the conditions obtaining on this side [*l'en deçà*], it very much proves that the world loses for it the structure of a horizon: inherence enables the passage to the limit that enables liturgy to have for its hermeneutic site the frontier between the world [44] (between the stronghold of *In-sein*) and the *eschaton*, or their outer extremities. It is too early to assign to liturgy its precise experiential contents (see §§ 19-20, 54-55). But it is not too early to point out that it superimposes onto being-in a being-at-the-limit. By speaking in terms of the limit, we are obviously not implying that our relationship is analogous to the relationship maintained with an ontic totality, and we must not lose sight of the fact that the limit separates two orders of experience, not two regions of being (the "this side" is not a region from which the Absolute is absent). We are suggesting, however, that the world ceases, in a liturgical sense, to envelop us. It is not something we might leave behind us. On the contrary, it is a structure of presence from which we withdraw the right to be the ultimate determinant. It is a field of experience that holds no more promise for us, and we lose interest in its play in a more than symbolical way (in a restricted sense of the term) when we show ourselves to be capable of accepting another structure of presence.

This lack of interest, as we have said, certainly does not come without its dangers. Whoever prays does not cease to be in the grip [être pris] of the play of the world. In particular, the experience of closure, and the liturgical proof that we can break through it, gives us no hold [nulle prise] over the Absolute: the border between the world and definitive or eschatological realities lies between what is accessible and what is not. Liturgy acts as the negation and the adoption of a position: it denies that the logic of inherence unveils all that we are, and it affirms our desire to exist before God. But to affirm this is to accept that we have no right over God. When we pray, we contest that being-in-the-world accounts entirely for our being; and we are proposing that a relation to the Absolute can have the first and last word on the question of who we are. On the other hand, from the fact that we are exposed to the Absolute, and from the fact that we freely expose ourselves to God's condescension, does it follow that, by breaking loose from the closed field of experience, we think in terms of the concept of "world," we accede to a novel mode of experience in which the Absolute comes to presence and to experience for us? To respond to this question, we are forced to examine a paradox: that which conjoins the expectation with the admission of a presence.

Existing before He Who Is to Come

Liturgy manifests itself primordially as an act of presence. But if man is essentially exposed to an Absolute for which there is no a priori [45] evidence, which he must unveil or have unveiled for him, and to which he must open himself up intentionally, we cannot understand the grammar of prayer without recognizing the perplexities introduced by the mention of God in any discourse that speaks of presence. What sense are we to attribute to the presence of God? Little acumen is needed to perceive that every concept of presence constructed by referring to a type of presence other than God's leads to ambiguities at best and to equivocations at worst. We cannot equate the presence of God with the presence of things or of people, or of the world that is the horizon in which all appearance unfolds. If the world is the measure of every presence, we would be obliged either to deny that God participated in any sensible way in an economy of presence or to propose that his participation is possible only if he puts himself in place in the world (which only the theology of the incarnation or the theology of the sacraments can think). If one denies the possibility of thinking his presence other than as the assumption of being-there or as a participation in the logic of being-there, must God therefore be thought of as absent? Would he come to be known as "the Absent" in the same way as he has come to be called "the Other"? Would we then have to understand liturgy as the hope that the present absence of God can "one day" be made whole? This last question makes a significant presupposition: it implies that, in contrast to the historial and worldly regimes of presence, the presence of God must first be understood as an eschatological reality or event. But, at the same time, it harbors a considerable conceptual weakness: it supposes in fact that the presence of God is only thinkable as Parousia, and that non-Parousia is identical to a nonpresence.

This is what we cannot concede, for, even if no eschatological proximity is granted to those who pray (except in the types of anticipation represented by certain forms of mystical experience), there nevertheless exists a historial mode through which God is present to us. The world that maintains God in the chiaroscuro, and which prohibits theophany (understood in the strict sense), does not doom liturgy to confronting nothing more than an absence. We will therefore first qualify liturgy as the *expectation or desire for Parousia in the certitude of the nonparousiacal presence of God.* By this we will understand that one can unite the affirmation of a divine omnipresence (such that one necessarily avoids interpreting the nonparticipation of the Absolute in the play of presence proper to the world in the way the Gnostic interprets it, that is, on the grounds of a radical refusal to compromise himself by engaging in the world) and the request for [46] God to come. Liturgy strives for more than history and the veiled presence [*inévidence*] in which history maintains God. But the desire for the *eschaton* obviously does not bring about the Parousia (even though, as we will see in § 24, a moment in the liturgical logic compels whoever prays to imagine that the Absolute is present to him in the mode of Parousia). To pray in that way, even though it breaks through the closure of the world, is to dwell at the limit and not in the beyond. Though itself a paradigm of unveiling [*évidence*] and of every presence, the world keeps God and his nonparousiacal presence veiled over [*dans l'inévidence*]. This does not, however, constitute the aporia of liturgy: it constitutes the tension that is its lifeblood and that enables us to existence in the world turned toward God, while waiting for the definitive order of things in which the "world" would no longer present us with the veiled presence of God. The man who prays confesses his historiality and calls for the *eschaton* by asking that the already present God "come" into the chiaroscuro order of the world.

The Nonevent

It is possible, then, to investigate with some precision the experiential contents of liturgy, not as an experience of the world, but as a hypothetical "experience" of the proximity or distance of God. The principal difficulty we encounter in liturgy is the following: author of his own presence before God [*présence à Dieu*] (even though theology might deem this act of presence itself to be the work of God in man), he who enters into prayer does not enter into a field of experience where the givens of consciousness would put the Absolute in question in any obvious way; rather, he does nothing but prepare the space of a possibility. For it may well be that nothing that could be described as the indisputable advent of God (subject to the theological condition already mentioned) occurs in liturgy, and that liturgy, in essence, reveals itself as a nonevent. The man who prays apparently "does" many things. These things-words uttered or phrases chanted, attention paid to what gets veiled over by the world at the expense of the attention we usually pay to what is unveiled in the world—have only the status of prolegomena (however much religious anthropology might think them to overflow with meaning). By demonstrating the ecstasy man feels toward God, they in no way prove God's condescension toward man (or, rather, they prove that this condescension is independent of every given of consciousness). [47] If liturgy rested on the single theoretical presupposition of the omnipresence of God, we could say that it is only man's gestures that need be considered real. And yet one prays only by presupposing more than the abstract omnipresence of God or his "general providence." Faced with an Absolute, whose freedom he recognizes, the man who prays first learns that, although he exposes himself to this Absolute or dwells at the limit between the historial and eschatological order, his expectation of God can never compel God's condescension. Insofar as the man who prays reveals his humanity, and reveals which conceptions of his humanity he exceeds, the proofs are not lacking–"religious anthropology" suffers, not from a dearth, but from too great an abundance of givens. But the man who prays does not do so in order to prove his existence or the possibility of a mode of existence: he prays, on the one hand, to subordinate what he and world and earth are unveiled as to God's veiled presence, while hoping, on the other hand, that the veiled and omnipresent God will provide proof of his presence. Despite the undeniable importance of a phenomenology of the expectation of God, liturgy must thus appear to us, first of all, as a human power to liberate a space where perhaps nothing can come to pass that, in the sphere of immanence of consciousness, would bear unequivocal witness to God's condescension. Insofar as the interpretation refers to words that commonly serve to speak to man, but which are also used by those who pray to speak to God, or to the silences we often keep in order to manifest the attention we are paying to things in the world, but which are also used by those who pray in order to direct their attention to God, liturgy assumes the character of an event. Moreover, it assumes it in a more radical fashion insofar as the interpretation makes itself the interpreter of the givens of a "consciousness." But it is also very much possible that the act of presence in which liturgy consists acknowledges in a more exacting fashion the intentions behind it, when man, having provided himself with a time and place to exist in the presence and in expectation of God, recognizes that God is in fact absent from his experience, or that the experience cannot ground itself in any content of consciousness to which the Gods condescension would be unequivocally linked. (Or, to put it more directly, it is very much possible that we can interpret liturgy only by marginalizing the concept of consciousness and those bound up with it. We will return to this later–in §§ 25, 56.)

Our self-presencing before God [présence à Dieu] and the expectation of God–by definition–open up the field of liturgy. But this [48] expectation can be frustrated, on the one hand (the Absolute may not come to conscious experience, a fact we acknowledge to be the daily bread on which prayer lives), and accords me no right over whatever it is I am expecting, on the other. Not even the most beautiful architecture can summon up a presence. Our historiality, moreover, leads us to be defined in terms of expectation rather than of the joy of a plenary and unambiguous presence free of ambiguity. This implies that no one prayers implies that no one prays without acknowledging the conditions in which he prays, and which, even though they enable a sketch of gestures of praise laden with an eschatological meaning, first qualify his relation to the Absolute as inexperience. He who prays does, of course, know in principle to whom he addresses his praise or his requests: liturgy is established in the element of knowledge. But knowledge and inexperience *do not contradict each other*. It is not, therefore, senseless to say that man's transcendence toward God can have no other experiential content than that which man himself makes manifest in it, and that the proximity of the God we know [*Dieu connu*] does not itself come to experience–or, if you prefer, that the knowledge [*le savoir*] is ordinarily the only experience to which liturgy can commend itself and the only one to which it absolutely must commend itself.

Nonevent and the Critique of Experience

In positing liturgy as being fundamentally determined by a nonexperiential dimension, we do not, of course, preclude the idea that the Absolute can enter into the field of experience, or that the contents of consciousness can bear truthful witness to its descension. But we thereby acquire the criterion of a distinction. We are all, of course, experts at linking the name of God to experiential certitude; and we make use of a concept, that of "religious experience," to thematize this link. And yet the ordinary usage of this concept–and this usage is the concept's destiny– suffers from an irreducible deficiency. Who (or what) is involved when we authorize ourselves on the basis of an *Erlebnis*, of a "consciously lived through" experience, to utter the name of God? Is it necessary, moreover, for him who wishes to exist before God to commend himself to an *Erlebnis*? Our initial response must be negative. For, if we cannot declare in an a priori sense that we necessarily remain in inexperience as regards the Absolute or, more precisely, that we exist in the absence of any experience other than knowledge, we can, nonetheless, know that all experience that takes place within the immediate sphere of consciousness is necessarily [49] bound up within a still greater inexperience. We are not investigating here the criteria for the veracity of experiential language, the experiential confirmation of true knowledge–which is not to say that such criteria do not exist, but simply that their interpretation belongs to another problematic. But we can emphasize the vulnerability of such a language, whatever the possibility of its veracity. The (historical) presence of God is not his Parousia. And yet this (patently true) proposition implies, among other things, that world and history shroud in ambiguity every appeal we make to this presence. Only the Parousia could provide us with apodeictic proof and bridge the gap between the element of knowledge and that of immediate certainty. Since we do not in fact enjoy possession of the parousiacal presence, the fundamentally nonexperiential character of liturgy permits us to criticize every theory in which experience governs knowledge [*connaissance*] of God, or in which the relation of man to God reaches its culmination in the field of conscious experience. Knowledge [*connaissance*] exceeds experience here, which it may confirm (this is the question of the "discerning of spirits") or refute; experience must in this case always take knowledge as its measure. Exposed to the Absolute, and free to expose ourselves to its condescension, we have no experiential hold over the Absolute that is not open to critique (a critique, moreover, that is a priori). Although it can be legitimate (but theoretically difficult) to appeal to conscious experience, this appeal can dissipate neither the veiled presence nor the ambiguity enshrouding the God that consciousness believes it recognizes as having entered into its sphere of immanence. Experience is a function of our historiality. This poses no problem insofar as only realities (presences) that take world and history as their measure come to experience. But it does pose problems if we contend that the Absolute itself comes to experience. The sole solution to the problem (outside of the case of mystical experience, which can only be interpreted as a suspension in the government of the world, and as a glimmer of the Parousia in advance of itself in the chiaroscuro of history) consists in not silencing inexperience, to which everyone who enters into liturgy must consent. ...

Existence as Vigil

Patience

[90] To both the embarrassment and the fecundation of liturgical theory, whoever prays is no longer nowhere; if the rationality at work in the liturgical vigil enables us to speak the language of the originary coherently, it in no way masks the fact that neither the gift (nor the restitution) of the origin nor the tension that ordains the absolute beginning an absolute future makes the Absolute available to us: liturgy does not cease to be determined as a nonexperience because [91] the philosopher uncovers its rationality. In attempting to bracket the claim the

world makes over him, whoever prays achieves a great deal but does not annul the world's irrepressible intrusion into his relation with God–and it must doubtless be said that forces of historiality appear more vividly to those who know (whether thematically or not) that although their being-in-vocation exceeds their being-in-fact, their access to the originary will always be mediated by the native conditions of experience. But how then can restlessness exist in a present between the origin and the accomplishment, in a meantime that is removed from the time of the world only in the eschatological symbolism of the vigil, and in which at bottom we merely pretend to be witnesses to the Parousia, knowing all the while that the Absolute is present to us in a historical rather than parousiacal mode? We can respond by uttering one word: "Patience."

Liturgy is inoperativity, which means that its logic is not that of the great theurgical work, of the force the religious man brings to bear on the divine. This is not to say that the one he expects is the Absent. But because it concerns itself with a presence while hoping for a beyond-to-presence, and because it hopes as one hopes for a gift rather than for the payment of a debt, its expectation must reckon with the possibility of perpetual frustration. It may be expedient here to recall that liturgy engages one as a "soul" more than as a "consciousness." No theoretical marginalization of consciousness can result in time not being a matter for consciousness. Whoever prays must learn that Hegel was right and Schleiermacher wrong on a point of major importance: man's relation to God takes place, not in the element of feeling (*Gefühl*) or of immediate "knowledge" ["*savoir*" *immédiat*] (*Wissen*), but in that of "knowledge" ["*connaissance*"] (*Erkenntnis*).[354] He must nevertheless also learn (though Hegel makes no contribution to this teaching) that no rationally acquired knowledge [*connaissance*] prevents the liturgical (and thus

---

[354] Hegel's polemic against Schleiermacher appears, of course, in the *Lectures on the Philosophy of Religion* and gained in importance after 1821 (the year when the first volume of Schleiermacher's *Die christliche Glaube: Nach den Grundsätzen der evangelischen Kirche im Zusammenhange dargestellt*, reprint (Berlin: de Gruyter, 1980); *The Christian Faith*, trans. H.R. Mackintosh (Edinburgh: T & T Clark, 1928) appeared and when Hegel taught the philosophy of religion for the first time in Berlin). See Hegel, *Vorlesungen*, 23-24 (Hegel's manuscript), 175-176 (Notes from the lectures of 18243), 285-286 (notes from the course of 1827); *Lectures*.

experiential) relation of man to God from being governed by a logic of inexperience, and that the liturgical vigil is the time, not in which man enjoys his theological knowledge [*connaissance*], but in which he awaits the morning when the experiential will confirm the conceptual contents of knowledge [*connaissance*]. But this wait ignores all the delays involved in the Absolute coming to experience—whether it comes on this side or the beyond of death. Thus, for consciousness, if we must speak of it, patience is a major liturgical virtue. The patient consciousness knows that its attentiveness and expectation [*son attention et son attente*] give it no hold over God. It is a confession of powerlessness. Impatience [92] is undoubtedly not a fault. We should, for example, impatiently desire the good to come about immediately, without delay. It is neither senseless nor probably unjustifiable for man to impatiently wish that "grace comes and that the world passes."[355] If we admit (and it would be irresponsible, both experientially and conceptually, not to do so) that the liturgical vigil provides the conditions for the hospitality man wishes to extend to the Absolute—but also that the guest will come in his own time; that he will, or perhaps already has, come incognito; and that no visit he makes to us in the time that leads us to death will grant us the definitive intimacy in which the immediate would be the nondeceiving and insuperable element of our relation, then impatience must yield to patience (for it is simply a question of respecting the logic intrinsic to liturgical experience).

This is confirmed for us by knowledge that we have not wished to call upon thus far—the theological knowledge grounded in divine self-manifestation—and which teaches us the good usage of faith. Theology knows and declares that, if the world is interposed between God and us, and that if there exists no clear alternative between a chiaroscuro omnipresence and the Parousia, it is because the world shelters a third presence by which the Absolute participates in the logic of inherence, namely, what Christology and the theology of the sacraments teach. And yet even the gift of the Eucharist, in which the Absolute occupies a place here and now, is made to us only on condition that the world interposes itself, and that a so-called "real" presence does not render it diaphanous and theophanic. This interposition is ontically the most tenuous there is: the breadth and tenuity of the

---

355 Didachē; "Didachē: The Teaching of the Twelve Apostles," in *Apostolic Fathers*, trans. Kirsopp Lake, Loeb classical Library (London: Heinemann, 1912), chapter 10, verse 6.

Eucharistic species, of bread and wine. But these tenuous realities bear within themselves all the ontological density of the world; and if they are the place of a presence that constitutes the joy of believing, they also constitute for him a constant reminder of his historiality. That is why this presence does not absolve us of the duty to be patient.)

What do we do when we are patient? We do not have to wait for the question of liturgy to be posed to know what it means to be patient. We can be patient while waiting for a train, for a visit, or for the mail. But the nocturnal patience that liturgy requires of us tells us more about this figure of consciousness. Liturgy never ceases to tell us that being-in-the-world is not the definitive, and that it represents the initial and not the originary. Moreover, the restlessness that is associated with knowledge (and which learns from this knowledge what it itself is), in order to guide the liturgical subversion of [93] being-in-the-world, constantly reminds us that we have not freed ourselves from the government of world or earth when liturgy has overdetermined being-in-the-world. Whoever is patient "does" nothing. Moral consciousness, if it radically wishes for the good, also wishes for the Kingdom (whether or not it knows it), and can–asymptotically–hasten its arrival. And yet it is to the asymptotic character that "doing" assumes when hastening the arrival of definitive realities that the inactivity proper to patience responds. We can go some way to assuming our responsibility to the *eschaton* by consenting to the call of the highest moral exigencies (on condition that we do not forget that our finitude tragically contradicts the infinite task set for goodwill). But the work of man will not bring it about; and between God and us the world remains that which we can neither leave nor abolish. It must be understood then that, in being patient, we *renounce* [*nous nous démettons*] *all pretentions to being the project managers of the definitive, and put ourselves in God's hands* [*nous en remettons à Dieu*] *as the giver of all that does not pass away*. We are free to open ourselves up to the Absolute's design. We are free to offer him our hospitality. But this hospitality can be accepted unbeknownst to us, on the one hand, and history maintains us far from the eschatological reversal by which the Absolute will offer us definitive hospitality, on the other. Our time must thus be lived in patience [*Il faut donc donner notre temps en patience*].

RICHARD KEARNEY (1954-)

Born in 1954 in Cork, Ireland, Kearney acquired a bachelor's from University College, Dublin in 1975, a master's from McGill University under Charles Taylor in 1976, and a doctorate at the University of Paris X, Nanterre under Paul Ricoeur in 1980. Kearney taught at the University College, Dublin from 1988 to 2005, and Boston College beginning in 1999. He was inducted into the Royal Irish Academy in 1998.

Among his writings one can mention *The Wake of the Imagination* (London: Routledge, 1998), *Poetics of Imagining* (New York: Fordham University Press, 1998), *The God Who May Be* (Bloomington: Indiana University Press, 2001), *Strangers, Gods and Monsters: Interpreting Otherness* (London: Routledge, 2003), *Anatheism: Returning to God after God* (New York: Columbia University Press, 2011).

For more on Kearney see Panteleimon, John M., *After God: Richard Kearney and the Religious Turn in Continental Philosophy* (New York: Fordham University Press, 2006) and Littlejohn, M.E., ed., *Imagination Now: A Richard Kearney Reader* (Lanham: Rowman and Littlefield, 2020).

Somewhat critical of the more radical postmodernists, Kearney enters into a "diacritical hermeneutics" which seeks the middle ground between the Romantic hermeneutics of Schleiermacher and the Radical hermeneutics of Derrida and Caputo. The following excerpt is from Kearney's *The God Who May Be* (Bloomington: Indiana University Press, 2001), chapter 2, pages 31-38 wherein Kearney criticizes the God without being of Marion and advocates a God who may be. He thus interprets the name of God in Exodus 3:14 to be neither purely ontological 'I am the one who is,' nor purely eschatological 'I am the one who is not,' but rather onto-eschatological, a possibilizing God who may be, a God who refuses to impose on us or abandon us, but instead traverses the present while opening up a future to come. Such a God is not a zealot who imposes a kingdom or an onto-theology of essence, nor remains wholly foreign to humans and demands quietism of us. Rather it is a God who may be, a God of possibility that offers us the possibility of realizing the kingdom by opening up to the transforming power of His transcendence.

The God Who May Be (2001)[356]

I Am Who May Be

Critical Considerations

[31] Transcendence can, however, become too transcendent. If removed entirely from historical being, God can become so unknowable and invisible as to escape all identification whatsoever. Such a numinous deity often takes the form of a "negative" or "apophatic" theology.

This tendency to construe the transfiguring God of Exodus as a God without being is especially evident in a contemporary thinker like Jean-Luc Marion.[357] Marion cites Dionysius and the apophatic tradition in his argument that the whole metaphysics of *naming* God must give way to a new understanding of God as pure *giving*. To subordinate the God of love to speculative distinctions of being and non-being is to resort to principles of reason which God radically transcends. Indeed for Marion the conceptual atheism of modern thinkers like Nietzsche and Heidegger is, curiously, one of the best weapons against the "conceptual idolatry" of onto-theology. Why? Because by deconstructing the old idols it can permit a new logic to emerge: that of superabundance and gratuity. The statement "God is One" may thus give way–for Marion, if not for Nietzsche and Heidegger–to the utterance "God loves."

[32] But there are problems with Marion's mystical theology when it comes to the name of God. In *God without Being,* Marion directly relates Exodus 3:14 to what he considers to be privileged mystical revelations in the Christian scriptures (John 8:24 and 8:58; or Luke 24:39 where Christ says "I am myself," *ego eimi autos*). So doing, Marion invokes the authority of a Eucharistic hermeneutic. The "hermeneutic of the text by the community," he

---

356 [Richard Kearney, *The God Who May Be: A Hermeneutics of Religion.* Copyright © 2001 by Indiana University Press. All rights reserved. Used with permission of Indiana University Press, https://iupress.org.]

357 Jean-Luc Marion, God without Being, trans. Thomas A. Carlson (Chicago: University of Chicago Press, 1991), p. 123. Marion is greatly indebted here to Levinas' discussion of transcendence in *Totality and Infinity* (Pittsburgh: Duquesne University Press, 1969), in *Otherwise Than Being* (The Hague: Martinus Nihoff, 1981), and in *De Dieu qui vient à l'idée* (Paris: Vrin, 1982).

writes, is conditioned by that community itself being "interpreted by the Word." But this can only be ultimately guaranteed "thanks to the liturgical service of the theologian *par excellence*, the bishop."[358] In the heel of the Marionesque hunt, "only the bishop merits, in the full sense, the title of theologian."[359] To remain true to such an ecclesiastical hermeneutic we must accept that the "saturation" of signs (words, names, texts, speech) by the "unspeakable Word" means that "we find all already given, gained, available."[360]

The transfiguring Word, in short, does not depend on us in any way. It does not really need our response in order to be more fully fulfilled. Once it is revealed through such a saturated phenomenon as the burning bush (or, Marion adds, the Eucharist), there is nothing further for us to think, say, or do to make the Word more fully alive in this world. We have little or no part to play in the transfiguring mission of the Word–e.g., the quest for historical justice. The referent of the religious sign is not, Marion makes plain, something to be "taught," and by extension debated or developed. No, it is encountered *as is* "by mystical union."[361] Consequently, only he who knows the "Word nonverbally," in mystical communion with the Eucharist, has the wisdom to subsequently interpret it.[362] (A confessional move which, on the face of it, does not seem very inclusive of non-communicant non-Catholics.)

But how does Marion come to such a conclusion? In his essay "In the Name," Marion clarifies the underlying implications of his thinking. Here he points to a God beyond both the affirmation and negation of names, where words assume a purely pragmatic function: "beyond every name and every denegation of the name ... the word says just as little as it negates–it acts by referring to the One who de-nominates (*de-nomme*)."[363] As such, Marion argues

---

[358] Ibid., p. 152.

[359] Ibid., p. 153.

[360] Ibid., pp. 156-158.

[361] Ibid., p. 155.

[362] Ibid, p. 155.

[363] Jean-Luc Marion, "In the Name: How to Avoid Speaking of Negative Theology," in Caputo, John, and Michael J. Scanlon eds., *God, the Gift, and Postmodernism* (Bloomington: Indiana University Press, 1999), pp. 20-53. The title and theme of this paper critically echoes Derrida's "Comment ne pas parler," in *Psyché: Inventions de l'autre* (Paris: Éditions Galilée, 1987), pp. 535-595. For the most pioneering and illuminating treatment of Derrida and Levinas on the God question and

that the "hyper" invoked by Dionysius and others to indicate the "ineffability" of God *(Divine Names* IV, 1, 865c), is not of the order of essence or knowledge but transgresses both in favor of a praise of that which precedes every essence. The "hyper" of negative theology would thus point to a God radically devoid of being and safely beyond the reaches of onto-theology understood as metaphysics of presence. Marion distills negative theology (as enunciated by Dionysius and Gregory of Nyssa) into an uncompromising "theology of absence." The "saturated phenomenon" of mystical eucharistic encounter with the divine is informed by such a *hyper-excess* that it cannot be seen, known, or understood. Its very superabundance surpasses all predication and narration. Or to put it in Marion's own words: this mystical experience takes the form of a certain "stupor" or "terror" which its very "incomprehensibility imposes on us."[364]

[33] We hit here upon a serious hermeneutic muddle. If the saturating phenomenon is really as bedazzling as Marion suggests, how can we tell the difference between the divine and its opposites? How are we to distinguish between enabling and disabling revelations? Who is it that speaks when God speaks from the burning bush? And if it is true indeed, as Saint Paul concedes, that the Messiah comes like a thief in the night, in the very same passage (1 Thessalonians 5), Paul, *pace* Marion, calls for sober and enlightened vigilance: "But you, beloved, are not in darkness, for that day to surprise you like a thief; for you are children of light and children of the day; we are not of the night or of darkness. ... So let us keep awake and be sober." Such Pauline sobriety seems a far cry from Marion's celebration of blind mystical rapture. Or as John Caputo adroitly inquires–when we are confronted with the saturated phenomenon of God how can we discriminate between excess and defect–"how do we know that we have been visited by a supereminent excess and not just invaded by *khora*"?[365] How

<hr>

negative theology, see John D. Caputo, *The Prayers and Tears of Jacques Derrida* (Bloomington: Indiana University Press, 1997).

[364] Ibid. Marion offers a more critical and discriminating account of the phenomenon of mystical manifestation and intuition in his essay "The Saturated Phenomenon," in Janicaud, Dominique, et al., eds., *Phenomenology and the Theological Turn* (New York: Fordham University Press, 2000), pp. 176-216.

[365] John D. Caputo, "Roundtable on the Gift," discussion on the phenomenology of the gift with Jacques Derrida, Jean-Luc Marion, and Richard Kearney, with response by John D. Caputo, Villanova University, in *God, the Gift, and Postmodernism* (Bloomington: Indiana University

indeed!

But in addition to conceptual atheists (like Nietzsche) and negative theologians (like Marion), there exists a further strand of mystical postmodernism which challenges attempts to reduce divine alterity to the level of human hermeneutics. This third approach I term–borrowing from medieval parlance–a *teratology of the sublime* in that it focuses on the "monstrous" character of God. One finds examples of this in certain New Age invocations of a neo-Jungian or neo-Gnostic "dark god"–an ambivalent deity which transcends our conventional moral notions of good and evil and summons us to rediscover our innermost unconscious selves, to "follow our bliss." A typical instance of this is Joseph Campbell's reference to the "monster God" whose very horrendousness explodes all categories of judgment and shatters our accredited "standards for harmony, order and ethical conduct."[366] In this order of spellbinding sublimity, "God is horrific."

Some postmodern advocates of the monstrous God find intellectual precedents in a particular strain of German idealist mysticism running from Schelling's writings on the "dark side of God" (the groundless ground of divme nature whose obverse is the burning bush epiphany) to the later Heidegger's "Last God."[367] Such Gods are considered monstrous in so far as their very sublimity reveals itself as ultimately indistinguishable from abjection and evil. In the realm of the sublime, vertical excess and abyssal excess easily collapse into one another. Alterity becomes the flip side of the void. And this reversibility of opposites prompts a provocative Slavoj Zizek to suggest that Judaism, as a cult of utterly unnameable, unimaginable, inaccessible transcendence, is itself a religion of the sublime: "Judaism is the religion of the Sublime (in that) it tries to render the suprasensible dimension ... in a purely negative way, by renouncing the images altogether."[368]

Press, 1999).

[366] Joseph Campbell, *The Power of Myth* (New York: Doubleday, 1988), p. 22.

[367] See Friedrich Schelling, *Of Human Freedom*, trans. James Gutmann (Chicago: Open Court, 1936); see George Seidel, "Heidegger's Last God and the Schelling Connection," in *Laval Théologique et Philosophique* 55, no. 1 (February 1999): 85-98, pp. 91ff. See also the section on Heidegger in chapter 5 and the conclusion below; and the chapter on Heidegger's "Last Gods," in my *Strangers, Gods, and Monsters* (London: Routledge, 2002), pp. 213-228. I am grateful to John Manoussakis for bringing this to my attention.

[368] Slavoj Zizek, *On Belief* (London: Routledge, 2001).

God becomes so unfamiliar and [34] ineffable as to be traumatic–
that is, *horrible*. So horrifying indeed as to assume the form of the
"Real of the primordial violent thing."[369] In other words, Zizek is
suggesting that the monotheistic God can sometimes appear so
alien as to be not just strange but radically estranging. Which
prompts certain critics to suggest that even Levinas's pursuit of a
radically other God can go to such extremes that he becomes a
master of the "literature of horror"![370]

But whatever the accuracy of such critiques, I remain
persuaded that it is still possible to respect the otherness of the
Exodic God without succumbing to the extremes of mystical
postmodernism, and in particular its dispensing with ethical and
historical judgment.

While acknowledging therefore how salutary it is to shock
theological orthodoxies and unsettle the self-righteous, I do
believe that certain postmodern teratologists revel in excess for its
own sake. By contrast, a rebel iconoclast like Moses already
showed us how we can break open a new order of existence
without dissolving into a void. He confronted the burning bush
without succumbing to the monstrous. His encounter with the
absolutely Other revealed a deity who, as noted, calls us to an
ethico-political task–the eschatological quest for liberty and
justice. To the cult of apocalyptic traumatism (and masochistic
fouissance) advanced by some of my postmodern colleagues, I
might oppose Rashi's radical reading of the burning-bush God as
mission and promise; a reading reinforced by Moses Hess's own
bracing version of Exodus 3:14: "As God has redeemed the people
from Egypt, so he will be the Redeemer from every other social
slavery (whether material or spiritual, bodily or moral) in the
future."[371]

In sum, the danger of God without being is that of an alterity so
"other" that it becomes impossible to distinguish it from
monstrosity–mystical or sublime. To avoid this, it may, I suggest,
be wiser to reinterpret the God of Exodus 3:14 as neither being nor
non-being, but as something before, between, and beyond the two:
an eschatological *may be?* Such a third way might help us eschew

---

[369] Ibid.

[370] See Simon Critchley, *Very Little ... Almost Nothing: Death,
Philosophy, Literature* (London: Routledge, 1997), p. 80. See also Paul
Ricoeur's suspicion of a certain masochism in Levinas's ethics,
Autrement (Paris: Presses Universitaires de France, 1997).

[371] Moses Hess, *Rome and Jerusalem* (New York: Bloch, 1943).

the excesses of both *ecclesiastical mysticism* on the one hand (Marion and certain negative theologians) and *apocalyptic postmodemism* on the other (Zizek and the prophets of the sublime).

The God Who May Be–A Via Tertia

In conclusion I will sketch a hermeneutic retrieval (*Wiederholung*) of the Exodic name with a view to charting an itinerary beyond the polar opposition between onto-theology and negative theology. My wager here is that at the chiasmus where *'ehyeh* meets *einai* a seismic shift occurs–with God putting being into question just as being gives flesh to God. At this border-crossing, the transfiguring Word struggles for carnal embodiment even as it dissolves into the flaming bush of its own desire.

From this onto-eschatological perspective, I will try, by way of a few final [35] tentative remarks, to reread some highpoints in the historical interpretations of Exodus 3:14.

When Philo invoked the Greek translation of the Exodus passage–*ego eimi ho on*–he insisted that God here reveals not his content (whatness–essence) but only *that* he exists (the verb *einai*). Christian commentators would later render this passage in the light of self-revelations of Jesus–e.g., "The one who is, and who was, and who is coming," or again, "Before Abraham was, I am" (John 8:58). This translation of the Hebrew into Greek (*einai*) and later into Latin (*esse*) was to radicalize the existing plurality of terms for being. It provoked an extraordinary variety of interpretations throughout the history of Western thought. Indeed, it is Paul Ricoeur's view that this very pluralism of interpretation actually safeguards against the danger of "conceptual idolatry" (so rightly feared by Marion and other postmoderns) and reinforces the enigmatic resonance of the original phrase heard by Moses and his Hebrew followers.[372] In

---

[372] Paul Ricoeur, "From Interpretation to Translation," in *Thinking Biblically: Exegetical and Hermeneutical Studies*, ed. André LaCocque and Paul Ricoeur (Chicago: University of Chicago Press, 1998), p. 341: "This resonance would already have at least a double sense: the enigma of a positive revelation giving rise to thought (about existence, efficacity, faithfulness, accompanying through history), and of a negative revelation dissociating the Name from those utilitarian and magical values concerning power that were ordinarily associated with it. And perhaps the even greater enigma of a revelation, in the usual sense of a theophany, or a non-revelation, in the sense of a withdrawal into the incognito."

short, why not assume that Exodus 3:14 was "ready from the very beginning to add a new region of significance to the rich polysemy of the verb being, explored in other terms by the Greeks and their Muslim, Jewish and Christian heirs?"373

The prefatory command of God to Moses to remove the sandals from his feet may now be seen in its original innovative implications. As also the fact that it is far from his own people, captured in Egypt, that Moses receives his revelation from God. For it is only in the solitary estrangement from Moses' native home that the Other shows itself to Moses as self-consuming fire. In this manner, the "dangerous liaisons" between being and God are, as Stanislas Breton suggests, a way of signaling God in his transcendence without neglecting his carnal desire. For if there was no burning bush to see or no voice, however riddling, to hear, there would be nothing to witness, and so nothing to remember or promise! There would only be regress to the chaos of pre-creation: the dark before the Word. *Tahu bohu.*

Revisiting Meister Eckhart's much neglected intervention in the Exodus 3:14 debate, one remarks how this subtle Dominican managed to skew ontological categories in the direction of eschatological intent. Under his gaze, the "I" of the Exodic tautology is seen to accentuate the sense of God's *difference*: for example, the epithet *discretivum,* with which Eckhart qualifies the "I," connotes a measure of distance.374 By extension, Eckhart's use of the term *substantia* may be understood in the curious sense of a "being that stands on its own, by its own energy"–the quasi-being encountered at the heart of nothingness, which "carries all things according to the Word." This pure separateness of the divine "I" declines all additions of "this or that" and outstrips the familiar Aristotelian categories of substance deployed by conventional scholasticism.

Eckhart's commentary on the verb *sum* also invites us to reinterpret the traditional being of God. "Being-as-copula" becomes being in "solitude and separation."375 Qua *sum,* God here absolves himself from all predication, [36] announcing both the ontological difference between Being and beings and the theological difference between divine and human. Here is a *sum* whose very burning-bush indeterminacy, in Breton's words,

---

373 Ibid., p. 341.

374 Stanislas Breton, "'Je Suis (celui) qui Suis," *Libres Commentaires* (Paris: Cerf, 1990), p. 59.

375 Ibid., p. 60.

"expresses the purificatory fire of a certain iconoclasm."[376]

And what, finally, of the *who?* Here, Eckhart may be seen as stressing the *dynamism* of the self-giving God: "The repetition which says twice 'I am who I am' is the purity of affirmation which excludes all negation ... it indicates a certain reflexive conversion in itself and on itself, a sanctuary or repose which holds in itself; what is more, it indicates a specific effervescence (or bubbling over) or birth of self: this being, in fact, conceals a fervor which expands within itself and onto itself in a sort of bubbling; light within light, it penetrates everything ... ."[377] By means of such

---

[376] Ibid., p. 64. See Derrida 's subtle and suggestive reading of Eckhart's negative theology in "Comment ne pas parler," from *Psyché*, trans. Ken Frieden, in *Languages of the Unsayahle: The Play of Negativity in Literature and Literary Theory*, ed. Sanford Budick and Wolfgang Iser (Stanford: Stanford University Press, 1996), pp. 3-70.

[377] Eckhart, *In Exodum 3:14, Lateinische Werke* II, 21. Cited in Breton, "Je Suis (celui) qui Suis," pp. 61-62. See Breton's suggestive gloss on this in ibid., p. 62: "L'acte d'être, sous la flamme du boisson ardent, deviant flamme à son tour, élan de vie, feu originel, déployé en un groupe d'opérations, de mouvements et de relations qu'entretient une énergie bouillonnante qui se répand au-dedans comme au-dehors. Le mot *ferveur* est ice décisif. Il projette sur l'abstrait dynamisme de la *causa sui* l'irradiation d'une source de lumière et de chaleur qui entraîne, en son tourbillon, le monde et la divinité elle-même. L'univers est un Buisson d'étincelles. Ephémères ou durables, ces 'fleurs du feu' naissent d'un espace festif qui n'est autre que la surabondance de l'acte pur." On this metaphor of the God of Exodus 3:14 as an overspilling, bubbling, superabundant source, see also Adolph Gesché, "Apprendre de Dieu ce qui'il est," in *Qu'est-ce que Dieu?* (Brussels: Publications des Facultés Universitaires Saint-Louis, 1985), p. 743: "La tradition chretienne parle de Dieu comme *pègè*, Source intarissable. C'est sans doute parce que Dieu est source débordante qu'il peut ainsi 'se vider' (Ph. 2:7) et donner sans rien perdre, se perdre sans rien perdre. Qu'il peut même donner 'ce qu'il n'est pas,' si l'on peut se permettre d'exprimer ainsi ce qu 'est la creation, position et surgissement d'une veritable alterité. La surabondance divine explique cette priorité de Dieu, d'un Dieu toujours en avance, jamais en retard sur l'être. 'Je suis qui je suis' (Ex 3:14). Superbe tautologie, qui signifie que Dieu n'est pas determine par une antériorité qui le limiterait, comme il en est des Idées éternelles incréées de Platon. Surtout, il n'est pas précédé par *nos* definitions. Dieu *est* 'dès-avant' (*prior*), il est *Sur-Sum.* Non-pas, comme l'être précédé ('cogito/ergo sum'), mais le precedent, puisqu'il y a infiniment plus dans le mot Dieu que dans le mot être.' Seigneur, ainsi que nous l'avons vu plus haut,—termes plus adéquats que celui de personne,—que Dieu peut ainsi prendre l'initiative d'une priorité et le risqué d'une premier pas, qui

hyperbole, Eckhart's rendering of the Exodic verse actually destabilizes and reworks traditional metaphysics. Behind their ostensible orthodoxy, the ontological proposition *esse est Deus* and the theological proposition *Deus est esse* mutually deconstruct each other. This bilateral deconstruction does not ignore the fundamental implication of God in flesh. On the contrary, it shows that God's self-nomination cannot dispense with the detour through amorous being, lest it become so unknowable as to pass us by unseen and unheard. There's more to God than being. Granted. But to pass *beyond* being you have to pass *through* it. Without the flesh of the world, there is no birth.

And I might add here that it is in this passing through flesh that God made flesh liberates and transfigures the *persona* in each one of us. Indeed Eckhart even goes so far (perhaps too far) as to suggest that "between the Son and the soul there is no distinction" and so "the eye by which I see God and the eye by which God sees me are one and the same."[378] But already in the transfiguring fire of the burning bush, Eckhart, like Rosenzweig, identifies a similar overlapping "of the distant God with the near."[379]

Thus the ontological commentaries on the *ego sum qui sum* found in Eckhart may be seen—from an eschatological viewpoint—to carry a presentiment of God as pure *gift* and *passage*. Pure gift in the sense of self-giving beyond the economic condition of return. "Being," as Eckhart put it, "is so superior in rank and purity and so much God's own that no one can give it but he—as he gives himself."[380] But God is also pure passage in the sense that while he always stays faithful to his promise, He never stays put. Eckhart's own best defense against the charges of onto-theology or

---

chez tout autre serait faux pas?"

[378] Eckhart, *Meister Eckhart: A Modern Translation*, ed. Raymond B. Blackney (New York: Harper, 1941), pp. 208 and 206.

[379] One might usefully compare and contrast this Eckhartian reading of Exodus 3:14 with Franz Rosenzweig's radical reading from a more Jewish perspective," see "The Eternal" (1929), in Martin Buber and Franz Rosenzweig, *Scripture and Translation*, trans. Lawrence Rosenwald and Everett Fox (Bloomington: Indiana University Press, 1994), p. 108.

[380] Meister Eckhart, *Meister Eckhart*, "The Sermons, 16," p. 171. This notion of a self-giving God in turn echoes Eriugena's view of the divine as a self-othering self-creation—a form of *kenosis-poesis-dunamis* whereby the world is created by God in and through the human. See Wayne Hankey, "Theoria versus Poesis: Neoplatonism and Trinitarian Difference in Aquinas, John Milbank, Jean-Luc Marion, and John Zizioulas," *Modern Theology* 15, no. 4 (199): 387-415.

mystical ontologism is the reminder that he deemed the dialogue between God and being to be *provisional* rather than final. God passes through being just as beings pass through God. But the primary verb is just that: *passage,* understood as transition and migration. Reinterpreted from an eschatological angle, God is the *imperative of transit.* "This is a God who disturbs, uproots, reiterates the call of Yahweh to Abraham to 'leave his house'; a God who shakes every edifice, even the venerable *esse subsistens.*"381 Which is surely why Eckhart takes his leave of being only after he has rendered homage to its imprescribable necessity as passage.

[37] His famous formula—"I pray God to rid me of God"—may be read consequently as an echo of the imperative to transit. The move beyond ontology has as corollary the move beyond essentialist theology, surpassing the essence of God toward God's ultimate promise. In this wise, the metaphysics of exodus (being-word-abyss) becomes an exodus of metaphysics. A self-emptying movement of metaphysics beyond itself. The revelation of God as traversal—or as what I have called in the opening chapter *transfiguration.*382

Transiting through and beyond metaphysics, God reveals himself, in keeping with his promissory note in Exodus, as a God that neither is nor is not but *may be.* And here I might add the intellectual dexterity of Cusanus to the deconstructive daring of Eckhart. God, as Nicholas of Cusa puts it, is best considered neither as *esse,* nor as *nihil,* but as *possest.* Transgressing the traditional scholastic capture of God as *esse,* Cusanus redefines God as *possest* (absolute possibility which includes all that is actual). "Existence (esse) presupposes possibility (posse)," writes Cusanus, "since it is not the case that anything exists unless there is possibility from which it exists." God alone, he concludes, "is what he is able to be."383 It is arguably this same hidden intellectual heritage which resurfaces, however obscurely, in

---

381 Breton, "'Je Suis (celui) qui Suis'," p. 66. He adds: "Having divinized being one must go beyond it by passing through it."

382 Ibid., p. 67.

383 Nicholas of Cusa, *Trialogus de Possest,* translated into English as On Actualized-Possibility by Jasper Hopkins, in *A Concise Introduction to the Philosophy of Nicholas of Cusa,* by Jasper Hopkins (Minneapolis: University of Minnesota Press, 1978), pp. 120, 69. See also my commentary on Nicholas of Cusa's discussion of God as *possest* in *The Wake of Imagination* (London: Routledge, 1994), pp. 74-78.

Schelling's definition of the God of Exodus 3:14 as the "possibility to-be" (*seyn wird*) or the "immediate can-be" (*unniittelbar Seyn-konnende*); or again in Heidegger's later understanding of the gift of being as a "loving-possibilizing" (*das Vermogen des Mogens*). Indeed we may even detect distant traces of it in Derrida's enigmatic description of the transfiguring power of the messianic Perhaps: "There will occur, perhaps, the event of that which arrives, and this will be the hour of joy, an hour of birth but also of resurrection ... the promise promises in that fundamental mode of perhaps. ... The possibilisation of the impossible possible must remain at one and the same time as undecidable–and therefore as decisive–as the future itself."[384] This counter-tradition of readings, which I will revisit in subsequent chapters, calls I believe for a new hermeneutic of God as May-Be. What I term an onto-eschatological hermeneutics. Or more simply, a *poetics of the possible*.[385]

Does all this amount to a *conditional* God? No. For if God's future being is indeed conditional on our actions in history, God's infinite love is not. As a gift, God is *unconditional* giving. Divinity is constantly waiting.

Let me conclude with the following surmises: In the circular words, I-am-who-may-be, God transfigures and exceeds being. His

---

[384] Jacques Derrida, "Loving in Friendship: Perhaps–the Noun and the Adverb," in *The Politics of Friendship,* trans. George Collins (London: Verso, 1997), pp. 28-29. See also Derrida's development of this notion of the "perhaps" as "impossible possibility" in "Comme si c'était possible, 'Within such Limits' ... ," *Revue Internationale de Philosophie* 3, no. 205 (1998): 497-529; and John Caputo's illuminating "Apology for the Impossible," in *God, the Gift, and Postmodernism,* ed. John D. Caputo and Michael J. Scanlon (Bloomington: Indiana University Press, 1999), pp. 11-19. Cf. my development of this theme in the fourth and final part of "Eschatology of the Possible God," in *The Religious: Blackwell Readings in Continental Philosophy,* ed. John D. Caputo (Oxford: Blackwell, 2001), pp. 175-196, and ch. 5 below.

[385] See my development of this notion of God as *possest*/possibility/may-be–in comparison and contrast with Heidegger's notion of Being as *Vermögen*/power/can-be–in *Poétique du possible* (Paris: Beauchesne, 1997) (in particular part 4, where I adumbrate a new eschatological hermeneutic of God as posse in critical comparison and contrast with Heidegger's ontological hermeneutic of being as *Vermögen- Mögende* in his "Letter on Humanism" and elsewhere). See also my development of this critical rapport in "Eschatology of the Possible God," in *The Religious,* and ch. 5 below.

esse reveals itself, surprisingly and dramatically, as *posse*. The Exodus 3:14 exchange between God and Moses might, I have been suggesting, be usefully reread not as the manifestation of some secret name but as a pledge to remain constant to a promise. God, transfiguring himself in the guise of an angel, speaks through (*persona*) a burning bush and seems to say something like this: I *am who may be if you* [38] *continue to keep my word and struggle for the coming of justice*. The God who reveals Himself on Mount Horeb is and is not, neither is nor is not. This is a God who puns and tautologizes, flares up and withdraws, promising always to return, to become again, to come to be what he is *not yet* for us. This God is the coming God who may-be. The one who resists quietism as much as zealotry, who renounces both the onto-theology of essence and the voluntarist impatience to appropriate promised lands. This Exodic God obviates the extremes of atheistic and theistic dogmatism in the name of a still small voice that whispers and cries in the wilderness: *perhaps*. Yes, perhaps if we remain faithful to the promise, one day, some day, we know not when, I-am-who-may-be will at last be. Be what? we ask. Be what is promised as it is promised. And what is that? we ask. A kingdom of justice and love. There and then to the human "Here I am," God may in turn respond, "Here I am." But not yet.

BIBLIOGRAPHY

Baring, Edward, *Converts to the Real: Catholicism and the Making of Continental Philosophy* (Cambridge: Harvard University Press, 2019).

Bettoni, Efrem, ed., *La situation actuelle de la philosophie parmi les catholiques dans divers pays* (Utrecht: Spectrum, 1948).

Cessario, Romanus, *A Short History of Thomism* (Washington: Catholic University of America, 2005).

Coreth, Emerich, Walter Neidl, and George Pfligersdorffer, eds., *Christliche Philosophie im katholischen Denken des 19. und 20. Jahrhunderts*, vols. 1-3 (Graz: Styria, 1987-1990).

Davies, Katherine, and Toby Garfitt, eds. *God's Mirror: Renewal and Engagement in French Catholic Intellectual Culture in the Mid-Twentieth Century* (New York: Fordham University Press, 2014).

De Laubier, Patrick, ed., *La philosophie d'inspiration chrétienne en France* (Paris: Desclée et Brouwer, 1988).

Florian Michel, *La pensée catholique en Amérique du Nord: Réseaux intellectuels et échanges culturels entre l'Europe, le Canada et les États-Unis (années 1920-1960)* (Paris: Desclée de Brouwer, 2010).

Floyd, Gregory, and Stephanie Rumpza, eds, *The Catholic Reception of Continental Philosophy in North America* (Toronto: University of Toronto Press, 2020).

Gschwandtner, Christina M., *Postmodern Apologetics: Arguments for God in Contemporary Philosophy* (New York: Fordham University Press, 2013).

John, Helen James, *The Thomist Spectrum* (New York: Fordham University Press, 1966).

Jonkers, Peter, and Rudd Welten, eds., *God in France: Eight Contemporary French Thinkers on God* (Leuven: Peeters, 2005).

Kerr, Fergus, *Twentieth-Century Catholic Theologians* (Oxford: Blackwell, 2007).

Knasas, John, *Being and Some Twentieth-Century Thomists* (New York: Fordham University Press, 2003).

Long, Eugene Thomas, *Twentieth Century Western Philosophy of Religion* (Dordrecht: Kluwer, 2003).

MacIntyre, Alasdair, *God, Philosophy, Universities: A Selective History of the Catholic Philosophical Tradition* (Lanham: Rowman & Littlefield, 2009).

Macquarrie, John, *Twentieth-Century Religious Thought* (London: SCM, 1988).

McCool, Gerard, *From Unity to Pluralism: The Internal Evolution of Thomism* (New York: Fordham University Press, 1989).

_____, *The Neo-Thomists* (Milwaukee: Marquette University Press, 1994).

_____, *Nineteenth-Century Scholasticism: The Search for a Unitary Method* (Fordham University Press, 1989).

Nichols, Aidan. *The Conversation of Faith and Reason: Modern Catholic Thought from Hermes to Benedict XVI* (Chicago: Liturgy Training Publications, 2009).

Royal, Robert, *A Deeper Vision: The Catholic Intellectual Tradition in the Twentieth Century* (San Francisco: Ignatius Press, 2015).

Swindal, James, and Harry Gensler, *The Sheed and Ward Anthology of Catholic Philosophy* (Lanham: Rowman & Littlefield, 2005).

Thompson, Phillip, *Between Science and Religion: The Engagement of Catholic Intellectuals with Science and Technology in the Twentieth Century* (Lanham: Lexington Books, 2009).

Van Riet, Georges, *Thomistic Epistemology*, 2 vols. (St. Louis: Herder, 1963-1965).

Vincelette, Alan, *Recent Catholic Philosophy: The Nineteenth Century* (Milwaukee: Marquette University Press, 2009).

_____, *Recent Catholic Philosophy: The Twentieth Century* (Milwaukee: Marquette University Press, 2011).

_____, *Recent Catholic Philosophy: The Twentieth Century*, 2nd edition (St. Louis: Enroute, 2020).

INDEX

ABOUT THE AUTHOR

Alan Vincelette is the Wilfred L. and Mary Jane Von der Ahe Chair of Philosophy at St. John's Seminary in Camarillo, California. In addition he serves as an Adjunct Professor of Philosophy at Holy Apostles College and Seminary in Cromwell, Connecticut. He specializes in ethics and the philosophy of love as well as the history of Catholic philosophy, having written on such topics for the *New Catholic Encyclopedia*, the *Continuum Encyclopedia of British Philosophy*, and the *Bloomsbury Encyclopedia of Philosophers*, among other works, and he continues to teach in these areas for seminarians and laity of the Archdiocese of Los Angeles, the Diocese of Norwich, and nearby dioceses.

www.ingramcontent.com/pod-product-compliance
Lightning Source LLC
Chambersburg PA
CBHW050545270326
41926CB00012B/1928